W9-AZV-947

TABLE OF CONTENTS

Publisher
James D. McNair III

Chief Operating Officer
Bradford J. Kidney

Staff Writers
Debra Cochran/Sue Barile

Front Cover Design & 4/C Layout
Paula Mennone

Back Cover Design & Illustration
Grant E. Copeland

Library of Congress No.: 97-77619
ISBN: 0-938-708-77 5

Submit all Canadian plan orders to:
The Garlinghouse Company
60 Baffin Place, Unit #5
Waterloo, Ontario N2V 1Z7

Canadian Orders Only: 1-800-561-4169
Fax No. 1-800-719-3291
Customer Service No.: 1-519-746-4169

GARLINGHOUSE

© 1998 by the L. F. Garlinghouse Company, Inc. of Middletown, Connecticut. Building a home from a design in this publication without first purchasing a set of home plans is a copyright violation. Printed in the USA. The cover plan may have been modified to suit individual tastes.

PLAN NO. 20161

Detailed Charmer

main floor	1,307 sq. ft.
basement	1,298 sq. ft.
garage	462 sq. ft.
foundation	bsmt, slab, crawl
bedrooms	three
bathrooms	(2)full
price code	a

TOTAL LIVING AREA
1,307 sq. ft.

Walk past the charming front porch, in through the foyer and you'll be struck by the exciting, spacious living room. Complete with high sloping ceilings and a beautiful fireplace flanked by large windows. The large master bedroom shows off a full wall of closet space, its own private bath, and an extraordinary decorative ceiling. Just down the hall are two more bedrooms and another full bath. Take advantage of the accessibility off the foyer and turn one of these rooms into a private den or office space. The dining room provides a feast for your eyes with its decorative ceiling details, and a full slider out to the deck. Along with great counter space, the kitchen includes a double sink and an attractive bump-out window. The adjacent laundry room, optional expanded pantry, and a two-car garage make this Ranch a charmer. The photographed home may have been modified to suit individual tastes.

PHOTOGRAPHY BY JOHN EHRENCLOU

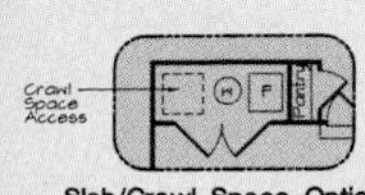
Crawl Space Access

Slab/Crawl Space Option

An EXCLUSIVE DESIGN
By Karl Kreeger

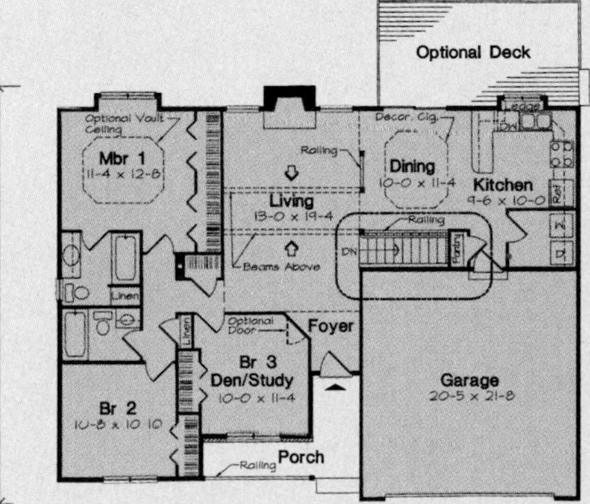
60'-0"
40'-0"
Optional Deck
Optional Vault Ceiling
Mbr 1
11-4 x 12-8
Railing
Decor. Clg.
Dining
10-0 x 11-4
Kitchen
9-6 x 10-0
Living
13-0 x 19-4
Railing
Beams Above
Linen
Optional Door
Foyer
Br 3
Den/Study
10-0 x 11-4
Br 2
10-8 x 10 10
Garage
20-5 x 21-8
Railing
Porch

MAIN AREA

3 4 6 0 0

Rustic Exterior

main floor	1,013 sq. ft.
upper floor	315 sq. ft.
basement	1,013 sq. ft.
foundation	bsmt, crawl, slb
bedrooms	three
bathrooms	(2)full

Although rustic in appearance, the interior of this cabin is quie modern and comfortable. Small in overall size, it still contains thre bedrooms and two baths in addition to a large, two-story living room with exposed beams. As a hunting/fishing lodge or mountain retreat, this compares well. The photographed home may have been modified to suit individual tastes.

1,328 Square Feet

PHOTOGRAPHY SUPPLIED BY BETTY STEELE

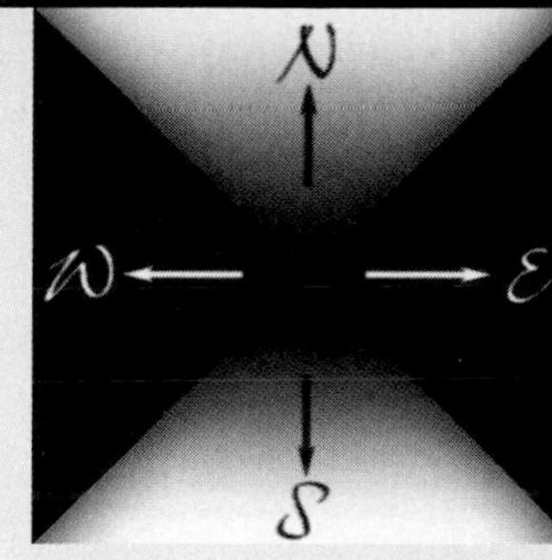
N
W
E
S

PRICE CODE A

Enjoy the outdoors. You'll never get cabin fever in this bright sunroom, perfect for bird watching and indoor gardening.

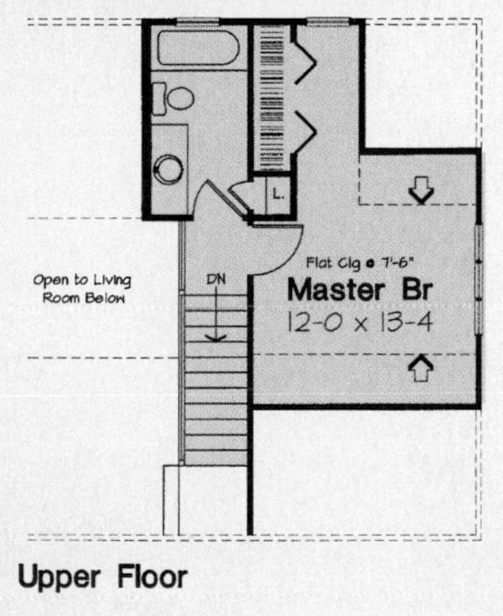
Open to Living Room Below
DN
Flat Clg @ 7'-6"
Master Br
12-0 x 13-4

Upper Floor

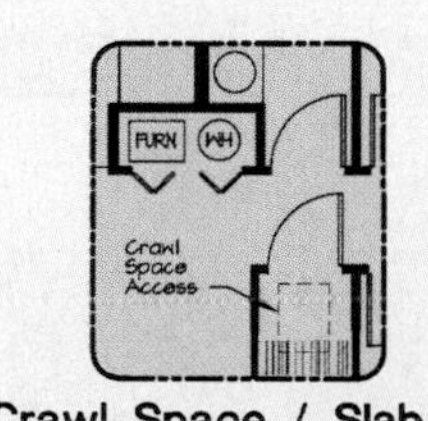
FURN
WH
Crawl Space Access

Crawl Space / Slab Plan

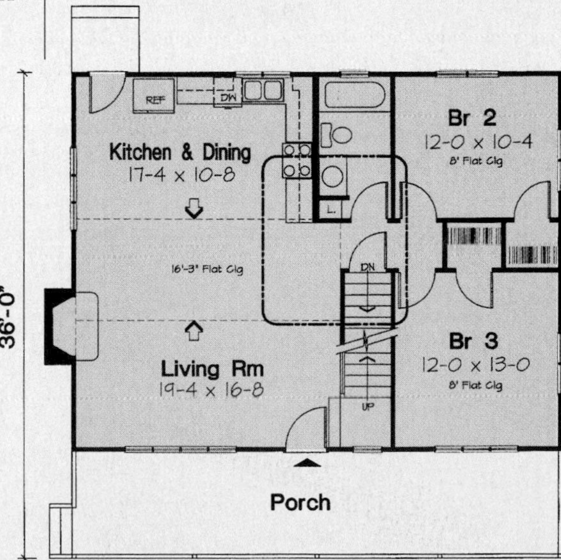
38'-0"
36'-0"
REF
DW
Kitchen & Dining
17-4 x 10-8
16'-3" Flat Clg
Living Rm
19-4 x 16-8
Br 2
12-0 x 10-4
8' Flat Clg
Br 3
12-0 x 13-0
8' Flat Clg
DN
UP
Porch

Main Floor

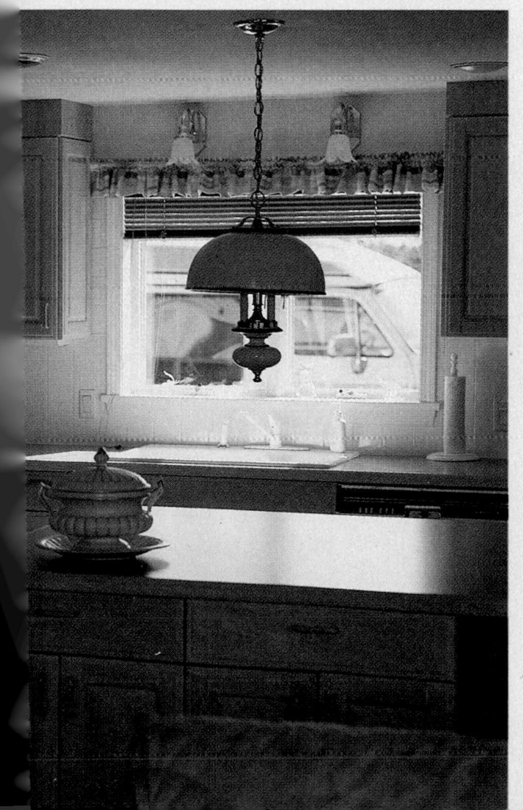

A sunny window and plenty of counter space make this a great kitchen design. The open layout of the floor plan will make entertaining a snap. Family and friends will feel right at home. Enjoy!

1 0 5 8 3

Opulent Foyer

lower floor	1,241 sq. ft.
first floor	2,367 sq. ft.
loft plan	295 sq. ft.
foundation	basement
bedrooms	four
bathrooms	(3)full

This hillside home, characterized by enormous rooms and two garages, is built on two levels. From the foyer, travel down one hall to a cozy bedroom, full bath, island kitchen, laundry and garage. Or, walk straight into the sun-filled Great and dining rooms with wrap-around deck. One room features a massive fireplace, built-in bookshelves, and access to the lofty study; the other contains a window greenhouse. For ultimate privacy, the master bedroom suite possesses a lavish skylit tub. On the lower level are two additional bedrooms, a bath, and a rec room with bar that opens onto an outdoor patio. The photographed home may have been modified to suit individual tastes.

3,903 Square Feet

HORSE

PHOTOGRAPHY BY BETH SINGER

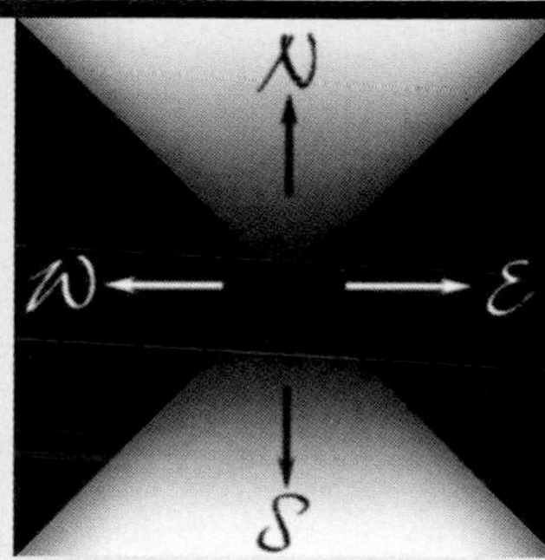
N
W
E
S

PRICE CODE F

Picture yourself looking out these windows to a perfect and peaceful view. This open plan will bring you closer to the outdoors within the comfort of your own home.

An EXCLUSIVE DESIGN By Karl Kreeger

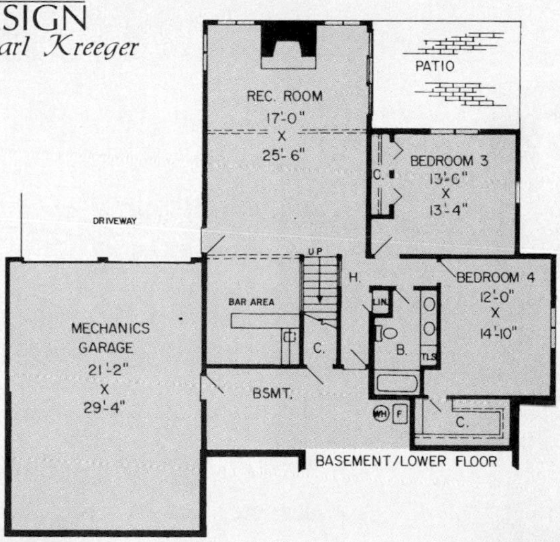

PATIO
REC. ROOM 17'-0" X 25'-6"
BEDROOM 3 13'-0" X 13'-4"
DRIVEWAY
MECHANICS GARAGE 21'-2" X 29'-4"
BAR AREA
UP
H.
LIN.
C.
B.
TLS
BEDROOM 4 12'-0" X 14'-10"
BSMT.
WH F
C.
BASEMENT/LOWER FLOOR

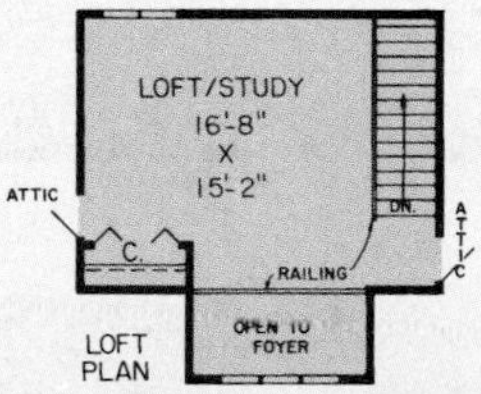

LOFT/STUDY 16'-8" X 15'-2"
ATTIC
C.
DN.
RAILING
ATTIC
OPEN TO FOYER
LOFT PLAN

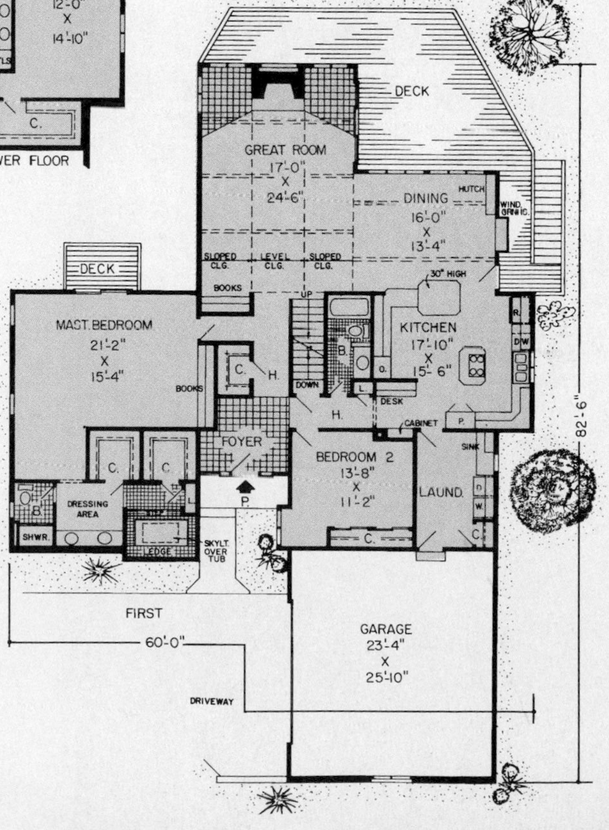

DECK
GREAT ROOM 17'-0" X 24'-6"
DINING 16'-0" X 13'-4"
HUTCH
WIND. GRNHS.
SLOPED CLG.
LEVEL CLG.
SLOPED CLG.
BOOKS
30" HIGH
UP
DECK
MAST. BEDROOM 21'-2" X 15'-4"
KITCHEN 17'-10" X 15'-6"
R.
DW
B.
C.
H.
BOOKS
DOWN
DESK
H.
CABINET
P.
SINK
FOYER
BEDROOM 2 13'-8" X 11'-2"
C.
C.
B
DRESSING AREA
SHWR.
LEDGE
SKYLT. OVER TUB
P
LAUND.
D
W
C.
C.
FIRST
60'-0"
82'-6"
GARAGE 23'-4" X 25'-10"
DRIVEWAY

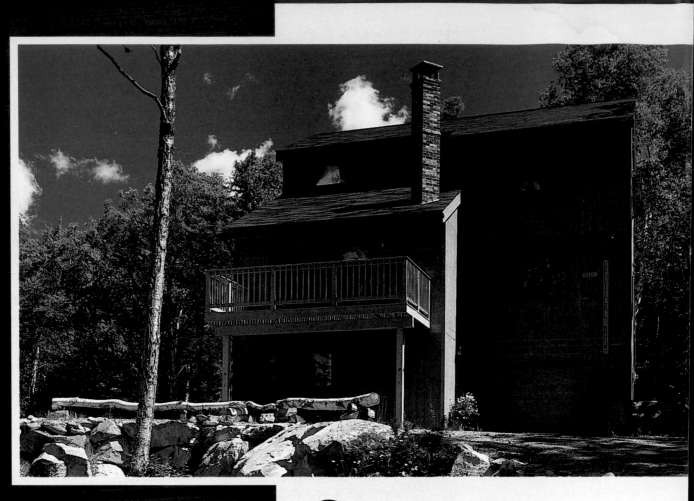

2 4 3 1 9

Vacation Haven

main floor	728 sq. ft.
upper floor	573 sq. ft.
lower floor	409 sq. ft.
garage	244 sq. ft
foundation	basement
bedrooms	three
bathrooms	(2)full

This home is a vacation haven with views from every room whether it is situated on a lake or a mountaintop. The main floor features a living room and dining room split by a fireplace. The kitchen flows into the dining room and is gracefully separated by a bar. There is a bedroom and a full bath on the main floor. The second floor has a bedroom or library loft, with clerestory windows, which opens above the living room. The master bedroom and bath are also on the top floor. The lower floor has a large recreation room with a whirlpool tub and a bar, a laundry room and a garage. This home has large decks and windows on one entire side. The photographed home may have been modified to suit individual tastes.

1,710 Square Feet

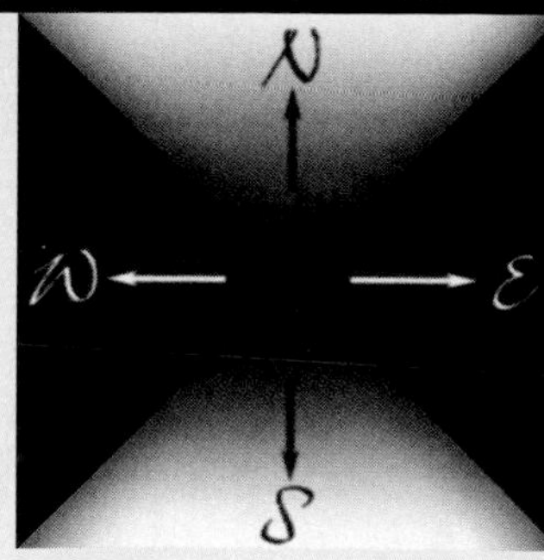
N
W
E
S

PRICE CODE B

PHOTOGRAPHY SUPPLIED BY JOHN EHRENCLOU

A cozy atmosphere is created when preparing meals in this work easy room. The cook can talk to the crowd while making last minute culinary adjustments.

An EXCLUSIVE DESIGN By Marshall Associates

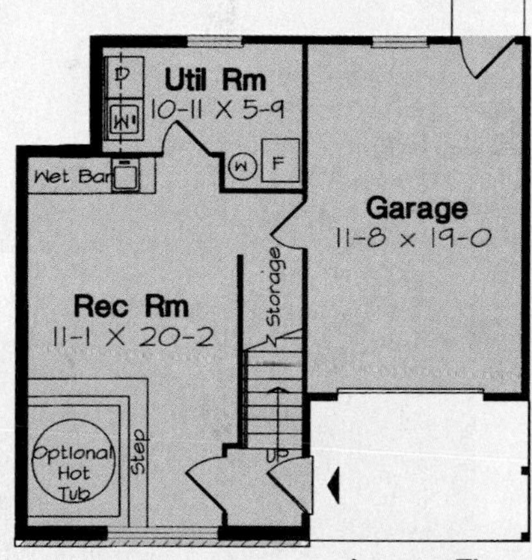
Util Rm
10-11 X 5-9
Wet Bar
Garage
11-8 x 19-0
Rec Rm
11-1 X 20-2
Storage
Optional Hot Tub
Step

Lower Floor

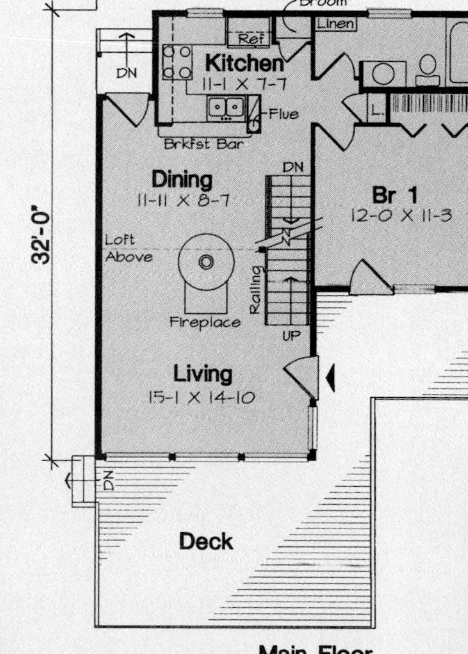
28'-0"
32'-0"
Broom
Linen
Ref
DN
Kitchen
11-1 X 7-7
Flue
Brkfst Bar
Dining
11-11 X 8-7
DN
Br 1
12-0 X 11-3
Loft Above
Railing
Fireplace
UP
Living
15-1 X 14-10
DN
Deck

Main Floor

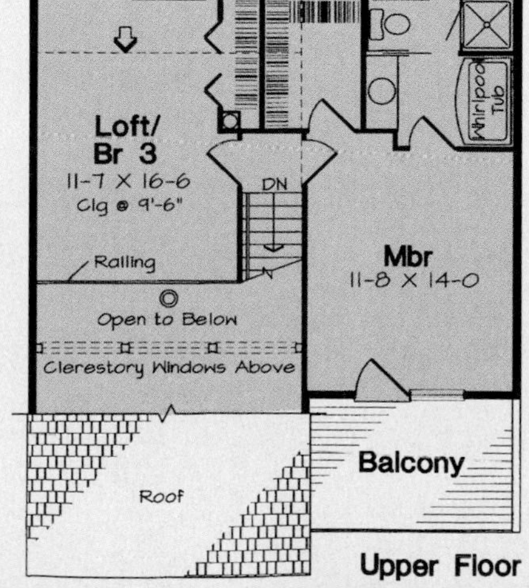
Loft/
Br 3
11-7 X 16-6
Clg @ 9'-6"
DN
Whirlpool Tub
Railing
Mbr
11-8 X 14-0
Open to Below
Clerestory Windows Above
Balcony
Roof

Upper Floor

10396

Spacious Living

first floor	886 sq. ft.
second floor	456 sq. ft.
basement	886 sq. ft.
foundation	basement
bedrooms	three
bathrooms	3(full)

This passive solar design is suitable for vacation or year round living. The rear or southern elevation of the home is highlighted by an abundance of decks and glass. A minimum of windows are found on the north, east and west sides. The basement level has a large shop, storage and recreation areas, plus a bedroom. The first level living room is two steps up from the rest of the first floor, with two stories of glass on its southern wall. An angled wall lends character to the kitchen/ dining area. The master suite occupies the entire second level with its own bath, dressing area, walk-in closet, storage nook and private deck. The photographed home may have been modified to suit individual tastes.

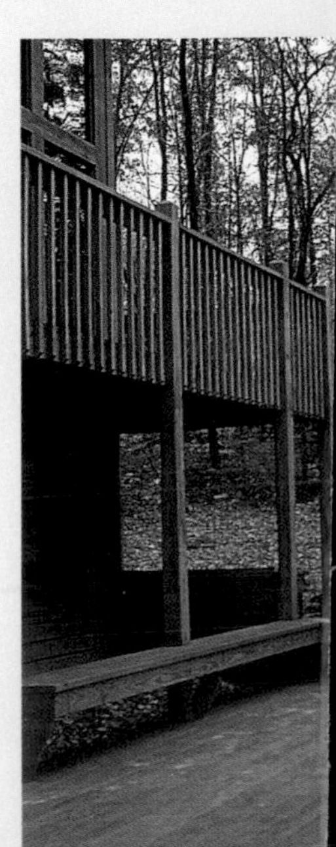

2,228 Square Feet

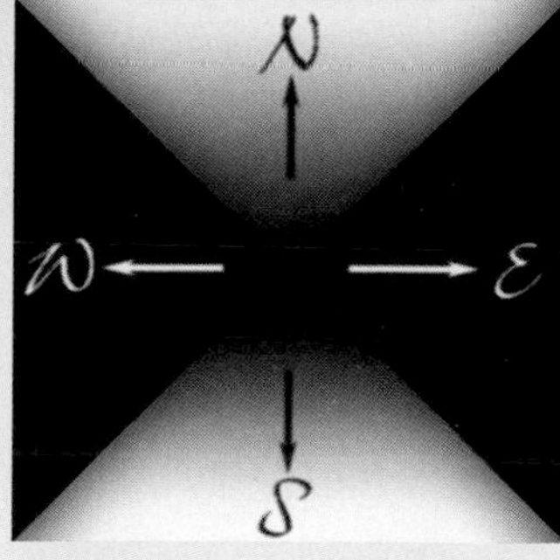

N
W
E
S

PRICE CODE D

PHOTOGRAPHY BY CARREN STROCK

Natural wood accents and interesting wall cuts compliment the abundant window walls that provide a pleasing glimpse of nature.

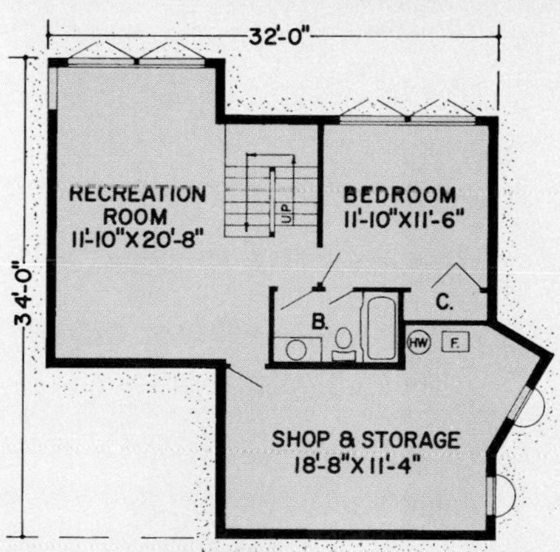

32'-0"
34'-0"
RECREATION ROOM 11'-10"X20'-8"
UP
BEDROOM 11'-10"X11'-6"
C.
B.
HW
F.
SHOP & STORAGE 18'-8"X11'-4"
BASEMENT

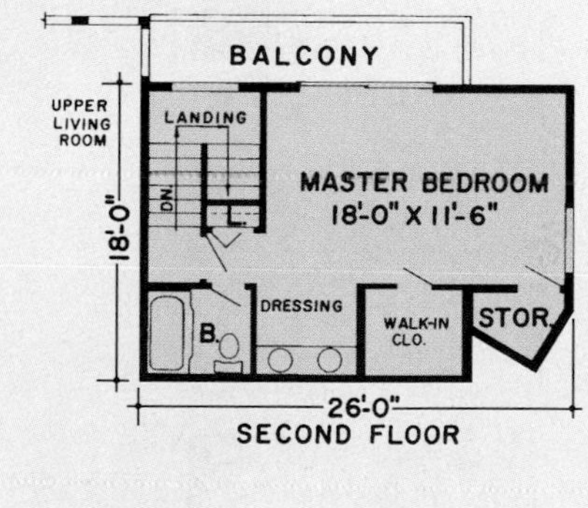

BALCONY
UPPER LIVING ROOM
LANDING
DN.
18'-0"
MASTER BEDROOM 18'-0" X 11'-6"
B.
DRESSING
WALK-IN CLO.
STOR.
26'-0"
SECOND FLOOR

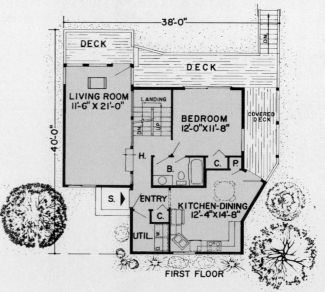

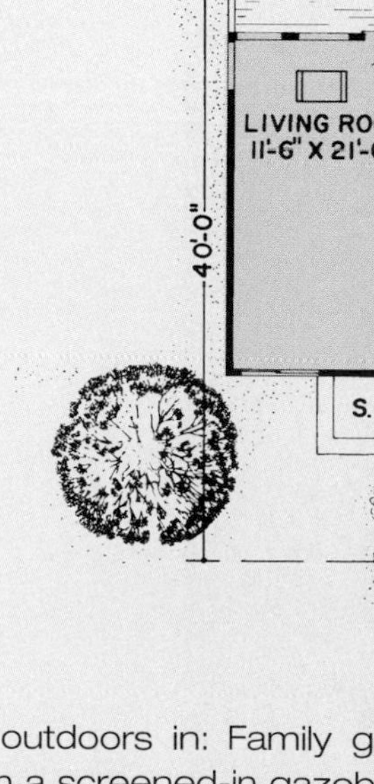

38'-0"
DECK
DECK
DN.
LIVING ROOM 11'-6" X 21'-0"
LANDING
DN.
UP
BEDROOM 12'-0"X11'-8"
COVERED DECK
40'-0"
H.
B.
C.
P.
S.
ENTRY
C.
KITCHEN-DINING 12'-4"X14'-8"
UTIL.
W.
D.
FIRST FLOOR

Bring the outdoors in: Family gatherings are even more special outdoors in a screened-in gazebo that's attached to an enormous wrap-around deck.

10515

Open Plan

first floor	1,280 sq. ft.
second floor	735 sq. ft.
greenhouse	80 sq. ft.
playhouse	80 sq. ft.
foundation	crawl space
bedrooms	three
bathrooms	(2)full, (1)half

The first floor living space of this inviting home blends the family room and the dining room for comfortable family living. The large kitchen shares a preparation/eating bar with the dining room. The ample utility room is designed with a pantry, plus room for a freezer, a washer and a dryer. Also on the first floor is the master suite with its two closets and five-piece bath which opens into a greenhouse. The second floor is highlighted by a loft which overlooks the first floor living area. The two upstairs bedrooms each have double closets and share a four-piece, compartmentalized bath. The photographed home may have been modified to suit individual tastes.

2,015 Square Feet

PHOTOGRAPHY BY JOHN EHRENCLOU

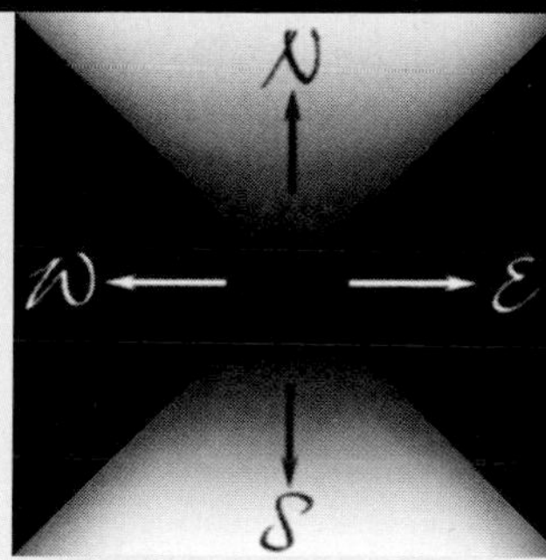
N
W
E
S

PRICE CODE C

This lovely stone fireplace adds a dramatic touch to this bright family room. Sliders lead out to an ample-sized deck with an attached playhouse (optional of course!).

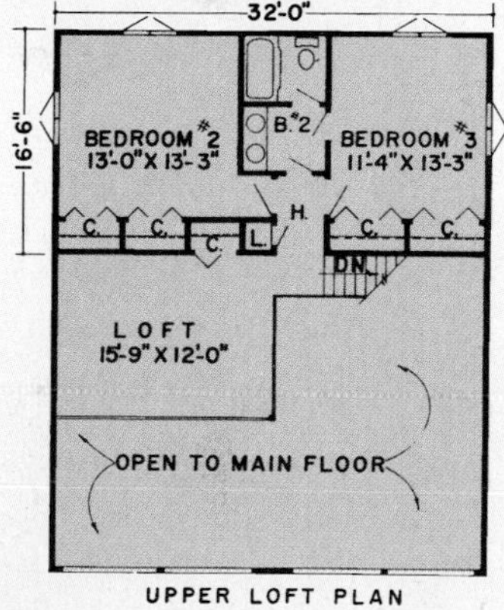
32'-0"
16'-6"
BEDROOM #2
13'-0" X 13'-3"
B. #2
BEDROOM #3
11'-4" X 13'-3"
H.
C.
L.
DN.
LOFT
15'-9" X 12'-0"
OPEN TO MAIN FLOOR

UPPER LOFT PLAN

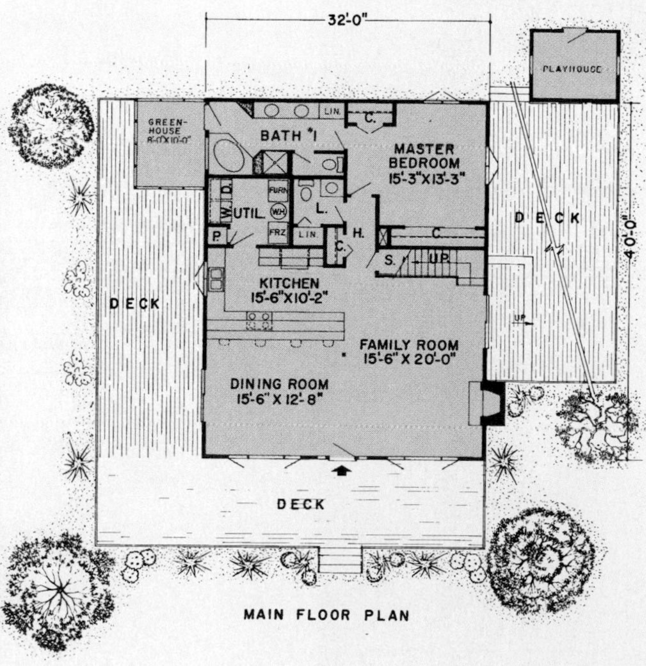
32'-0"
PLAYHOUSE
GREEN-HOUSE
8'-0" X 10'-0"
BATH #1
LIN.
C.
MASTER
BEDROOM
15'-3" X 13'-3"
W.D.
UTIL.
FURN.
WH
FRZ
LIN
L.
H.
P.
S.
UP
DECK
KITCHEN
15'-6" X 10'-2"
DECK
40'-0"
FAMILY ROOM
15'-6" X 20'-0"
DINING ROOM
15'-6" X 12'-8"
DECK

MAIN FLOOR PLAN

If bright and airy kitchens are what you're looking for, look no further. This well-lit unique window treatment makes entertaining a treat.

1,174 Square Feet

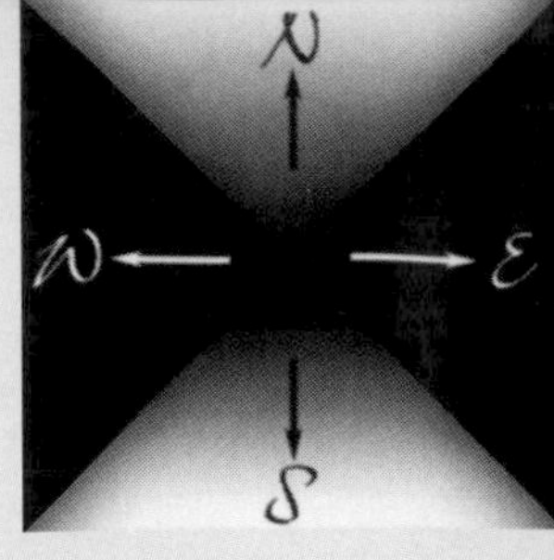
N
W
E
S

Perfect for vacation living, this chalet beach home features several worksaving ideas, including a breakfast bar which divides the living room and kitchen. The ample living/dining room spills out onto the attractive 24 foot deck. Four closeted bedrooms include two upstairs, favored with balconies and reached by a spiral staircase off the living room. The home is built on treated pilings, but might also be constructed on a conventional foundation. The photographed home may have been modified to suit individual tastes.

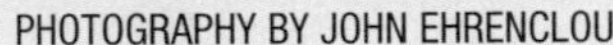
PHOTOGRAPHY BY JOHN EHRENCLOU

1 0 0 5 4

Chalet Living

first floor	768 sq. ft.
second floor	406 sq. ft.
foundation	pier, post
bedrooms	four
bathrooms	1(full)
Price code	a

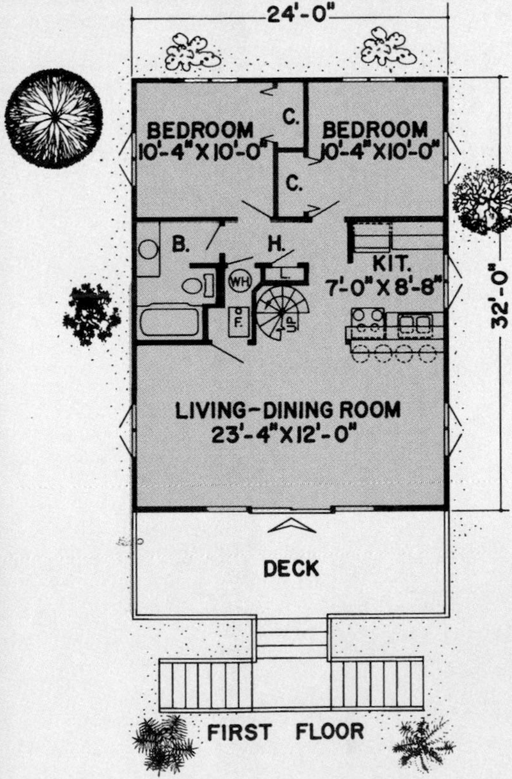
24'-0"
BEDROOM
10'-4"X10'-0"
C.
BEDROOM
10'-4"X10'-0"
C.
B.
H.
KIT.
7'-0"X8'-8"
32'-0"
LIVING-DINING ROOM
23'-4"X12'-0"
DECK
FIRST FLOOR

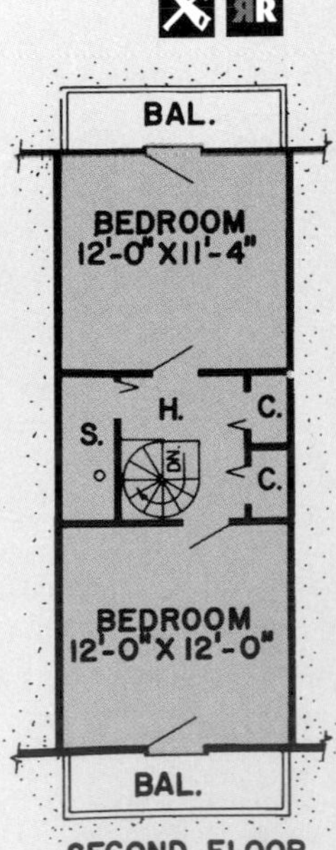
BAL.
BEDROOM
12'-0"X11'-4"
H.
S.
C.
C.
BEDROOM
12'-0"X12'-0"
BAL.
SECOND FLOOR

1,821 Square Feet

N W E S

PHOTOGRAPHY BY JOHN EHRENCLOU

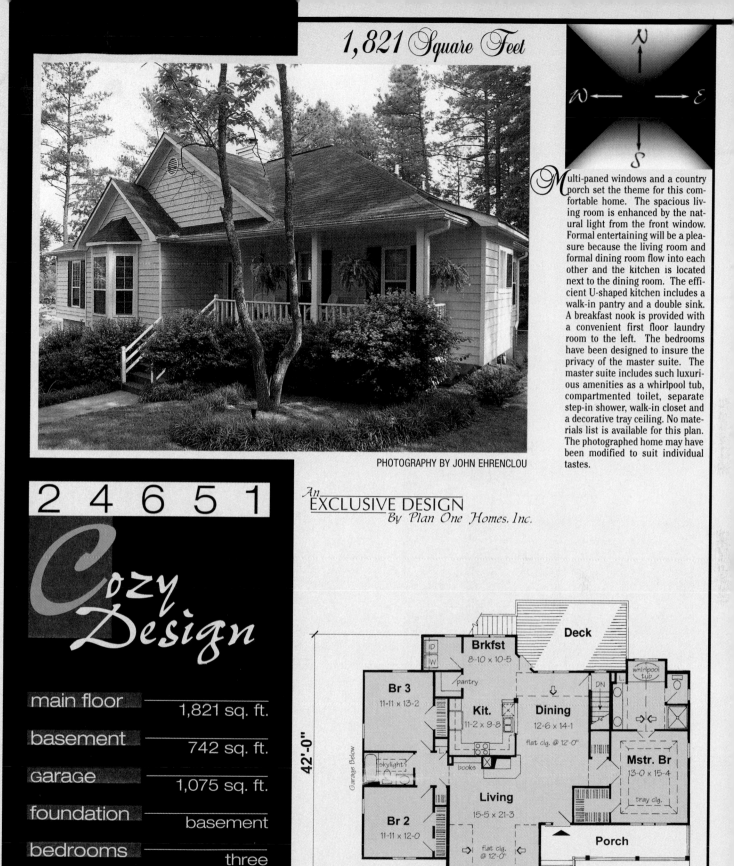

Multi-paned windows and a country porch set the theme for this comfortable home. The spacious living room is enhanced by the natural light from the front window. Formal entertaining will be a pleasure because the living room and formal dining room flow into each other and the kitchen is located next to the dining room. The efficient U-shaped kitchen includes a walk-in pantry and a double sink. A breakfast nook is provided with a convenient first floor laundry room to the left. The bedrooms have been designed to insure the privacy of the master suite. The master suite includes such luxurious amenities as a whirlpool tub, compartmented toilet, separate step-in shower, walk-in closet and a decorative tray ceiling. No materials list is available for this plan. The photographed home may have been modified to suit individual tastes.

2 4 6 5 1

Cozy Design

main floor	1,821 sq. ft.
basement	742 sq. ft.
garage	1,075 sq. ft.
foundation	basement
bedrooms	three
bathrooms	(2)full
price code	c

An EXCLUSIVE DESIGN By Plan One Homes, Inc.

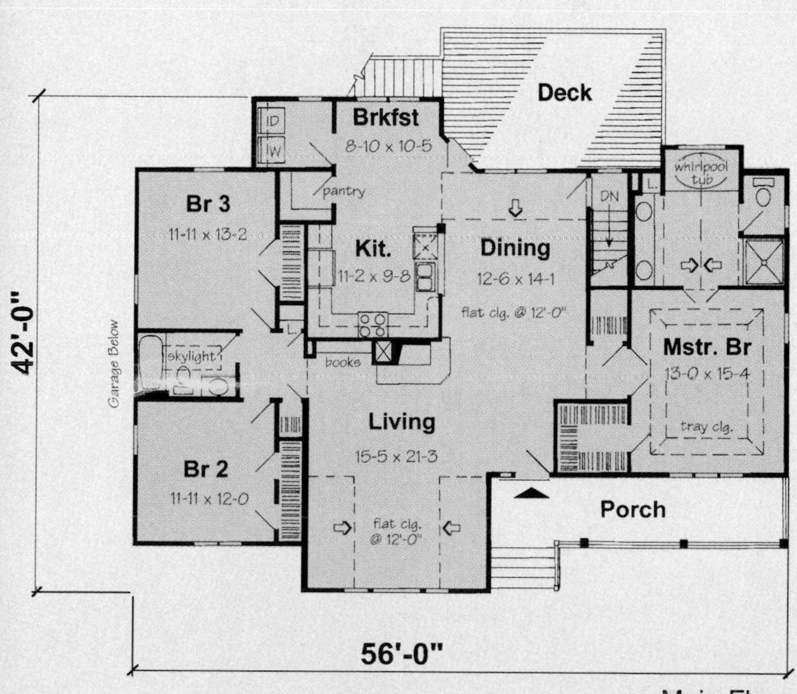
Deck
Brkfst
8-10 x 10-5
D
W
pantry
whirlpool tub
DN
Br 3
11-11 x 13-2
Kit.
11-2 x 9-8
Dining
12-6 x 14-1
flat clg. @ 12'-0"
Mstr. Br
13-0 x 15-4
tray clg.
Garage Below
skylight
books
Living
15-5 x 21-3
flat clg. @ 12'-0"
Br 2
11-11 x 12-0
Porch
42'-0"
56'-0"

Main Floor

1,341 Square Feet

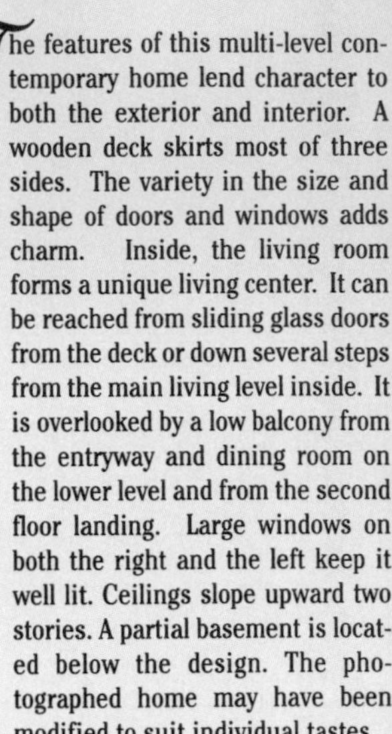
N
W
E
S

The features of this multi-level contemporary home lend character to both the exterior and interior. A wooden deck skirts most of three sides. The variety in the size and shape of doors and windows adds charm. Inside, the living room forms a unique living center. It can be reached from sliding glass doors from the deck or down several steps from the main living level inside. It is overlooked by a low balcony from the entryway and dining room on the lower level and from the second floor landing. Large windows on both the right and the left keep it well lit. Ceilings slope upward two stories. A partial basement is located below the design. The photographed home may have been modified to suit individual tastes.

PHOTOGRAPHY BY JOHN EHRENCLOU

26111

Multi Level

first floor	769 sq. ft.
second floor	572 sq. ft.
basement	546 sq. ft.
foundation	basement
bedrooms	three
bathrooms	(2)full
Price code	a

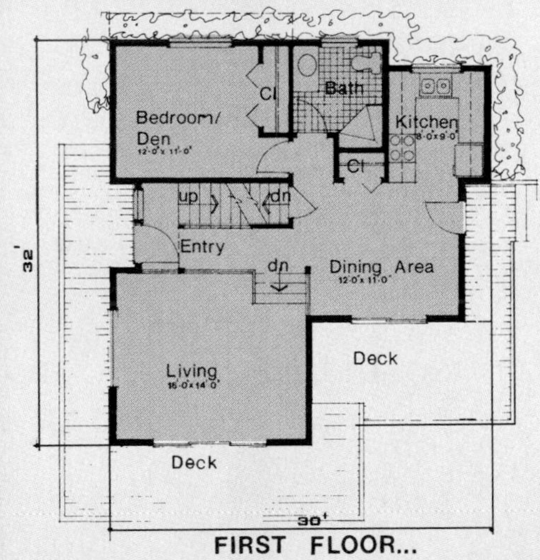
Bedroom/
Den
12·0"x 11·0"
Cl
Bath
Kitchen
8·0"x9·0"
Cl
up
dn
Entry
32'
dn
Dining Area
12·0"x 11·0"
Living
16·0"x14·0"
Deck
Deck
30'

FIRST FLOOR...

Bedroom
12·0"x 13·0"
Cl
Bath
Cl
dn
Skylights
Bedroom
12·0"x 20·0"
Balcony
Cl
Open to Living
30'

SECOND FLOOR...

786 Square Feet

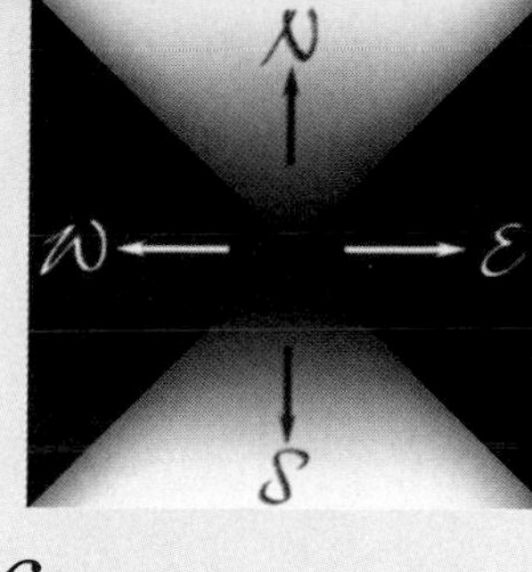
N
W
E
S

Your scenic surroundings will be enjoyed in this perfect vacation home. The deck wraps around the left side of the home expanding living space to the outdoors. A fireplace adds warmth to the atmosphere and the temperature in the great room. There is a sloped ceiling in the great room. The kitchen area flows into the great room creating a feeling of spaciousness. The master bedroom includes direct access to a three quarter bath. The secondary bedroom is located in close proximity to another three quarter bath. No materials list is available for this plan.

94307

Enjoy the View

main area	786 sq. ft.
deck	580 sq. ft.
foundation	crawl space
bedrooms	two
bathrooms	(2)three-quarter
Price code	z

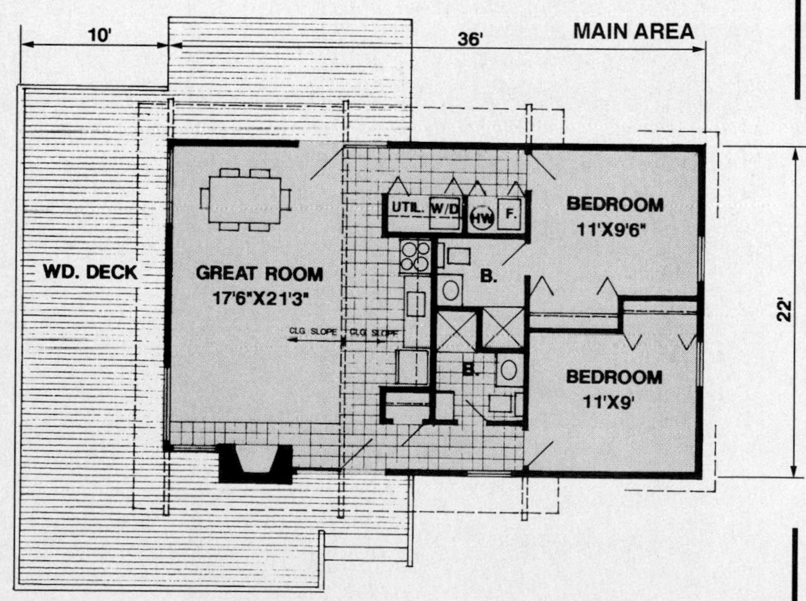
10'
36'
MAIN AREA
WD. DECK
GREAT ROOM
17'6"X21'3"
CLG. SLOPE
CLG. SLOPE
UTIL.
W/D
HW
F.
B.
B.
BEDROOM
11'X9'6"
BEDROOM
11'X9'
22'

An EXCLUSIVE DESIGN By Marshall Associates

576 Square Feet

This cute little cabin in the woods is a respite from the hectic pace of your life. Take off for the weekend and relax here on your deck. In the winter a roaring fire in the wood stove will keep you warm and cozy. Store firewood in the convenient storage bin on the deck. The large living room has double doors that open out to the deck. The kitchen contains ample counter and cabinet space, a double sink, a 32" refrigerator, and a 30" oven/range. A full bath serves the two large bedrooms. A mechanical room houses the water heater and furnace. The crawl space is accessed through a bedroom closet. This little cabin will reward you handsomely throughout the years that you own it.

20002

Cabin in The Woods

first floor	576 sq. ft.
deck	344 sq. ft.
foundation	crawl, slab
bedrooms	two
bathrooms	(1)full
price code	z

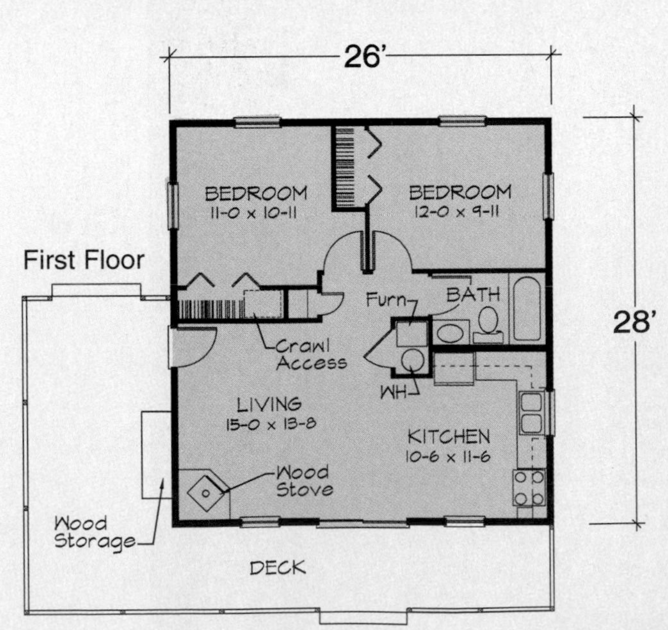
26'
28'
First Floor
BEDROOM
11-0 x 10-11
BEDROOM
12-0 x 9-11
Furn
BATH
Crawl Access
WH
LIVING
15-0 x 13-8
KITCHEN
10-6 x 11-6
Wood Stove
Wood Storage
DECK

1,249 Square Feet

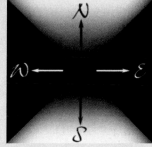

This compact house has plenty of closets and storage areas where you can stow away the gear you usually need on vacation. The utility room is also larger than most, and opens directly outside, so there's no reason for anyone to track in dirt. Sliding glass doors lead from the two-story living room and dining room out to a paved patio. Tucked into a corner, the kitchen is both out of the way and convenient. A handsome stone fireplace adds a functional and decorative element to both the interior and exterior of the home. A downstairs bedroom will sleep either children or guests. Beyond the railed loft, a master suite with a full bath and a walk-in closet provides the owner of this home with every comfort. This plan is available with a basement or crawl space foundation. Please specify when ordering.

9 1 0 3 3

Neat & Tidy

first floor	952 sq. ft.
second floor	297 sq. ft.
foundation	bsmt, crawl
bedrooms	two
bathrooms	(2)full
Price code	a

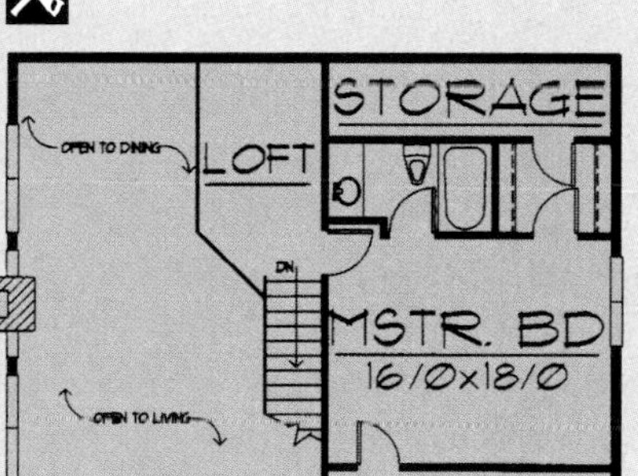
STORAGE
LOFT
OPEN TO DINING
MSTR. BD
16/0x18/0
OPEN TO LIVING
STORAGE

Second Floor

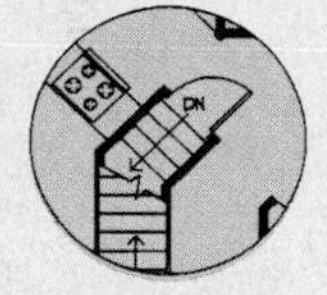

Optional Basement Plan

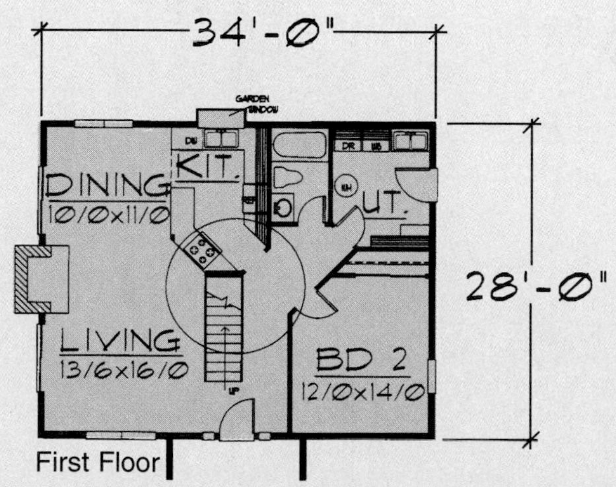
34'-0"
28'-0"
GARDEN WINDOW
DINING
10/0x11/0
KIT.
UT.
LIVING
13/6x16/0
BD 2
12/0x14/0

First Floor

1,400 Square Feet

B LeBold

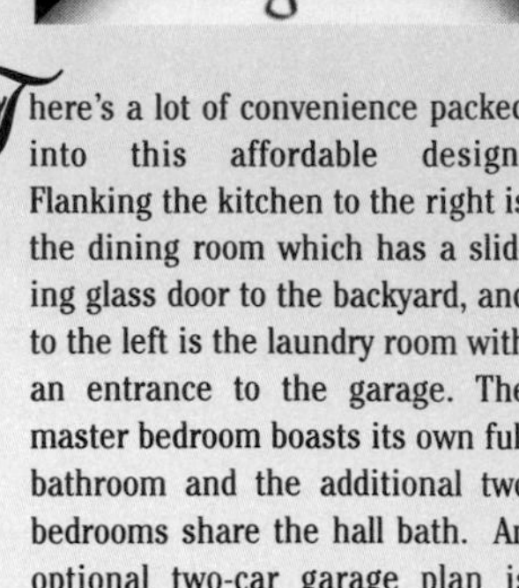
N
W
E
S

There's a lot of convenience packed into this affordable design. Flanking the kitchen to the right is the dining room which has a sliding glass door to the backyard, and to the left is the laundry room with an entrance to the garage. The master bedroom boasts its own full bathroom and the additional two bedrooms share the hall bath. An optional two-car garage plan is included.

34054

Great Kitchen

main floor	1,400 sq. ft.
basement	1,400 sq. ft.
garage	528 sq. ft.
foundation	bsmt, slb, crawl
bedrooms	three
bathrooms	(2)full
Price code	a

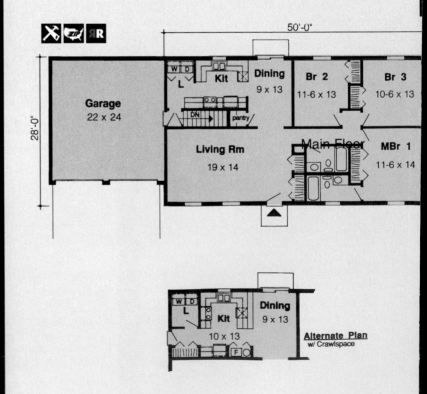

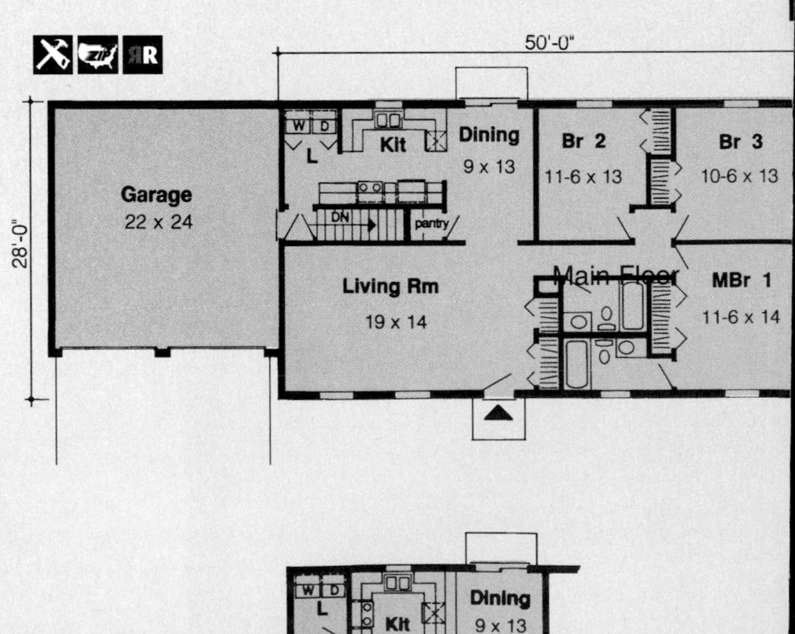
50'-0"
28'-0"
Garage
22 x 24
W D
L
Kit
DN
pantry
Dining
9 x 13
Br 2
11-6 x 13
Br 3
10-6 x 13
Living Rm
19 x 14
Main Floor
MBr 1
11-6 x 14
W D
L
Kit
10 x 13
F
Dining
9 x 13
Alternate Plan
w/ Crawlspace

1,127 Square Feet

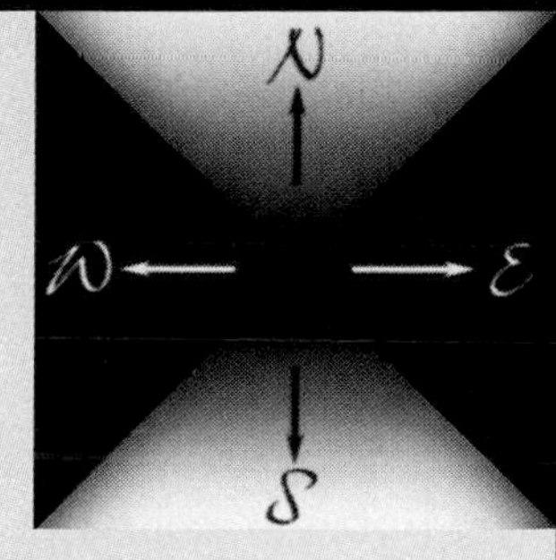
N
W
E
S

Family vacations are memories in the making. This home will help to make those precious times. Three bedrooms give private space to all. If you don't have a large family, make one bedroom into a study or maybe a hobby room, the possibilities are endless. The living room with a fireplace is large and open and can extend your living area out of the home with access to two decks. The efficient kitchen opens to the dining area. The master bedroom features a private bath with corner tub. There are also two closets in this room. Looking forward to retirement? This home may be what you are looking for. All the living area is on one floor, yet it is spacious and layed out with convenience in mind.

An EXCLUSIVE DESIGN By Marshall Associates

2 4 3 1 1

Room for More

main floor	1,127 sq. ft.
foundation	bsmt, slb, crawl
bedrooms	two
bathrooms	(2)full
Price code	a

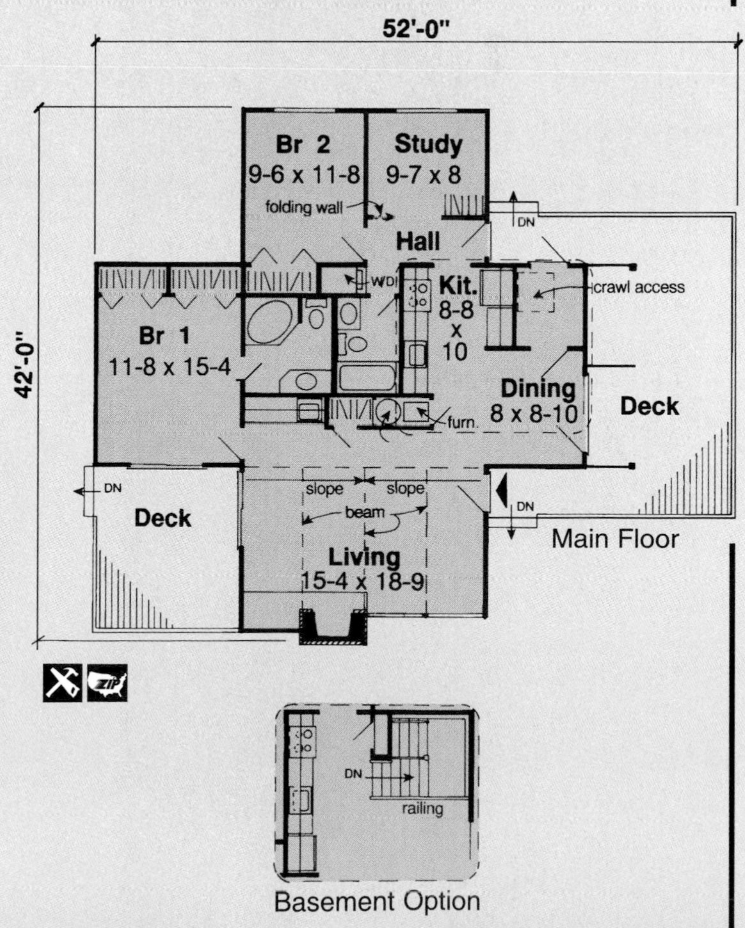
52'-0"
42'-0"
Br 2
9-6 x 11-8
Study
9-7 x 8
folding wall
Hall
DN
Kit.
8-8 x 10
crawl access
W/D
Br 1
11-8 x 15-4
Dining
8 x 8-10
Deck
furn.
DN
Deck
slope
slope
beam
Living
15-4 x 18-9
DN
Main Floor
DN
railing
Basement Option

1,146 Square Feet

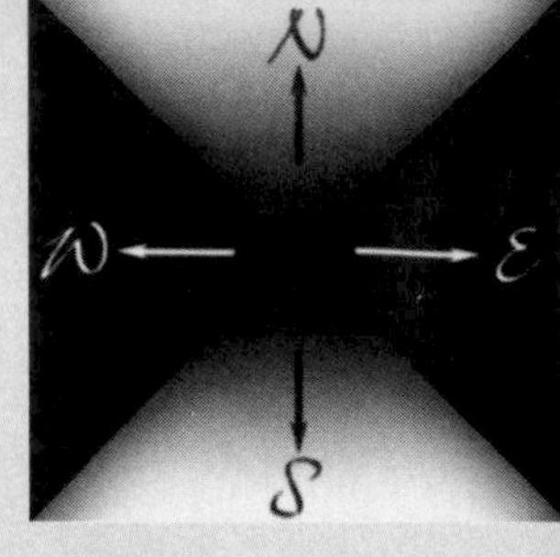
N
W
E
S

Hanging plants would make for a magnificent entrance to this charming home. Walk into the fire-placed living room brightened by a wonderful picture window. The kitchen and dining area are separated by a counter island featuring double sinks. In the hallway, toward the bedrooms, is a linen closet and full bath. The master bedroom features its own private bath and double closets. The two other bedrooms have good-sized closets, keeping clutter to a minimum. Many windows throughout this home lighten up each room, creating a warm cozy atmosphere.

3 4 0 0 3

Compact Home

main floor	1,146 sq. ft.
foundation	bsmt, slb, crawl
bedrooms	three
bathrooms	(2)full
Price code	a

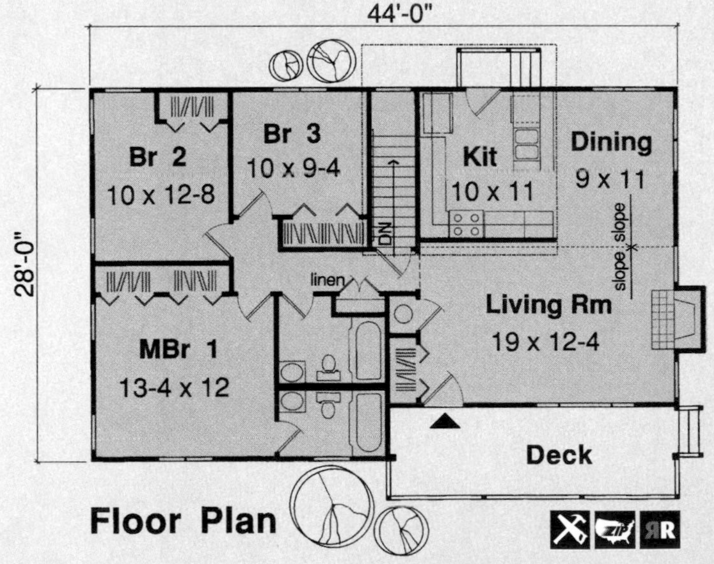
44'-0"
28'-0"
Br 2
10 x 12-8
Br 3
10 x 9-4
Kit
10 x 11
Dining
9 x 11
DN
linen
slope
slope
Living Rm
19 x 12-4
MBr 1
13-4 x 12
Deck

Floor Plan

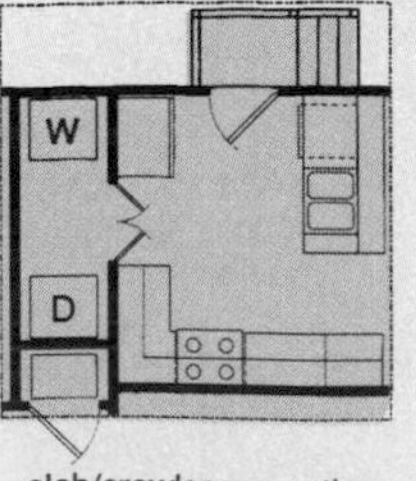
W
D

slab/crawlspace option

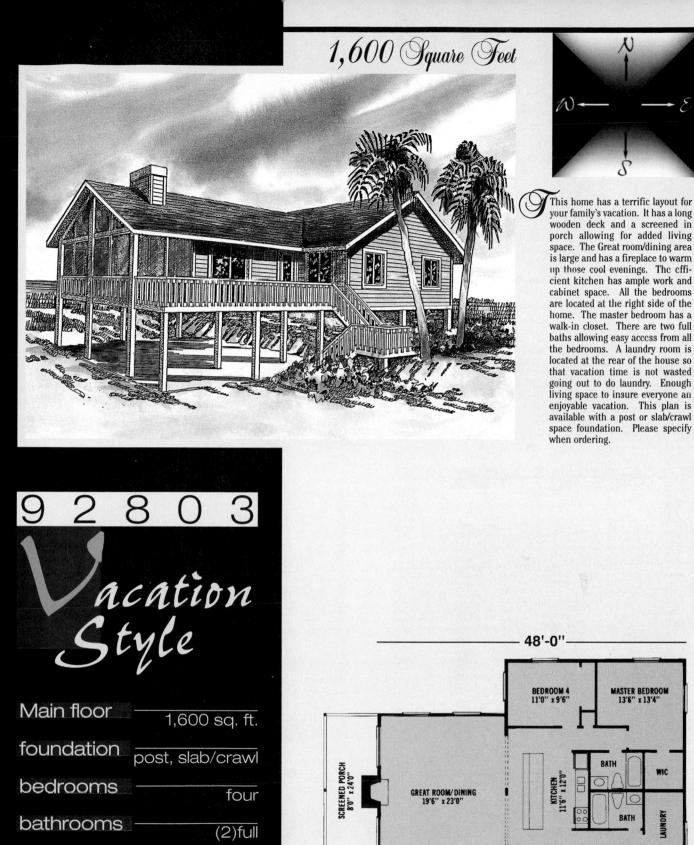

1,600 Square Feet

This home has a terrific layout for your family's vacation. It has a long wooden deck and a screened in porch allowing for added living space. The Great room/dining area is large and has a fireplace to warm up those cool evenings. The efficient kitchen has ample work and cabinet space. All the bedrooms are located at the right side of the home. The master bedroom has a walk-in closet. There are two full baths allowing easy access from all the bedrooms. A laundry room is located at the rear of the house so that vacation time is not wasted going out to do laundry. Enough living space to insure everyone an enjoyable vacation. This plan is available with a post or slab/crawl space foundation. Please specify when ordering.

92803

Vacation Style

Main floor	1,600 sq. ft.
foundation	post, slab/crawl
bedrooms	four
bathrooms	(2)full
Price code	b

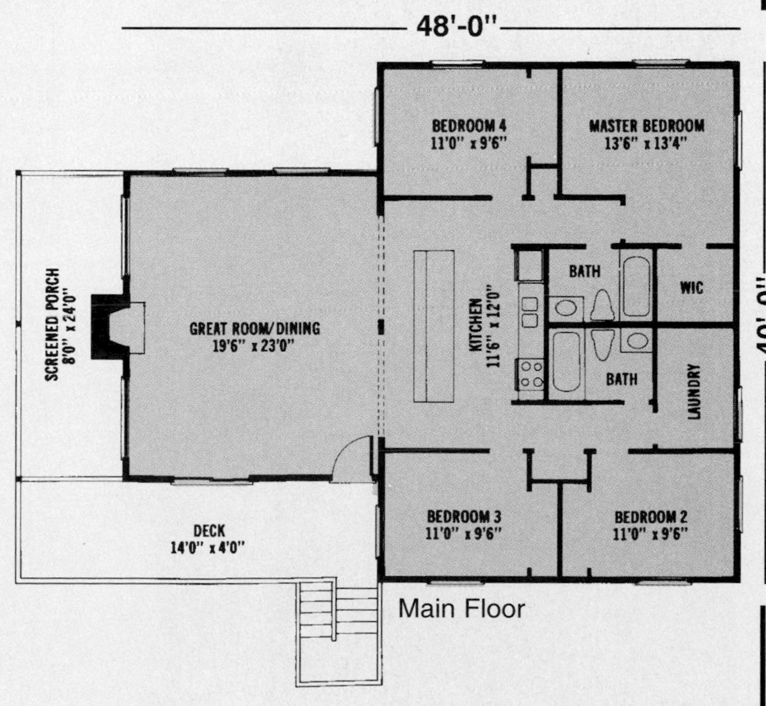
48'-0"
40'-0"
BEDROOM 4
11'0" x 9'6"
MASTER BEDROOM
13'6" x 13'4"
SCREENED PORCH
8'0" x 24'0"
GREAT ROOM/DINING
19'6" x 23'0"
KITCHEN
11'6" x 12'0"
BATH
WIC
BATH
LAUNDRY
DECK
14'0" x 4'0"
BEDROOM 3
11'0" x 9'6"
BEDROOM 2
11'0" x 9'6"

Main Floor

1,354 Square Feet

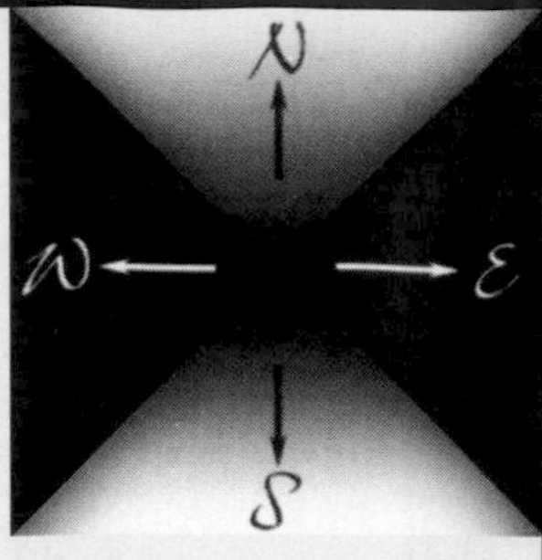
N
W
E
S

Built into a hill, this vacation house takes advantage of your wonderful view. It features a Great room that opens out on a deck and brings earth and sky into the home through sweeping panels of glass. The open plan draws the kitchen into the celebration of the outdoors and shares the warmth of the sturdy wood stove. Two bedrooms on the main level share a bath. Two large, upstairs lofts, one overlooking the Great room, have a full bath all to themselves. This house feels as airy and delightful as a tree house.

91026

Hill House

main floor	988 sq. ft.
upper floor	366 sq. ft.
basement	988 sq. ft.
foundation	bsmt
bedrooms	three
bathrooms	(2)full
price code	a

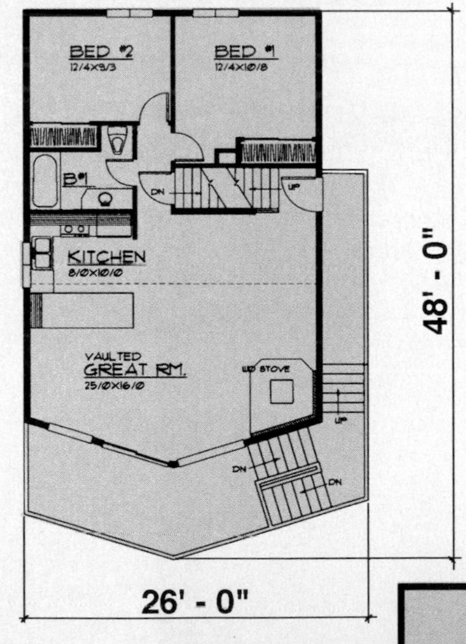
BED #2
12/4X9/3
BED #1
12/4X10/8
B#1
DN
UP
KITCHEN
8/0X10/0
VAULTED
GREAT RM.
25/0X16/0
WD STOVE
48' - 0"
26' - 0"

MAIN FLOOR PLAN

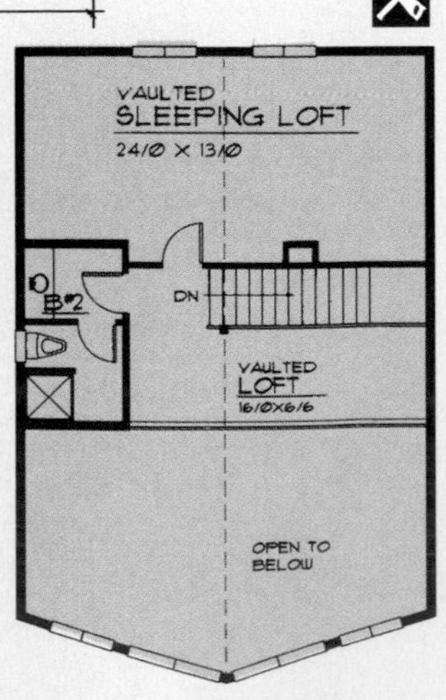
VAULTED
SLEEPING LOFT
24/0 X 13/0
B#2
DN
VAULTED
LOFT
16/0X6/6
OPEN TO
BELOW

UPPER FLOOR PLAN

2,477 Square Feet

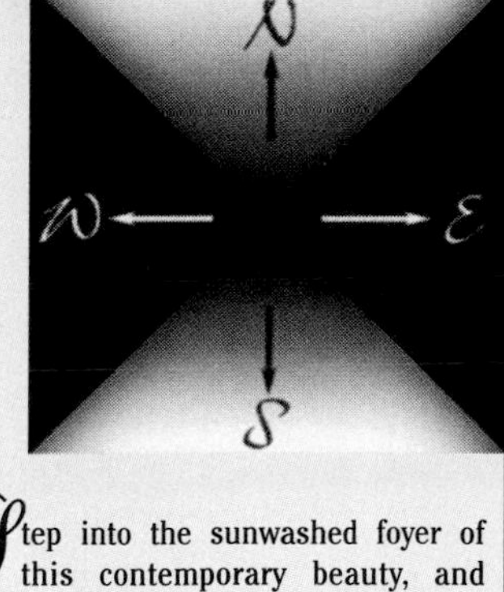
N
W
E
S

Step into the sunwashed foyer of this contemporary beauty, and you'll be faced with a choice. You can walk downstairs into a huge, fireplaced rec room with built-in bar and adjoining patio. Or, you can ascend the stairs to a massive living room with sloping ceilings, a tiled fireplace, and a commanding view of the backyard. Sharing the view, the breakfast nook with sunny bay opens to an outdoor deck. The adjoining kitchen is just steps away from the formal dining room, which features recessed ceilings and overlooks the foyer. You'll also find the master suite on this level, just past the powder room off the living room. Three more bedrooms and a full bath are located on the lower level.

An EXCLUSIVE DESIGN By Karl Kreeger

20095

Enjoy the View

first floor	1,029 sq. ft.
lower floor	1,448 sq. ft.
garage	504 sq. ft.
foundation	bsmt, slab
bedrooms	four
bathrooms	(2)full, (1)half
price code	d

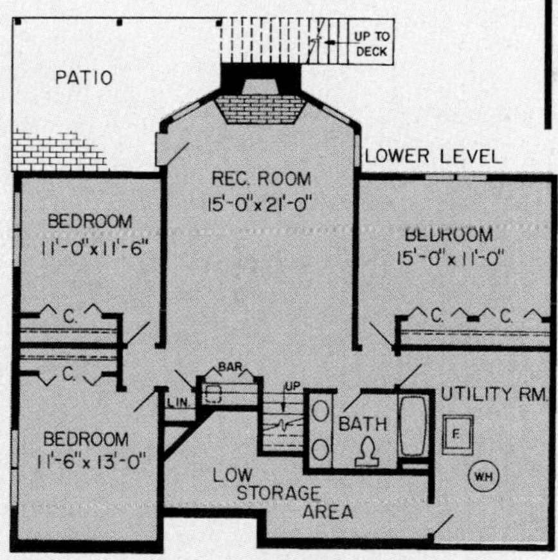
PATIO
UP TO DECK
REC. ROOM 15'-0"x 21'-0"
LOWER LEVEL
BEDROOM 11'-0"x 11'-6"
BEDROOM 15'-0"x 11'-0"
C.
C.
C.
C.
BAR
LIN.
UP
BATH
UTILITY RM.
F.
WH
BEDROOM 11'-6"x 13'-0"
LOW STORAGE AREA

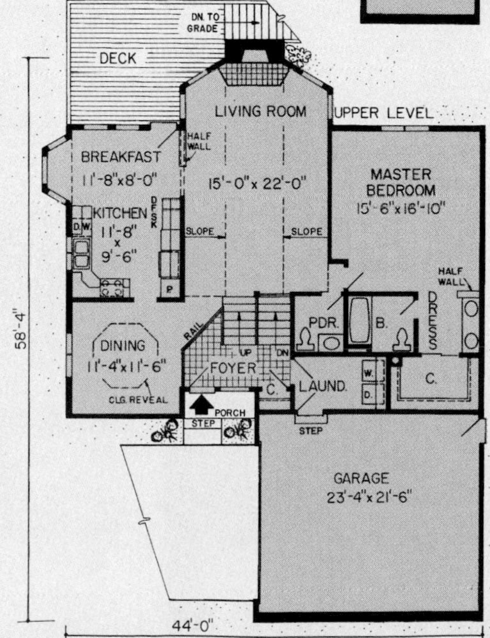
DN. TO GRADE
DECK
LIVING ROOM
UPPER LEVEL
BREAKFAST 11'-8"x 8'-0"
HALF WALL
15'-0"x 22'-0"
MASTER BEDROOM 15'-6"x 16'-10"
KITCHEN 11'-8" x 9'-6"
DESK
D.W.
SLOPE
SLOPE
P
HALF WALL
PDR.
B.
DRESS
DINING 11'-4"x 11'-6"
CLG. REVEAL
RAIL
UP
DN
FOYER
C.
LAUND.
W.
D.
C.
PORCH
STEP
STEP
GARAGE 23'-4"x 21'-6"
58'-4"
44'-0"

1,011 Square Feet

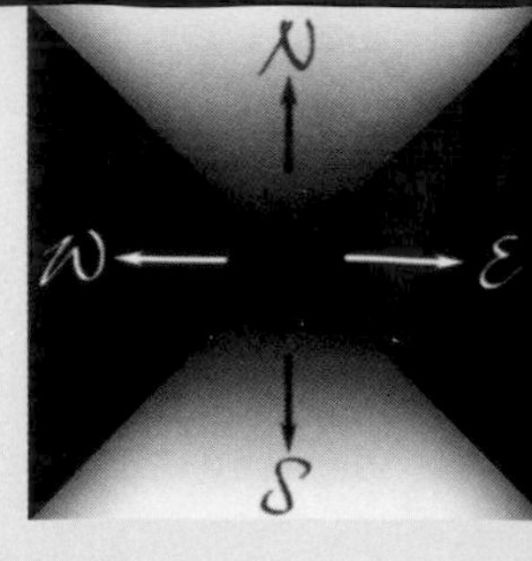
N
W
E
S

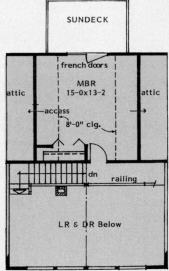

Nothing was missed when this charming little A-frame was designed. Starting at the rear entrance, there is a stacked washer and dryer, a large closet for coats and skis and even a bench to make putting on inter footwear easier. Two good sized bedrooms with plenty of closet space are in close proximity to the family bathroom. A very roomy family area at the front features an island kitchen and a spectacular vaulted ceiling. The open staircase leads up to the sleeping loft which can be either closed off as shown or open to the living area below.

9 0 9 9 5

Nothing Missed

first floor	768 sq. ft.
second floor	243 sq. ft.
foundation	crawl space
bedrooms	three
bathrooms	(1)full
Price code	a

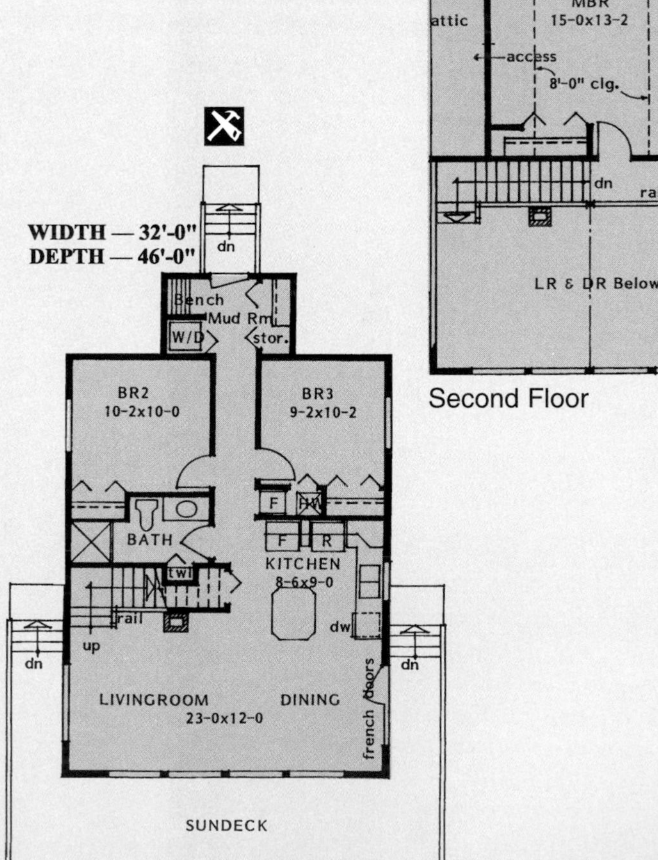
SUNDECK
french doors
MBR
15-0x13-2
attic
attic
access
8'-0" clg.
dn
railing
LR & DR Below
Second Floor
WIDTH — 32'-0"
DEPTH — 46'-0"
dn
Bench
Mud Rm
W/D
stor.
BR2
10-2x10-0
BR3
9-2x10-2
BATH
KITCHEN
8-6x9-0
rail
up
dw
dn
dn
LIVINGROOM
23-0x12-0
DINING
french doors
SUNDECK
First Floor

An EXCLUSIVE DESIGN By Westhome Planners, Ltd.

576 Square Feet

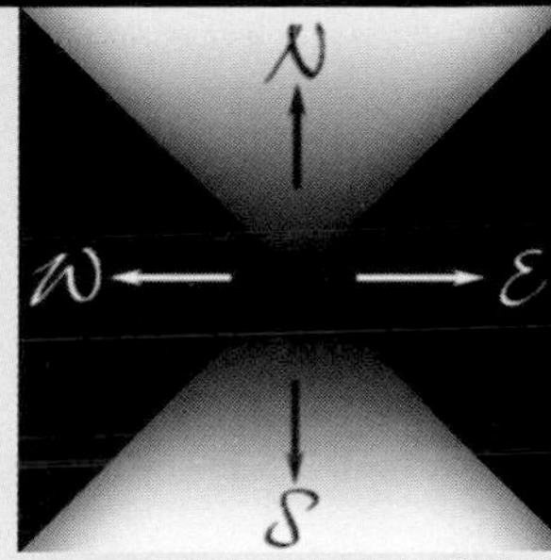

N
W
E
S

This small cabin is big on being a "homey" weekend get-away. This plan is compact yet serves four to six people comfortably. Two bedrooms share a full bathroom while each has its own closet. There is a living room that is connected to the kitchen and dining area that gives this plan an open feeling.

34075

Cozy Cabin

main floor	576 sq. ft.
foundation	slab, crawl
bedrooms	two
bathrooms	(1)full
Price code	Z

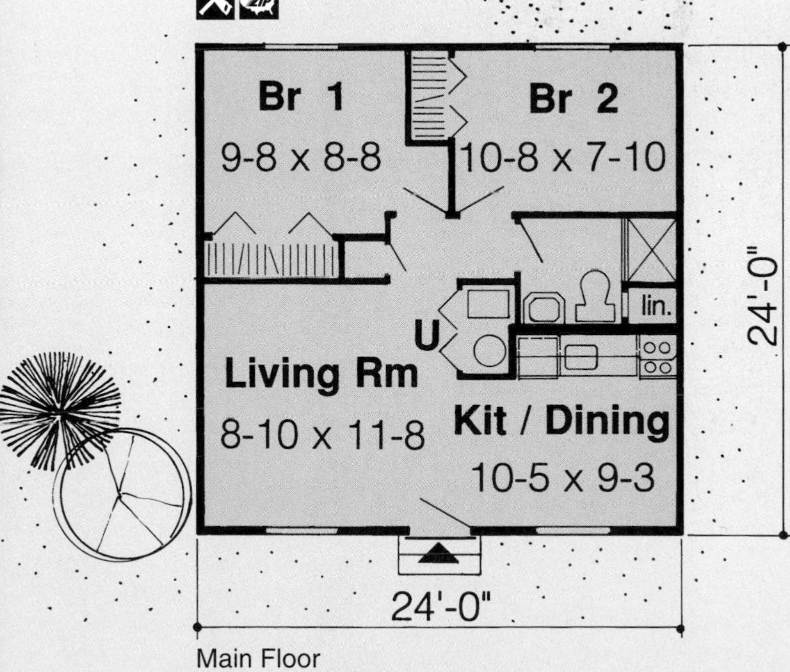

Br 1
9-8 x 8-8
Br 2
10-8 x 7-10
lin.
U
Living Rm
8-10 x 11-8
Kit / Dining
10-5 x 9-3
24'-0"
24'-0"

Main Floor

1,908 Square Feet

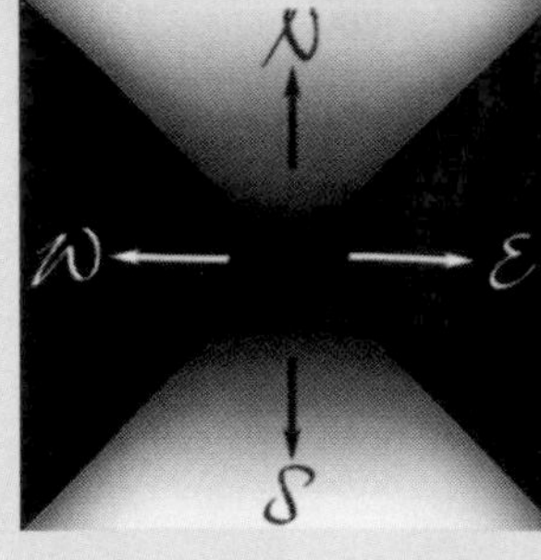

N
W
E
S

Your hillside lot is no problem if you choose this spectacular, multi-level sun-catcher. Window walls combine with sliders to unite active areas with a huge outdoor deck. Interior spaces flow together for an open feeling that's accentuated by the sloping ceilings and towering fireplace in the living room. Thanks to the island kitchen, even the cook can stay involved in the action. Walk up a short flight to reach the laundry room, a full bath, and two bedrooms, each with a walk-in closet. Up a separate staircase, you'll find the master suite, truly a private retreat complete with a garden spa, abundant closets, and balcony.

20501

Home on a Hill

first floor	1,316 sq. ft.
upper floor	592 sq. ft.
foundation	bsmt, crawl, post
bedrooms	three
bathrooms	(2)full
price code	C

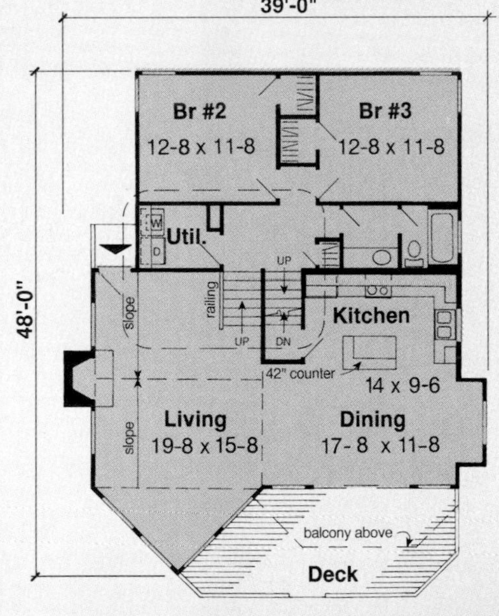

39'-0"
48'-0"
Br #2
12-8 x 11-8
Br #3
12-8 x 11-8
Util.
UP
railing
slope
UP
DN
Kitchen
42" counter
14 x 9-6
Living
19-8 x 15-8
Dining
17- 8 x 11-8
balcony above
Deck

First Floor

Pier/ Crawl Space Option

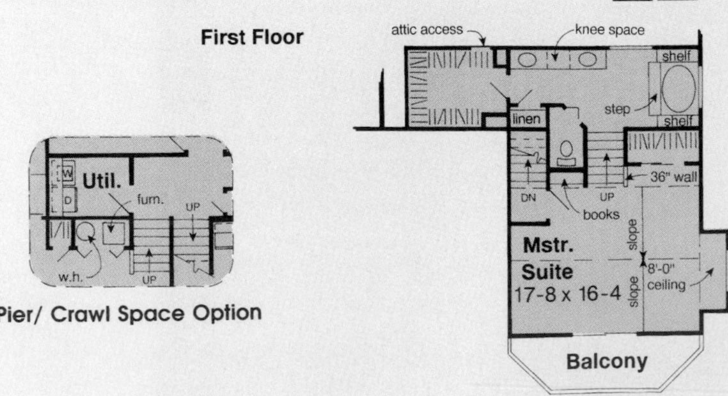

Util.
furn.
UP
w.h.
UP
attic access
knee space
shelf
step
shelf
linen
36" wall
DN
UP
books
slope
Mstr. Suite
17-8 x 16-4
8'-0" ceiling
slope
Balcony

Second Floor

1,231 Square Feet

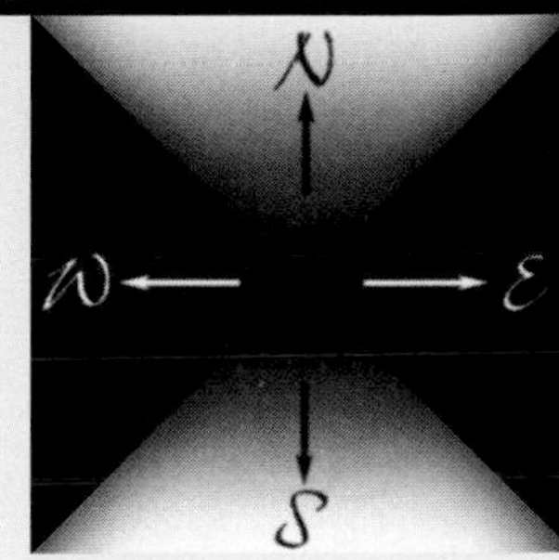
N
W
E
S

This compact vacation or retirement home packs a lot of living space into its modest square footage. The kitchen and living room are wide open for a spacious feeling when relaxing by the fire. The master bedroom enjoys privacy on the first floor while the second floor offers an additional bedroom and a loft area that can be converted to a third bedroom. There is a full bath on each floor for convenience and lots of windows or sliders to let the sun shine in.

3 4 6 2 5

Lakeside Luxury

first floor	780 sq. ft.
second floor	451 sq. ft.
basement	780 sq. ft.
foundation	bsmt, crawl, slb
bedrooms	three
bathrooms	(2)full
price code	a

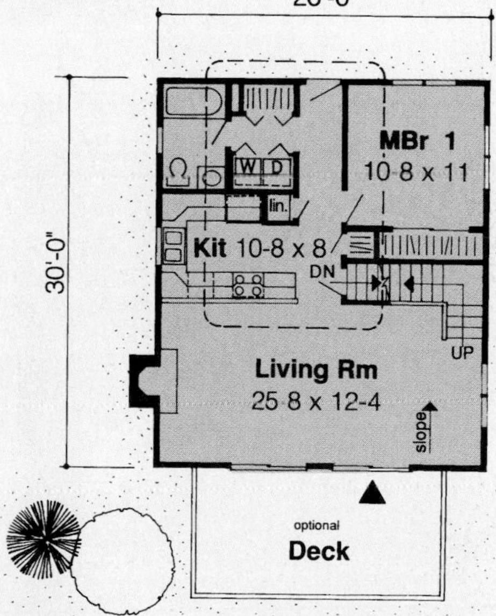
26'-0"
30'-0"
MBr 1
10-8 x 11
W D
lin.
Kit 10-8 x 8
DN
UP
Living Rm
25-8 x 12-4
slope
optional
Deck

Main Level

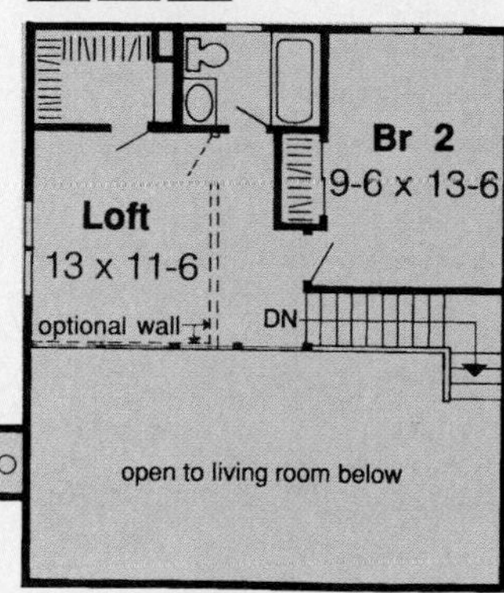
Br 2
9-6 x 13-6
Loft
13 x 11-6
optional wall
DN
open to living room below

Upper Level

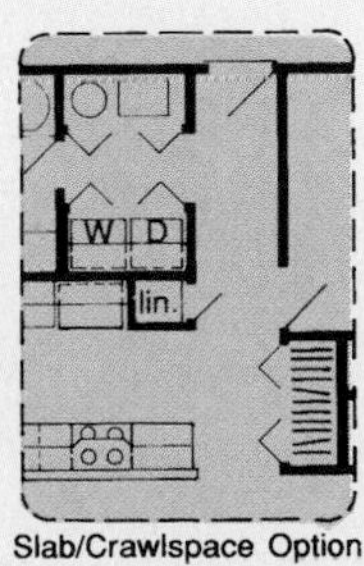
W D
lin.

Slab/Crawlspace Option

1,855 Square Feet

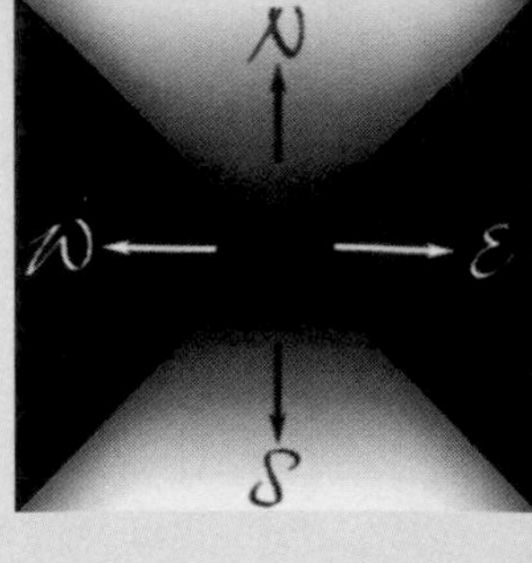
N
W
E
S

A large deck area and huge windows help this home owner to enjoy their surroundings effortlessly. Inside, the center fireplace in the Great room enhances the area with warmth and atmosphere. The dining room adjoins the Great room and the kitchen. A peninsula counter extends the work space and offers a snack bar arrangement. The master suite includes a walk-in closet, a double vanity and a shower. There is direct access to a private terrace from the bath area. Two additional, roomy bedrooms on the second floor, share the use of a full double vanity bath. A loft area over looks the Great room below. The lower level includes a recreation room, a mechanical room and unfinished storage space. No materials list is available for this plan.

24704

Good Life

first floor	913 sq. ft.
upper floor	516 sq. ft.
lower floor	426 sq. ft.
foundation	basement
bedrooms	three
bathrooms	(2)full, (1)half
Price code	C

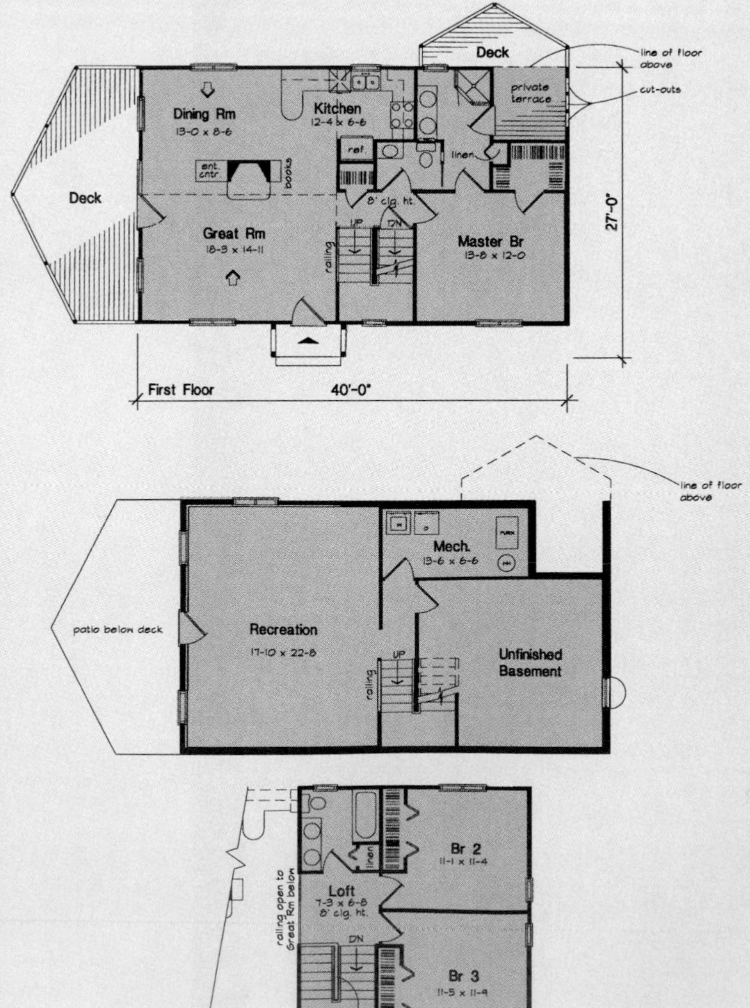
Deck
line of floor above
private terrace
cut-outs
Dining Rm
13-0 x 8-6
Kitchen
12-4 x 6-6
ref.
linen
ent. cntr.
books
Deck
8' clg. ht.
UP
DN
Great Rm
18-3 x 14-11
railing
Master Br
13-8 x 12-0
27'-0"
First Floor
40'-0"
line of floor above
Mech.
13-6 x 6-6
patio below deck
Recreation
17-10 x 22-8
UP
railing
Unfinished Basement
Br 2
11-1 x 11-4
linen
Loft
7-3 x 6-8
8' clg. ht.
railing open to Great Rm below
DN
Br 3
11-5 x 11-4
1/2 wall
Second Floor

1,440 Square Feet

Wrap-around decks, sliding glass doors, and lots of windows accent this coastal styled design. The sliding glass doors provide the entrance and the great view on two sides of the home. The efficient kitchen runs in an L-shape to the living room and dining area providing an open, spacious feeling with lots of natural light flowing in. The three bedrooms are to the right of the living/dining area. The master bedroom has its own private bath and the secondary bedrooms share the hall bath. Upstairs, the loft area provides extra living space or perhaps a studio or hobby room. This plan is available with a pole, slab or crawl space foundation. Please specify when ordering.

92801

Beach Bound

first floor	1,296 sq. ft.
loft	144 sq. ft.
foundation	pole, slab, crawl
bedrooms	three
bathrooms	(2)full
price code	a

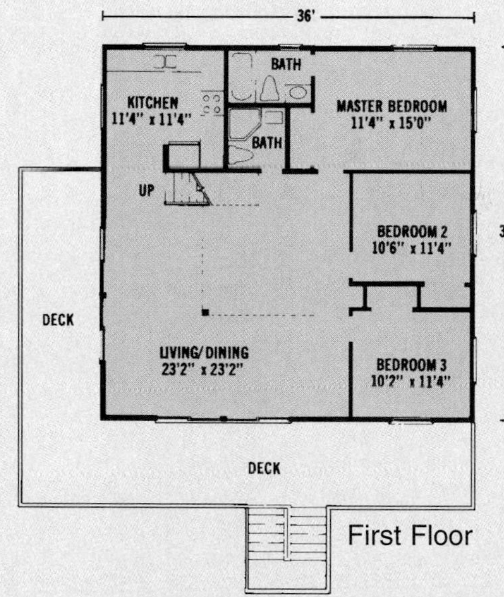
36'
BATH
KITCHEN
11'4" x 11'4"
MASTER BEDROOM
11'4" x 15'0"
BATH
UP
BEDROOM 2
10'6" x 11'4"
36'
DECK
LIVING/DINING
23'2" x 23'2"
BEDROOM 3
10'2" x 11'4"
DECK

First Floor

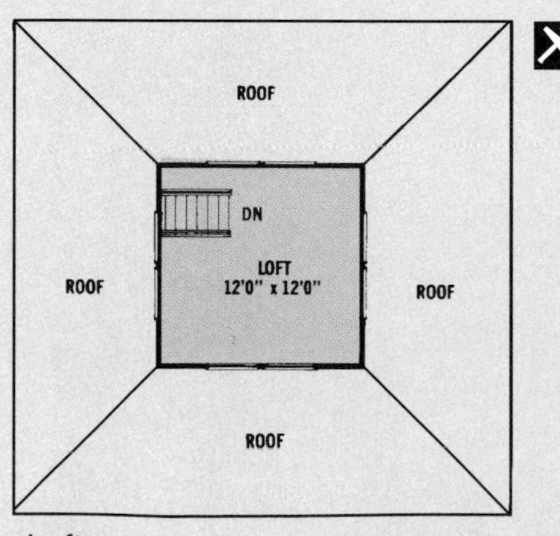
ROOF
DN
LOFT
12'0" x 12'0"
ROOF
ROOF
ROOF

Loft

966 Square Feet

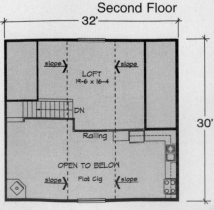

This cabin will be your home away from home in all seasons. A large deck wraps around the cabin, and is perfect for sitting and enjoying the scenery. The deck has a convenient wood storage bin located in close proximity to the wood stove inside. The large living room has a sloped ceiling and is open to the loft above. The L-shaped kitchen is fully appointed with everything that you would expect from your kitchen at home. Downstairs find two large bedrooms with closets. A full bath rounds out the main level. There is a utility closet for the mechanicals and a separate access for the crawl space. Upstairs find a spacious loft with a sloped ceiling. You and your family will surely enjoy vacationing in this home.

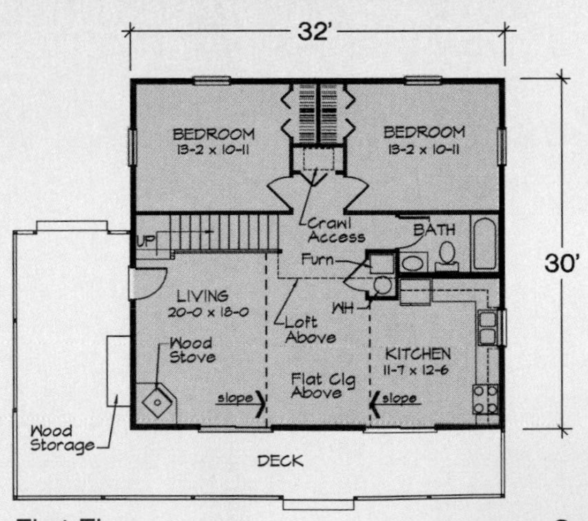

2001

Lakeside Leisure

first floor	728 sq. ft.
upper floor	238 sq. ft.
deck	378 sq. ft.
foundation	crawl, slab
bedrooms	two
bathrooms	(1)full
Price code	Z

32'

30'

BEDROOM 13-2 x 10-11

BEDROOM 13-2 x 10-11

Crawl Access

BATH

UP

Furn

WH

LIVING 20-0 x 18-0

Loft Above

Wood Stove

KITCHEN 11-7 x 12-6

Flat Clg Above

slope

slope

Wood Storage

DECK

First Floor

Second Floor

32'

30'

slope

slope

LOFT 19-6 x 16-4

DN

Railing

OPEN TO BELOW

slope

Flat Clg

slope

1,469 Square Feet

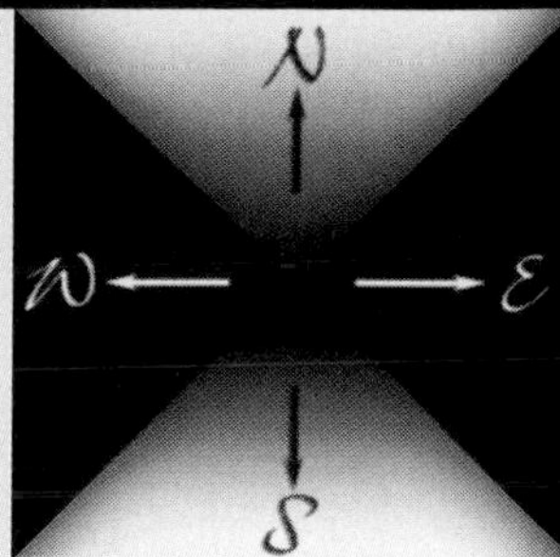

N
W
E
S

Numerous south-facing glass doors and windows, skylights and a greenhouse clue the exterior viewer to this passive solar contemporary design. For minimum heat loss, 2x6 studs for R-19 insulation are used in exterior walls, and R-33 insulation is used in all sloping ceilings. The living room employs a concrete slab floor for solar gain. Basement space is located under the kitchen, dining room, lower bedroom and den. A northern entrance through a vestibule and French doors channels you upward to the first floor living area. A unique feature on this level is the skylit living room ceiling which slants two stories. Second story rooms are lit by clerestory windows. Two balconies are on this level: an exterior one off the bedroom and an interior one overlooking the living room.

26110

Passive Solar

first floor	902 sq. ft.
second floor	567 sq. ft.
foundation	basement
bedrooms	three
bathrooms	(1)full, (1)half
price code	a

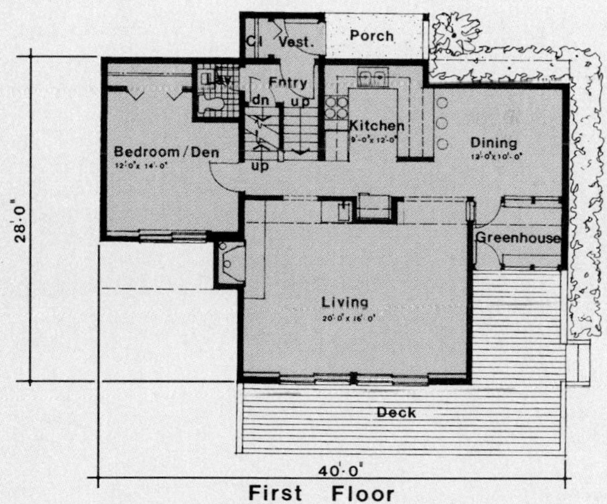

Cl
Vest.
Porch
Lav
Entry
dn
up
Kitchen
Dining
Bedroom/Den
up
28'-0"
Greenhouse
Living
Deck
40'-0"
First Floor

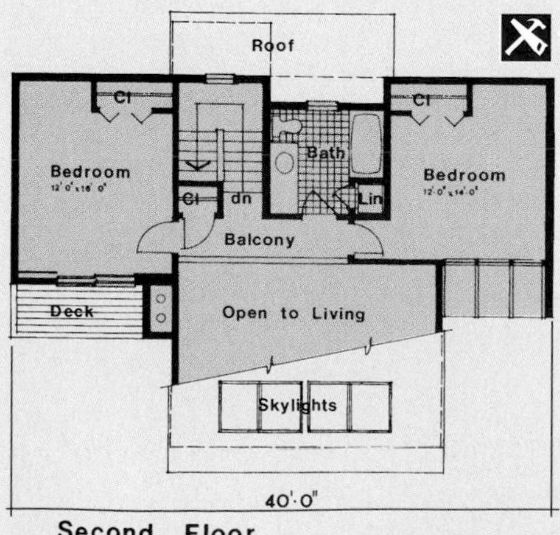

Roof
Cl
Cl
Bedroom
Bath
Bedroom
Cl
dn
Lin
Balcony
Deck
Open to Living
Skylights
40'-0"
Second Floor

1,956 Square Feet

This romantic chalet design would be equally appealing along an ocean beach or mountain stream. Restful log fires will add atmosphere in the sizable recreation room bordering the patio of this chalet. Upstairs, another fireplace warms the living and dining rooms which are accessible to the large wooden sun deck. Four bedrooms and two baths are outlined. The home is completely insulated for year round convenience and contains washer and dryer space.

9964

Welcoming Chalet

first floor	906 sq. ft.
second floor	456 sq. ft.
lower floor	594 sq. ft.
basement	279 sq. ft.
foundation	basement
bedrooms	four
bathrooms	(2)full
price code	C

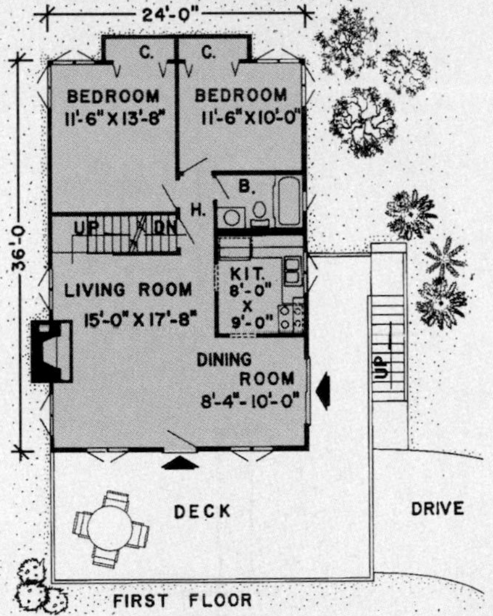

24'-0"
C.
C.
BEDROOM 11'-6" X 13'-8"
BEDROOM 11'-6" X 10'-0"
B.
H.
UP
DN
36'-0
KIT. 8'-0" X 9'-0"
LIVING ROOM 15'-0" X 17'-8"
DINING ROOM 8'-4"- 10'-0"
UP
DECK
DRIVE
FIRST FLOOR

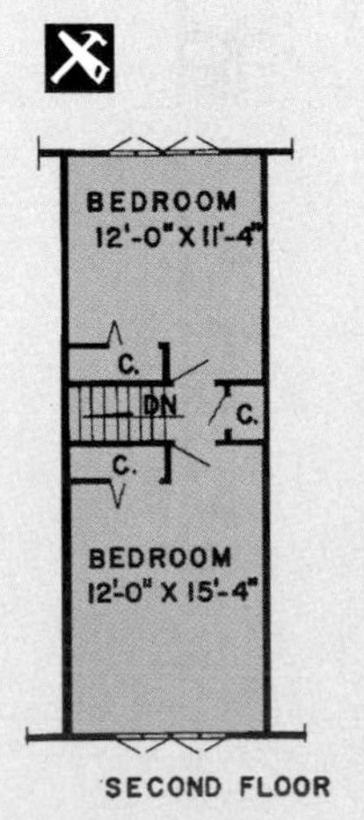

BEDROOM 12'-0" X 11'-4"
C.
DN.
C.
C.
BEDROOM 12'-0" X 15'-4"
SECOND FLOOR

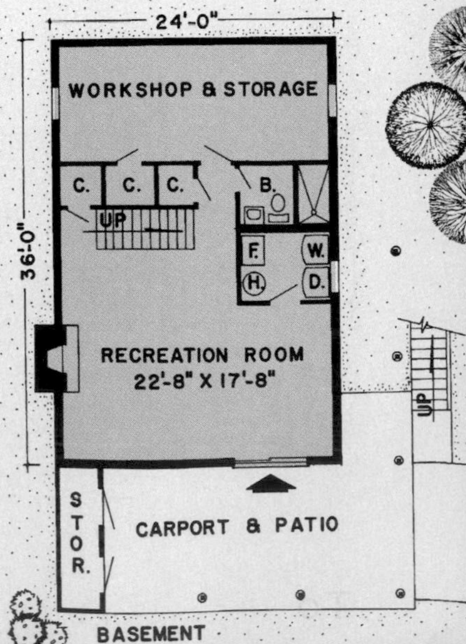

24'-0"
WORKSHOP & STORAGE
C.
C.
C.
B.
UP
36'-0"
F.
W.
H.
D.
RECREATION ROOM 22'-8" X 17'-8"
UP
STOR.
CARPORT & PATIO
BASEMENT

Refer to **Pricing Schedule C** on the order form for pricing information

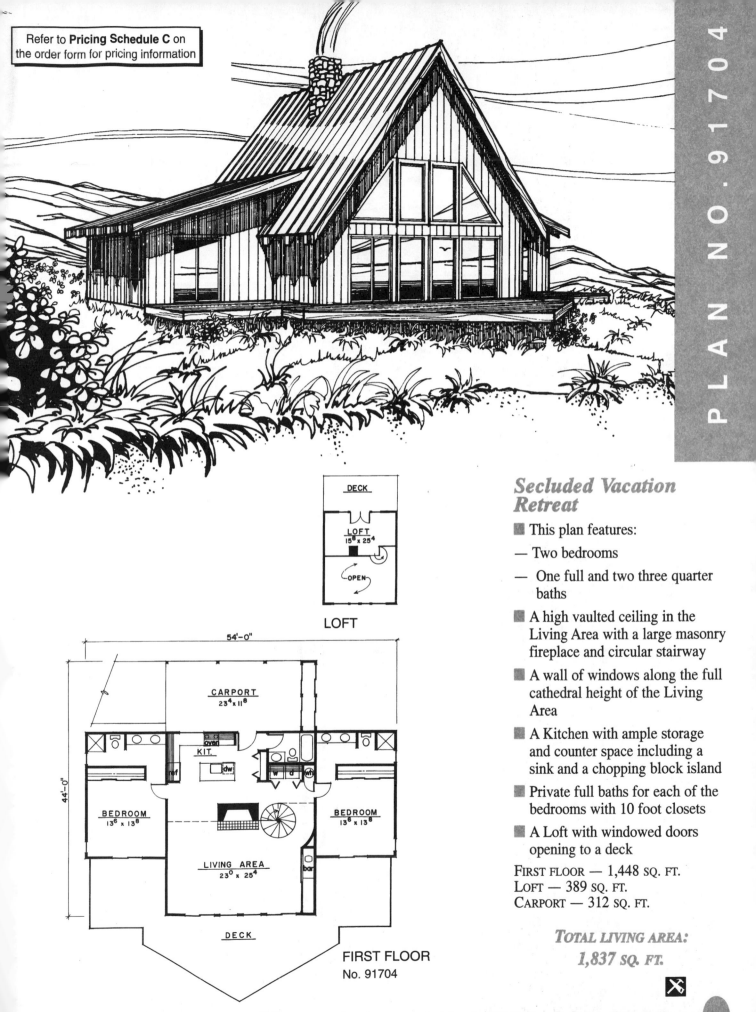

PLAN NO. 91704

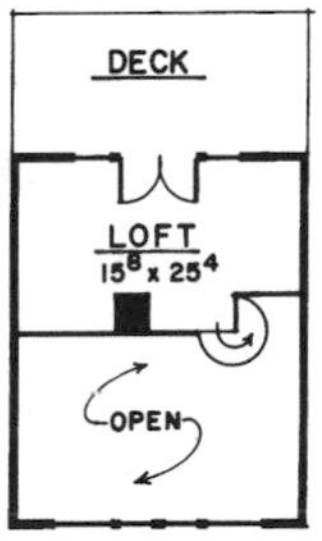

LOFT

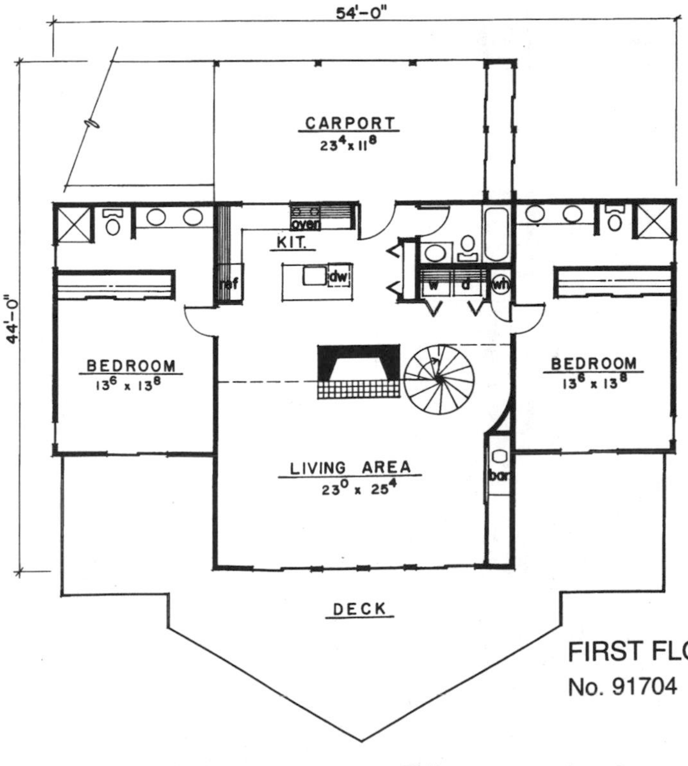

FIRST FLOOR
No. 91704

Secluded Vacation Retreat

- This plan features:

— Two bedrooms

— One full and two three quarter baths

- A high vaulted ceiling in the Living Area with a large masonry fireplace and circular stairway
- A wall of windows along the full cathedral height of the Living Area
- A Kitchen with ample storage and counter space including a sink and a chopping block island
- Private full baths for each of the bedrooms with 10 foot closets
- A Loft with windowed doors opening to a deck

FIRST FLOOR — 1,448 SQ. FT.
LOFT — 389 SQ. FT.
CARPORT — 312 SQ. FT.

TOTAL LIVING AREA: 1,837 SQ. FT.

Refer to **Pricing Schedule A** on the order form for pricing information

PLAN NO. 24304

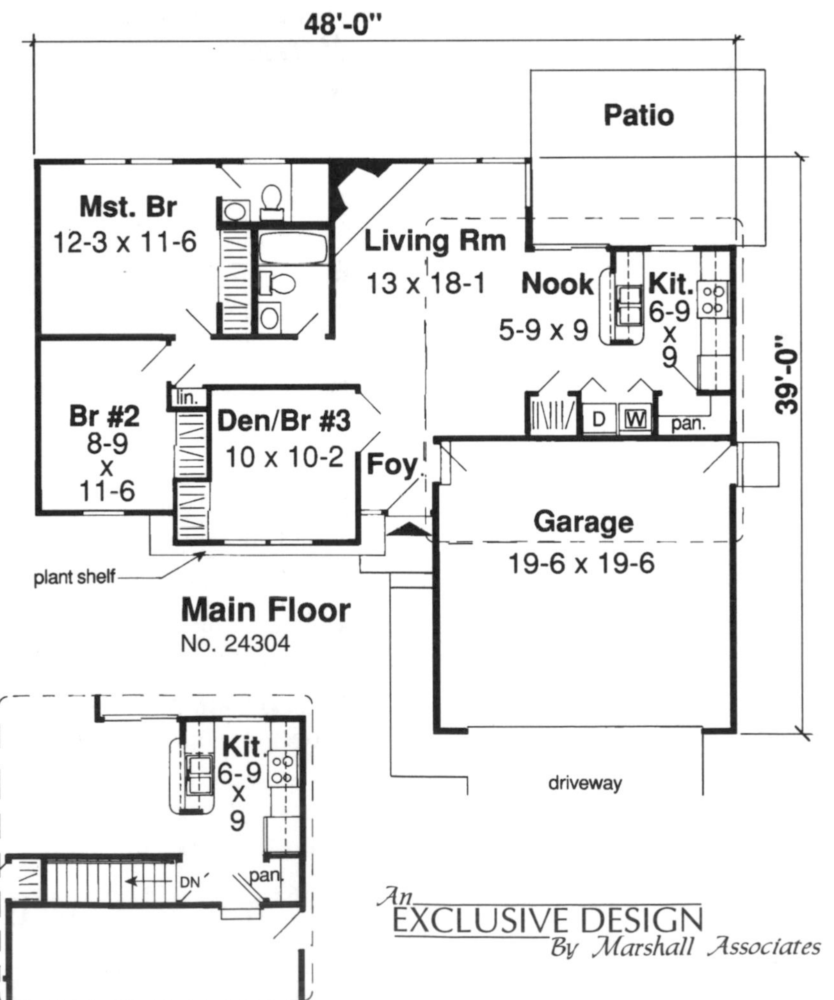

48'-0"
Patio
Mst. Br
12-3 x 11-6
Living Rm
13 x 18-1
Nook
5-9 x 9
Kit.
6-9
x
9
39'-0"
lin.
Br #2
8-9
x
11-6
Den/Br #3
10 x 10-2
Foy
D
W
pan.
Garage
19-6 x 19-6
plant shelf
Main Floor
No. 24304
driveway
Kit.
6-9
x
9
DN
pan.
Basement Option
An
EXCLUSIVE DESIGN
By Marshall Associates

Large Living in a Small Space

- This plan features:
  - — Three bedrooms
  - — Two full baths
- A sheltered entrance leads into an open Living Room with a corner fireplace and a wall of windows
- A well-equipped Kitchen features a peninsula counter with a Nook, a laundry and clothes closet, and a built-in pantry
- A Master Bedroom with a private bath
- Two additional bedrooms that share full hall bath

MAIN FLOOR — 993 SQ. FT.
GARAGE — 390 SQ. FT.
BASEMENT — 987 SQ. FT.

TOTAL LIVING AREA:
993 SQ. FT.

Refer to **Pricing Schedule B** on the order form for pricing information

PLAN NO. 34055

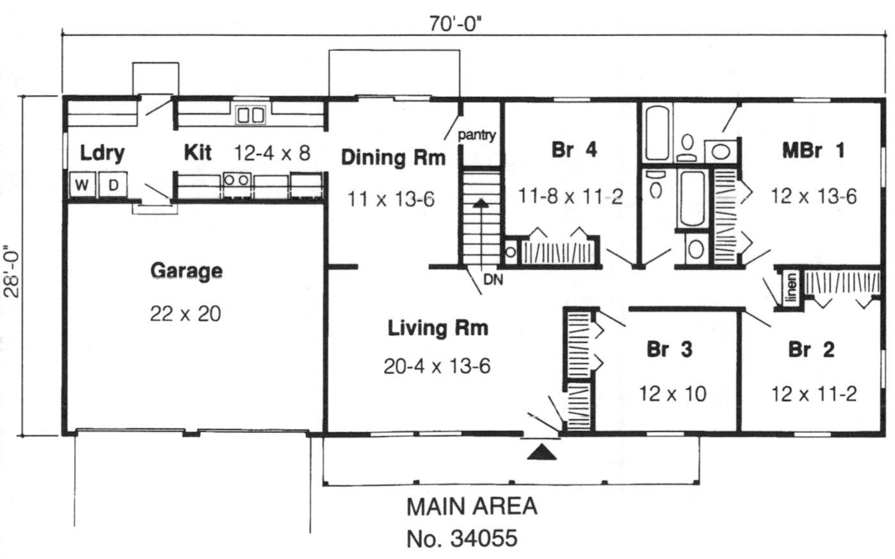

70'-0"
28'-0"
Ldry
W D
Kit 12-4 x 8
Dining Rm
11 x 13-6
pantry
Br 4
11-8 x 11-2
MBr 1
12 x 13-6
Garage
22 x 20
DN
linen
Living Rm
20-4 x 13-6
Br 3
12 x 10
Br 2
12 x 11-2
MAIN AREA
No. 34055

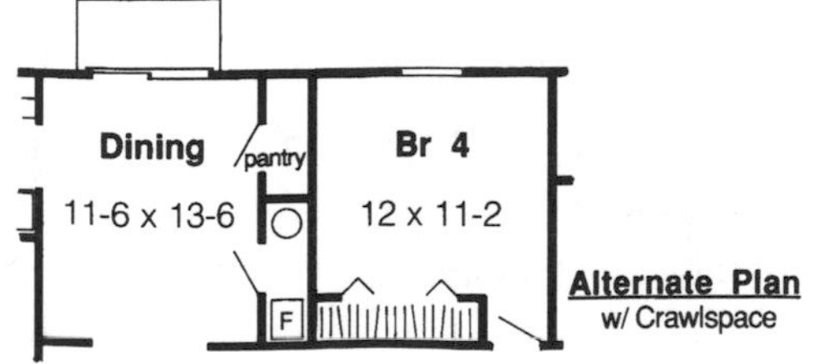

Dining
11-6 x 13-6
pantry
Br 4
12 x 11-2
F
Alternate Plan
w/ Crawlspace

Ranch Provides Great Floor Plan

- This plan features:
  - — Four bedrooms
  - — Two full baths
- A large Living Room and Dining Room flowing together into one open space for perfect entertaining
- A Laundry area, which doubles as a mudroom, off the Kitchen
- A Master Suite including a private bath
- A two-car Garage

MAIN AREA — 1,527 SQ. FT.
BASEMENT — 1,344 SQ. FT.
GARAGE — 425 SQ. FT.

TOTAL LIVING AREA:
1,527 SQ. FT.

PLAN NO. 20156

Refer to **Pricing Schedule A** on the order form for pricing information

Family Favorite

- This plan features:
- — Three bedrooms
- — Two full baths
- An open arrangement with the Dining Room that combines with ten foot ceilings to make the Living Room seem more spacious
- Glass on three sides of the Dining Room which overlooks the deck
- An efficient, compact Kitchen with a built-in pantry and peninsula counter
- A Master Suite with a window seat, a compartmentalized private bath and a walk-in closet
- Two additional bedrooms that share a full hall closet

MAIN AREA — 1,359 SQ. FT.
BASEMENT — 1,359 SQ. FT.
GARAGE — 501 SQ. FT.

An EXCLUSIVE DESIGN By Karl Kreeger

TOTAL LIVING AREA:
1,359 SQ. FT.

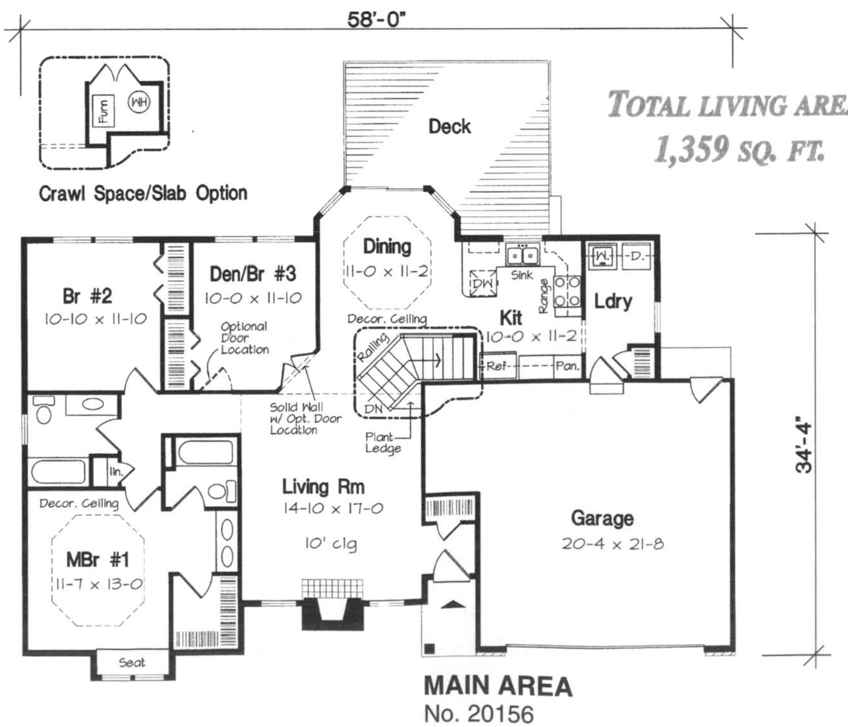

58'-0"
Deck
Crawl Space/Slab Option
Furn
WH
Dining
11-0 x 11-2
Den/Br #3
10-0 x 11-10
Br #2
10-10 x 11-10
Optional Door Location
Decor. Ceiling
Railing
DN
Sink
DW
Range
Kit
10-0 x 11-2
Ref
Pan.
Ldry
Solid Wall w/ Opt. Door Location
Plant Ledge
lin.
Decor. Ceiling
Living Rm
14-10 x 17-0
10' clg
MBr #1
11-7 x 13-0
Seat
Garage
20-4 x 21-8
34'-4"

MAIN AREA
No. 20156

To order your Blueprints, call 1-800-235-5700

Refer to **Pricing Schedule A** on the order form for pricing information

PLAN NO. 34328

Compact Ranch Loaded with Living Space

- This plan features:

— Three bedrooms

— One full bath

- A central entrance, opening to the Living Room with ample windows
- A Kitchen, featuring a Breakfast area with sliding doors to the backyard and an optional deck

MAIN AREA — 1,092 SQ. FT.
BASEMENT — 1,092 SQ. FT.

TOTAL LIVING AREA:
1,092 SQ. FT.

ALTERNATE FLOOR PLAN
for Crawl Space

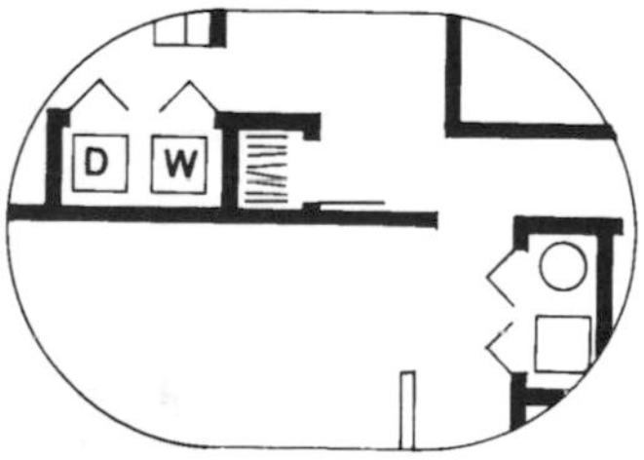

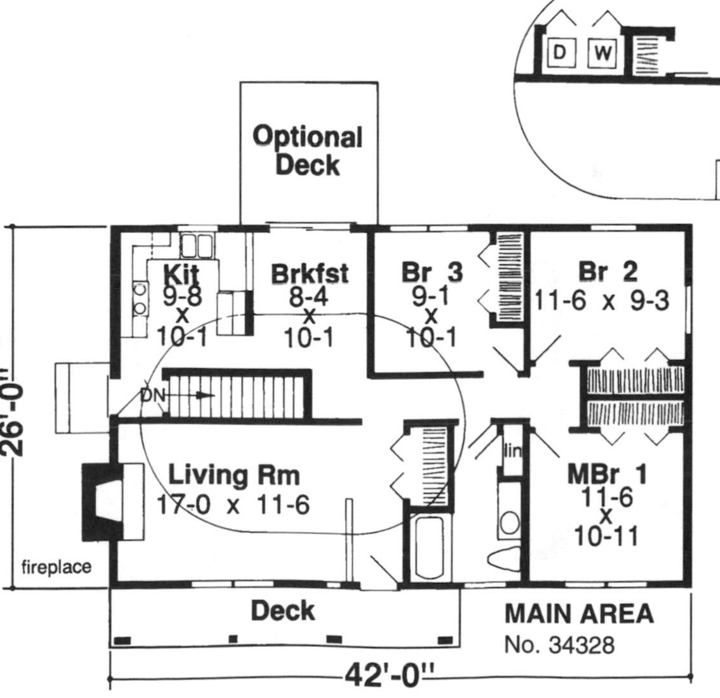

Optional Deck
Kit 9-8 x 10-1
Brkfst 8-4 x 10-1
Br 3 9-1 x 10-1
Br 2 11-6 x 9-3
DN
Living Rm 17-0 x 11-6
lin
MBr 1 11-6 x 10-11
26'-0"
fireplace
Deck
42'-0"
MAIN AREA
No. 34328

PLAN NO. 9107

Refer to **Pricing Schedule C** on the order form for pricing information

Angled for Views

- This plan features:

— Four bedrooms

— Two full baths

- A large Foyer leading into the Living Room, the Family Room and the Kitchen
- A spacious Living Room with large windows and a sliding glass door to the Balcony, shared by the Family Room with the same features
- An efficient, U-shaped Kitchen with a laundry and eating space
- A Master Bedroom suite with an over-sized closet and a vanity bath
- Two additional bedrooms with ample closets, sharing a full hall bath

MAIN FLOOR — 2,051 SQ. FT.
BASEMENT — 1,380 SQ. FT.
GARAGE — 671 SQ. FT.

TOTAL LIVING AREA:
2,051 SQ. FT.

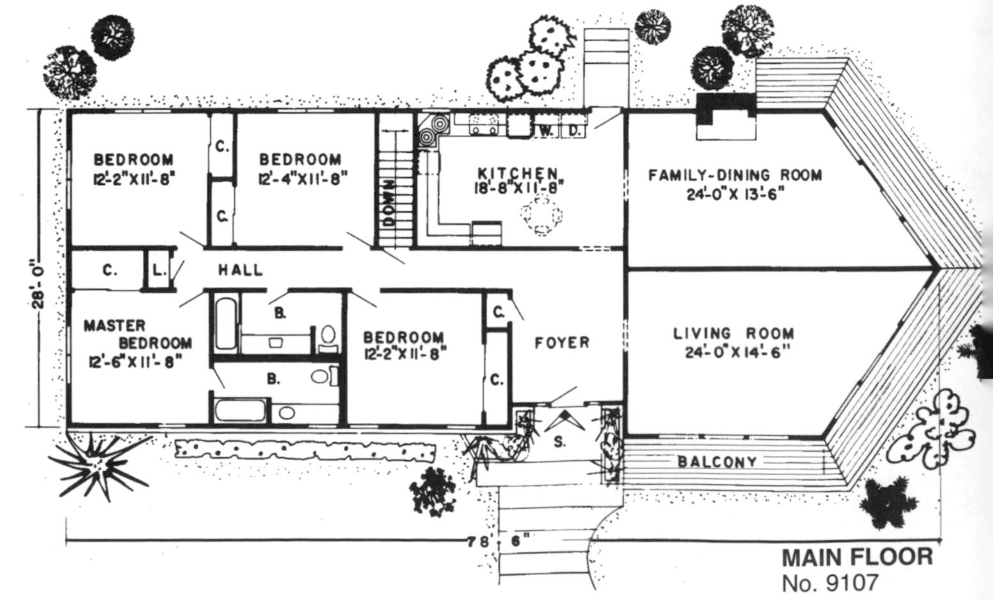
BEDROOM
12'-2"X11'-8"
C.
C.
BEDROOM
12'-4"X11'-8"
DOWN
KITCHEN
18'-8"X11'-8"
W. D.
FAMILY-DINING ROOM
24'-0"X 13'-6"
C.
L.
HALL
28'-0"
MASTER BEDROOM
12'-6"X 11'-8"
B.
B.
BEDROOM
12'-2"X 11'-8"
C.
C.
FOYER
LIVING ROOM
24'-0"X 14'-6"
S.
BALCONY
78'-6"

MAIN FLOOR
No. 9107

To order your Blueprints, call 1-800-235-5700

Refer to **Pricing Schedule A** on the order form for pricing information

PLAN NO. 10228

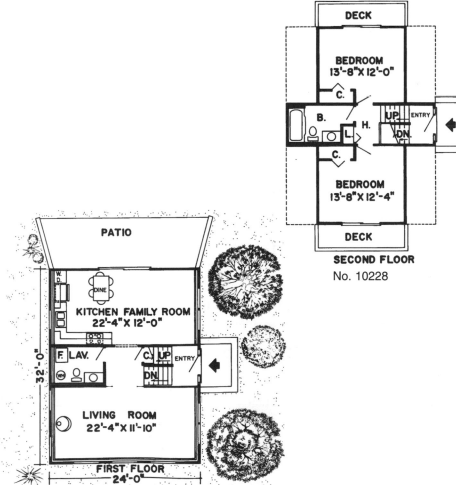

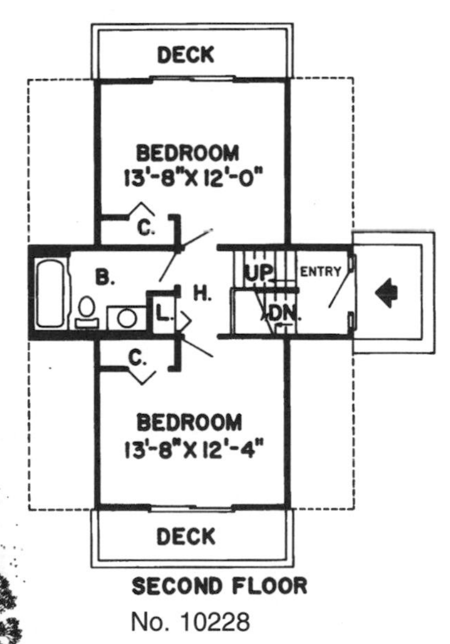
DECK
BEDROOM
13'-8"X 12'-0"
C.
B.
H.
L.
UP
DN.
ENTRY
C.
BEDROOM
13'-8"X 12'-4"
DECK
SECOND FLOOR

No. 10228

PATIO

W. D.

DINE

KITCHEN FAMILY ROOM
22'-4"X 12'-0"

F. LAV.

WH

C. UP

ENTRY

DN.

32'-0"

LIVING ROOM
22'-4"X 11'-10"

FIRST FLOOR
24'-0"

Unusual A-Frame

- This plan features:
  - — Two bedrooms
  - — One and a half baths
- A covered Entry leading down to a large Living Room with a cheerful, metal fircplace
- An L-shaped Kitchen opening into a Family Room with sliding glass doors to the Patio
- An upper level with two spacious bedrooms and private Decks sharing a full hall bath

FIRST FLOOR — 768 SQ. FT.
SECOND FLOOR — 521 SQ. FT.

TOTAL LIVING AREA:
1,289 SQ. FT.

PLAN NO. 34029

Refer to **Pricing Schedule B** on the order form for pricing information

Skylight Brightens Master Bedroom

- This plan features:
- — Three bedrooms
- — Two full baths
- A covered-porch entry
- A foyer separating the Dining Room from the Breakfast area and Kitchen
- A Living Room enhanced by a vaulted beam ceiling and a fireplace
- A Master Bedroom with a decorative ceiling and a skylight in the private bath
- An optional deck accessible through sliding doors off the Master Bedroom

MAIN FLOOR — 1,686 SQ. FT.
GARAGE — 484 SQ. FT.
BASEMENT — 1,676 SQ. FT.

TOTAL LIVING AREA:
1,686 SQ. FT.

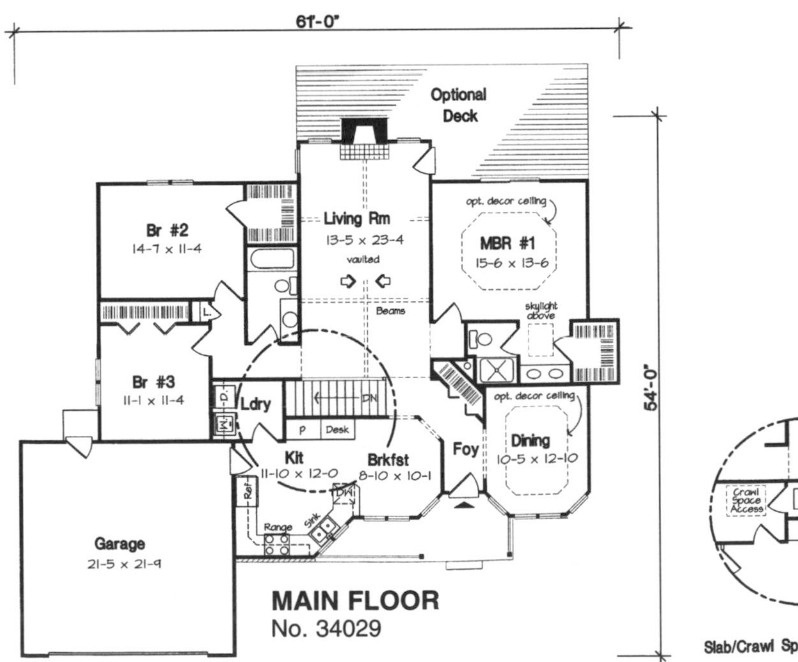
61'-0"
Optional Deck
Living Rm
13-5 x 23-4
vaulted
Beams
Br #2
14-7 x 11-4
opt. decor ceiling
MBR #1
15-6 x 13-6
skylight above
Br #3
11-1 x 11-4
Ldry
DN
P Desk
opt. decor ceiling
Kit
11-10 x 12-0
Brkfst
8-10 x 10-1
Foy
Dining
10-5 x 12-10
Ref
Range
Sink
DW
Garage
21-5 x 21-9
54'-0"
Crawl Space Access
Furn
HH
P Desk
Slab/Crawl Space Option

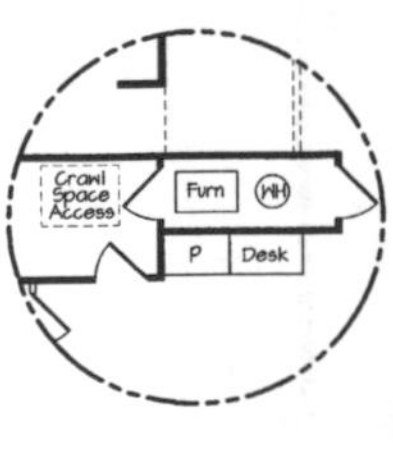

MAIN FLOOR
No. 34029

An
EXCLUSIVE DESIGN
By Karl Kreeger

To order your Blueprints, call 1-800-235-5700

Refer to **Pricing Schedule B** on the order form for pricing information

PLAN NO. 20110

An EXCLUSIVE DESIGN *By Karl Kreeger*

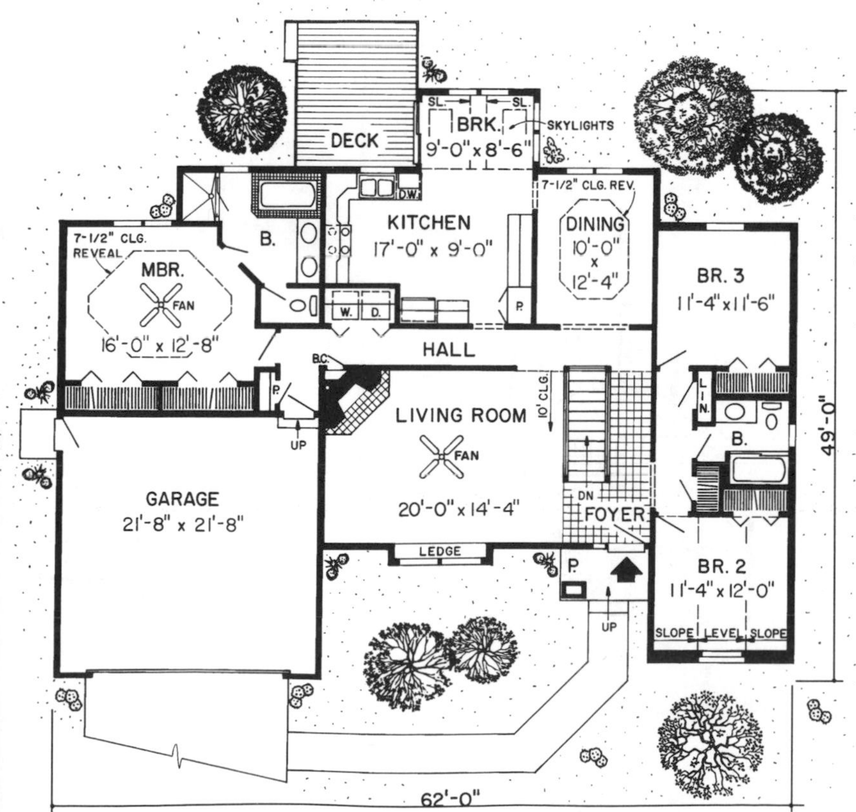

DECK
BRK.
9'-0" x 8'-6"
SL
SKYLIGHTS
DW
KITCHEN
17'-0" x 9'-0"
7-1/2" CLG. REV.
DINING
10'-0" x 12'-4"
7-1/2" CLG. REVEAL
MBR.
FAN
16'-0" x 12'-8"
B.
W.
D.
P.
HALL
B.C.
BR. 3
11'-4" x 11'-6"
LIN.
B.
LIVING ROOM
10' CLG.
FAN
20'-0" x 14'-4"
LEDGE
UP
GARAGE
21'-8" x 21'-8"
DN
FOYER
BR. 2
11'-4" x 12'-0"
SLOPE
LEVEL
SLOPE
49'-0"
62'-0"

MAIN FLOOR
No. 20110

Classic and Convenient

- This plan features:
  - — Three bedrooms
  - — Two full baths
- Clapboard and brick lending curbside appeal
- A spacious Living Room dominated by a corner fireplace
- A hallway off the foyer, leading to the two additional bedrooms
- A formal Dining Room and a sky-lit Breakfast Nook adjoining the Kitchen
- A rear deck perfect for summer barbecues or relaxing
- A Master Suite with a double vanity, a raised bath and a walk-in shower

MAIN AREA — 1,786 SQ. FT.
BASEMENT — 1,786 SQ. FT.
GARAGE — 484 SQ. FT.

TOTAL LIVING AREA:
1,786 SQ. FT.

PLAN NO. 26113

Refer to **Pricing Schedule A** on the order form for pricing information

Roof Lines Attract the Eye

- This plan features:
- — Three bedrooms
- — One full and three quarter bath
- Unusual roof lines which are both pleasing and balanced
- An open floor plan shared by the Kitchen, Dining Room, Living Room and split entry spaces
- An optional Den/Bedroom on the first floor
- A wrap-around deck and two-car Garage adding the finishing touches to this design

FIRST FLOOR — 846 SQ. FT.
SECOND FLOOR — 492 SQ. FT.
BASEMENT — 846 SQ. FT.
GARAGE — 540 SQ. FT.
DECK — 423 SQ. FT.

TOTAL LIVING AREA:
1,338 SQ. FT.

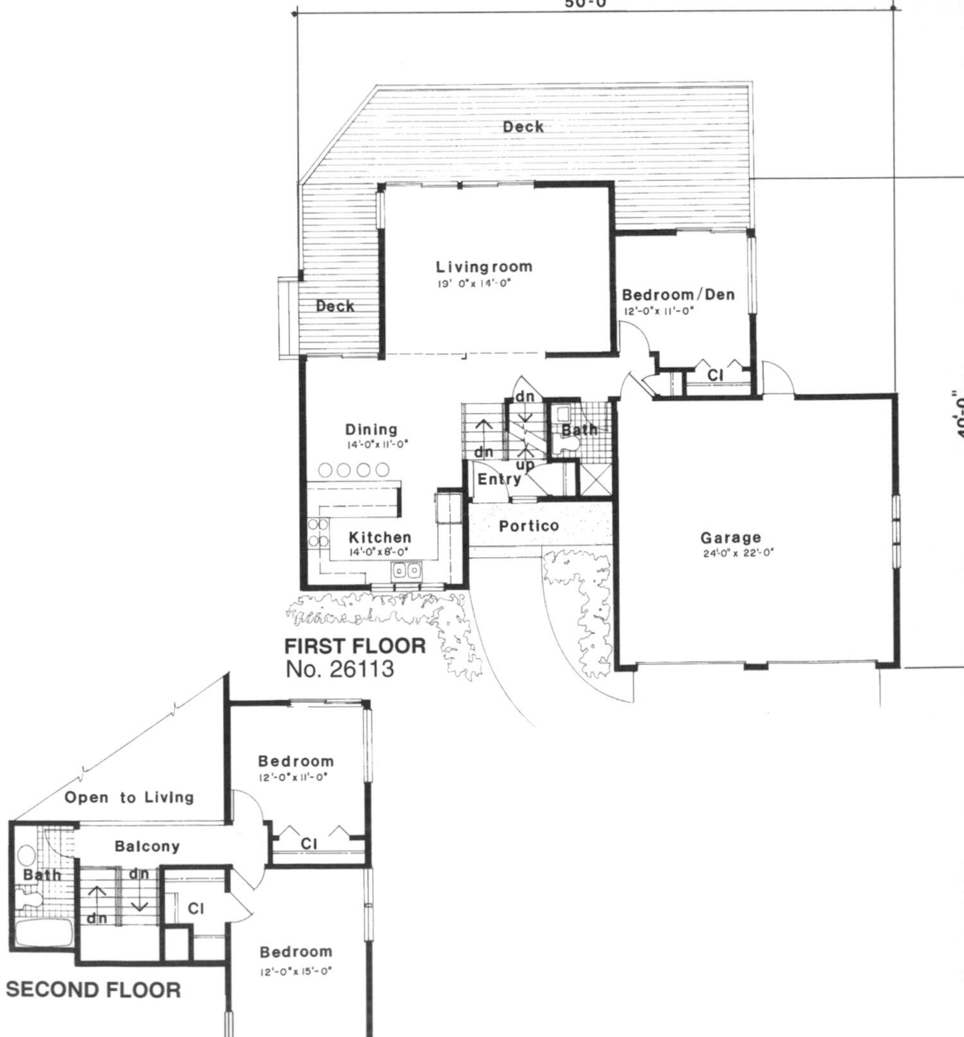
50'-0"
40'-0"
Deck
Deck
Livingroom
19' 0" x 14'-0"
Bedroom/Den
12'-0" x 11'-0"
Cl
dn
Dining
14'-0" x 11'-0"
Bath
dn
up
Entry
Kitchen
14'-0" x 8'-0"
Portico
Garage
24'-0" x 22'-0"
FIRST FLOOR
No. 26113
Open to Living
Bedroom
12'-0" x 11'-0"
Balcony
Cl
Bath
dn
dn
Cl
Bedroom
12'-0" x 15'-0"
SECOND FLOOR

To order your Blueprints, call 1-800-235-5700

Refer to **Pricing Schedule A** on the order form for pricing information

PLAN NO. 90288

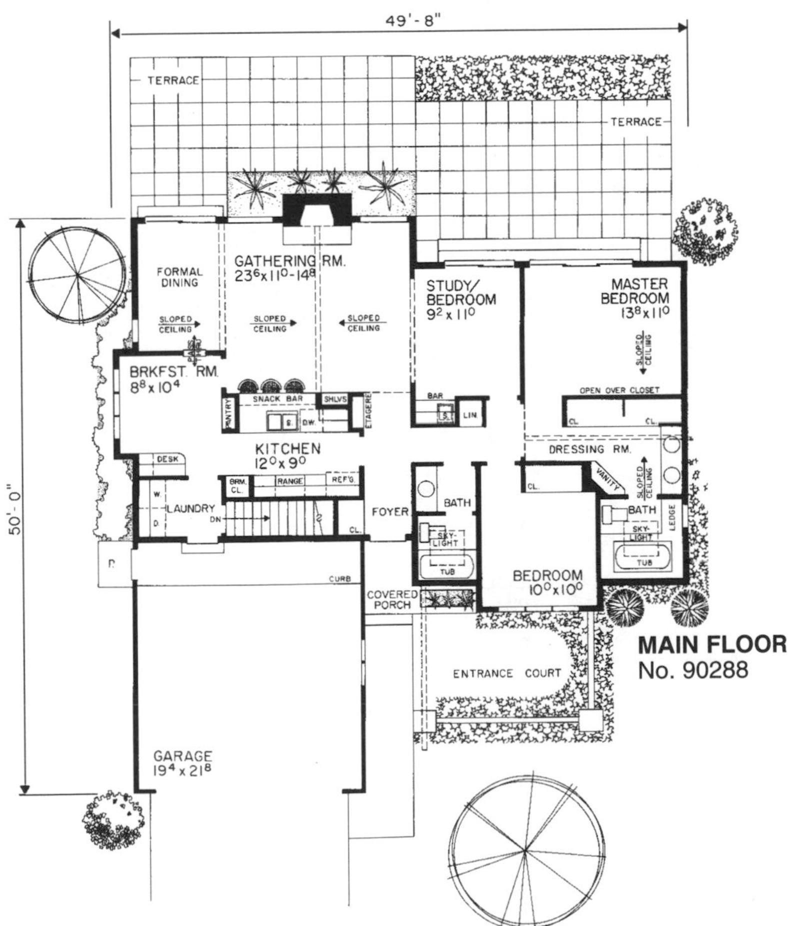

49'-8"
TERRACE
TERRACE
FORMAL DINING
GATHERING RM.
$23^6 \times 11^0$-14^8
SLOPED CEILING
SLOPED CEILING
SLOPED CEILING
STUDY/ BEDROOM
$9^2 \times 11^0$
MASTER BEDROOM
$13^8 \times 11^0$
SLOPED CEILING
OPEN OVER CLOSET
BRKFST RM.
$8^8 \times 10^4$
SNACK BAR
SHLVS
PANTRY
ETAGERE
BAR
LIN
CL
CL
KITCHEN
$12^0 \times 9^0$
DESK
RANGE
REF'G.
DRESSING RM.
VANITY
CL.
LAUNDRY
DN
FOYER
BATH
CL
SKY-LIGHT
TUB
BATH
SKY-LIGHT
TUB
LEDGE
50'-0"
CURB
COVERED PORCH
BEDROOM
$10^0 \times 10^0$
ENTRANCE COURT
GARAGE
$19^4 \times 21^8$

MAIN FLOOR
No. 90288

Soaring Ceilings Add Space and Drama

- This plan features:
- — Two bedrooms (with optional third bedroom)
- — Two full baths
- A sunny Master Suite with a sloping ceiling, private terrace entry, and luxurious garden bath with an adjoining Dressing Room
- A Gathering Room with a fireplace, study and formal Dining Room, flowing together for a more spacious feeling
- A convenient pass-through that adds to the efficiency of the galley Kitchen and adjoining Breakfast Room

MAIN FLOOR — 1,387 SQ. FT.
Garage —460 SQ. FT.

TOTAL LIVING AREA:
1,387 SQ. FT.

Refer to **Pricing Schedule B** on the order form for pricing information

Carefree Comfort

TOTAL LIVING AREA:
1,665 SQ. FT.

- This plan features:
  — Three bedrooms
  — Two full baths
- A dramatic vaulted Foyer
- A range top island Kitchen with a sunny eating Nook surrounded by a built-in planter
- A vaulted ceiling in the Great Room with a built-in bar and corner fireplace
- A bayed Dining Room that combines with the Great Room for a spacious feeling
- A Master Bedroom with a private reading nook, vaulted ceiling, walk-in closet, and a well-appointed private Bath
- Two additional bedrooms sharing a full hall bath
- This plan is available with a basement, slab or crawl space foundation— please specify

MAIN AREA — 1,665 SQ. FT.
GARAGE — 2-CAR

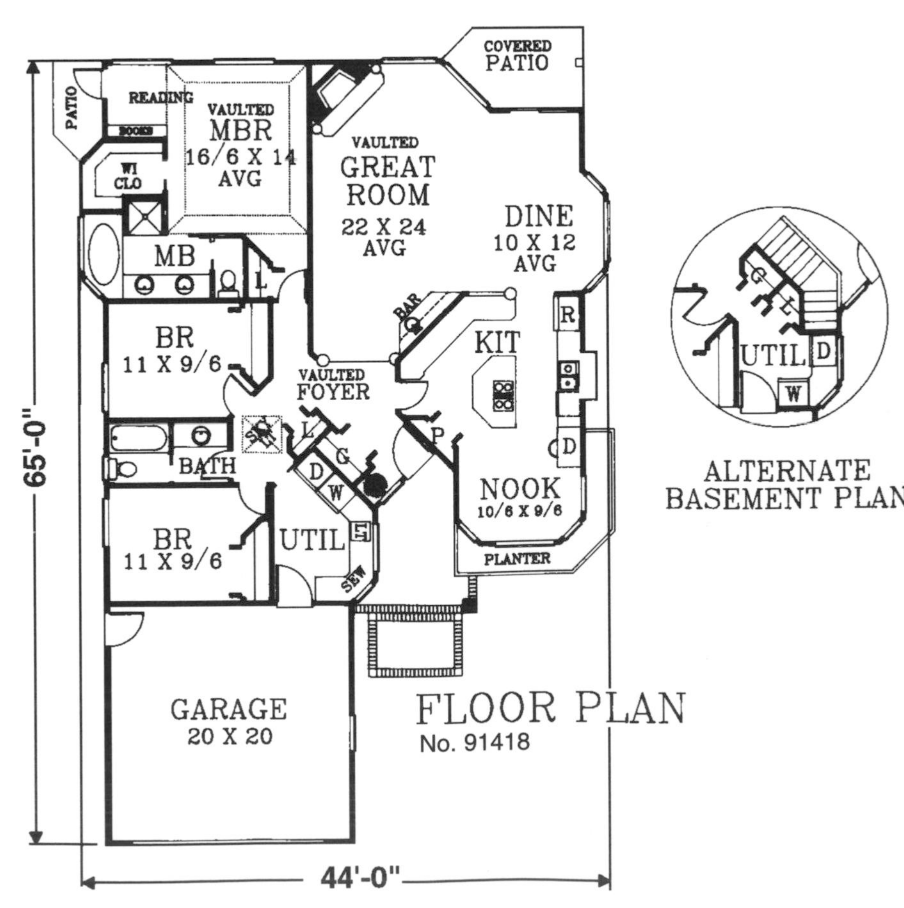
COVERED PATIO
PATIO
READING
BOOKS
VAULTED MBR 16/6 X 14 AVG
WI CLO
VAULTED GREAT ROOM 22 X 24 AVG
DINE 10 X 12 AVG
MB
L
BR 11 X 9/6
BAR
KIT
R
VAULTED FOYER
BATH
D
W
G
P
NOOK 10/6 X 9/6
PLANTER
BR 11 X 9/6
UTIL
SEW
GARAGE 20 X 20
65'-0"
44'-0"
ALTERNATE BASEMENT PLAN
UTIL

FLOOR PLAN
No. 91418

To order your Blueprints, call 1-800-235-5700

Refer to **Pricing Schedule Z** on the order form for pricing information

An EXCLUSIVE DESIGN *By Marshall Associates*

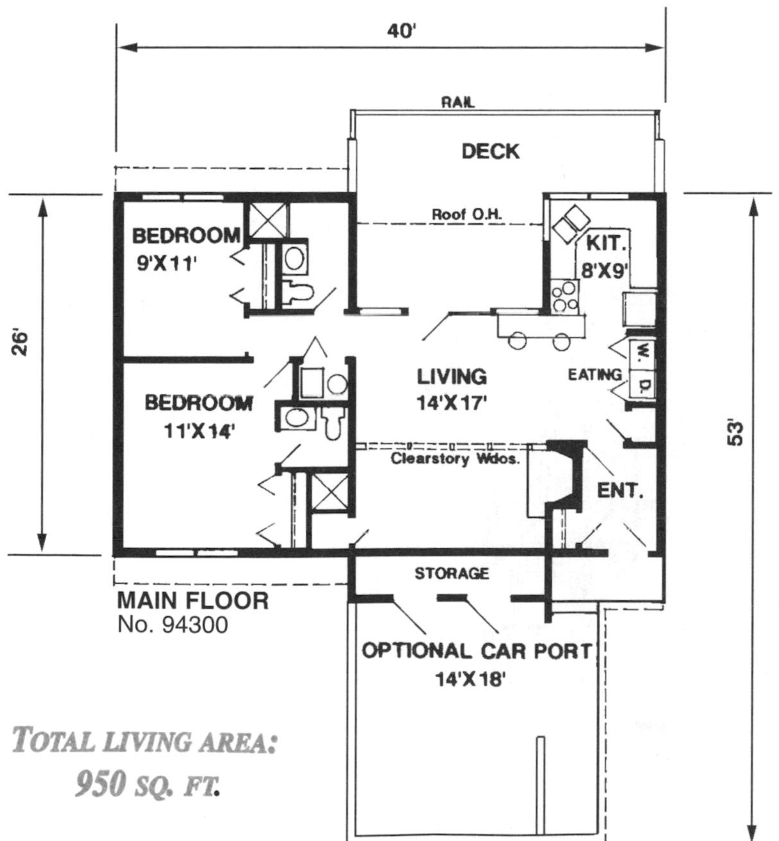
40'
RAIL
DECK
Roof O.H.
BEDROOM
9'X11'
KIT.
8'X9'
26'
LIVING
14'X17'
EATING
W. D.
BEDROOM
11'X14'
53'
Clearstory Wdos.
ENT.
STORAGE
MAIN FLOOR
No. 94300
OPTIONAL CAR PORT
14'X18'

TOTAL LIVING AREA:
950 SQ. FT.

Vacation Retreat

- This plan features;
  - Two bedrooms
  - Two full baths
- A welcoming Porch into an air-lock Entry
- Open Living/Dining room with a circular fireplace and a wall of windows with Deck access
- Private Deck with covered and open areas, offers comfortable outdoor living space
- Compact Kitchen with a wonderful view, easily serves Dining and Deck areas
- Two bedrooms, one with a walk-in closet and private bath, have double windows
- An optional Carport offers sheltered space and Storage access
- No materials list is available

MAIN FLOOR — 950 SQ. FT.

Refer to **Pricing Schedule C** on the order form for pricing information

Secluded Master Suite

- This plan features:
  - — Three bedrooms
  - — Two full baths
- A convenient one-level design with an open floor plan between the Kitchen, Breakfast area and Great Room
- A vaulted ceiling and a large cozy fireplace in the Great Room
- A well-equipped Kitchen using a peninsula counter as an eating bar
- A Master Suite with a luxurious Master Bath
- Two additional bedrooms having use of a full hall bath
- This plan is available with a crawl space or slab foundation — please specify when ordering

MAIN AREA — 1,680 SQ. FT.
GARAGE — 538 SQ. FT.

TOTAL LIVING AREA:
1,680 SQ. FT.

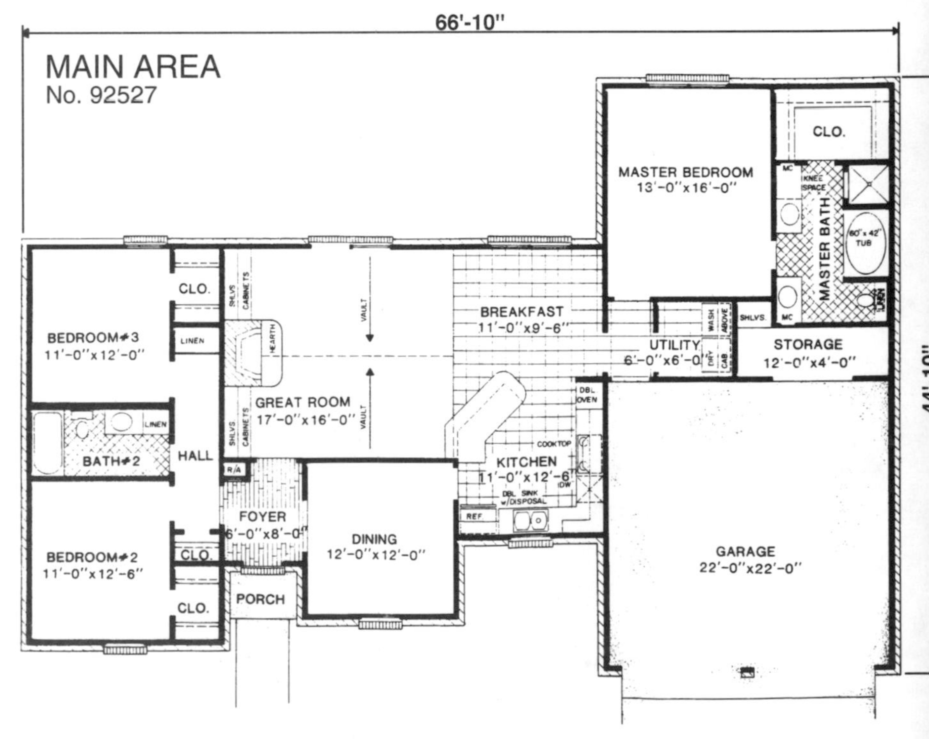
66'-10"
MAIN AREA
No. 92527
MASTER BEDROOM
13'-0"x16'-0"
CLO.
MASTER BATH
BEDROOM#3
11'-0"x12'-0"
CLO.
LINEN
GREAT ROOM
17'-0"x16'-0"
BREAKFAST
11'-0"x9'-6"
UTILITY
6'-0"x6'-0"
STORAGE
12'-0"x4'-0"
BATH#2
HALL
KITCHEN
11'-0"x12'-6"
FOYER
6'-0"x8'-0"
DINING
12'-0"x12'-0"
BEDROOM#2
11'-0"x12'-6"
CLO.
PORCH
GARAGE
22'-0"x22'-0"

To order your Blueprints, call 1-800-235-5700

PLAN NO. 94302

Refer to **Pricing Schedule A** on the order form for pricing information

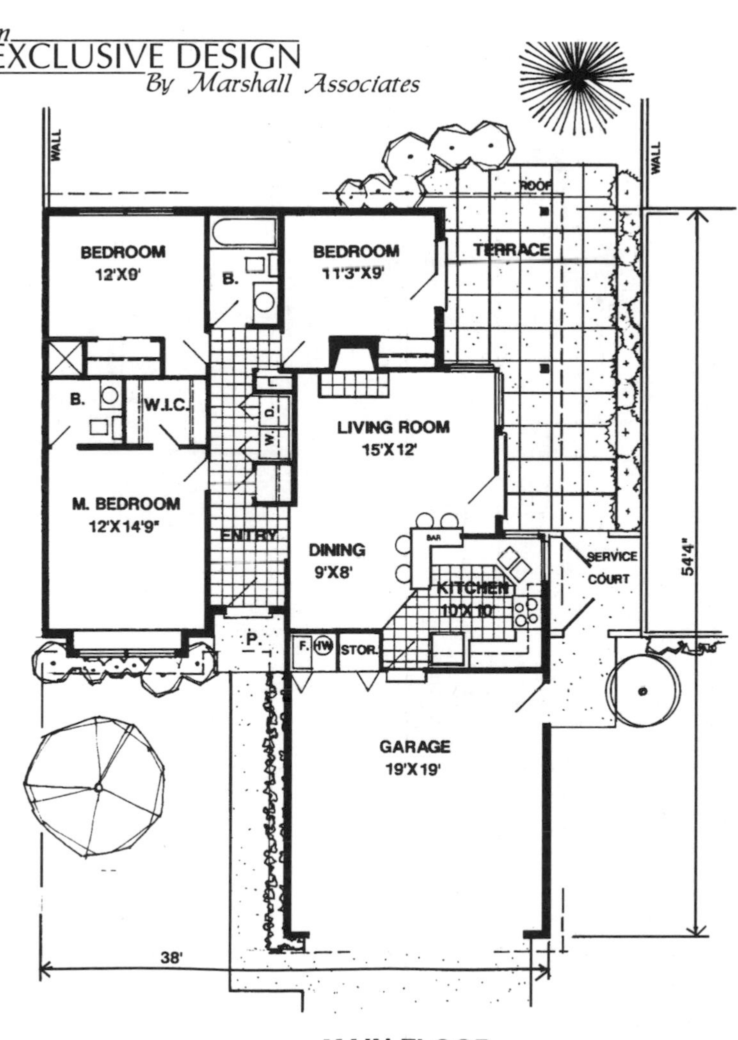

An EXCLUSIVE DESIGN By Marshall Associates
WALL
ROOF
BEDROOM
12'X9'
B.
BEDROOM
11'3"X9'
TERRACE
B.
W.I.C.
LIVING ROOM
15'X12'
M. BEDROOM
12'X14'9"
ENTRY
DINING
9'X8'
BAR
KITCHEN
10'X10'
SERVICE
COURT
P.
F.
HW
STOR.
GARAGE
19'X19'
54'4"
38'

MAIN FLOOR
No. 94302

Two Choices for Courtyard Home

- This plan features:
  - — Two or Three bedrooms
  - — Two full baths
- A tiled Entry leading to an open Dining/Living Room area with hearth fireplace and a wall of windows with an atrium door to Terrace
- Kitchen with a corner window and eating bar adjoins Dining area, Garage and Terrace
- A Master Bedroom with walk-in closet and private bath featuring either recessed, decorative window or atrium door to Terrace
- One or two additional bedrooms with ample closets near full bath
- No materials list available for this plan

MAIN FLOOR —
1,013 OR 1,137 SQ. FT.
GARAGE — 390 SQ. FT.

TOTAL LIVING AREA:
1,013 OR 1,137 SQ. FT.

PLAN NO. 91349

Refer to **Pricing Schedule B** on the order form for pricing information

Two Separate Dining Areas to Chose From

- This plan features:
  - — Two bedrooms
  - — One full and one three quarter baths
- A vaulted ceiling entry
- A Living Room with a vaulted ceiling, accented by a bay window and an optional fireplace
- A garden window, eating bar, and an abundance of storage space in the efficient Kitchen
- A Master Bedroom with its own bath, a double sink vanity and a walk-in closet
- A Library with a vaulted ceiling option and a window seat

MAIN AREA — 1,694 SQ. FT.

TOTAL LIVING AREA:
1,694 SQ. FT.

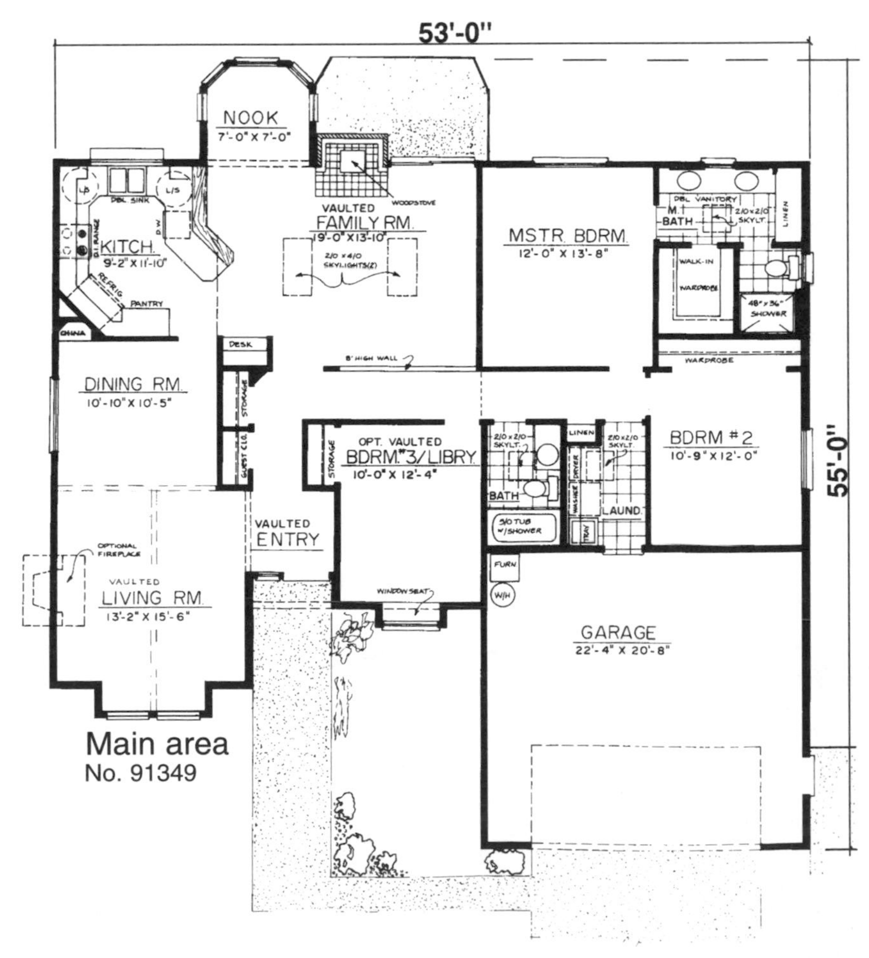
53'-0"
55'-0"
NOOK
7'-0" X 7'-0"
VAULTED
FAMILY RM.
19'-0" X 13'-10"
WOODSTOVE
KITCH.
9'-2" X 11'-10"
PANTRY
REFRIG
DINING RM.
10'-10" X 10'-5"
DESK
STORAGE
8' HIGH WALL
MSTR. BDRM.
12'-0" X 13'-8"
M. BATH
DBL. VANITORY
WALK-IN
WARDROBE
48" x 36" SHOWER
WARDROBE
LINEN
OPT. VAULTED
BDRM.#3/LIBRY.
10'-0" X 12'-4"
STORAGE
BATH
LINEN
LAUND.
BDRM #2
10'-9" X 12'-0"
VAULTED
ENTRY
OPTIONAL FIREPLACE
VAULTED
LIVING RM.
13'-2" X 15'-6"
WINDOW SEAT
FURN
W/H
GARAGE
22'-4" X 20'-8"

Main area
No. 91349

To order your Blueprints, call 1-800-235-5700

Refer to **Pricing Schedule B** on the order form for pricing information

PLAN NO. 91731

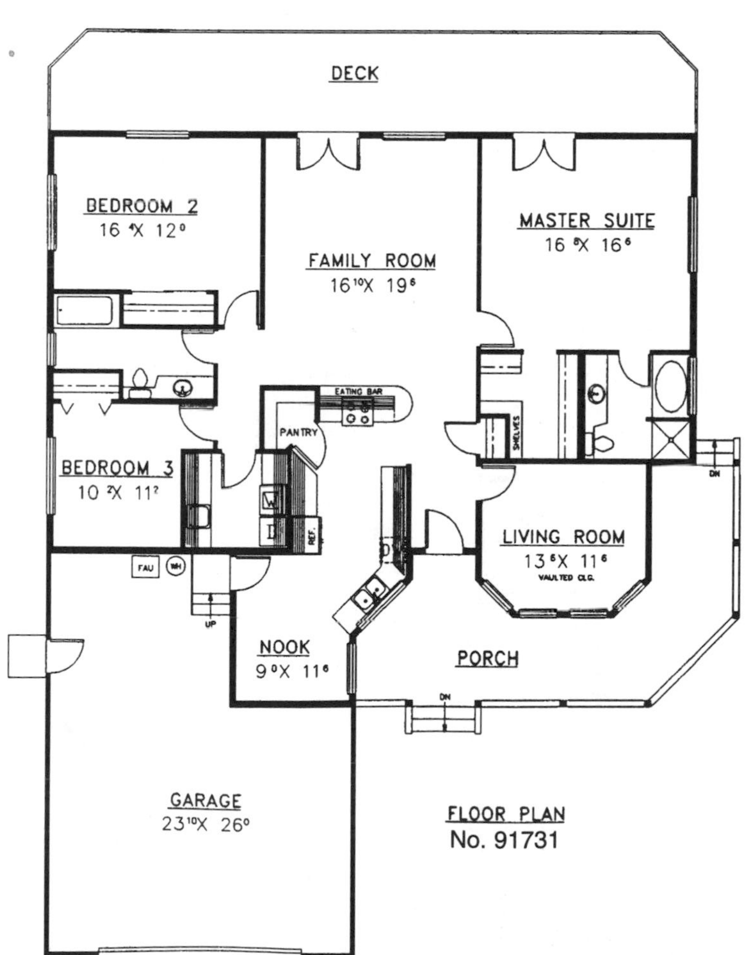

DECK
BEDROOM 2
16 4X 12 0
FAMILY ROOM
16 10X 19 6
MASTER SUITE
16 6X 16 6
EATING BAR
PANTRY
SHELVES
BEDROOM 3
10 2X 11 7
REF.
LIVING ROOM
13 6X 11 6
VAULTED CLG.
FAU
WH
UP
DN
NOOK
9 0X 11 6
PORCH
GARAGE
23 10X 26 0
FLOOR PLAN
No. 91731

Country Style & Charm

- This plan features:
  - — Three bedrooms
  - — Two full baths
- Brick accents, front facing gable, and railed wrap-around covered porch
- A built-in range and oven in a dog-leg shaped Kitchen
- A Nook with garage access for convenient unloading of groceries and other supplies
- A bay window wrapping around the front of the formal Living Room
- A Master Suite with French doors opening to the deck

MAIN AREA — 1,857 SQ. FT.
GARAGE — 681 SQ. FT.
WIDTH — 51′-6″
DEPTH — 65′-0″

TOTAL LIVING AREA:
1,857 SQ. FT.

PLAN NO. 34150

Refer to **Pricing Schedule A** on the order form for pricing information

An EXCLUSIVE DESIGN *By Karl Kreeger*

Simple Lines Enhanced by Elegant Window Treatment

TOTAL LIVING AREA:
1,492 SQ. FT.

- This plan features:
  - Two bedrooms (optional third)
  - Two full baths
- A huge, arched window that floods the front room with natural light
- A homey, well-lit Office or Den
- Compact, efficient use of space
- An efficient Kitchen with easy access to the Dining Room
- A fireplaced Living Room with a sloping ceiling and a window wall
- A Master Bedroom sporting a private Master Bath with a roomy walk-in closet

MAIN AREA — 1,492 SQ. FT.
BASEMENT — 1,486 SQ. FT.
GARAGE — 462 SQ. FT.

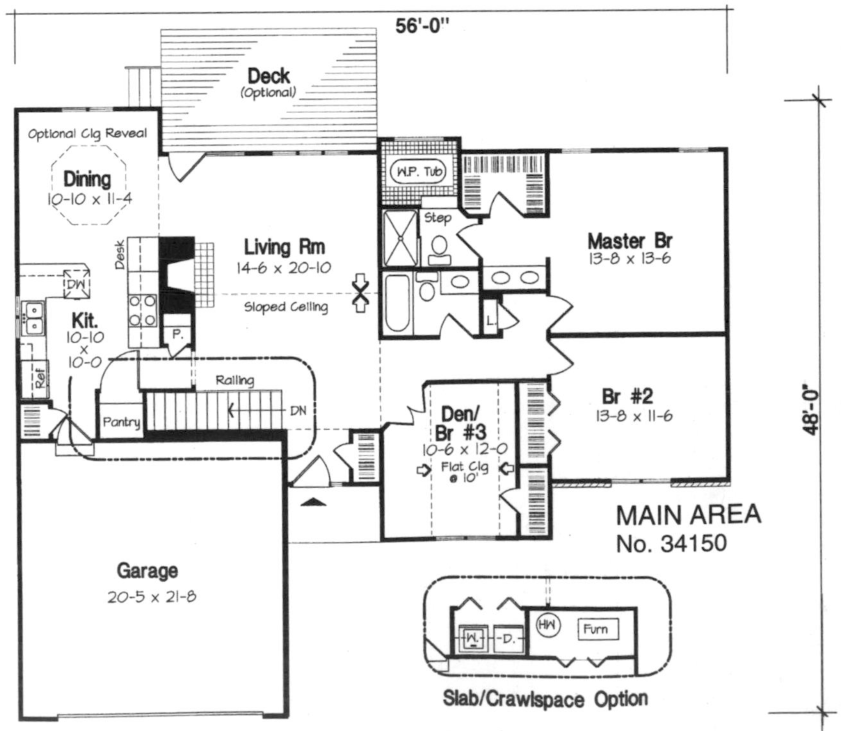
56'-0"
Deck
(Optional)
Optional Clg Reveal
Dining
10-10 x 11-4
Desk
DW
Living Rm
14-6 x 20-10
Sloped Ceiling
Kit.
10-10 x 10-0
Ref
P.
Railing
Pantry
DN
W.P. Tub
Step
Master Br
13-8 x 13-6
L
Br #2
13-8 x 11-6
Den/ Br #3
10-6 x 12-0
Flat Clg @ 10'
48'-0"
MAIN AREA
No. 34150
Garage
20-5 x 21-8
W.
D.
HW
Furn
Slab/Crawlspace Option

To order your Blueprints, call 1-800-235-5700

Refer to **Pricing Schedule B** on the order form for pricing information

PLAN NO. 20150

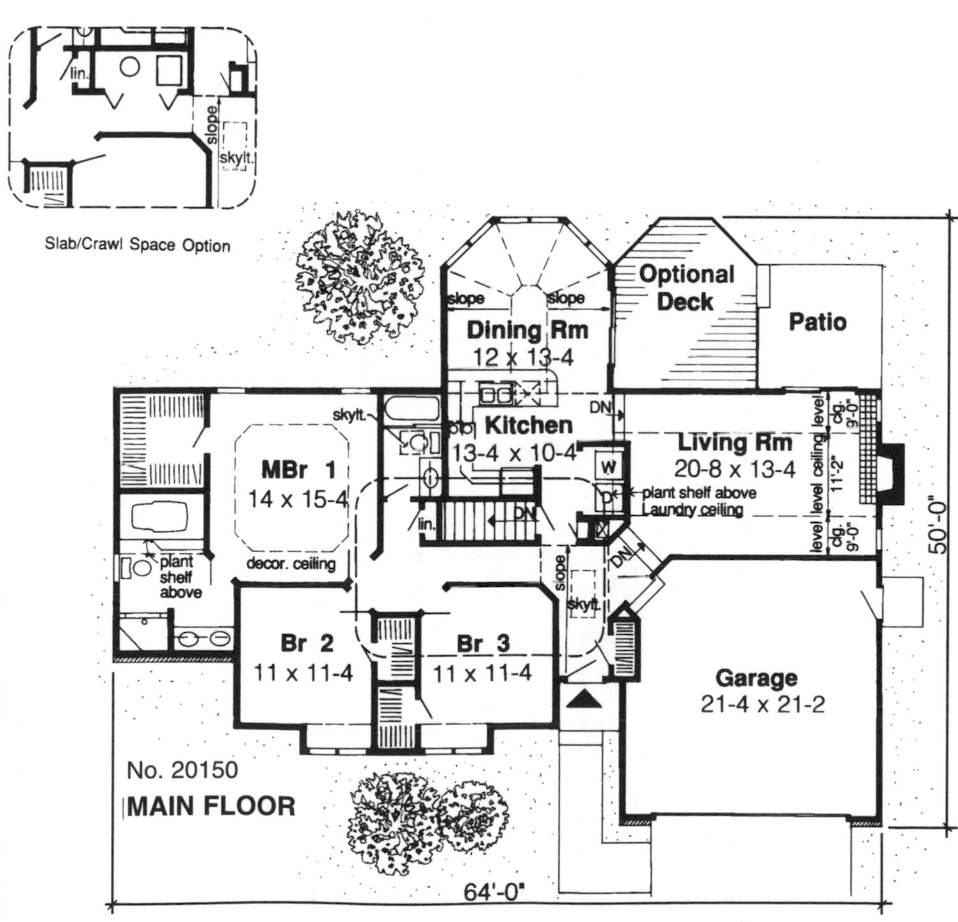

lin.
slope
skylt.
Slab/Crawl Space Option
slope
slope
Dining Rm
12 x 13-4
Optional
Deck
Patio
skylt.
Kitchen
13-4 x 10-4
DN
Living Rm
20-8 x 13-4
level ceiling level
clg. 9'-0"
11'-2"
clg. 9'-0"
W
D
plant shelf above
Laundry ceiling
MBr 1
14 x 15-4
decor. ceiling
lin.
DN
plant shelf above
slope
skylt.
DN
Br 2
11 x 11-4
Br 3
11 x 11-4
Garage
21-4 x 21-2
50'-0"
No. 20150
MAIN FLOOR
64'-0"

Sunshine Special

- This plan features:
  - — Three bedrooms
  - — Two full baths
- A Living Room with a large fireplace and a sloped ceiling.
- A walk-in closet in each bedroom
- A Master Suite including a luxury bath and a decorative ceiling

MAIN FLOOR — 1,638 SQ. FT.
BASEMENT — 1,320 SQ. FT.
GARAGE — 462 SQ. FT.

TOTAL LIVING AREA:
1,638 SQ. FT.

An EXCLUSIVE DESIGN
By Karl Kreeger

To order your Blueprints, call 1-800-235-5700

PLAN NO. 26114

Refer to **Pricing Schedule A** on the order form for pricing information

High Windows Add Natural Light

- This plan features:
- — Three bedrooms
- — One full and one half baths
- A covered Entry steps down into the spacious Living/Dining Room featuring a vaulted ceiling, a fireplace and sliding glass doors to expansive Deck area
- An efficient, U-shaped Kitchen with a peninsula counter adjoining the Dining Room
- A first floor Bedroom/Den with a triple window and a walk-in closet
- Two additional bedrooms on the second floor share a balcony and a full bath

FIRST FLOOR — 696 SQ. FT.
SECOND FLOOR — 416 SQ. FT.
BASEMENT — 696 SQ. FT.

TOTAL LIVING AREA:
1,112 SQ. FT.

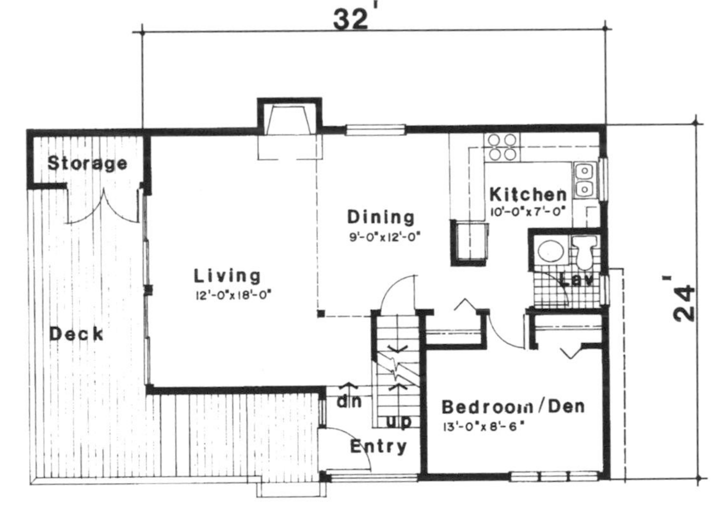

32'
24'
Storage
Dining
9'-0"x12'-0"
Kitchen
10'-0"x7'-0"
Living
12'-0"x18'-0"
Lav
Deck
dn
up
Entry
Bedroom/Den
13'-0"x8'-6"

FIRST FLOOR
No. 26114

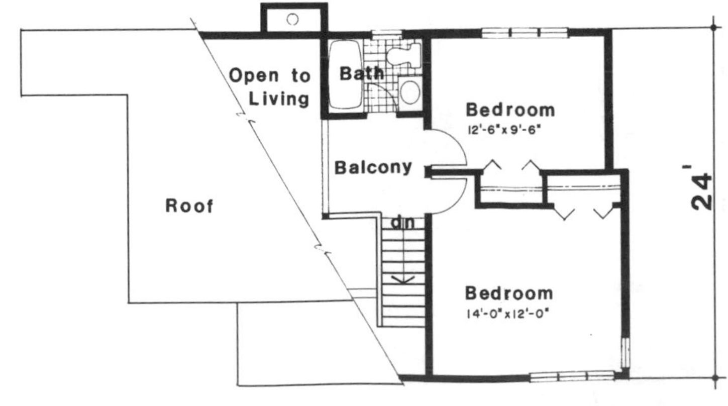

Open to Living
Bath
Bedroom
12'-6"x9'-6"
Balcony
Roof
dn
24'
Bedroom
14'-0"x12'-0"

SECOND FLOOR

To order your Blueprints, call 1-800-235-5700

Refer to **Pricing Schedule Z** on the order form for pricing information

PLAN NO.10306

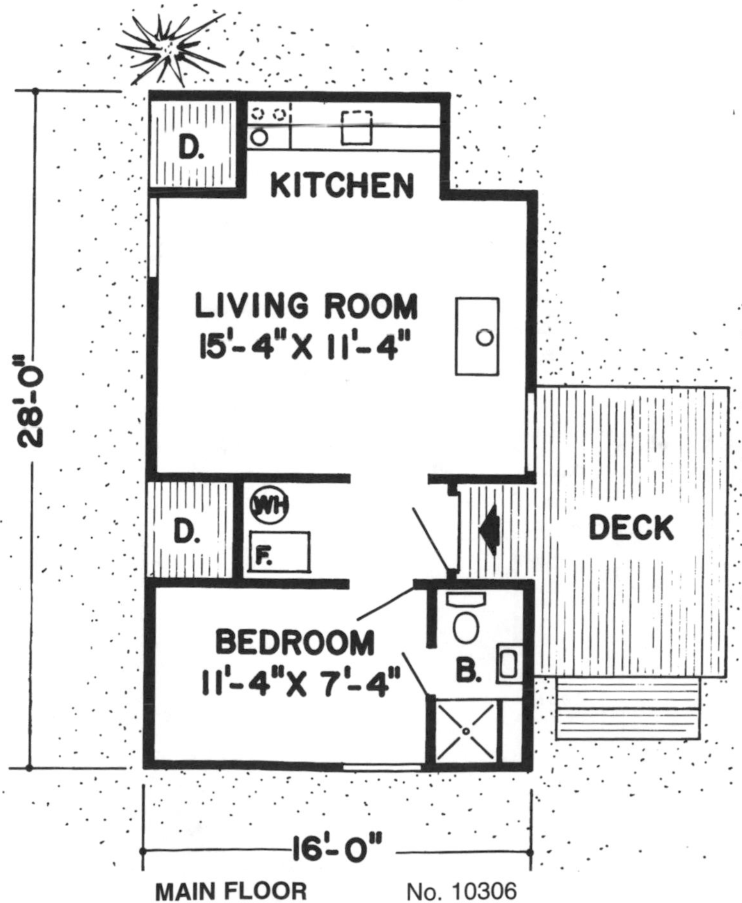

D.
KITCHEN
LIVING ROOM
15'-4"X 11'-4"
28'-0"
D.
WH
F.
DECK
BEDROOM
11'-4"X 7'-4"
B.
16'-0"

MAIN FLOOR No. 10306

Deck Enlarges and Enhances Cottage

- This plan features:
  - — One bedroom
  - — One full bath
- A large wood deck for dining, sunbathing or relaxing with friends
- A one wall Kitchen open to the Living Room, creating simplicity and warmth.
- A look that is ideal for both beach and mountain enthusiasts

MAIN FLOOR — 408 SQ. FT.

TOTAL LIVING AREA:
408 SQ. FT.

PLAN NO. 10619

Refer to **Pricing Schedule D** on the order form for pricing information

An EXCLUSIVE DESIGN By Karl Kreeger

Deck Doubles Outdoor Living Space

- This plan features:
- — Three bedrooms
- — Two full and one three quarter baths
- A design made for the sun lover with a front deck and patio
- A sunken Living Room with three window walls and a massive fireplace.
- A hot tub with skylight, a vaulted Master Suite and a utility area

MAIN AREA — 2,352 SQ. FT.
BASEMENT — 2,352 SQ. FT.
GARAGE — 696 SQ. FT.

TOTAL LIVING AREA:
2,352 SQ. FT.

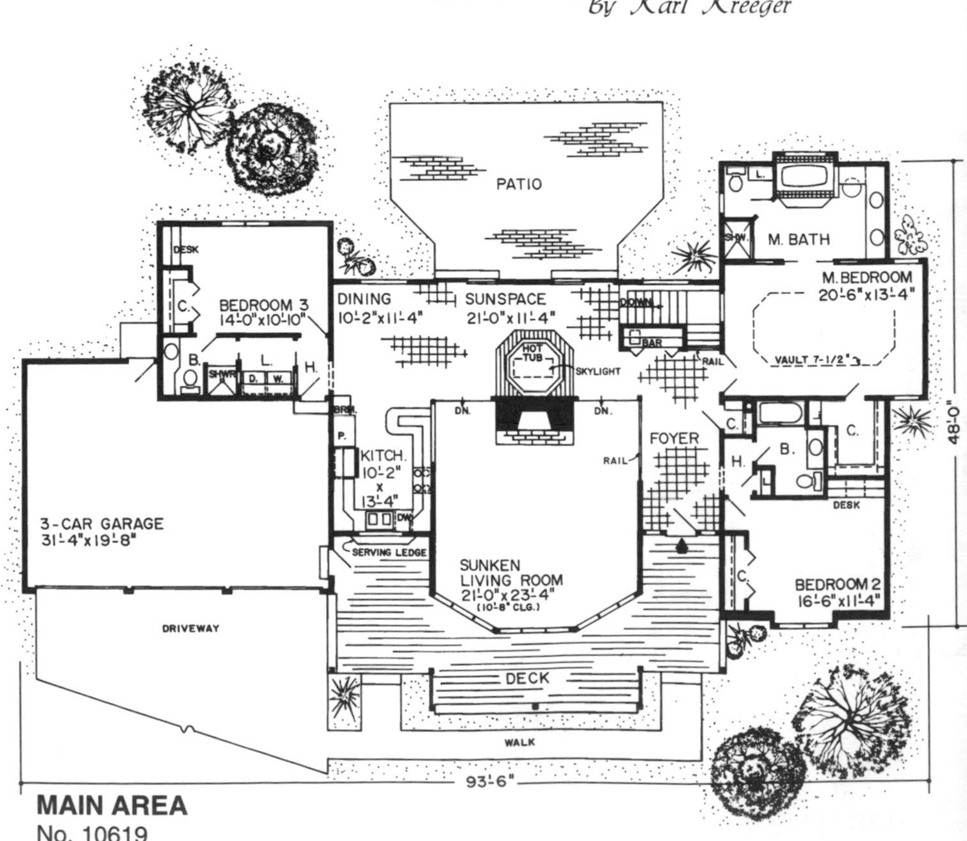

PATIO
DESK
BEDROOM 3
14'-0"x10'-10"
C.
B.
SHWR
L.
D.
W.
H.
DINING
10'-2"x11'-4"
SUNSPACE
21'-0"x11'-4"
HOT TUB
SKYLIGHT
DOWN
BAR
RAIL
SHW.
M. BATH
M.BEDROOM
20'-6"x13'-4"
VAULT 7-1/2"
48'-0"
3-CAR GARAGE
31'-4"x19'-8"
P.
KITCH.
10'-2" x 13'-4"
DW
SERVING LEDGE
DN.
SUNKEN LIVING ROOM
21'-0"x23'-4"
(10'-8" CLG.)
FOYER
DESK
BEDROOM 2
16'-6"x11'-4"
DRIVEWAY
DECK
WALK
93'-6"

MAIN AREA
No. 10619

To order your Blueprints, call 1-800-235-5700

Refer to **Pricing Schedule A** on the order form for pricing information

PLAN NO. 90309

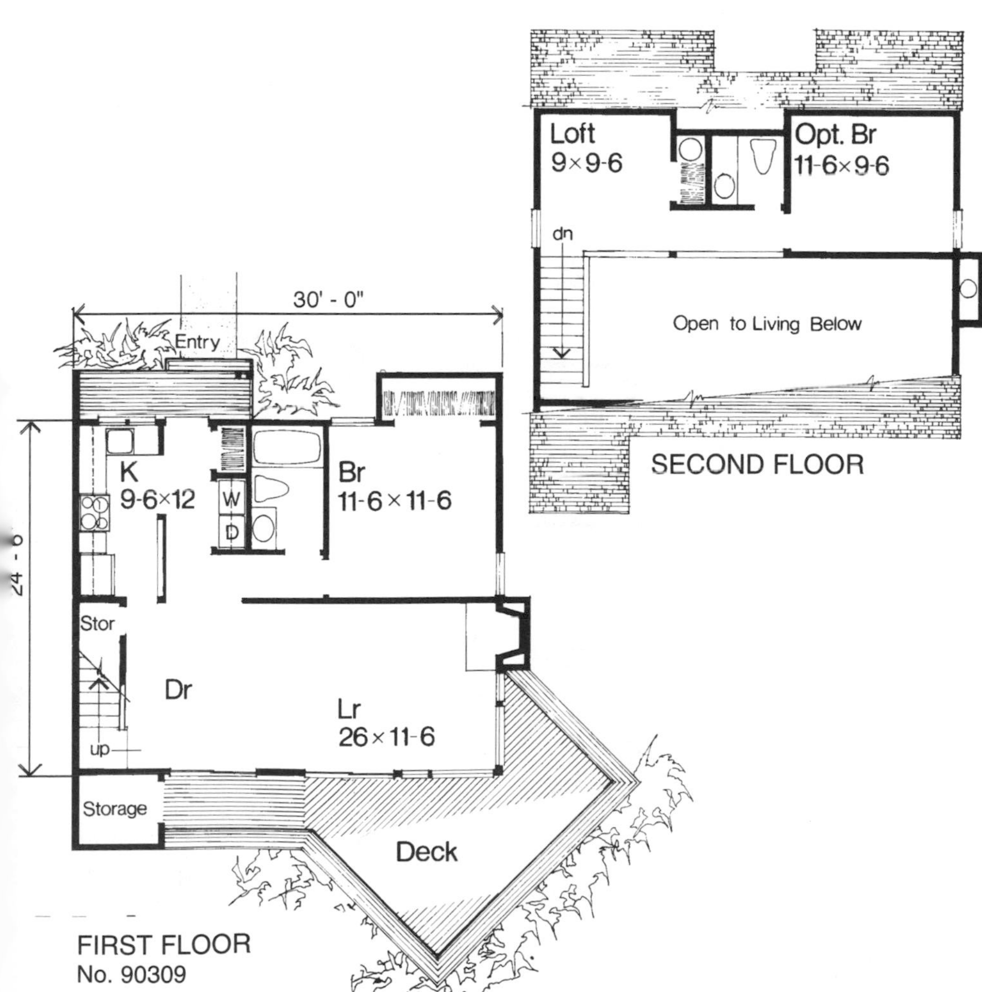

Loft
9×9-6
Opt. Br
11-6×9-6
dn
Open to Living Below
SECOND FLOOR
30' - 0"
Entry
K
9-6×12
W
D
Br
11-6×11-6
24' - 6"
Stor
Dr
Lr
26×11-6
up
Storage
Deck
FIRST FLOOR
No. 90309

Modified A-Frame at Home Anywhere

- This plan features:
- — One or two bedrooms
- — One full and one half bath
- A combined Living Room/Dining Room with a ceiling that reaches to the second floor loft
- A galley-styled Kitchen conveniently arranged and open to the Dining Room
- A fireplace in the Living Room area with sliding glass doors to the Deck
- A loft with a half bath and an optional bedroom

FIRST FLOOR — 735 SQ. FT.
SECOND FLOOR — 304 SQ. FT.

TOTAL LIVING AREA:
1,039 SQ. FT.

PLAN NO. 91342

Refer to **Pricing Schedule A** on the order form for pricing information

Easy Living Design

- This plan features:
  - Three bedrooms
  - Two full baths
- A handicaped Master Bath plan is available
- Vaulted Great Room, Dining Room and Kitchen areas
- A Kitchen accented with angles and an abundance of cabinets for storage
- A Master Bedroom with an ample sized wardrobe, large covered private deck, and private bath

MAIN AREA — 1,345 SQ. FT.
WIDTH — 47′-8″
DEPTH — 56′-0″

TOTAL LIVING AREA:
1,345 SQ. FT.

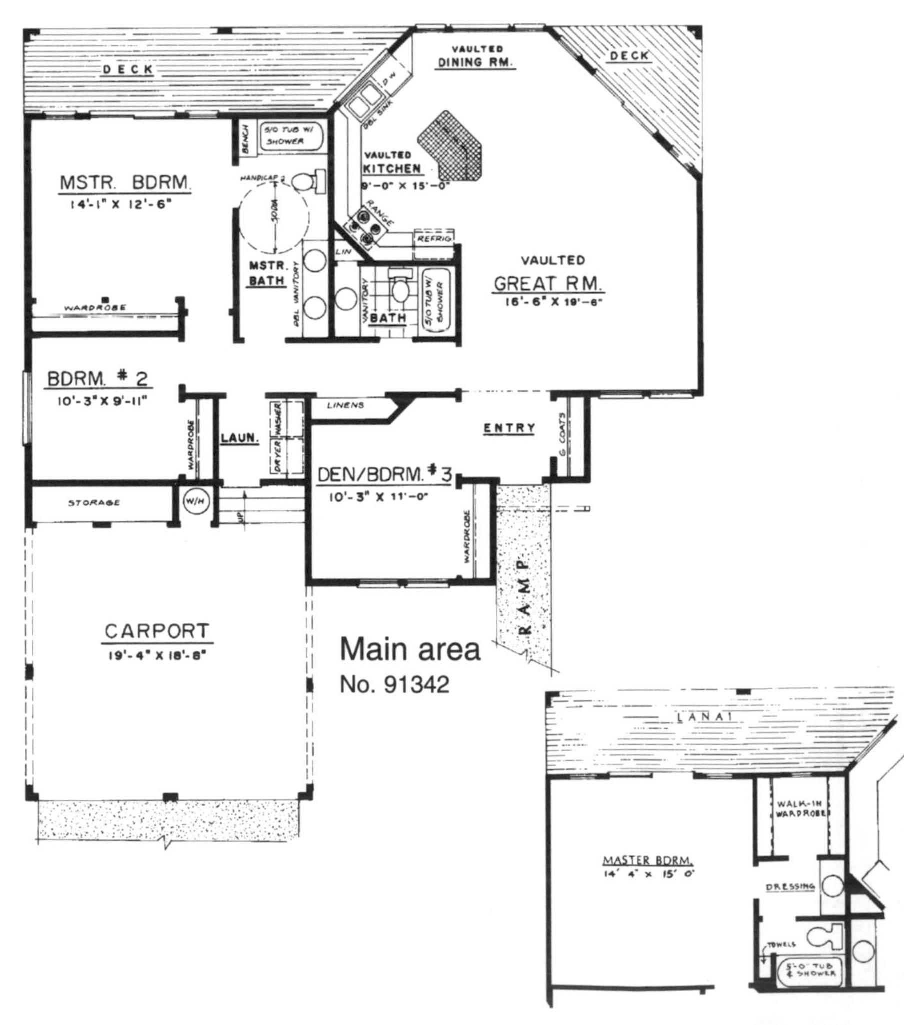

DECK
VAULTED DINING RM.
DECK
MSTR. BDRM.
14'-1" X 12'-6"
VAULTED KITCHEN
9'-0" X 15'-0"
MSTR. BATH
BATH
VAULTED
GREAT RM.
16'-6" X 19'-6"
WARDROBE
BDRM. # 2
10'-3" X 9'-11"
LINENS
LAUN.
ENTRY
DEN/BDRM. # 3
10'-3" X 11'-0"
STORAGE
W/H
WARDROBE
RAMP
CARPORT
19'-4" X 18'-8"
Main area
No. 91342
LANAI
WALK-IN WARDROBE
MASTER BDRM.
14' 4" x 15' 0"
DRESSING
TOWELS
5'-0" TUB & SHOWER

ALTERNATE BATH

To order your Blueprints, call 1-800-235-5700

Refer to **Pricing Schedule A** on the order form for pricing information

PLAN NO. 91063

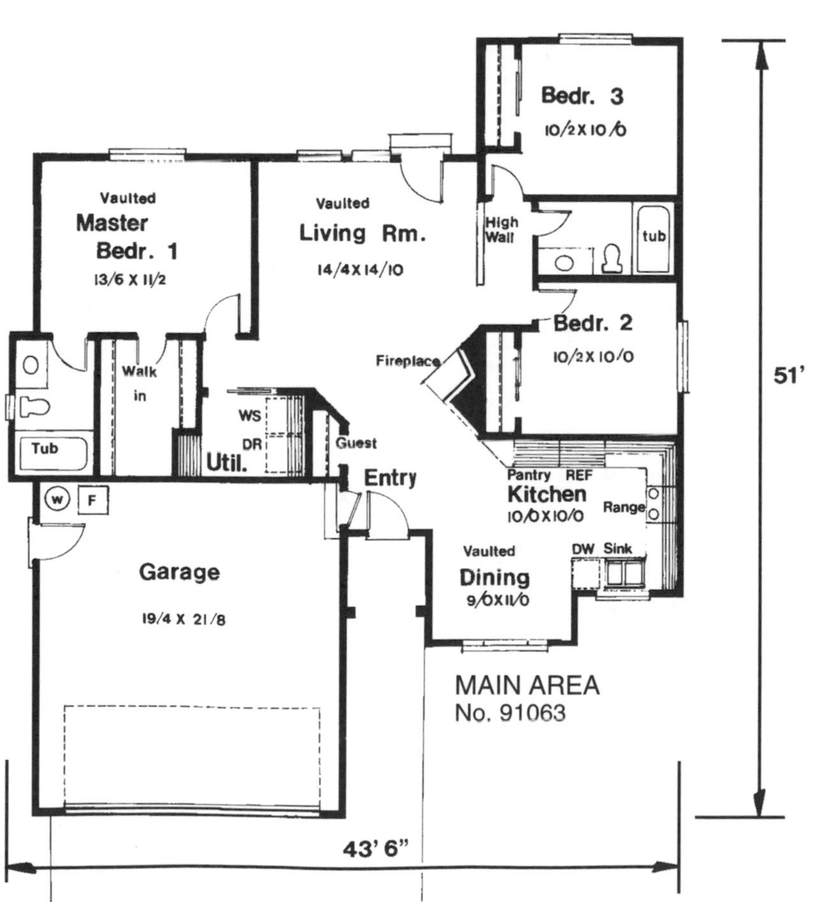
Bedr. 3
10/2 X 10/0
Vaulted
Master
Bedr. 1
13/6 X 11/2
Vaulted
Living Rm.
14/4 X 14/10
High
Wall
tub
Bedr. 2
10/2 X 10/0
Fireplace
Walk
in
WS
DR
Util.
Guest
Tub
Entry
Pantry REF
Kitchen
10/0 X 10/0
Range
Vaulted
Dining
9/0 X 11/0
DW Sink
W F
Garage
19/4 X 21/8
MAIN AREA
No. 91063
51'
43' 6"

Gabled Roofline and Arched Windows Enhance Exterior

- This plan features:
- — Three bedrooms
- — Two full baths
- Vaulted ceilings and an open interior creating a spacious feeling
- A private Master Bedroom with a generous closet and Master Bath
- Two additional bedrooms sharing the second full bath
- A Kitchen with ample storage, countertops, and a built-in pantry
- No materials list available for this plan.

MAIN AREA — 1,207 SQ. FT.
GARAGE — 440 SQ. FT.

TOTAL LIVING AREA:
1,207 SQ. FT.

PLAN NO. 34043

Refer to **Pricing Schedule B** on the order form for pricing information

A Home for Today and Tomorrow

- This plan features:

— Three bedrooms

— Two full baths

- An intriguing Breakfast nook off the Kitchen
- A wide open, fireplaced Living Room with glass sliders to an optional deck
- A step-saving arrangement of the Kitchen between the Breakfast area and formal Dining Room
- A handsome Master Bedroom with sky-lit compartmentalized bath

MAIN AREA — 1,583 SQ. FT.
BASEMENT — 1,573 SQ. FT.
GARAGE — 484 SQ. FT.

TOTAL LIVING AREA:
1,583 SQ. FT.

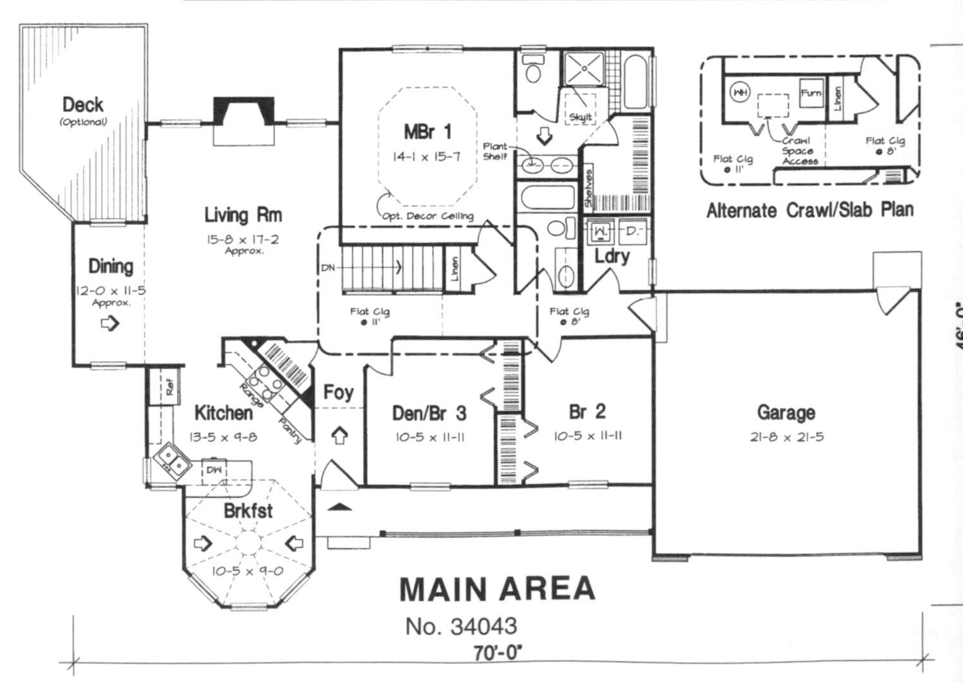
Deck
(Optional)
Living Rm
15-8 x 17-2
Approx.
MBr 1
14-1 x 15-7
Plant Shelf
Skylt
Opt. Decor Ceiling
Dining
12-0 x 11-5
Approx.
DN
Linen
Shelves
Ldry
Flat Clg @ 11'
Flat Clg @ 8'
Ref
Range
Pantry
Kitchen
13-5 x 9-8
DW
Foy
Den/Br 3
10-5 x 11-11
Br 2
10-5 x 11-11
Garage
21-8 x 21-5
Brkfst
10-5 x 9-0
Alternate Crawl/Slab Plan
WH
Furn
Crawl Space Access
Flat Clg @ 11'
Flat Clg @ 8'
46'-0"
MAIN AREA
No. 34043
70'-0"

An EXCLUSIVE DESIGN By Karl Kreeger

To order your Blueprints, call 1-800-235-5700

Refer to **Pricing Schedule B** on the order form for pricing information

PLAN NO. 10548

An EXCLUSIVE DESIGN *By Karl Kreeger*

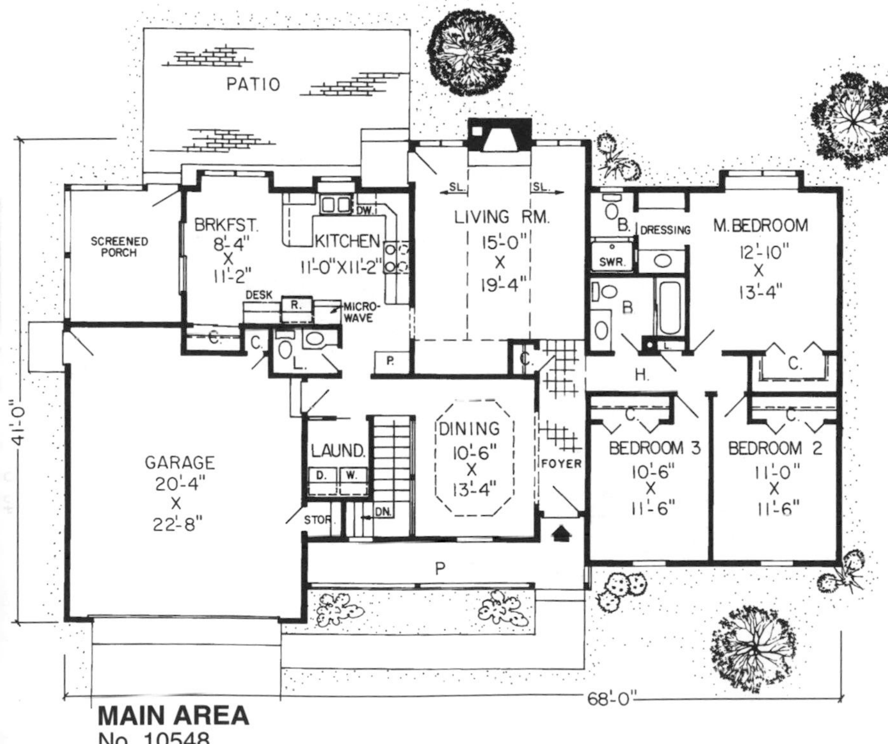

PATIO
SCREENED PORCH
BRKFST. 8'-4" X 11'-2"
KITCHEN 11'-0"X11'-2"
DW.
DESK
R.
MICRO-WAVE
LIVING RM. 15'-0" X 19'-4"
SL.
SL.
B.
DRESSING
SWR.
M. BEDROOM 12'-10" X 13'-4"
B
H.
C.
L.
P.
GARAGE 20'-4" X 22'-8"
LAUND.
D.
W.
STOR.
DN.
DINING 10'-6" X 13'-4"
FOYER
BEDROOM 3 10'-6" X 11'-6"
BEDROOM 2 11'-0" X 11'-6"
P
41'-0"
68'-0"

MAIN AREA
No. 10548

Sloped Ceiling Attractive Feature of Ranch Design

- This plan features:
- — Three bedrooms
- — Two and one half baths
- A fireplace and sloped ceiling in the Living Room
- A Master Bedroom complete with a full bath, shower and dressing area
- A decorative ceiling in the Dining Room

MAIN AREA — 1,688 SQ. FT.
BASEMENT — 1,688 SQ. FT.
SCREENED PORCH — 120 SQ. FT.
GARAGE — 489 SQ. FT.

TOTAL LIVING AREA:
1,688 SQ. FT.

PLAN NO. 90004

Refer to **Pricing Schedule A** on the order form for pricing information

Rustic Vacation House

- This plan features:
  - — Three bedrooms
  - — One full and one half baths
- Two porches and an outdoor balcony for entertaining, relaxing or just enjoying a sunset
- A spiral stairway leading to the balcony and upstairs bedroom
- A Living Room with a massive stone fireplace, floor-to-ceiling windows at the gable end, and sliding glass doors to a rear porch
- A pantry adjoining the Kitchen which has a small bay window over the sink

FIRST FLOOR — 1,020 SQ. FT.
SECOND FLOOR — 265 SQ. FT.

TOTAL LIVING AREA:
1,285 SQ. FT.

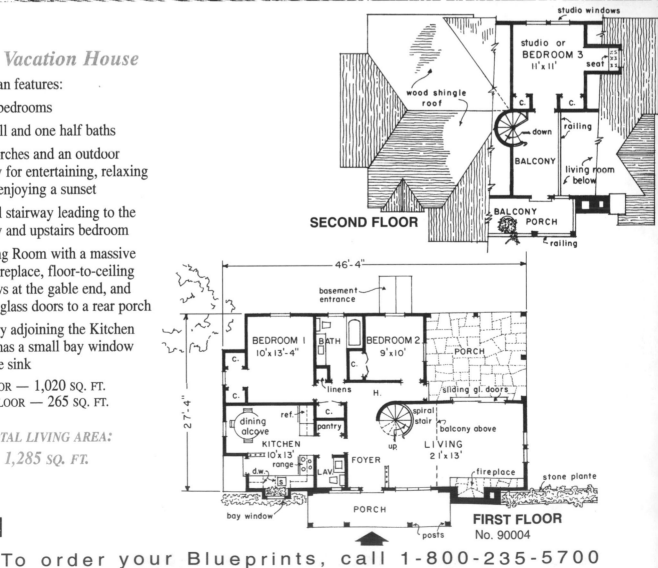

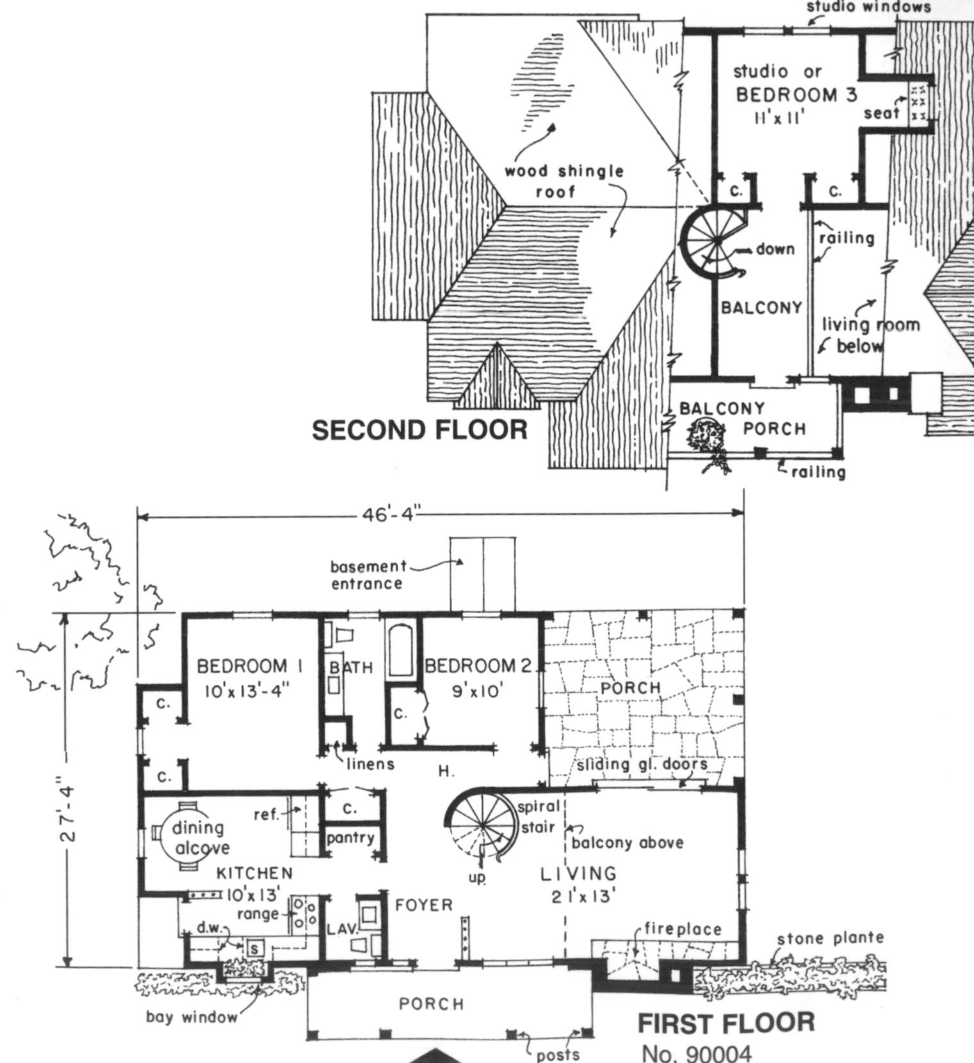

studio windows
studio or
BEDROOM 3
11'x11'
seat
wood shingle roof
C.
C.
railing
down
BALCONY
living room below
BALCONY PORCH
railing
SECOND FLOOR
46'-4"
basement entrance
27'-4"
BEDROOM 1
10'x13'-4"
BATH
BEDROOM 2
9'x10'
PORCH
C.
C.
C.
linens
H.
sliding gl. doors
C.
ref.
pantry
dining alcove
spiral stair
balcony above
KITCHEN
10'x13'
range
up
LIVING
21'x13'
d.w.
S
LAV.
FOYER
fireplace
stone plante
PORCH
bay window
posts
FIRST FLOOR
No. 90004

To order your Blueprints, call 1-800-235-5700

Refer to **Pricing Schedule C** on the order form for pricing information

PLAN NO.10569

An EXCLUSIVE DESIGN *By Karl Kreeger*

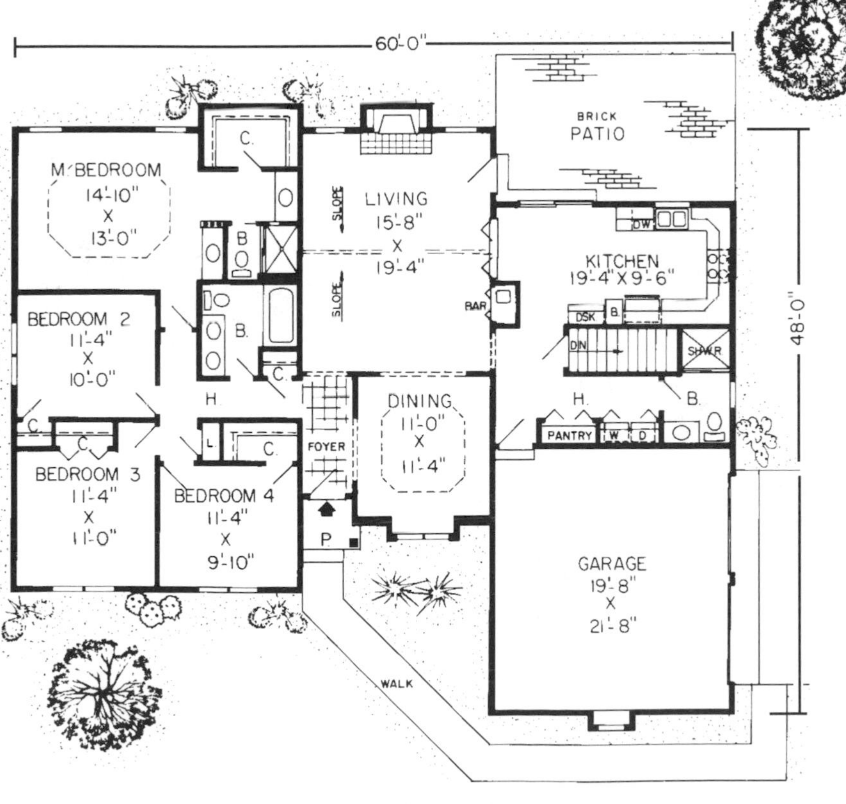

60'-0"
48'-0"
BRICK PATIO
M-BEDROOM 14'-10" X 13'-0"
LIVING 15'-8" X 19'-4"
SLOPE
KITCHEN 19'-4" X 9'-6"
DW
BAR
DSK
DIN
SHWR
BEDROOM 2 11'-4" X 10'-0"
DINING 11'-0" X 11'-4"
FOYER
PANTRY
W
D
BEDROOM 3 11'-4" X 11'-0"
BEDROOM 4 11'-4" X 9'-10"
GARAGE 19'-8" X 21'-8"
WALK

MAIN AREA
No. 10569

Ranch Offers Attractive Window Facade

- This plan features:
- — Four bedrooms
- — Three full baths
- A Living Room with sloping, open-beamed ceilings and a fireplace with built-in bookshelves
- A Dining Room with a vaulted ceiling, adding a feeling of spaciousness
- A Master Bath with ample closet space and a private bath
- A two-car garage

FIRST FLOOR — 1,840 SQ. FT.
BASEMENT — 1,803 SQ. FT.
GARAGE — 445 SQ. FT.

TOTAL LIVING AREA: 1,840 SQ. FT.

PLAN NO. 90048

Refer to **Pricing Schedule A** on the order form for pricing information

Three Porches Offer Outdoor Charm

- This plan features:
  - — Three bedrooms
  - — Two full baths
- An oversized log burning fireplace in the spacious Living/Dining area which is two stories high with sliding glass doors
- Three porches offering the maximum in outdoor living space
- A private bedroom located on the second floor
- An efficient Kitchen including an eating bar and access to the covered Dining Porch

FIRST FLOOR — 974 SQ. FT.
SECOND FLOOR — 300 SQ. FT.

TOTAL LIVING AREA:
1,274 SQ. FT.

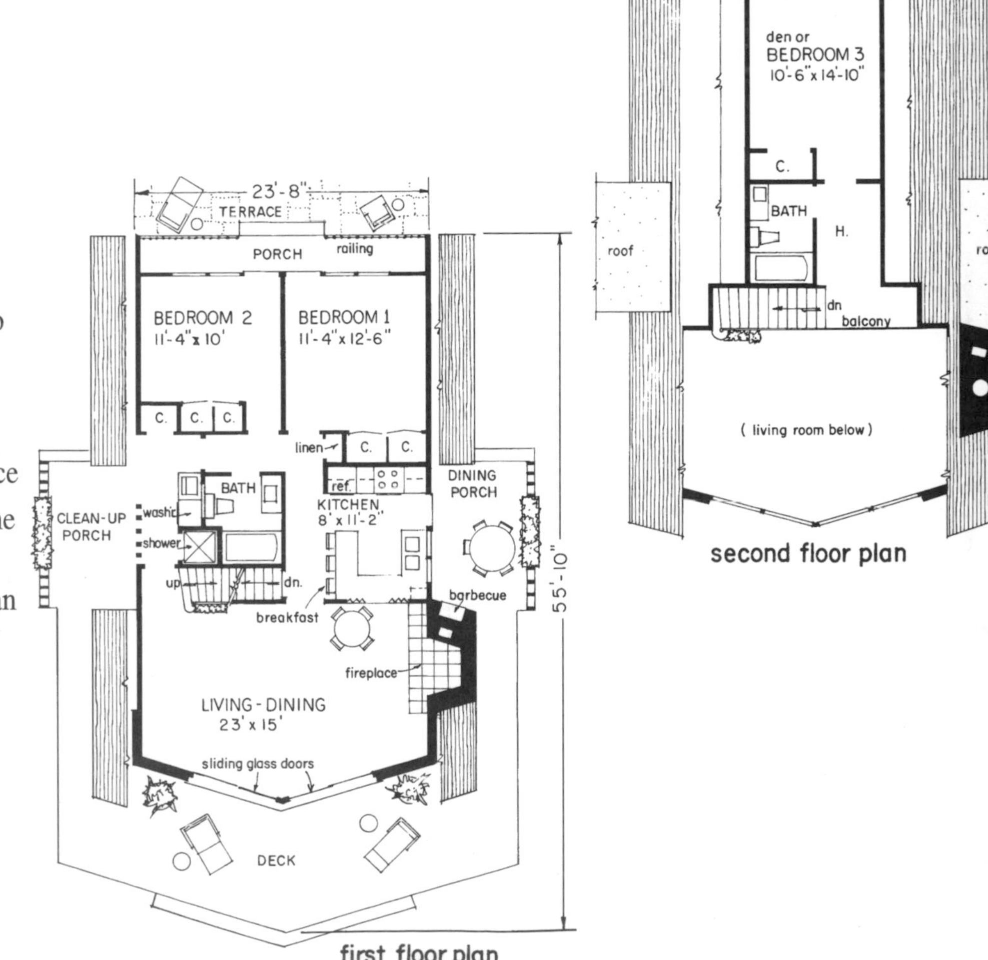

23'-8"
TERRACE
PORCH
railing
BEDROOM 2
11'-4" x 10'
BEDROOM 1
11'-4" x 12'-6"
C.
linen
BATH
washer
shower
CLEAN-UP PORCH
ref.
KITCHEN
8' x 11'-2"
DINING PORCH
up
dn.
breakfast
barbecue
fireplace
LIVING - DINING
23' x 15'
sliding glass doors
DECK
55'-10"
den or
BEDROOM 3
10'-6" x 14'-10"
BATH
H.
roof
dn
balcony
(living room below)
second floor plan

first floor plan
No. 90048

To order your Blueprints, call 1-800-235-5700

Refer to **Pricing Schedule A** on the order form for pricing information

PLAN NO. 24305

Contemporary Living

■ This plan features:

— Three bedrooms

— Two full baths

■ A split-level with an open living area, so that the Kitchen, Living Room and Dining Room flow into each other

■ A U-shaped Kitchen with double sink and plenty of storage and counter area

■ A spacious Living Room, with a large multi-paned window offering natural light, and a view of the front yard

■ A Dining Room convenient to the Kitchen, with direct access to the patio

■ A Master Suite with a private bath that includes a step-in shower

■ Two additional bedrooms that share a full hall bath

MAIN AREA — 984 SQ. FT.
BASEMENT — 442 SQ. FT.
GARAGE — 393 SQ. FT.

TOTAL LIVING AREA:
984 SQ. FT.

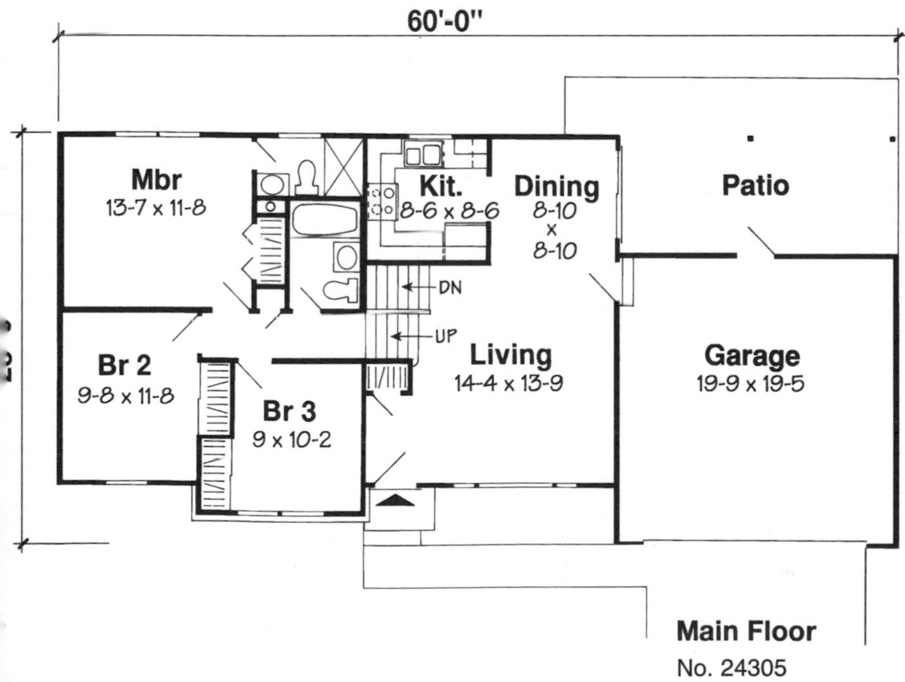

60'-0"
Mbr
13-7 x 11-8
Kit.
8-6 x 8-6
Dining
8-10 x 8-10
Patio
DN
UP
Br 2
9-8 x 11-8
Br 3
9 x 10-2
Living
14-4 x 13-9
Garage
19-9 x 19-5
Main Floor
No. 24305

An EXCLUSIVE DESIGN *By Marshall Associates*

PLAN NO. 90360

Refer to **Pricing Schedule A** on the order form for pricing information

Detailed Ranch Design

- This plan features:
- — Three bedrooms
- — Two full baths
- A Breakfast area with a vaulted ceiling and access to the deck
- An efficient Kitchen with built-in pantry and appliances
- A Master bedroom with private bath and ample closet space
- A large Great Room with a vaulted ceiling and cozy fireplace

MAIN AREA — 1,283 SQ. FT.

TOTAL LIVING AREA:
1,283 SQ. FT.

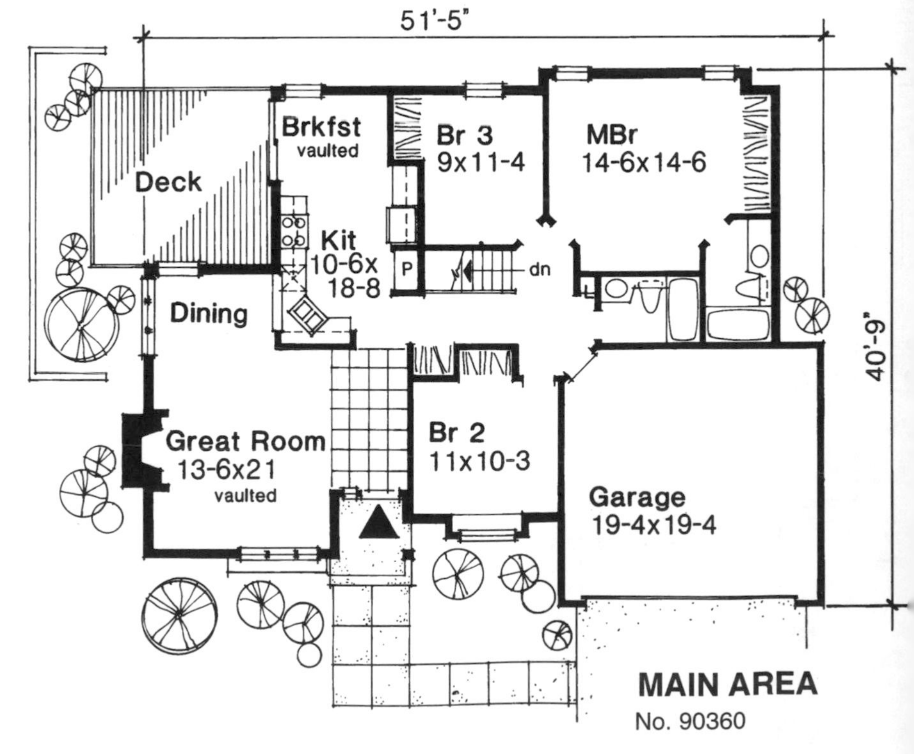

51'-5"
Brkfst
vaulted
Br 3
9x11-4
MBr
14-6x14-6
Deck
Kit
10-6x
18-8
P
dn
Dining
Great Room
13-6x21
vaulted
Br 2
11x10-3
Garage
19-4x19-4
40'-9"

MAIN AREA
No. 90360

To order your Blueprints, call 1-800-235-5700

Refer to **Pricing Schedule A** on the order form for pricing information

PLAN NO. 20164

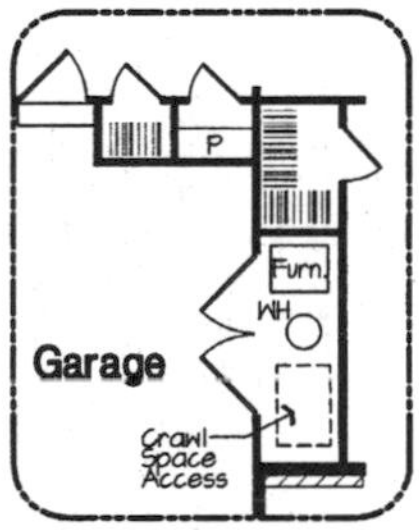

Slab/Crawl Space Option

Garage

Furn.

WH

Crawl Space Access

P

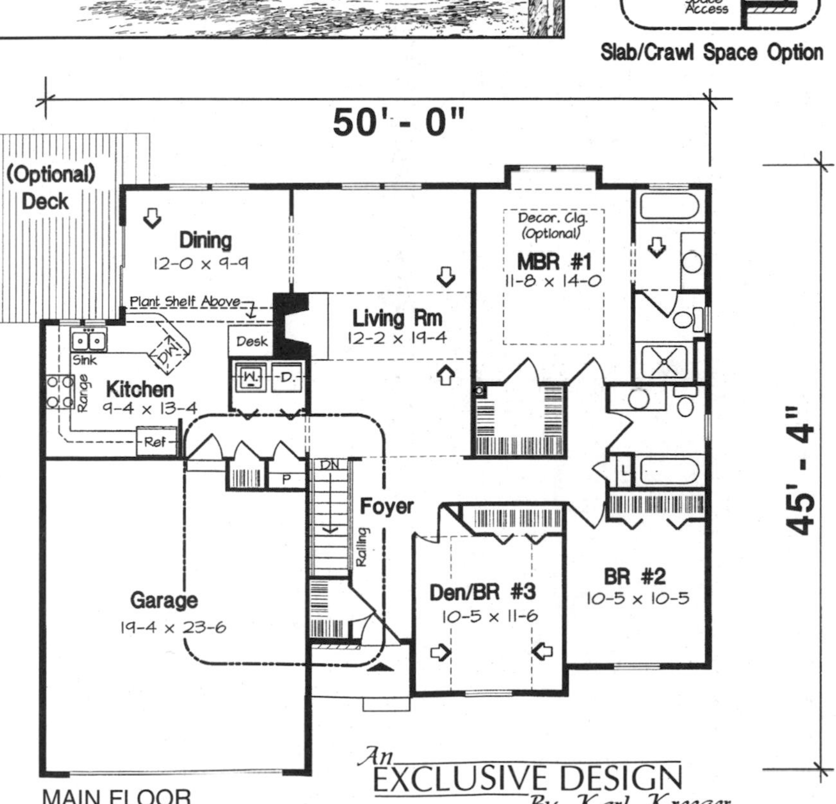

50'-0"
45'-4"
(Optional) Deck
Dining
12-0 x 9-9
Plant Shelf Above
Living Rm
12-2 x 19-4
Decor. Clg. (Optional)
MBR #1
11-8 x 14-0
Desk
Sink
Kitchen
9-4 x 13-4
Range
DW
W
D
Ref
P
DN
Foyer
Railing
L
Garage
19-4 x 23-6
Den/BR #3
10-5 x 11-6
BR #2
10-5 x 10-5
MAIN FLOOR
No. 20164
An EXCLUSIVE DESIGN
By Karl Kreeger

Easy Living

- This plan features:
  - — Three bedrooms
  - — Two full baths
- A dramatic sloped ceiling and a massive fireplace in the Living Room
- A Dining Room crowned by a sloping ceiling and a plant shelf also having sliding doors to the deck
- A U-shaped Kitchen with abundant cabinets, a window over the sink and a walk-in pantry
- A Master Suite with a private full bath, decorative ceiling and walk-in closet
- Two additional bedrooms that share a full bath

MAIN FLOOR — 1,456 SQ. FT.
BASEMENT — 1,448 SQ. FT.
GARAGE — 452 SQ. FT.

TOTAL LIVING AREA:
1,456 SQ. FT.

To order your Blueprints, call 1-800-235-5700

PLAN NO. 26760

Refer to **Pricing Schedule C** on the order form for pricing information

Natural Light & Views

- This plan features:
- — Three bedrooms
- — Two full and one half baths
- A sheltered entrance enhanced by skylight
- An adjoining Living and Dining Room for easy entertaining
- A prow-shaped Family Room highlighted by beamed ceiling, cozy fireplace and sliding glass door to multi-level Deck
- An open Kitchen with a cook island and Breakfast area with access to Deck
- A Master Bedroom with private Deck and bath with a dressing area walk-in closet
- Two additional bedrooms near full bath

MAIN FLOOR — 2,023 SQ. FT.
DECKS — 589 SQ. FT.

TOTAL LIVING AREA:
2,023 SQ. FT.

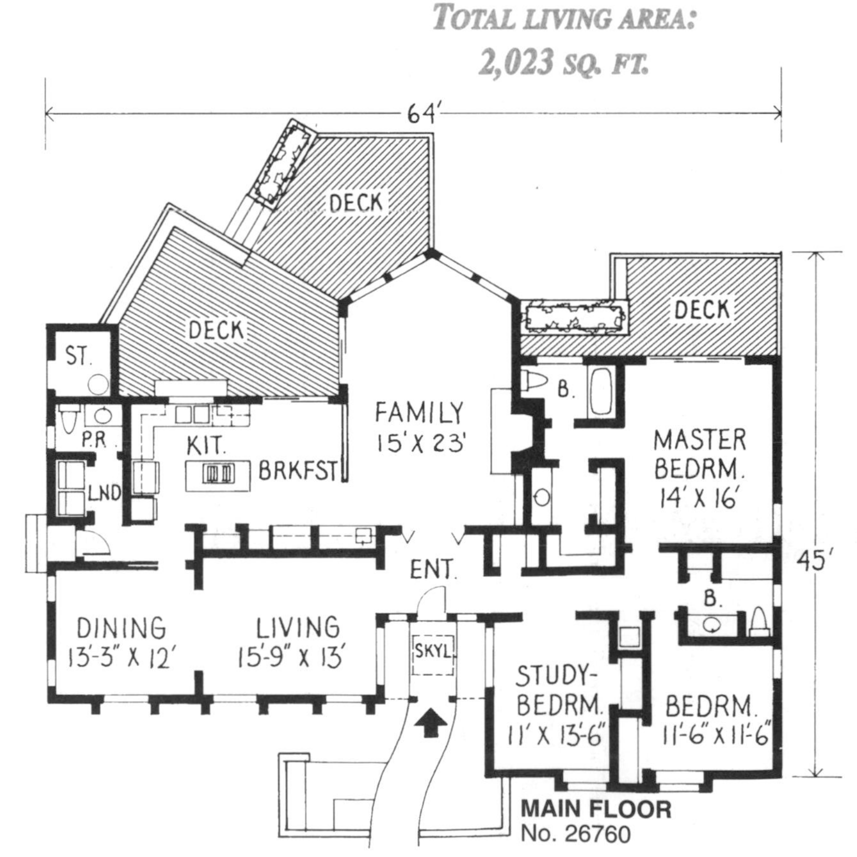
64'
DECK
DECK
DECK
ST.
P.R.
KIT.
BRKFST
LND
FAMILY
15' X 23'
B.
MASTER
BEDRM.
14' X 16'
45'
ENT.
B.
DINING
13'-3" X 12'
LIVING
15'-9" X 13'
SKYL.
STUDY-
BEDRM.
11' X 13'-6"
BEDRM.
11'-6" X 11'-6"

MAIN FLOOR
No. 26760

Refer to **Pricing Schedule A** on the order form for pricing information

PLAN NO. 90307

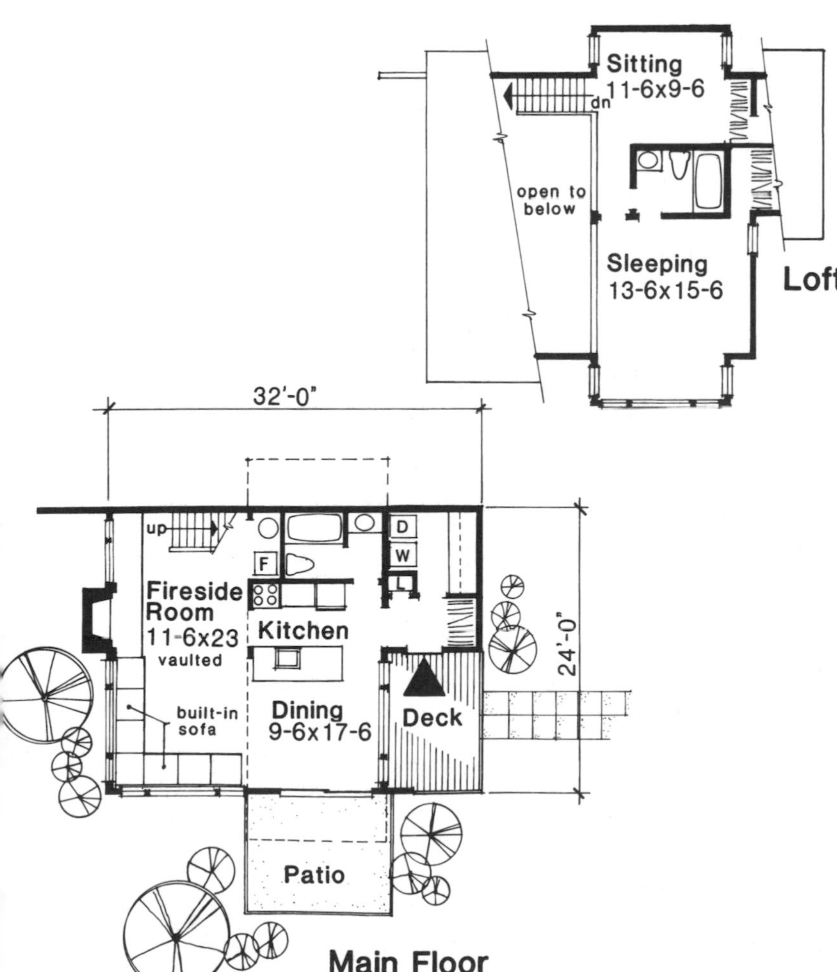
Sitting
11-6x9-6
dn
open to below
Sleeping
13-6x15-6
Loft
32'-0"
24'-0"
up
F
D
W
Fireside Room
11-6x23
vaulted
Kitchen
built-in sofa
Dining
9-6x17-6
Deck
Patio
Main Floor
No. 90307

Open Floor Plan Enhances Home

- This plan features:
  - — One bedroom
  - — Two full baths
- A Fireside Room with a vaulted ceiling and a unique built-in sofa enclosed in glass with a focal point fireplace
- A centrally-located island Kitchen efficiently laid out and flowing into the Dining Room
- A second floor bedroom incorporating a bump-out window and a sitting room

FIRST FLOOR — 768 SQ. FT.
SECOND FLOOR — 419 SQ. FT.

TOTAL LIVING AREA:
1,187 SQ. FT.

PLAN NO. 10464

Refer to **Pricing Schedule D** on the order form for pricing information

Central Atrium Highlights Plan

- This plan features:
- — Three bedrooms
- — Two and a half baths
- A tiled entry hall continuing into the Family Room offers easy maintenance and access to all the living areas and the Garage
- A unique Atrium in the center of the home offers outdoor living inside
- A spacious Living Room with a fireplace flanked by bookcases
- An efficient Kitchen featuring a peninsula counter/snackbar dividing the Family Room, Nook and Utility areas
- A Master Bedroom suite offering a plush, double vanity bath
- Two additional bedrooms with walk-in closets and private access to a full bath

MAIN FLOOR — 2,222 SQ. FT.
GARAGE — 468 SQ. FT.

TOTAL LIVING AREA:
2,222 SQ. FT.

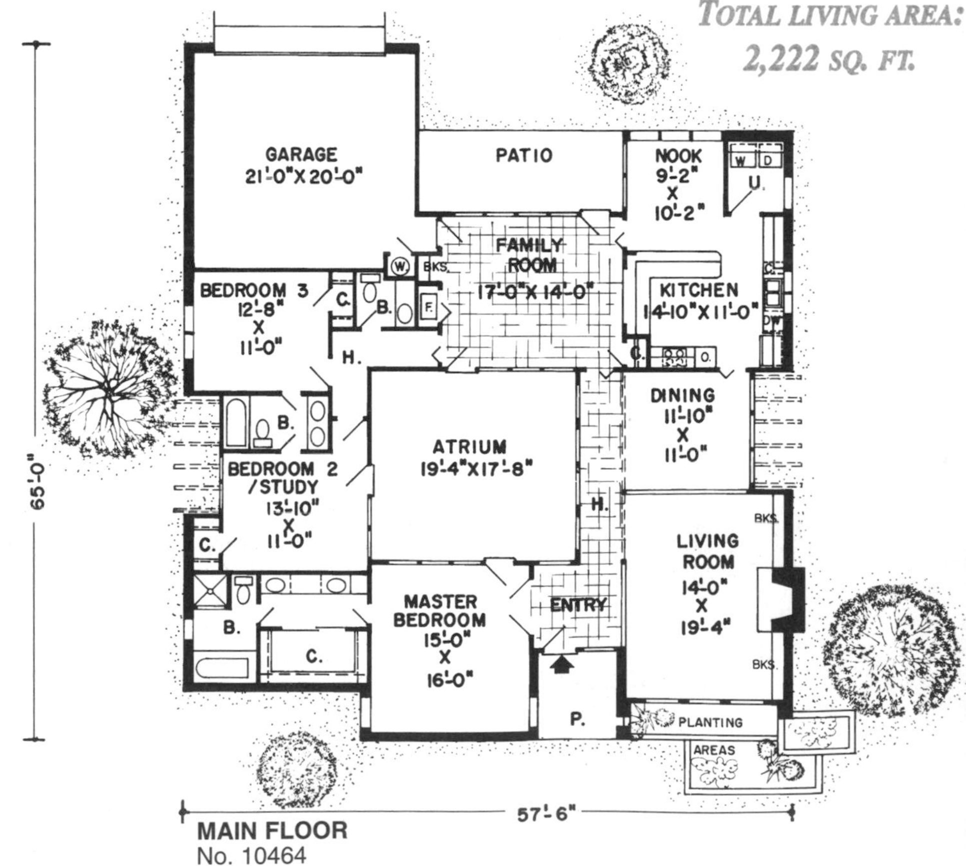
GARAGE
21'-0"X20'-0"
PATIO
NOOK
9'-2" X 10'-2"
W
D
U.
FAMILY ROOM
17'-0"X14'-0"
KITCHEN
14'-10"X11'-0"
DW
BKS.
BEDROOM 3
12'-8" X 11'-0"
C.
B.
F.
H.
C.
O.
DINING
11'-10" X 11'-0"
B.
ATRIUM
19'-4"X17'-8"
BEDROOM 2 /STUDY
13'-10" X 11'-0"
C.
H.
LIVING ROOM
14'-0" X 19'-4"
BKS.
BKS.
MASTER BEDROOM
15'-0" X 16'-0"
ENTRY
B.
C.
P.
PLANTING AREAS
65'-0"
57'-6"
MAIN FLOOR
No. 10464

To order your Blueprints, call 1-800-235-5700

Refer to **Pricing Schedule C** on the order form for pricing information

PLAN NO. 92560

Covered Front and Rear Porches

TOTAL LIVING AREA:
1,660 SQ. FT.

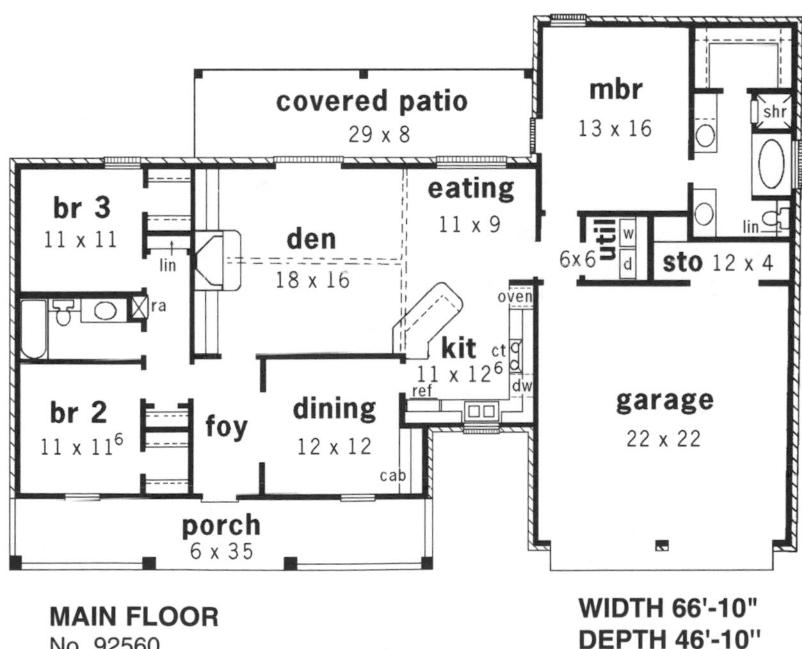

covered patio
29 x 8
mbr
13 x 16
shr
lin
br 3
11 x 11
lin
den
18 x 16
eating
11 x 9
util
w
d
6x6
sto 12 x 4
oven
ra
kit
11 x 12^6
ct
dw
ref
br 2
11 x 11^6
foy
dining
12 x 12
cab
garage
22 x 22
porch
6 x 35

MAIN FLOOR
No. 92560

WIDTH 66'-10"
DEPTH 46'-10"

- This plan features:
- —Three bedrooms
- —Two full baths
- Traditional country styling with front and rear covered porches
- Peninsula counter/eating bar in Kitchen for meals on the go
- Informal Breakfast area and formal Dining room with built-in cabinet
- Vaulted ceiling and cozy fireplace highlighting Den
- Master Bedroom suite in private corner pampered by five-piece bath
- Split bedroom plan with additional bedrooms at the opposite of home sharing full bath
- Optional Slab or Crawl space foundation — please specify when ordering

MAIN FLOOR — 1,660 SQ. FT.
GARAGE — 544 SQ. FT.

PLAN NO. 20075

Refer to **Pricing Schedule B** on the order form for pricing information

Compact and Appealing

- This plan features:
- — Three bedrooms
- — Two full baths
- A fireplaced Living Room and formal Dining Room with extra wide doorways
- A centrally-located Kitchen for maximum convenience
- A Master Bedroom with a vaulted ceiling and a private Master Bath and walk-in closet

MAIN AREA — 1,682 SQ. FT.
BASEMENT — 1,682 SQ. FT.
GARAGE — 484 SQ. FT.

TOTAL LIVING AREA:
1,682 SQ. FT.

An EXCLUSIVE DESIGN *By Karl Kreeger*

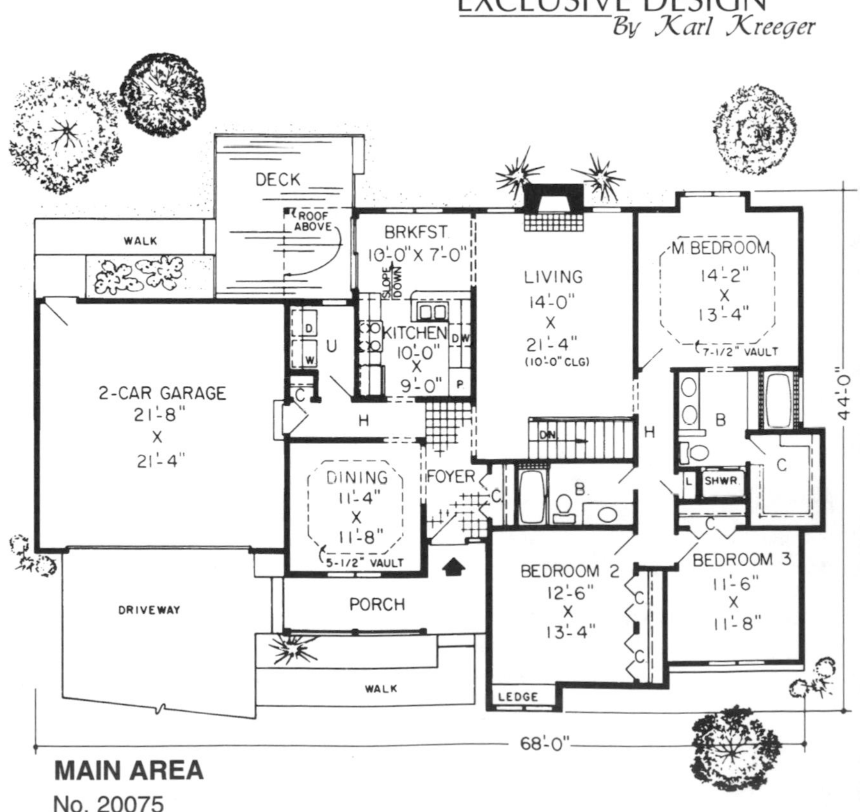

DECK
ROOF ABOVE
WALK
BRKFST
10'-0" X 7'-0"
SLOPE DOWN
LIVING
14'-0"
X
21'-4"
(10'-0" CLG)
M BEDROOM
14'-2"
X
13'-4"
7-1/2" VAULT
KITCHEN
10'-0"
X
9'-0"
DW
P
D
W
U
C
H
DN
2-CAR GARAGE
21'-8"
X
21'-4"
DINING
11'-4"
X
11'-8"
5-1/2" VAULT
FOYER
B
L
SHWR
BEDROOM 2
12'-6"
X
13'-4"
BEDROOM 3
11'-6"
X
11'-8"
DRIVEWAY
PORCH
WALK
LEDGE
44'-0"
68'-0"

MAIN AREA
No. 20075

To order your Blueprints, call 1-800-235-5700

Refer to **Pricing Schedule Z** on the order form for pricing information

PLAN NO. 84020

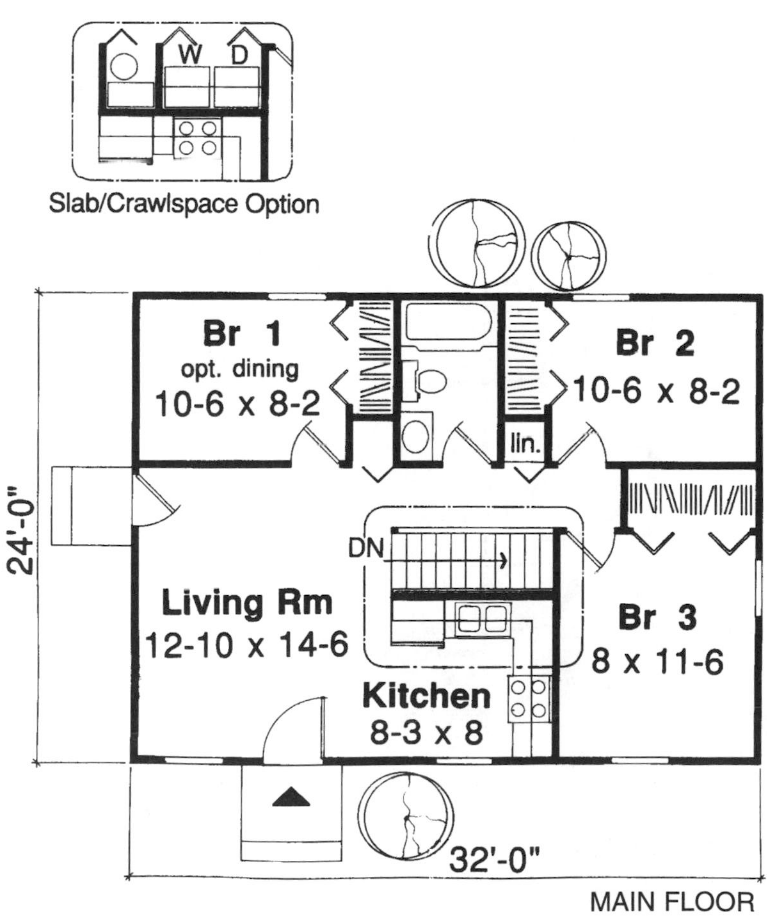

W
D
Slab/Crawlspace Option
Br 1
opt. dining
10-6 x 8-2
Br 2
10-6 x 8-2
lin.
DN
Living Rm
12-10 x 14-6
Br 3
8 x 11-6
Kitchen
8-3 x 8
24'-0"
32'-0"

MAIN FLOOR
No. 84020

Compact, Open Cabin

- This plan features:
  - — Three bedrooms
  - — One full bath
- An open Living Room leading into an efficient Kitchen
- Three bedrooms, with ample closets, sharing a full hall bath
- A full basement option or a separate washer and dryer area
- No materials list is available for this plan

MAIN FLOOR — 768 SQ. FT.

TOTAL LIVING AREA:
768 SQ. FT.

P L A N N O . 9 0 3 4 8

Refer to **Pricing Schedule A** on the order form for pricing information

Window Design Highlights Plan

- This plan features:
- — Two bedrooms plus loft
- — Two full baths
- An airy Living Room with glass on three sides and a fireplace tucked into corner
- An efficient Kitchen serving the Living and Dining Rooms easily
- First floor Bedrooms featuring a private bath and a walk-in closet connected to Storage area
- A landing staircase leading to a second bedroom with a walk-in closet, a Laundry and a full Bath
- A ladder to top-of-the-tower Loft with loads of light and multiple uses

FIRST FLOOR — 729 SQ. FT.
SECOND FLOOR — 420 SQ. FT.

TOTAL LIVING AREA:
1,149 SQ. FT

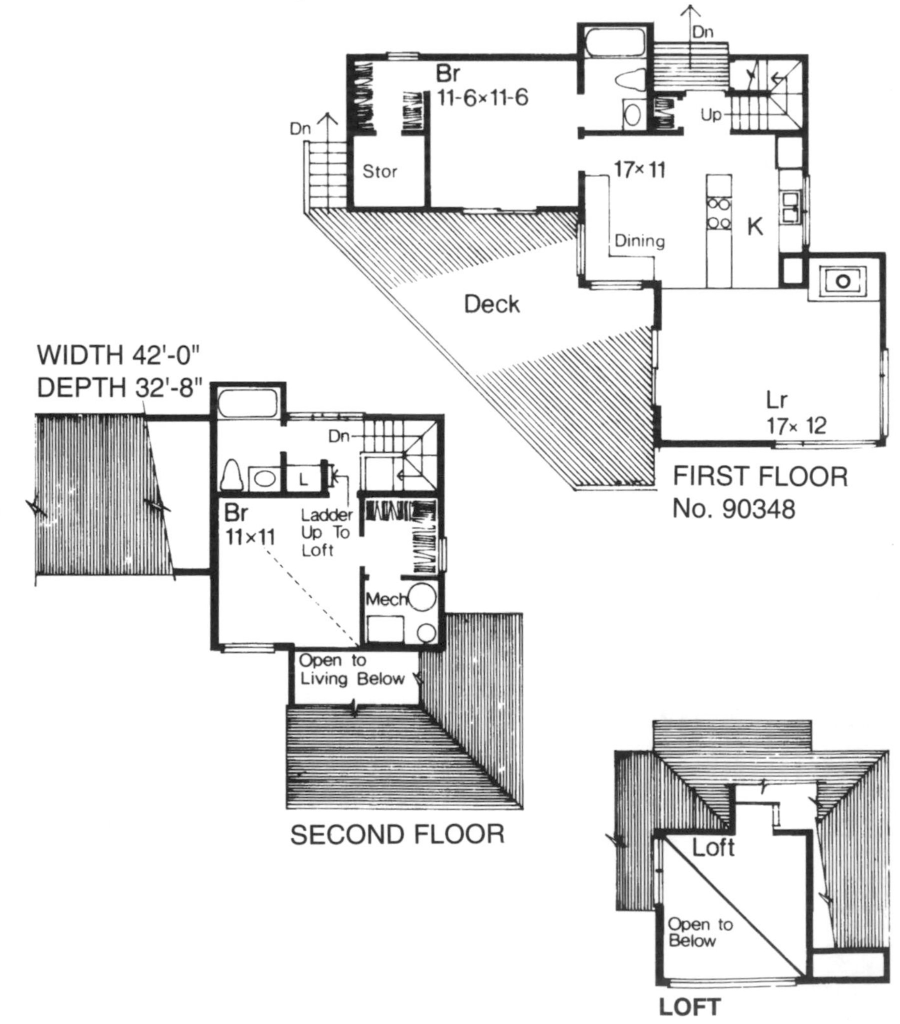

WIDTH 42'-0"
DEPTH 32'-8"
Br
11-6×11-6
Dn
Stor
Up
17×11
Dining
K
Deck
Lr
17× 12
FIRST FLOOR
No. 90348
Dn
L
Br
11×11
Ladder
Up To
Loft
Mech
Open to
Living Below
SECOND FLOOR
Loft
Open to
Below
LOFT

Refer to **Pricing Schedule E** on the order form for pricing information

PLAN NO. 10542

An EXCLUSIVE DESIGN *By Karl Kreeger*

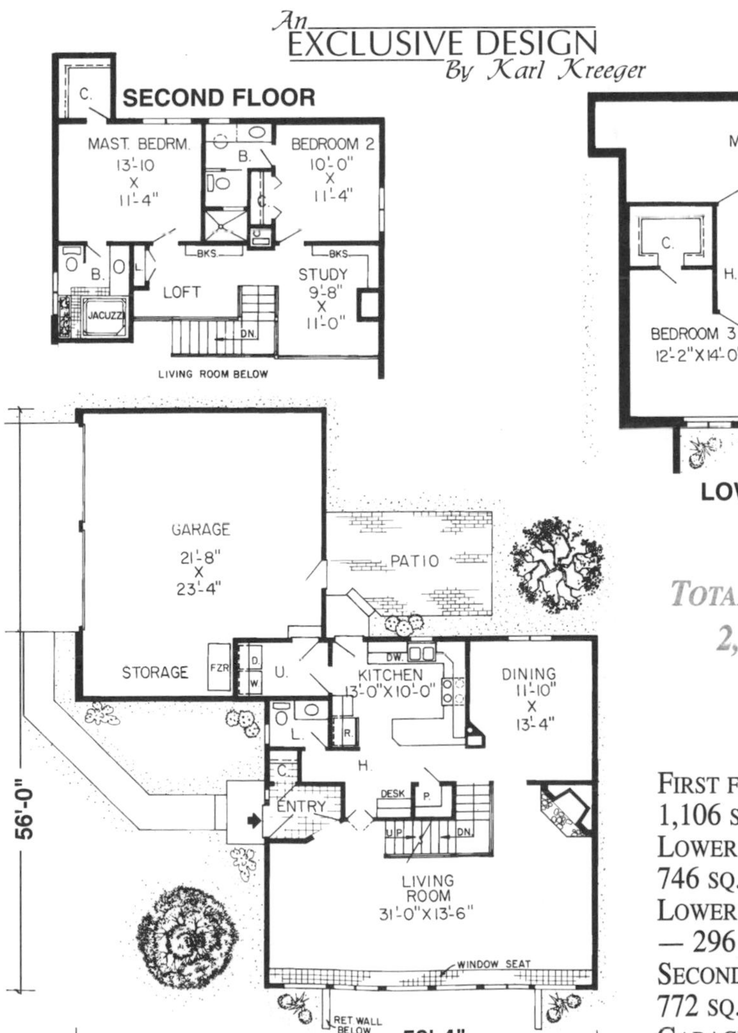

SECOND FLOOR
C.
MAST. BEDRM. 13'-10 X 11'-4"
B.
BEDROOM 2 10'-0" X 11'-4"
BKS
B.
JACUZZI
LOFT
STUDY 9'-8" X 11'-0"
DN
LIVING ROOM BELOW
GARAGE 21'-8" X 23'-4"
PATIO
STORAGE
FZR
D
W
U.
DW
KITCHEN 13'-0"X10'-0"
DINING 11'-10" X 13'-4"
L.
R
C.
H.
DESK
P.
ENTRY
UP
DN
LIVING ROOM 31'-0"X13'-6"
WINDOW SEAT
RET WALL BELOW
56'-0"
50'-4"
FIRST FLOOR
No. 10542

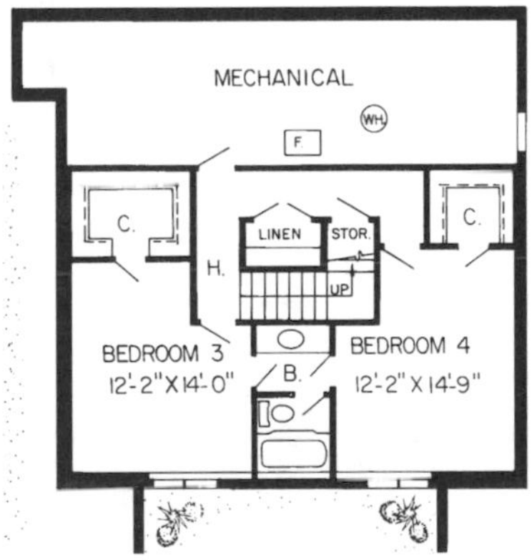

MECHANICAL

WH

F

C.

LINEN

STOR

UP

C.

H.

BEDROOM 3 12'-2"X14'-0"

B.

BEDROOM 4 12'-2"X14'-9"

LOWER LEVEL

Clerestory Windows above Window Seat

- This plan features:
- — Four bedrooms
- — Three and a half baths
- A tile Entry leading into a two-story Living Room with a corner fireplace and two levels of windows above the Window Seat
- A central Kitchen with a peninsula counter, a double sink, a built-in desk, and direct access to the Dining Room, Patio, Utility Room and Garage
- A Master Bedroom suite with a walk-in closet and a plush bath with a Jacuzzi
- On the upper level, another Bedroom with a private bath, a Study and a Loft overlooking Living Room
- Two additional bedrooms, with walk-in closets, share a full bath on the lower level.

TOTAL LIVING AREA:
2,624 SQ. FT.

FIRST FLOOR —
1,106 SQ. FT.
LOWER LEVEL (FINISHED) —
746 SQ. FT.
LOWER LEVEL (UNFINISHED)
— 296 SQ. FT.
SECOND FLOOR —
772 SQ. FT.
GARAGE — 645 SQ. FT.

PLAN NO. 10328

Refer to **Pricing Schedule B** on the order form for pricing information

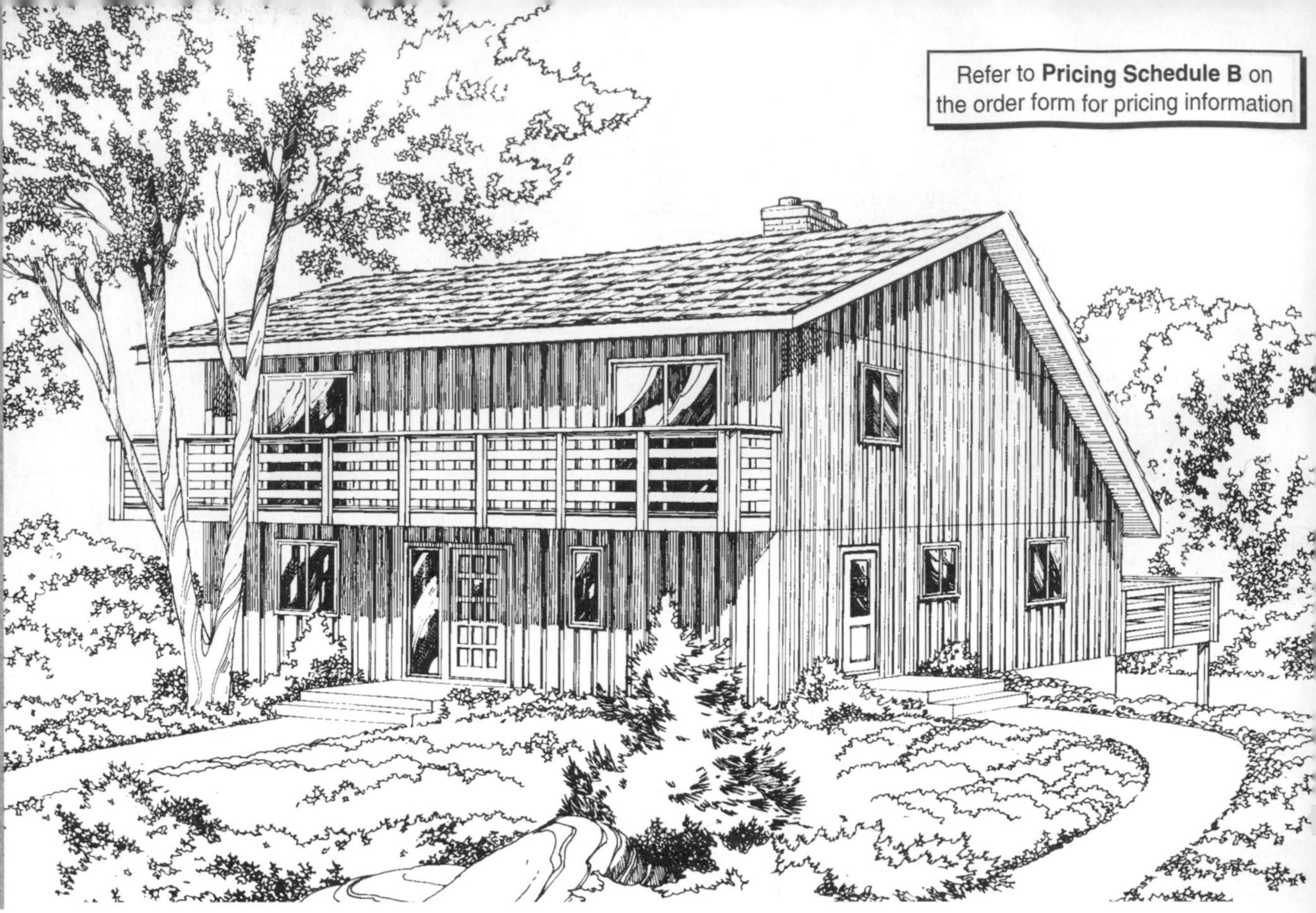

Living Room Focus of Spacious Home

- This plan features:
  - — Three bedrooms
  - — One full and one three quarter bath
- A well planned traffic pattern connecting the Dining Area, the Kitchen, the laundry niche and the bath
- A balcony overlooking the open Living Room second floor
- Sliding glass doors opening to the deck, a fireplace and a sizable Living Room

FIRST FLOOR — 1,024 SQ. FT.
SECOND FLOOR — 576 SQ. FT.
BASEMENT — 1,024 SQ. FT.

TOTAL LIVING AREA:
1,600 SQ. FT.

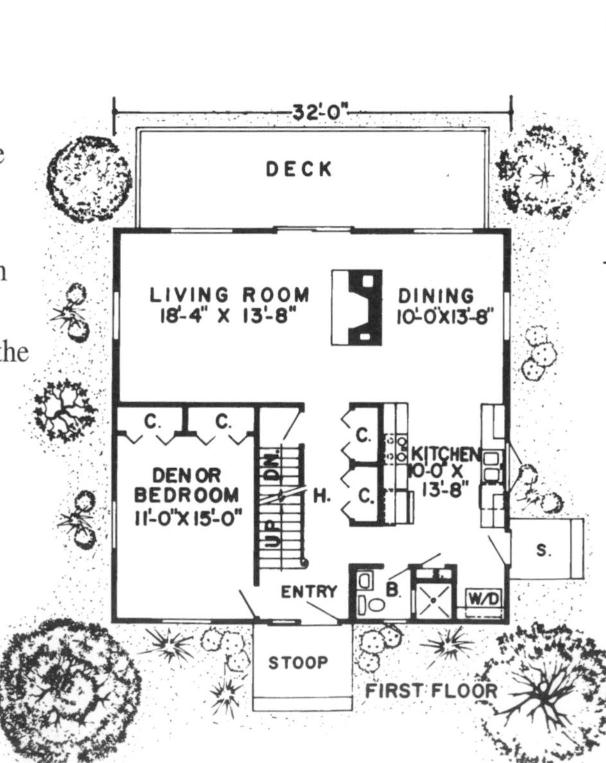
32'-0"
DECK
LIVING ROOM
18'-4" X 13'-8"
DINING
10'-0"X13'-8"
C.
C.
C.
C.
DEN OR
BEDROOM
11'-0"X15'-0"
UP
DN
H.
KITCHEN
10'-0" X
13'-8"
S.
B.
ENTRY
W/D
STOOP
FIRST FLOOR

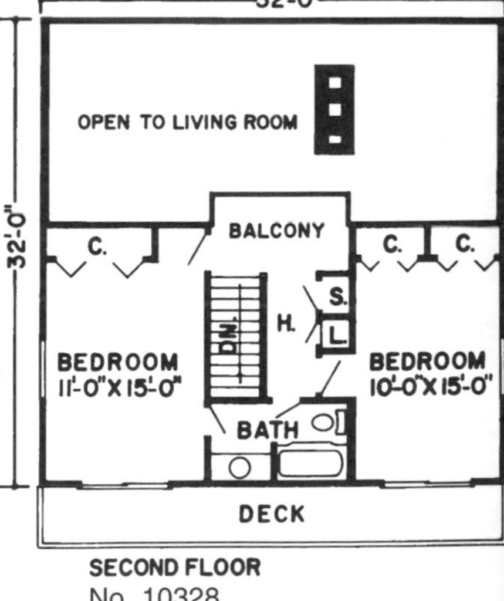
32'-0"
32'-0"
OPEN TO LIVING ROOM
BALCONY
C.
C.
C.
S.
H.
L
DN
BEDROOM
11'-0"X15'-0"
BEDROOM
10'-0"X15'-0"
BATH
DECK

SECOND FLOOR
No. 10328

Refer to **Pricing Schedule A** on the order form for pricing information

PLAN NO. 84058

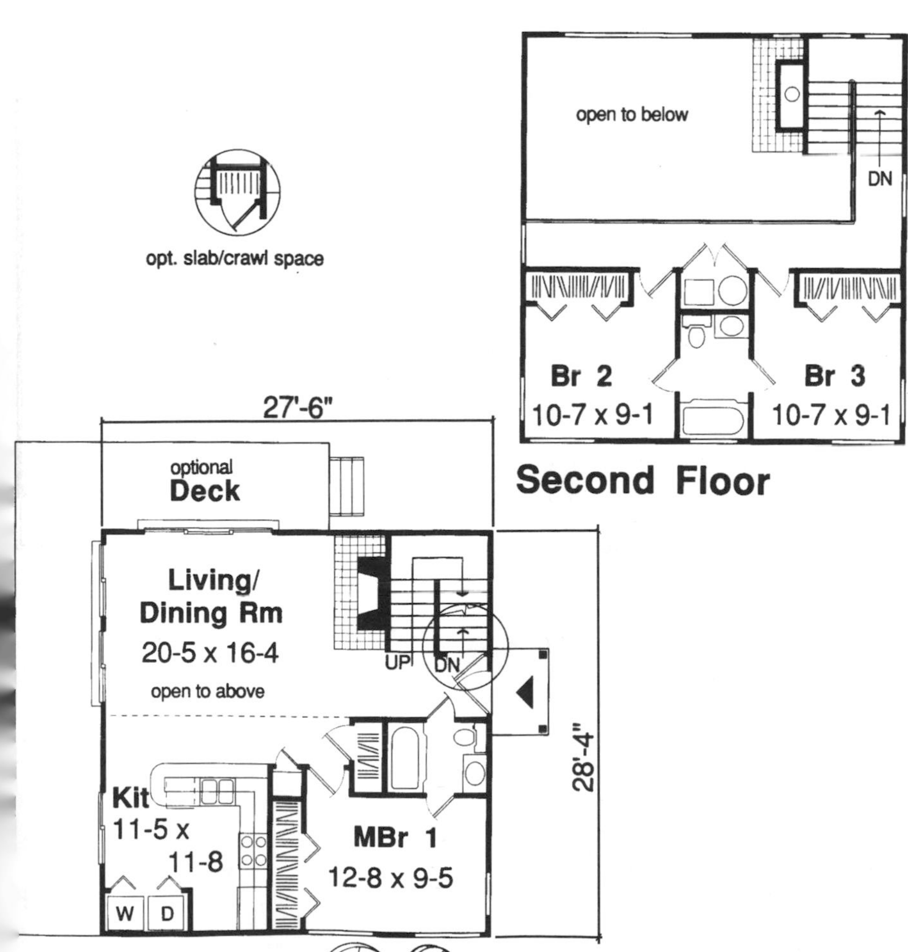

open to below
DN
opt. slab/crawl space
Br 2
10-7 x 9-1
Br 3
10-7 x 9-1
Second Floor
27'-6"
optional
Deck
Living/
Dining Rm
20-5 x 16-4
open to above
UP
DN
28'-4"
Kit
11-5 x
11-8
W
D
MBr 1
12-8 x 9-5
No. 84058
First Floor

Well Planned Saltbox has Rustic Charm

- This plan features:
  - — Three bedrooms
  - — Two full baths
- Efficient use of living space creating a spacious feeling
- A Living/Dining area occupying more than half of the lower level
- A central chimney housing a built-in fireplace
- An optional deck
- No materials list available for this plan

FIRST FLOOR — 779 SQ. FT.
SECOND FLOOR — 519 SQ. FT.

TOTAL LIVING AREA:
1,298 SQ. FT.

PLAN NO. 26810

Refer to **Pricing Schedule E** on the order form for pricing information

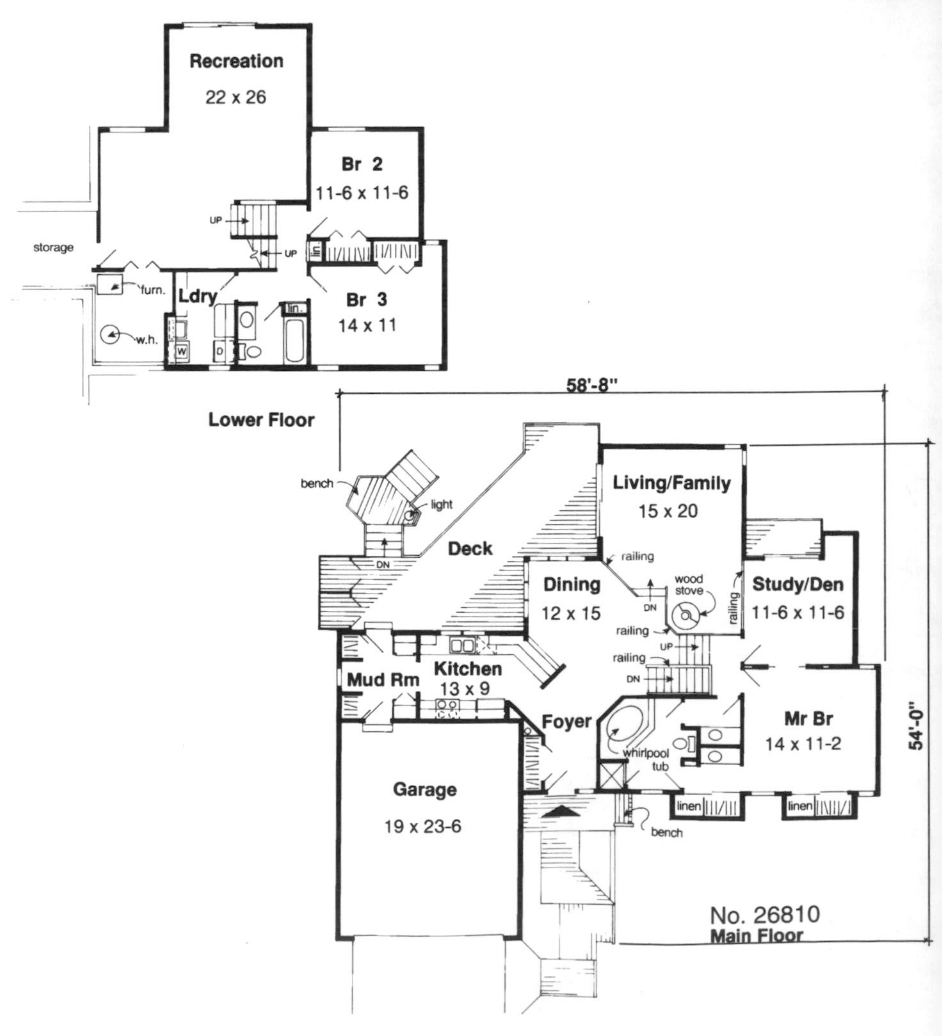

Recreation
22 x 26
Br 2
11-6 x 11-6
UP
UP
storage
furn.
Ldry
w.h.
W
D
lin.
Br 3
14 x 11
Lower Floor
58'-8"
bench
light
DN
Deck
Living/Family
15 x 20
railing
Dining
12 x 15
wood stove
DN
railing
railing
Study/Den
11-6 x 11-6
railing
UP
DN
Mud Rm
Kitchen
13 x 9
Foyer
whirlpool tub
Mr Br
14 x 11-2
54'-0"
Garage
19 x 23-6
linen
linen
bench
No. 26810
Main Floor

Master Suite on a Private Level

- This plan features:
  - — Three bedrooms
  - — Two full baths
- A Dining Room and sunken Living Room on a space-expanding diagonal
- A corridor Kitchen extending into a traffic-free space open to the living areas
- A deck, making the outdoors a natural part of all social areas
- A Master Bedroom connecting to a Study and deck
- A recreation area in the Basement level

FIRST FLOOR — 1,423 SQ. FT.
LOWER FLOOR — 1,420 SQ. FT.
GARAGE — 478 SQ. FT.

TOTAL LIVING AREA:
2,843 SQ. FT.

To order your Blueprints, call 1-800-235-5700

Refer to **Pricing Schedule B** on the order form for pricing information

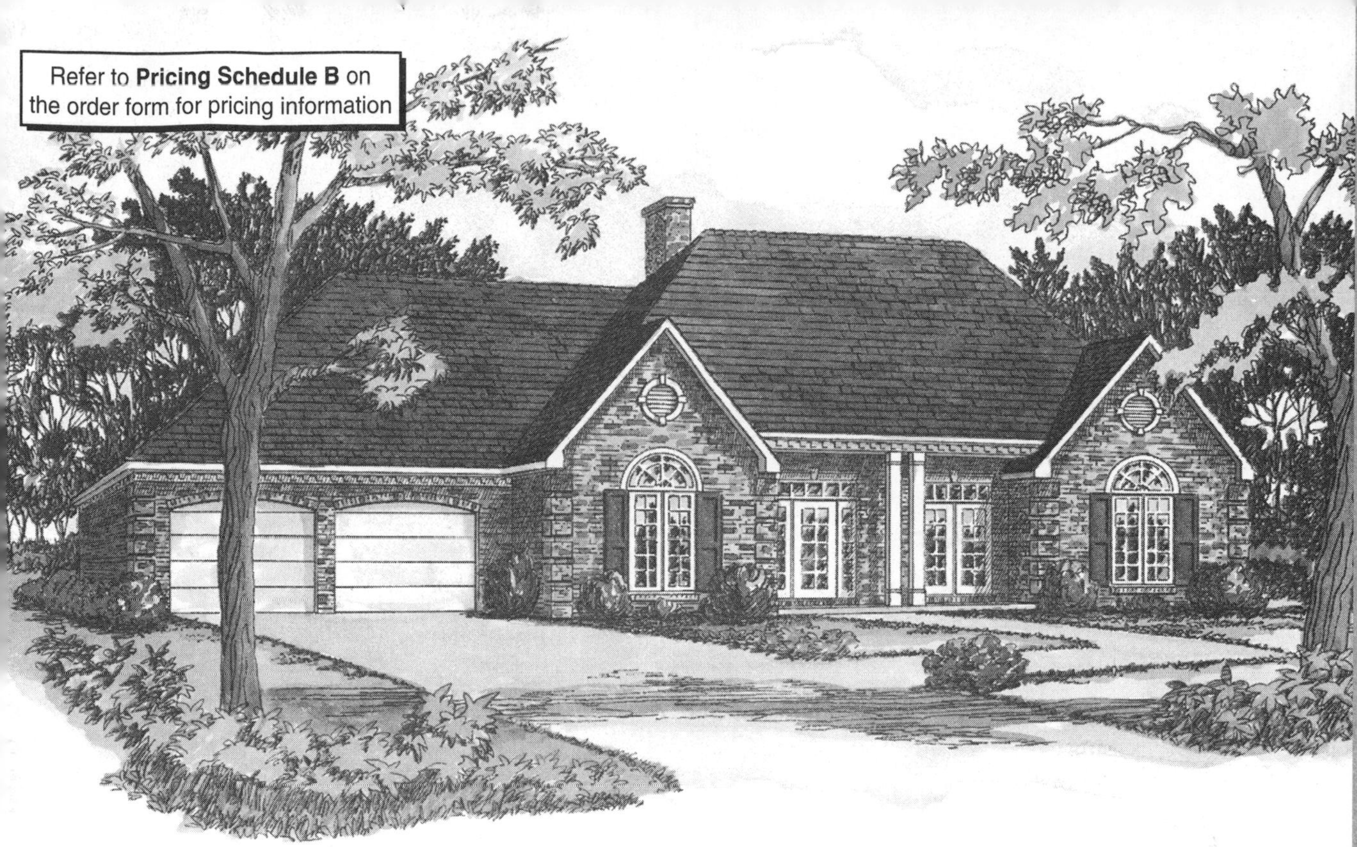

PLAN NO. 92557

Elegant Brick Exterior

- This plan features:

—Three bedrooms

—Two full baths

- Detailing and accenting columns highlighting the covered front porch
- Den is enhanced by a corner fireplace and adjoining with Dining Room
- Efficient Kitchen well-appointed and with easy access to the utility/laundry room
- Master Bedroom topped by a vaulted ceiling and a private bath and a walk-in closet
- Two secondary bedrooms are located at the opposite end of home sharing a full bath
- Optional slab or crawl space foundation — Please specify when ordering

MAIN FLOOR — 1,390 SQ. FT.
GARAGE — 590 SQ. FT.

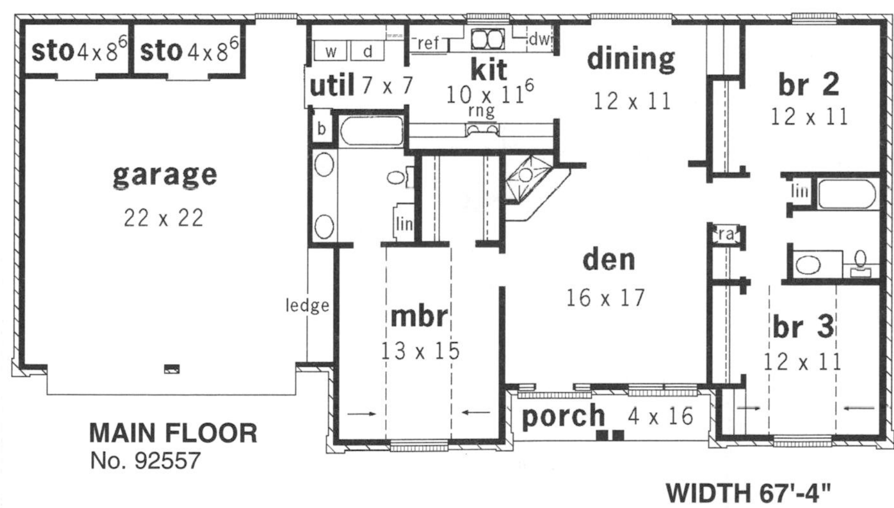

sto 4 x 8⁶
sto 4 x 8⁶
garage
22 x 22
util 7 x 7
w
d
ref
dw
kit
10 x 11⁶
rng
dining
12 x 11
br 2
12 x 11
b
lin
lin
ra
den
16 x 17
ledge
mbr
13 x 15
br 3
12 x 11
porch 4 x 16
MAIN FLOOR
No. 92557
WIDTH 67'-4"
DEPTH 32'-10"

TOTAL LIVING AREA:
1,390 SQ. FT.

PLAN NO. 1078

Refer to **Pricing Schedule A** on the order form for pricing information

Vacation Retreat or Year Round Living

- This plan features:
- — Two bedrooms
- — One full bath
- A long hallway dividing bedrooms and living areas assuring privacy
- A centrally located utility room and bath
- An open Living/Dining Room area with exposed beams, sloping ceilings and optional fireplace

FIRST FLOOR — 1,024 SQ. FT.
CARPORT & STORAGE — 387 SQ. FT.
DECK — 411 SQ. FT.

TOTAL LIVING AREA:
1,024 SQ. FT.

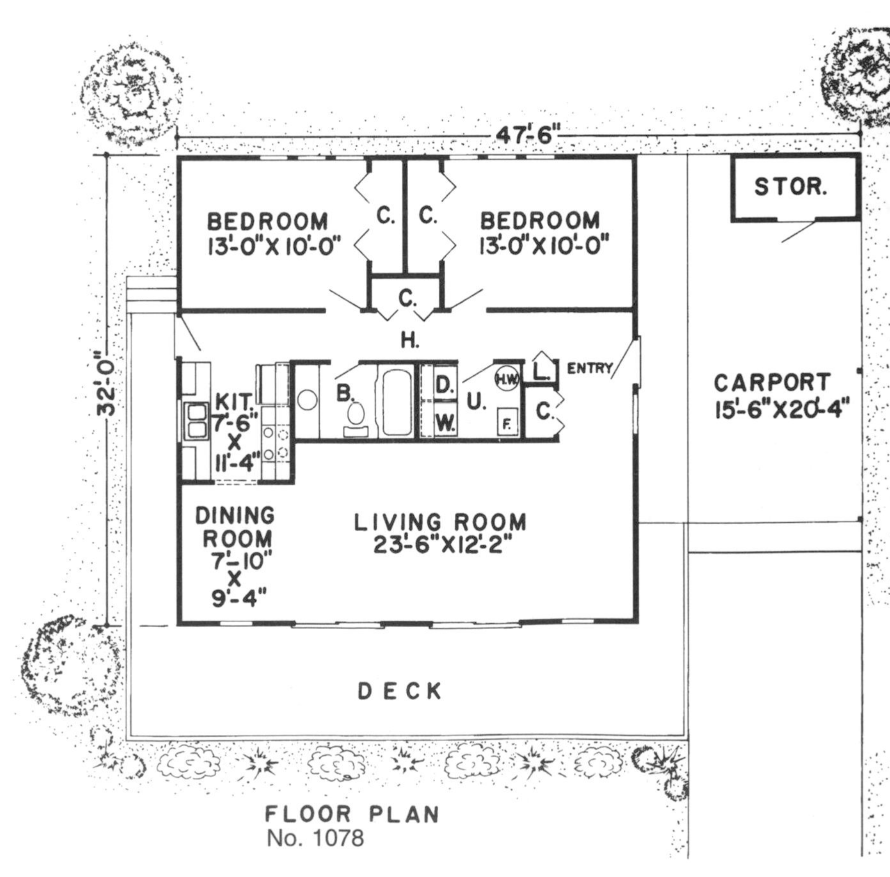
47'-6"
32'-0"
BEDROOM
13'-0"X10'-0"
C.
C.
BEDROOM
13'-0"X10'-0"
STOR.
C.
H.
KIT.
7'-6"
X
11'-4"
B.
D.
W.
U.
H.W.
L.
ENTRY
F.
C.
CARPORT
15'-6"X20'-4"
DINING
ROOM
7'-10"
X
9'-4"
LIVING ROOM
23'-6"X12'-2"
DECK

FLOOR PLAN
No. 1078

To order your Blueprints, call 1-800-235-5700

Refer to **Pricing Schedule B** on the order form for pricing information

PLAN NO. 84056

Convenient Single Level Living

- This plan features:
  - — Three bedrooms
  - — Two full baths
- A well-appointed U-shaped Kitchen that includes a view of the front yard and a built-in pantry
- An expansive Great Room with direct access to the rear yard, expanding the living space
- A Master Bedroom equipped with two closets—one is a walk-in—and a private bath
- Two additional bedrooms that share a full hall bath
- A step-saving, centrally located laundry center
- No materials list available for this plan

MAIN FLOOR — 1,644 SQ. FT.
GARAGE — 576 SQ. FT.

TOTAL LIVING AREA:
1,644 SQ. FT.

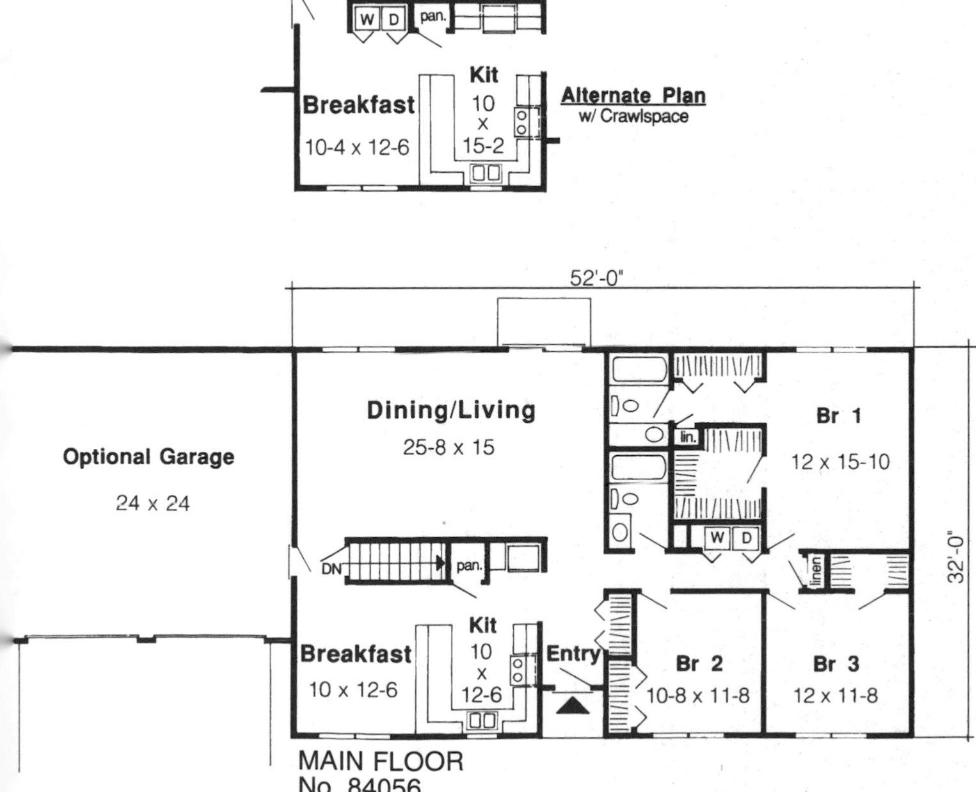
W
D
pan.
Kit
10 x 15-2
Breakfast
10-4 x 12-6
Alternate Plan
w/ Crawlspace
52'-0"
Dining/Living
25-8 x 15
Optional Garage
24 x 24
Br 1
12 x 15-10
lin.
W
D
linen
DN
pan.
32'-0"
Kit
10 x 12-6
Breakfast
10 x 12-6
Entry
Br 2
10-8 x 11-8
Br 3
12 x 11-8
MAIN FLOOR
No. 84056

PLAN NO. 26870

Refer to **Pricing Schedule E** on the order form for pricing information

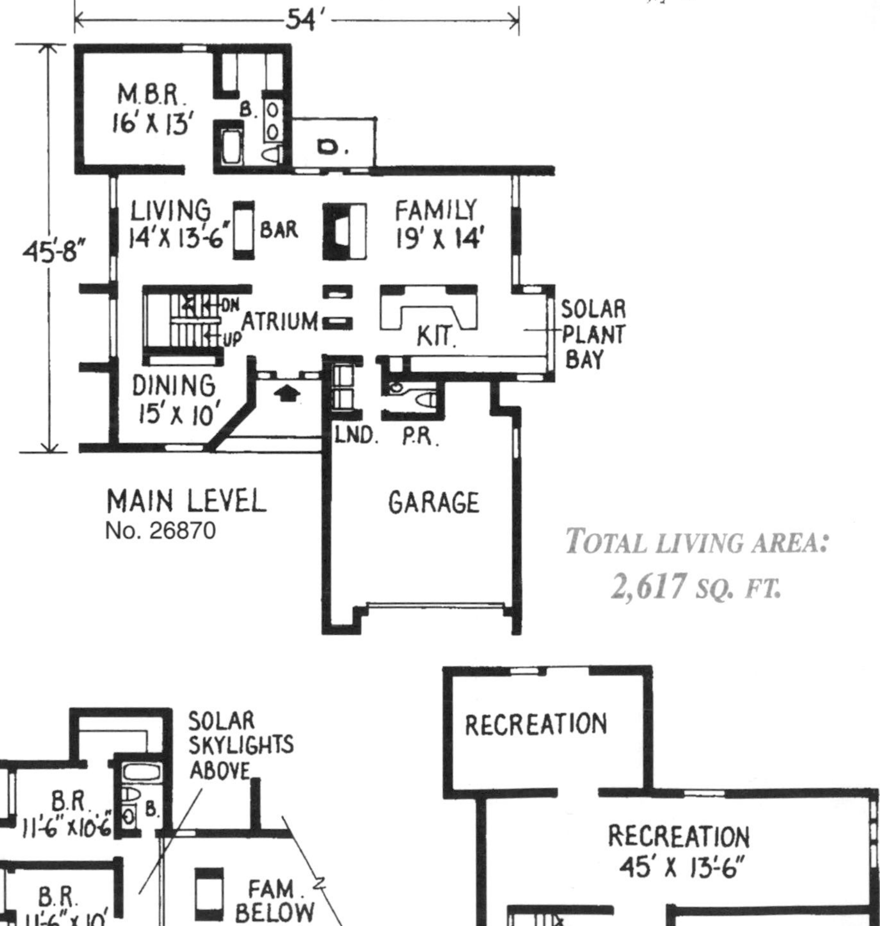
54'
45'-8"
M.B.R.
16' X 13'
B.
D.
LIVING
14' X 13'-6"
BAR
FAMILY
19' X 14'
DN
UP
ATRIUM
KIT.
SOLAR
PLANT
BAY
DINING
15' X 10'
LND.
P.R.
GARAGE
MAIN LEVEL
No. 26870
SOLAR
SKYLIGHTS
ABOVE
B.R.
11'-6" X 10'-6"
B.
B.R.
11'-6" X 10'
FAM.
BELOW
DN
BALC./
STUDY
STOR.
DIN.
BELOW
UPPER LEVEL
RECREATION
RECREATION
45' X 13'-6"
UP
MECH.
STOR.
LOWER LEVEL

Two-Story Atrium

- This plan features:
  - Three bedrooms
  - Two full and one half baths
- A two story Atrium entrance leading into open layout of Living, Family and Kitchen areas
- A spacious Living Room with a quiet Dining Room nearby
- A Family Room with a cozy fireplace and direct access to Deck and Kitchen
- An airy Kitchen with a unique Solar Plant Bay
- A private Master Suite wing with a double vanity bath
- Two additional bedrooms on upper level sharing a Balcony Study and full bath
- Loads of Recreation space and Storage on lower level

FIRST FLOOR — 1,641 SQ. FT.
SECOND FLOOR — 976 SQ. FT.
LOWER FLOOR — 1,632 SQ. FT.

TOTAL LIVING AREA:
2,617 SQ. FT.

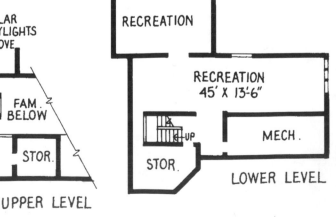

To order your Blueprints, call 1-800-235-5700

Refer to **Pricing Schedule C** on the order form for pricing information

PLAN NO. 92617

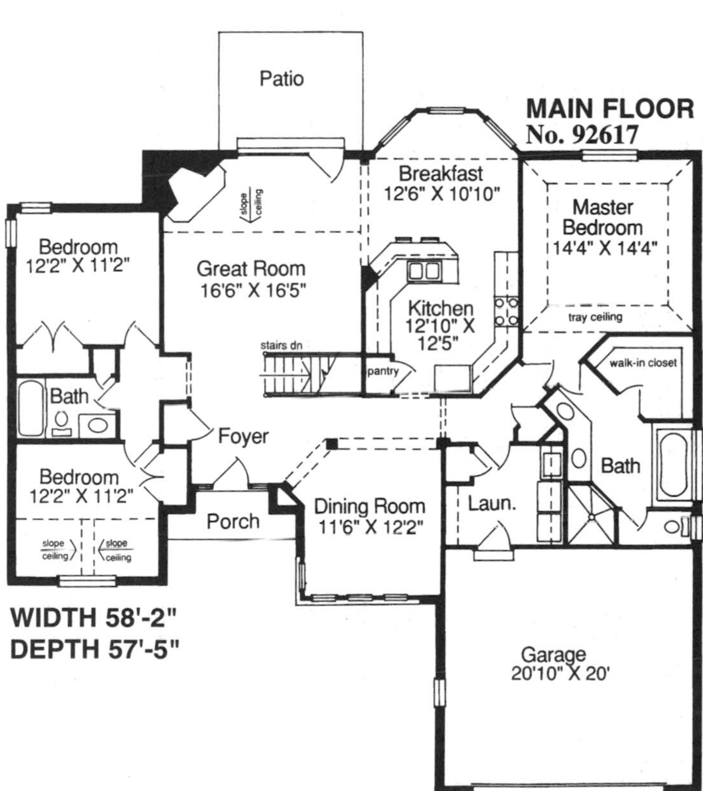

Patio
MAIN FLOOR
No. 92617
Breakfast
12'6" X 10'10"
Master
Bedroom
14'4" X 14'4"
tray ceiling
walk-in closet
slope ceiling
Bedroom
12'2" X 11'2"
Great Room
16'6" X 16'5"
Kitchen
12'10" X
12'5"
stairs dn
pantry
Bath
Foyer
Bath
Bedroom
12'2" X 11'2"
Porch
Dining Room
11'6" X 12'2"
Laun.
slope ceiling
slope ceiling
WIDTH 58'-2"
DEPTH 57'-5"
Garage
20'10" X 20'

Step Saving Convenience

- This plan features:
  - — Three bedrooms
  - — Two full baths
- A covered Porch leading into the Foyer
- A corner fireplace and a wall of windows with an atrium door to the Patio in the Great Room
- An efficient Kitchen with a built-in pantry, a peninsula counter/snack bar separating it from the Breakfast alcove
- Topped by a tray ceiling, a private Master Bedroom offers an ultra bath with a walk-in closet, a double vanity and a window tub
- Two additional bedrooms, one with a sloped ceiling, sharing a full hall bath
- No materials list available

MAIN FLOOR — 1,955 SQ. FT.

TOTAL LIVING AREA:
1,955 SQ. FT.

PLAN NO. 1074

Refer to **Pricing Schedule A** on the order form for pricing information

Design Features
Six Sides

- This plan features:
  - — Three bedrooms
  - — One full and one three quarter bath
- Active living areas centrally located between two quiet bedroom and bath areas
- A Living Room that can be closed off from bedroom wings giving privacy to both areas
- A bath located behind a third bedroom
- A bedroom complete with washer/dryer facilities.

MAIN AREA — 1,040 SQ. FT.
STORAGE — 44 SQ. FT.
DECK — 258 SQ. FT.
CARPORT — 230 SQ. FT.

TOTAL LIVING AREA:
1,040 SQ. FT.

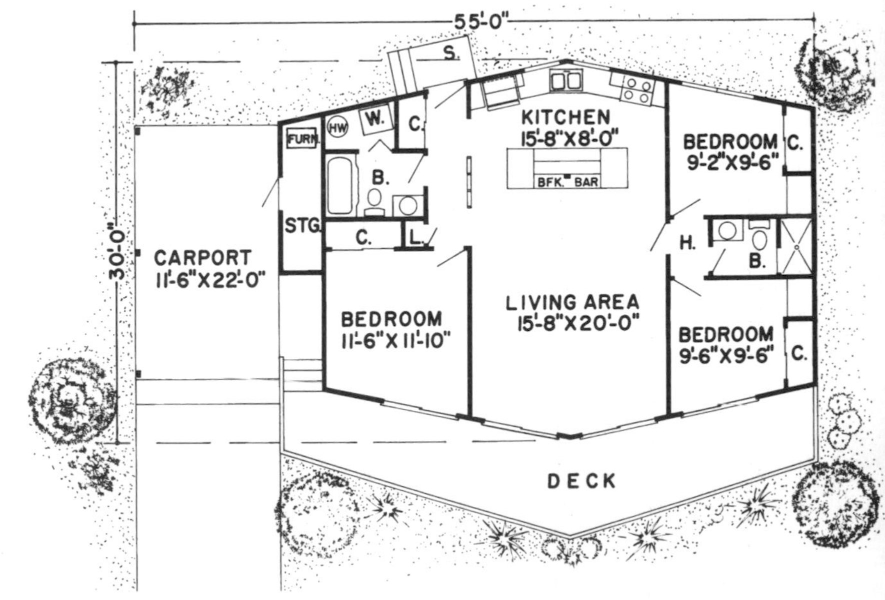
55'-0"
30'-0"
S.
KITCHEN
15'-8"X8'-0"
BFK. BAR
FURN.
HW
W.
C.
B.
STG.
C.
L.
CARPORT
11'-6"X22'-0"
BEDROOM
11'-6"X11'-10"
LIVING AREA
15'-8"X20'-0"
BEDROOM
9'-2"X9'-6"
C.
H.
B.
BEDROOM
9'-6"X9'-6"
C.
DECK

MAIN AREA
No. 1074

To order your Blueprints, call 1-800-235-5700

Refer to **Pricing Schedule Z** on the order form for pricing information

PLAN NO. 24309

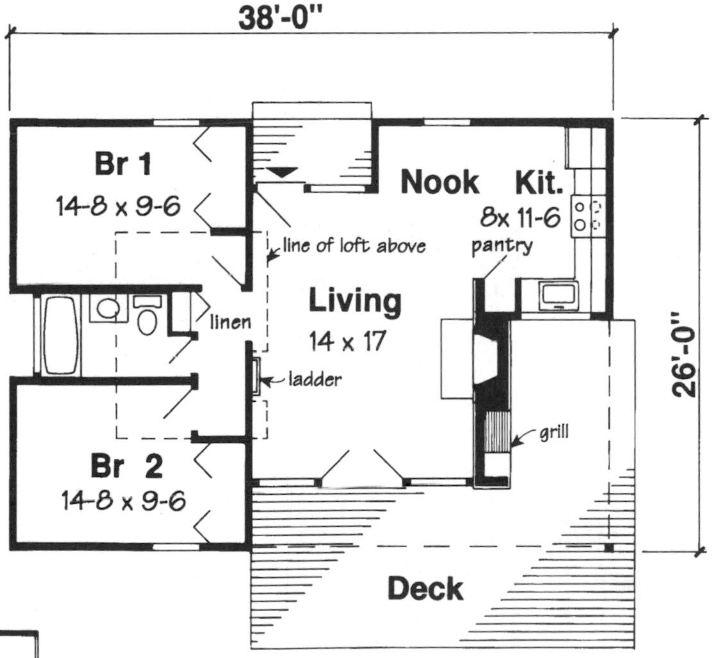

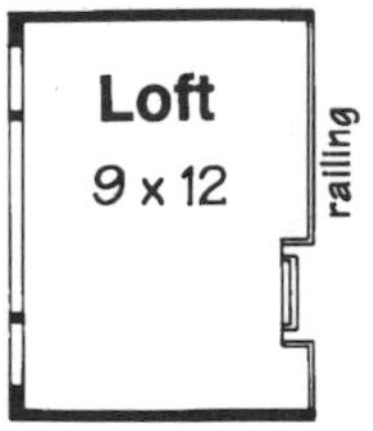

Rustic Retreat

- This plan features:
  - — Two bedrooms
  - — One full bath
- A wrap-around deck equipped with a built-in bar-b-que for easy outdoor living
- An entry, in a wall of glass, opens the Living area to the outdoors
- A large fireplace in the Living area opens into an efficient Kitchen, with a built-in pantry, that serves the Nook area
- Two bedrooms share a centrally located full bath with a window tub
- A loft area ready for multiple uses

MAIN FLOOR — 789 SQ. FT.
LOFT — 108 SQ. FT.

TOTAL LIVING AREA: 897 SQ. FT.

38'-0"
26'-0"
Br 1
14-8 x 9-6
Nook
Kit.
8x 11-6
pantry
line of loft above
Living
14 x 17
linen
ladder
grill
Br 2
14-8 x 9-6
Deck
Loft
9 x 12
railing

Main Floor
No. 24309

An EXCLUSIVE DESIGN By Marshall Associates

PLAN NO. 34601

Refer to **Pricing Schedule A** on the order form for pricing information

Large Front Porch Adds a Country Touch

- This plan features:
- — Three bedrooms
- — Two full baths
- A country-styled front porch
- Vaulted ceiling in the Living Room which includes a fireplace
- An efficient Kitchen with double sinks and peninsula counter that may double as an eating bar
- Two first floor bedrooms with ample closet space
- A second floor Master Suite with sloped ceiling, walk-in closet and private master Bath

FIRST FLOOR — 1,007 SQ. FT.
SECOND FLOOR — 408 SQ. FT.
BASEMENT — 1,007 SQ. FT.

TOTAL LIVING AREA: 1,415 SQ. FT.

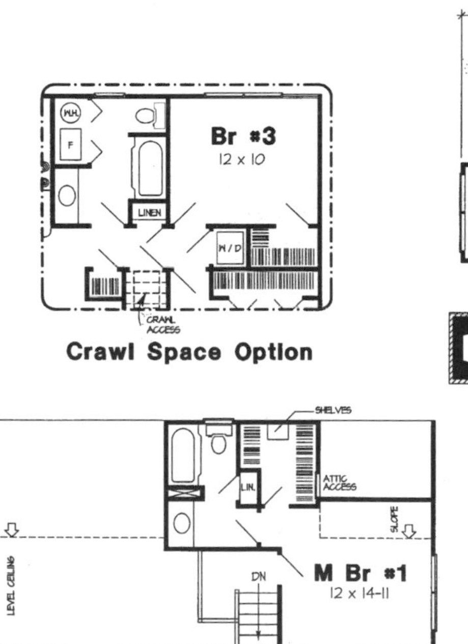
Br #3
12 x 10
LINEN
W/D
CRAWL ACCESS
Crawl Space Option
SHELVES
LIN.
ATTIC ACCESS
SLOPE
M Br #1
12 x 14-11
DN
LEVEL CEILING
OPEN TO BELOW
HANDRAIL
Second Floor

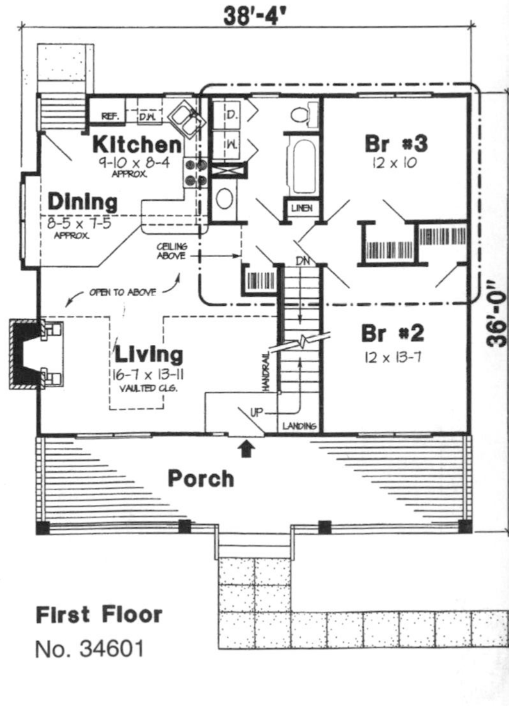
38'-4"
REF.
D.W.
Kitchen
9-10 x 8-4
APPROX.
Dining
8-5 x 7-5
APPROX.
CEILING ABOVE
OPEN TO ABOVE
Br #3
12 x 10
LINEN
DN
Br #2
12 x 13-7
Living
16-7 x 13-11
VAULTED CLG.
HANDRAIL
UP
LANDING
Porch
36'-0"
First Floor
No. 34601

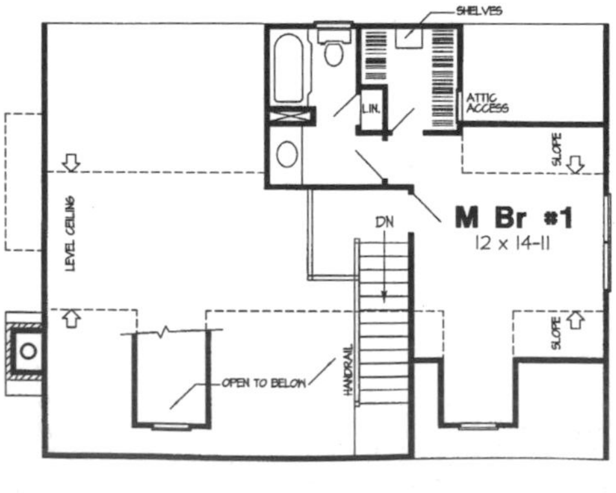

To order your Blueprints, call 1-800-235-5700

Refer to **Pricing Schedule A** on the order form for pricing information

PLAN NO. 20062

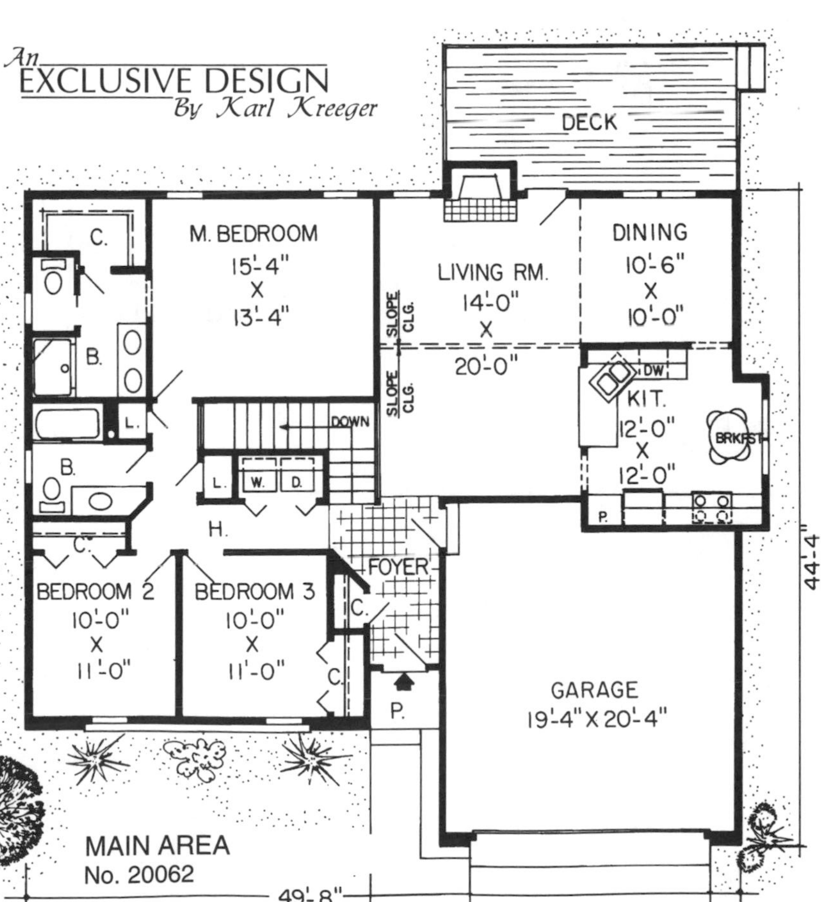

An EXCLUSIVE DESIGN By Karl Kreeger
DECK
C.
M. BEDROOM
15'-4"
X
13'-4"
LIVING RM.
14'-0"
X
20'-0"
SLOPE CLG.
SLOPE CLG.
DINING
10'-6"
X
10'-0"
B.
L.
DOWN
DW
KIT.
12'-0"
X
12'-0"
BRKFST
B.
L.
W.
D.
P.
H.
C.
FOYER
BEDROOM 2
10'-0"
X
11'-0"
BEDROOM 3
10'-0"
X
11'-0"
C.
C.
P.
GARAGE
19'-4" X 20'-4"
44'-4"
MAIN AREA
No. 20062
49'-8"

Inexpensive Ranch Design

- This plan features:
  - — Three bedrooms
  - — Two full baths
- A large picture window brightening the Breakfast area
- A well planned Kitchen
- A Living Room which is accented by an open beam across the sloping ceiling and wood burning fireplace
- A Master Bedroom with an extremely large bath area

MAIN AREA — 1,500 SQ. FT.
BASEMENT — 1,500 SQ. FT.
GARAGE — 482 SQ. FT.

TOTAL LIVING AREA:
1,500 SQ. FT.

PLAN NO. 34602

Refer to **Pricing Schedule B** on the order form for pricing information

Family Get-Away

- This plan features:
- — Three bedrooms
- — Two and one half baths
- A wrap-around porch for views and visiting provides access into the Great Room and Dining area
- A spacious Great Room with a two-story ceiling and dormer window above a massive fireplace
- A combination Dining/Kitchen with an island work area and breakfast bar opening to a Great Room and adjacent to the laundry/storage and half-bath area
- A private two-story Master Bedroom with a dormer window, walk-in closet, double vanity bath and optional deck with hot tub
- Two second floor bedrooms sharing a full bath

FIRST FLOOR — 1,061 SQ. FT.
SECOND FLOOR — 499 SQ. FT.
BASEMENT — 1,061 SQ. FT.

TOTAL LIVING AREA:
1,560 SQ. FT.

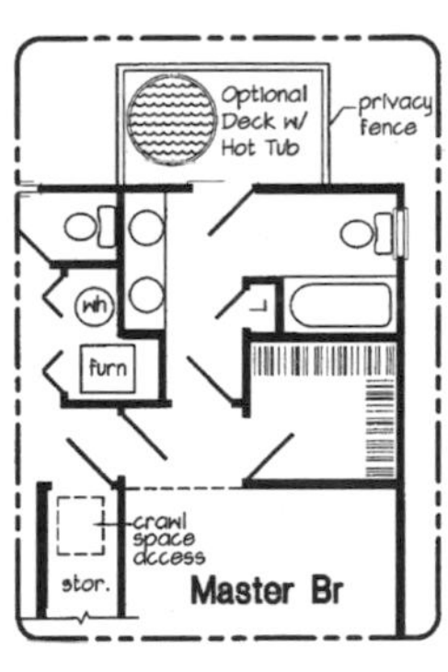
Optional Deck w/ Hot Tub
privacy fence
wh
furn
crawl space access
stor.
Master Br

Alternate Foundation Plan

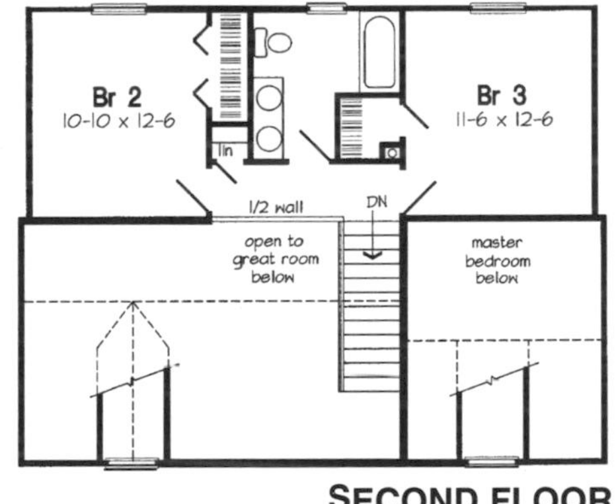
Br 2
10-10 x 12-6
Br 3
11-6 x 12-6
lin
1/2 wall
DN
open to great room below
master bedroom below

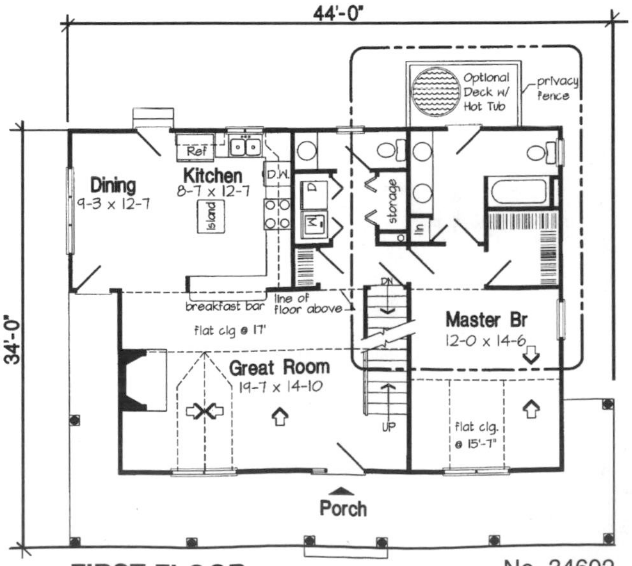

SECOND FLOOR

44'-0"
34'-0"
Optional Deck w/ Hot Tub
privacy fence
Dining
9-3 x 12-7
Kitchen
8-7 x 12-7
Ref
DW
island
D
W
storage
lin
breakfast bar
line of floor above
flat clg @ 17'
Master Br
12-0 x 14-6
Great Room
14-7 x 14-10
UP
DN
Flat clg. @ 15'-7"
Porch

FIRST FLOOR

No. 34602

To order your Blueprints, call 1-800-235-5700

Refer to **Pricing Schedule A** on the order form for pricing information

PLAN NO. 10012

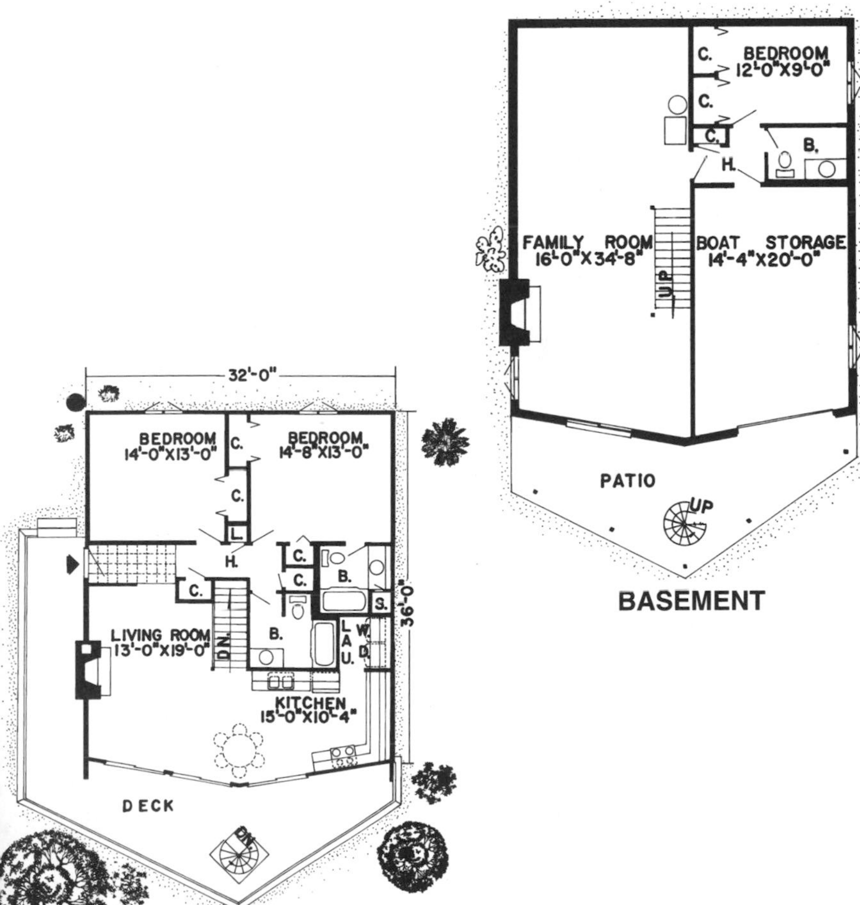

BEDROOM
12'-0"X9'-0"
C.
C.
C.
B.
H.
FAMILY ROOM
16'-0"X34'-8"
UP
BOAT STORAGE
14'-4"X20'-0"
PATIO
UP
BASEMENT
32'-0"
BEDROOM
14'-0"X13'-0"
C.
BEDROOM
14'-8"X13'-0"
C.
L
H.
C.
C.
B.
C.
S.
LIVING ROOM
13'-0"X19'-0"
DN
B.
LAU.
W.
D.
36'-0"
KITCHEN
15'-0"X10'-4"
DECK
DN
MAIN AREA
No. 10012

Rustic Design Blends into Hillside

- This plan features:
- — Three bedrooms
- — Two and one half baths
- A redwood deck that adapts equally to both lake and ocean settings
- A Family Room measuring 36 feet long and leading out to a shaded patio
- Fireplaces in both the Living Room and Family Room
- An open Kitchen with a laundry room for convenience

MAIN AREA — 1,198 SQ. FT.
BASEMENT — 1,198 SQ. FT.

TOTAL LIVING AREA:
1,198 SQ. FT.

PLAN NO. 90357

Refer to **Pricing Schedule A** on the order form for pricing information

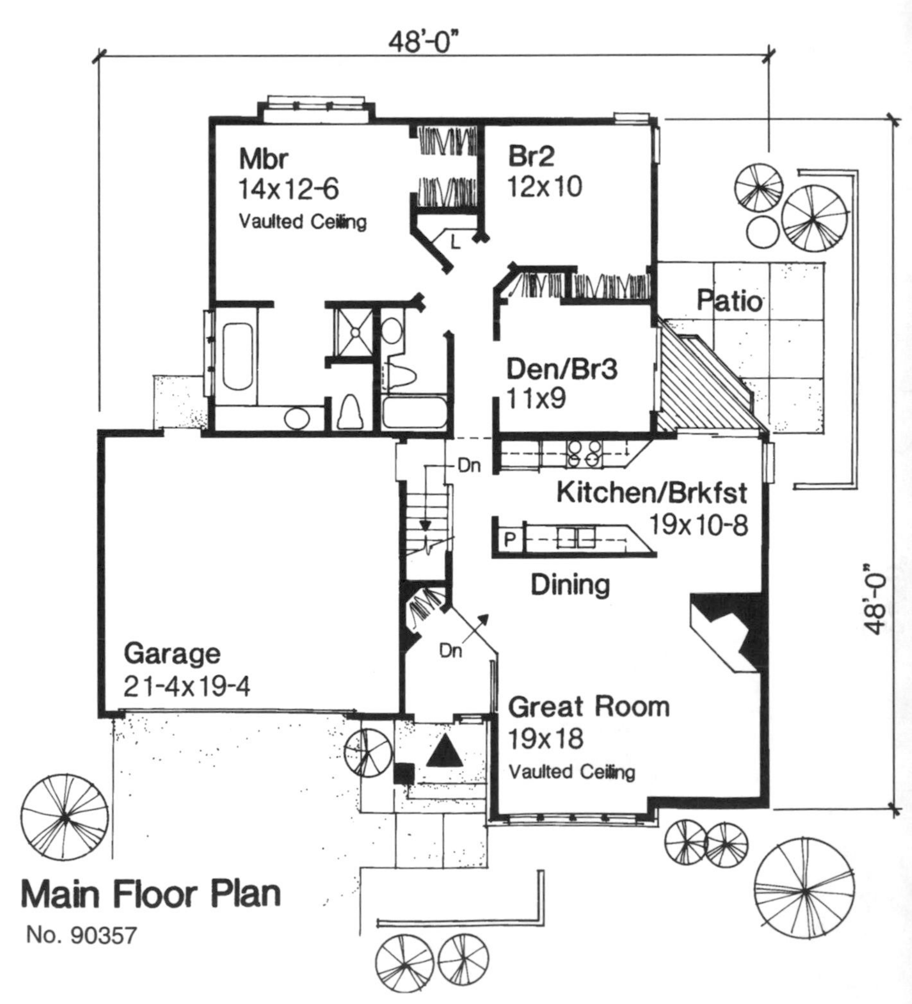

48'-0"
Mbr
14x12-6
Vaulted Ceiling
Br2
12x10
L
Patio
Den/Br3
11x9
Dn
Kitchen/Brkfst
19x10-8
P
Dining
Garage
21-4x19-4
Dn
Great Room
19x18
Vaulted Ceiling
48'-0"

Main Floor Plan
No. 90357

High Impact Angles

- This plan features:
- — Three bedrooms
- — Two full baths
- Soaring ceilings to give the house a spacious, contemporary feeling
- A fireplaced Great Room adjoining a convenient Kitchen, with a sunny Breakfast Nook
- Sliding glass doors opening onto an angular deck
- A Master Suite with vaulted ceilings and a private bath

MAIN AREA — 1,368 SQ. FT.

TOTAL LIVING AREA:
1,368 SQ. FT.

To order your Blueprints, call 1-800-235-5700

Refer to **Pricing Schedule Z** on the order form for pricing information

PLAN NO. 10220

TOTAL LIVING AREA:
888 SQ. FT.

50'-0"
WALK
S.
B.
W. D.
LAU.
F. W.H.
KITCHEN 9'-8"X8'-0"
C.
BEDROOM 11'-4"X 11'-4"
L.
FAMILY AREA 23'-4"X 15'-4"
C.
C.
BEDROOM 9'-4"X11'-4"
24'-0"
DECK

MAIN AREA
No. 10220

Bedrooms Sliders Open Onto Wooden Deck

- This plan features:
- — Two bedrooms
- — One full bath
- A fifty foot deck setting the stage for a relaxing lifestyle encouraged by this home
- A simple, yet complete floor plan centering around the large Family Area, warmed by a prefab fireplace sliders to the deck
- An efficient L-shaped Kitchen that includes a double sink with a window above, and direct access to the rear yard and the Laundry Room
- Two bedrooms privately located, each outfitted with sliding doors to the deck and a large window for plenty of light

MAIN AREA — 888 SQ. FT.

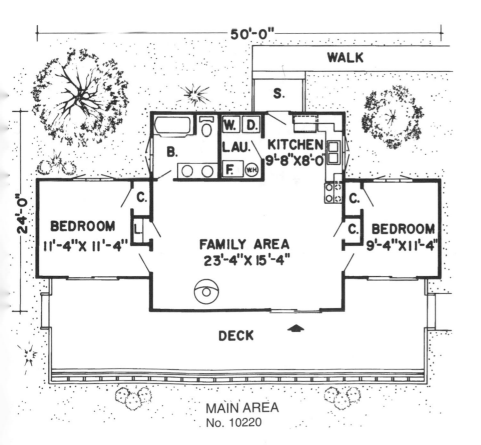

PLAN NO.10594

Refer to **Pricing Schedule B** on the order form for pricing information

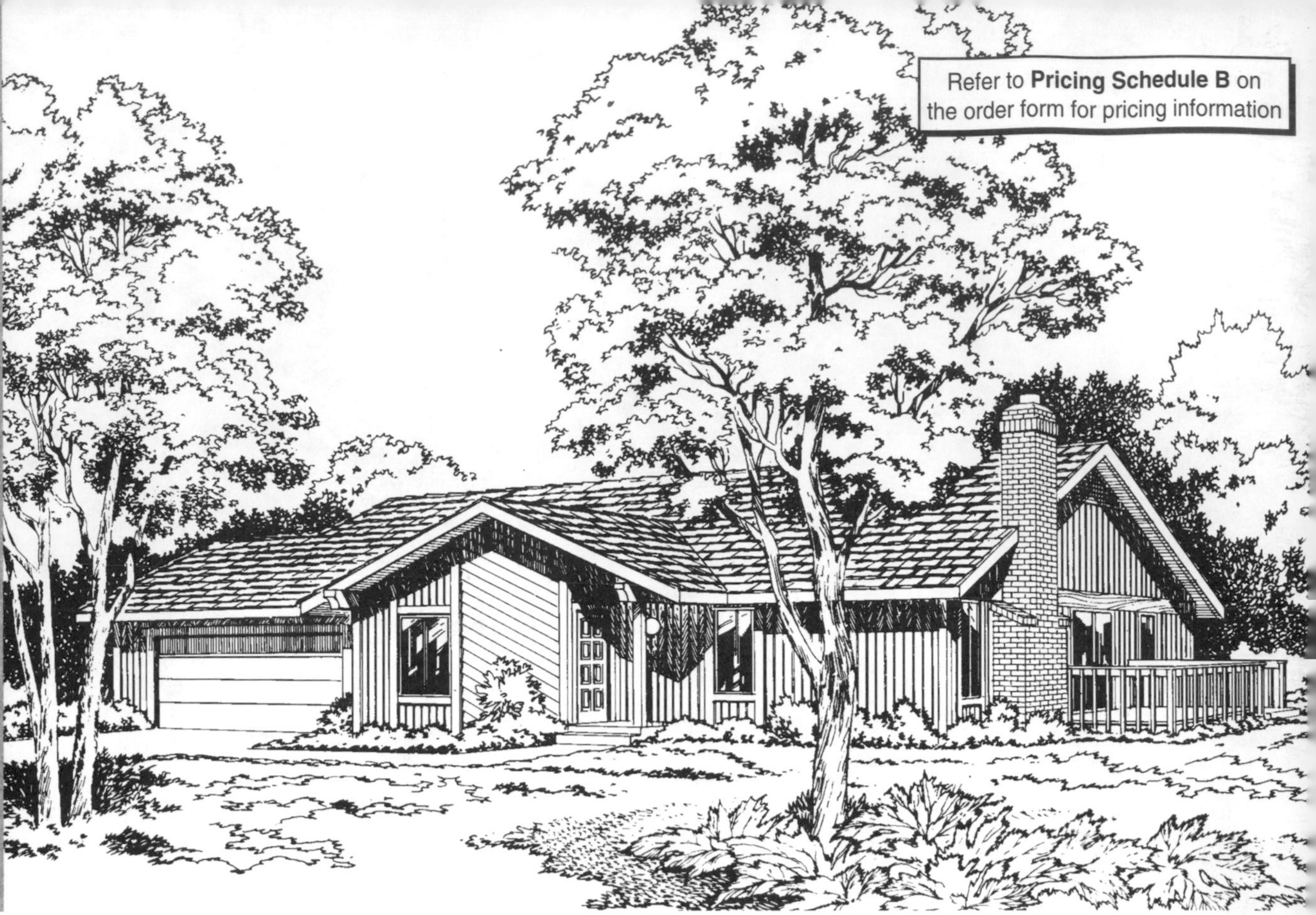

Lots of Room in Ranch Design

- This plan features:
- — Two bedrooms with optional third bedroom
- — Two full baths
- A sloping, open-beamed ceiling and a wood-burning fireplace in the Great Room
- A Dining Room with sliding glass doors leading onto a large wooden deck
- A laundry room near the Kitchen and Dining Room

MAIN FLOOR — 1,565 SQ. FT.
BASEMENT — 1,576 SQ. FT.
GARAGE — 430 SQ. FT.

TOTAL LIVING AREA:
1,565 SQ. FT.

An EXCLUSIVE DESIGN *By Karl Kreeger*

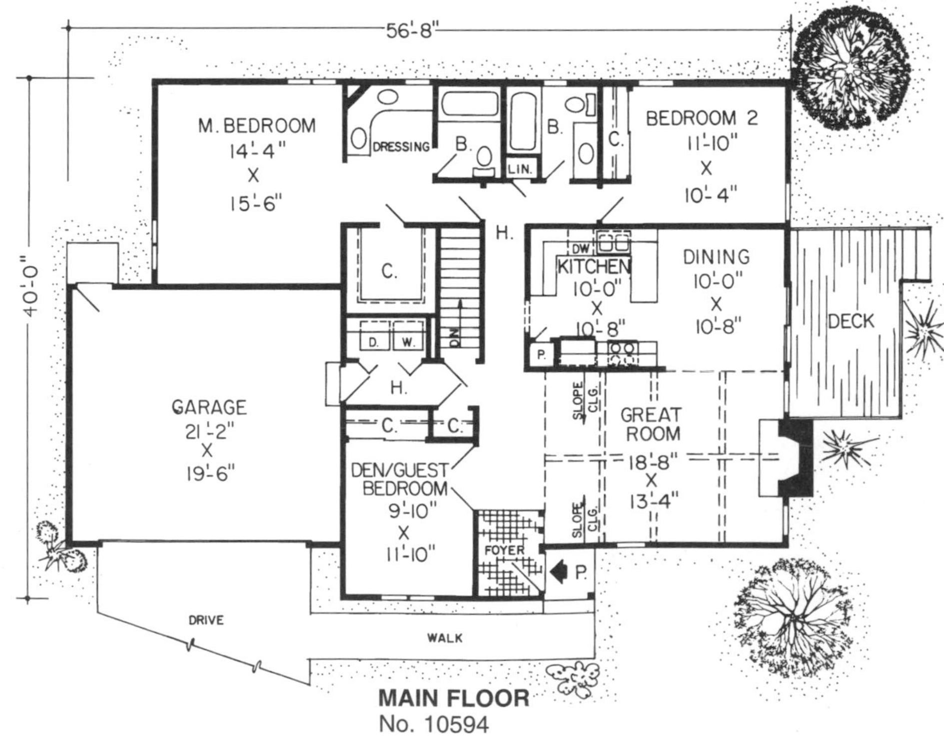

56'-8"
40'-0"
M. BEDROOM 14'-4" X 15'-6"
DRESSING
B.
LIN.
B.
C.
BEDROOM 2 11'-10" X 10'-4"
H.
C.
DW
KITCHEN 10'-0" X 10'-8"
DINING 10'-0" X 10'-8"
DECK
D. W.
DN
P.
GARAGE 21'-2" X 19'-6"
H.
C. C.
SLOPE CLG.
GREAT ROOM 18'-8" X 13'-4"
DEN/GUEST BEDROOM 9'-10" X 11'-10"
FOYER
P.
DRIVE
WALK

MAIN FLOOR
No. 10594

Refer to **Pricing Schedule A** on the order form for pricing information

PLAN NO. 90390

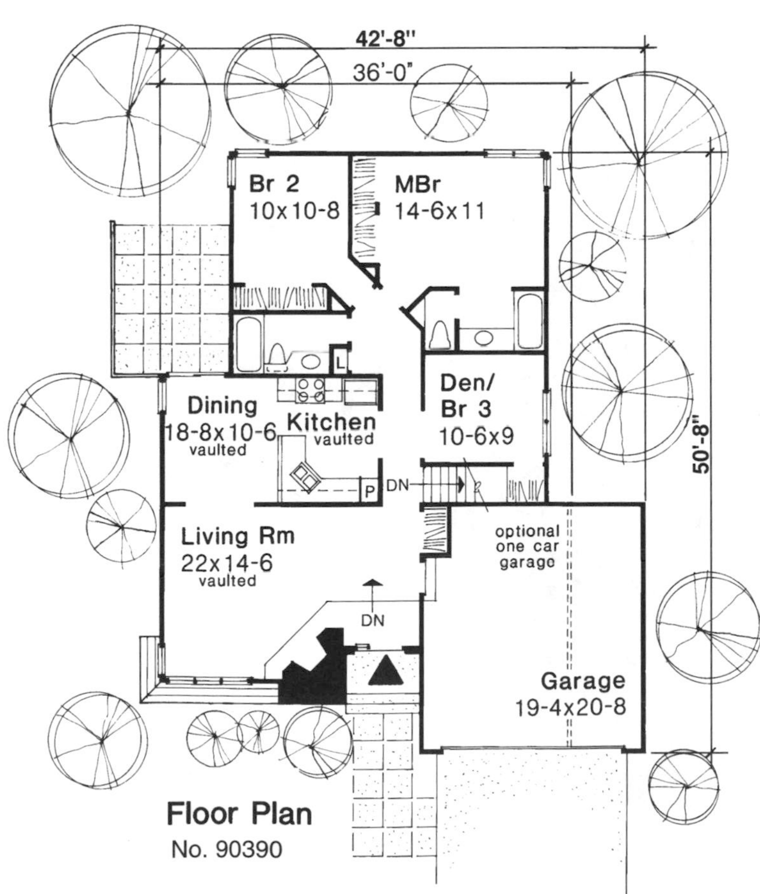

42'-8"
36'-0"
Br 2
10x10-8
MBr
14-6x11
L
Dining
18-8x10-6
vaulted
Kitchen
vaulted
Den/
Br 3
10-6x9
P
DN
50'-8"
Living Rm
22x14-6
vaulted
optional
one car
garage
DN
Garage
19-4x20-8

Floor Plan
No. 90390

Small Scale, Lots of Space

- This plan features:
- — Two bedrooms with optional third bedroom/den
- — Two full baths
- Vaulted ceilings and corner windows
- A Living Room enhanced by a cozy corner fireplace
- A Master Suite featuring interesting angles and corner window treatments

MAIN FLOOR — 1,231 SQ. FT.

TOTAL LIVING AREA:
1,231 SQ. FT.

PLAN NO. 90398

Refer to **Pricing Schedule B** on the order form for pricing information

Interior and Exterior Unity Enhances Plan

- This plan features:
- — Three bedrooms
- — Two full baths
- A vaulted ceiling Living Room with cozy fireplace
- Columns dividing the Living and Dining Rooms, and half-walls separating the Kitchen and Breakfast Room
- A luxurious Master Suite with a private sky-lit bath, double vanities and a generous walk-in closet

MAIN AREA — 1,630 SQ. FT.

TOTAL LIVING AREA:
1,630 SQ. FT.

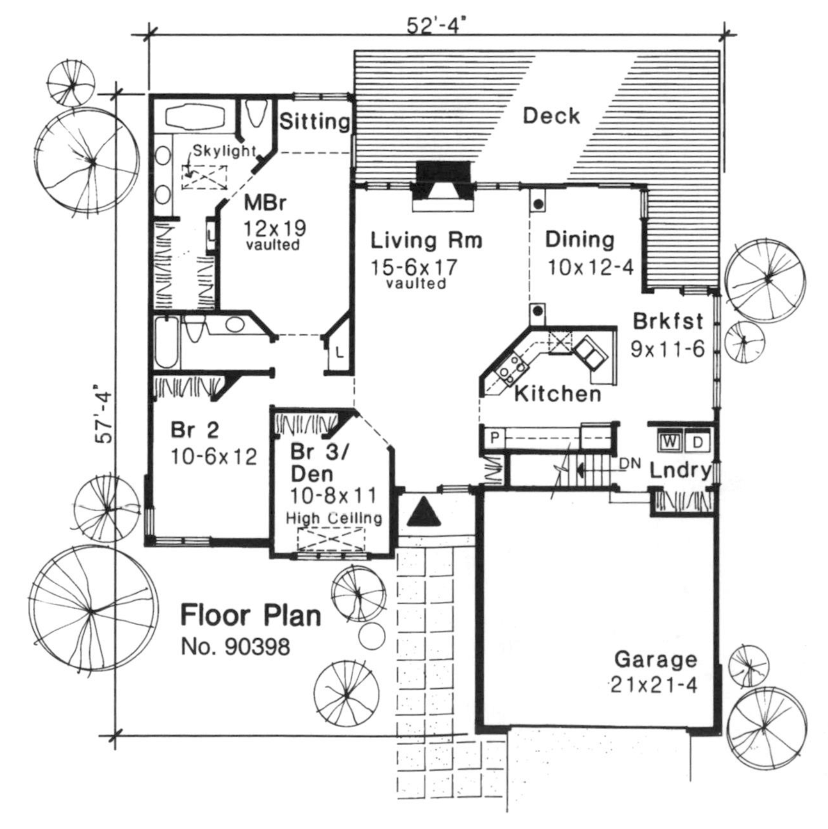

52'-4"
57'-4"
Deck
Sitting
Skylight
MBr
12x19
vaulted
Living Rm
15-6x17
vaulted
Dining
10x12-4
Brkfst
9x11-6
Kitchen
L
Br 2
10-6x12
Br 3/
Den
10-8x11
High Ceiling
P
DN
Lndry
W
D
Garage
21x21-4

Floor Plan
No. 90398

To order your Blueprints, call 1-800-235-5700

Refer to **Pricing Schedule B** on the order form for pricing information

PLAN NO. 10674

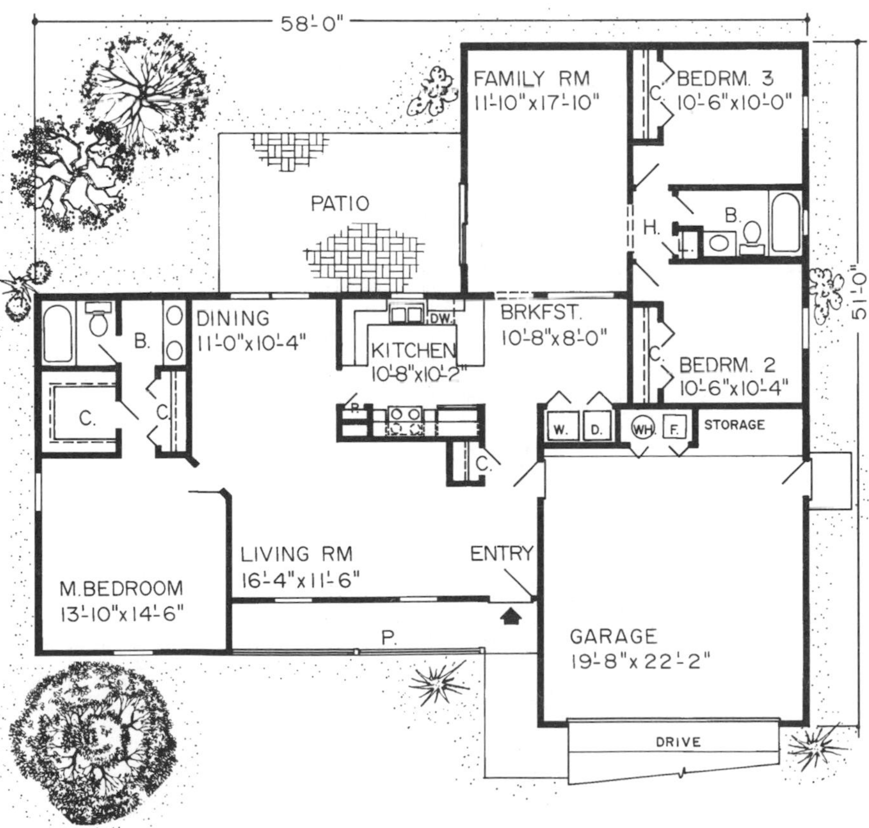

58'-0"
51'-0"
FAMILY RM
11'-10"x17'-10"
BEDRM. 3
10'-6"x10'-0"
PATIO
B.
H.
C.
DINING
11'-0"x10'-4"
KITCHEN
10'-8"x10'-2"
DW.
BRKFST.
10'-8"x8'-0"
BEDRM. 2
10'-6"x10'-4"
W.
D.
WH.
F.
STORAGE
LIVING RM
16'-4"x11'-6"
ENTRY
M.BEDROOM
13'-10"x14'-6"
P.
GARAGE
19'-8"x22'-2"
DRIVE

MAIN AREA
No. 10674

Carefree Convenience

- This plan features:
  - — Three bedrooms
  - — Two full baths
- A galley Kitchen, centrally located between the Dining, Breakfast and Living Room areas
- A huge Family Room which exits onto the patio
- A Master Suite with double closets and vanities with two additional bedrooms share a full-half bath

MAIN AREA — 1,600 SQ. FT.
GARAGE — 465 SQ. FT.

TOTAL LIVING AREA:
1,600 SQ. FT.

PLAN NO. 92531

Refer to **Pricing Schedule C** on the order form for pricing information

Enhanced by a Columned Porch

- This plan features:
- — Three bedrooms
- — Two full baths
- A Great Room with a fireplace and decorative ceiling
- A large efficient Kitchen with Breakfast area
- A Master Bedroom with a private Master Bath and walk-in closet
- A formal Dining Room located near the Kitchen
- Two additional bedrooms with walk-in closets and use of full hall bath
- This plan is available with a crawl space or slab foundation — please specify when ordering

MAIN FLOOR — 1,754 SQ. FT.
GARAGE — 552 SQ. FT.

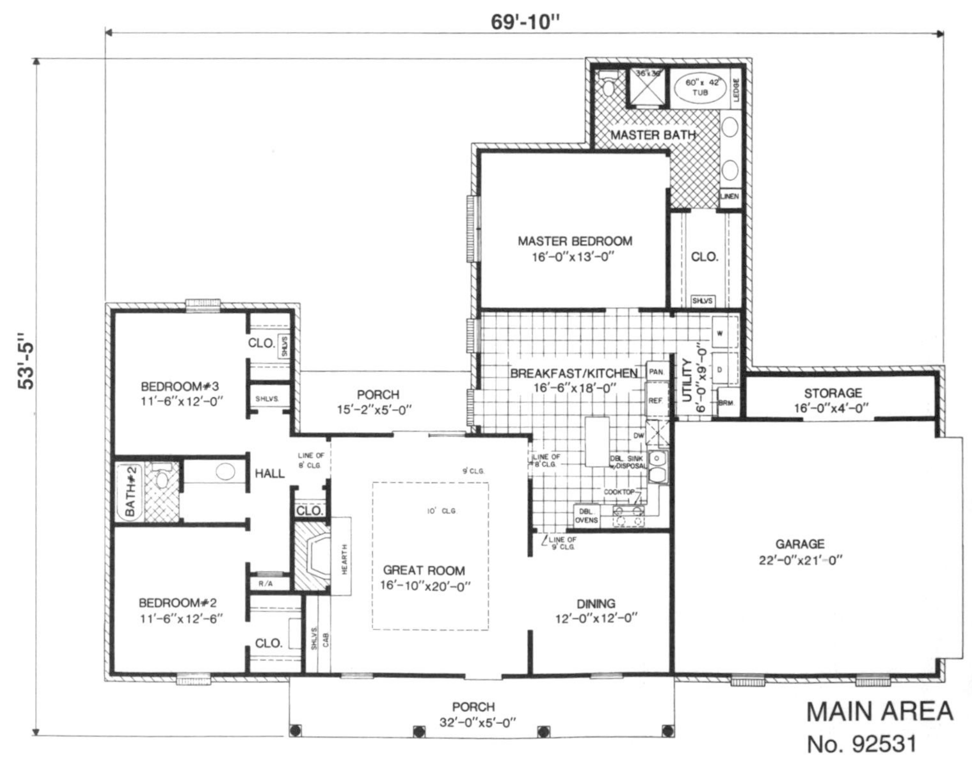

69'-10"
53'-5"
MASTER BATH
60" x 42" TUB
LEDGE
LINEN
MASTER BEDROOM
16'-0"x13'-0"
CLO.
SHLVS
BEDROOM#3
11'-6"x12'-0"
CLO.
SHLVS
PORCH
15'-2"x5'-0"
BREAKFAST/KITCHEN
16'-6"x18'-0"
PAN
REF
UTILITY
6'-0"x9'-0"
STORAGE
16'-0"x4'-0"
HALL
BATH#2
CLO.
HEARTH
10' CLG.
9' CLG.
LINE OF 8' CLG.
GREAT ROOM
16'-10"x20'-0"
DW
DBL SINK DISPOSAL
COOKTOP
DBL OVENS
LINE OF 9' CLG.
GARAGE
22'-0"x21'-0"
BEDROOM#2
11'-6"x12'-6"
R/A
CLO.
SHLVS
CAB
DINING
12'-0"x12'-0"
PORCH
32'-0"x5'-0"

MAIN AREA
No. 92531

TOTAL LIVING AREA:
1,754 SQ. FT.

To order your Blueprints, call 1-800-235-5700

Refer to **Pricing Schedule B** on the order form for pricing information

PLAN NO. 10745

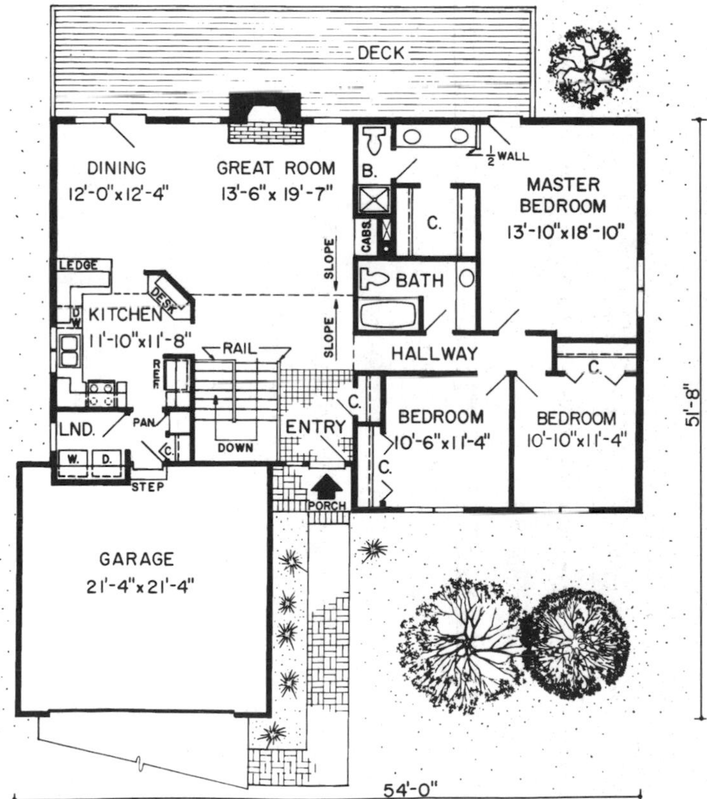
DECK
DINING
12'-0"x12'-4"
GREAT ROOM
13'-6"x 19'-7"
B.
½ WALL
MASTER
BEDROOM
13'-10"x18'-10"
C.
CABS.
BATH
LEDGE
DESK
KITCHEN
11'-10"x11'-8"
SLOPE
SLOPE
RAIL
HALLWAY
REF
C.
BEDROOM
10'-6"x11'-4"
BEDROOM
10'-10"x11'-4"
C.
LND.
PAN.
C.
ENTRY
DOWN
C.
W.
D.
STEP
PORCH
GARAGE
21'-4"x21'-4"
51'-8"
54'-0"

MAINFLOOR
No. 10745

Light and Airy

- This plan features:
  - — Three bedrooms
  - — Two full baths
- An open plan with cathedral ceilings
- A fireplaced Great Room flowing into the Dining Room
- A Master Bedroom with a private Master Bath
- An efficient Kitchen, with Laundry area and pantry in close proximity

MAIN FLOOR — 1,643 SQ. FT.
BASEMENT — 1,643 SQ. FT.
GARAGE — 484 SQ. FT.

TOTAL LIVING AREA:
1,643 SQ. FT.

PLAN NO. 20191

Refer to **Pricing Schedule B** on the order form for pricing information

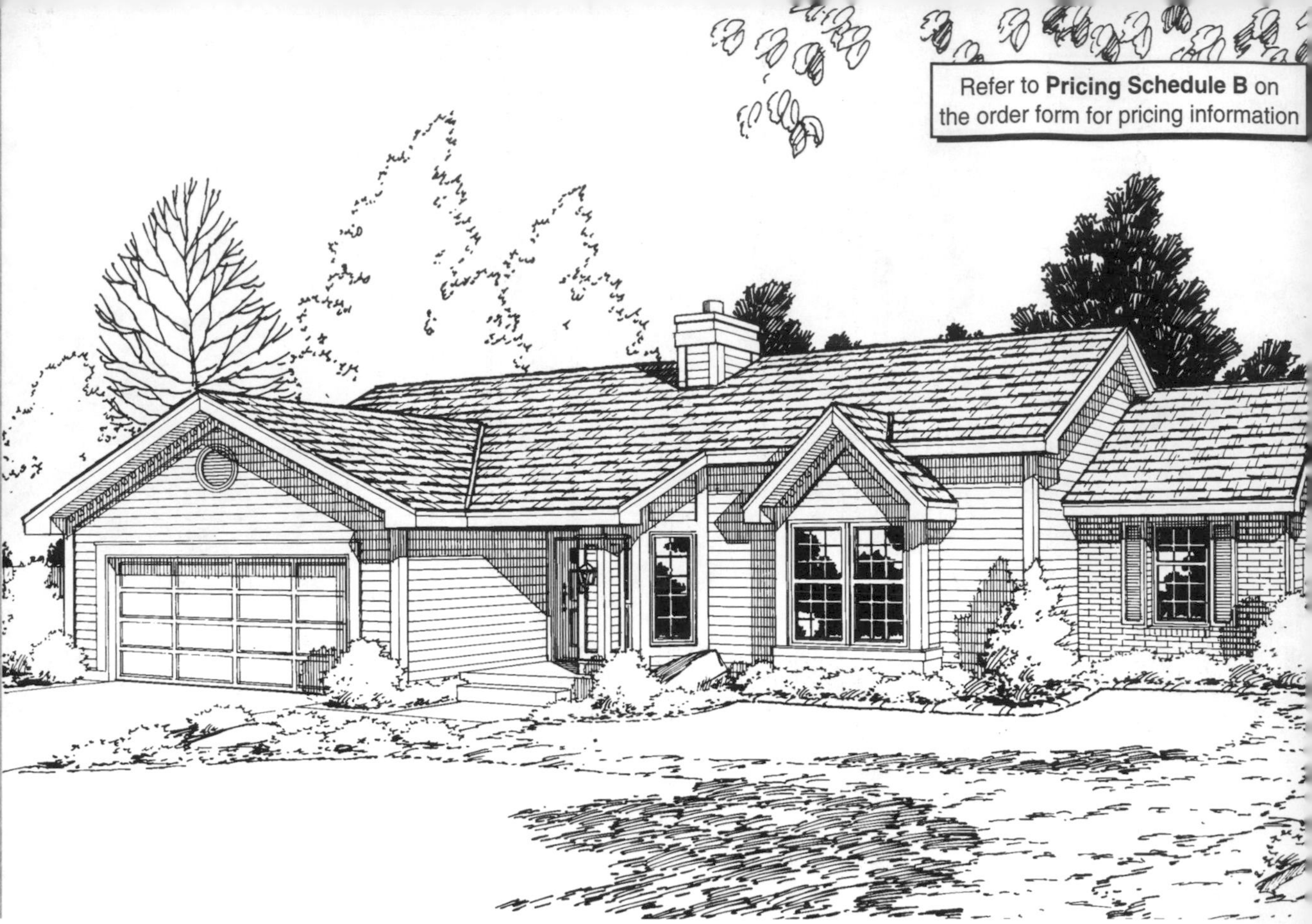

Exciting Ceilings

- This plan features:
  - — Three bedrooms
  - — Two full baths
- A brick hearth fireplace in the Living Room
- An efficient Kitchen, with an island and double sinks, that flows into the Dining Room, which features a lovely decorative ceiling
- A private Master Suite with another decorative ceiling and a pampering Master Bath
- Two additional bedrooms that share a full bath

MAIN FLOOR — 1,606 SQ. FT.
BASEMENT — 1,575 SQ. FT.
GARAGE — 545 SQ. FT.

TOTAL LIVING AREA:
1,606 SQ. FT.

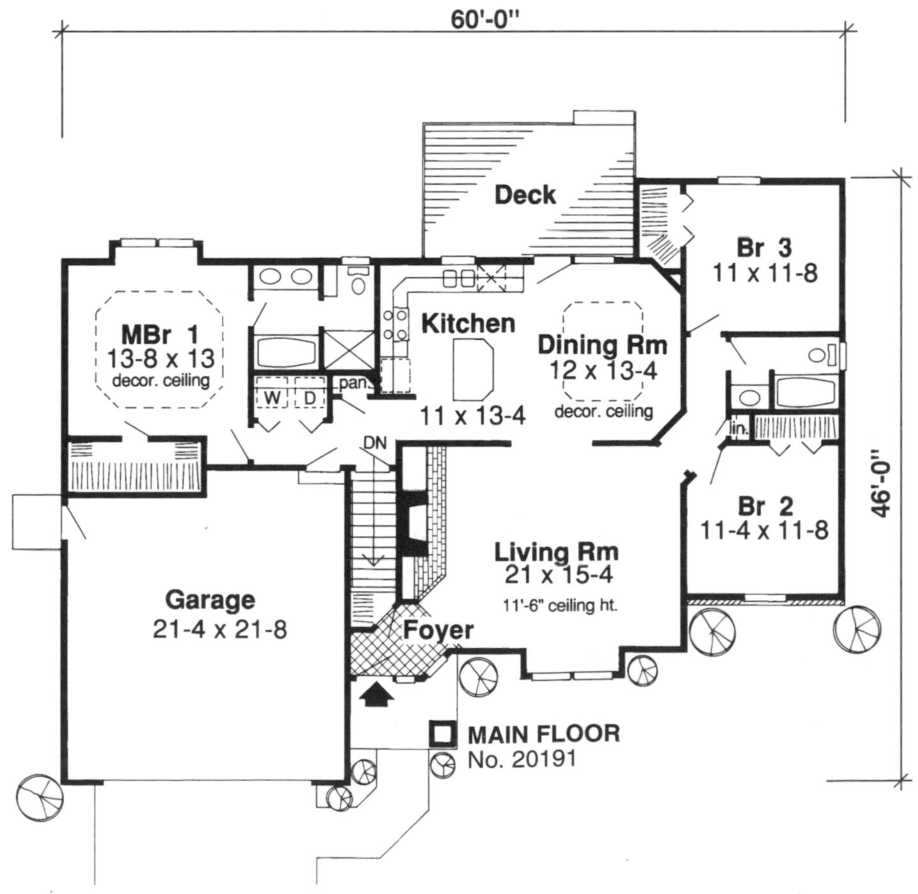

60'-0"
Deck
Br 3
11 x 11-8
MBr 1
13-8 x 13
decor. ceiling
Kitchen
11 x 13-4
Dining Rm
12 x 13-4
decor. ceiling
W
D
pan.
DN
lin.
Br 2
11-4 x 11-8
46'-0"
Living Rm
21 x 15-4
11'-6" ceiling ht.
Garage
21-4 x 21-8
Foyer
MAIN FLOOR
No. 20191

Refer to **Pricing Schedule C** on the order form for pricing information

PLAN NO. 90407

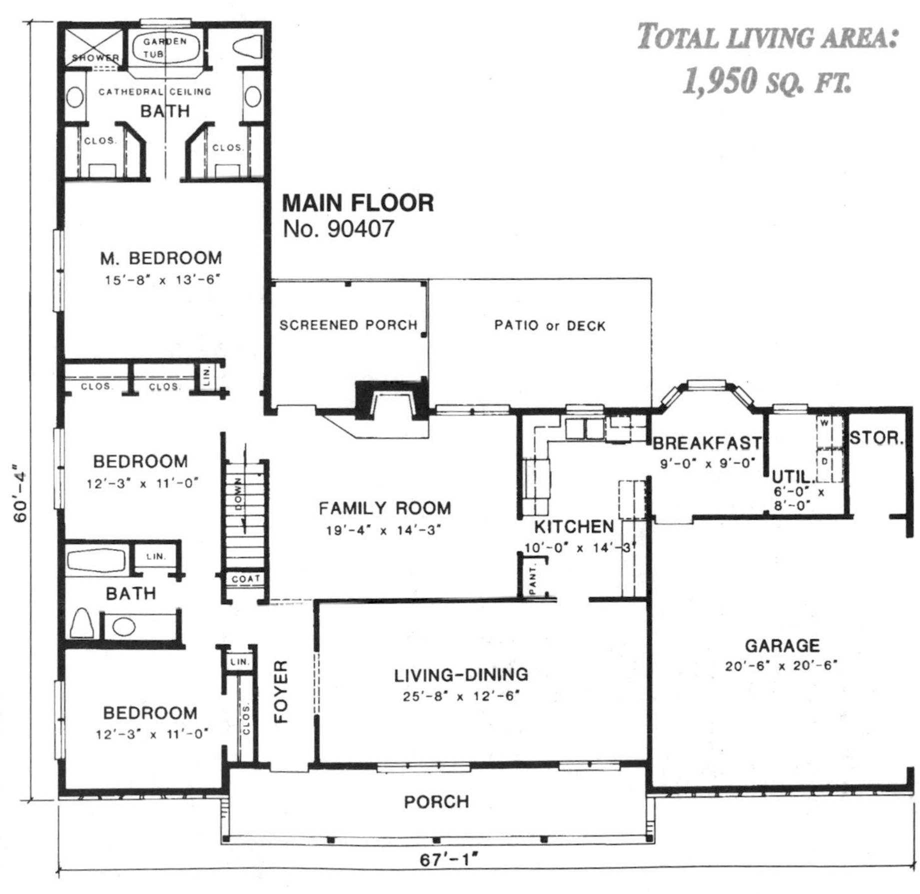

GARDEN TUB
SHOWER
CATHEDRAL CEILING
BATH
CLOS.
CLOS.
MAIN FLOOR
No. 90407
M. BEDROOM
15'-8" x 13'-6"
SCREENED PORCH
PATIO or DECK
CLOS.
CLOS.
LIN.
BEDROOM
12'-3" x 11'-0"
DOWN
FAMILY ROOM
19'-4" x 14'-3"
BREAKFAST
9'-0" x 9'-0"
W
D
UTIL.
6'-0" x 8'-0"
STOR.
KITCHEN
10'-0" x 14'-3"
PANT.
60'-4"
LIN.
BATH
COAT
GARAGE
20'-6" x 20'-6"
LIN.
FOYER
LIVING-DINING
25'-8" x 12'-6"
BEDROOM
12'-3" x 11'-0"
CLOS.
PORCH
67'-1"

TOTAL LIVING AREA:
1,950 SQ. FT.

L-Shaped Bungalow With Two Porches

- This plan features:
  - — Three bedrooms
  - — Two full baths
- A Master Suite with a lavish Master Bath including a garden tub, shower, his-n-her vanities and separate walk-in closets
- Two additional bedrooms having ample closet space and sharing a full hall bath
- A large Family Room accentuated by a fireplace
- A U-shaped Kitchen with a built-in pantry, double sink and ample storage and counter space
- A sunny, bay Breakfast Nook for informal eating
- An optional basement, slab or crawl space foundation — please specify when ordering

MAIN FLOOR — 1,950 SQ. FT.

PLAN NO. 20083

Refer to **Pricing Schedule B** on the order form for pricing information

One-Level with a Twist

- This plan features:
  - — Three bedrooms
  - — Two full baths
- Wide-open active areas that are centrally-located
- A spacious Dining, Living, and Kitchen area
- A Master Suite at the rear of the house with a full bath
- Two additional bedrooms that share a full hall bath and the quiet atmosphere that results from an intelligent design

MAIN AREA — 1,575 SQ. FT.
BASEMENT —1,575 SQ. FT.
GARAGE — 475 SQ. FT.

TOTAL LIVING AREA:
1,575 SQ. FT.

An EXCLUSIVE DESIGN *By Karl Kreeger*

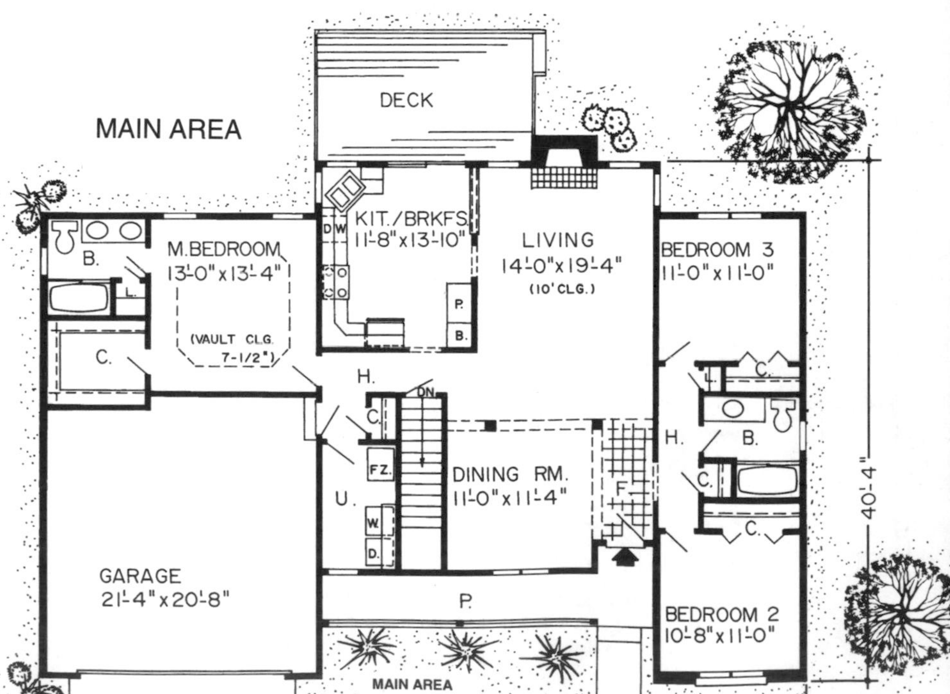
MAIN AREA
DECK
KIT./BRKFS.
11'-8"x13'-10"
LIVING
14'-0"x19'-4"
(10' CLG.)
BEDROOM 3
11'-0"x11'-0"
M.BEDROOM
13'-0"x13'-4"
(VAULT CLG. 7-1/2")
DINING RM.
11'-0"x11'-4"
GARAGE
21'-4"x20'-8"
BEDROOM 2
10'-8"x11'-0"
40'-4"
60'-0"
DRIVE
MAIN AREA

No. 20083

Refer to **Pricing Schedule A** on the order form for pricing information

PLAN NO. 90325

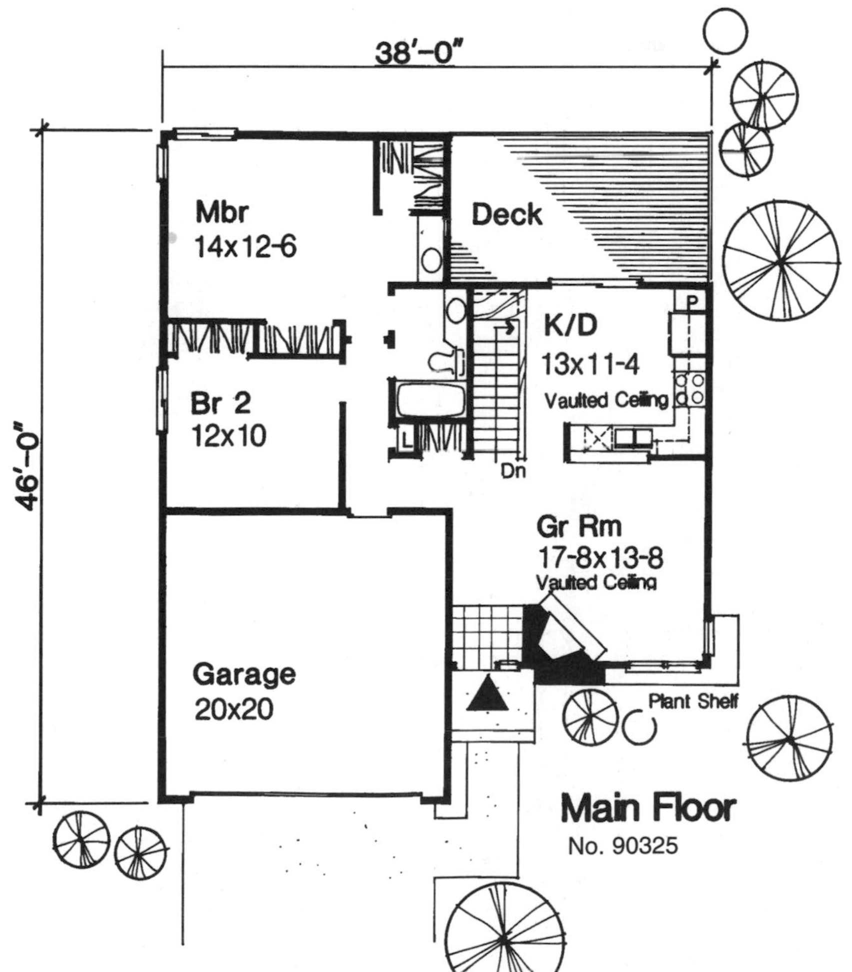

38'-0"
46'-0"
Mbr
14x12-6
Deck
K/D
13x11-4
Vaulted Ceiling
Br 2
12x10
Dn
Gr Rm
17-8x13-8
Vaulted Ceiling
Garage
20x20
Plant Shelf
Main Floor
No. 90325

Designed for Informal Life Style

- This plan features:
  - — Two bedrooms
  - — One full bath
- A Great Room and Kitchen accented by vaulted ceilings
- A conveniently arranged L-shaped food preparation center
- A Dining Room overlooking a deck through sliding doors
- A Great Room highlighted by a corner fireplace
- A Master Bedroom including a separate vanity and dressing area

FIRST FLOOR — 988 SQ. FT.
BASEMENT — 988 SQ. FT.
GARAGE — 400 SQ. FT.

TOTAL LIVING AREA:
988 SQ. FT.

PLAN NO. 92625

Refer to **Pricing Schedule B** on the order form for pricing information

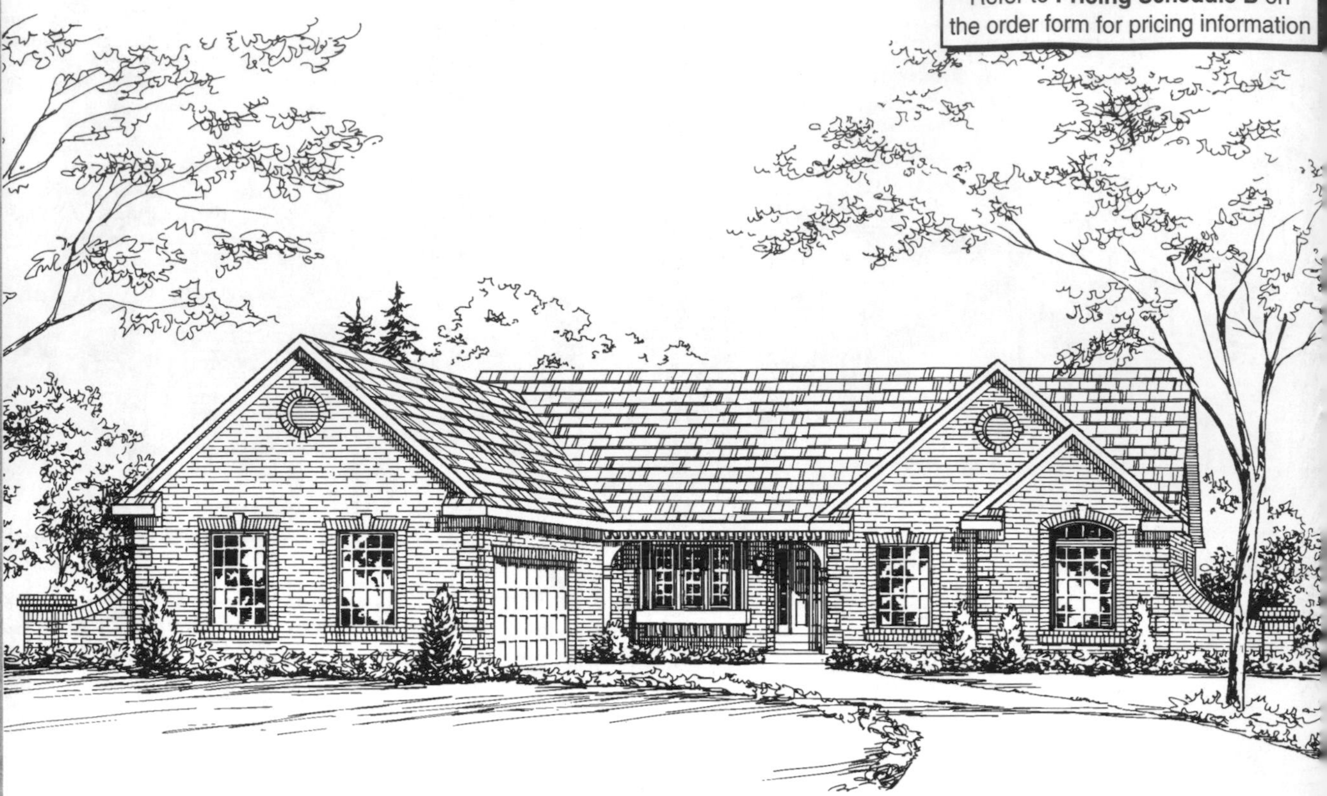

Home For the Discriminating Buyer

- This plan features:
  - — Three bedrooms
  - — Two full baths
- A sloped ceiling and a corner fireplace enhancing the Great Room
- A Kitchen with a garden window above the double sink
- A peninsula counter joins the Kitchen and the Breakfast Room in an open layout
- A Master Suite with a large walk-in closet, a private bath with an oval corner tub, and a separate shower and double vanity
- Two additional bedrooms that share a full hall bath
- No materials list available for this plan

MAIN AREA — 1,710 SQ. FT.
BASEMENT — 1,560 SQ. FT.
GARAGE — 455 SQ. FT.

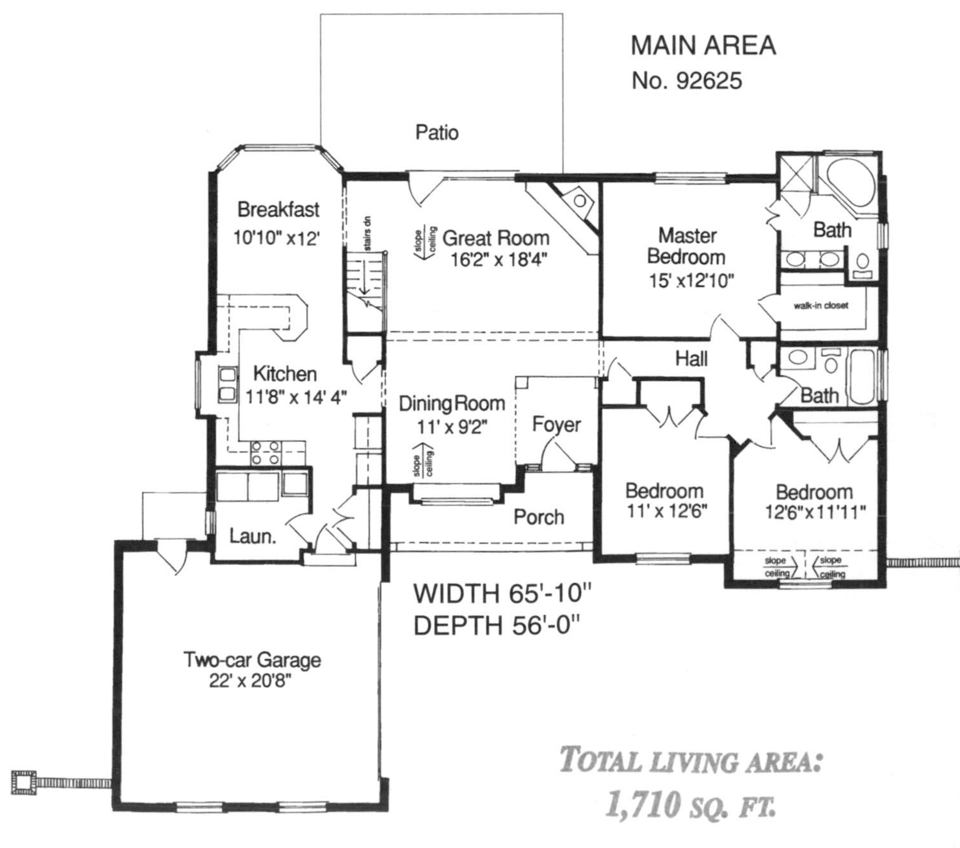

MAIN AREA
No. 92625
Patio
Breakfast
10'10" x12'
stairs dn
slope ceiling
Great Room
16'2" x 18'4"
Master Bedroom
15' x12'10"
Bath
walk-in closet
Kitchen
11'8" x 14' 4"
Hall
Bath
Dining Room
11' x 9'2"
slope ceiling
Foyer
Bedroom
11' x 12'6"
Bedroom
12'6"x11'11"
slope ceiling
slope ceiling
Porch
Laun.
WIDTH 65'-10"
DEPTH 56'-0"
Two-car Garage
22' x 20'8"

TOTAL LIVING AREA:
1,710 SQ. FT.

Refer to **Pricing Schedule B** on the order form for pricing information

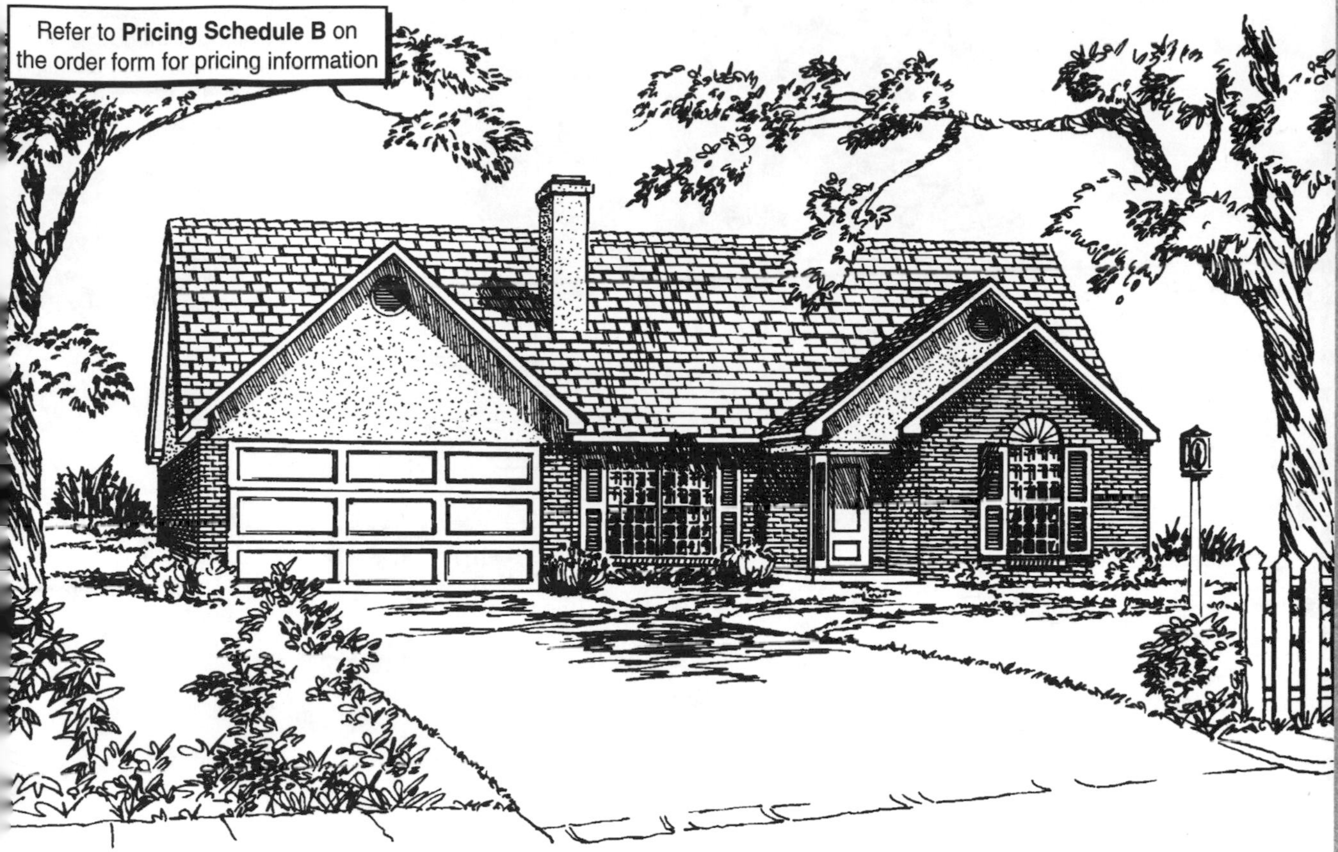

PLAN NO. 92502

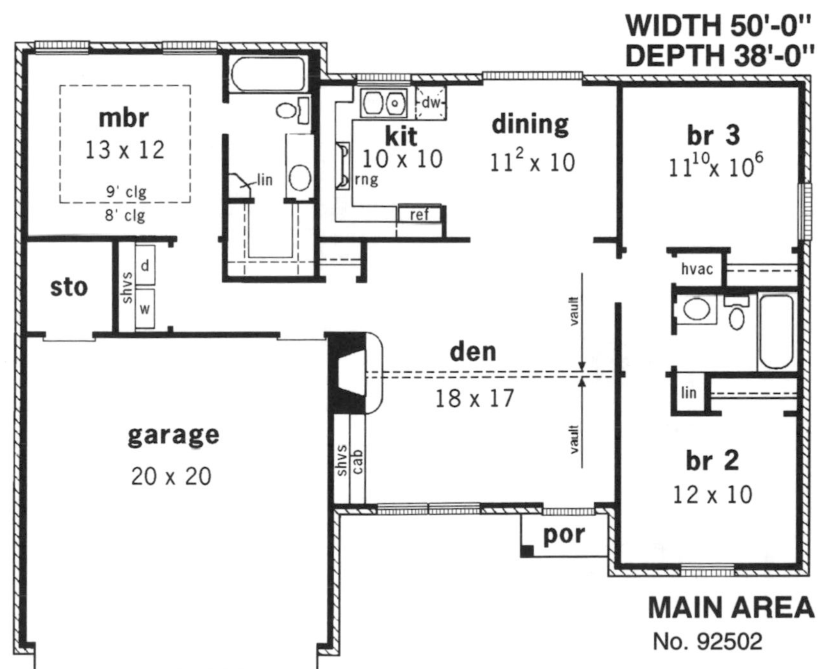

WIDTH 50'-0"
DEPTH 38'-0"
mbr
13 x 12
9' clg
8' clg
lin
kit
10 x 10
dw
rng
ref
dining
11^2 x 10
br 3
11^{10} x 10^6
hvac
lin
sto
shvs
d
w
den
18 x 17
vault
vault
shvs
cab
garage
20 x 20
br 2
12 x 10
por
MAIN AREA
No. 92502

Spectacular Traditional

- This plan features:
  - — Three bedrooms
  - — Two full baths
- The use of gable roofs and the blend of stucco and brick to form a spectacular exterior
- A high vaulted ceiling and a cozy fireplace, with built-in cabinets in the Dcn
- An efficient, U-shaped Kitchen with an adjacent Dining Area
- A Master Bedroom, with a raised ceiling, that includes a private bath and a walk-in closet
- Two family bedrooms that share a full hall bath
- This plan is available with a crawl space or slab foundation — please specify when ordering

MAIN AREA — 1,237 SQ. FT.
GARAGE — 436 SQ. FT.

TOTAL LIVING AREA:
1,237 SQ. FT.

PLAN NO. 20087

Refer to **Pricing Schedule B** on the order form for pricing information

An EXCLUSIVE DESIGN By Karl Kreeger

Foyer Isolates Bedroom Wing

- This plan features:

— Three bedrooms

— Two full baths

- A Living Room complete with a window wall, flanking a massive fireplace
- A Dining Room with recessed ceilings and a pass-through for convenience
- A Master Suite tucked behind the two-car garage for maximum noise protection
- A spacious Kitchen with built-ins and access to the two-car garage

MAIN AREA — 1,568 SQ. FT.
BASEMENT — 1,568 SQ. FT.
GARAGE — 484 SQ. FT.

TOTAL LIVING AREA:
1,568 SQ. FT.

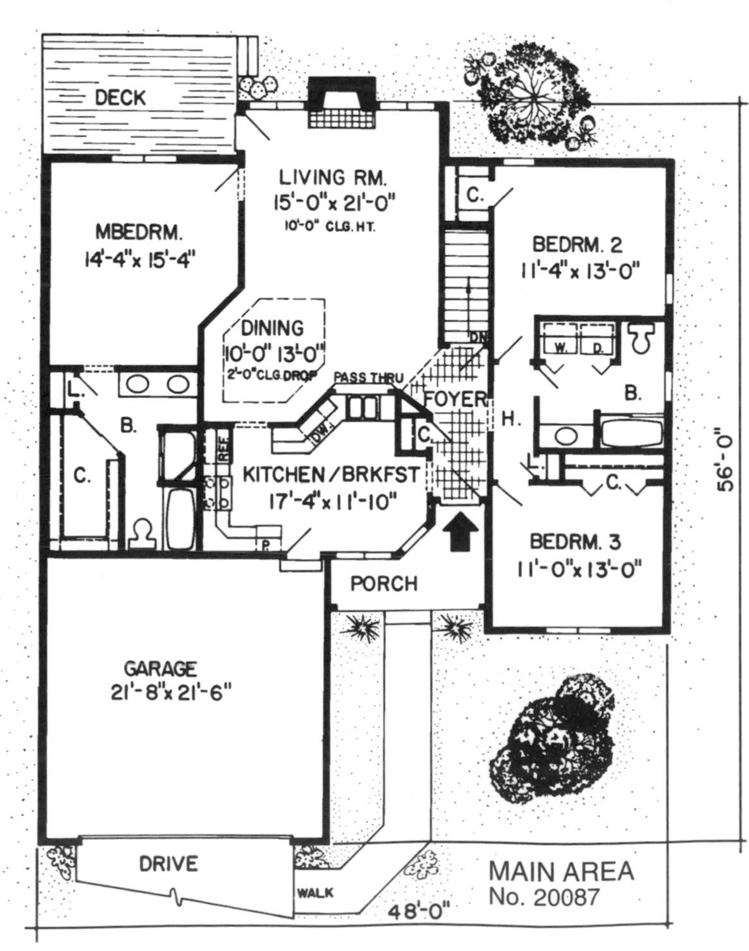
DECK
LIVING RM.
15'-0"x 21'-0"
10'-0" CLG. HT.
MBEDRM.
14'-4"x 15'-4"
DINING
10'-0" 13'-0"
2'-0" CLG. DROP
PASS THRU
C.
BEDRM. 2
11'-4"x 13'-0"
W.
D.
B.
FOYER
H.
L.
B.
C.
DW
REF.
KITCHEN / BRKFST
17'-4"x 11'-10"
C.
P.
BEDRM. 3
11'-0"x 13'-0"
PORCH
56'-0"
GARAGE
21'-8"x 21'-6"
DRIVE
WALK
48'-0"
MAIN AREA
No. 20087

To order your Blueprints, call 1-800-235-5700

Refer to **Pricing Schedule B** on
the order form for pricing information

PLAN NO. 90409

STORAGE
8'-4"x7'-6"
UTILITY
8'-2"x7'-6"
W.
D.
BREAKFAST
10'-0"x9'-6"
KITCHEN
9'-8"x8'-8"
PATIO
14'-0"x10'-0"
DINING RM.
19'-8"x11'-2"
BEDROOM
12'-10"x12'-0"
CL.
CL.
PAN.
DRESS.
CL.
BATH
LIN.
BATH
30'-0"
GARAGE
21'-2"x20'-2"
CATHEDRAL CLG.
M. BEDROOM
15'-8"x13'-10"
GREAT RM.
19'-8"x18'-2"
CL.
CL.
BEDROOM
13'-0"x11'-0"
PORCH
21'-0"x6'-0"
73'-8"

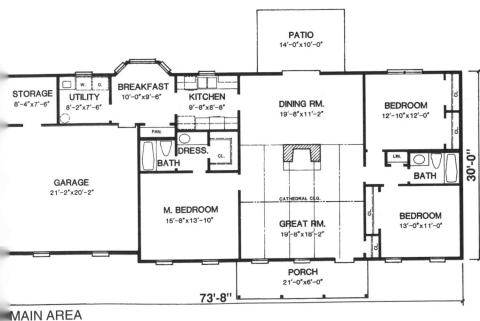

MAIN AREA
No. 90409

Rocking Chair Living

- This plan features:
  - — Three bedrooms
  - — Two full baths
- A massive fireplace separating Living and Dining Rooms
- An isolated Master Suite with a walk-in closet and a helpful compartmentalized bath
- A galley-type Kitchen between the Breakfast Room and Dining Room
- An optional basement, slab or crawl space foundation — please specify when ordering

MAIN AREA — 1,670 SQ. FT.

TOTAL LIVING AREA:
1,670 SQ. FT.

PLAN NO. 91785

Refer to **Pricing Schedule B** on the order form for pricing information

Barn With A Balcony

- This plan features:
- — Three bedrooms
- — Two full baths
- A gambrel roof and wrap-around deck to expand the living space inside and out
- A L-shaped Living/Dining Area with a tile fireplace and windows on three sides
- An efficient galley Kitchen with ample counter and storage space
- A first floor Bedroom with a private access to a full hall bath
- Two large bedrooms on the second floor, one with a private balcony, sharing a full hall bath

FIRST FLOOR — 960 SQ. FT.
SECOND FLOOR — 720 SQ. FT.

TOTAL LIVING AREA;
1,680 SQ. FT.

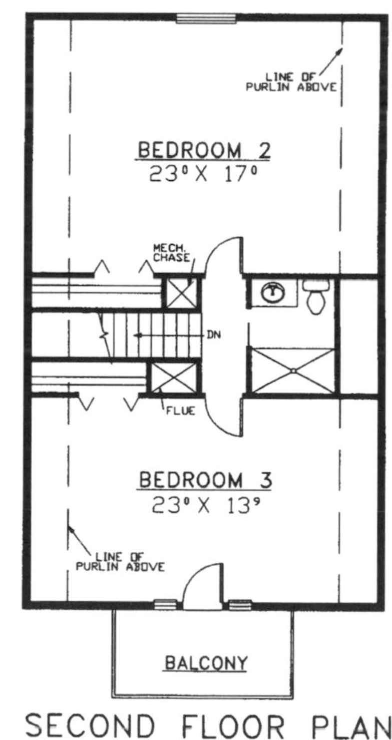

LINE OF PURLIN ABOVE
BEDROOM 2
23⁰ X 17⁰
MECH. CHASE
DN
FLUE
BEDROOM 3
23⁰ X 13⁹
LINE OF PURLIN ABOVE
BALCONY

SECOND FLOOR PLAN
No. 91785

WIDTH 40'-0"
DEPTH 24'-0"

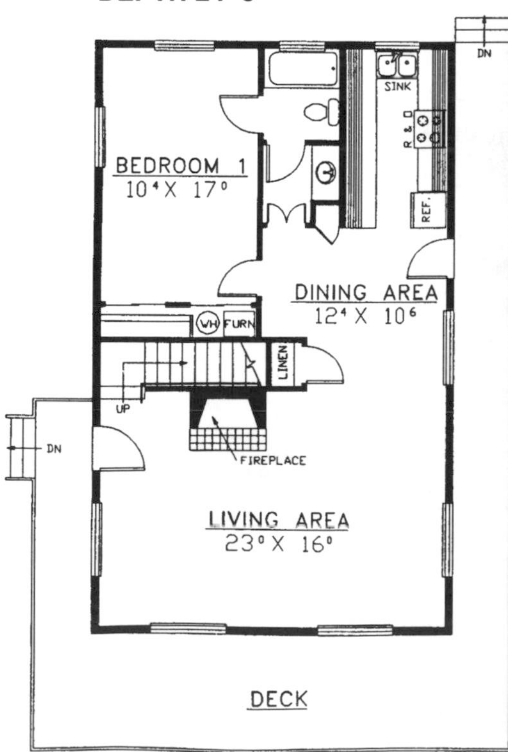

DN
SINK
R&O
REF.
BEDROOM 1
10⁴ X 17⁰
DINING AREA
12⁴ X 10⁶
VH
FURN
LINEN
UP
DN
FIREPLACE
LIVING AREA
23⁰ X 16⁰
DECK

FIRST FLOOR PLAN

To order your Blueprints, call 1-800-235-5700

Refer to **Pricing Schedule B** on the order form for pricing information

PLAN NO. 24250

Clever Design Packs in Plenty of Living Space

- This plan features:
- — Three bedrooms
- — Two full baths
- Custom, volume ceilings
- A sunken Living Room that includes a vaulted ceiling and a fireplace with oversized windows framing it
- A center island and an eating nook in the Kitchen that has more than ample counter space
- A formal Dining Room that adjoins the Kitchen, allowing for easy entertaining
- A spacious Master Suite including a vaulted ceiling and lavish bath
- Secondary bedrooms with custom ceiling treatments and use of full hall bath

MAIN AREA — 1,700 SQ. FT.

TOTAL LIVING AREA:
1,700 SQ. FT.

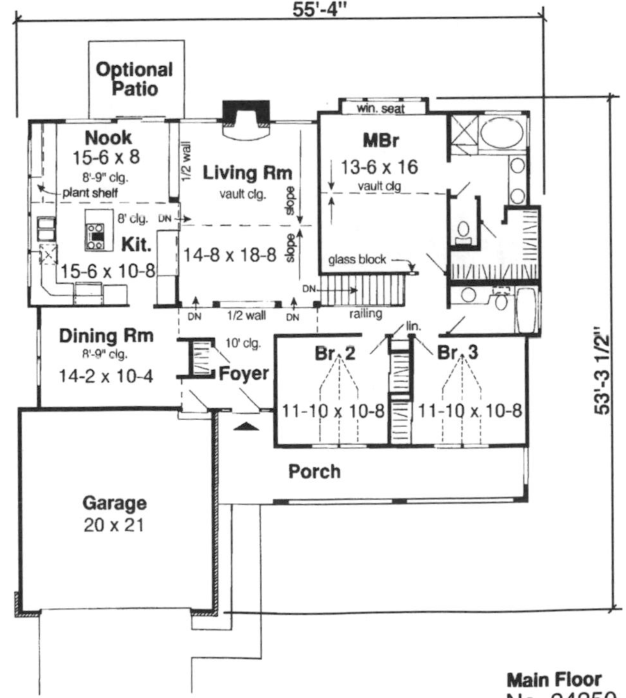
55'-4"
53'-3 1/2"
Optional Patio
Nook
15-6 x 8
8'-9" clg.
plant shelf
1/2 wall
Living Rm
vault clg.
slope
win. seat
MBr
13-6 x 16
vault clg
8' clg.
DN
Kit.
15-6 x 10-8
14-8 x 18-8
glass block
DN
1/2 wall
railing
Dining Rm
8'-9" clg.
14-2 x 10-4
10' clg.
Foyer
lin.
Br. 2
11-10 x 10-8
Br. 3
11-10 x 10-8
Porch
Garage
20 x 21

Main Floor
No. 24250

An
EXCLUSIVE DESIGN
By Energetic Enterprises

PLAN NO. 91797

Refer to **Pricing Schedule A** on the order form for pricing information

Country Ranch

- This plan features:
- — Three bedrooms
- — Two full baths
- A railed and covered wrap-around porch, adding charm to this country-styled home
- A high vaulted ceiling in the Living Room
- A smaller Kitchen with ample cupboard and counter space, that is augmented by a large pantry
- An informal Family Room with access to the wood deck
- A private Master Suite with a spa tub and a walk-in closet
- Two family bedrooms that share a full hall bath
- A shop and storage area in the two-car garage

MAIN AREA — 1,485 SQ. FT.
GARAGE — 701 SQ. FT.

TOTAL LIVING AREA:
1,485 SQ. FT.

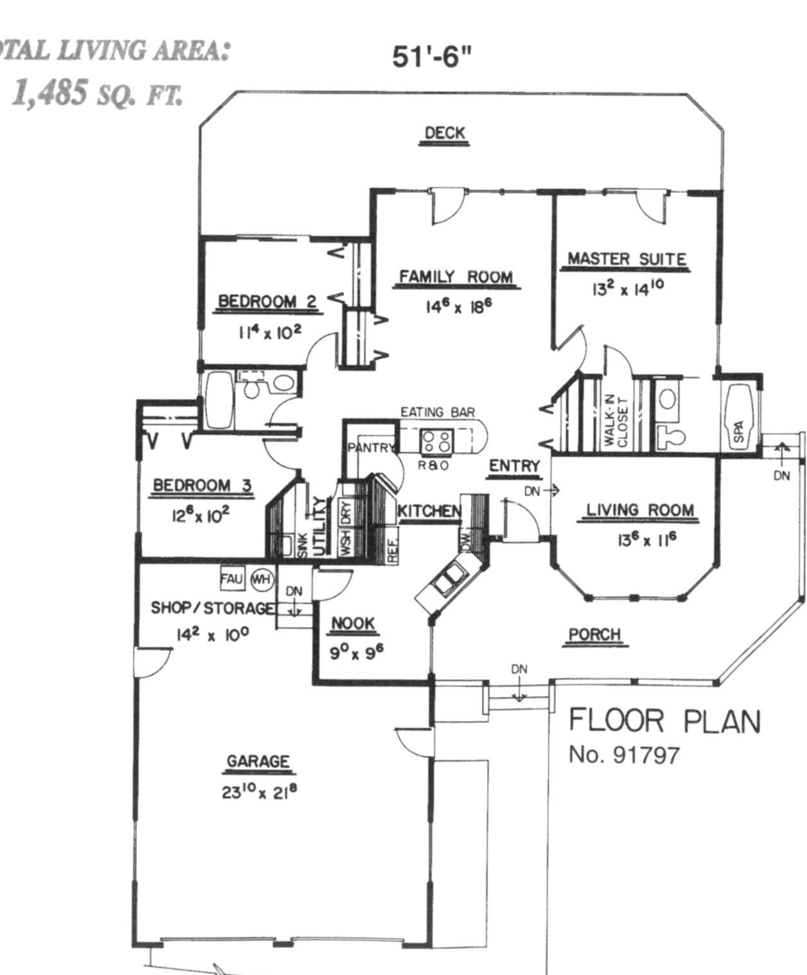
51'-6"
63'-0"
DECK
FAMILY ROOM
14^6 x 18^6
MASTER SUITE
13^2 x 14^{10}
BEDROOM 2
11^4 x 10^2
EATING BAR
PANTRY
R&O
ENTRY
DN
WALK-IN CLOSET
SPA
BEDROOM 3
12^6 x 10^2
SINK
UTILITY
DRY
WSH
REF.
KITCHEN
DW
LIVING ROOM
13^6 x 11^6
FAU
WH
SHOP/STORAGE
14^2 x 10^0
NOOK
9^0 x 9^6
PORCH
GARAGE
23^{10} x 21^8

FLOOR PLAN
No. 91797

To order your Blueprints, call 1-800-235-5700

Refer to **Pricing Schedule B** on the order form for pricing information

PLAN NO. 90418

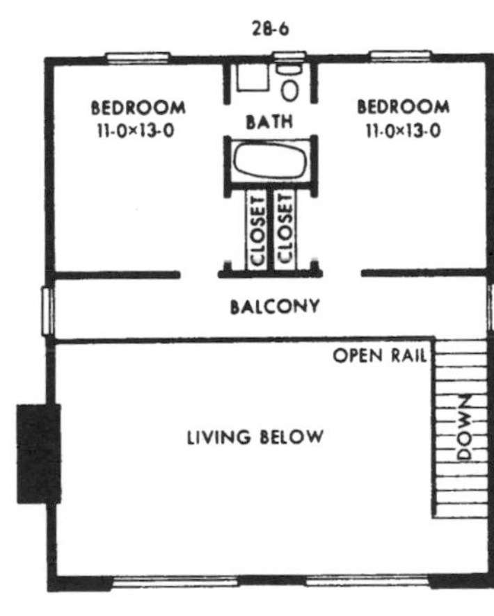
28-6
BEDROOM
11-0×13-0
BATH
BEDROOM
11-0×13-0
CLOSET
CLOSET
BALCONY
OPEN RAIL
LIVING BELOW
DOWN
SECOND FLOOR

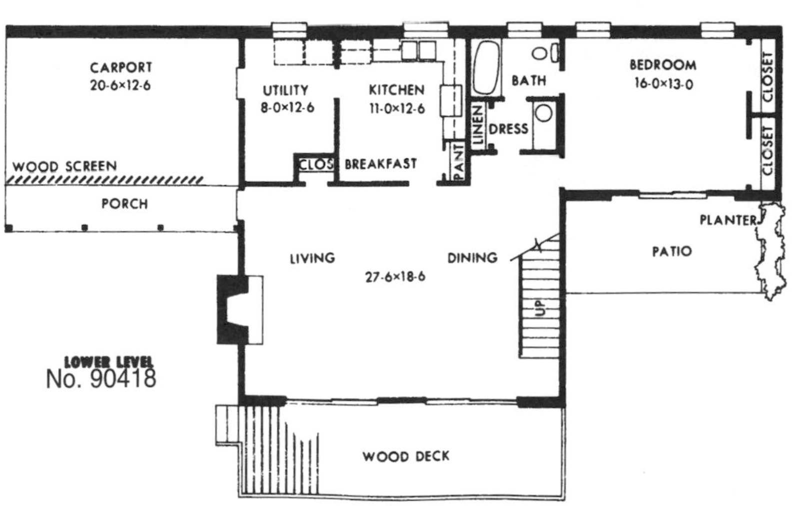
CARPORT
20-6×12-6
UTILITY
8-0×12-6
KITCHEN
11-0×12-6
BATH
BEDROOM
16-0×13-0
CLOSET
CLOSET
LINEN
DRESS
PANT
CLOS
BREAKFAST
WOOD SCREEN
PORCH
LIVING
27-6×18-6
DINING
PLANTER
PATIO
UP
LOWER LEVEL
WOOD DECK
68-0

No. 90418

House with a View

- This plan features:
- — Three bedrooms
- — Two full baths
- A large, open Living Room accented by a fireplace and open stairs to the second floor
- Access to the Garage through the Utility Room which adjoins Kitchen
- A large Master Bedroom with a private bath and dressing area, one wall of closets, and access to a private patio
- An optional basement, slab or crawl space foundation — please specify when ordering

LOWER LEVEL — 1,304 SQ. FT.
UPPER LEVEL — 303 SQ. FT.

TOTAL LIVING AREA:
1,607 SQ. FT.

PLAN NO.10274

Refer to **Pricing Schedule B** on the order form for pricing information

Fireplace Center of Circular Living Area

- This plan features:
- — Three bedrooms
- — One full and one three quarter bath
- A dramatically positioned fireplace as a focal point for the main living area
- The Kitchen, Dining and Living Rooms form a circle that allows work areas to flow into living areas
- Sliding glass doors accessible to wood a Deck
- A convenient Laundry Room located off the Kitchen
- A double Garage providing excellent storage

MAIN AREA— 1,783 SQ. FT.
GARAGE — 576 SQ. FT.

TOTAL LIVING AREA:
1,783 SQ. FT.

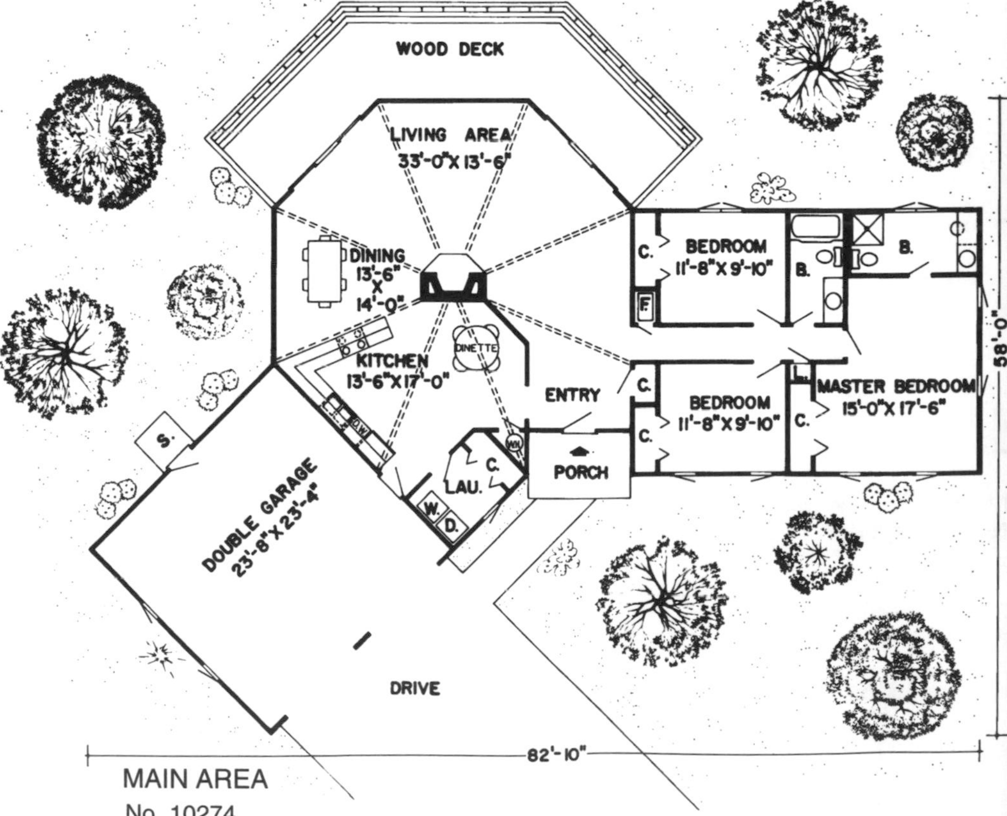

WOOD DECK
LIVING AREA
33'-0"X 13'-6"
DINING
13'-6"
X
14'-0"
KITCHEN
13'-6"X 17'-0"
DINETTE
BEDROOM
11'-8"X 9'-10"
BEDROOM
11'-8"X 9'-10"
MASTER BEDROOM
15'-0"X 17'-6"
ENTRY
PORCH
LAU.
DOUBLE GARAGE
23'-8"X 23'-4"
DRIVE
58'-0"
82'-10"

MAIN AREA
No. 10274

To order your Blueprints, call 1-800-235-5700

Refer to **Pricing Schedule B** on the order form for pricing information

PLAN NO. 90423

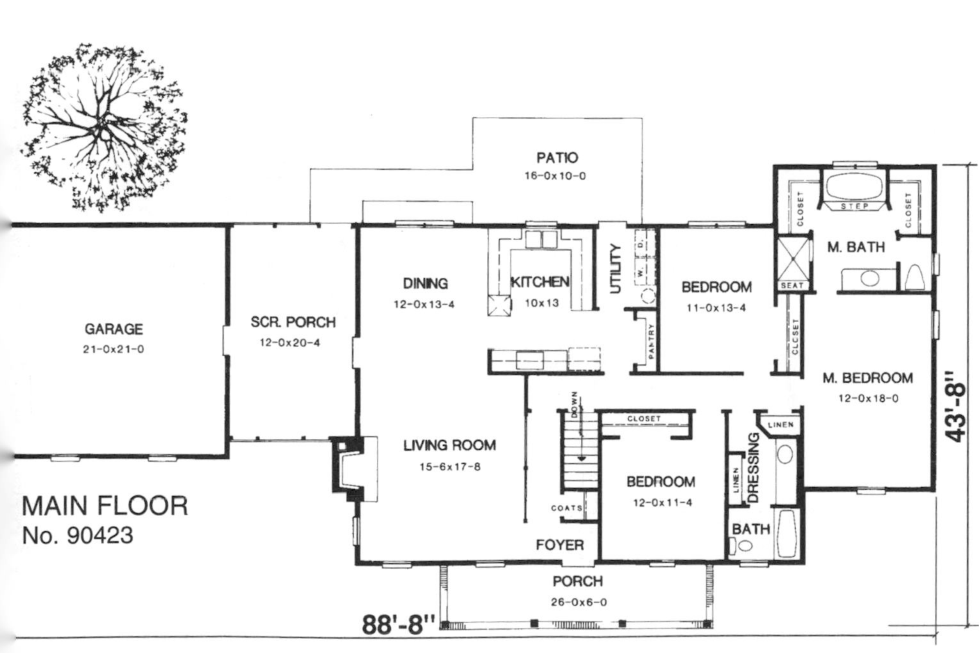
PATIO
16-0x10-0
GARAGE
21-0x21-0
SCR. PORCH
12-0x20-4
DINING
12-0x13-4
KITCHEN
10x13
UTILITY
W. D.
PANTRY
BEDROOM
11-0x13-4
CLOSET
STEP
CLOSET
M. BATH
SEAT
CLOSET
M. BEDROOM
12-0x18-0
43'-8"
DOWN
CLOSET
LINEN
LIVING ROOM
15-6x17-8
BEDROOM
12-0x11-4
LINEN
DRESSING
COATS
BATH
FOYER
PORCH
26-0x6-0
88'-8"
MAIN FLOOR
No. 90423

Expansive, Not Expensive

- This plan features:
- — Three bedrooms
- — Two full baths
- A Master Suite with his-n-her closets and a private Master Bath
- Two additional bedrooms that share a full hall closet
- A pleasant Dining Room that overlooks a rear garden
- A well-equipped Kitchen with a built-in planning corner and eat-in space
- This plan is available with a basement, slab or crawl space foundation — please specify

MAIN FLOOR — 1,773 SQ. FT.

TOTAL LIVING AREA:
1,773 SQ. FT.

PLAN NO. 92655

Refer to **Pricing Schedule B** on the order form for pricing information

Back Yard Views

- This plan features:
  - — Three bedrooms
  - — Two full baths
- Front Porch accesses open Foyer, and spacious Dining Room and Great Room with sloped ceilings
- Corner fireplace, windows and atrium door to Patio enhance Great Room
- Convenient Kitchen with a pantry, peninsula serving counter for bright Breakfast area and nearby Laundry/Garage entry
- Luxurious bath, walk-in closet and back yard view offered in Master Bedroom
- Two additional bedrooms, one with an arched window, share full bath
- No materials list available for this plan

MAIN FLOOR — 1,746 SQ. FT.
GARAGE — 480 SQ. FT.
BASEMENT — 1,697 SQ. FT.

TOTAL LIVING AREA:
1,746 SQ. FT.

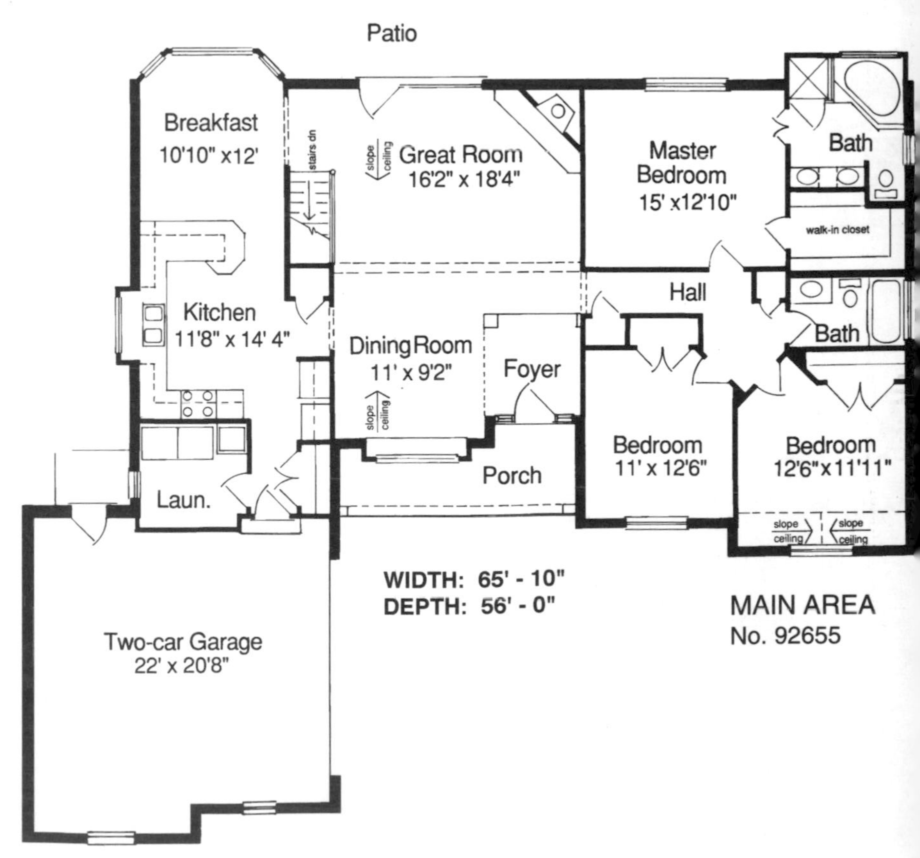

Patio
Breakfast
10'10" x12'
stairs dn
slope ceiling
Great Room
16'2" x 18'4"
Master Bedroom
15' x12'10"
Bath
walk-in closet
Kitchen
11'8" x 14' 4"
Hall
Dining Room
11' x 9'2"
Foyer
Bath
slope ceiling
Porch
Bedroom
11' x 12'6"
Bedroom
12'6"x11'11"
Laun.
slope ceiling
slope ceiling
WIDTH: 65' - 10"
DEPTH: 56' - 0"
MAIN AREA
No. 92655
Two-car Garage
22' x 20'8"

To order your Blueprints, call 1-800-235-5700

Refer to **Pricing Schedule Z** on the order form for pricing information

PLAN NO. 24308

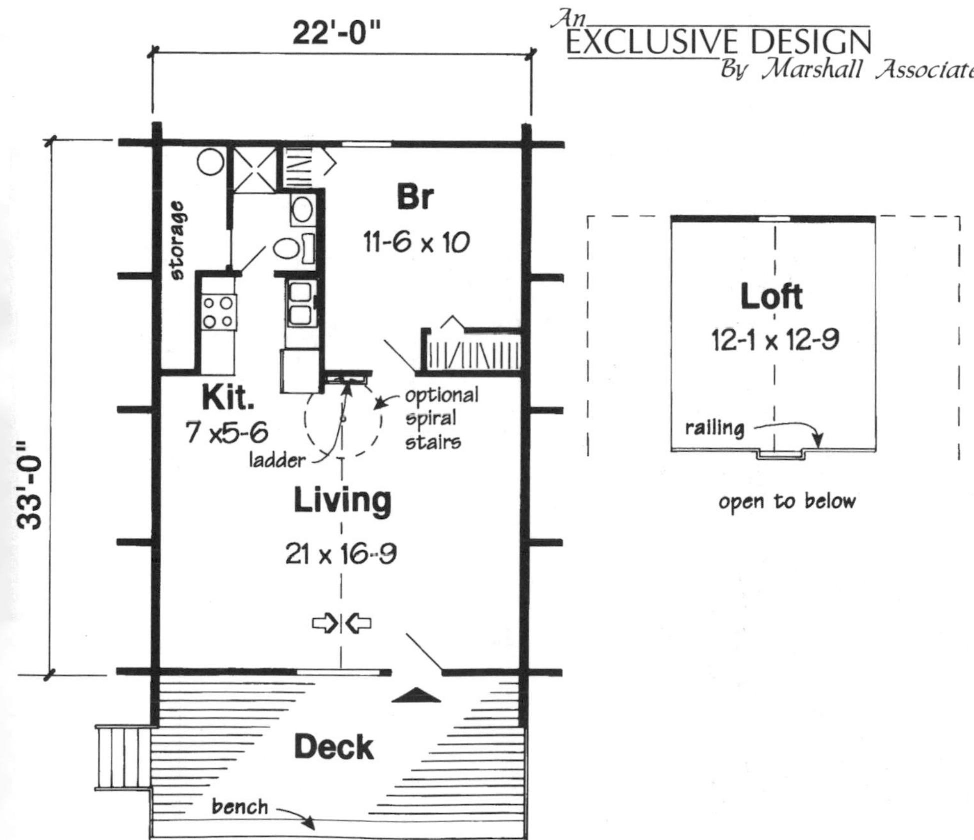

An EXCLUSIVE DESIGN By Marshall Associates
22'-0"
33'-0"
storage
Br
11-6 x 10
Kit.
7 x5-6
optional spiral stairs
ladder
Living
21 x 16-9
Deck
bench
Loft
12-1 x 12-9
railing
open to below
Main Floor
No. 24308

Leisure Time Getaway

- This plan features:
  - — One bedroom
  - — One full bath
- The simplicity of an A-frame with a spacious feeling achieved by the large, two-story Living Room
- An entrance deck leads into the open Living Room accented by a spiral staircase to the Loft
- A small, but efficient Kitchen serves the Living area easily, and provides access to the full bath with a shower and a storage area
- A first floor bedroom and a Loft area provide the sleeping quarters

MAIN FLOOR — 660 SQ. FT.
LOFT — 163 SQ. FT.

TOTAL LIVING AREA:
823 SQ. FT.

PLAN NO. 90692

Refer to **Pricing Schedule A** on the order form for pricing information

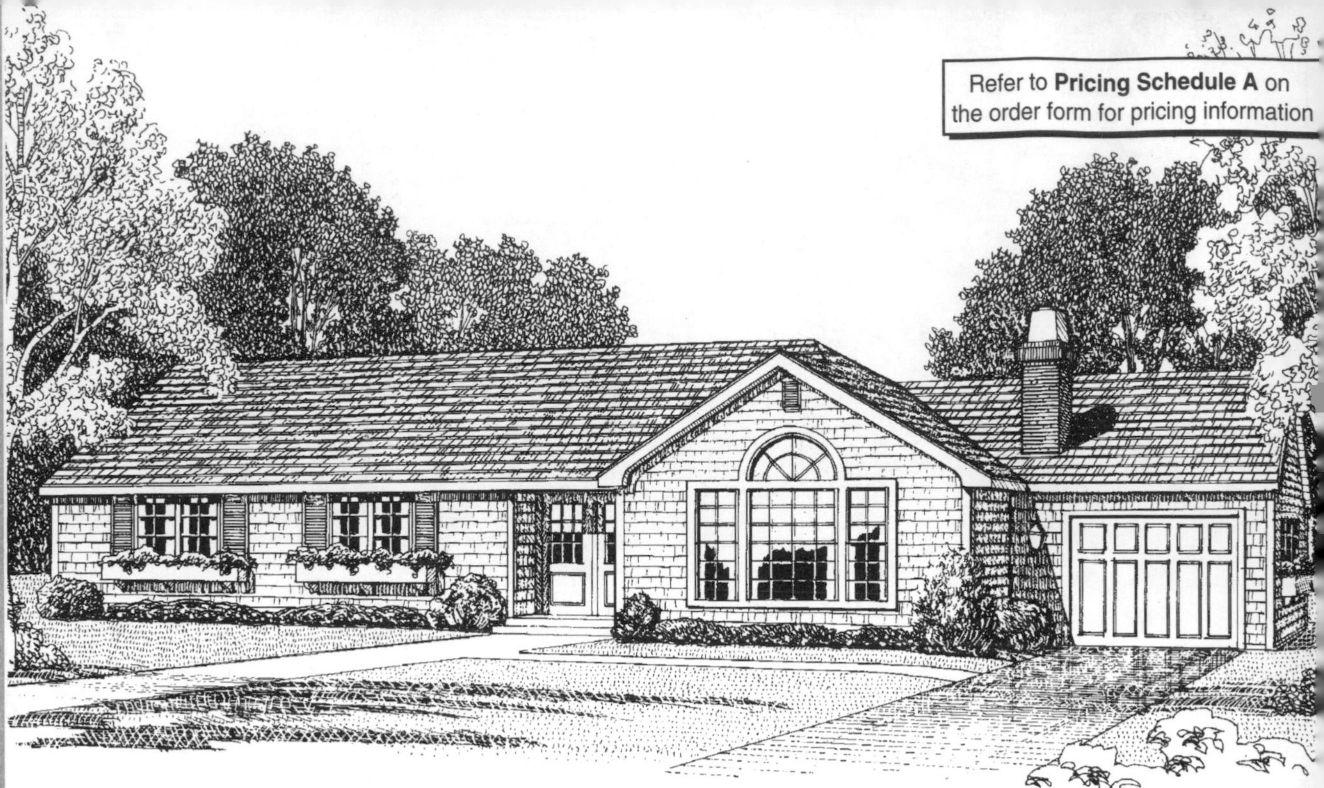

Carefree Comfort

- This plan features:
- — Three bedrooms
- — Two full baths
- Cedar shingle siding and flowerboxes
- A heat-circulating fireplace
- A central Foyer separating active areas from the bedroom wing
- A sunny Living Room with an arched window, fireplace, and soaring cathedral ceilings
- A formal Dining Room adjoining the Living Room

MAIN AREA — 1,492 SQ. FT.

TOTAL LIVING AREA:
1,492 SQ. FT.

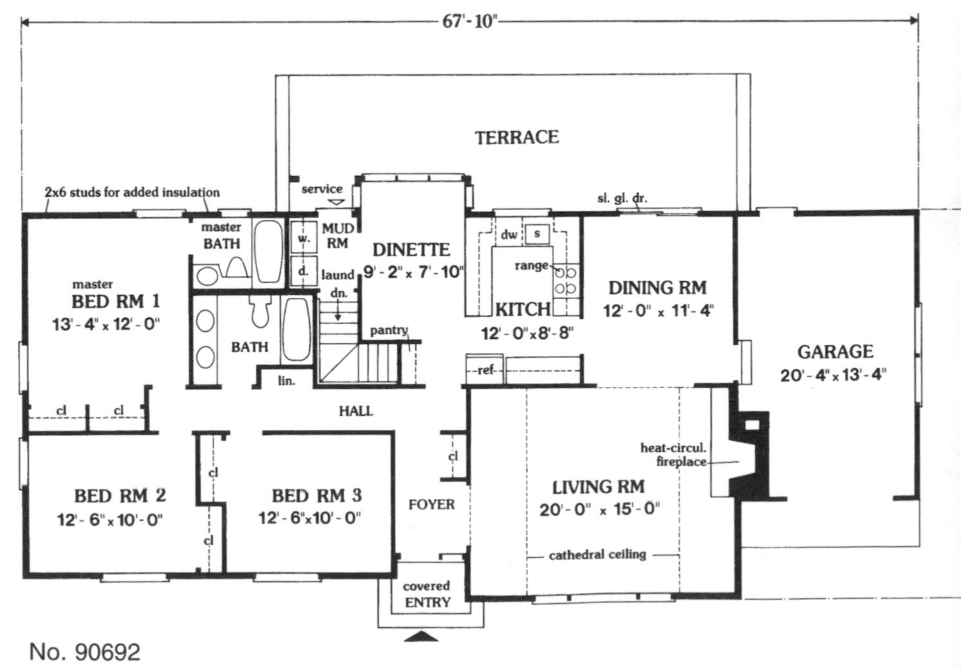

67'-10"
TERRACE
2x6 studs for added insulation
service
sl. gl. dr.
master BATH
w.
d.
MUD RM
laund
dn.
DINETTE
9'-2" x 7'-10"
dw
s
range
master
BED RM 1
13'-4" x 12'-0"
KITCH
12'-0"x8'-8"
DINING RM
12'-0" x 11'-4"
pantry
BATH
ref
GARAGE
20'-4"x13'-4"
lin.
cl
cl
HALL
cl
heat-circul. fireplace
cl
BED RM 2
12'-6"x10'-0"
BED RM 3
12'-6"x10'-0"
FOYER
LIVING RM
20'-0" x 15'-0"
cl
cathedral ceiling
covered ENTRY

No. 90692

FLOOR PLAN

Refer to **Pricing Schedule Z** on the order form for pricing information

PLAN NO. 90821

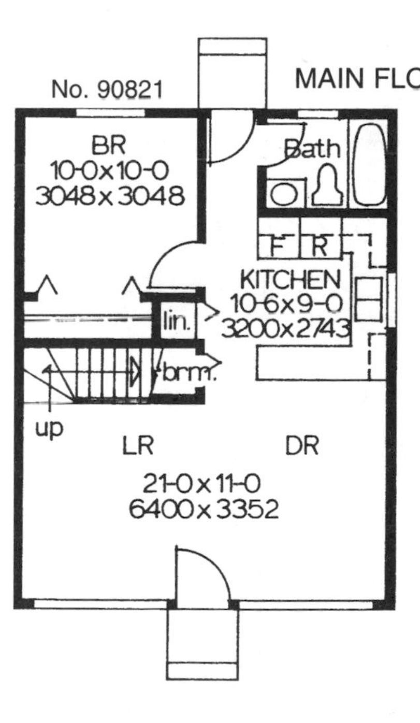

No. 90821
MAIN FLOOR
BR
10-0x10-0
3048x3048
Bath
F R
KITCHEN
10-6x9-0
3200x2743
lin.
brm.
up
LR
DR
21-0x11-0
6400x3352

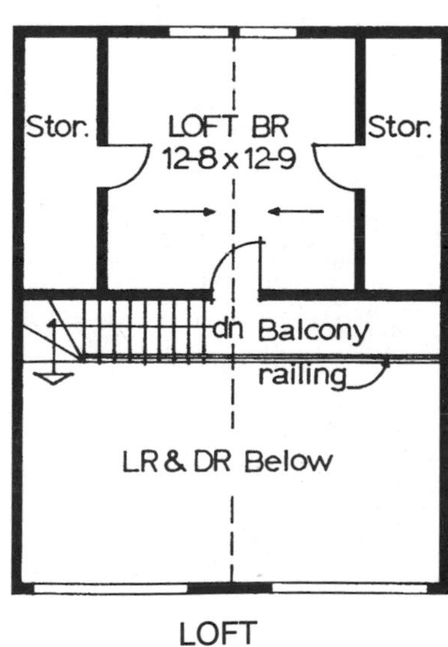

Stor.
LOFT BR
12-8x12-9
Stor.
dn Balcony
railing
LR & DR Below
LOFT

An EXCLUSIVE DESIGN
By Westhome Planners, Ltd.

Vacation Cottage

- This plan features:
  - — Two bedrooms
  - — One full bath
- An economical, neat and simple design
- Two picture windows in the Living/Dining Room
- An efficient Kitchen design
- A large, cozy loft bedroom flanked by big storage rooms
- This plan is available with a basement or crawl space foundation — please specify

MAIN FLOOR — 616 SQ. FT.
LOFT — 180 SQ. FT.
WIDTH — 22'-0"
DEPTH — 28'-0"

TOTAL LIVING AREA:
796 SQ. FT.

PLAN NO. 24313

Refer to **Pricing Schedule A** on the order form for pricing information

Cozy Rustic Exterior

- This plan features:
  - — Two bedrooms
  - — Two full baths
- An front deck with a double glass door entrance and large windows to either side
- An open layout creates space and efficiency between the Kitchen and the Living Room which boasts a fireplace
- A first floor bedroom with a double closet and a full bath
- A second floor bedroom with double closets and a Loft area share a full bath

FIRST FLOOR — 781 SQ. FT.
SECOND FLOOR — 429 SQ. FT.

TOTAL LIVING AREA:
1,210 SQ. FT.

An EXCLUSIVE DESIGN
By Marshall Associates

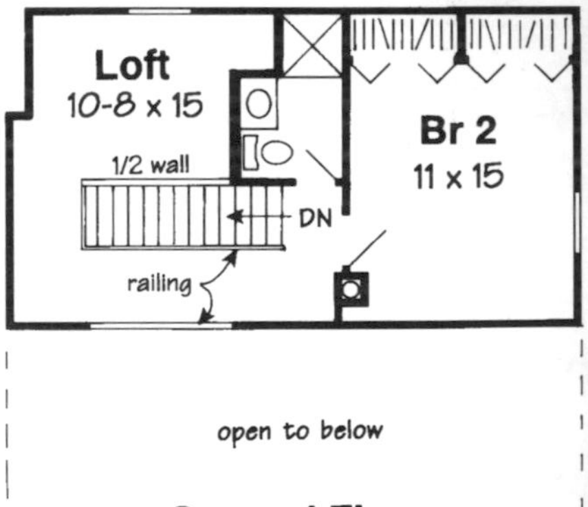

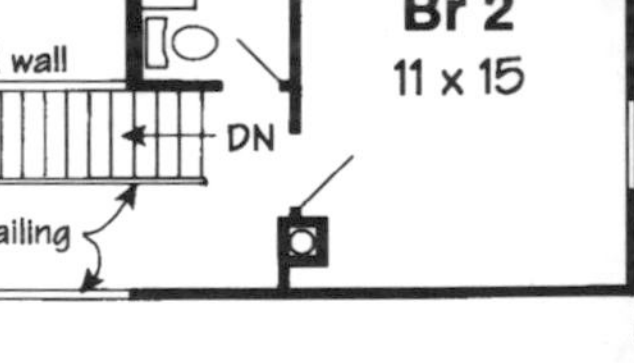

Loft
10-8 x 15
Br 2
11 x 15
1/2 wall
DN
railing
open to below

Second Floor

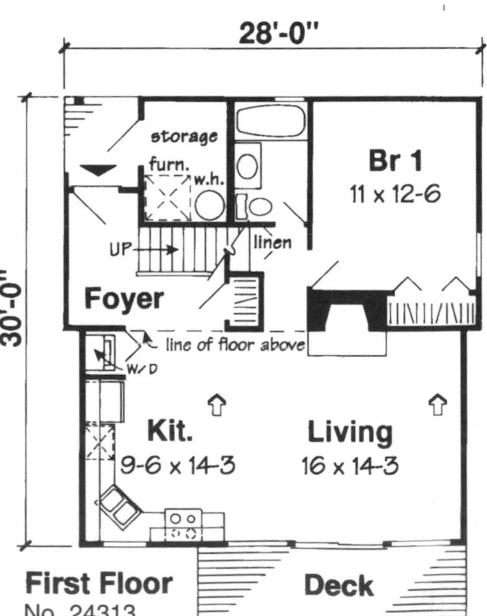

28'-0"
30'-0"
storage
furn.
w.h.
Br 1
11 x 12-6
UP
linen
Foyer
line of floor above
W/D
Kit.
9-6 x 14-3
Living
16 x 14-3
Deck

First Floor
No. 24313

To order your Blueprints, call 1-800-235-5700

Refer to **Pricing Schedule A** on the order form for pricing information

PLAN NO. 90354

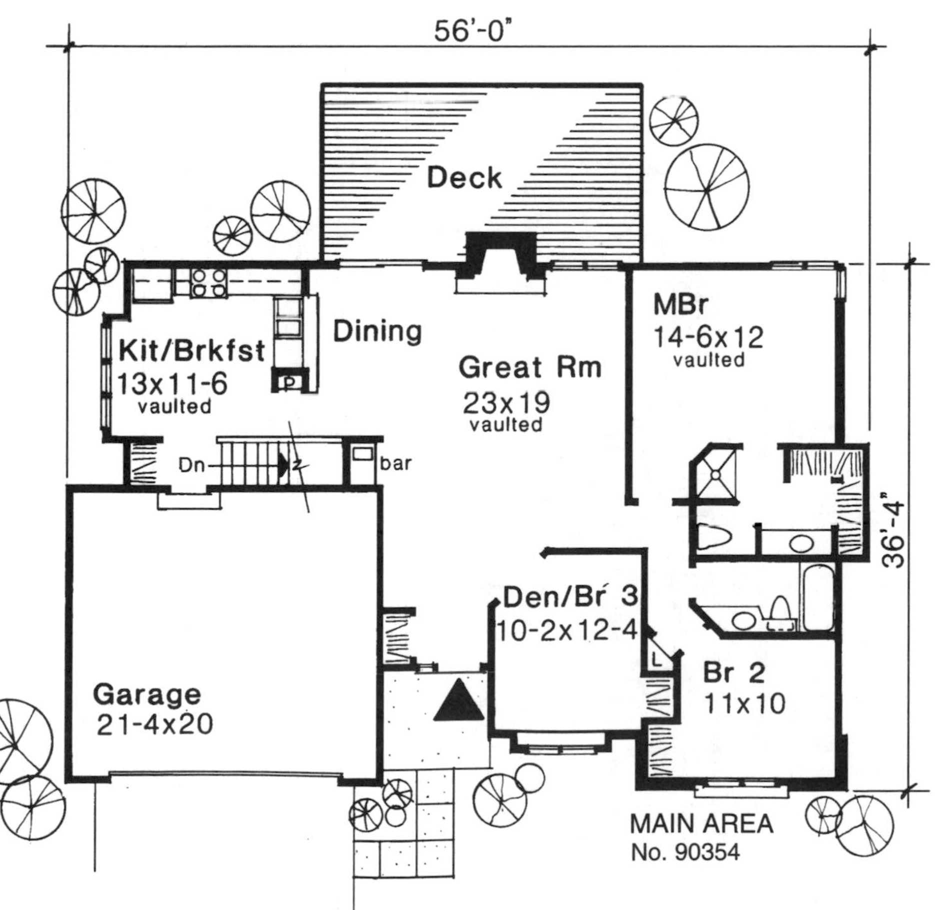

56'-0"
Deck
Kit/Brkfst
13x11-6
vaulted
Dining
Great Rm
23x19
vaulted
MBr
14-6x12
vaulted
Dn
bar
36'-4"
Den/Br 3
10-2x12-4
Br 2
11x10
Garage
21-4x20
MAIN AREA
No. 90354

Another Efficient Ranch Design

- This plan features:
  - — Three bedrooms
  - — One full and one three quarter baths
- A vaulted ceiling in the Great Room, that includes a fireplace and access to the rear deck
- Double door entrance into the Den/third bedroom
- A Kitchen and breakfast area with a vaulted ceiling and an efficient layout
- A Master Suite crowned by a vaulted ceiling and pampered by a private bath and dressing area
- A full hall bath that serves the two additional bedrooms

MAIN AREA — 1,360 SQ. FT.

TOTAL LIVING AREA:
1,360 SQ. FT.

PLAN NO. 93279

Refer to **Pricing Schedule A** on the order form for pricing information

Wonderful Open Spaces

An EXCLUSIVE DESIGN By *Jannis Vann & Associates, Inc.*

- This plan features:
  - — Three bedrooms
  - — Two full baths
- A Family Room, Kitchen and Breakfast Area that all connects to form a great space
- A central, double fireplace adding warmth and atmosphere to the Family Room, Kitchen and the Breakfast area
- An efficient Kitchen that is highlighted by a peninsula counter and doubles as a snack bar
- A Master Suite that includes a walk-in closet, a double vanity, separate shower and tub bath
- Two additional bedrooms sharing a full hall bath
- A wooden deck that can be accessed from the Breakfast Area
- This plan is available with a crawl space or slab foundation — please specify when ordering

MAIN FLOOR — 1,388 SQ. FT.
GARAGE — 400 SQ. FT.

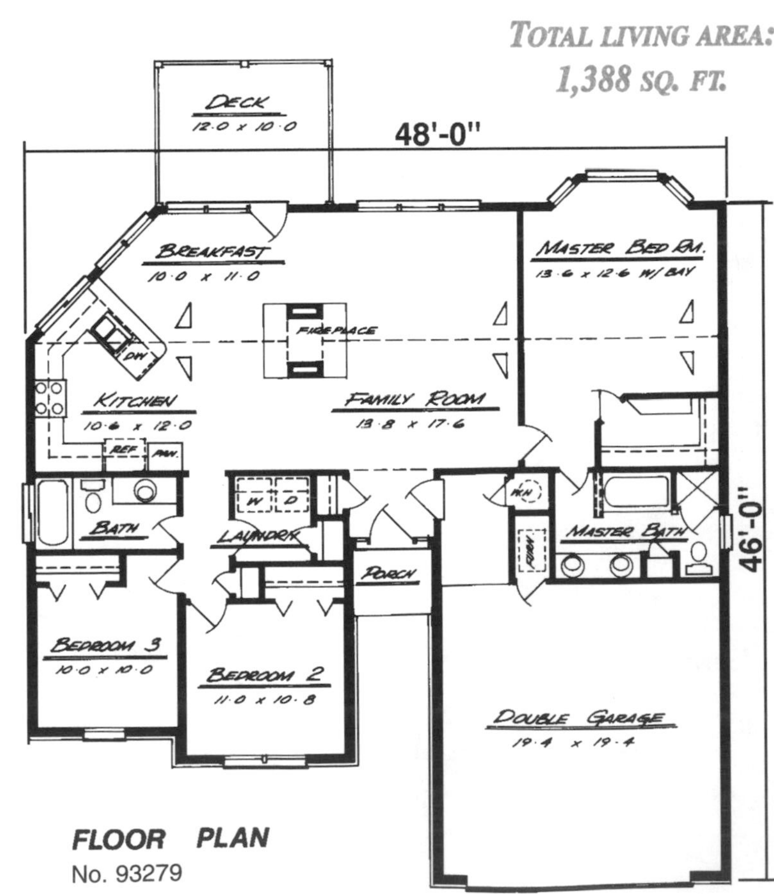
TOTAL LIVING AREA:
1,388 SQ. FT.
DECK
12·0 x 10·0
48'-0"
BREAKFAST
10·0 x 11·0
MASTER BED RM.
13·6 x 12·6 W/ BAY
FIREPLACE
KITCHEN
10·6 x 12·0
FAMILY ROOM
13·8 x 17·6
DW
REF.
PAN.
BATH
W D
LAUNDRY
W/H
MASTER BATH
46'-0"
PORCH
BEDROOM 3
10·0 x 10·0
BEDROOM 2
11·0 x 10·8
DOUBLE GARAGE
19·4 x 19·4

FLOOR PLAN
No. 93279

To order your Blueprints, call 1-800-235-5700

Refer to **Pricing Schedule B** on the order form for pricing information

PLAN NO. 92630

Charming Brick Ranch

TOTAL LIVING AREA:
1,7 82 SQ. FT.

- This plan features:
- — Three bedrooms
- — Two full baths
- Sheltered entrance leads into open Foyer and Dining Room defined by columns
- Vaulted ceiling spans Foyer, Dining Room, and Great Room with corner fireplace and atrium door to rear year
- Central Kitchen with separate Laundry and pantry easily serves Dining Room, Breakfast area and Screened Porch
- Luxurious Master bedroom offers tray ceiling and French doors to double vanity, walk-in closet and whirlpool tub
- Two additional bedrooms, one easily converted to a Study, share a full bath
- No mateials list available for this plan

MAIN FLOOR —1,782 SQ. FT.
GARAGE — 407 SQ. FT.
BASEMENT — 1,735 SQ. FT.

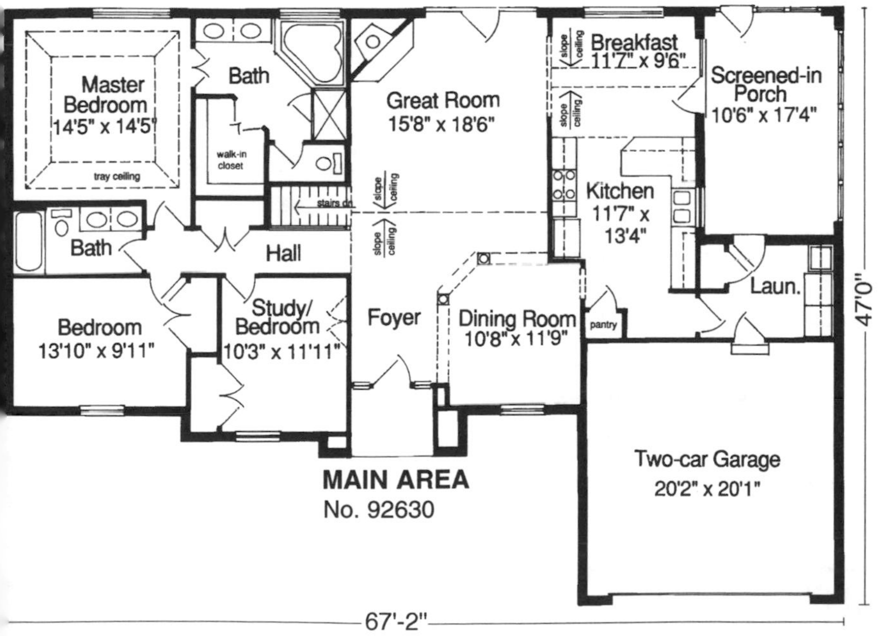
Master Bedroom
14'5" x 14'5"
tray ceiling
Bath
walk-in closet
Great Room
15'8" x 18'6"
Breakfast
11'7" x 9'6"
slope ceiling
Screened-in Porch
10'6" x 17'4"
Kitchen
11'7" x 13'4"
stairs dn
Bath
Hall
Laun.
Bedroom
13'10" x 9'11"
Study/ Bedroom
10'3" x 11'11"
Foyer
Dining Room
10'8" x 11'9"
pantry
47'0"
Two-car Garage
20'2" x 20'1"
MAIN AREA
No. 92630
67'-2"

PLAN NO. 90689

Refer to **Pricing Schedule A** on the order form for pricing information

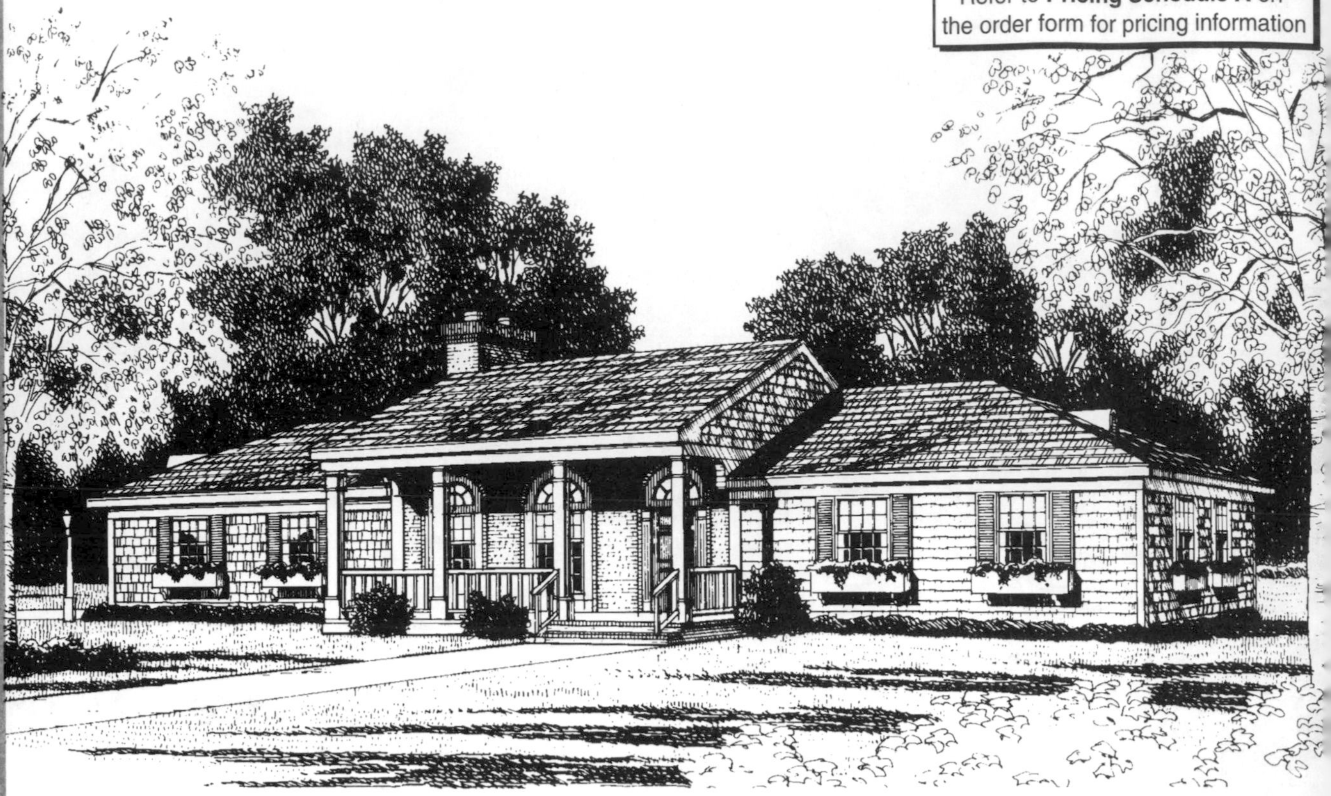

Formal Balance

- This plan features:

— Three bedrooms

— Two full baths

- A cathedral ceiling in the Living Room with a heat-circulating fireplace as the focal point
- A bow window in the Dining Room that adds elegance as well as natural light
- A well-equipped Kitchen that serves both the Dinette and the formal Dining Room efficiently
- A Master Bedroom with three closets and a private Master Bath with sliding glass doors to the Master Deck with a hot tub

MAIN FLOOR — 1,476 SQ. FT.
BASEMENT — 1,361 SQ. FT.
GARAGE — 548 SQ. FT.

TOTAL LIVING AREA:* *1,476 SQ. FT.

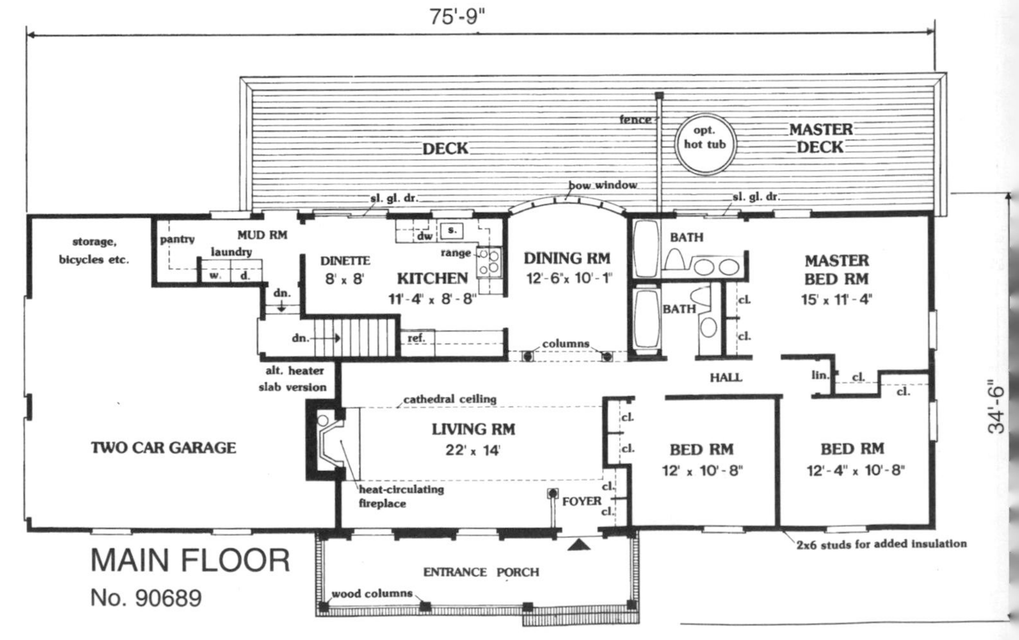
75'-9"
34'-6"
DECK
fence
opt. hot tub
MASTER DECK
bow window
sl. gl. dr.
sl. gl. dr.
storage, bicycles etc.
pantry
MUD RM
laundry
w.
d.
DINETTE 8' x 8'
KITCHEN 11'-4" x 8'-8"
dw
s.
range
ref.
dn.
dn.
DINING RM 12'-6" x 10'-1"
columns
BATH
BATH
cl.
cl.
MASTER BED RM 15' x 11'-4"
alt. heater slab version
HALL
lin.
cl.
cl.
cathedral ceiling
LIVING RM 22' x 14'
TWO CAR GARAGE
heat-circulating fireplace
FOYER
cl.
cl.
cl.
cl.
BED RM 12' x 10'-8"
BED RM 12'-4" x 10'-8"
2x6 studs for added insulation
ENTRANCE PORCH
wood columns
MAIN FLOOR
No. 90689

Refer to **Pricing Schedule D** on the order form for pricing information

PLAN NO. 10549

An EXCLUSIVE DESIGN *By Karl Kreeger*

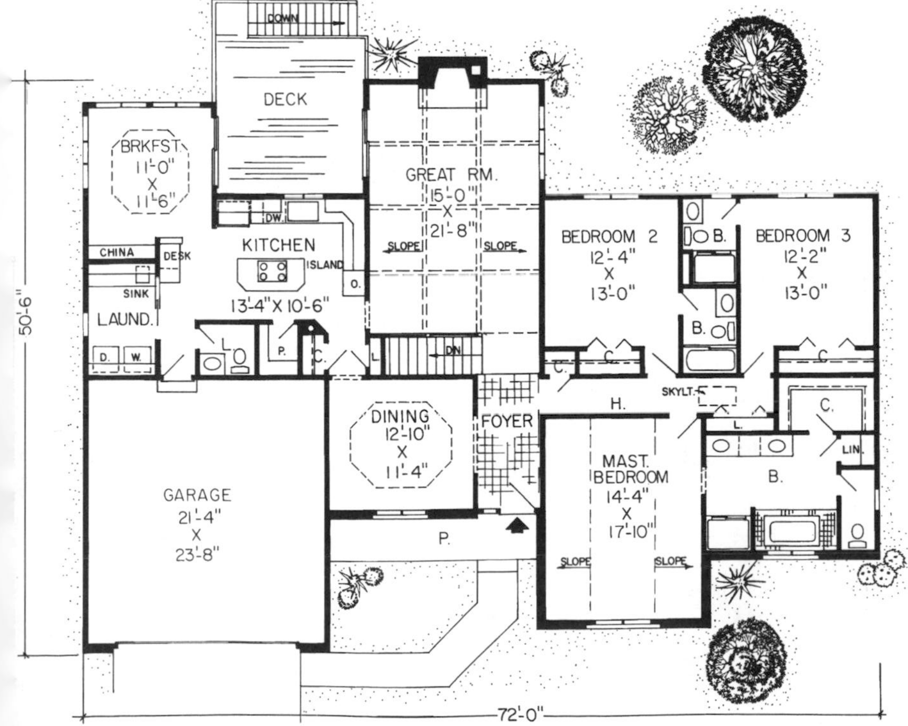

DOWN
DECK
BRKFST.
11'-0" X 11'-6"
GREAT RM.
15'-0" X 21'-8"
SLOPE
SLOPE
BEDROOM 2
12'-4" X 13'-0"
B.
BEDROOM 3
12'-2" X 13'-0"
CHINA
DESK
DW
KITCHEN
ISLAND
O.
SINK
13'-4" X 10'-6"
LAUND.
D.
W.
L.
P.
C.
L.
DN
C.
C.
C.
B.
SKYLT.
H.
L.
C.
DINING
12'-10" X 11'-4"
FOYER
MAST. BEDROOM
14'-4" X 17'-10"
LIN.
B.
GARAGE
21'-4" X 23'-8"
P.
SLOPE
SLOPE
50'-6"
72'-0"

MAIN AREA
No. 10549

Brick Design has Striking Exterior

- This plan features:
  - — Three bedrooms
  - — Three full and one half baths
- A circle-head window that sets off a striking exterior
- A Master Bedroom including a sloping ceiling, large closet space, and a private bath with both a tub and shower
- A Great Room with impressive open-crossed beams and a wood-burning fireplace
- A Kitchen with access to the Dining Room and Breakfast Room

FIRST FLOOR — 2,280 SQ. FT.
BASEMENT — 2,280 SQ. FT.
GARAGE — 528 SQ. FT.

TOTAL LIVING AREA: 2,280 SQ. FT.

PLAN NO. 94301

Refer to **Pricing Schedule C** on the order form for pricing information

Multi-Level View

- This plan features:
- — Three bedrooms
- — Two full baths
- A Deck surrounding three sides to expand living outdoors
- A cozy fireplace surrounded by windows in Living/Dining area
- An efficient, U-shaped Kitchen with an eating bar and more windows
- Two first floor bedrooms sharing a full bath
- A spacious Master Bedroom on the second floor with a walk-in closet, plush bath with raised tub and double sink vanity
- A Loft/Study with a second fireplace and private Deck
- No materials list is available

FIRST FLOOR — 1,145 SQ. FT.
SECOND FLOOR — 726 SQ. FT.
GARAGE — 433 SQ. FT.

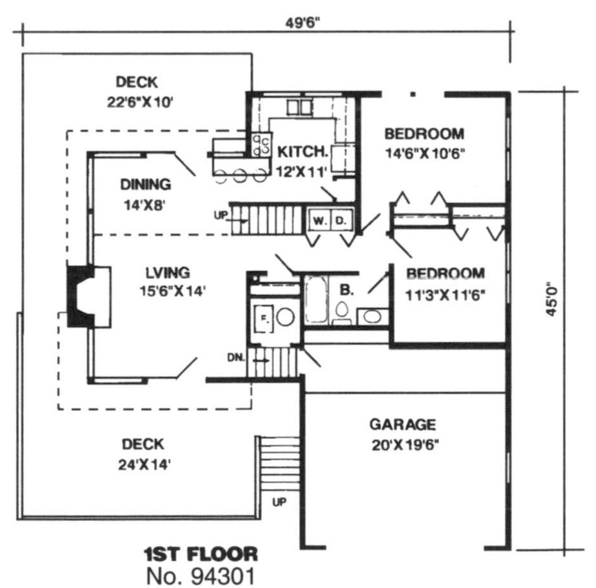

49'6"
DECK
22'6"X10'
KITCH.
12'X11'
BEDROOM
14'6"X10'6"
DINING
14'X8'
UP
W. D.
LVING
15'6"X14'
B.
BEDROOM
11'3"X11'6"
F.
DN.
45'0"
GARAGE
20'X19'6"
DECK
24'X14'
UP

1ST FLOOR
No. 94301

TOTAL LIVING AREA:
1,871 SQ. FT.

An
EXCLUSIVE DESIGN
By Marshall Associates

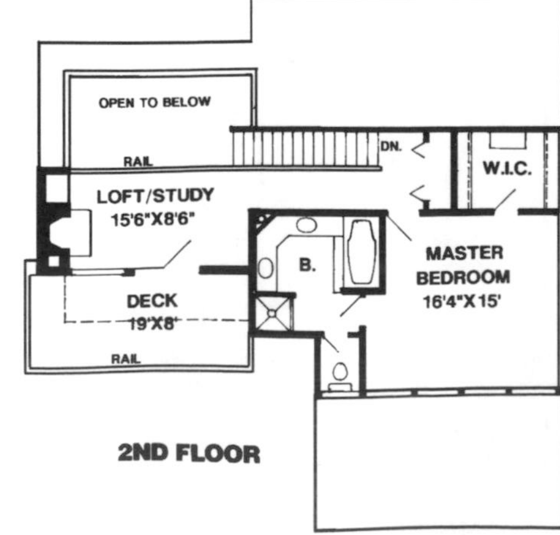

OPEN TO BELOW
RAIL
DN.
W.I.C.
LOFT/STUDY
15'6"X8'6"
B.
MASTER
BEDROOM
16'4"X15'
DECK
19'X8'
RAIL

2ND FLOOR

To order your Blueprints, call 1-800-235-5700

Refer to **Pricing Schedule B** on the order form for pricing information

PLAN NO. 92649

Multiple Gables Galore

- This plan features:
  - Three bedrooms
  - Two full baths
- Multiple gables and a cozy front porch
- Cheery Great Room capped by a sloped ceiling and a fireplace
- The Dining Area includes double hung windows and angles adding light and dimension to the room
- A functional Kitchen providing an abundance of counter space and a breakfast bar
- A Master Bedroom Suite including a walk-in closet and private bath
- Two additional bedrooms share a full bath in the hall
- No materials list available for this plan

MAIN FLOOR — 1,508 SQ. FT.
BASEMENT — 1,429 SQ. FT.
GARAGE — 440 SQ. FT.

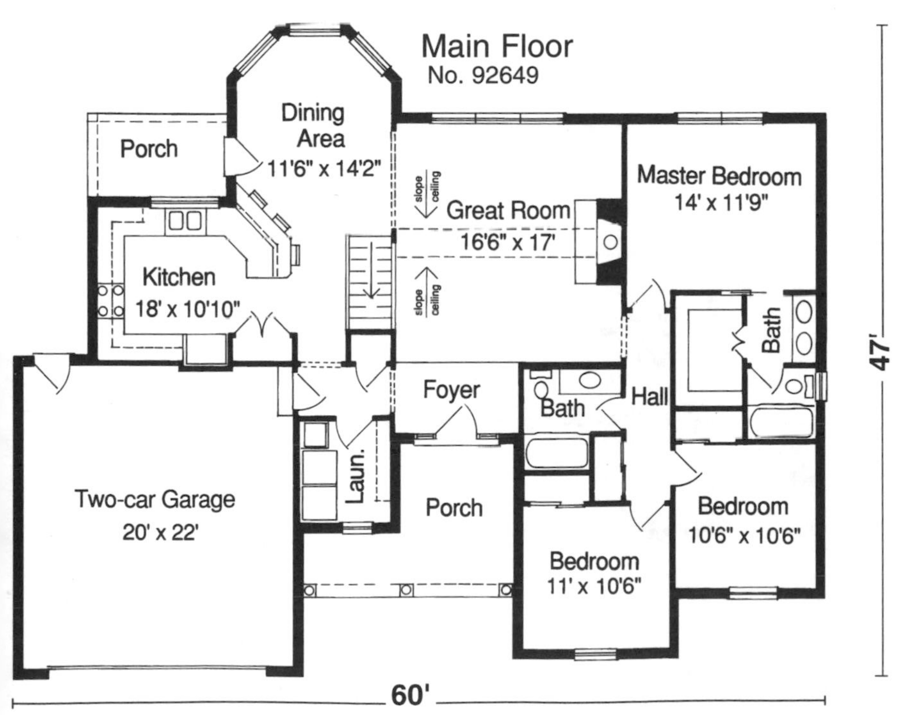

Main Floor
No. 92649
Dining Area
11'6" x 14'2"
Porch
Great Room
16'6" x 17'
slope ceiling
slope ceiling
Master Bedroom
14' x 11'9"
Kitchen
18' x 10'10"
Bath
47'
Foyer
Bath
Hall
Two-car Garage
20' x 22'
Laun.
Porch
Bedroom
10'6" x 10'6"
Bedroom
11' x 10'6"
60'

TOTAL LIVING AREA:
1,508 SQ. FT.

To order your Blueprints, call 1-800-235-5700

PLAN NO. 90412

Refer to **Pricing Schedule A** on the order form for pricing information

No Wasted Space

- This plan features:
- — Three bedrooms
- — Two full baths
- A centrally located Great Room with a cathedral ceiling, exposed wood beams, and large areas of fixed glass
- The Living and Dining areas separated by a massive stone fireplace
- A secluded Master Suite with a walk-in closet and private Master Bath
- An efficient Kitchen with a convenient laundry area
- An optional basement, slab or crawl space foundation — please specify when ordering

MAIN AREA — 1,454 SQ. FT.

TOTAL LIVING AREA:
1,454 SQ. FT.

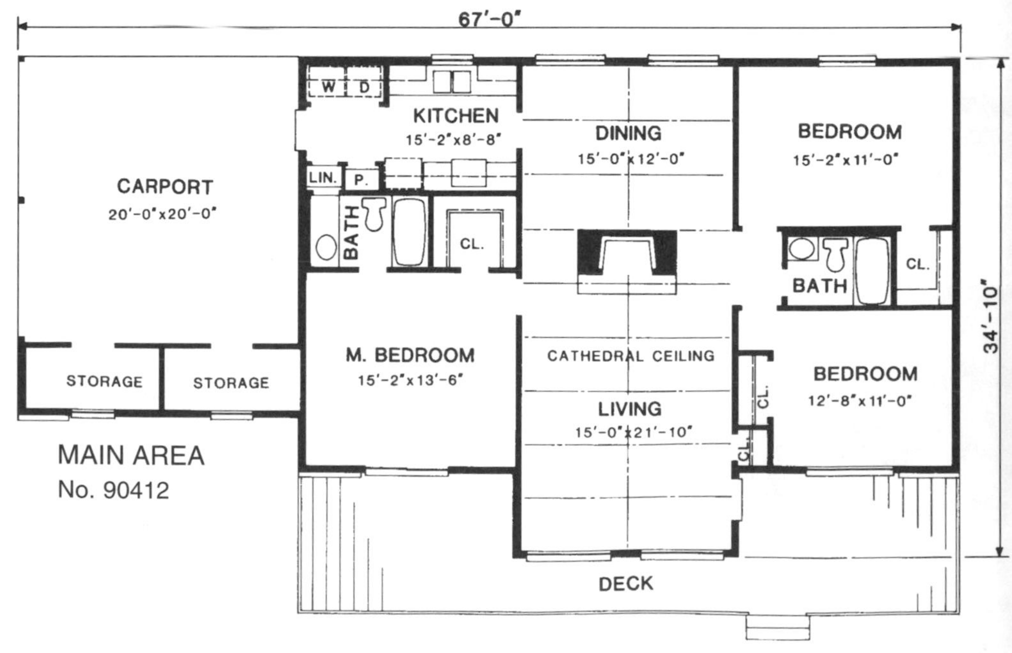
67'-0"
34'-10"
W
D
KITCHEN
15'-2"x8'-8"
DINING
15'-0"x12'-0"
BEDROOM
15'-2"x11'-0"
CARPORT
20'-0"x20'-0"
LIN.
P.
BATH
CL.
BATH
CL.
M. BEDROOM
15'-2"x13'-6"
CATHEDRAL CEILING
LIVING
15'-0"x21'-10"
BEDROOM
12'-8"x11'-0"
STORAGE
STORAGE
CL.
CL.
DECK
MAIN AREA
No. 90412

Refer to **Pricing Schedule B** on the order form for pricing information

PLAN NO. 20198

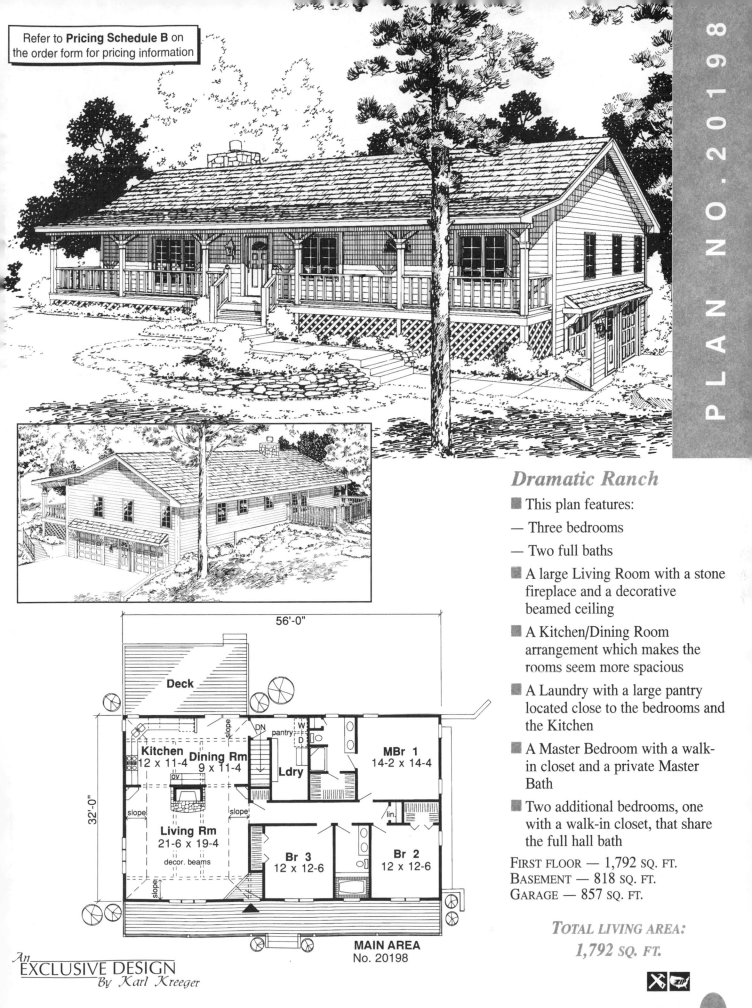

Dramatic Ranch

- This plan features:
- — Three bedrooms
- — Two full baths
- A large Living Room with a stone fireplace and a decorative beamed ceiling
- A Kitchen/Dining Room arrangement which makes the rooms seem more spacious
- A Laundry with a large pantry located close to the bedrooms and the Kitchen
- A Master Bedroom with a walk-in closet and a private Master Bath
- Two additional bedrooms, one with a walk-in closet, that share the full hall bath

FIRST FLOOR — 1,792 SQ. FT.
BASEMENT — 818 SQ. FT.
GARAGE — 857 SQ. FT.

***TOTAL LIVING AREA:* 1,792 SQ. FT.**

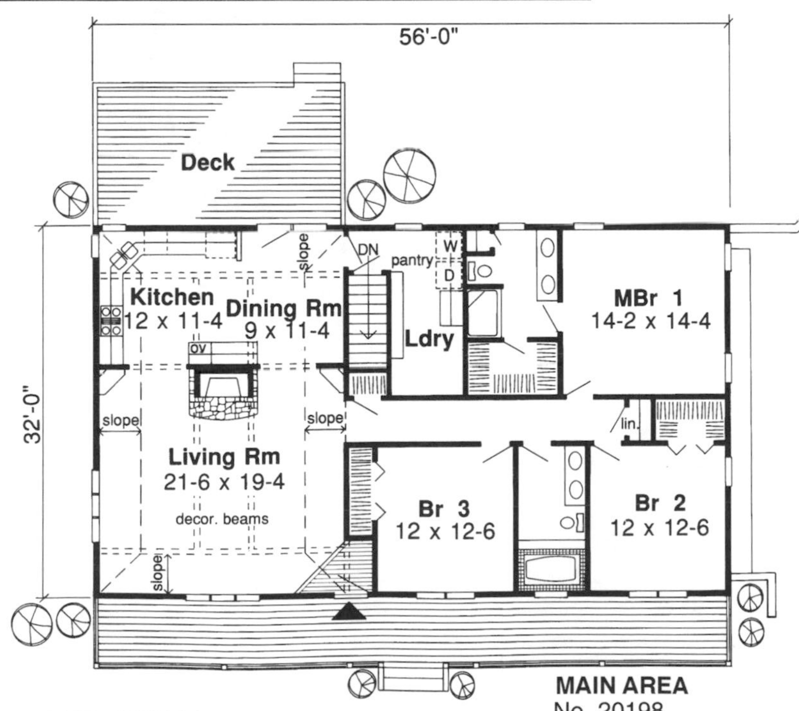
56'-0"
32'-0"
Deck
slope
DN
pantry
W
D
Kitchen
12 x 11-4
Dining Rm
9 x 11-4
Ldry
MBr 1
14-2 x 14-4
ov
slope
slope
lin.
Living Rm
21-6 x 19-4
decor. beams
Br 3
12 x 12-6
Br 2
12 x 12-6
slope

MAIN AREA
No. 20198

An EXCLUSIVE DESIGN *By Karl Kreeger*

PLAN NO. 94116

Refer to **Pricing Schedule C** on the order form for pricing information

Small, But Not Lacking

- This plan features:

—Three bedrooms

— One full and one three quarter baths

- Great Room adjoining the Dining Room for ease in entertaining
- Kitchen highlighted by a peninsula counter/snack bar extending work space and offering convenience in serving informal meals or snacks
- Split bedroom plan allowing for privacy for the Master Bedroom suite with a private bath and a walk-in closet
- Two additional bedrooms sharing the full family bath in the hall
- Garage entry convenient to the kitchen

FIRST FLOOR — 1,546 SQ. FT.
GARAGE — 440 SQ. FT.
BASEMENT — 1,530 SQ. FT.

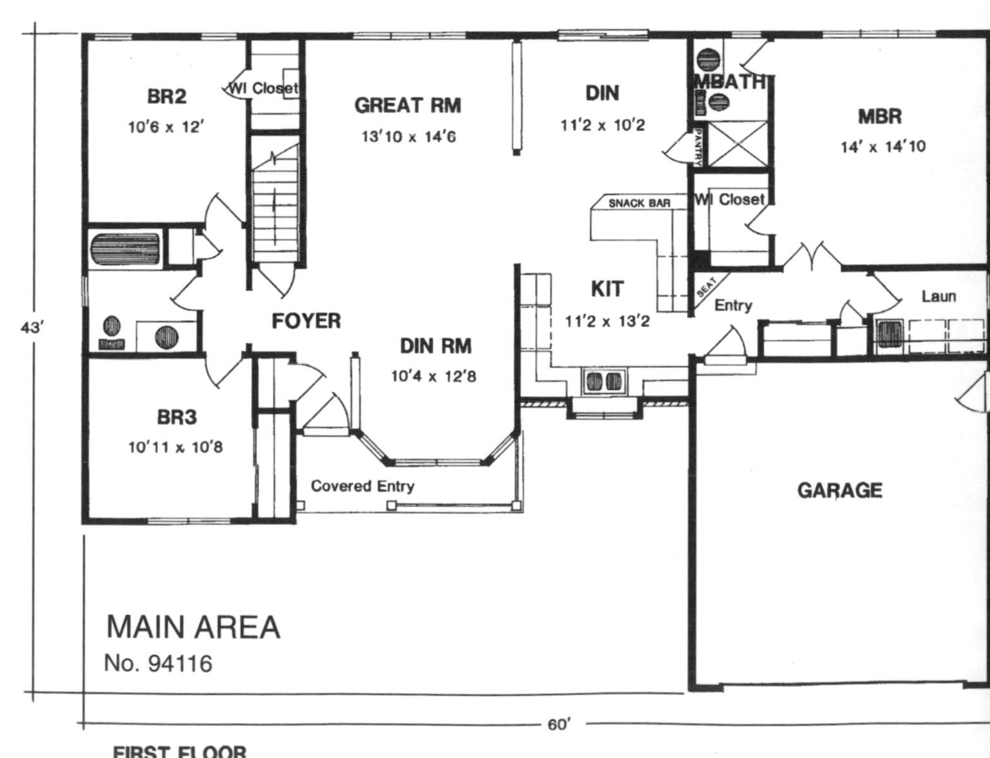
BR2
10'6 x 12'
WI Closet
GREAT RM
13'10 x 14'6
DIN
11'2 x 10'2
MBATH
PANTRY
MBR
14' x 14'10
SNACK BAR
WI Closet
KIT
11'2 x 13'2
SEAT
Entry
Laun
43'
FOYER
DIN RM
10'4 x 12'8
BR3
10'11 x 10'8
Covered Entry
GARAGE
MAIN AREA
No. 94116
60'
FIRST FLOOR

TOTAL LIVING AREA:
1,546 SQ. FT.

To order your Blueprints, call 1-800-235-5700

Refer to **Pricing Schedule A** on the order form for pricing information

PLAN NO. 24306

An EXCLUSIVE DESIGN *By Marshall Associates*

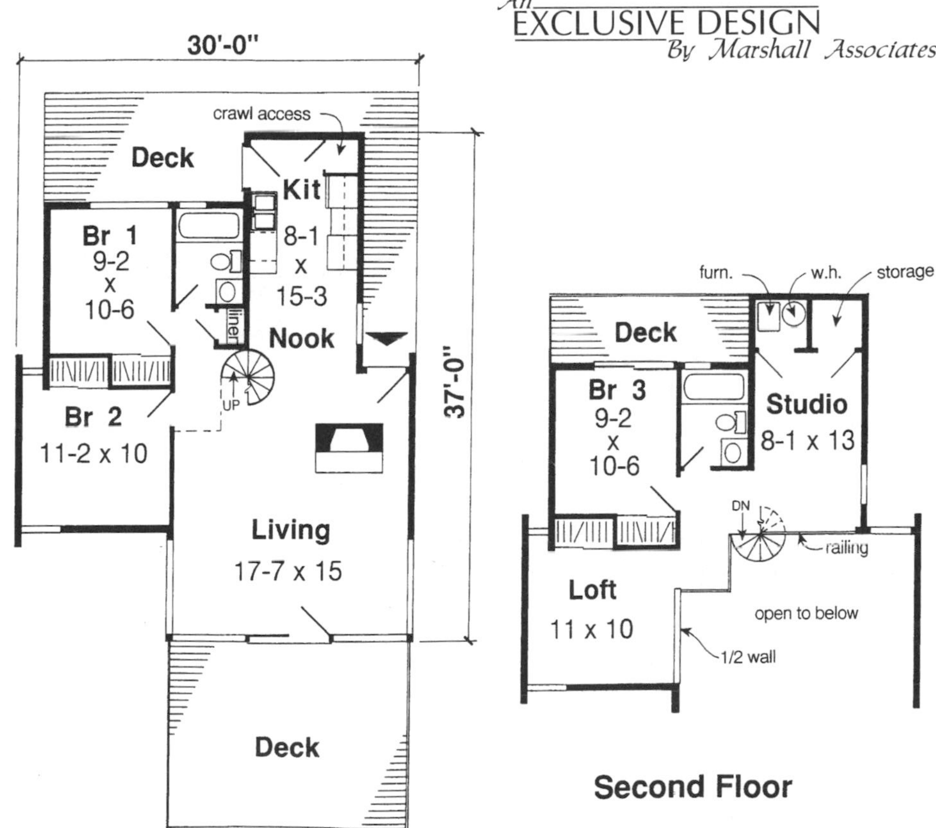

30'-0"
37'-0"
crawl access
Deck
Kit
8-1 x 15-3
Br 1
9-2 x 10-6
liner
Nook
UP
Br 2
11-2 x 10
Living
17-7 x 15
Deck
First Floor
No. 24306
furn.
w.h.
storage
Deck
Br 3
9-2 x 10-6
Studio
8-1 x 13
DN
railing
Loft
11 x 10
open to below
1/2 wall
Second Floor

Deck Defies Gravity

- This plan features:
  - Three bedrooms
  - Two full baths
- Perfect layout for a mountain side with a far reaching view
- Fireplace in a large and sunny Living room
- Spiral staircase to the second floor adding style
- Galley Kitchen with access to rear deck
- Loft area, with closet, overlooking the living room
- Third Bedroom with a private deck and bathroom

FIRST FLOOR — 841 SQ. FT.
SECOND FLOOR — 489 SQ. FT.

TOTAL LIVING AREA
1,330 SQ. FT.

PLAN NO. 94303

Refer to **Pricing Schedule A** on the order form for pricing information

Attractive Tiled Entry

- This plan features:
  - — Two bedrooms
  - — One full and one three quarter baths
- A tiled entry leading to an open Dining/Living Room area with a hearth fireplace and a wall of windows with an atrium door to Terrace
- An efficient Kitchen with a corner window and eating bar adjoining Dining Area, Garage and Terrace
- A Master Bedroom with walk-in closet and private bath and an atrium door to the Terrace
- One additional bedroom with ample closet near the full bath
- No materials list is available

MAIN FLOOR — 1,013 SQ. FT.
GARAGE — 390 SQ. FT.

TOTAL LIVING AREA 1,013 SQ. FT.

An EXCLUSIVE DESIGN By Marshall Associates

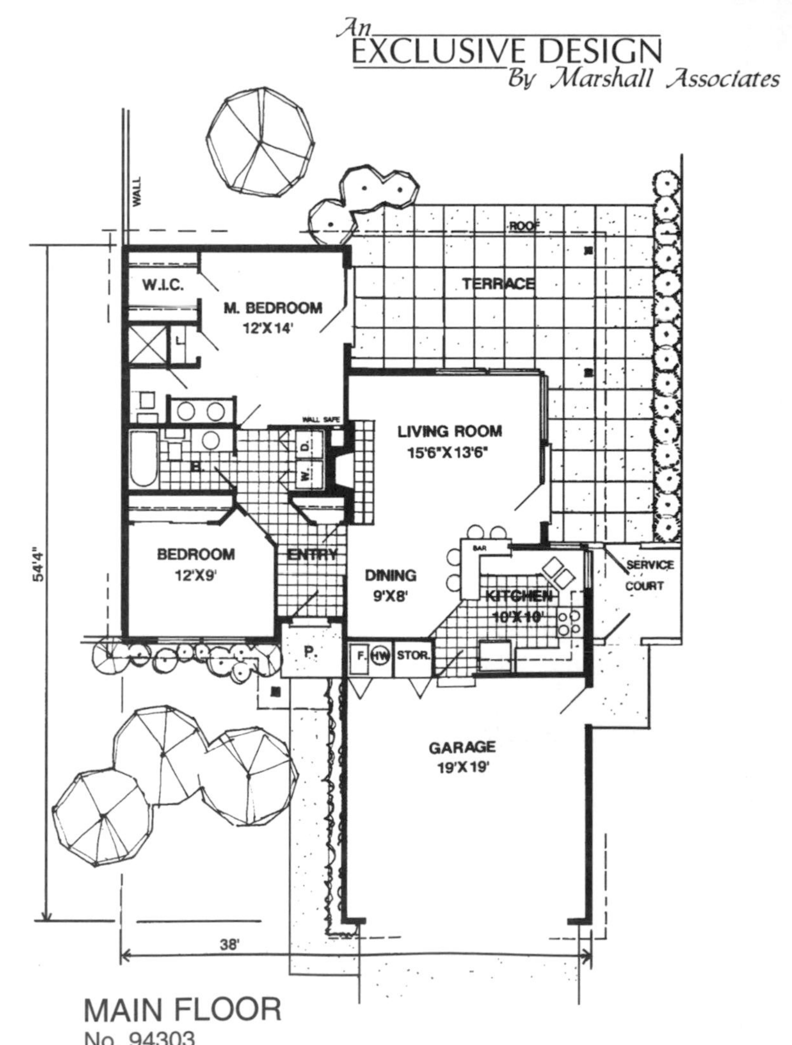
WALL
ROOF
TERRACE
W.I.C.
M. BEDROOM
12'X14'
WALL SAFE
LIVING ROOM
15'6"X13'6"
BEDROOM
12'X9'
ENTRY
DINING
9'X8'
BAR
KITCHEN
10'X10'
SERVICE
COURT
P.
F.
HW
STOR.
GARAGE
19'X19'
54'4"
38'

MAIN FLOOR
No. 94303

To order your Blueprints, call 1-800-235-5700

Refer to **Pricing Schedule B** on the order form for pricing information

PLAN NO. 92503

Charming Southern Traditional

TOTAL LIVING AREA:
1,271 SQ. FT.

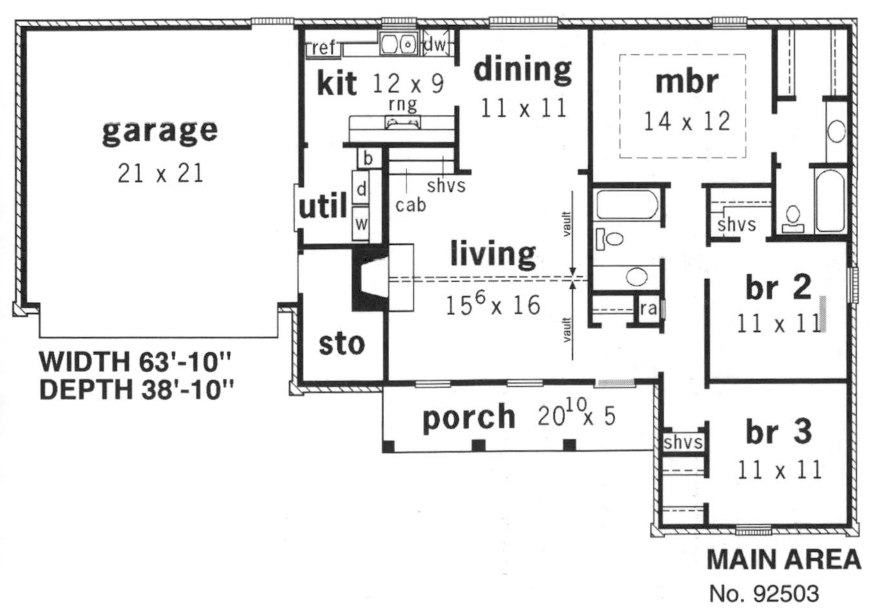

garage
21 x 21
ref
dw
kit 12 x 9
rng
dining
11 x 11
mbr
14 x 12
b
d
w
util
shvs
cab
vault
living
15⁶ x 16
shvs
br 2
11 x 11
ra
sto
porch 20¹⁰ x 5
shvs
br 3
11 x 11
WIDTH 63'-10"
DEPTH 38'-10"
MAIN AREA
No. 92503

- This plan features:
  - — Three bedrooms
  - — Two full baths
- A covered front porch with striking columns, brick quoins, and dentil molding
- A spacious Great Room with vaulted ceilings, a fireplace, and built-in cabinets
- A Utility Room adjacent to the Kitchen which leads to the two- car Garage and Storage Rooms
- A Master Bedroom including a large walk-in closet and a compartmentalized bath
- This plan is available with a crawl space or slab foundation — please specify when ordering

MAIN AREA — 1,271 SQ. FT.
GARAGE — 506 SQ. FT.

PLAN NO. 92804

Refer to **Pricing Schedule B** on the order form for pricing information

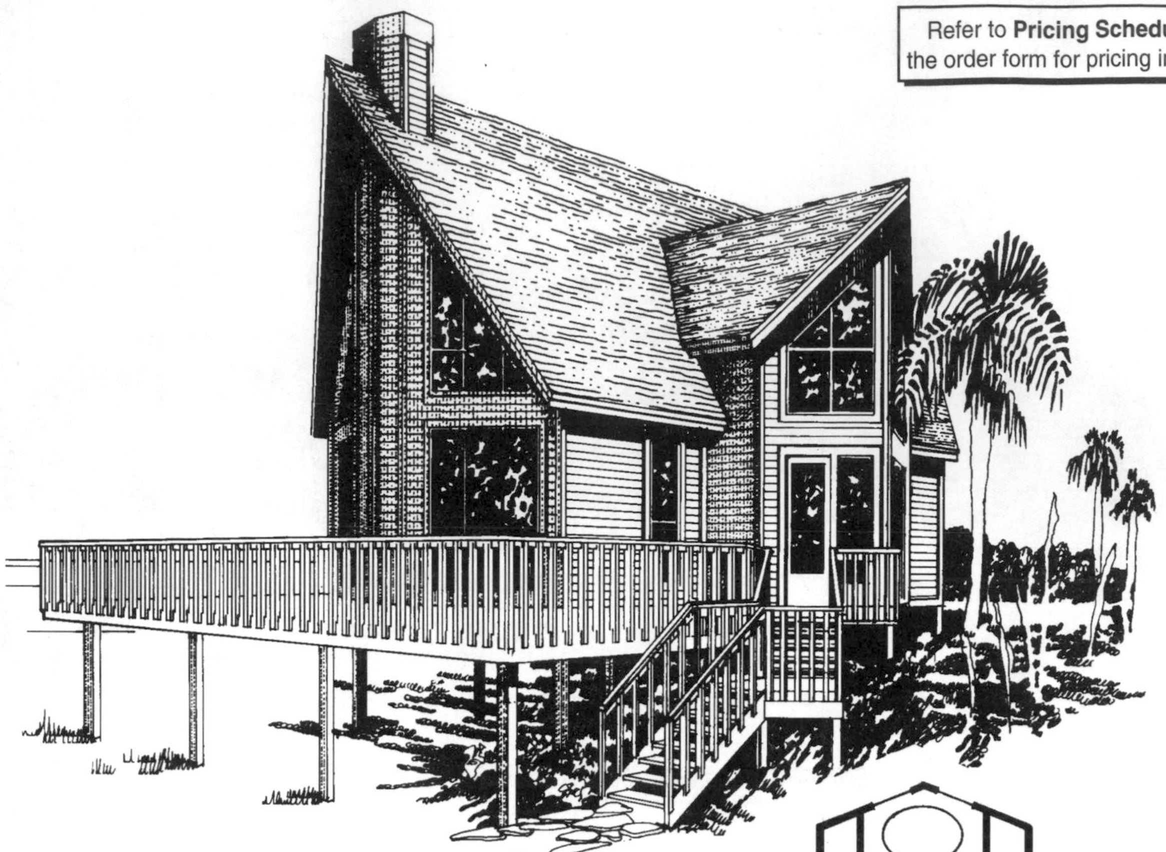

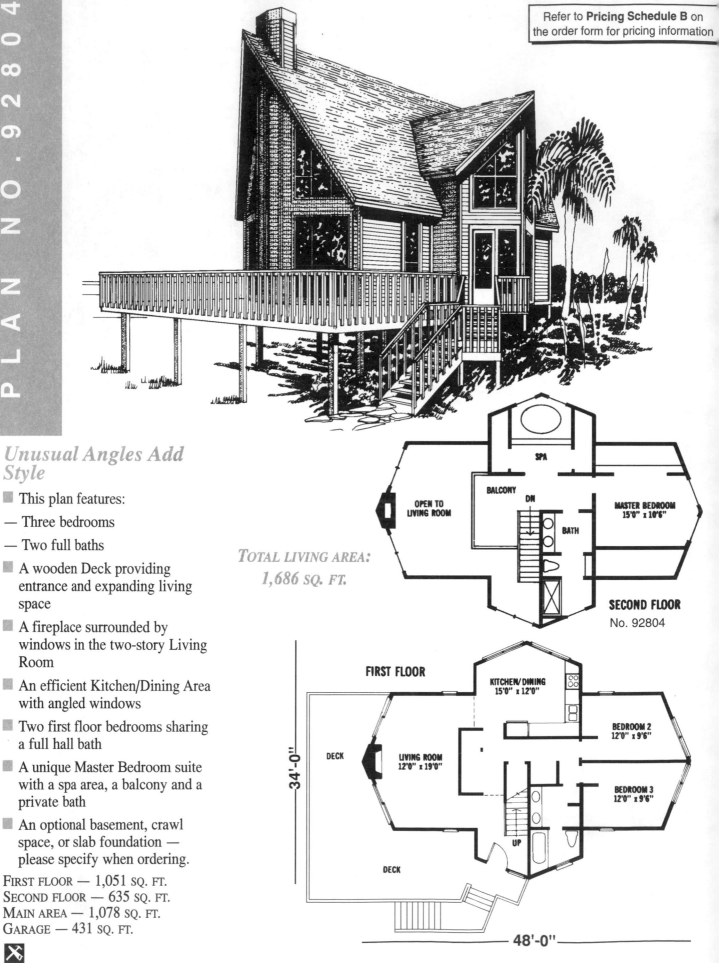

Unusual Angles Add Style

- This plan features:
  - — Three bedrooms
  - — Two full baths
- A wooden Deck providing entrance and expanding living space
- A fireplace surrounded by windows in the two-story Living Room
- An efficient Kitchen/Dining Area with angled windows
- Two first floor bedrooms sharing a full hall bath
- A unique Master Bedroom suite with a spa area, a balcony and a private bath
- An optional basement, crawl space, or slab foundation — please specify when ordering.

FIRST FLOOR — 1,051 SQ. FT.
SECOND FLOOR — 635 SQ. FT.
MAIN AREA — 1,078 SQ. FT.
GARAGE — 431 SQ. FT.

TOTAL LIVING AREA:
1,686 SQ. FT.

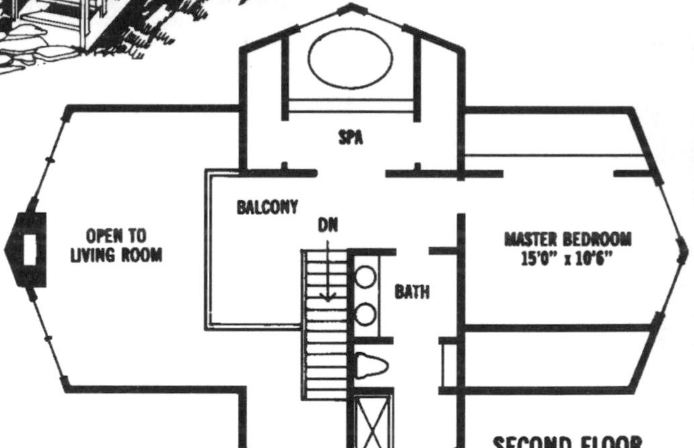

SPA
BALCONY
DN
OPEN TO LIVING ROOM
MASTER BEDROOM 15'0" x 10'6"
BATH

SECOND FLOOR
No. 92804

FIRST FLOOR
KITCHEN/DINING 15'0" x 12'0" 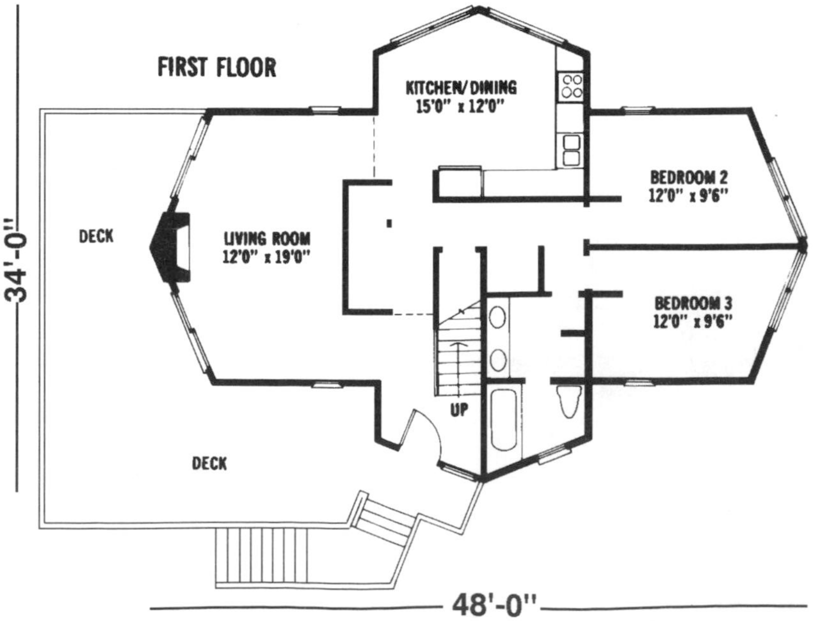
BEDROOM 2 12'0" x 9'6"
DECK
LIVING ROOM 12'0" x 19'0"
BEDROOM 3 12'0" x 9'6"
UP
DECK
34'-0"
48'-0"

Refer to **Pricing Schedule A** on the order form for pricing information

PLAN NO. 91807

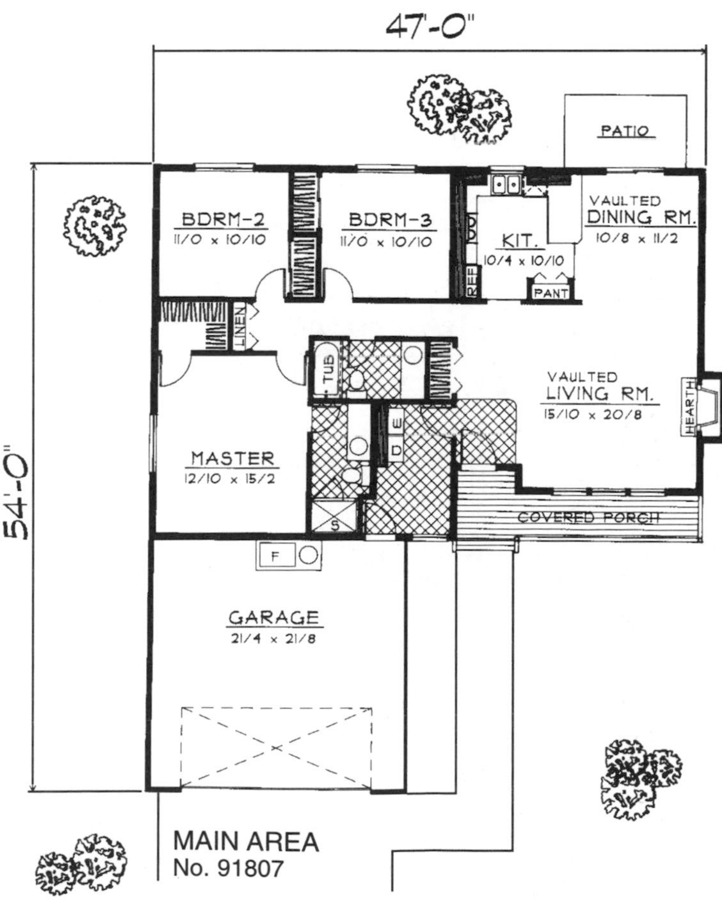

47'-0"
54'-0"
PATIO
BDRM-2
11/0 x 10/10
BDRM-3
11/0 x 10/10
KIT.
10/4 x 10/10
VAULTED
DINING RM.
10/8 x 11/2
REF
PANT
LINEN
TUB
VAULTED
LIVING RM.
15/10 x 20/8
HEARTH
MASTER
12/10 x 15/2
COVERED PORCH
F
GARAGE
21/4 x 21/8
MAIN AREA
No. 91807

An Affordable, Stylish Floor Plan

- This plan features:
  - — Three bedrooms
  - — One full and one three quarter baths
- A covered porch entry
- An old-fashioned hearth fireplace in the vaulted ceiling Living Room
- A handy Kitchen with U-shaped counter that is accessible from the Dining Room
- A Master Bedroom with a large walk-in closet and private bath
- This plan is available with a crawl space or slab foundation — please specify when ordering

MAIN FLOOR — 1,410 SQ. FT.
GARAGE — 484 SQ. FT.

TOTAL LIVING AREA: 1,410 SQ. FT.

PLAN NO. 94304

Refer to **Pricing Schedule A** on the order form for pricing information

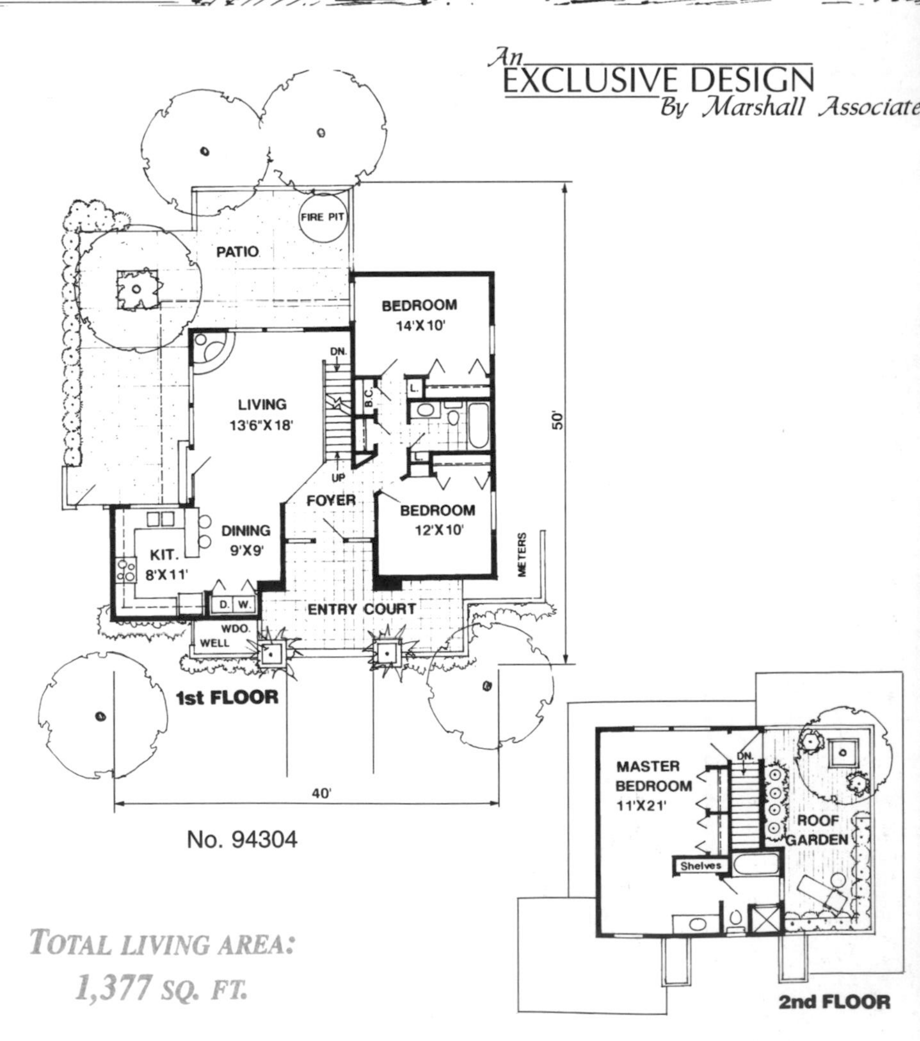

An EXCLUSIVE DESIGN
By Marshall Associates
FIRE PIT
PATIO
BEDROOM
14'X10'
DN.
LIVING
13'6"X18'
B.C.
L
UP
FOYER
BEDROOM
12'X10'
DINING
9'X9'
KIT.
8'X11'
D. W.
METERS
ENTRY COURT
WDO.
WELL
50'
40'
1st FLOOR
MASTER
BEDROOM
11'X21'
DN.
ROOF
GARDEN
Shelves
2nd FLOOR

No. 94304

TOTAL LIVING AREA:
1,377 SQ. FT.

Roof Garden Delight

- This plan features:
— Three bedrooms
— Two full baths
- A tiled Entry Court leading into the Foyer and setting a southwestern theme
- A Living/Dining area with a corner fireplace, window walls and access to a Patio
- An efficient, U-shaped Kitchen with an eating bar and laundry area
- Two first floor bedrooms sharing a full bath
- A second floor Master Bedroom with a double closet, built-in shelves, a private bath and direct access to the Roof Garden
- No materials list is available

FIRST FLOOR — 981 SQ. FT.
SECOND FLOOR — 396 SQ. FT.

To order your Blueprints, call 1-800-235-5700

Refer to **Pricing Schedule Z** on the order form for pricing information

PLAN NO. 24310

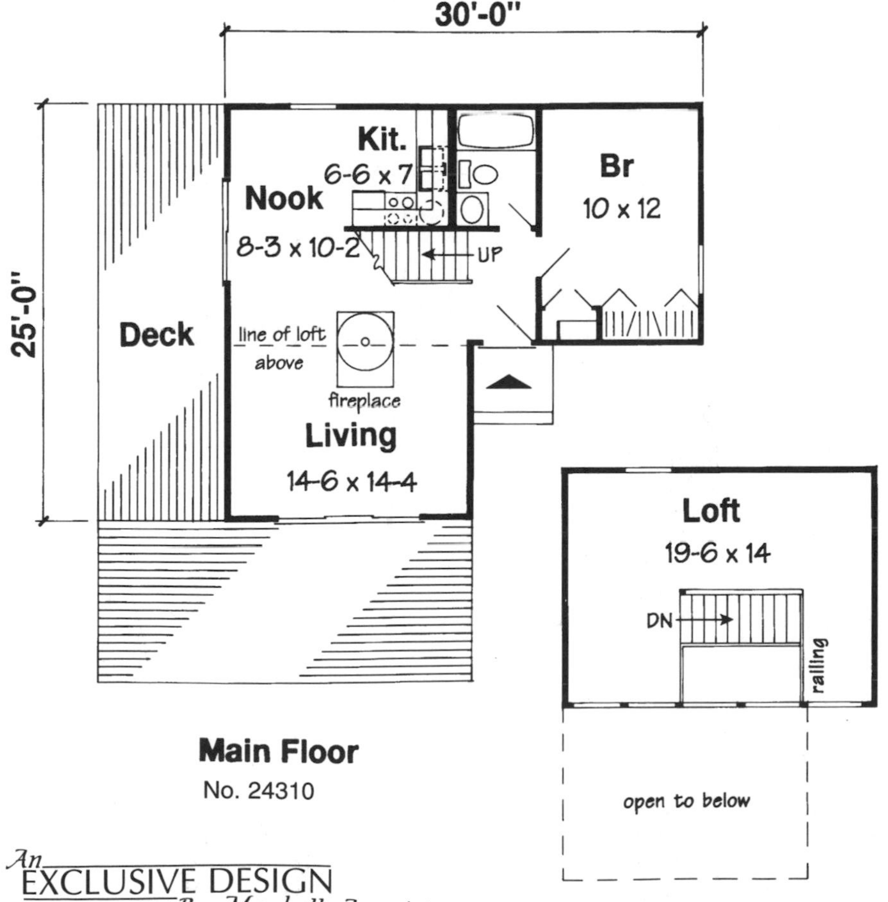

30'-0"
25'-0"
Kit.
6-6 x 7
Nook
8-3 x 10-2
Br
10 x 12
UP
Deck
line of loft above
fireplace
Living
14-6 x 14-4
Loft
19-6 x 14
DN
railing
open to below

Main Floor

No. 24310

An EXCLUSIVE DESIGN By Marshall Associates

Upper Floor

For the View

- This plan features:
  - — Onc bedroom
  - — One full bath
- An abundance of glass enabling homeowners to view their scenic surroundings
- Living Room with a circular fireplace and an entire wall of windows
- Dining and Kitchen area flowing off the Living Room
- Dining area accesses deck for added living space
- Studio area in Loft easily transformed into a second bedroom

MAIN FLOOR — 598 SQ. FT.
LOFT — 290 SQ. FT.

TOTAL LIVING AREA
888 SQ. FT.

PLAN NO. 20204

Refer to **Pricing Schedule B** on the order form for pricing information

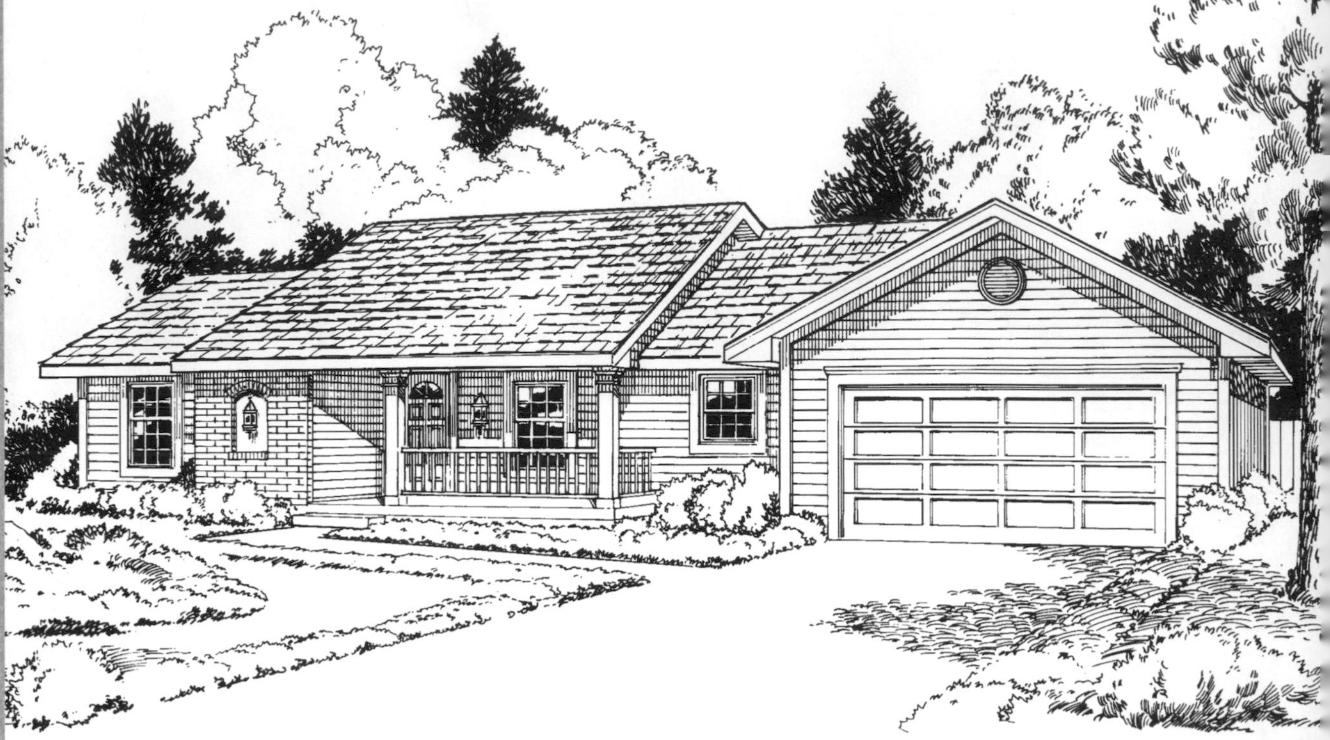

An
EXCLUSIVE DESIGN
By Karl Kreeger

Abundance of Closet Space

- This plan features:
  - — Three bedrooms
  - — Two full baths
- Roomy walk-in closets in all the bedrooms
- A Master Bedroom with a decorative ceiling and a private full bath
- A fireplaced Living Room with sloped ceilings and sliders to the deck
- An efficient Kitchen, with plenty of cupboard space and a pantry

MAIN AREA —1,532 SQ. FT.
GARAGE — 484 SQ. FT.

TOTAL LIVING AREA:
1,532 SQ. FT.

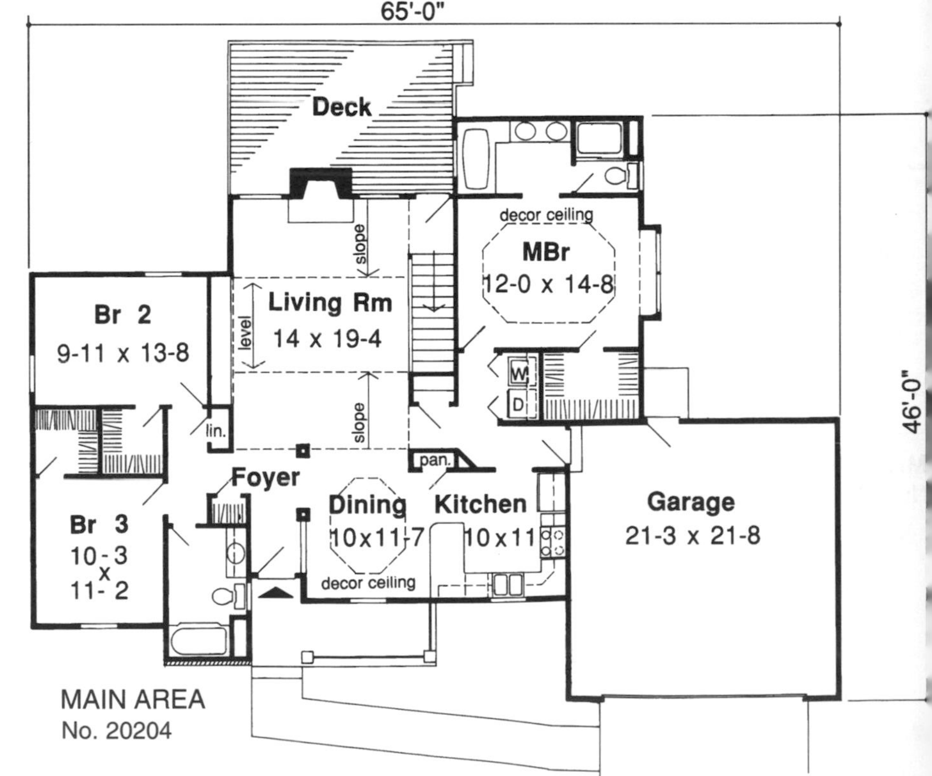

65'-0"
46'-0"
Deck
decor ceiling
MBr
12-0 x 14-8
slope
Living Rm
14 x 19-4
level
slope
Br 2
9-11 x 13-8
lin.
W
D
pan.
Foyer
Dining
10x11-7
decor ceiling
Kitchen
10x11
Garage
21-3 x 21-8
Br 3
10-3
x
11-2

MAIN AREA
No. 20204

Refer to **Pricing Schedule B** on the order form for pricing information

PLAN NO. 90601

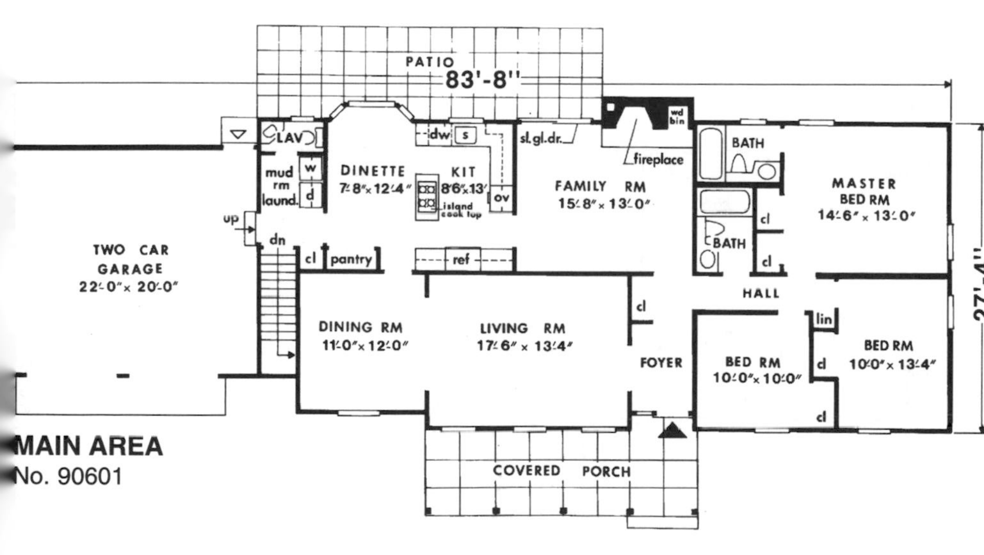

PATIO
83'-8"
LAV
dw
s
sl.gl.dr.
wd bin
fireplace
BATH
MASTER BED RM 14'6" x 13'0"
mud rm laund.
w
d
DINETTE 7'8"x12'4"
KIT 8'6"x13'
island cook top
ov
FAMILY RM 15'8"x13'0"
cl
BATH
up
dn
TWO CAR GARAGE 22'0"x 20'0"
cl
pantry
ref
HALL
27'-4"
DINING RM 11'0"x12'0"
LIVING RM 17'6" x 13'4"
FOYER
lin
BED RM 10'0"x10'0"
BED RM 10'0"x 13'4"
COVERED PORCH

MAIN AREA
No. 90601

Varied Roof Heights Create Interesting Lines

- This plan features:
- — Three bedrooms
- — Two full and one half baths
- A spacious Family Room with a heat-circulating fireplace, which is visible from the Foyer
- A large Kitchen with a cooktop island, opening into the dinette bay
- A Master Suite with his-n-her closets and a private Master Bath
- Two additional bedrooms which share a full hall bath
- Formal Dining and Living Rooms, flowing into each other for easy entertaining

MAIN AREA — 1,613 SQ. FT.

TOTAL LIVING AREA: 1,613 SQ. FT.

PLAN NO. 90441

Refer to **Pricing Schedule C** on the order form for pricing information

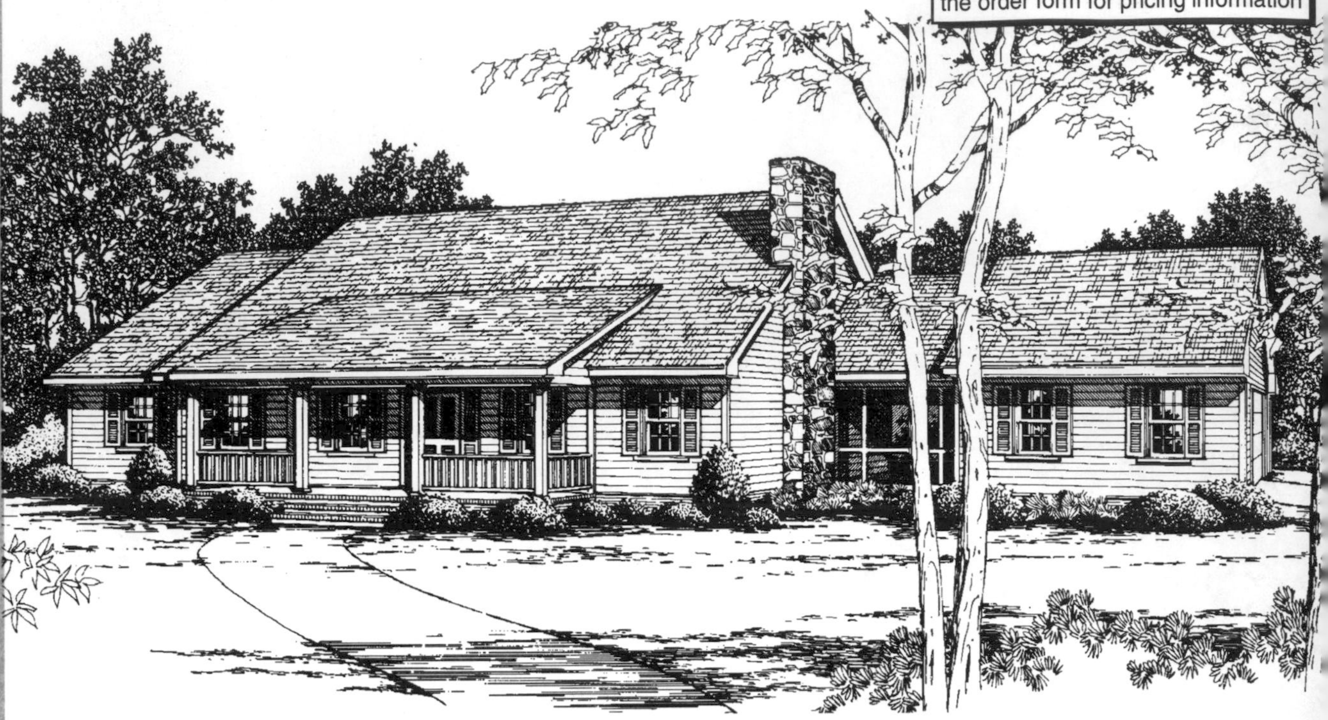

Moderate Ranch Has Features of Much Larger Plan

- This plan features:
- — Three bedrooms
- — Two full baths
- A large Great Room with a vaulted ceiling and a stone fireplace with bookshelves on either side
- A spacious Kitchen with ample cabinet space conveniently located next to the large Dining Room
- A Master Suite having a large bath with a garden tub, double vanity and a walk-in closet
- Two other large bedrooms, each with a walk-in closet and access to the full bath
- This plan is available with a basement, slab or crawl space foundation — please specify

MAIN FLOOR — 1,811 SQ. FT.

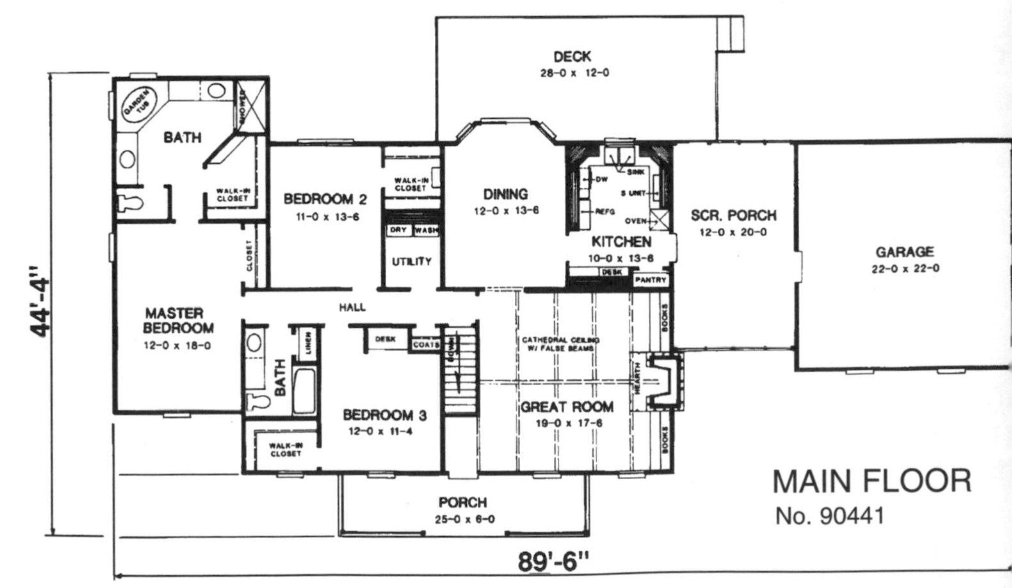

DECK
28-0 x 12-0
BATH
WALK-IN CLOSET
BEDROOM 2
11-0 x 13-6
WALK-IN CLOSET
DINING
12-0 x 13-6
DW
SINK
S UNIT
REFG
OVEN
KITCHEN
10-0 x 13-6
DESK
PANTRY
SCR. PORCH
12-0 x 20-0
GARAGE
22-0 x 22-0
CLOSET
DRY
WASH
UTILITY
MASTER BEDROOM
12-0 x 18-0
HALL
DESK
COATS
LINEN
BATH
CATHEDRAL CEILING W/ FALSE BEAMS
BOOKS
HEARTH
BEDROOM 3
12-0 x 11-4
GREAT ROOM
19-0 x 17-6
BOOKS
WALK-IN CLOSET
PORCH
25-0 x 6-0
44'-4"
89'-6"
MAIN FLOOR
No. 90441

TOTAL LIVING AREA:
1,811 SQ. FT.

Refer to **Pricing Schedule B** on the order form for pricing information

PLAN NO. 10455

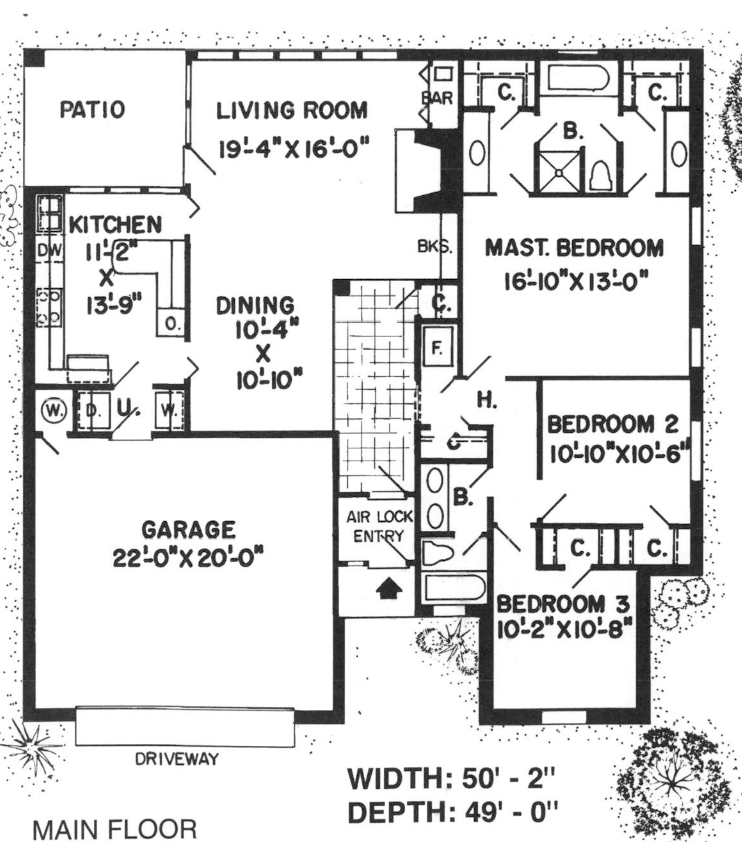

PATIO
LIVING ROOM
19'-4"X16'-0"
BAR
C.
B.
C.
KITCHEN
11'-2"
X
13'-9"
DW
O.
BKS.
MAST. BEDROOM
16'-10"X13'-0"
DINING
10'-4"
X
10'-10"
C.
F.
H.
W.
D.
U.
W.
BEDROOM 2
10'-10"X10'-6"
GARAGE
22'-0"X20'-0"
AIR LOCK
ENTRY
B.
C.
C.
BEDROOM 3
10'-2"X10'-8"
DRIVEWAY
WIDTH: 50' - 2"
DEPTH: 49' - 0"
MAIN FLOOR
No. 10455

Compact Home Design

- This plan features:
  - — Three bedrooms
  - — Two full baths
- An energy saving airlock Entry
- A Living Room with an entire wall of windows, fireplace, built-in bookcases, and a wetbar
- A step-saver Kitchen with an abundance of storage and a convenient peninsula
- A Master Bedroom with separate vanities and walk-in closets

MAIN AREA — 1,643 SQ. FT.
GARAGE — 500 SQ. FT.

TOTAL LIVING AREA:
1,643 SQ. FT.

PLAN NO. 24312

Refer to **Pricing Schedule A** on the order form for pricing information

Spacious Simplicity

An
EXCLUSIVE DESIGN
By Marshall Associates

- This plan features:
- — Three bedrooms
- — Two three quarter baths
- Spacious Living Room with wood burning stove or fireplace
- Open layout between the Living Room and the Dining Room for an open and airy atmosphere
- Efficient Kitchen is larger than what is usually found in a vacation home
- First floor Bedroom with direct access to a three-quarter bath
- Master Bedroom has a private deck and direct access to three quarter bath

FIRST FLOOR — 813 SQ. FT.
SECOND FLOOR — 485 SQ. FT.

TOTAL LIVING AREA
1,298 SQ. FT.

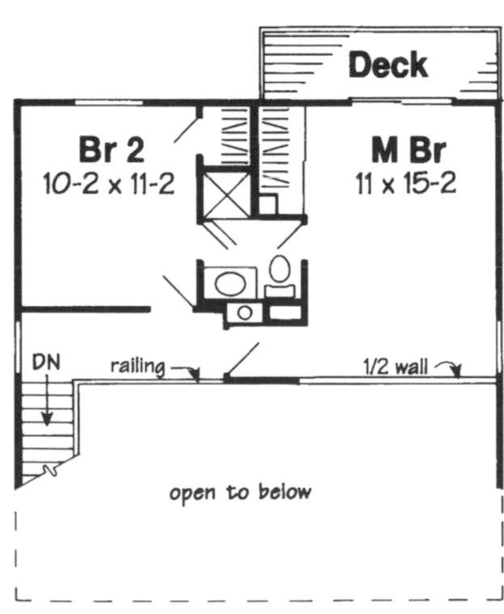

Deck
Br 2
10-2 x 11-2
M Br
11 x 15-2
DN
railing
1/2 wall
open to below

Second Floor

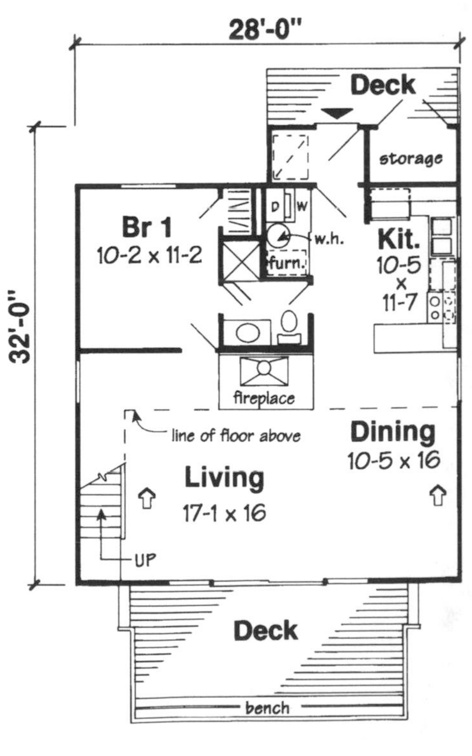

28'-0"
32'-0"
Deck
storage
Br 1
10-2 x 11-2
w.h.
furn.
Kit.
10-5
x
11-7
fireplace
line of floor above
Dining
10-5 x 16
Living
17-1 x 16
UP
Deck
bench

First Floor
No. 24312

To order your Blueprints, call 1-800-235-5700

Refer to **Pricing Schedule D** on the order form for pricing information

PLAN NO. 92516

Distinctive European Design

- This plan features:
- — Three bedrooms
- — Two full baths
- A spacious Foyer leading into a grand Living Room, topped by a vaulted ceiling, with a fireplace between built-in cabinets and a wall of glass leading
- A gourmet Kitchen with a peninsula counter/snackbar and a built-in pantry
- A large Master Bedroom, crowned by a raised ceiling, with French doors leading to a covered Porch, a luxurious bath and a walk-in closet
- Two additional bedrooms with decorative windows and over-sized closets share a full hall bath
- This plan is available with a crawl space or slab foundation — please specify when ordering

MAIN FLOOR — 1,887 SQ. FT.
GARAGE & STORAGE — 524 SQ. FT.

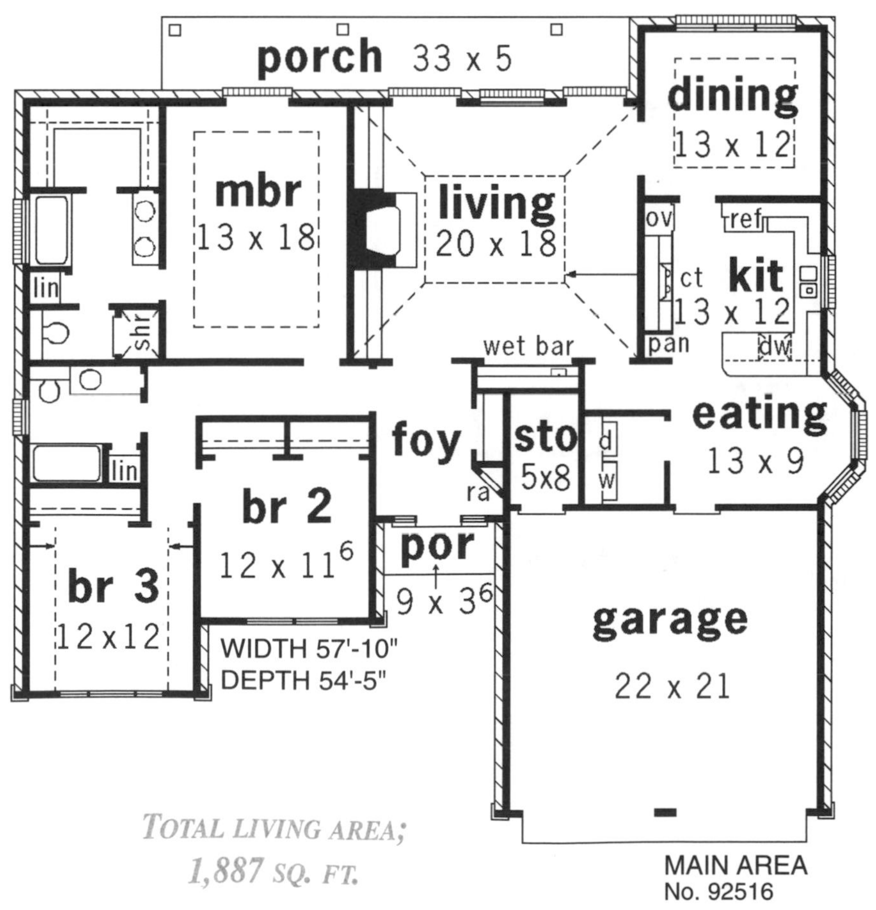

porch 33 x 5
dining 13 x 12
mbr 13 x 18
living 20 x 18
ov
ref
ct
kit 13 x 12
pan
dw
lin
shr
wet bar
eating 13 x 9
foy
sto 5x8
d
w
ra
lin
br 2 12 x 11⁶
por 9 x 3⁶
br 3 12x12
garage 22 x 21
WIDTH 57'-10"
DEPTH 54'-5"

TOTAL LIVING AREA; 1,887 SQ. FT.

MAIN AREA
No. 92516

PLAN NO. 94305

Refer to **Pricing Schedule A** on the order form for pricing information

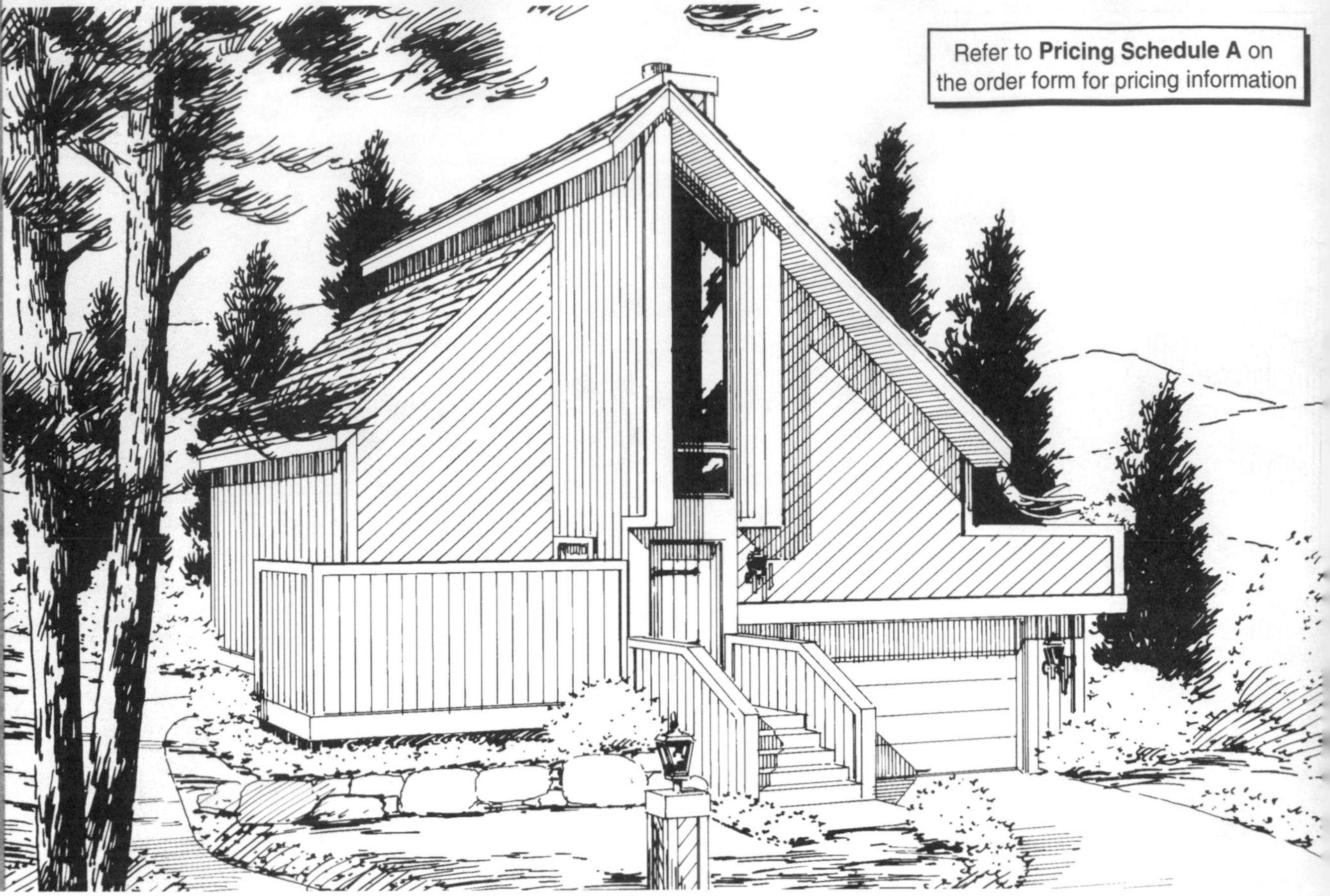

Eye-Catching Elevation

- This plan features:
- — Two bedrooms
- — Two 3/4 baths
- An entrance to a Spa Deck with hot tub and a few steps down to an open Living area with a cozy fireplace, a vaulted ceiling and atrium door to the side Deck
- An efficient Kitchen with a peninsula counter/eating bar opens to Living area
- A first floor bedroom next to the full bath and Utility area
- A second floor Master Bedroom with an over-sized and private bath
- No material list is available

LOWER/MID LEVELS — 680 SQ. FT.
UPPER LEVEL — 345 SQ. FT.

TOTAL LIVING AREA:
1,025 SQ. FT.

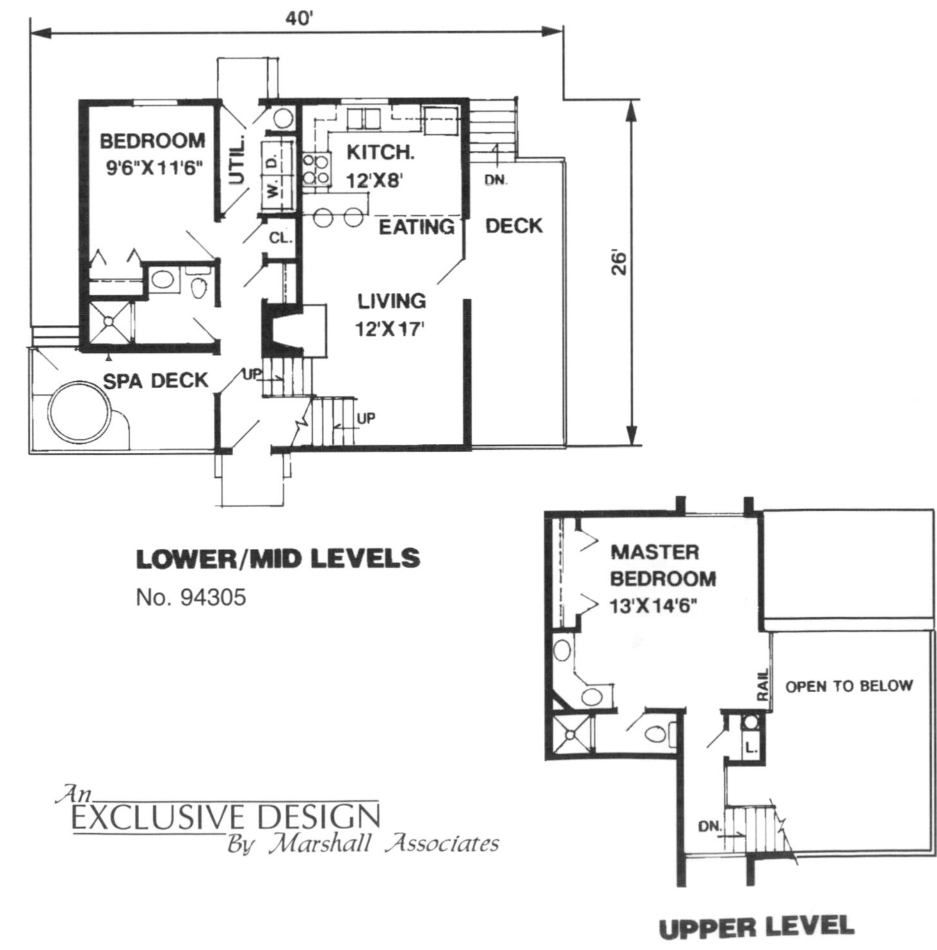

40'
26'
BEDROOM
9'6"X11'6"
UTIL.
W. D.
KITCH.
12'X8'
DN.
CL.
EATING
DECK
LIVING
12'X17'
SPA DECK
UP
UP
LOWER/MID LEVELS
No. 94305
An EXCLUSIVE DESIGN By Marshall Associates
MASTER
BEDROOM
13'X14'6"
RAIL
OPEN TO BELOW
L.
DN.
UPPER LEVEL

Refer to **Pricing Schedule B** on the order form for pricing information

PLAN NO. 92703

TOTAL LIVING AREA:
1,772 SQ. FT.

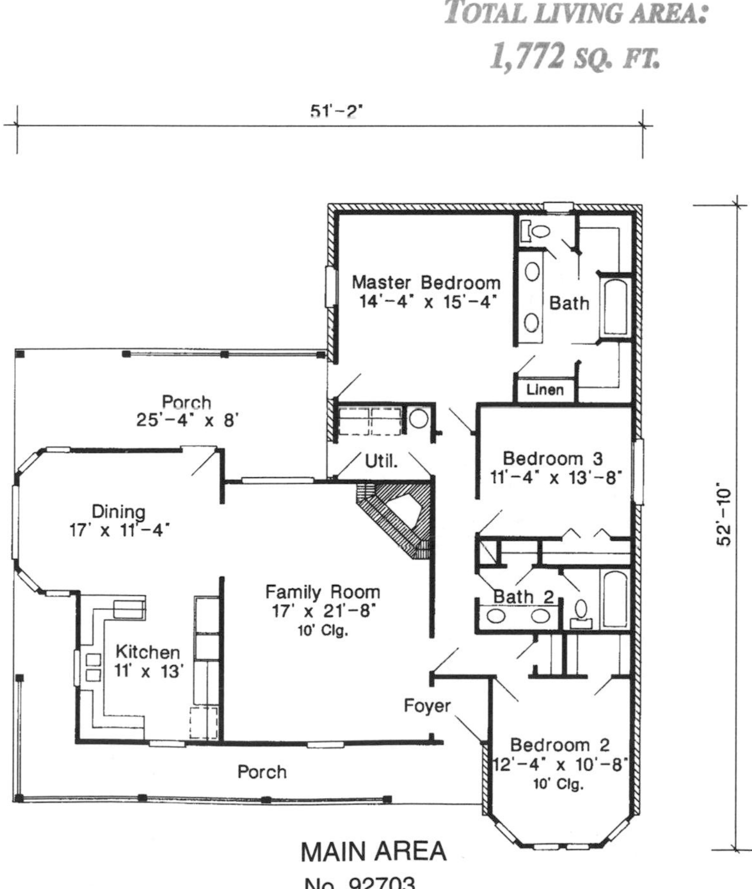

51'-2"
52'-10"
Master Bedroom
14'-4" x 15'-4"
Bath
Linen
Porch
25'-4" x 8'
Util.
Bedroom 3
11'-4" x 13'-8"
Dining
17' x 11'-4"
Family Room
17' x 21'-8"
10' Clg.
Bath 2
Kitchen
11' x 13'
Foyer
Bedroom 2
12'-4" x 10'-8"
10' Clg.
Porch
MAIN AREA
No. 92703

Casual Living Both Inside and Out

- This plan features:
- — Three bedrooms
- — Two full baths
- A Living Room with a ten foot ceiling and a cozy corner fireplace
- An enormous Dining Area that is able to handle even the largest family dinners
- A large rear Porch that is perfect for outdoor dining
- A conveniently placed Laundry Room
- His-n-her walk-in closets and a double vanity in the Master Bath
- Secondary bedrooms that share a full hall bath with a double vanity
- No materials list available for this plan

MAIN AREA — 1,772 SQ. FT.

PLAN NO. 94316

Refer to **Pricing Schedule B** on the order form for pricing information

Popular Floor Plan For Young Families

- This plan features:
  - — Four bedrooms
  - — Two and a half baths
- All the bedrooms on one floor, perfect for families with small children
- Private Master Bath and a walk-in closet in Master Bedroom suite
- Open layout between the Kitchen and Living room affording a spacious and airy feeling
- Convenient laundry center in the hall outside Kitchen
- Expansive family room with a cozy fireplace and access to the rear patio
- No Material List available

FIRST FLOOR — 736 SQ. FT.
SECOND FLOOR — 788 SQ. FT.
GARAGE — 400 SQ. FT.

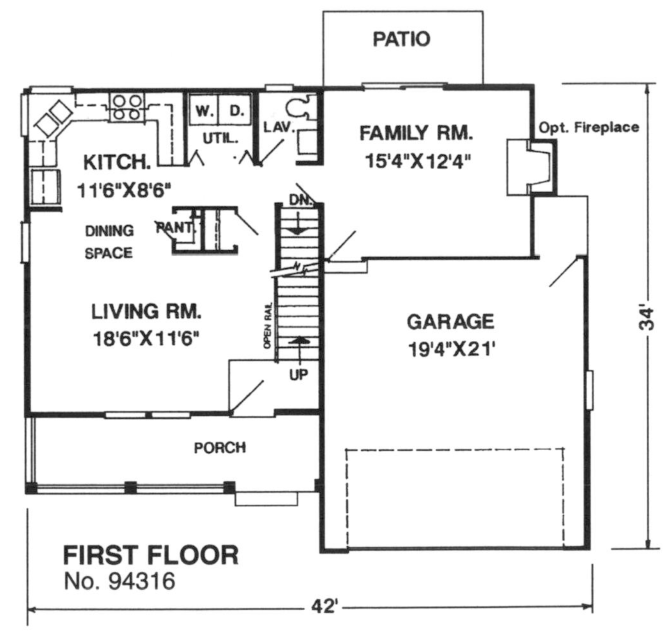
PATIO
W.
D.
UTIL.
LAV.
FAMILY RM.
15'4"X12'4"
Opt. Fireplace
KITCH.
11'6"X8'6"
DN.
DINING SPACE
PANT.
LIVING RM.
18'6"X11'6"
OPEN RAIL
UP
GARAGE
19'4"X21'
34'
PORCH
FIRST FLOOR
No. 94316
42'

TOTAL LIVING AREA
1,524 SQ. FT.

An EXCLUSIVE DESIGN By Marshall Associates

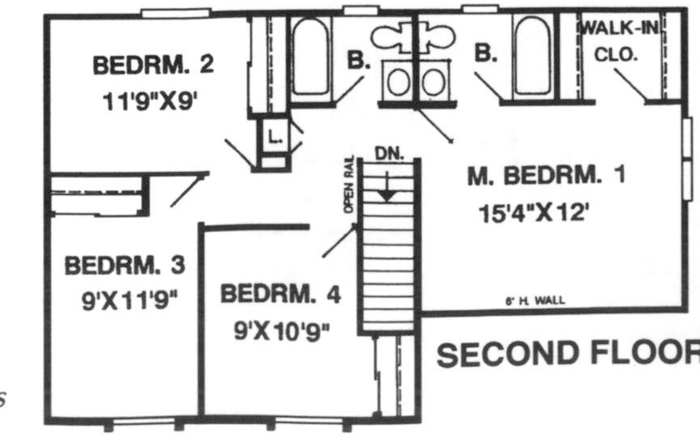
BEDRM. 2
11'9"X9'
B.
B.
WALK-IN CLO.
L.
DN.
OPEN RAIL
M. BEDRM. 1
15'4"X12'
BEDRM. 3
9'X11'9"
BEDRM. 4
9'X10'9"
6' H. WALL
SECOND FLOOR

To order your Blueprints, call 1-800-235-5700

Refer to **Pricing Schedule B** on the order form for pricing information

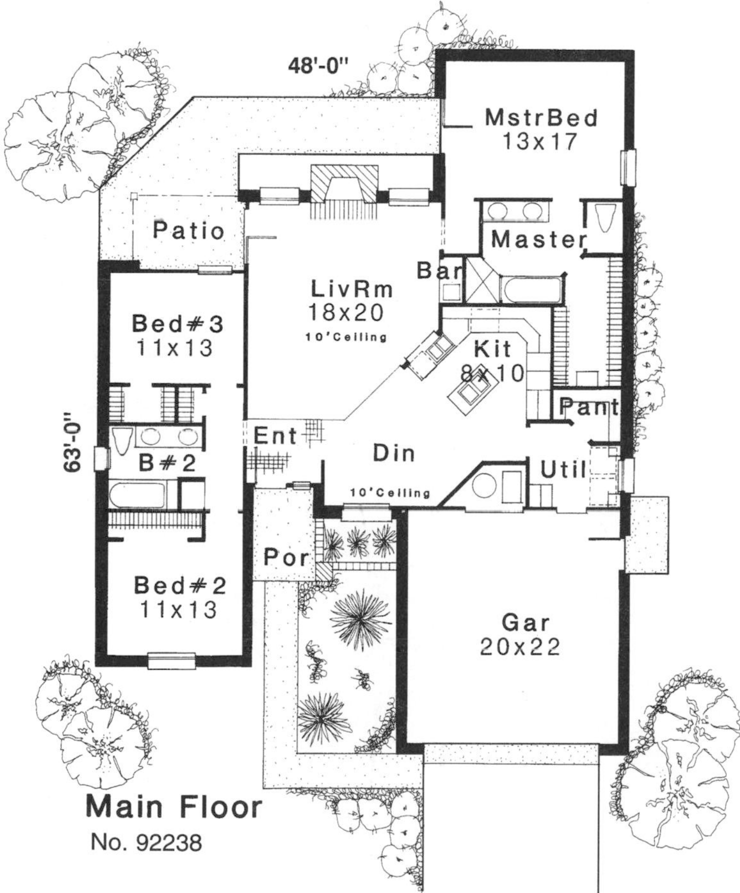
48'-0"
MstrBed
13x17
Master
Patio
Bar
LivRm
18x20
10'Ceiling
Bed#3
11x13
Kit
8x10
Pant
63'-0"
B#2
Ent
Din
10'Ceiling
Util
Por
Bed#2
11x13
Gar
20x22

Main Floor
No. 92238

TOTAL LIVING AREA:
***1,664** SQ. FT.*

Easy Everyday Living

- This plan features:
  - Three bedrooms
  - Two full baths
- Front entrance accented by segmented arches, sidelight and transom windows
- Open Living Room with focal point fireplace, wet bar and acccss to Patio
- Dining area open to both the Living Room and the Kitchen
- Efficient Kitchen with a cooktop island, walk-in pantry and Utility area with a Garage entry
- Large walk-in closet, double vanity bath and access to Patio featured in the Master Bedroom suite
- Two additional bedrooms share a double vanity bath
- No materials list available for this plan

MAIN FLOOR — 1,664 SQ. FT.
BASEMENT — 1,600 SQ. FT.
GARAGE — 440 SQ. FT

PLAN NO. 93027

Refer to **Pricing Schedule A** on the order form for pricing information

For Today's Sophisticated Homeowner

- This plan features:
- — Three bedrooms
- — Two full baths
- A formal Dining Room that opens off the foyer and has a classic bay window
- A Kitchen notable for its' angled eating bar that opens to the Living Room
- A cozy fireplace in the Living Room that can be seen from the Kitchen
- A Master Suite that includes a whirlpool tub/shower combination and a walk-in closet
- Ten foot ceilings in the major living areas, including the Master Bedroom
- No materials list available for this plan

MAIN AREA — 1,500 SQ. FT.
GARAGE — 437 SQ. FT.

WIDTH 59–10

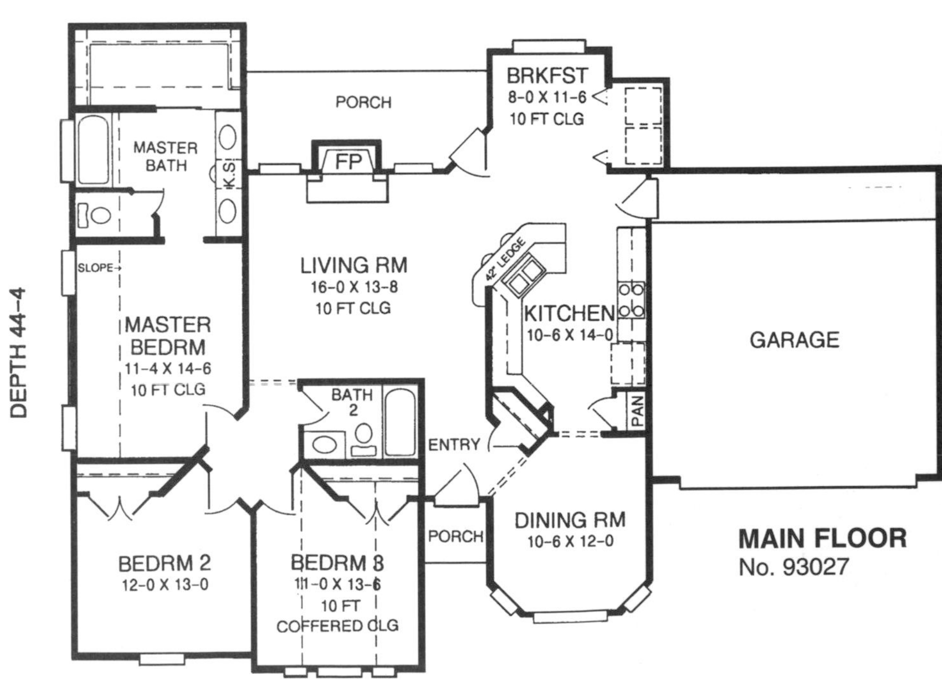

DEPTH 44–4
PORCH
BRKFST
8-0 X 11-6
10 FT CLG
MASTER BATH
K.S.
FP
SLOPE
LIVING RM
16-0 X 13-8
10 FT CLG
42" LEDGE
KITCHEN
10-6 X 14-0
GARAGE
MASTER BEDRM
11-4 X 14-6
10 FT CLG
BATH 2
PAN
ENTRY
PORCH
DINING RM
10-6 X 12-0
BEDRM 2
12-0 X 13-0
BEDRM 8
11-0 X 13-6
10 FT
COFFERED CLG

MAIN FLOOR
No. 93027

TOTAL LIVING AREA:
1,500 SQ. FT.

To order your Blueprints, call 1-800-235-5700

Refer to **Pricing Schedule C** on the order form for pricing information

PLAN NO. 24314

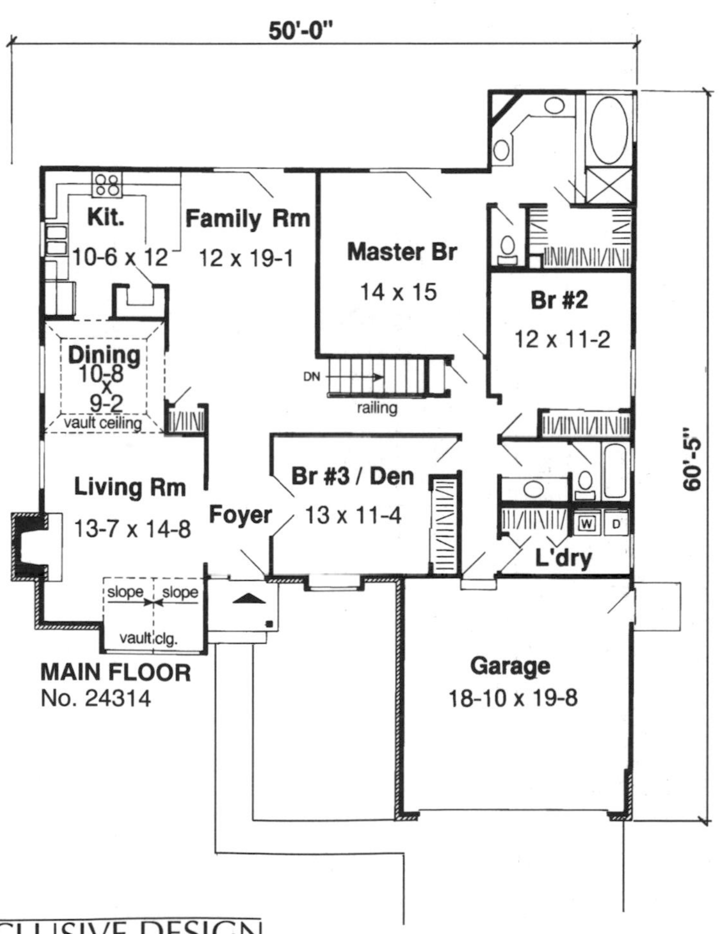

50'-0"
60'-5"
Kit.
10-6 x 12
Family Rm
12 x 19-1
Master Br
14 x 15
Br #2
12 x 11-2
Dining
10-8
x
9-2
vault ceiling
DN
railing
Living Rm
13-7 x 14-8
Foyer
Br #3 / Den
13 x 11-4
W
D
L'dry
slope
slope
vault clg.
Garage
18-10 x 19-8
MAIN FLOOR
No. 24314

An EXCLUSIVE DESIGN By Marshall Associates

Rambling Ranch

- This plan features:
  - — Three bedrooms
  - — Two full baths
- A cozy Living Room that flows into an elegant Dining Room with a vaulted ceiling
- A well-appointed Kitchen that includes double sink and a walk-in pantry that conveniently serves the Dining Room and the Family Room's eating bar
- A Family Room with direct access to the rear yard
- A Master Suite with a lavish private bath retreat and a walk-in closet
- Two additional bedrooms that share a full hall bath

MAIN FLOOR — 1,850 SQ. FT.

TOTAL LIVING AREA:
1,850 SQ. FT.

PLAN NO. 91071

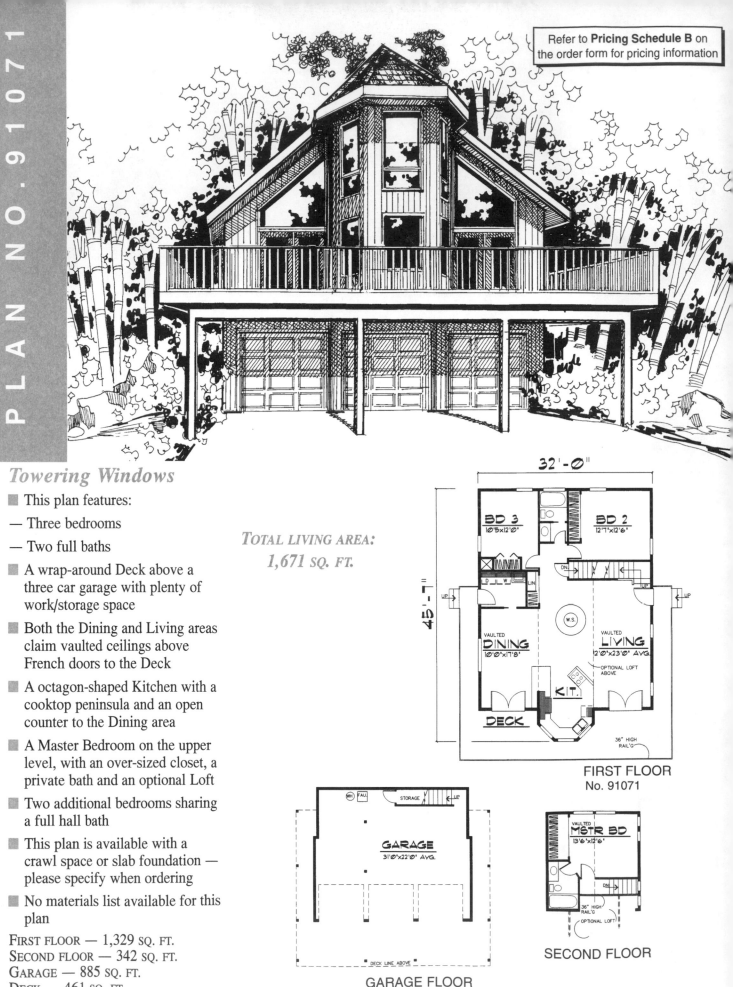

Refer to **Pricing Schedule B** on the order form for pricing information

Towering Windows

- This plan features:
- — Three bedrooms
- — Two full baths
- A wrap-around Deck above a three car garage with plenty of work/storage space
- Both the Dining and Living areas claim vaulted ceilings above French doors to the Deck
- A octagon-shaped Kitchen with a cooktop peninsula and an open counter to the Dining area
- A Master Bedroom on the upper level, with an over-sized closet, a private bath and an optional Loft
- Two additional bedrooms sharing a full hall bath
- This plan is available with a crawl space or slab foundation — please specify when ordering
- No materials list available for this plan

FIRST FLOOR — 1,329 SQ. FT.
SECOND FLOOR — 342 SQ. FT.
GARAGE — 885 SQ. FT.
DECK — 461 SQ. FT.

TOTAL LIVING AREA:
1,671 SQ. FT.

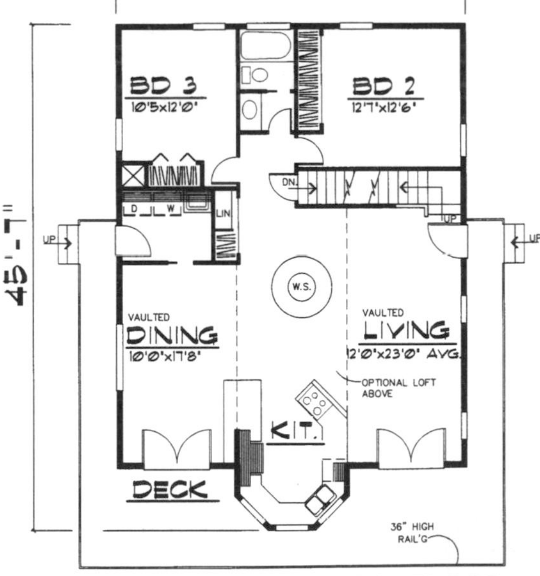
32'-0"
45'-7"
BD 3
10'5x12'0'
BD 2
12'7'x12'6'
DN.
UP
D
W
LIN
W.S.
VAULTED
DINING
10'0'x17'8'
VAULTED
LIVING
12'0'x23'0' AVG.
OPTIONAL LOFT ABOVE
KIT.
DECK
36" HIGH RAIL'G

FIRST FLOOR
No. 91071

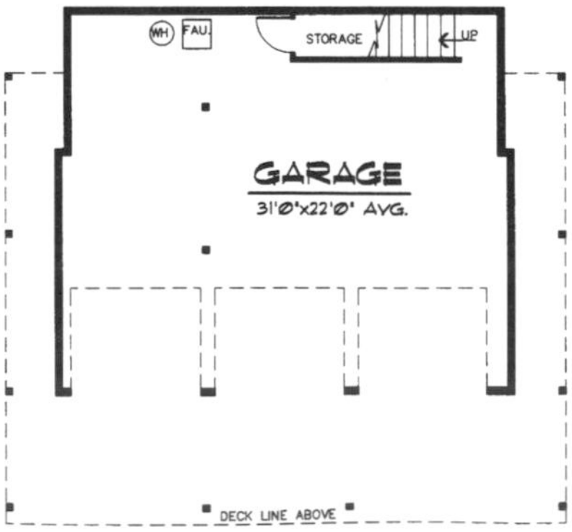

WH FAU STORAGE UP
GARAGE
31'0'x22'0' AVG.
DECK LINE ABOVE

GARAGE FLOOR

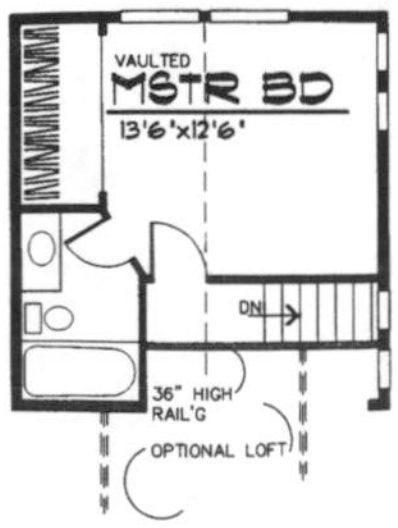

VAULTED
MSTR BD
13'6'x12'6'
DN
36" HIGH RAIL'G
OPTIONAL LOFT

SECOND FLOOR

To order your Blueprints, call 1-800-235-5700

Refer to **Pricing Schedule A** on the order form for pricing information

PLAN NO. 90822

An
EXCLUSIVE DESIGN
By Westhome Planners, Ltd.

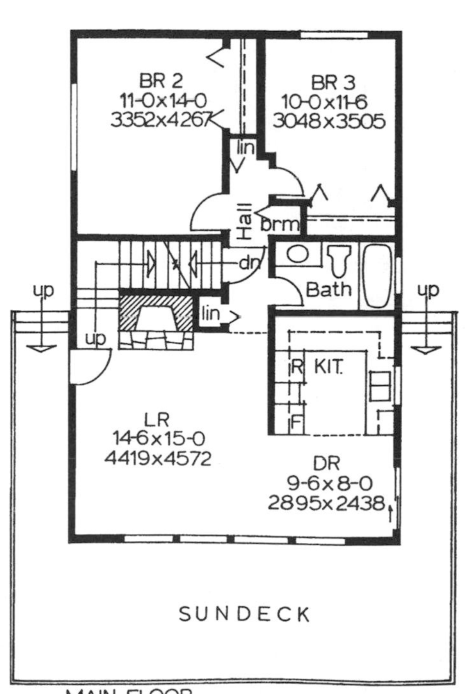

BR 2
11-0x14-0
3352x4267
BR 3
10-0x11-6
3048x3505
lin
Hall
brm
dn
Bath
up
lin
up
up
KIT.
R
F
LR
14-6x15-0
4419x4572
DR
9-6x8-0
2895x2438
SUNDECK

MAIN FLOOR

No. 90822

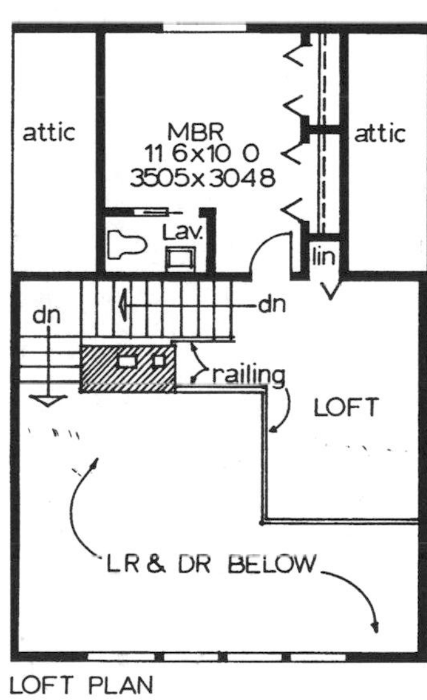

attic
MBR
11 6x10 0
3505x3048
attic
Lav.
lin
dn
dn
railing
LOFT
LR & DR BELOW

LOFT PLAN

Total Living Area:
1,263 sq. ft.

Suited for a Hill

- This plan features:
- — Three bedrooms
- — One and a half baths
- Vaulted ceilings and a fieldstone fireplace in the Living/Dining Room
- Two first floor bedrooms that have ample closet space and share a full hall bath
- A Master Bedroom on the loft level including a private bath
- A wrap-around sun deck offering an abundance of outdoor living space

Main floor — 925 sq. ft.
Loft — 338 sq. ft.
Basement — 864 sq. ft.
Width — 33'-0"
Depth — 47'-0"

PLAN NO. 93021

Refer to **Pricing Schedule A** on the order form for pricing information

A Stylish, Open Concept Home

- This plan features:
- — Three bedrooms
- — Two full baths
- An angled Entry creating the illusion of space
- Two square columns that flank the bar and separate the Kitchen from the Living Room
- A Dining Room that may service both formal and informal occasions
- A Master Bedroom with a large walk-in closet
- A large Master Bath with double vanities, linen closet and whirlpool tub/shower combination
- Two additional bedrooms that share a full bath
- No materials list available for this plan

MAIN FLOOR — 1,282 SQ. FT.
GARAGE — 501 SQ. FT.

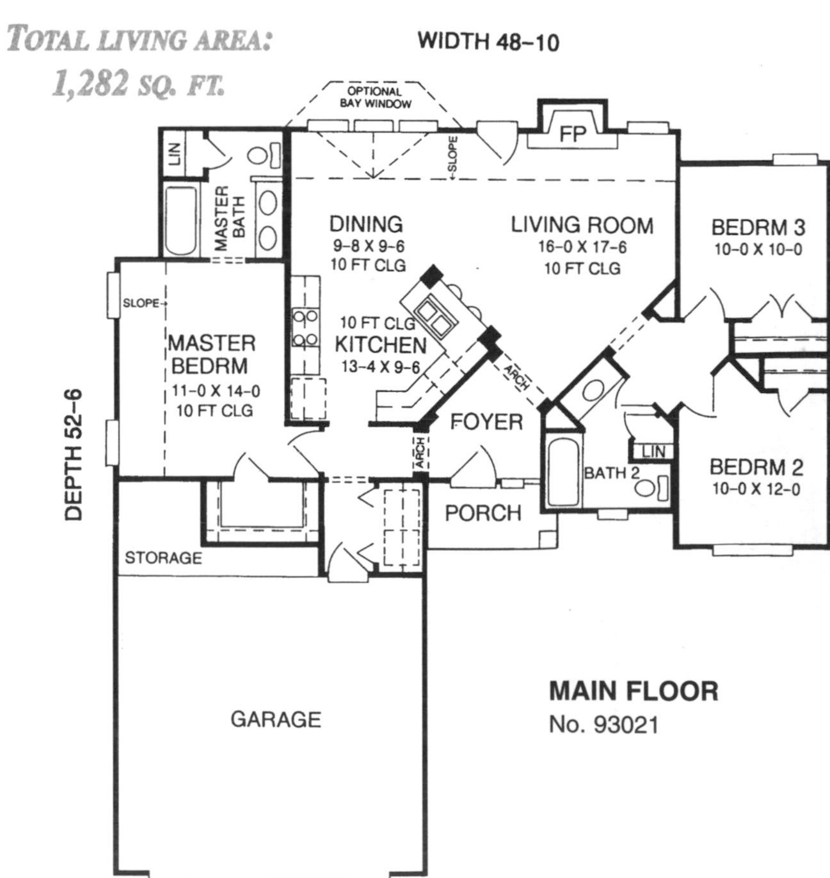

TOTAL LIVING AREA:
1,282 SQ. FT.
WIDTH 48-10
DEPTH 52-6
OPTIONAL BAY WINDOW
SLOPE
FP
LIN
MASTER BATH
DINING
9-8 X 9-6
10 FT CLG
LIVING ROOM
16-0 X 17-6
10 FT CLG
BEDRM 3
10-0 X 10-0
SLOPE
MASTER BEDRM
11-0 X 14-0
10 FT CLG
10 FT CLG
KITCHEN
13-4 X 9-6
ARCH
FOYER
ARCH
LIN
BATH 2
BEDRM 2
10-0 X 12-0
PORCH
STORAGE
GARAGE
MAIN FLOOR
No. 93021

To order your Blueprints, call 1-800-235-5700

Refer to **Pricing Schedule A** on the order form for pricing information

PLAN NO. 92704

TOTAL LIVING AREA:
1,078 SQ. FT.

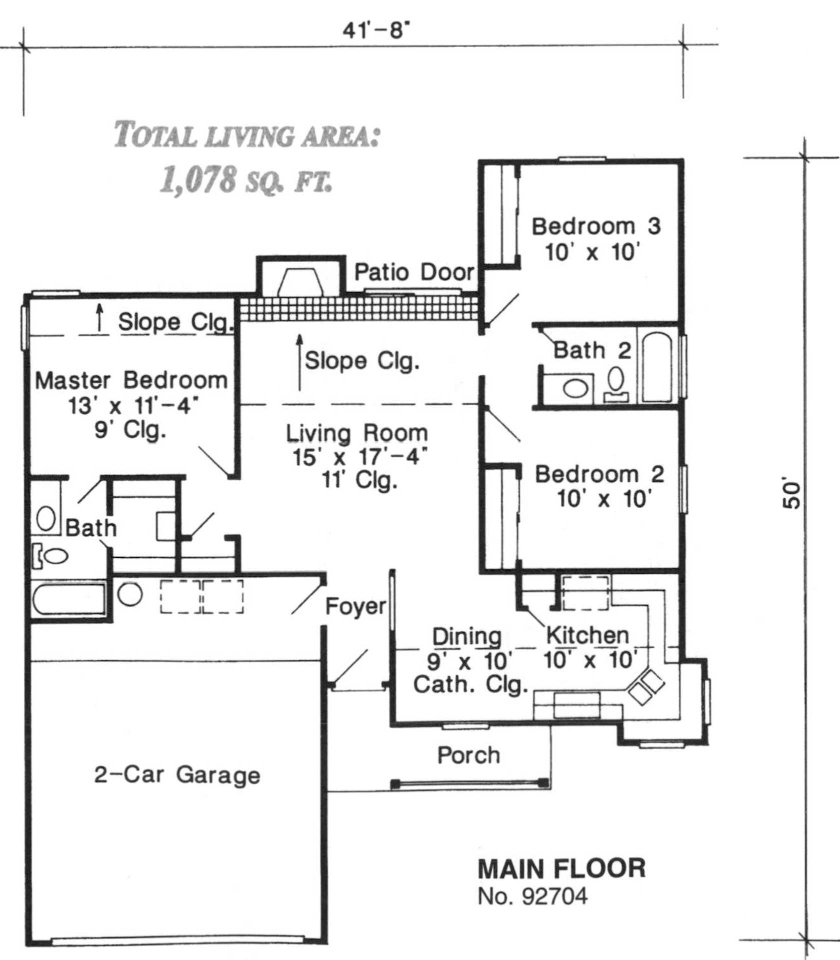

41'-8"
50'
Bedroom 3
10' x 10'
Patio Door
Slope Clg.
Slope Clg.
Master Bedroom
13' x 11'-4"
9' Clg.
Bath 2
Living Room
15' x 17'-4"
11' Clg.
Bedroom 2
10' x 10'
Bath
Foyer
Dining
9' x 10'
Cath. Clg.
Kitchen
10' x 10'
Porch
2-Car Garage

MAIN FLOOR
No. 92704

Perfect First Home

- This plan features:
  - — Three bedrooms
  - — Two full baths
- A front porch with turned posts and railing, and a corner box window
- A large Living Room with an 11 foot ceiling, sloping towards the sliding glass doors to the rear yard
- A cathedral ceiling in the Dining Area, with a view of the porch through an elegant window
- A corner double sink below the corner box window in the efficient Kitchen
- A secluded Master Bedroom that includes a private bath and a walk-in closet
- Two additional bedrooms that share a full hall bath
- No materials list available for this plan

MAIN AREA — 1,078 SQ. FT.
GARAGE — 431 SQ. FT.

PLAN NO. 94917

Refer to **Pricing Schedule B** on the order form for pricing information

Attractive Gables and Arches

- This plan features:
- — Three bedrooms
- — Two full baths
- Entry opens to formal Dining Room with arched window
- Angles and transom windows add interest to the Great Room
- Bright Hearth area expands Breakfast/Kitchen area and shares three-sided fireplace
- Efficient Kitchen offers an angled snack bar, a large pantry and nearby laundry/Garage entry
- Secluded Master Bedroom suite crowned by decorative ceiling, a large walk-in closet and a plush bath with a whirlpool tub
- Secondary bedrooms located separately from master suite

MAIN FLOOR — 1,782 SQ. FT.
BASEMENT — 1,782 SQ. FT.
GARAGE — 466 SQ. FT.

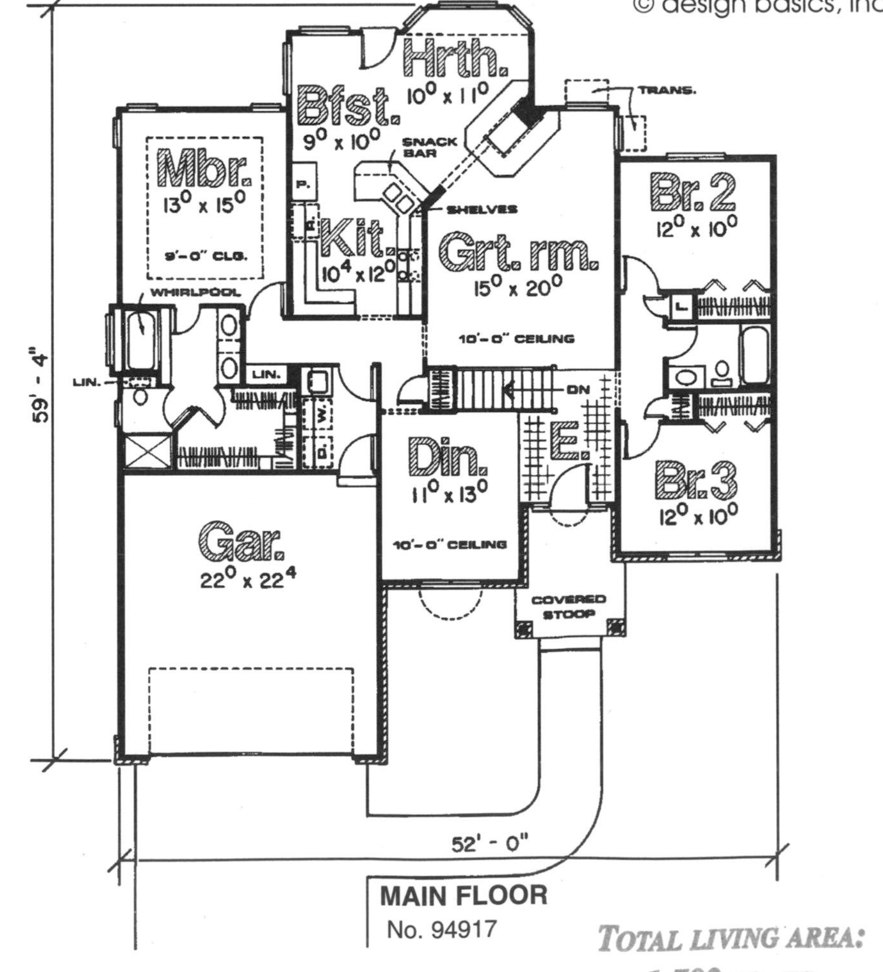

© design basics, inc.
Hrth. 10⁰ x 11⁰
Bfst. 9⁰ x 10⁰
SNACK BAR
TRANS.
Mbr. 13⁰ x 15⁰
9'-0" CLG.
SHELVES
Kit. 10⁴ x 12⁰
Grt. rm. 15⁰ x 20⁰
10'-0" CEILING
Br. 2 12⁰ x 10⁰
WHIRLPOOL
LIN.
LIN.
DN
E.
Din. 11⁰ x 13⁰
10'-0" CEILING
Br. 3 12⁰ x 10⁰
Gar. 22⁰ x 22⁴
COVERED STOOP
59' - 4"
52' - 0"
MAIN FLOOR
No. 94917

TOTAL LIVING AREA: 1,782 SQ. FT.

To order your Blueprints, call 1-800-235-5700

Refer to **Pricing Schedule E** on the order form for pricing information

PLAN NO. 91319

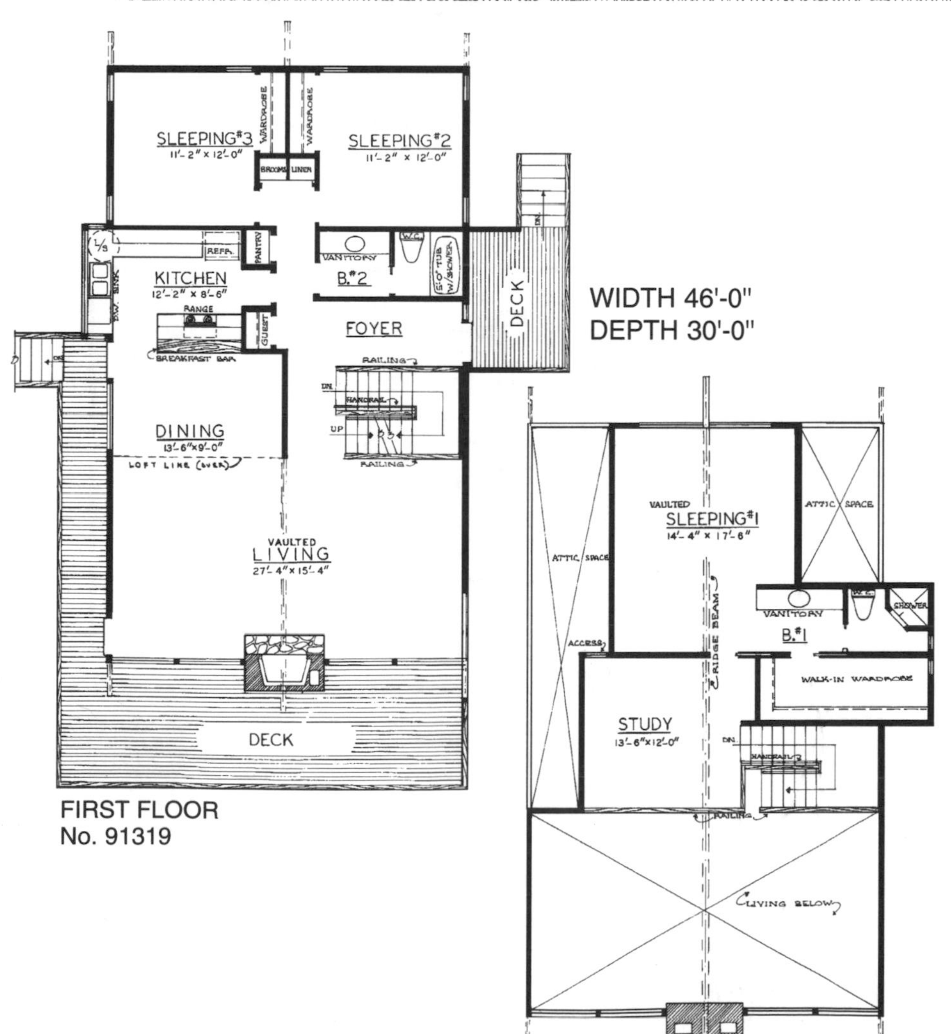

SLEEPING#3
11'-2" x 12'-0"
SLEEPING#2
11'-2" x 12'-0"
WARDROBE
WARDROBE
BROOMS
LINEN
REFR.
PANTRY
KITCHEN
12'-2" x 8'-6"
RANGE
BREAKFAST BAR
GUEST
VANITORY
B.#2
W.C.
5'-0" TUB W/SHOWER
DECK
FOYER
RAILING
HANDRAIL
UP
DN.
DINING
13'-6"x9'-0"
LOFT LINE (OVER)
VAULTED
LIVING
27'-4"x15'-4"
DECK
WIDTH 46'-0"
DEPTH 30'-0"
VAULTED
SLEEPING#1
14'-4" x 17'-6"
ATTIC SPACE
ATTIC SPACE
ACCESS
RIDGE BEAM
VANITORY
W.C.
SHOWER
B.#1
WALK-IN WARDROBE
STUDY
13'-6"x12'-0"
HANDRAIL
RAILING
LIVING BELOW

FIRST FLOOR
No. 91319

SECOND FLOOR

All Seasons

- This plan features:
  - Three bedrooms
  - One full, one half and one three quarter baths
- A wall of windows taking full advantage of the front view
- An open stairway to the upstairs study and the Master Bedroom
- A Master Bedroom with a private master Bath and a walk-in wardrobe
- An efficient Kitchen including a breakfast bar that opens into the Dining Area
- A formal Living Room with a vaulted ceiling and a stone fireplace

FIRST FLOOR — 1,306 SQ. FT.
SECOND FLOOR — 598 SQ. FT.
BASEMENT — 1,288 SQ. FT.

TOTAL LIVING AREA:
3,192 SQ. FT.

PLAN NO. 20220

Refer to **Pricing Schedule B** on the order form for pricing information

Traditional Ranch

- This plan features:
— Three bedrooms
— Two full baths
- A large front palladium window that gives this home great curb appeal, and allows a view of the front yard from the Living Room
- A vaulted ceiling in the Living Room, adding to the architectural interest and the spacious feel of the room
- Sliding glass doors in the Dining Room that lead to a wood deck
- A built-in pantry, double sink and breakfast bar in the efficient Kitchen
- A Master Suite that includes a walk-in closet and a private bath with a double vanity
- Two additional bedrooms that share a full hall bath

MAIN AREA — 1,568 SQ. FT.
BASEMENT — 1,568 SQ. FT.
GARAGE — 509 SQ. FT.

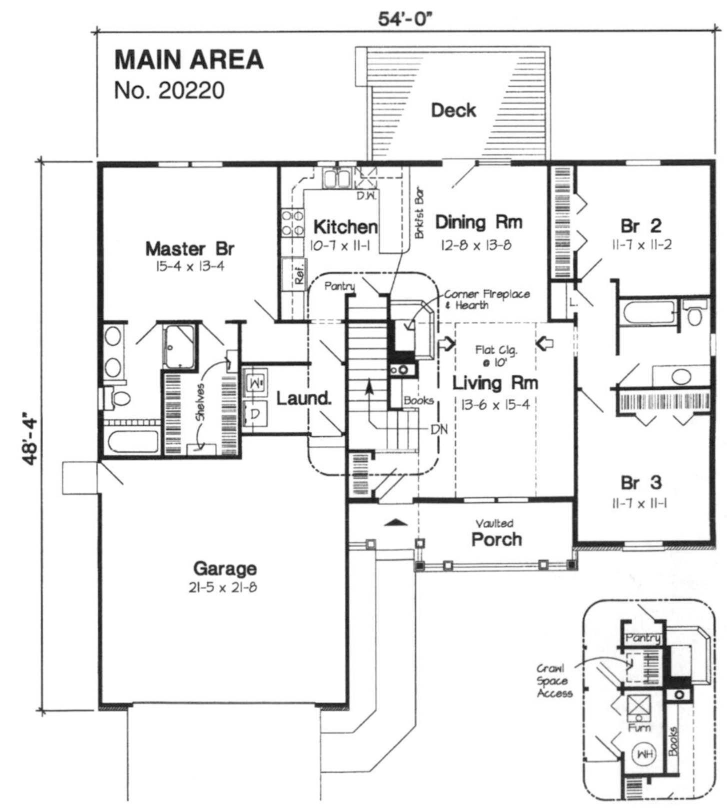

54'-0"
MAIN AREA
No. 20220
Deck
Master Br
15-4 x 13-4
Kitchen
10-7 x 11-1
D.W.
Ref.
Brkfst Bar
Dining Rm
12-8 x 13-8
Br 2
11-7 x 11-2
Pantry
Corner Fireplace & Hearth
Flat Clg. @ 10'
Living Rm
13-6 x 15-4
Books
DN
Laund.
Shelves
Br 3
11-7 x 11-1
Vaulted
Porch
Garage
21-5 x 21-8
48'-4"
Crawl Space Access
Pantry
Furn
WH
Books

An
EXCLUSIVE DESIGN
By Karl Kreeger

TOTAL LIVING AREA:
1,568 SQ. FT.

To order your Blueprints, call 1-800-235-5700

Refer to **Pricing Schedule Z** on the order form for pricing information

PLAN NO. 90433

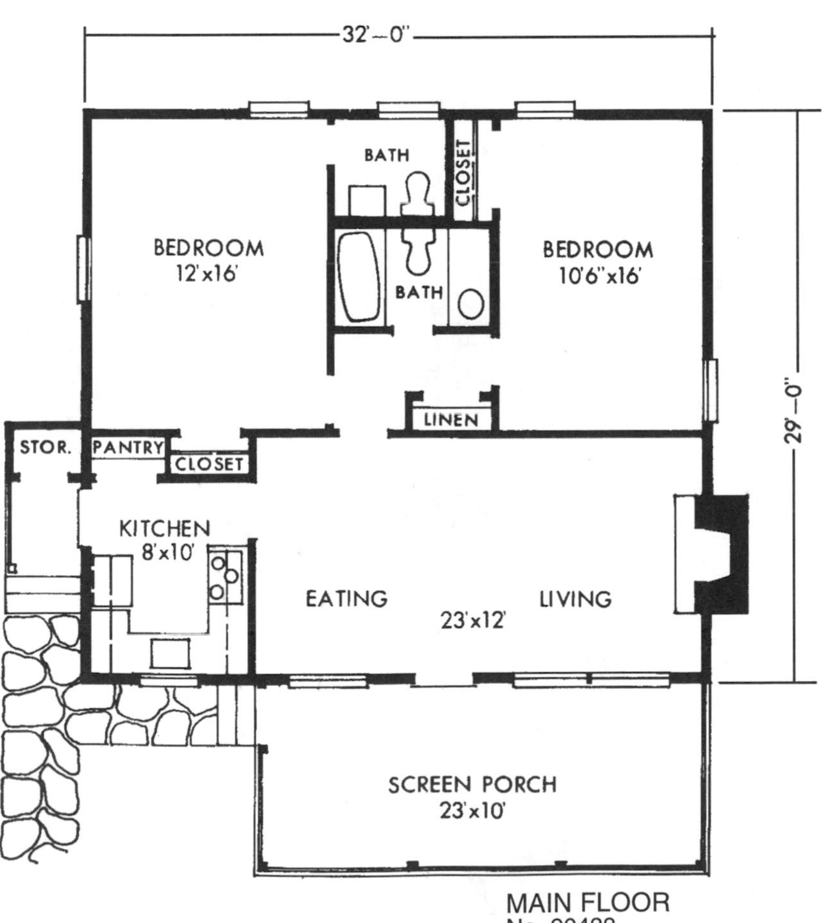

32'—0"
29'—0"
BATH
CLOSET
BEDROOM
12'x16'
BATH
BEDROOM
10'6"x16'
LINEN
STOR.
PANTRY
CLOSET
KITCHEN
8'x10'
EATING
23'x12'
LIVING
SCREEN PORCH
23'x10'

MAIN FLOOR
No. 90433

Cabin in the Country

- This plan features:
  - — Two bedrooms
  - — One full and one half baths
- A screened porch for enjoyment of your outdoor surroundings
- A combination Living and Dining area with cozy fireplace for added warmth
- An efficiently laid out Kitchen with a built-in pantry
- Two large bedrooms located at the rear of the home
- An optional slab or crawl space foundation — please specify when ordering

MAIN FLOOR — 928 SQ. FT.
SCREENED PORCH — 230 SQ. FT.
STORAGE — 14 SQ. FT.

TOTAL LIVING AREA:
928 SQ. FT.

PLAN NO. 94923

Refer to **Pricing Schedule B** on the order form for pricing information

Keystone Arches and Decorative Windows

© design basics, inc.

- This plan features:
- — Three bedrooms
- — One full and one three quarter baths
- Brick and stucco enhance the dramatic front elevation and volume entrance
- Inviting Entry leads into expansive Great Room with hearth fireplace framed by transom window
- Bay window Dining Room topped by decorative ceiling convenient to the Great Room and the Kitchen/Breakfast area
- Corner Master Suite enjoys a tray ceiling, roomy walk-in closet and a plush bath with a double vanity and whirlpool window tub
- Two additional bedrooms with large closets, share a full bath

MAIN FLOOR — 1,666 SQ. FT.
BASEMENT — 1,666 SQ. FT.
GARAGE — 496 SQ. FT.

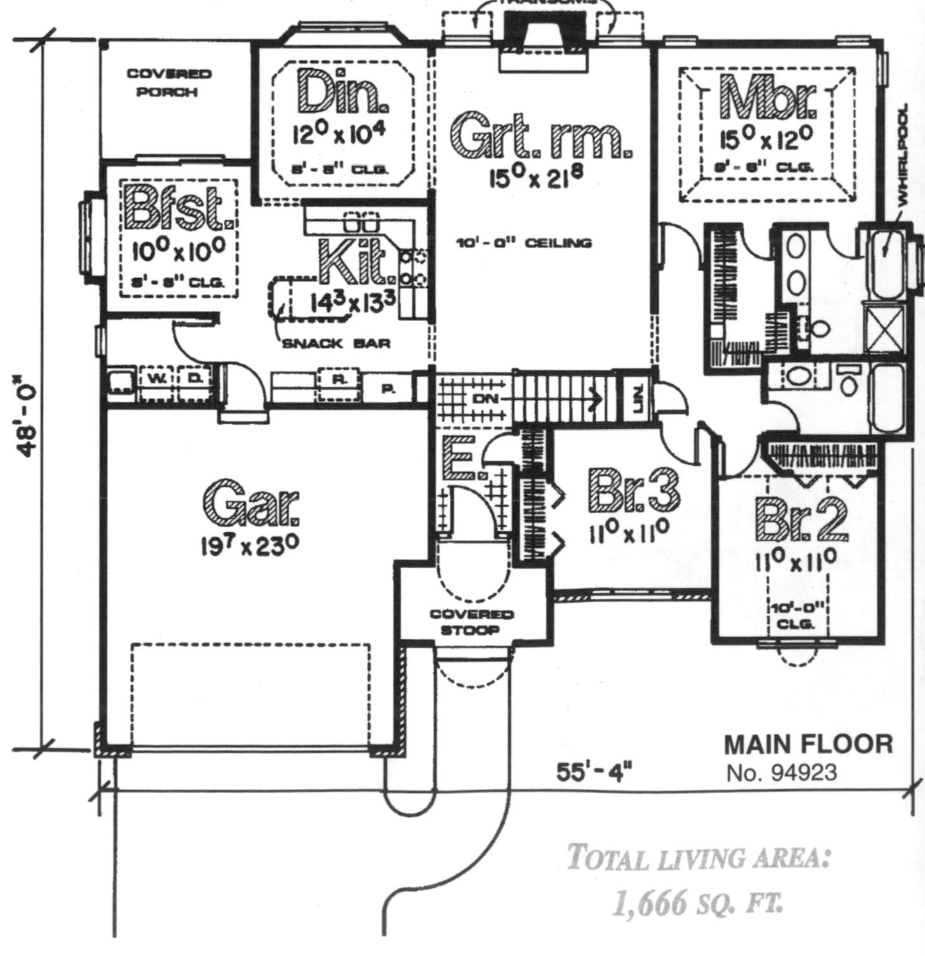
TRANSOMS
COVERED PORCH
Din.
12⁰ x 10⁴
8'-8" CLG.
Grt. rm.
15⁰ x 21⁸
10'-0" CEILING
Mbr.
15⁰ x 12⁰
8'-8" CLG.
WHIRLPOOL
Bfst.
10⁰ x 10⁰
8'-8" CLG.
Kit.
14³ x 13³
SNACK BAR
W. D.
R. P.
DN
LIN.
E.
Gar.
19⁷ x 23⁰
Br.3
11⁰ x 11⁰
Br.2
11⁰ x 11⁰
10'-0" CLG.
COVERED STOOP
48'-0"
55'-4"
MAIN FLOOR
No. 94923

TOTAL LIVING AREA: 1,666 SQ. FT.

To order your Blueprints, call 1-800-235-5700

Refer to **Pricing Schedule A** on the order form for pricing information

PLAN NO. 92026

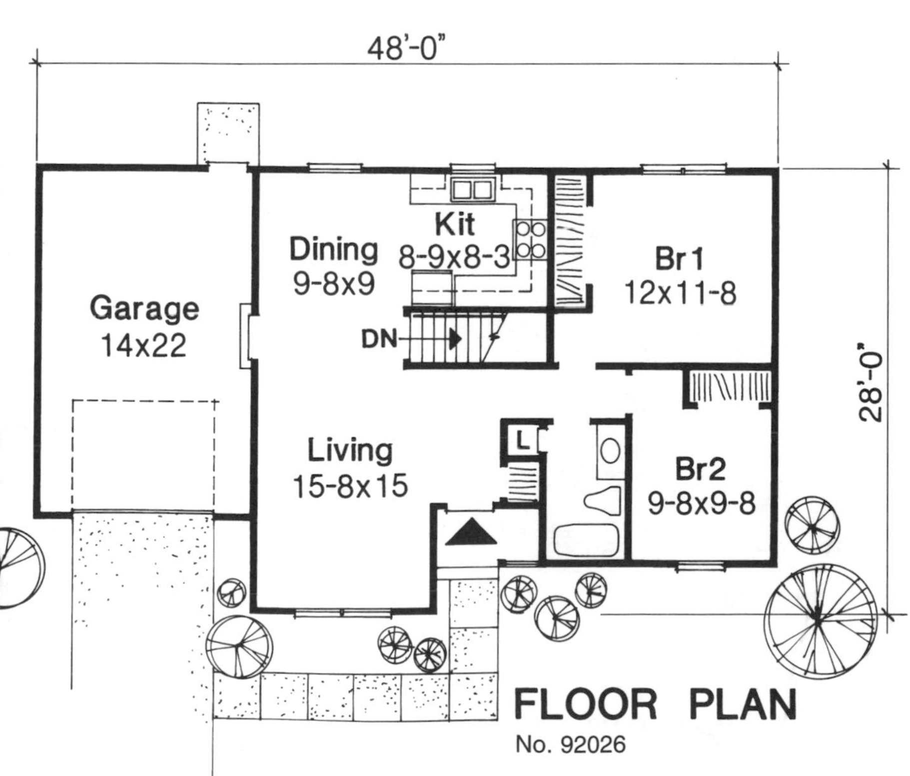

48'-0"
28'-0"
Kit
8-9x8-3
Dining
9-8x9
Br1
12x11-8
Garage
14x22
DN
L
Living
15-8x15
Br2
9-8x9-8

FLOOR PLAN
No. 92026

Inviting Entrance Welcomes All

- This plan features:
- — Two bedrooms
- — One full bath
- A covered front porch
- A large Living Room/Dining Room combination
- An efficient U-shaped Kitchen with a double sink and ample cabinet and counter space
- Two bedrooms that share the full hall bath and have ample storage space

MAIN FLOOR — 863 SQ. FT.

TOTAL LIVING AREA:
863 SQ. FT.

PLAN NO. 94306

Refer to **Pricing Schedule A** on the order form for pricing information

An EXCLUSIVE DESIGN By Marshall Associates

Relaxing Retreat

- This plan features:
  - — Three bedrooms
  - — Two 3/4 baths
- A wood Deck, expanding living space, leads into a tiled Entry and the open layout of the Living/Dining area and Kitchen
- A central fireplace warming both temperature and atmosphere in the Living/Dining area
- An efficient Kitchen with a side entry and a convenient closet
- A roomy Master Bedroom with a private bath and second floor Deck
- A first floor bedroom next to the full bath
- A Loft Bedroom with clerestory windows and an oversized closet
- No materials list is available

FIRST FLOOR — 598 SQ. FT.
SECOND FLOOR — 414 SQ. FT.

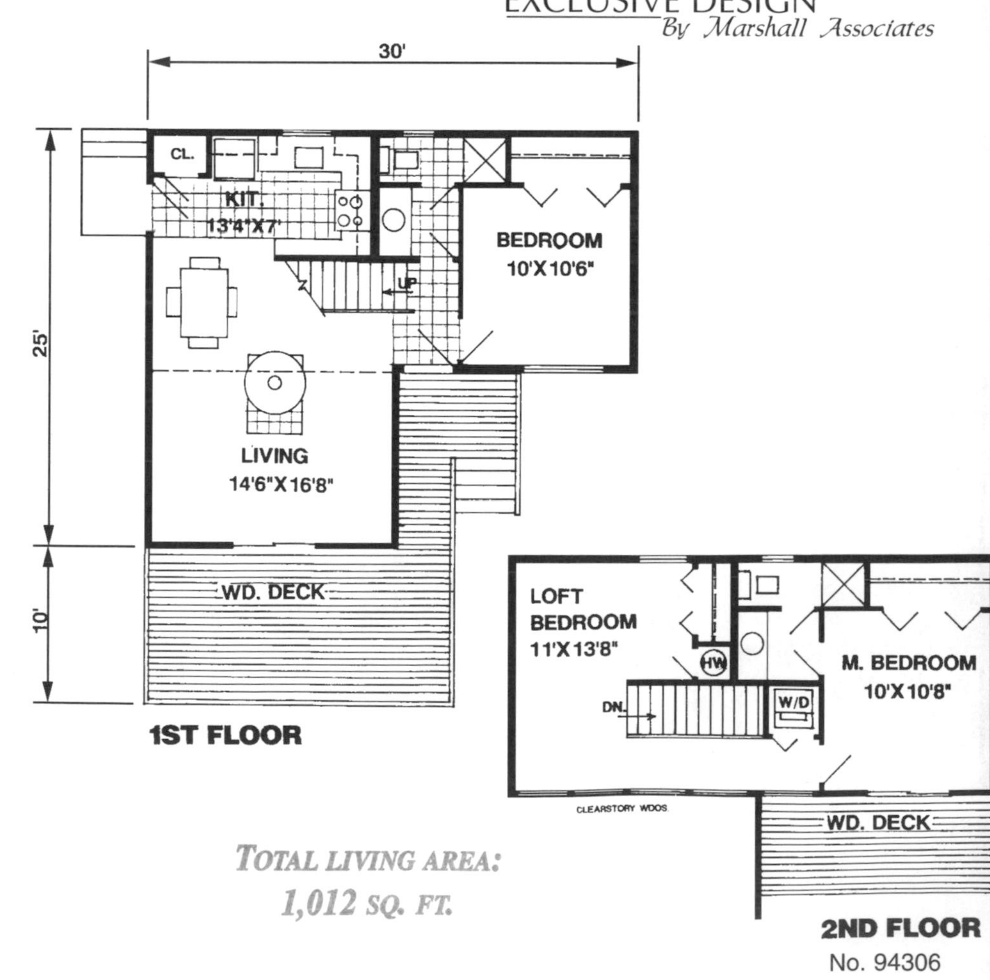

30'
CL.
KIT.
13'4"X7'
BEDROOM
10'X10'6"
UP
25'
LIVING
14'6"X16'8"
WD. DECK
10'
1ST FLOOR
LOFT
BEDROOM
11'X13'8"
HW
W/D
DN.
M. BEDROOM
10'X10'8"
CLEARSTORY WDOS.
WD. DECK
2ND FLOOR
No. 94306

TOTAL LIVING AREA:
1,012 SQ. FT.

Refer to **Pricing Schedule D** on the order form for pricing information

PLAN NO. 24315

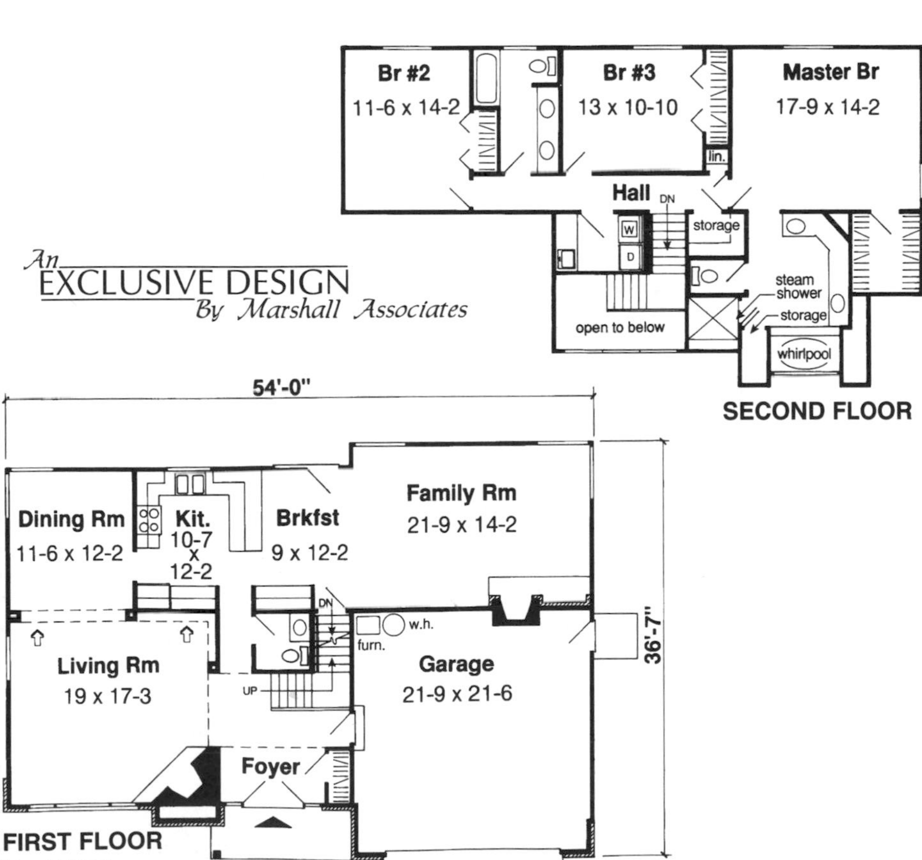

Br #2
11-6 x 14-2
Br #3
13 x 10-10
Master Br
17-9 x 14-2
lin.
Hall
DN
W
D
storage
open to below
steam shower
storage
whirlpool
SECOND FLOOR
An EXCLUSIVE DESIGN By Marshall Associates
54'-0"
36'-7"
Dining Rm
11-6 x 12-2
Kit.
10-7 x 12-2
Brkfst
9 x 12-2
Family Rm
21-9 x 14-2
DN
w.h.
furn.
Living Rm
19 x 17-3
UP
Garage
21-9 x 21-6
Foyer
FIRST FLOOR
No. 24315

Luxury Bath In Master Suite

- This plan features:
- — Three bedrooms
- — Two full and one half baths
- Sloped ceiling and angled fireplace in spacious Living Room
- Formal dining room in proximity to kitchen
- Family room with second fireplace
- Master Suite with lavish, private, whirlpool bath
- Two good sized secondary bedrooms with full, dual vanity bath between

FIRST FLOOR — 1,322 SQ. FT.
SECOND FLOOR — 1,223 SQ. FT.

TOTAL LIVING AREA
2,545 SQ. FT.

PLAN NO. 24317

Refer to **Pricing Schedule B** on the order form for pricing information

Natural Light Gives Bright Living Spaces

An EXCLUSIVE DESIGN
By Marshall Associates

- This plan features:
- — Three bedrooms
- — Two full baths
- A generous use of windows throughout the home, creating a bright living space
- A center work island and a built-in pantry in the Kitchen
- A sunny Eating Nook for informal eating and a formal Dining Room for entertaining
- A large Living Room with a cozy fireplace to add atmosphere to the room as well as warmth
- A Master Bedroom with a private bath and double closets
- Two additional bedrooms that share a full, compartmented hall bath

MAIN AREA — 1,620 SQ. FT.

TOTAL LIVING AREA:
1,620 SQ. FT.

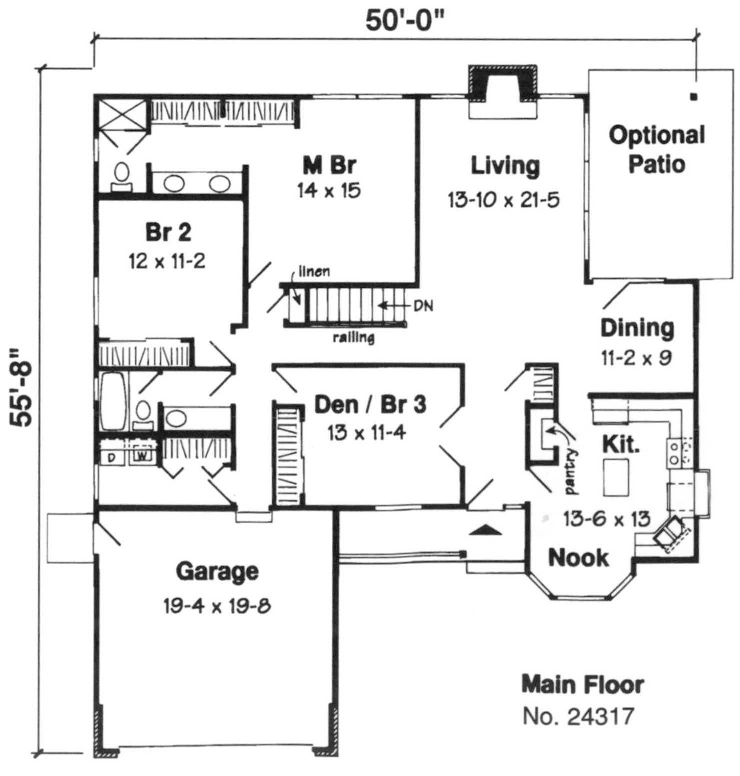
50'-0"
55'-8"
M Br
14 x 15
Living
13-10 x 21-5
Optional Patio
Br 2
12 x 11-2
linen
DN
railing
Dining
11-2 x 9
Den / Br 3
13 x 11-4
Kit.
pantry
13-6 x 13
Nook
Garage
19-4 x 19-8
D
W

Main Floor
No. 24317

To order your Blueprints, call 1-800-235-5700

Refer to **Pricing Schedule A** on the order form for pricing information

B.N.

PLAN NO. 90630

DINING
KIT 8'6" × 12'10"
table
MUD RM
BATH
BATH
MASTER BED RM 14'4"× 12'10"
LIVING RM 15'0"× 24'0" cathedral ceil.
exposed beam
Heat circulating fireplace
DECK
bench
sl.gl.drs
HALL
FOYER
BED RM 9'0"× 11'0"
BED RM 12'4" × 10'6"
roof overh'g
12'0"
45'4"
36'4"

FLOOR PLAN

No. 90630

Year Round Leisure

- This plan features:
  - — Three bedrooms
  - — One full and one three quarter baths
- A cathedral ceiling with exposed beams and a stone wall with heat-circulating fireplace in the Living Room
- Three sliding glass doors leading from the Living Room to a large deck
- A built-in Dining area that separates the Kitchen from the far end of the Living Room
- A Master Suite with his and her closets and a private bath
- Two additional bedrooms, one double sized, sharing a full hall bath

MAIN FLOOR — 1,207 SQ. FT.

TOTAL LIVING AREA:* *1,207 SQ. FT.

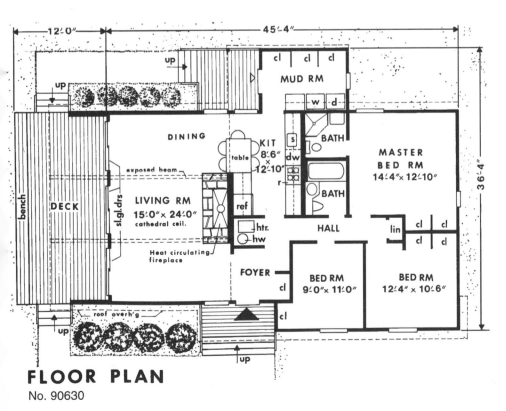

PLAN NO. 90844

Refer to **Pricing Schedule B** on the order form for pricing information

Open Space Living

- This plan features:
  - — Three bedrooms
  - — Two full and one half baths
- A wrap-around Deck providing outdoor living space, ideal for a sloping lot
- Two and a half-story glass wall and two separate atrium doors providing natural light for the Living/Dining Room area
- An efficient galley Kitchen with easy access to the Dining area
- A Master Bedroom suite with a half bath and ample closet space
- Another bedroom on the first floor adjoins a full hall bath
- A second floor Bedroom/Studio, with a private Deck, adjacent to a full hall bath and a Loft area

FIRST FLOOR — 1,086 SQ. FT.
SECOND FLOOR — 466 SQ. FT.
BASEMENT — 1,080 SQ. FT.

An EXCLUSIVE DESIGN *By Westhome Planners, Ltd.*

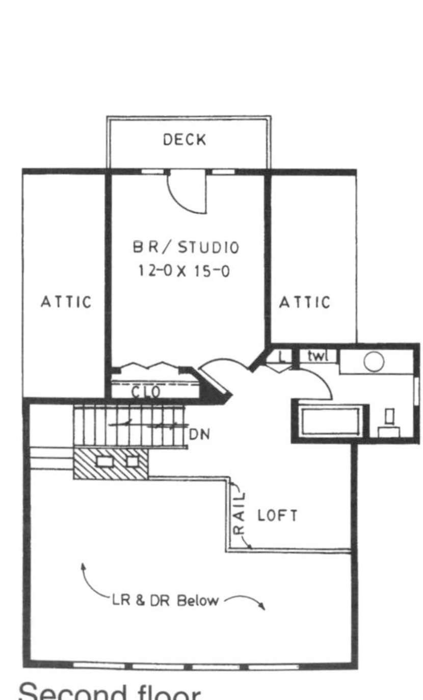
DECK
BR/STUDIO
12-0 X 15-0
ATTIC
ATTIC
CLO
twl
DN
RAIL
LOFT
LR & DR Below

Second floor

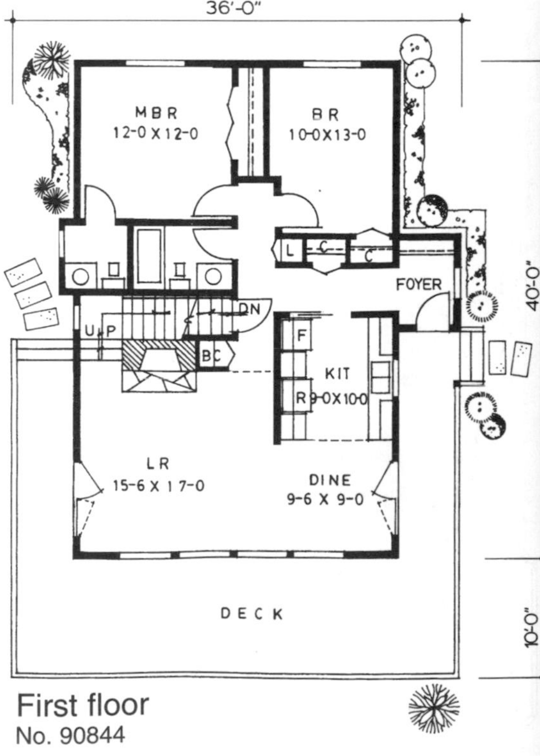
36'-0"
MBR
12-0 X 12-0
BR
10-0 X 13-0
FOYER
40'-0"
UP
DN
BC
F
KIT
R 9-0 X 10-0
LR
15-6 X 17-0
DINE
9-6 X 9-0
DECK
10'-0"

First floor
No. 90844

TOTAL LIVING AREA:* 1,552 *SQ. FT.

To order your Blueprints, call 1-800-235-5700

Refer to **Pricing Schedule D** on the order form for pricing information

PLAN NO. 91304

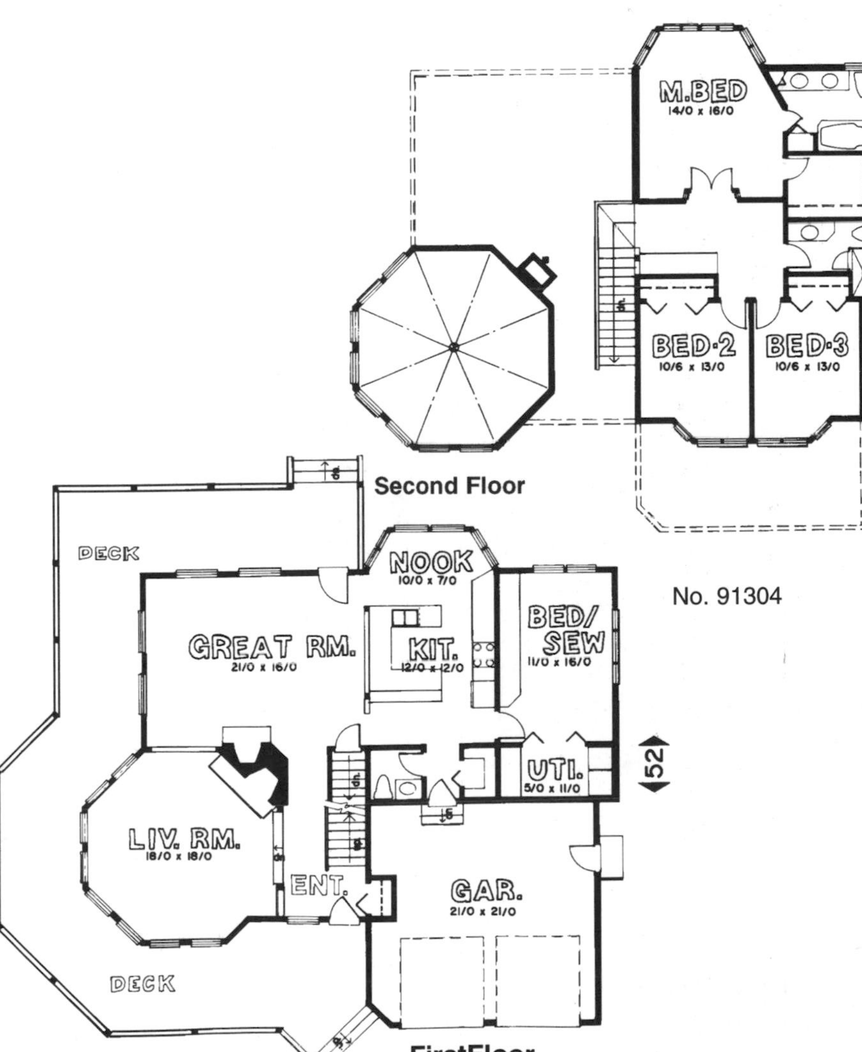

M.BED
14/0 x 16/0
BED-2
10/6 x 13/0
BED-3
10/6 x 13/0
Second Floor
DECK
NOOK
10/0 x 7/0
GREAT RM.
21/0 x 16/0
KIT.
12/0 x 12/0
BED/SEW
11/0 x 16/0
UTI.
5/0 x 11/0
52
LIV. RM.
18/0 x 18/0
ENT.
GAR.
21/0 x 21/0
DECK
No. 91304
FirstFloor
59-10

Deck Surrounds House on Three Sides

- This plan features:
- — Three bedrooms
- — One full and one three quarter baths
- A sunken, circular Living Room with windows on four sides and a vaulted clerestory for a wide-open feeling
- Back-to-back fireplaces in the Living Room and the adjoining Great Room
- A convenient, efficient Kitchen with a sunny eating Nook
- A Master Suite with a walk-in closet and a private Master Bath
- Two additional bedrooms that share a full hall bath

FIRST FLOOR — 1,439 SQ. FT.
SECOND FLOOR — 873 SQ. FT.

TOTAL LIVING AREA:
2,312 SQ. FT.

PLAN NO. 94986

Refer to **Pricing Schedule B** on the order form for pricing information

Ten Foot Entry

- This plan features:

—Three bedrooms

—Two full baths

- Large volume Great Room highlighted by a fireplace flanked by windows
- See-through wetbar enhancing the Breakfast area and the Dining Room
- Decorative ceiling treatment giving elegance to the Dining Room
- Fully equipped Kitchen with a planning desk and a pantry
- Roomy Master Bedroom suite has a volume ceiling and special amenities; a skylighted dressing bath area, plant shelf, a large walk-in closet, a double vanity and a whirlpool tub
- Secondary bedrooms with ample closets sharing a convenient hall bath

MAIN FLOOR — 1,604 SQ. FT.
GARAGE — 466 SQ. FT.

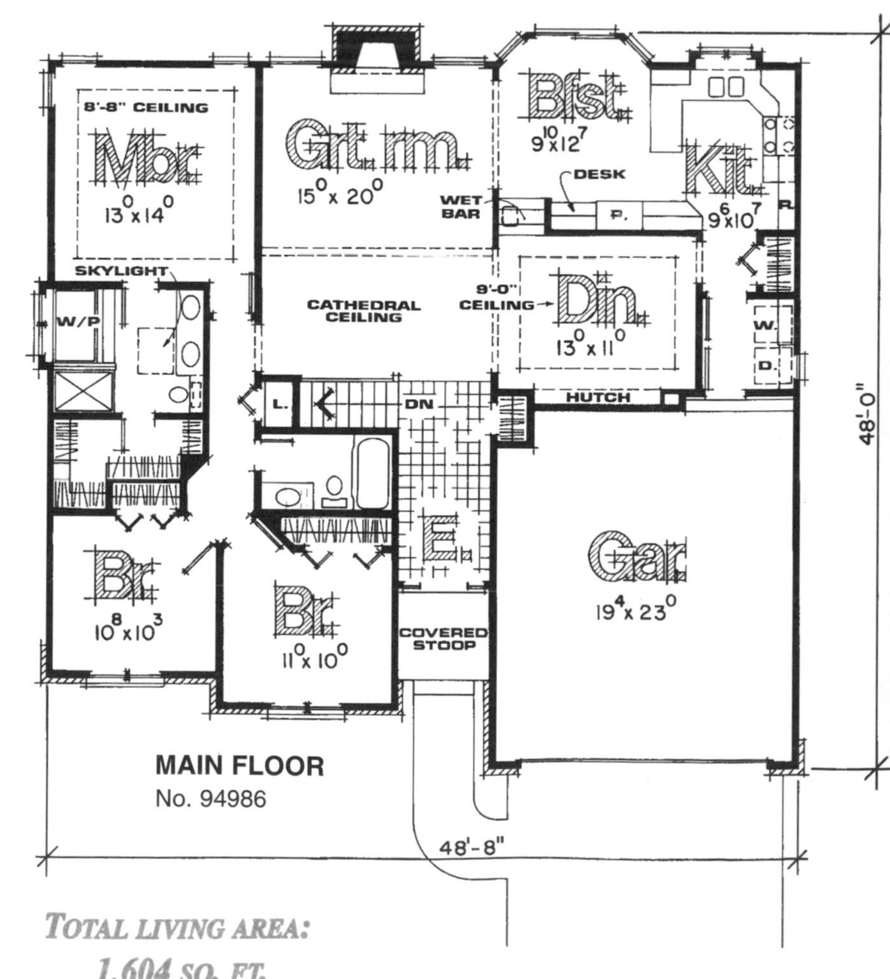

8'-8" CEILING
Mbr.
13⁰x14⁰
Grt.rm.
15⁰ x 20⁰
Bfst.
9¹⁰x12⁷
DESK
Kit.
9⁶x10⁷
WET BAR
P.
R.
SKYLIGHT
W/P
CATHEDRAL CEILING
9'-0" CEILING
Din.
13⁰x11⁰
W.
D.
L.
DN
HUTCH
48'-0"
E.
Gar.
19⁴x23⁰
Br.
10⁸x10³
Br.
11⁰x10⁰
COVERED STOOP
MAIN FLOOR
No. 94986
48'-8"

TOTAL LIVING AREA:
1,604 SQ. FT.

Refer to **Pricing Schedule A** on the order form for pricing information

PLAN NO. 90905

An EXCLUSIVE DESIGN By Westhome Planners, Ltd.

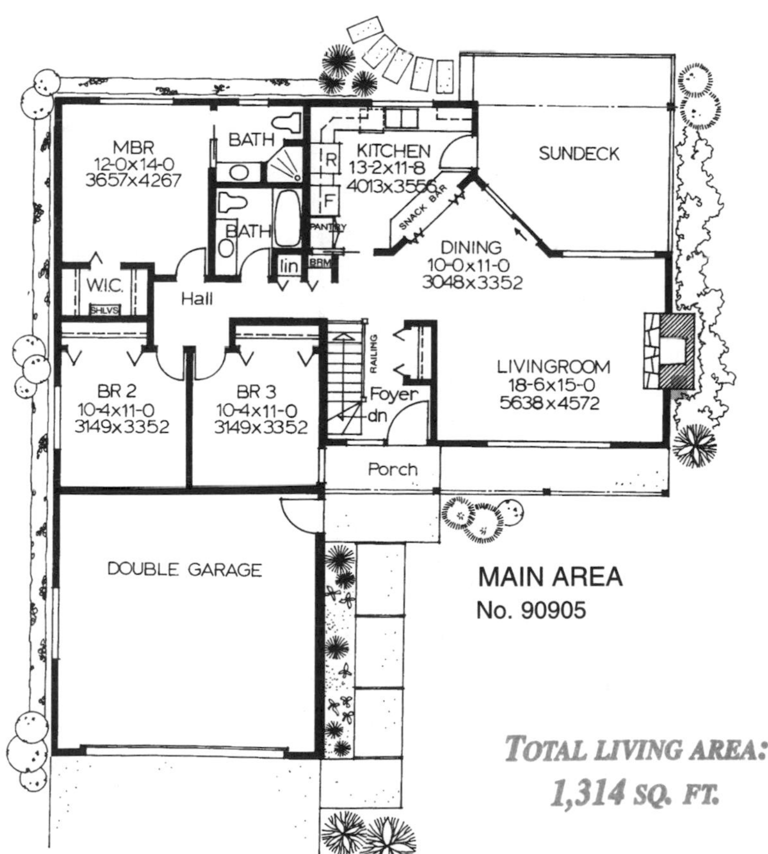

MBR
12-0x14-0
3657x4267
BATH
KITCHEN
13-2x11-8
4013x3556
SUNDECK
R
F
SNACK BAR
BATH
PANTRY
DINING
10-0x11-0
3048x3352
lin
BRM
W.I.C.
SHLVS
Hall
RAILING
Foyer
dn
LIVINGROOM
18-6x15-0
5638x4572
BR 2
10-4x11-0
3149x3352
BR 3
10-4x11-0
3149x3352
Porch
DOUBLE GARAGE
MAIN AREA
No. 90905

TOTAL LIVING AREA:
1,314 SQ. FT.

Compact Home is Surprisingly Spacious

- This plan features:
  - — Three bedrooms
  - — One full and one three quarter baths
- A spacious Living Room warmed by a fireplace
- A Dining Room flowing off the Living Room, with sliding glass doors to the deck
- An efficient, well-equipped Kitchen with a snack bar, double sink, and ample cabinet and counter space
- A Master Suite with a walk-in closet and private full bath
- Two additional, roomy bedrooms with ample closet space and protection from street noise from the two-car garage

MAIN AREA — 1,314 SQ. FT.
BASEMENT — 1,488 SQ. FT.
GARAGE — 484 SQ. FT.
WIDTH — 50'-0"
DEPTH — 54'-0"

PLAN NO. 96417

Refer to **Pricing Schedule C** on the order form for pricing information

© 1995 Donald A. Gardner Architects, Inc.

Casually Elegant

- This plan features:
  - — Three bedrooms
  - — Two full baths
- Arched windows, dormers and charming front and back porches with columns creating country flavoring
- Central Great Room topped by a cathedral ceiling, a fireplace and a clerestory window
- Breakfast bay for casual dining is open to the Kitchen
- Columns accenting the entryway into the formal Dining Room
- Cathedral ceiling crowning the Master Bedroom
- Master Bath with skylights, whirlpool tub, shower, and a double bowl vanity
- Two additional bedrooms sharing a bath located between the rooms

MAIN FLOOR — 1,561 SQ. FT.
GARAGE & STORAGE — 346 SQ. FT.

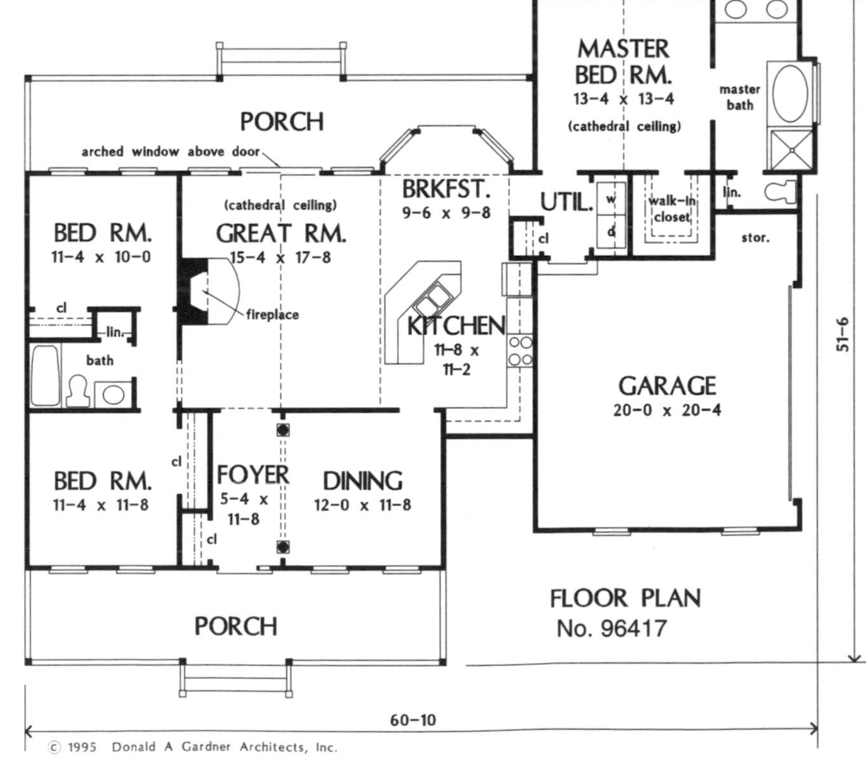

MASTER BED RM.
13–4 x 13–4
(cathedral ceiling)
master bath
PORCH
arched window above door
BRKFST.
9–6 x 9–8
UTIL.
w
d
walk-in closet
lin.
cl
stor.
BED RM.
11–4 x 10–0
(cathedral ceiling)
GREAT RM.
15–4 x 17–8
fireplace
cl
lin.
bath
KITCHEN
11–8 x
11–2
GARAGE
20–0 x 20–4
51–6
BED RM.
11–4 x 11–8
cl
FOYER
5–4 x
11–8
cl
DINING
12–0 x 11–8
PORCH
FLOOR PLAN
No. 96417
60–10
© 1995 Donald A Gardner Architects, Inc.

TOTAL LIVING AREA:
1,561 SQ. FT.

To order your Blueprints, call 1-800-235-5700

Refer to **Pricing Schedule A** on the order form for pricing information

PLAN NO. 92400

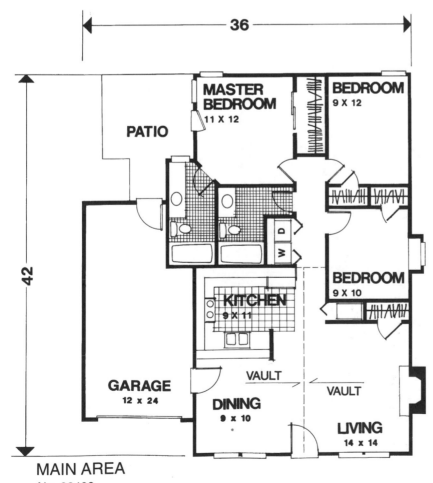

36

42

MASTER BEDROOM
11 X 12

BEDROOM
9 X 12

PATIO

D

W

BEDROOM
9 X 10

KITCHEN
9 X 11

VAULT

VAULT

GARAGE
12 x 24

DINING
9 x 10

LIVING
14 x 14

MAIN AREA
No. 92400

Quaint Starter Home

- This plan features:
  - — Three bedrooms
  - — Two full baths
- A vaulted ceiling giving an airy feeling to the Dining and Living Rooms
- A streamlined Kitchen with a comfortable work area, a double sink and ample cabinet space
- A cozy fireplace in the Living Room
- A Master Suite with a large closet, French doors leading to the patio and a private bath
- Two additional bedrooms sharing a full bath
- No materials list available for this plan

MAIN AREA — 1,050 SQ. FT.

TOTAL LIVING AREA:
1,050 SQ. FT.

To order your Blueprints, call 1-800-235-5700

PLAN NO. 24301

Refer to **Pricing Schedule C** on the order form for pricing information

An EXCLUSIVE DESIGN *By Marshall Associates*

From Times Gone By

- This plan features:
- — Four bedrooms
- — Two and one half baths
- A Family Room opening to a large deck in rear
- A Master Bedroom with a private bath and ample closet space
- A large Living Room with a bay window
- A modern Kitchen with many amenities

FIRST FLOOR — 987 SQ. FT.
SECOND FLOOR — 970 SQ. FT.
BASEMENT — 985 SQ. FT.

TOTAL LIVING AREA:
1,957 SQ. FT.

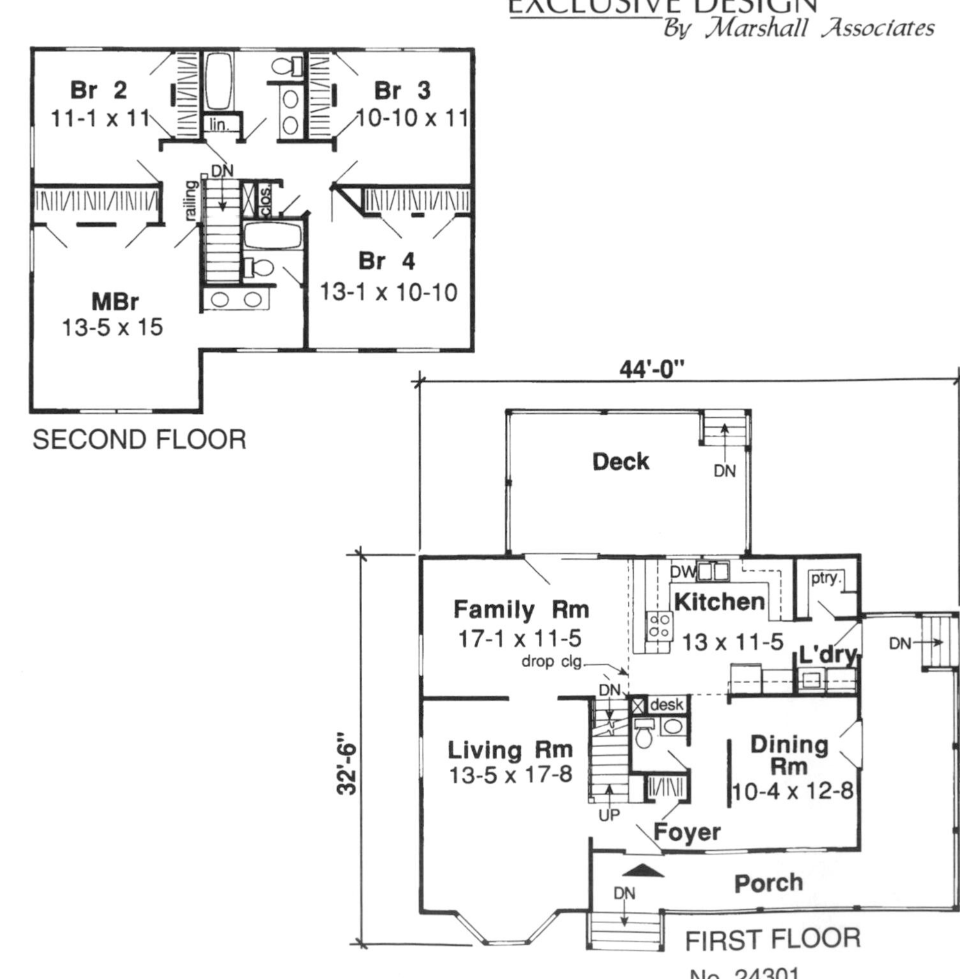

Br 2
11-1 x 11
lin.
Br 3
10-10 x 11
DN
railing
clos.
MBr
13-5 x 15
Br 4
13-1 x 10-10
SECOND FLOOR
44'-0"
Deck
DN
DW
ptry.
Family Rm
17-1 x 11-5
drop clg.
Kitchen
13 x 11-5
L'dry
DN
DN
desk
Living Rm
13-5 x 17-8
Dining Rm
10-4 x 12-8
32'-6"
UP
Foyer
Porch
DN
FIRST FLOOR
No. 24301

To order your Blueprints, call 1-800-235-5700

Refer to **Pricing Schedule A** on the order form for pricing information

PLAN NO. 90623

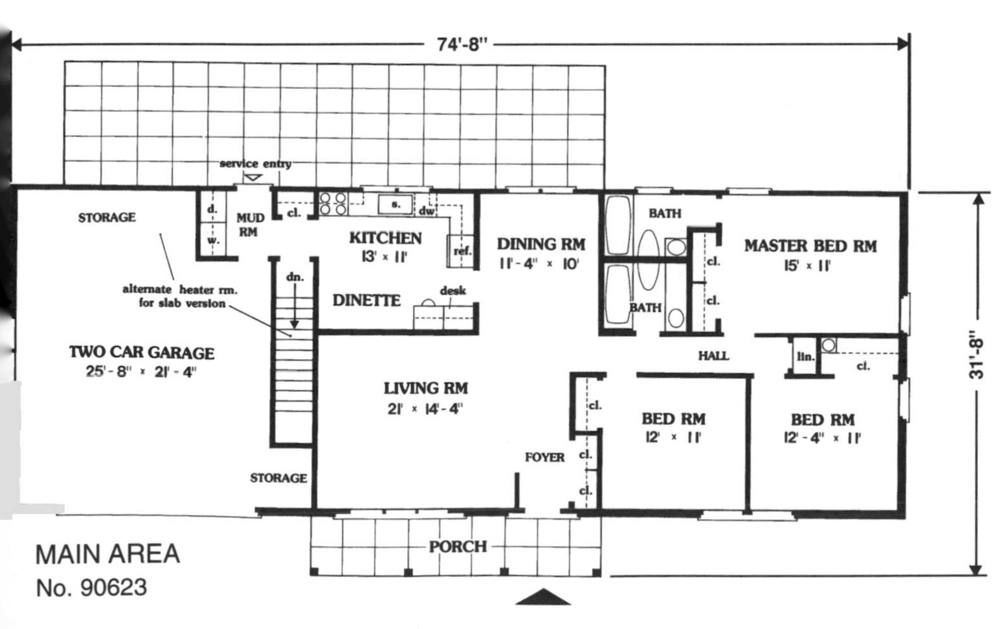

74'-8"
service entry
STORAGE
d.
w.
MUD RM
cl.
s.
dw
KITCHEN 13' x 11'
ref.
DINING RM 11'-4" x 10'
BATH
BATH
cl.
cl.
MASTER BED RM 15' x 11'
alternate heater rm. for slab version
dn.
desk
DINETTE
TWO CAR GARAGE 25'-8" x 21'-4"
HALL
lin.
cl.
31'-8"
LIVING RM 21' x 14'-4"
cl.
BED RM 12' x 11'
BED RM 12'-4" x 11'
FOYER
cl.
cl.
STORAGE
PORCH

MAIN AREA
No. 90623

Expansive, Not Expensive

- This plan features:
- — Three bedrooms
- — Two full baths
- A Master Suite with his and her closets and a private Master Bath
- Two additional bedrooms that share a full hall closet
- A pleasant Dining Room that overlooks a rear garden
- A well-equipped Kitchen with a built-in planning corner and eat-in space
- A basement foundation only

MAIN FLOOR — 1,474 SQ. FT.

TOTAL LIVING AREA:
1,474 SQ. FT.

PLAN NO. 24318

Refer to **Pricing Schedule A** on the order form for pricing information

Master Suite Offers Privacy

- This plan features:
- — Four bedrooms
- — Two full baths
- A large covered porch and dormer windows, creating a friendly invitation to enter
- A Living Room with a beamed ceiling and access to the patio through an atrium door
- A Dining Room adjoining the Living Room and Kitchen making entertaining easy
- A efficient, U-shaped Kitchen with a curved counter that serves as a pass-through and a snack bar
- A exclusive Master Suite, with a double vanity Bath, on the second floor offering a quiet place
- Three bedrooms on the first floor sharing a full hall bath.

FIRST FLOOR — 1,044 SQ. FT.

SECOND FLOOR — 354 SQ. FT.

TOTAL LIVING AREA:
1,398 SQ. FT

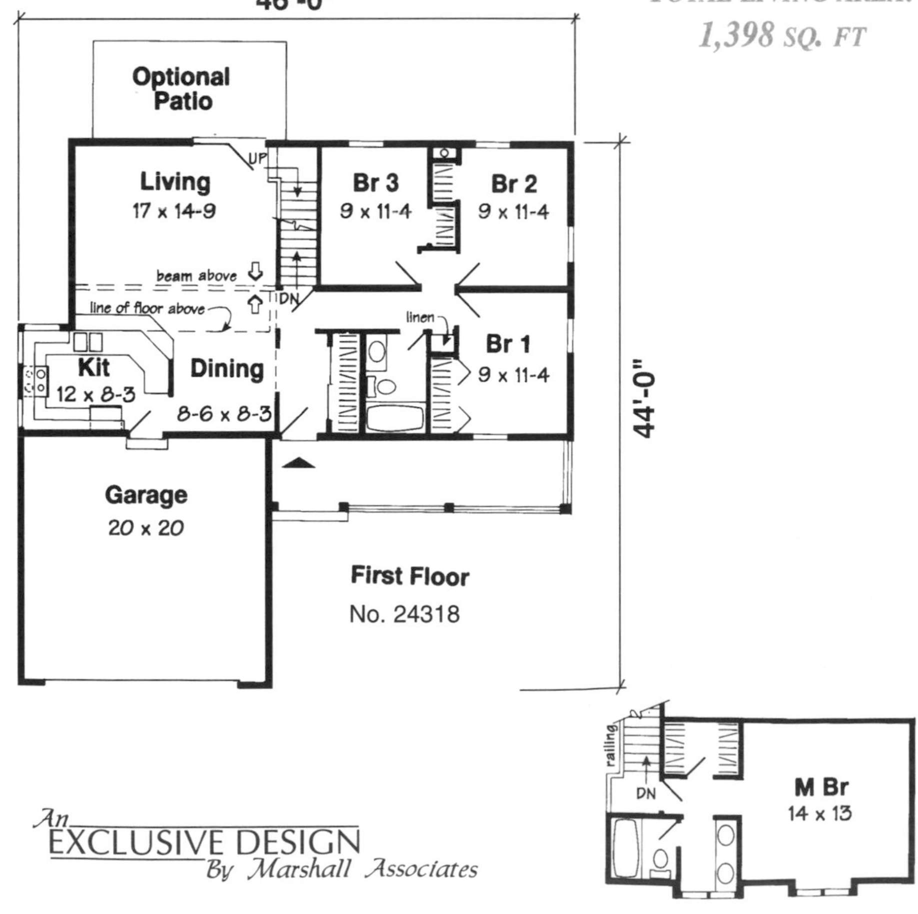

46'-0"
Optional Patio
Living
17 x 14-9
UP
beam above
line of floor above
DN
Br 3
9 x 11-4
Br 2
9 x 11-4
linen
Br 1
9 x 11-4
Kit
12 x 8-3
Dining
8-6 x 8-3
Garage
20 x 20
44'-0"
First Floor
No. 24318
railing
DN
M Br
14 x 13
Second Floor

An EXCLUSIVE DESIGN By Marshall Associates

To order your Blueprints, call 1-800-235-5700

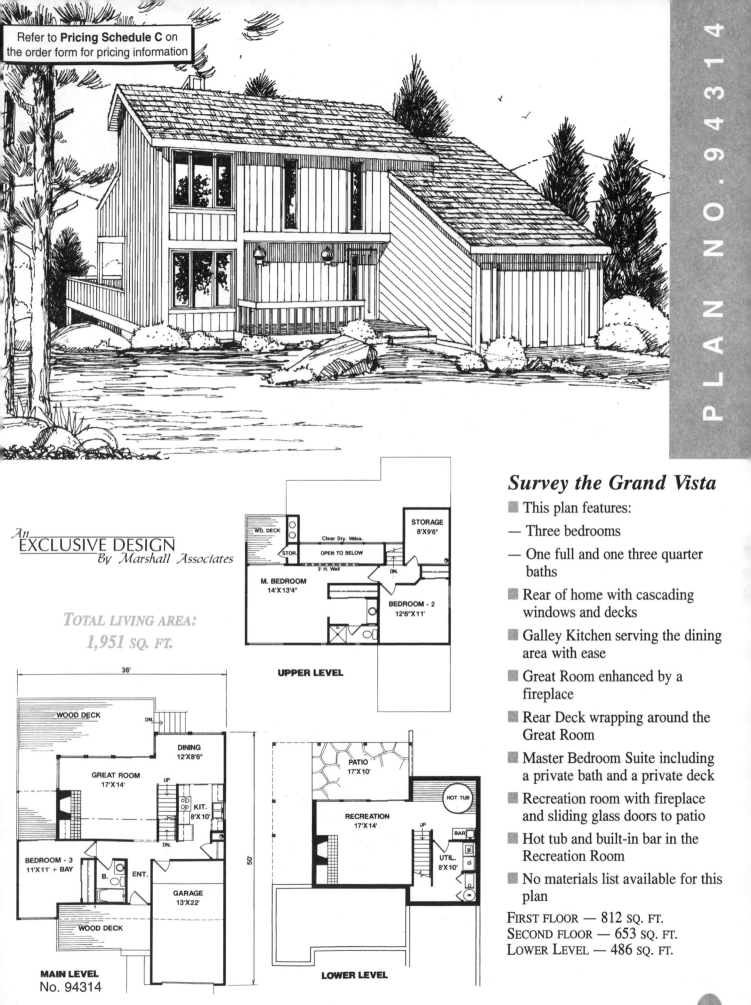

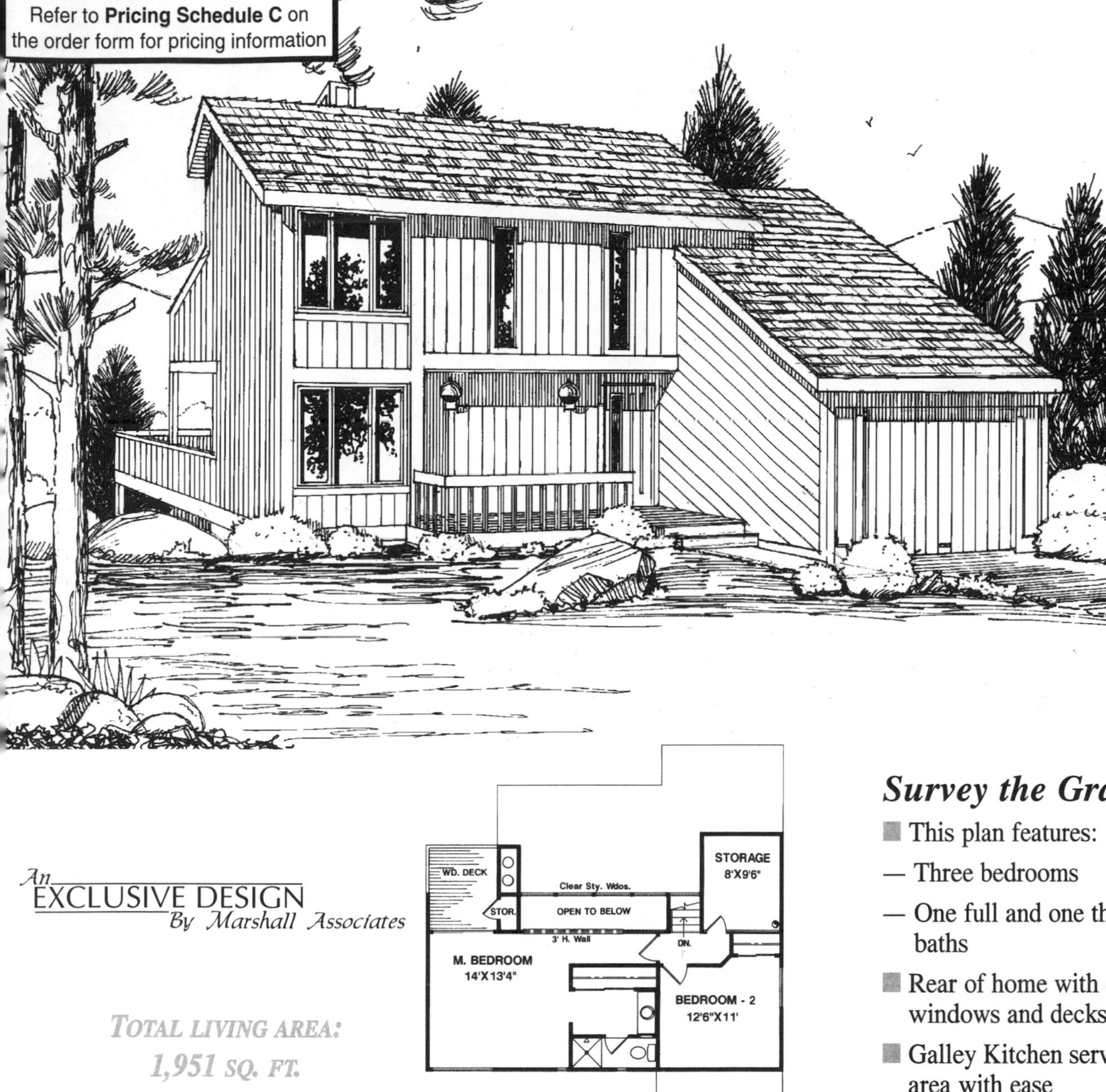
Refer to **Pricing Schedule C** on
the order form for pricing information

PLAN NO. 94314

An
EXCLUSIVE DESIGN
By Marshall Associates

TOTAL LIVING AREA:
1,951 SQ. FT.

Survey the Grand Vista

- This plan features:
  - — Three bedrooms
  - — One full and one three quarter baths
- Rear of home with cascading windows and decks
- Galley Kitchen serving the dining area with ease
- Great Room enhanced by a fireplace
- Rear Deck wrapping around the Great Room
- Master Bedroom Suite including a private bath and a private deck
- Recreation room with fireplace and sliding glass doors to patio
- Hot tub and built-in bar in the Recreation Room
- No materials list available for this plan

FIRST FLOOR — 812 SQ. FT.
SECOND FLOOR — 653 SQ. FT.
LOWER LEVEL — 486 SQ. FT.

WD. DECK
STOR.
Clear Sty. Wdos.
OPEN TO BELOW
3' H. Wall
STORAGE 8'X9'6"
DN.
M. BEDROOM 14'X13'4"
BEDROOM - 2 12'6"X11'

UPPER LEVEL

36'
WOOD DECK
DN.
DINING 12'X8'6"
GREAT ROOM 17'X14'
UP
KIT. 8'X10'
DN.
BEDROOM - 3 11'X11' + BAY
B.
ENT.
GARAGE 13'X22'
WOOD DECK
50'

MAIN LEVEL
No. 94314

PATIO 17'X10'
HOT TUB
RECREATION 17'X14'
UP
BAR
W.
D.
UTIL. 8'X10'

LOWER LEVEL

PLAN NO. 90930

Refer to **Pricing Schedule B** on the order form for pricing information

A-Frame for Year-Round Living

- This plan features:
- — Three bedrooms
- — One full and one three quarter baths
- A vaulted ceiling in the Living Room with a massive fireplace
- A wrap-around sun deck that gives you a lot of outdoor living space
- A luxurious Master Suite complete with a walk-in closet, full bath and private deck
- Two additional bedrooms that share a full hall bath

MAIN FLOOR — 1,238 SQ. FT.
LOFT — 464 SQ. FT.
BASEMENT — 1,175 SQ. FT.
WIDTH — 34'-0"
DEPTH — 56'-0"

TOTAL LIVING AREA:
1,702 SQ. FT.

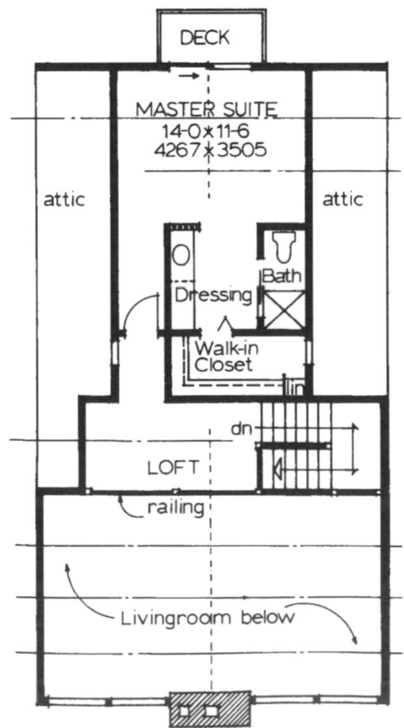
DECK
MASTER SUITE
14-0x11-6
4267x3505
attic
attic
Bath
Dressing
Walk-in Closet
lin
dn
LOFT
railing
Livingroom below
LOFT PLAN

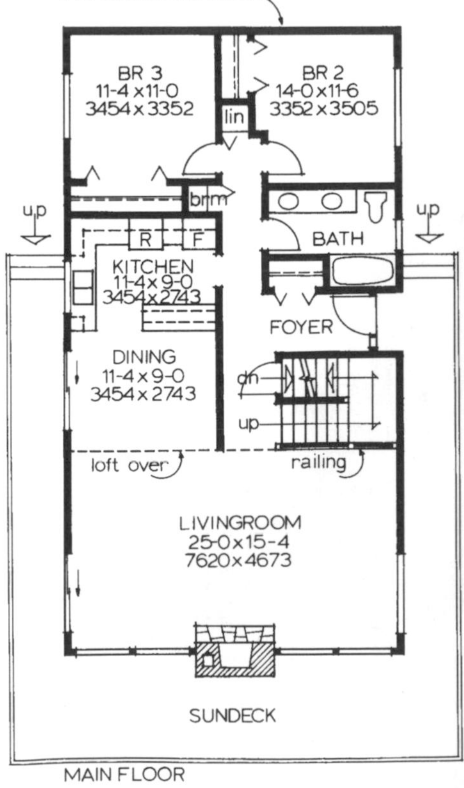
Full Basement under
BR 3
11-4 x11-0
3454x3352
BR 2
14-0x11-6
3352x3505
lin
brm
up
up
R
F
KITCHEN
11-4x9-0
3454x2743
BATH
FOYER
DINING
11-4x9-0
3454x2743
dn
up
loft over
railing
LIVINGROOM
25-0x15-4
7620x4673
SUNDECK
MAIN FLOOR
No. 90930

An EXCLUSIVE DESIGN
By Westhome Planners, Ltd.

To order your Blueprints, call 1-800-235-5700

Refer to **Pricing Schedule A** on the order form for pricing information

PLAN NO. 90847

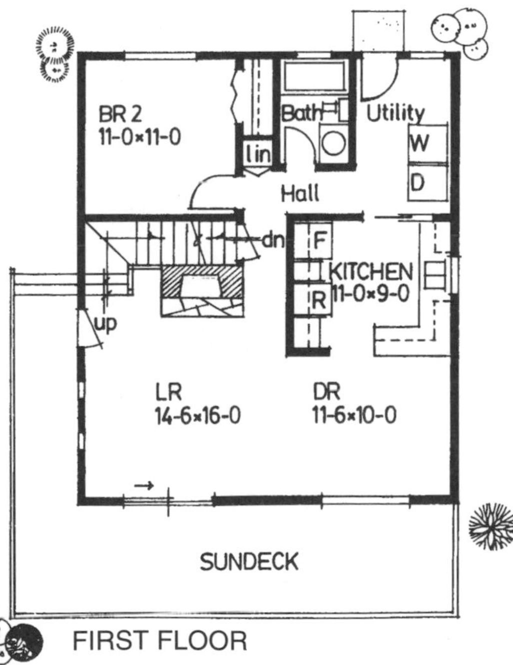

BR 2
11-0×11-0
Bath
Utility
lin
W
D
Hall
dn
F
KITCHEN
11-0×9-0
R
up
LR
14-6×16-0
DR
11-6×10-0
SUNDECK
FIRST FLOOR

WIDTH 27'-0"
DEPTH 32'-0"

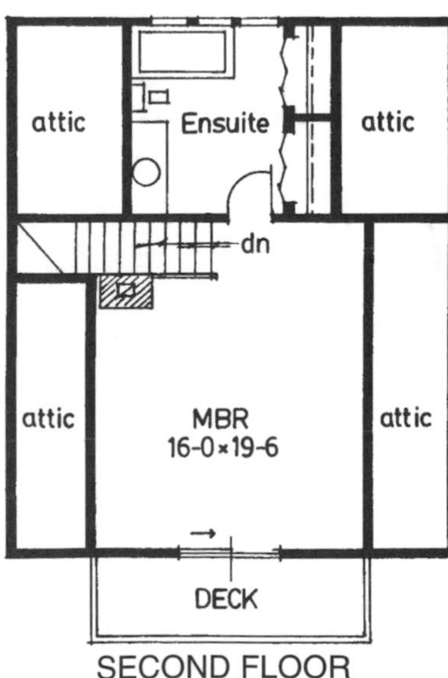

attic
Ensuite
attic
dn
attic
MBR
16-0×19-6
attic
DECK
SECOND FLOOR

No. 90847

An EXCLUSIVE DESIGN *By Westhome Planners, Ltd.*

Versatile Chalet

- This plan features:
  - — Two bedrooms
  - — Two full baths
- A Sun deck entry into a spacious Living Room/Dining Room with a fieldstone fireplace, a large window and a sliding glass door
- A well-appointed Kitchen with extended counter space and easy access to the Dining Room and the Utility area
- A first floor bedroom adjoins a full hall bath
- A spacious Master Bedroom, with a private Deck, a Suite bath and plenty of storage

FIRST FLOOR — 864 SQ. FT.
SECOND FLOOR — 496 SQ. FT.

TOTAL LIVING AREA:
1,360 SQ. FT.

PLAN NO. 24701

Refer to **Pricing Schedule B** on the order form for pricing information

Convenient Floor Plan

- This plan features:
  - — Three bedrooms
  - — Two full baths
- Central Foyer leads to Den/Guest room with arched window below vaulted ceiling and Living Room accented by two-sided fireplace
- Efficient, U-shaped Kitchen with peninsula counter/breakfast bar serving Dining Room and adjacent Utility/Pantry
- Master Suite features large walk-in closet and private bath with double vanity and whirlpool tub
- Two additional bedrooms with ample closet space share full bath

MAIN FLOOR — 1,625 SQ. FT.
GARAGE — 455 SQ. FT.
BASEMENT — 1,625 SQ. FT.

TOTAL LIVING AREA :
1,625 SQ. FT.

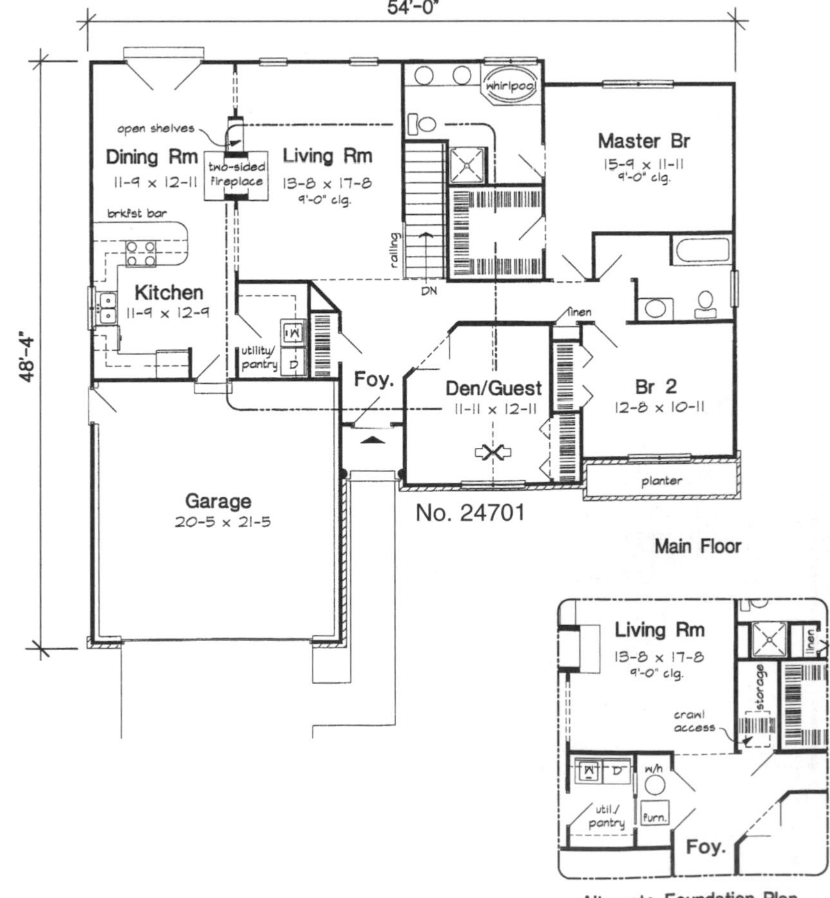

54'-0"
48'-4"
open shelves
Dining Rm
11-9 x 12-11
two-sided fireplace
Living Rm
13-8 x 17-8
9'-0" clg.
whirlpool
Master Br
15-9 x 11-11
9'-0" clg.
brkfst bar
Kitchen
11-9 x 12-9
railing
DN
linen
utility/ pantry
Foy.
Den/Guest
11-11 x 12-11
Br 2
12-8 x 10-11
planter
Garage
20-5 x 21-5
No. 24701
Main Floor
Living Rm
13-8 x 17-8
9'-0" clg.
storage
linen
crawl access
w/h
util/ pantry
furn.
Foy.
Alternate Foundation Plan

To order your Blueprints, call 1-800-235-5700

Refer to **Pricing Schedule A** on the order form for pricing information

PLAN NO. 24700

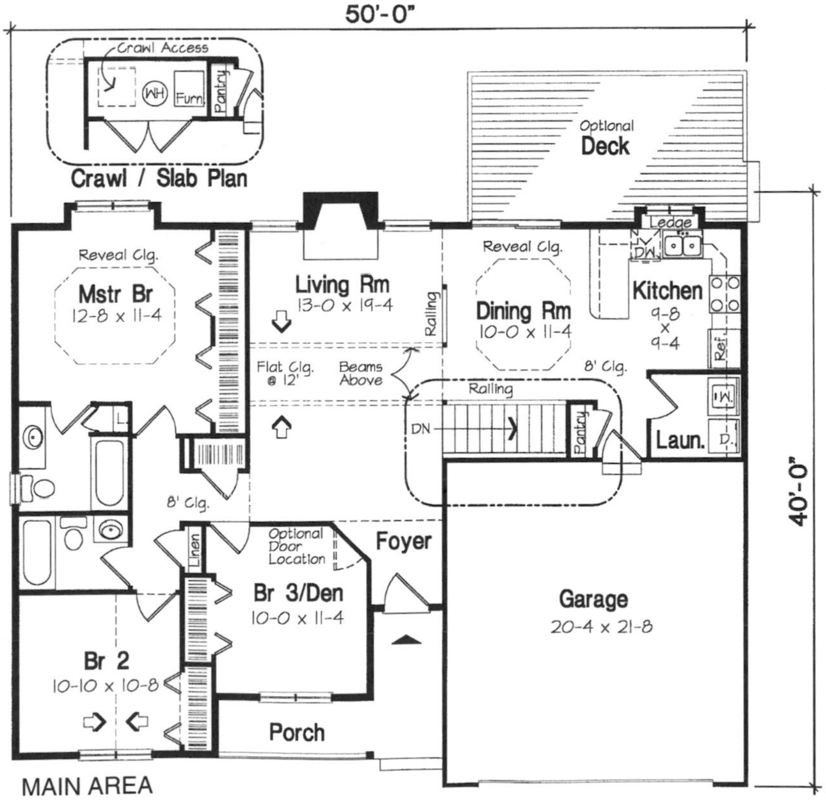

Fan-lights Highlight Facade

- This plan features:
  - — Three bedrooms
  - — Two full baths
- Front Porch entry leads into an open Living Room, accented by a hearth fireplace below a sloped ceiling
- Efficient Kitchen with a peninsula counter convenient to the Laundry, Garage, Dining area and Deck
- Master Bedroom accented by a decorative ceiling, a double closet and a private bath
- Two additional bedrooms with decorative windows and ample closets share a full bath

MAIN FLOOR — 1,312 SQ. FT.
BASEMENT — 1,293 SQ. FT.
GARAGE — 459 SQ. FT.

TOTAL LIVING AREA: 1,312 SQ. FT.

50'-0"
40'-0"
Crawl Access
WH
Furn.
Pantry
Crawl / Slab Plan
Optional Deck
Reveal Clg.
Mstr Br 12-8 x 11-4
Living Rm 13-0 x 19-4
Railing
Dining Rm 10-0 x 11-4
Ledge
DW
Kitchen 9-8 x 9-4
Ref.
Flat Clg. @ 12'
Beams Above
8' Clg.
Railing
DN
Pantry
W
D
Laun.
8' Clg.
Linen
Optional Door Location
Foyer
Br 3/Den 10-0 x 11-4
Garage 20-4 x 21-8
Br 2 10-10 x 10-8
Porch

MAIN AREA
No. 24700

PLAN NO. 94308

Refer to **Pricing Schedule Z** on the order form for pricing information

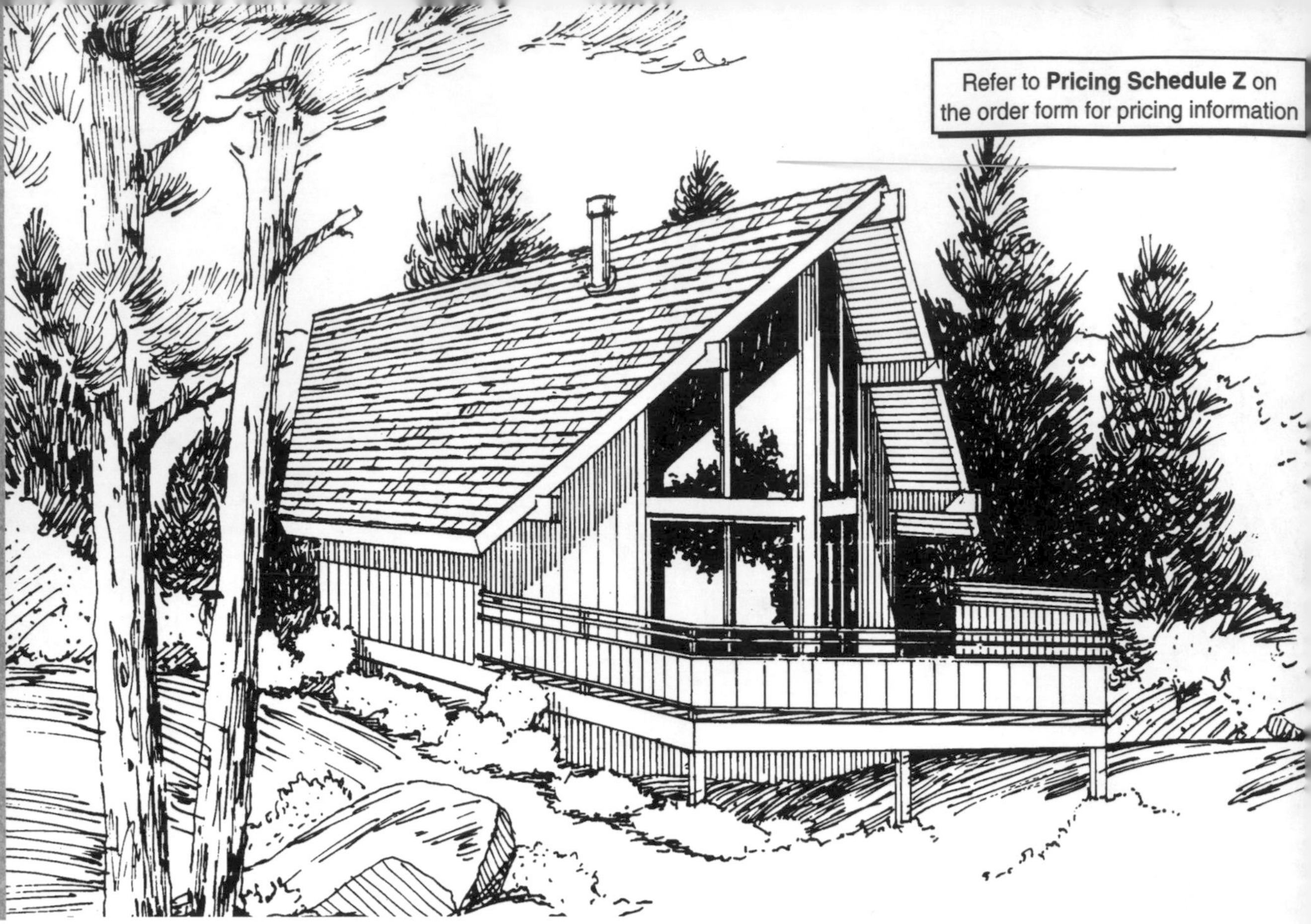

Cozy Hideaway

- This plan features:
- — One bedroom
- — One full bath
- Two levels of window to enjoy the surroundings
- Kitchen and living room with vaulted ceilings give a spacious feel
- Efficient kitchen layout which is highlighted by a corner sink.
- Living Room equipped with a sofa sleeper
- Loft overlooks the living room with added storage

MAIN FLOOR — 950 SQ. FT.

TOTAL LIVING AREA: 950 SQ. FT.

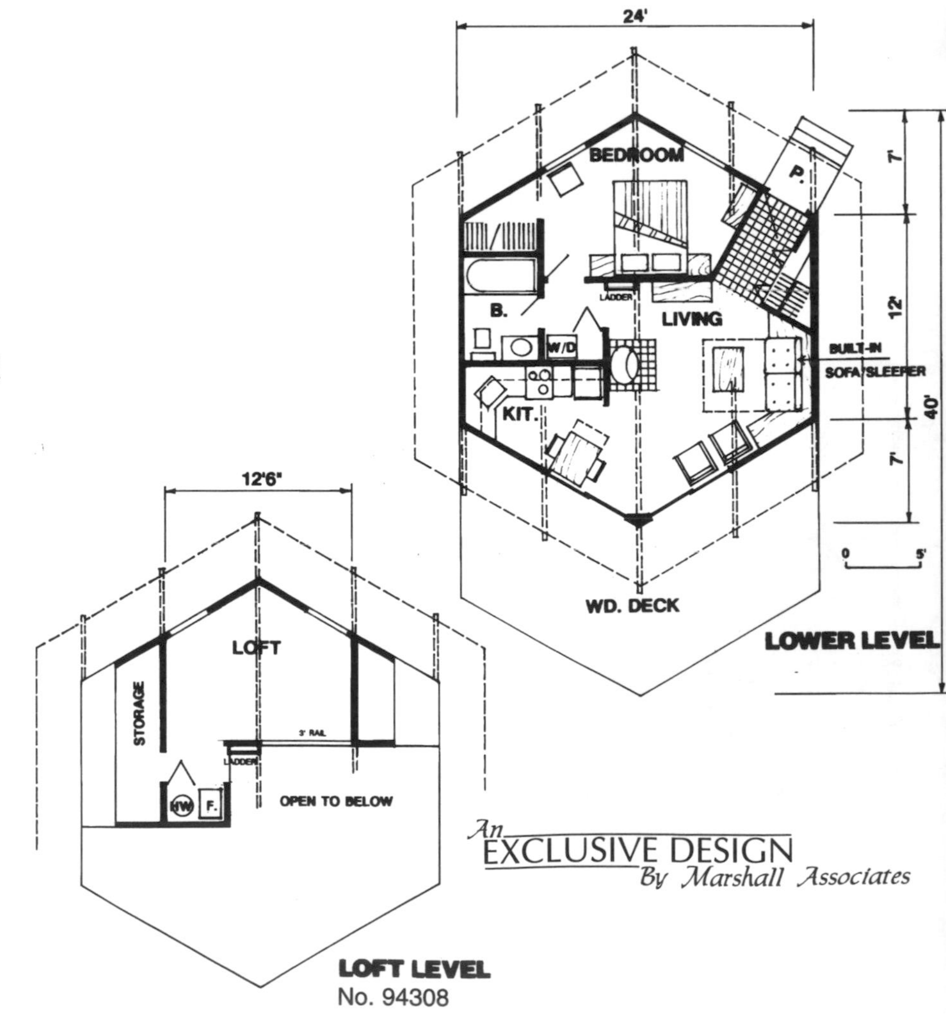
24'
BEDROOM
P.
B.
LADDER
LIVING
W/D
BUILT-IN SOFA/SLEEPER
KIT.
7'
12'
7'
40'
0
5'
WD. DECK
LOWER LEVEL
12'6"
LOFT
STORAGE
3' RAIL
LADDER
HW
F.
OPEN TO BELOW
LOFT LEVEL
No. 94308

An EXCLUSIVE DESIGN By Marshall Associates

Refer to **Pricing Schedule A** on the order form for pricing information

PLAN NO. 24320

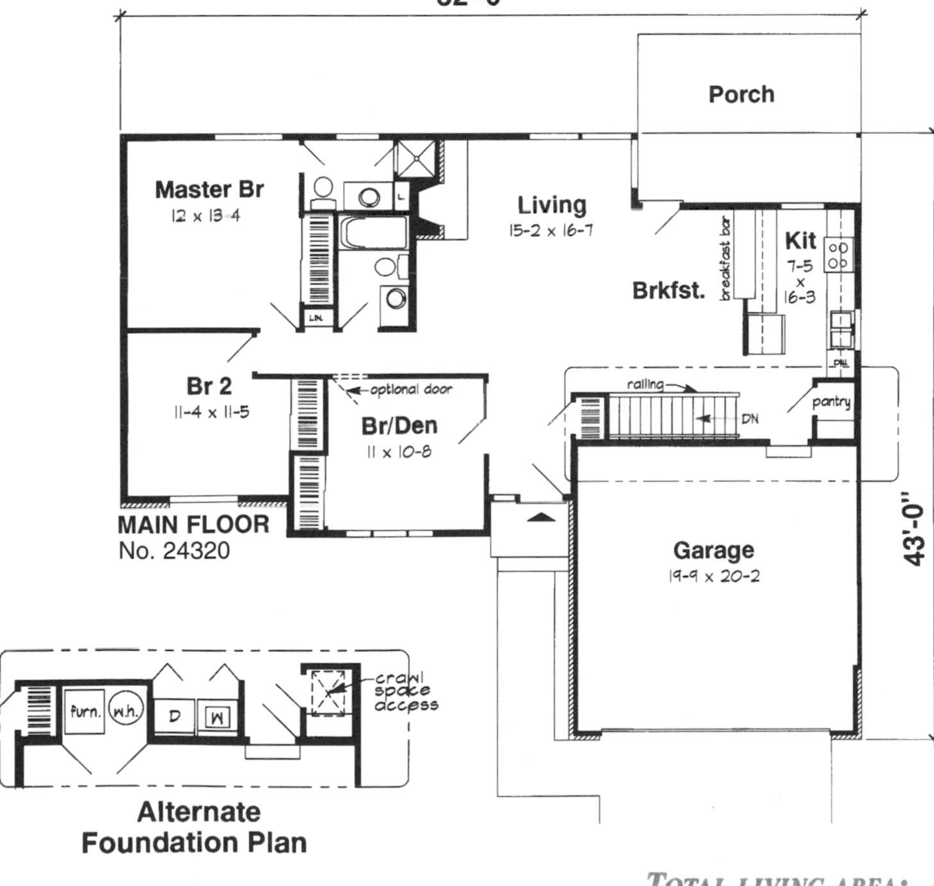

52'-0"
Porch
Master Br
12 x 13-4
Living
15-2 x 16-7
breakfast bar
Kit
7-5
x
16-3
Brkfst.
Br 2
11-4 x 11-5
optional door
Br/Den
11 x 10-8
railing
DN
pantry
Garage
19-9 x 20-2
43'-0"
furn.
w.h.
D
W
crawl space access

MAIN FLOOR
No. 24320

Alternate Foundation Plan

Step Saving One-Floor Living

- This plan features:
  - — Three bedrooms
  - — Two full baths
- A covered entrance leads to the Foyer and opens into the Living, Breakfast and Kitchen areas
- A fireplace and corner windows in Living area
- A galley Kitchen offers a breakfast bar, a built-in pantry and easy access to the covered Porch and Garage
- The Master Bedroom features a double closet and a private bath
- Two additional bedrooms sharing a full hall bath
- No materials list available

MAIN FLOOR — 1,235 SQ. FT.
GARAGE — 425 SQ. FT.

TOTAL LIVING AREA:
1,235 SQ. FT.

An EXCLUSIVE DESIGN
By Marshall Associates

Refer to **Pricing Schedule B** on the order form for pricing information

PLAN NO. 94315

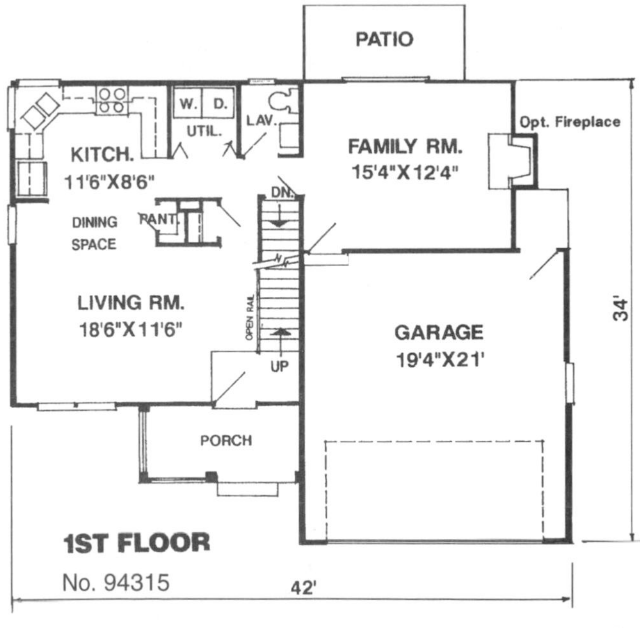

PATIO
W.
D.
UTIL.
LAV.
Opt. Fireplace
KITCH.
11'6"X8'6"
FAMILY RM.
15'4"X12'4"
DN.
DINING SPACE
PANT.
LIVING RM.
18'6"X11'6"
OPEN RAIL
GARAGE
19'4"X21'
34'
UP
PORCH
1ST FLOOR
No. 94315
42'

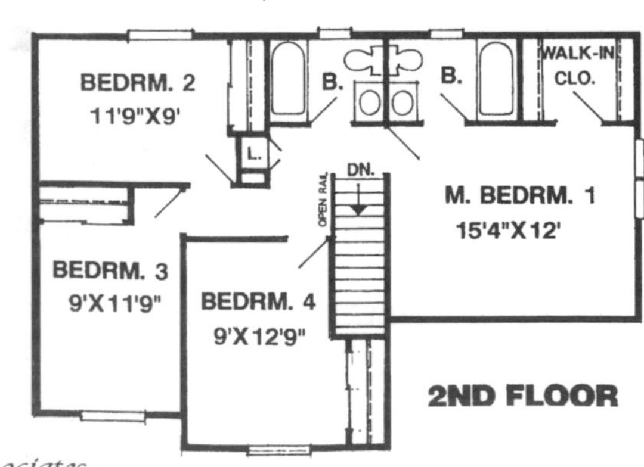

BEDRM. 2
11'9"X9'
B.
B.
WALK-IN CLO.
L.
DN.
OPEN RAIL
M. BEDRM. 1
15'4"X12'
BEDRM. 3
9'X11'9"
BEDRM. 4
9'X12'9"
2ND FLOOR

An EXCLUSIVE DESIGN By Marshall Associates

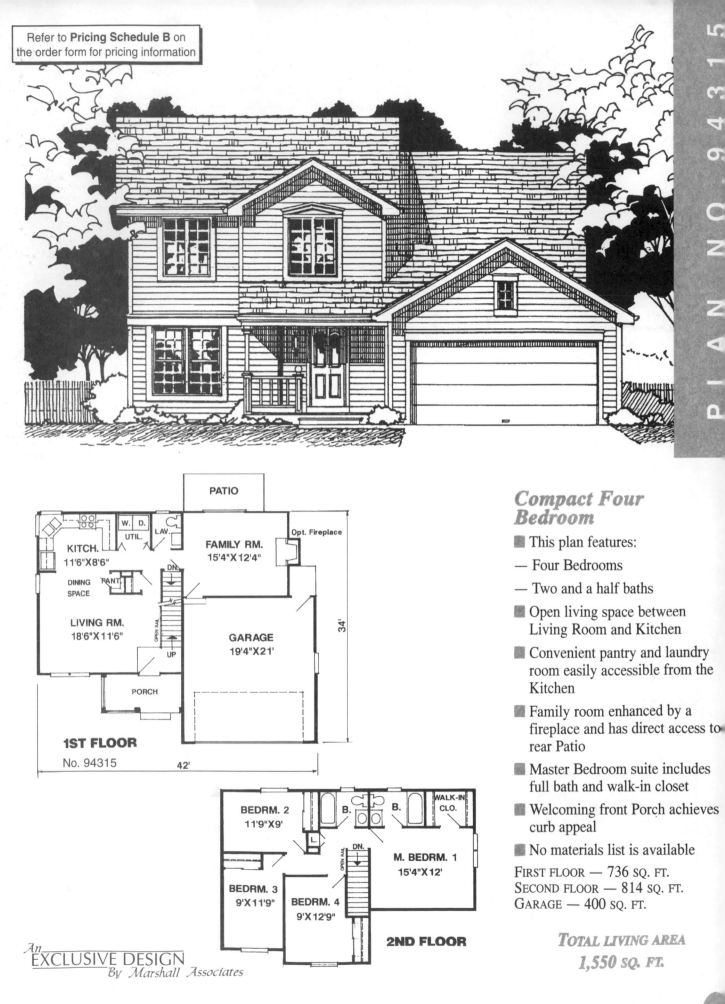

Compact Four Bedroom

- This plan features:
  - — Four Bedrooms
  - — Two and a half baths
- Open living space between Living Room and Kitchen
- Convenient pantry and laundry room easily accessible from the Kitchen
- Family room enhanced by a fireplace and has direct access to rear Patio
- Master Bedroom suite includes full bath and walk-in closet
- Welcoming front Porch achieves curb appeal
- No materials list is available

FIRST FLOOR — 736 SQ. FT.
SECOND FLOOR — 814 SQ. FT.
GARAGE — 400 SQ. FT.

TOTAL LIVING AREA 1,550 SQ. FT.

Refer to **Pricing Schedule B** on the order form for pricing information

PLAN NO. 92523

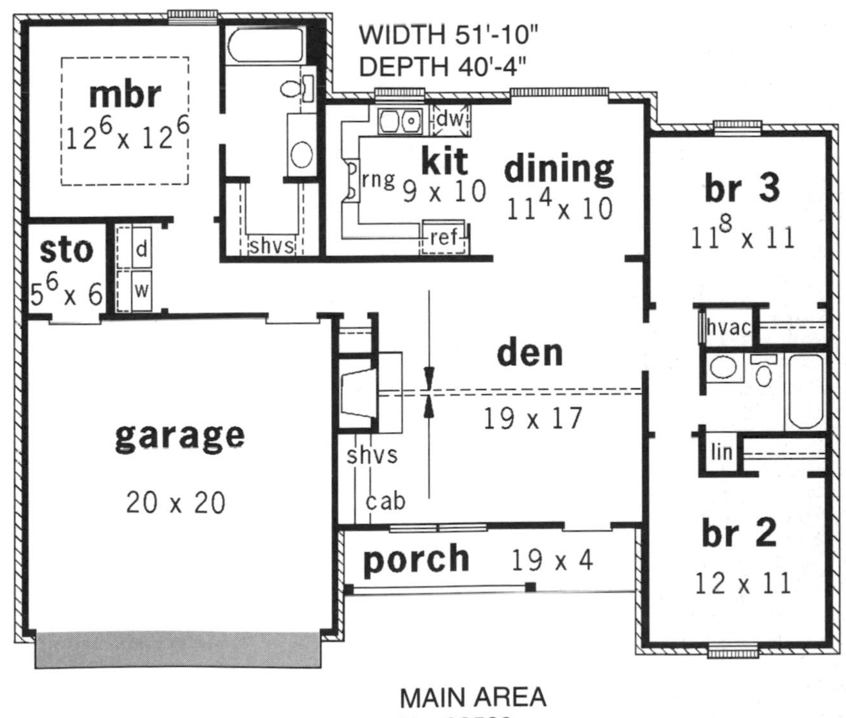
WIDTH 51'-10"
DEPTH 40'-4"
mbr
12^6 x 12^6
shvs
kit
9 x 10
rng
dw
ref
dining
11^4 x 10
br 3
11^8 x 11
sto
5^6 x 6
d
w
hvac
den
19 x 17
garage
20 x 20
shvs
cab
lin
br 2
12 x 11
porch
19 x 4

MAIN AREA
No. 92523

Private Master Suite

- This plan features:
- — Three bedrooms
- — Two full baths
- A spacious Great Room enhanced by a vaulted ceiling and fireplace
- A well-equipped Kitchen with windowed double sink
- A secluded Master Suite with decorative ceiling, private Master Bath, and walk-in closet
- Two additional bedrooms sharing hall bath
- This plan is available with a crawl space or slab foundation — please specify when ordering

MAIN FLOOR — 1,293 SQ. FT.
GARAGE — 433 SQ. FT.

TOTAL LIVING AREA:
1,293 SQ. FT.

PLAN NO. 24302

Refer to **Pricing Schedule A** on the order form for pricing information

An
EXCLUSIVE DESIGN
By Marshall Associates

Champagne Style on a Soda-Pop Budget

- This plan features:
  - Three bedrooms
  - Two full baths
- Multiple gables, circle-top windows, and a unique exterior setting this delightful Ranch apart in any neighborhood
- Living and Dining Rooms flowing together to create a very roomy feeling
- Sliding doors leading from the Dining Room to a covered patio
- A Master Bedroom with a private Bath

MAIN AREA — 988 SQ. FT.
BASEMENT — 988 SQ. FT.
GARAGE — 280 SQ. FT
OPTIONAL 2-CAR GARAGE — 384 SQ. FT.

TOTAL LIVING AREA: 988 SQ. FT.

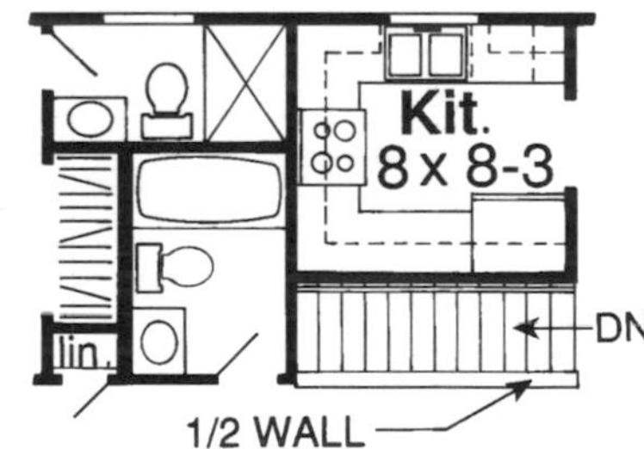
Kit.
8 x 8-3
DN
lin.
1/2 WALL

Basement Option

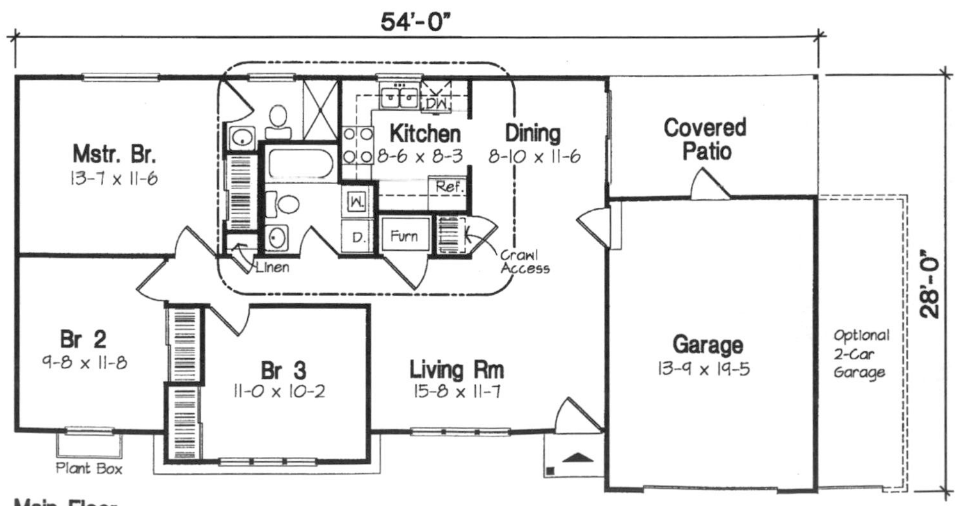
54'-0"
28'-0"
Mstr. Br.
13-7 x 11-6
Kitchen
8-6 x 8-3
Dining
8-10 x 11-6
DW
Ref.
W.
D.
Furn
Linen
Crawl Access
Covered Patio
Br 2
9-8 x 11-8
Br 3
11-0 x 10-2
Living Rm
15-8 x 11-7
Garage
13-9 x 19-5
Optional 2-Car Garage
Plant Box

Main Floor
No. 24302

Refer to **Pricing Schedule A** on the order form for pricing information

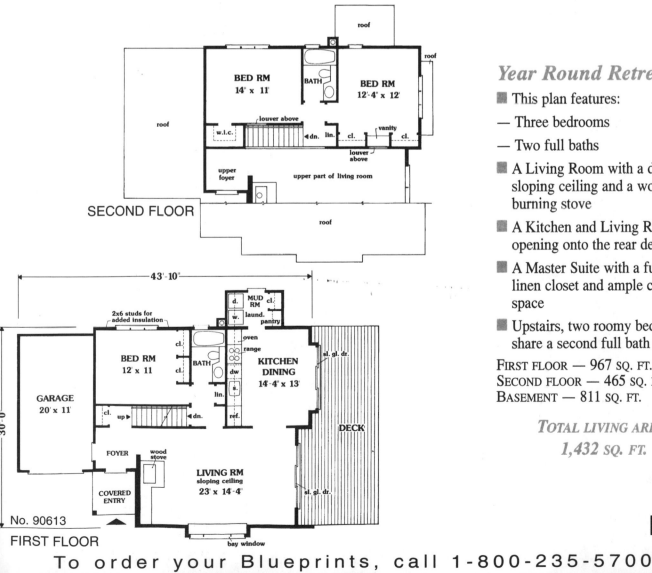

PLAN NO. 90613

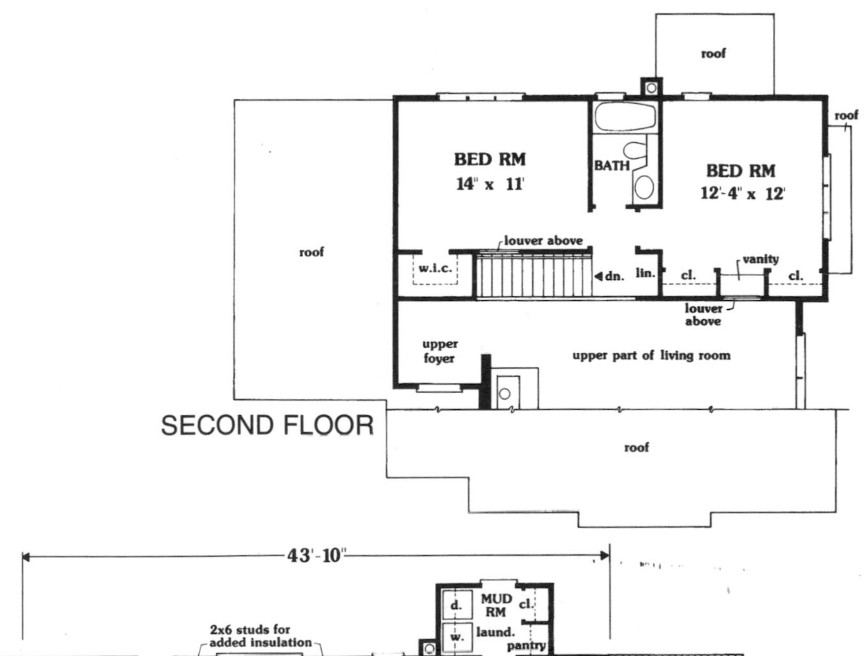

roof
roof
BED RM
14" x 11'
BATH
BED RM
12'-4" x 12'
louver above
w.i.c.
dn.
lin.
cl.
vanity
cl.
louver above
upper foyer
upper part of living room
SECOND FLOOR 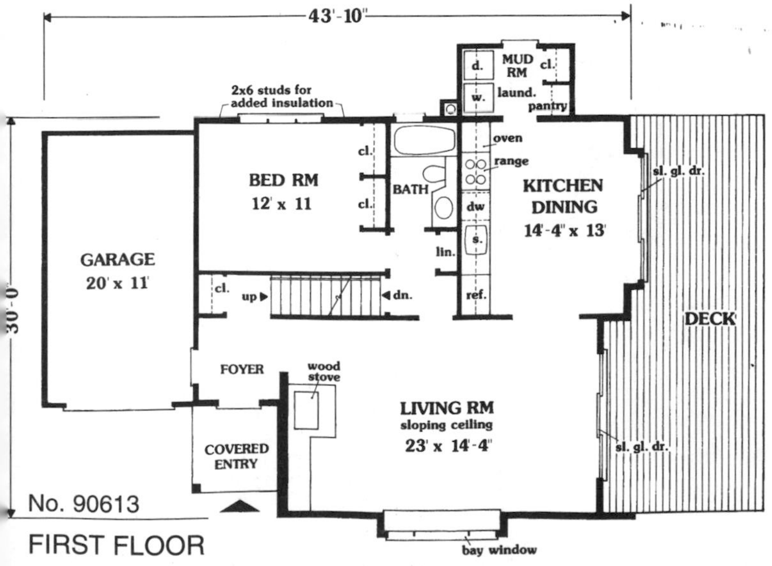
roof
43'-10"
MUD RM
d.
w.
cl.
laund.
pantry
2x6 studs for added insulation
oven
range
BED RM
12' x 11
cl.
cl.
BATH
dw
s.
KITCHEN DINING
14'-4" x 13'
sl. gl. dr.
lin.
GARAGE
20' x 11'
cl.
up
dn.
ref.
DECK
30'-0"
FOYER
wood stove
LIVING RM
sloping ceiling
23' x 14'-4"
sl. gl. dr.
COVERED ENTRY
No. 90613
FIRST FLOOR
bay window

Year Round Retreat

- This plan features:
  - — Three bedrooms
  - — Two full baths
- A Living Room with a dramatic sloping ceiling and a wood burning stove
- A Kitchen and Living Room opening onto the rear deck
- A Master Suite with a full bath, linen closet and ample closet space
- Upstairs, two roomy bedrooms share a second full bath

FIRST FLOOR — 967 SQ. FT.
SECOND FLOOR — 465 SQ. FT.
BASEMENT — 811 SQ. FT.

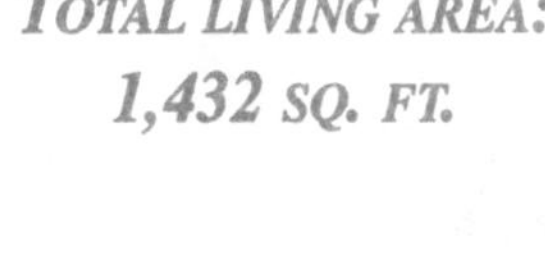

TOTAL LIVING AREA:
1,432 SQ. FT.

PLAN NO. 94309

Refer to **Pricing Schedule A** on the order form for pricing information

An EXCLUSIVE DESIGN By Marshall Associates

Cozy Vacation Hide-Away

- This plan features:
- —Two bedrooms
- —One and three quarter baths
- Highly windowed Living Room offering a unrestricted view of surroundings
- Spacious deck expanding living space to the outdoors with a built-in grill
- Efficient Kitchen highlighted by a corner double sink and an eating bar
- Master Bedroom suite equipped with a walk-in closet and private three quarter bath
- Spiral staircase gaining access to loft area overlooking the Living Room
- No Material List available

MAIN FLOOR — 1,028 SQ. FT.
LOFT — 187 SQ. FT.

TOTAL LIVING AREA
1,215 SQ. FT.

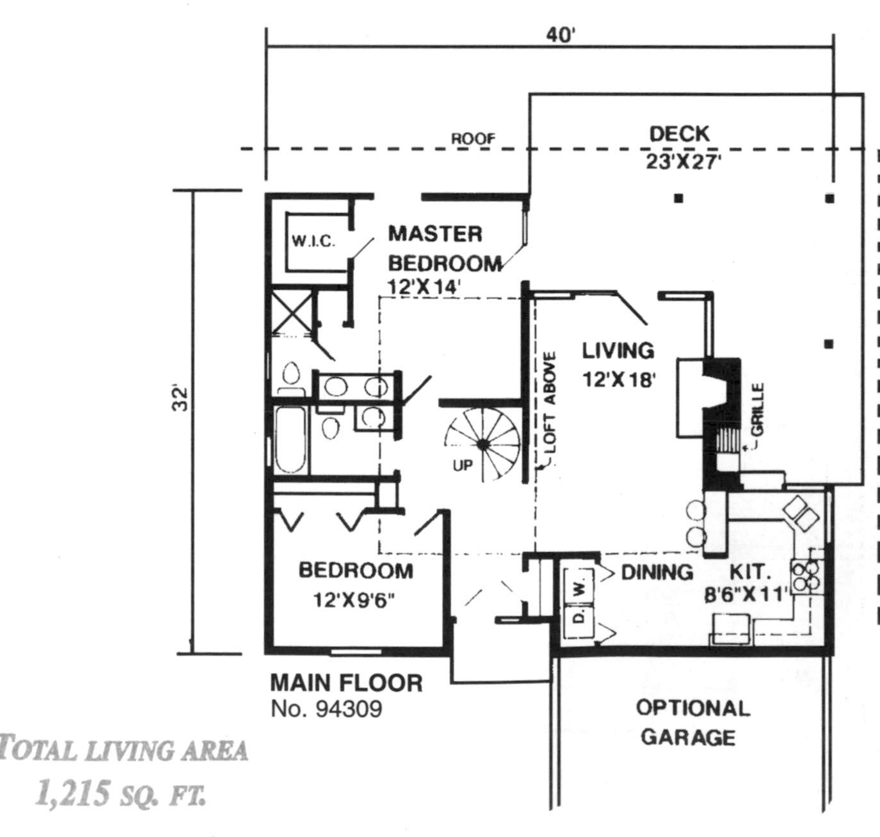
40'
ROOF
DECK
23'X27'
32'
W.I.C.
MASTER
BEDROOM
12'X14'
LIVING
12'X18'
LOFT ABOVE
GRILLE
UP
BEDROOM
12'X9'6"
D. W.
DINING
KIT.
8'6"X11'
MAIN FLOOR
No. 94309
OPTIONAL
GARAGE

Refer to **Pricing Schedule B** on the order form for pricing information

PLAN NO. 94801

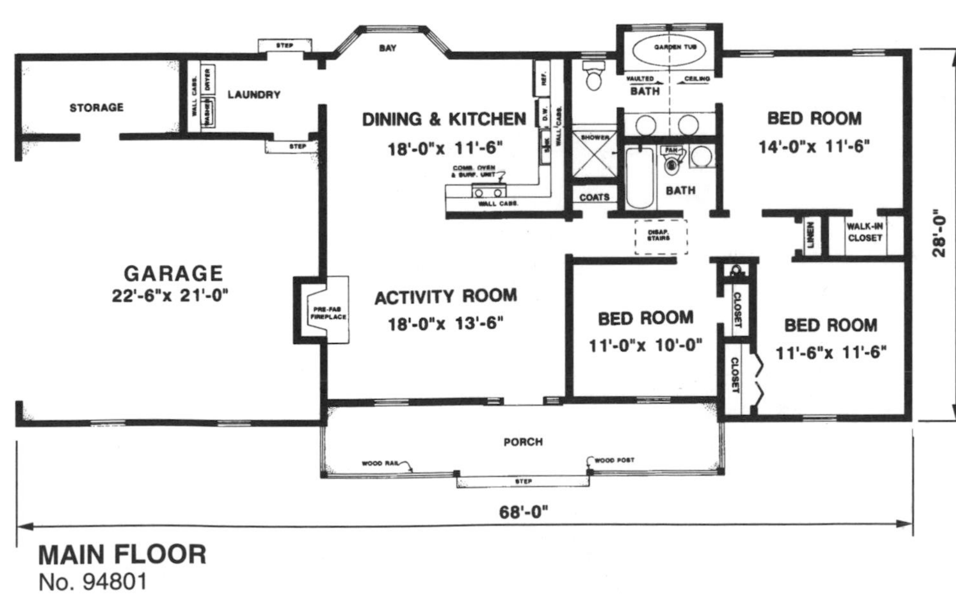

STORAGE
LAUNDRY
STEP
BAY
DINING & KITCHEN
18'-0"x 11'-6"
GARDEN TUB
BATH
SHOWER
COATS
BATH
BED ROOM
14'-0"x 11'-6"
LINEN
WALK-IN CLOSET
GARAGE
22'-6"x 21'-0"
PRE-FAB FIREPLACE
ACTIVITY ROOM
18'-0"x 13'-6"
BED ROOM
11'-0"x 10'-0"
CLOSET
CLOSET
BED ROOM
11'-6"x 11'-6"
28'-0"
PORCH
WOOD RAIL
WOOD POST
STEP
68'-0"

MAIN FLOOR
No. 94801

A Comfortable Informal Design

- This plan features:
  - — Three bedrooms
  - — Two full baths
- Warm, country front Porch with wood details
- Spacious Activity Room enhanced by a pre-fab fireplace
- Open and efficient Kitchen/Dining area highlighted by bay window, adjacent to Laundry and Garage entry
- Corner Master Bedroom offers a pampering bath with a garden tub and double vanity topped by a vaulted ceiling
- Two additional bedrooms with ample closets, share a full bath
- This plan is available with a slab or crawl space foundation — please specify when ordering

MAIN FLOOR — 1,300 SQ. FT.
GARAGE — 576 SQ. FT.

TOTAL LIVING AREA:
1,300 SQ. FT.

PLAN NO. 24321

Refer to **Pricing Schedule C** on the order form for pricing information

Sunny Breakfast Bay

- This plan features:
- — Three bedrooms
- — Three full baths
- Three sides of windows fill breakfast bay with natural light
- Formal Dining Room located to the other side of the kitchen for ease in serving
- Living Room open to the Dining Room highlighted by a cozy, corner fireplace
- Den/Guest Room with easy access to full bath
- Master Bedroom suite with large whirlpool private bath and walk-in closet
- No Materials List available

FIRST FLOOR — 1,013 SQ. FT.
SECOND FLOOR — 948 SQ. FT.
GARAGE — 393 SQ. FT.

TOTAL LIVING AREA
1,961 SQ. FT.

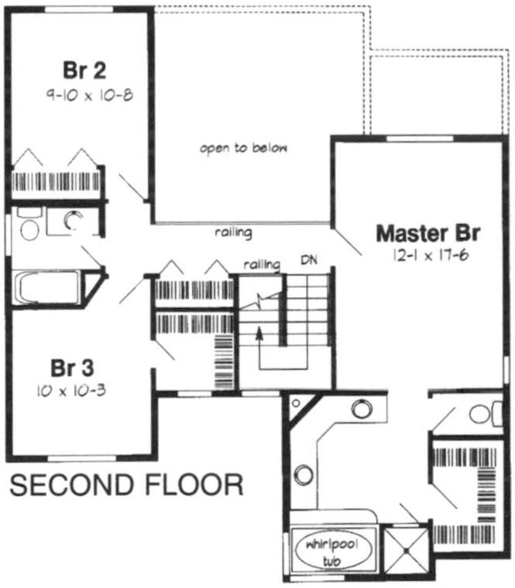

An EXCLUSIVE DESIGN By Marshall Associates

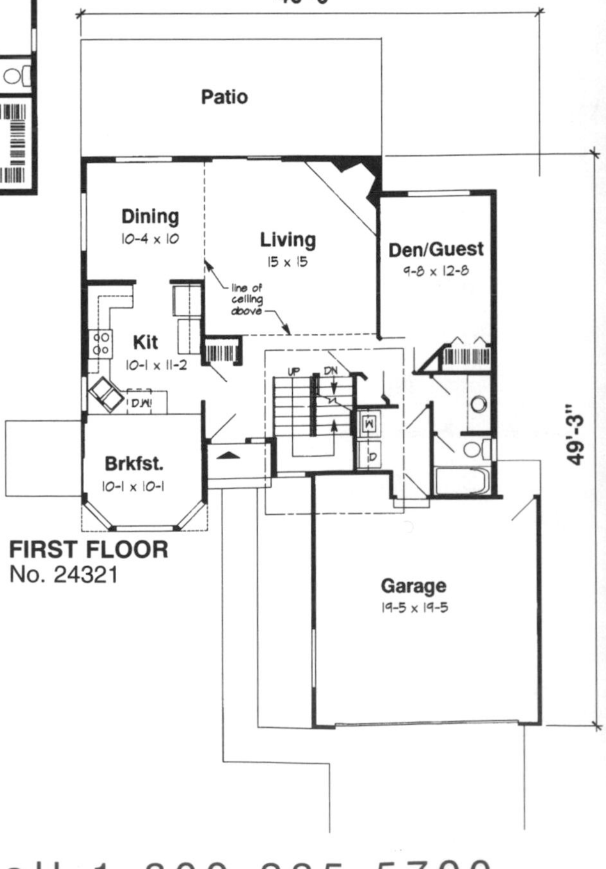

Br 2 9-10 x 10-8
open to below
railing
railing DN
Master Br 12-1 x 17-6
Br 3 10 x 10-3
whirlpool tub
SECOND FLOOR

40'-0"
Patio
Dining 10-4 x 10
Living 15 x 15
Den/Guest 9-8 x 12-8
line of ceiling above
Kit 10-1 x 11-2
DW
UP DN
Brkfst. 10-1 x 10-1
49'-3"
Garage 19-5 x 19-5
FIRST FLOOR
No. 24321

To order your Blueprints, call 1-800-235-5700

Refer to **Pricing Schedule A** on the order form for pricing information

PLAN NO. 90983

An EXCLUSIVE DESIGN By Westhome Planners, Ltd.

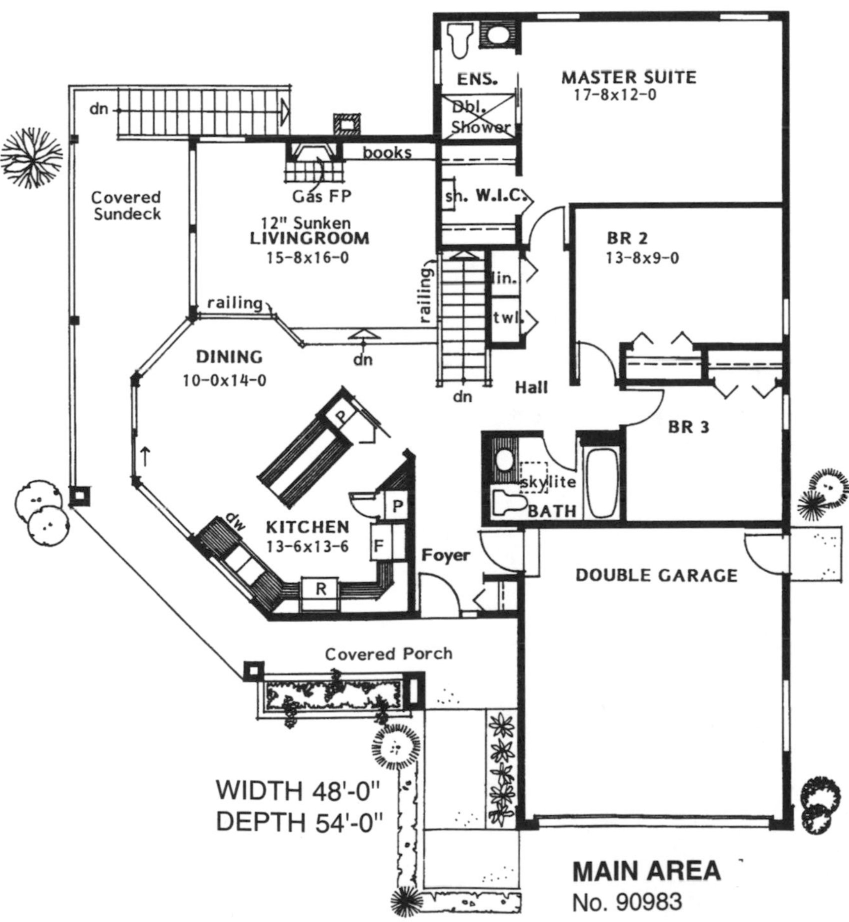

ENS.
Dbl. Shower
MASTER SUITE
17-8x12-0
dn
books
Covered Sundeck
Gas FP
12" Sunken
LIVINGROOM
15-8x16-0
sh. W.I.C.
BR 2
13-8x9-0
railing
lin.
twl.
DINING
10-0x14-0
dn
Hall
BR 3
skylite
BATH
KITCHEN
13-6x13-6
dw
P
F
R
Foyer
DOUBLE GARAGE
Covered Porch
WIDTH 48'-0"
DEPTH 54'-0"
MAIN AREA
No. 90983

Attractive Roof Lines

- This plan features:
- — Three bedrooms
- — One full and one three quarter baths
- An open floor plan shared by the sunken Living Room, Dining and Kitchen areas
- An unfinished daylight Basement which will provide future bedrooms, a bathroom and laundry facilities
- A Master Suite with a big walk-in closet and a private bath featuring a double shower

FIRST FLOOR — 1,396 SQ. FT.
BASEMENT — 1,396 SQ. FT.
GARAGE — 389 SQ. FT.

TOTAL LIVING AREA:
1,396 SQ. FT.

PLAN NO. 90611

Refer to **Pricing Schedule B** on the order form for pricing information

Solar Room More Than Just a Greenhouse

- This plan features:
- — Three bedrooms
- — Two full baths
- A passive design that will save on heating costs
- A heat-circulating fireplace in the Living Room adding atmosphere as well as warmth
- A Master Suite, with lofty views of the living area
- Two additional bedrooms with ample closet space and a shared full hall bath
- A slab foundation only

FIRST FLOOR — 1,120 SQ. FT.
SECOND FLOOR — 490 SQ. FT.
UTILITY ROOM — 122 SQ. FT.

TOTAL LIVING AREA:
1,732 SQ. FT.

roof
storage
cl
storage
cl
BATH
dn
MASTER BED RM
15'-4" x 14'-4"
roof
railing
SITTING RM
11'-4" x 8'-10'
balcony
sl. gl. dr.
balcony
upper part of living dining
SECOND FLOOR
8'-6"
28'-0"
40'-0"
BED RM
12'-8" x 10'-10"
cl
cl
cl
lin.
BED RM
14'-2" x 12'-0"
UTILITY
BATH
cl
cl
cl
ENTRY
d.
w.
laundry
stor
MUD RM
KITCH
9'-0" x 8'-4"
dw
storage
ref.
up
upper level over
LIVING RM
22'-6" x 18'-4"
DINING RM
No. 90611
heat-circulating fireplace
sl. gl. dr.
sl. gl. dr.
SOLAR RM
13'-8" x 9'-8"
DECK

FIRST FLOOR

To order your Blueprints, call 1-800-235-5700

Refer to **Pricing Schedule A** on the order form for pricing information

PLAN NO. 24240

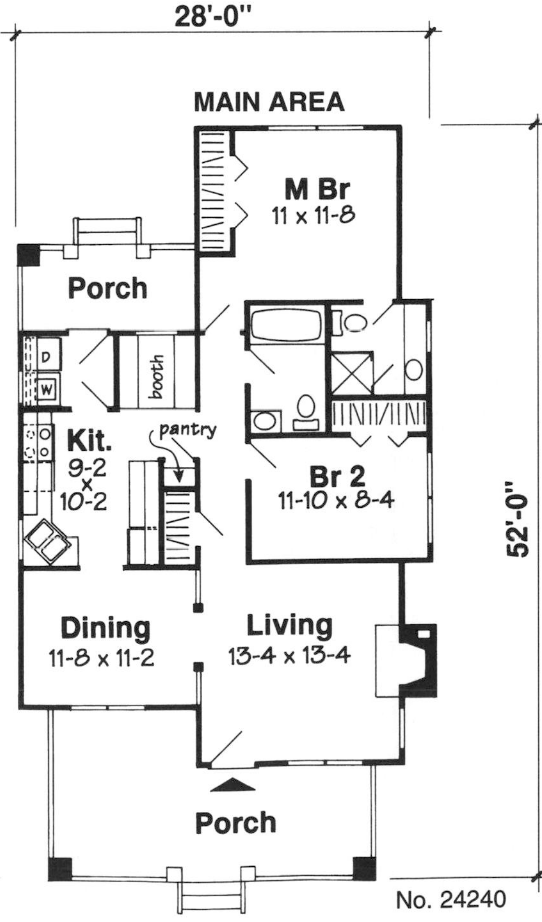

28'-0"
MAIN AREA
M Br
11 x 11-8
Porch
booth
D
W
pantry
Kit.
9-2
x
10-2
Br 2
11-10 x 8-4
52'-0"
Dining
11-8 x 11-2
Living
13-4 x 13-4
Porch
No. 24240

Be in Tune with the Elements

- This plan features:
  - — Two bedrooms
  - — One full baths and one three quarter bath
- Cozy front porch to enjoy three seasons
- A simple design allowing breezes to flow from front to back, heat to rise to the attic and cool air to settle
- A fireplaced Living Room
- A formal Dining Room next to the Kitchen
- A compact Kitchen with a breakfast nook and a pantry
- A rear entrance with a covered porch
- A Master Suite with a private bath

MAIN AREA — 964 SQ. FT.

TOTAL LIVING AREA:
964 SQ. FT.

PLAN NO. 93048

Refer to **Pricing Schedule A** on the order form for pricing information

For First Time Buyers

- This plan features:
- — Three bedrooms
- — Two full baths
- An efficiently designed Kitchen with a corner sink, ample counter space and a peninsula counter
- A sunny Breakfast Room with a convenient hide-away laundry center
- An expansive Family Room that includes a corner fireplace and direct access to the Patio
- A private Master Suite with a walk-in closet and a double vanity Bath
- Two additional bedrooms, both with walk-in closets, that share a full hall bath
- No materials list available for this plan

MAIN FLOOR — 1,310 SQ. FT.
GARAGE — 449 SQ. FT.

TOTAL LIVING AREA:
1,310 SQ. FT.

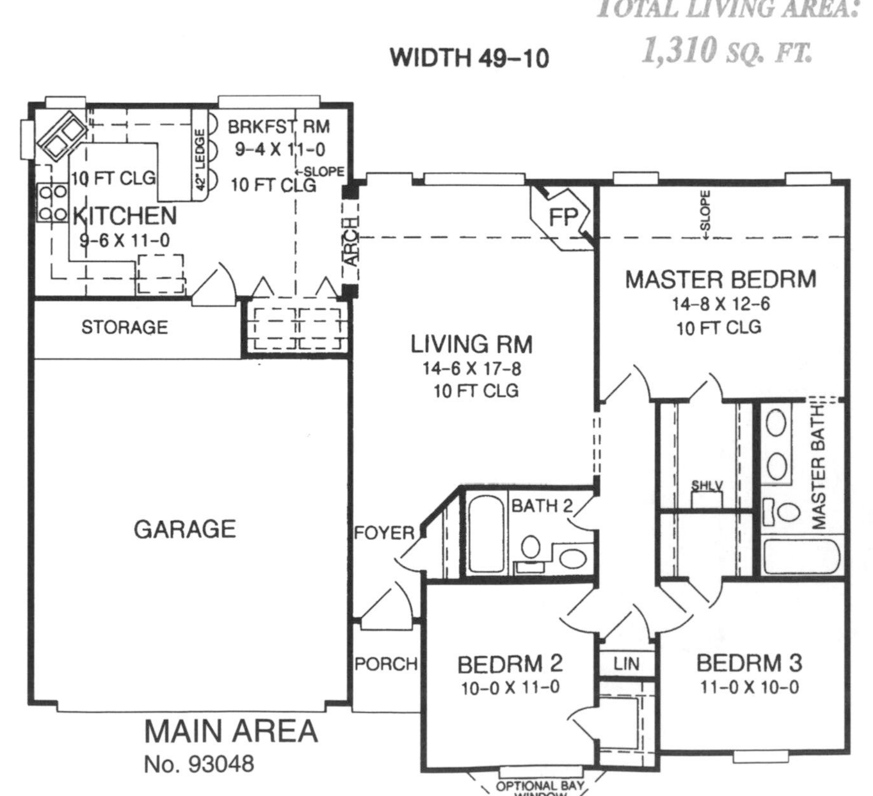

WIDTH 49–10
BRKFST RM
9–4 X 11–0
10 FT CLG
SLOPE
42" LEDGE
10 FT CLG
KITCHEN
9–6 X 11–0
ARCH
FP
SLOPE
MASTER BEDRM
14–8 X 12–6
10 FT CLG
STORAGE
LIVING RM
14–6 X 17–8
10 FT CLG
SHLV
MASTER BATH
GARAGE
BATH 2
FOYER
PORCH
BEDRM 2
10–0 X 11–0
LIN
BEDRM 3
11–0 X 10–0
MAIN AREA
No. 93048
OPTIONAL BAY WINDOW
DEPTH 40–6

To order your Blueprints, call 1-800-235-5700

Refer to **Pricing Schedule C** on the order form for pricing information

PLAN NO. 98316

54'–0"
57'–0"
Brkfst
10x12
10' Ceiling
Lanai
10' Ceiling
desk
Great Room
23x14
13' Ceiling
Master Suite
16-4x12-4
10' Ceiling
high glass
Kitchen
P
halfwall
D
W
F
niche
L
Den/Br3
10–8x14
Br 2
12-8x12-8
Garage
19-4x20-4
Courtyard

Floor Plan
No. 98316

For the Empty-Nester

- This plan features:
  - — Two bedrooms
  - — Two full baths
- A Great Room with a 13′ ceiling and access to the Lanai
- An island Kitchen with a built-in pantry, desk, and an open layout to the Breakfast area
- A Master Suite with walk-in closets and a private Master Bath
- A Den that can function as a third bedroom

FIRST FLOOR — 1,859 SQ. FT.
GARAGE — 393 SQ. FT.

TOTAL LIVING AREA:
1,859 SQ. FT.

PLAN NO. 90941

Refer to **Pricing Schedule E** on the order form for pricing information

Exciting Vaulted Sunken Living Room

- This plan features:

— Four bedrooms

— Two full and one half baths

- A dramatic, sunken Living Room with a vaulted ceiling, fireplace, and glass walls to enjoy the view
- A well-appointed, Kitchen with a peninsula counter and direct access to the Family Room, Dining Room or the sun deck
- A Master Suite with a walk-in closet and a private full bath
- A Family Room with direct access to the rear sun deck

FIRST FLOOR — 1,464 SQ. FT.
BASEMENT FLOOR— 1,187 SQ. FT.
GARAGE — 418 SQ. FT.

TOTAL LIVING AREA:
2,651 SQ. FT.

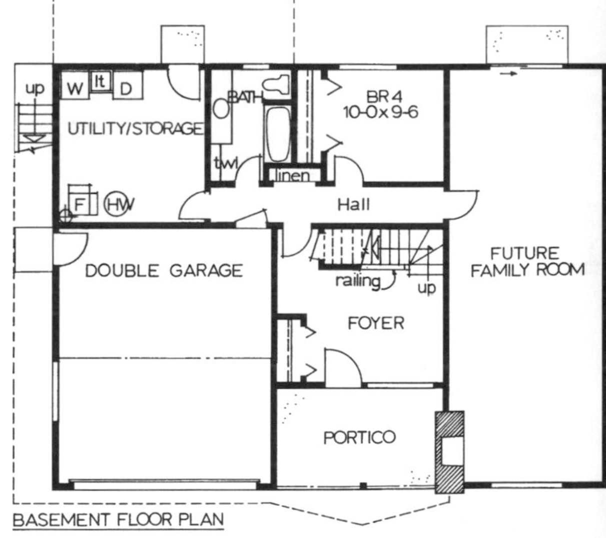

up
W
lt
D
UTILITY/STORAGE
BATH
twl
linen
BR 4
10-0x9-6
F
HW
Hall
DOUBLE GARAGE
railing
up
FUTURE
FAMILY ROOM
FOYER
PORTICO

BASEMENT FLOOR PLAN

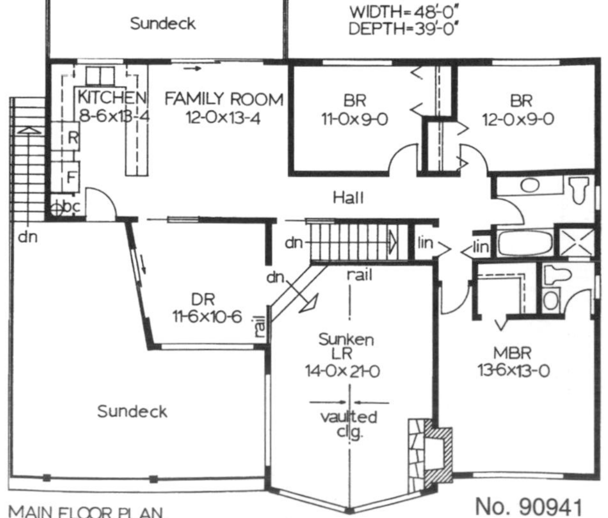

Sundeck
WIDTH=48'-0"
DEPTH=39'-0"
KITCHEN
8-6x13-4
FAMILY ROOM
12-0x13-4
BR
11-0x9-0
BR
12-0x9-0
R
F
bbc
Hall
dn
dn
lin
lin
dn
rail
DR
11-6x10-6
rail
Sunken
LR
14-0x21-0
MBR
13-6x13-0
Sundeck
vaulted
clg.

MAIN FLOOR PLAN

No. 90941

An EXCLUSIVE DESIGN
By Westhome Planners, Ltd.

To order your Blueprints, call 1-800-235-5700

Refer to **Pricing Schedule B** on the order form for pricing information

PLAN NO. 90859

An EXCLUSIVE DESIGN
By Westhome Planners, Ltd.

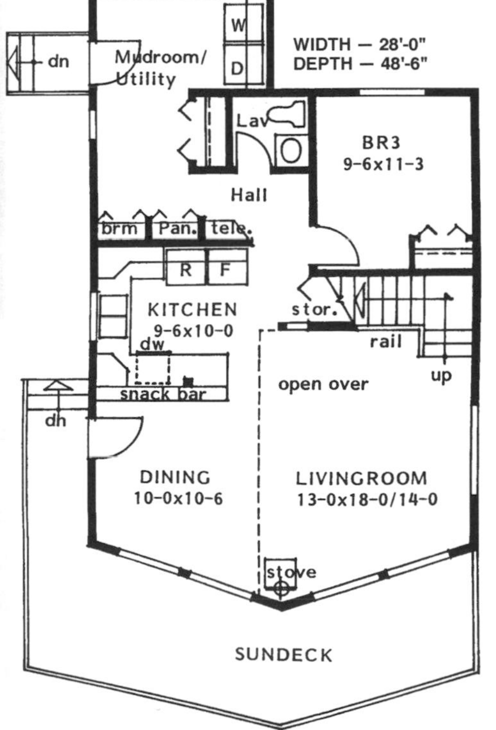

dn
Mudroom/ Utility
W
D
WIDTH — 28'-0"
DEPTH — 48'-6"
Lav
BR3
9-6x11-3
Hall
brm
Pan.
tele.
R
F
KITCHEN
9-6x10-0
dw
stor.
rail
snack bar
open over
up
dh
DINING
10-0x10-6
LIVINGROOM
13-0x18-0/14-0
stove
SUNDECK

FIRST FLOOR
No. 90859

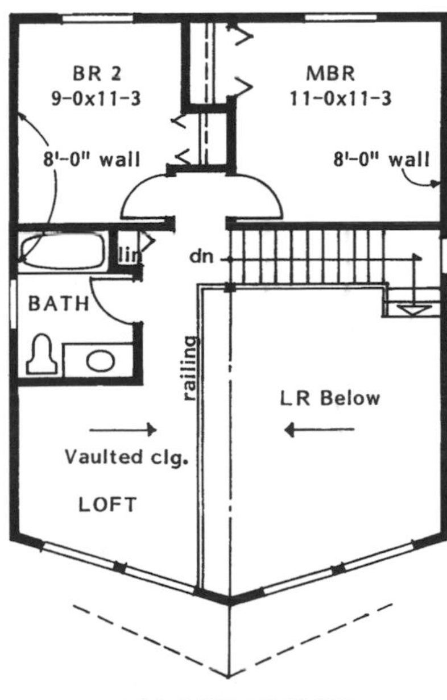

BR 2
9-0x11-3
MBR
11-0x11-3
8'-0" wall
8'-0" wall
lin
dn
BATH
railing
LR Below
Vaulted clg.
LOFT

SECOND FLOOR

Enjoy The View

- This plan features:
  - — Three bedrooms
  - — One and a half baths
- A wrap-around Sundeck
- A spacious Living/Dining Room with a vaulted ceiling and a wood stove flanked by a wall of glass
- A Mudroom/Utility entrance with a laundry area and ample closets
- An efficient, U-shaped Kitchen with a snack bar separating the Dining area
- A first floor bedroom adjacent to a half bath
- A second floor Master Bedroom, Loft and secondary bedroom sharing the full hall bath

FIRST FLOOR — 843 SQ. FT.
SECOND FLOOR — 768 SQ. FT.

TOTAL LIVING AREA:
1,611 SQ. FT.

PLAN NO. 24322

Refer to **Pricing Schedule E** on the order form for pricing information

Two-Story Entry Adds Elegance

- This plan features:
  - — Four or five bedrooms
  - — Three full baths
- A two-story entry with elegant curved staircase
- Formal Living and Dining Room with convenient built-ins
- A spacious Family Room with direct access to rear yard
- A well-appointed Kitchen with access to both Dining Room and Breakfast area
- A lavish Master Suite with a private Master Bath and walk-in closet
- Three additional bedrooms share a full bath
- No materials list available

FIRST FLOOR — 1,499 SQ. FT.
SECOND FLOOR — 1,168 SQ. FT.
GARAGE — 473 SQ. FT.

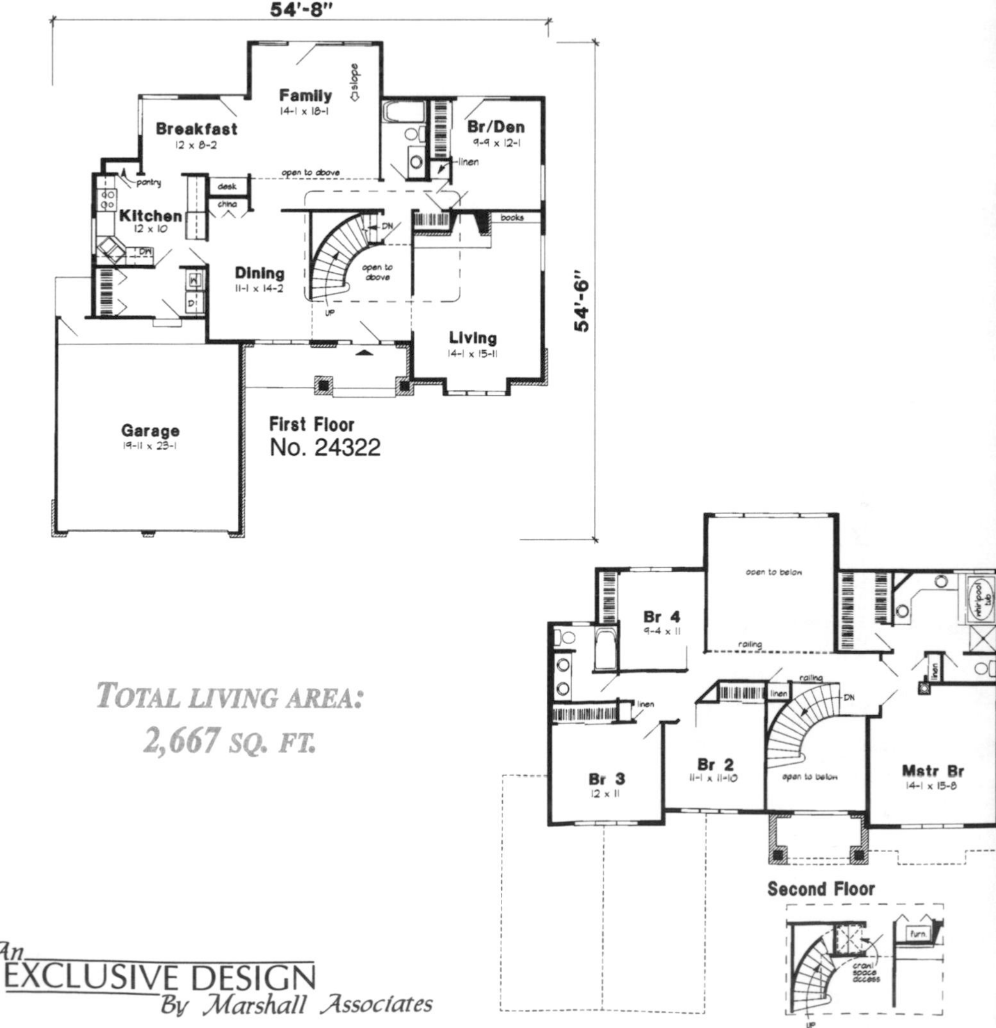
54'-8"
54'-6"
Family
14-1 x 18-1
Breakfast
12 x 8-2
Br/Den
9-9 x 12-1
Kitchen
12 x 10
Dining
11-1 x 14-2
Living
14-1 x 15-11
Garage
19-11 x 23-1
First Floor
No. 24322
Br 4
9-4 x 11
Br 3
12 x 11
Br 2
11-1 x 11-10
Matr Br
14-1 x 15-8
Second Floor

TOTAL LIVING AREA:
2,667 SQ. FT.

An EXCLUSIVE DESIGN By Marshall Associates

To order your Blueprints, call 1-800-235-5700

Refer to **Pricing Schedule B** on the order form for pricing information

PLAN NO. 92283

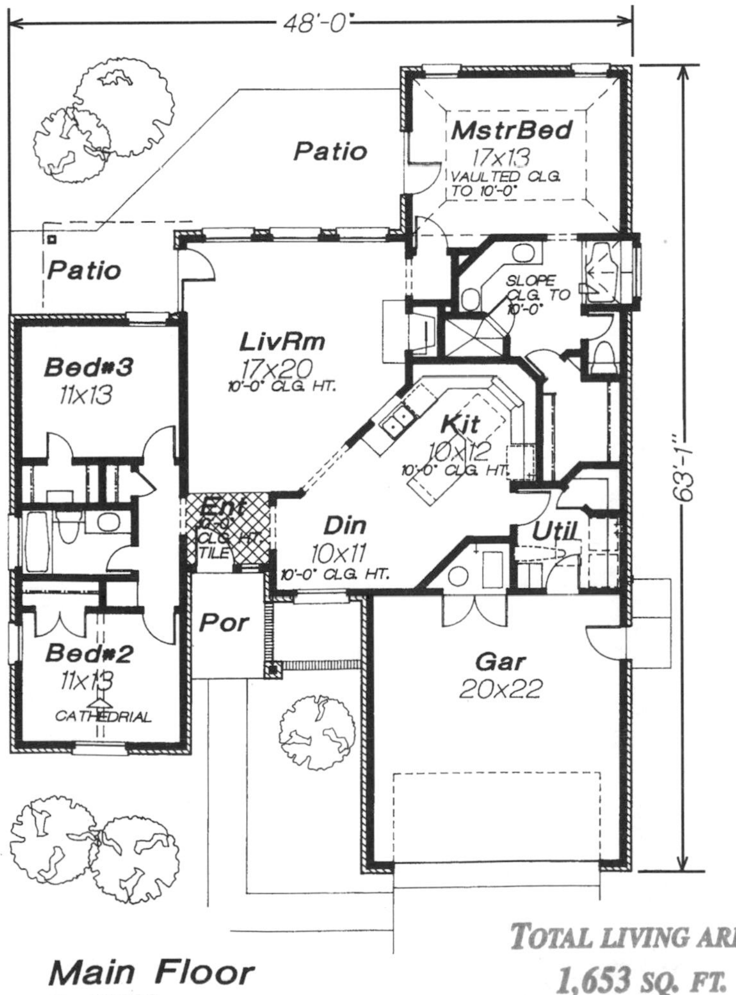

48'-0"
63'-1"
Patio
MstrBed
17x13
VAULTED CLG. TO 10'-0"
Patio
SLOPE CLG. TO 10'-0"
LivRm
17x20
10'-0" CLG. HT.
Bed#3
11x13
Kit
10x12
10'-0" CLG. HT.
Ent
10'-0" CLG. HT. TILE
Din
10x11
10'-0" CLG. HT.
Util
Por
Gar
20x22
Bed#2
11x13
CATHEDRAL

Main Floor
No. 92283

TOTAL LIVING AREA:
1,653 SQ. FT.

Style and Convenience

- This plan features:
- — Three bedrooms
- — Two full baths
- A sheltered Porch leads into an easy-care tile Entry
- Spacious Living Room offers a cozy fireplace, triple window and access to Patio
- An efficient Kitchen with a skylight, work island, Dining area, walk-in pantry and Utility/Garage entry
- Secluded Master Bedroom highlighted by a vaulted ceiling, access to Patio and a lavish bath
- Two additional bedrooms, one with a cathedral ceiling, share a full bath
- No materials list available for this plan

MAIN FLOOR — 1,653 SQ. FT.
GARAGE — 420 SQ. FT.

PLAN NO. 90629

Refer to **Pricing Schedule C** on the order form for pricing information

A Home For All Seasons

- This plan features:
- — Three bedrooms
- — Three full and one half baths
- All rooms with outdoor decks
- A Living Room with a heat-circulating fireplace
- A Kitchen with ample counter and cabinet space and easy access to the Dining Room and outdoor dining area
- A Master Bedroom with a heat-circulating fireplace, plush Master Bath and a walk-in closet
- A basement foundation only

FIRST FLOOR — 1,001 SQ. FT.
SECOND FLOOR — 712 SQ. FT.
LOWER FLOOR — 463 SQ. FT.

TOTAL LIVING AREA:
2,176 SQ. FT.

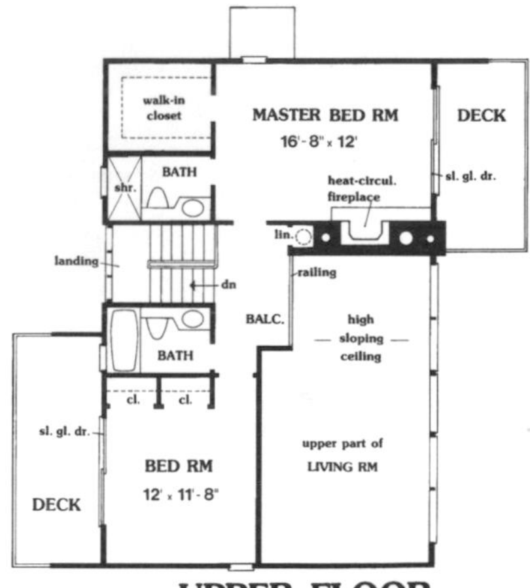
walk-in closet
MASTER BED RM
16'-8" x 12'
DECK
BATH
shr.
heat-circul. fireplace
sl. gl. dr.
lin.
landing
railing
dn
BALC.
high sloping ceiling
BATH
cl.
cl.
sl. gl. dr.
upper part of LIVING RM
BED RM
12' x 11'-8"
DECK

UPPER FLOOR

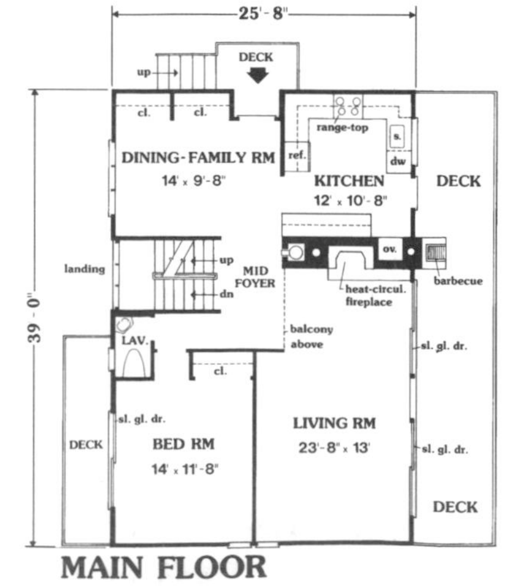
25'-8"
DECK
up
cl.
cl.
range-top
s.
ref.
dw
DINING-FAMILY RM
14' x 9'-8"
KITCHEN
12' x 10'-8"
DECK
landing
up
MID FOYER
dn
ov.
heat-circul. fireplace
barbecue
39'-0"
LAV.
balcony above
sl. gl. dr.
cl.
sl. gl. dr.
DECK
BED RM
14' x 11'-8"
LIVING RM
23'-8" x 13'
sl. gl. dr.
DECK

MAIN FLOOR
No. 90629

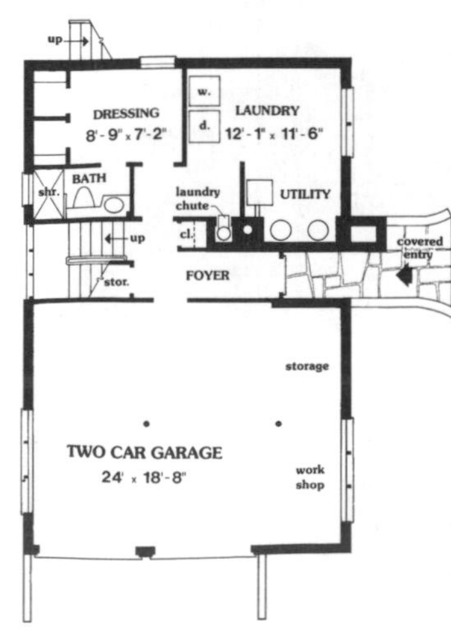
up
DRESSING
8'-9" x 7'-2"
w.
d.
LAUNDRY
12'-1" x 11'-6"
shr.
BATH
laundry chute
UTILITY
cl.
up
stor.
FOYER
covered entry
storage
TWO CAR GARAGE
24' x 18'-8"
work shop

LOWER FLOOR

To order your Blueprints, call 1-800-235-5700

Refer to **Pricing Schedule B** on the order form for pricing information

PLAN NO. 24326

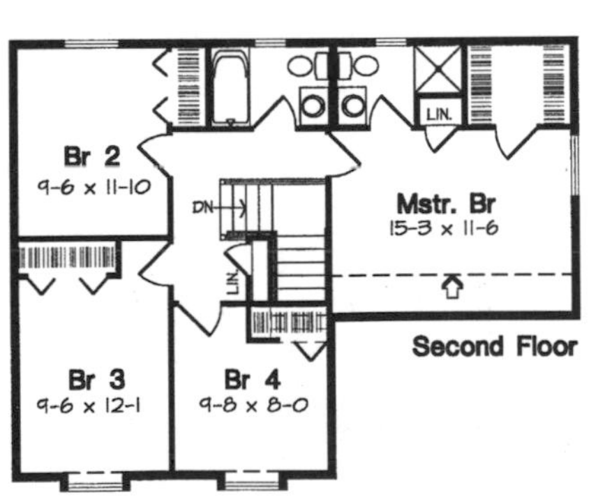

Br 2
9-6 x 11-10
Mstr. Br
15-3 x 11-6
LIN.
DN
LIN
Br 3
9-6 x 12-1
Br 4
9-8 x 8-0
Second Floor

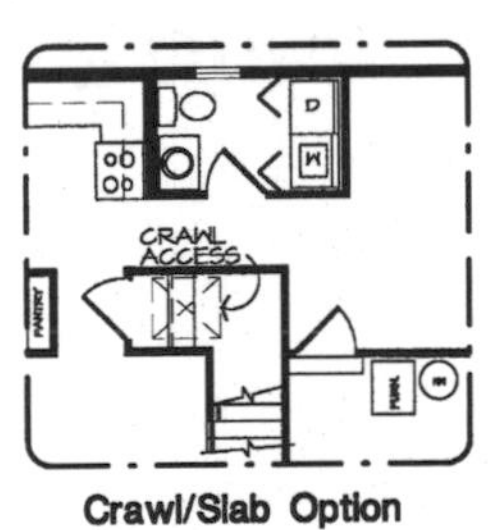

CRAWL ACCESS
PANTRY
Crawl/Slab Option

TOTAL LIVING AREA:
1,505 SQ. FT.

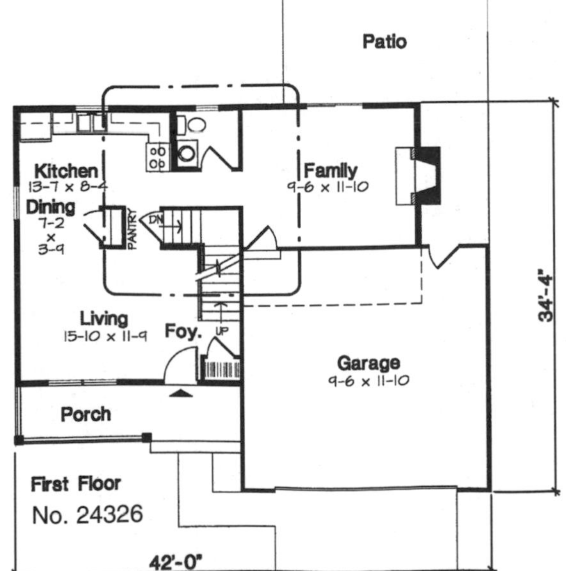

Patio
Kitchen
13-7 x 8-4
Dining
7-2 x 3-9
PANTRY
DN
Family
9-6 x 11-10
Living
15-10 x 11-9
Foy.
UP
Garage
9-6 x 11-10
34'-4"
Porch
First Floor
No. 24326
42'-0"

Fireplace-Equipped Family Room

- This plan features:
  - Four bedrooms
  - Two full baths and one half bath
- A lovely front porch shading the entrance
- A spacious Living Room that opens into the Dining Area which flows into the efficient Kitchen
- A Family Room equipped with a cozy fireplace and sliding glass doors to a patio
- A Master Suite with a large walk-in closet and a private bath with a step-in shower
- Three additional bedrooms that share a full hall bath

FIRST FLOOR — 692 SQ. FT.
SECOND FLOOR — 813 SQ. FT.
BASEMENT — 699 SQ. FT.
GARAGE — 484 SQ. FT.

An EXCLUSIVE DESIGN By Marshall Associates

PLAN NO. 96418

Refer to **Pricing Schedule B** on the order form for pricing information

B. NATHAN

© 1990 Donald A. Gardner Architects, Inc.

Compact Three Bedroom

- This plan features:
—Three bedrooms
—Two full baths
- Contemporary interior punctuated by elegant columns
- Dormers above the covered porch light the foyer leading to the dramatic Great Room crowned in a cathedral ceiling and enhanced by a fireplace
- Great Room opens to the island Kitchen with Breakfast area and access to a spacious rear deck
- Tray ceilings adding interest to the Bedroom/Study, Dining Room and the Master Bedroom
- Luxurious Master Bedroom suite highlighted by a walk-in closet and a bath with dual vanity, separate shower and a pampering whirlpool tub

MAIN FLOOR — 1,452 SQ. FT.
GARAGE AND STORAGE — 427 SQ. FT.

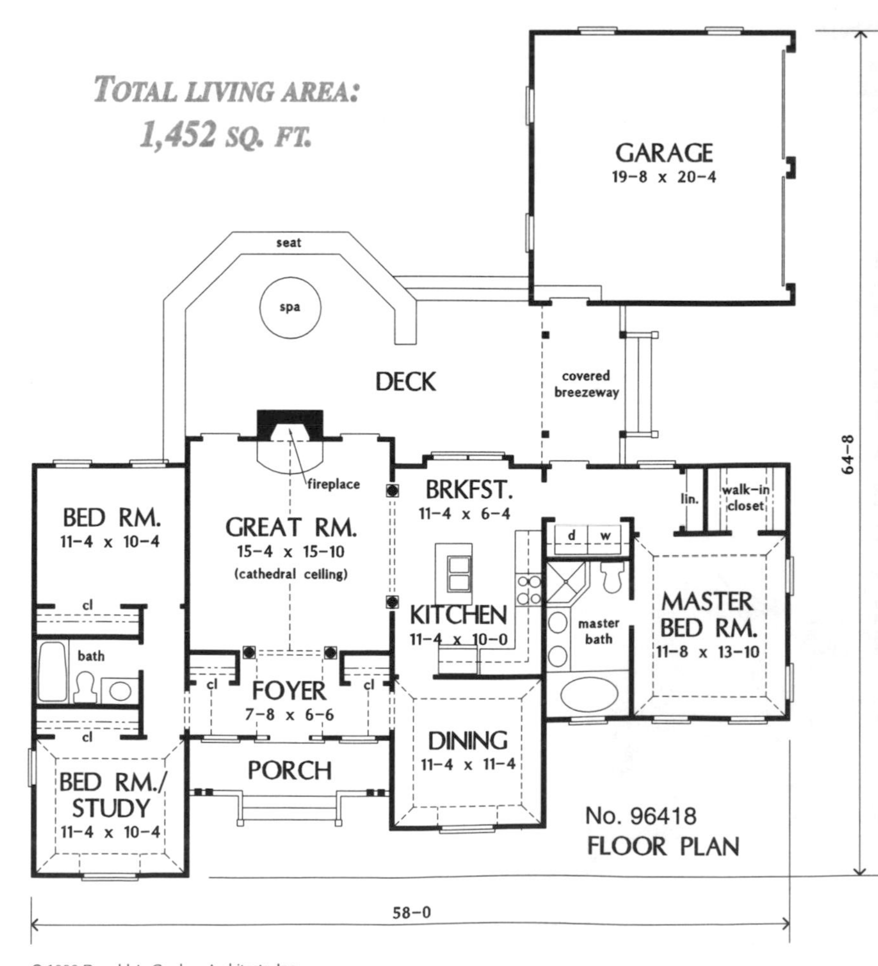

TOTAL LIVING AREA:
1,452 SQ. FT.
GARAGE
19–8 x 20–4
seat
spa
DECK
covered breezeway
fireplace
BRKFST.
11–4 x 6–4
BED RM.
11–4 x 10–4
GREAT RM.
15–4 x 15–10
(cathedral ceiling)
lin.
walk-in closet
d
w
KITCHEN
11–4 x 10–0
master bath
MASTER BED RM.
11–8 x 13–10
cl
bath
cl
cl
FOYER
7–8 x 6–6
cl
DINING
11–4 x 11–4
PORCH
BED RM./ STUDY
11–4 x 10–4
No. 96418
FLOOR PLAN
64–8
58–0

© 1990 Donald A. Gardner Architects, Inc.

To order your Blueprints, call 1-800-235-5700

Refer to **Pricing Schedule C** on the order form for pricing information

PLAN NO.94313

Country Spirit

- This plan features:
- – Three bedrooms
- – Two full & one half baths
- An old fashioned wrap-around porch extending to a large Patio
- Two-story Entry accented by a curved staircase
- Formal Living Room enhanced by decorative windows and an open fireplace
- Expansive Family area with Patio access and Dining area with a glass alcove
- Kitchen with a serving counter, Utility area and Garage entry
- Corner Master Bedroom with large walk-in closet, corner window tub and double vanity
- Two additional bedrooms with large closets share a full bath
- No materials list is available

IRST FLOOR — 967 SQ. FT.
ECOND FLOOR — 869 SQ. FT.
ARAGE — 462 SQ. FT.

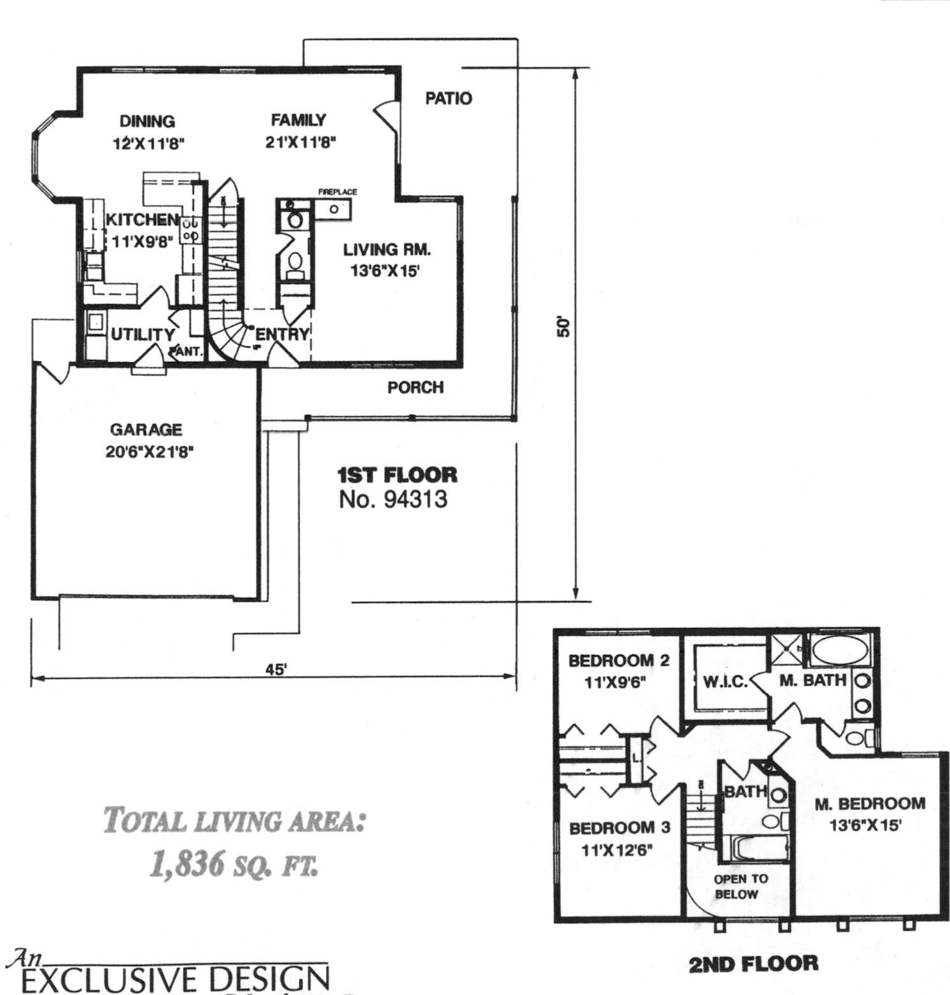

DINING
12'X11'8"
FAMILY
21'X11'8"
PATIO
FIREPLACE
KITCHEN
11'X9'8"
LIVING RM.
13'6"X15'
UTILITY
PANT.
ENTRY
PORCH
GARAGE
20'6"X21'8"
1ST FLOOR
No. 94313
50'
45'
BEDROOM 2
11'X9'6"
W.I.C.
M. BATH
BATH
M. BEDROOM
13'6"X15'
BEDROOM 3
11'X12'6"
OPEN TO BELOW
2ND FLOOR

TOTAL LIVING AREA:
1,836 SQ. FT.

An EXCLUSIVE DESIGN By Marshall Associates

To order your Blueprints, call 1-800-235-5700

PLAN NO. 93222

Refer to **Pricing Schedule A** on the order form for pricing information

For an Established Neighborhood

- This plan features:
  - — Three bedrooms
  - — Two full baths
- A covered entrance sheltering and welcoming visitors
- A Living Room enhanced by natural light streaming in from the large front window
- A bayed formal Dining Room with direct access to the Sun Deck and the Living Room
- An efficient, galley Kitchen
- An informal Breakfast Room with direct access to the Sun Deck
- A large Master Suite equipped with a walk-in closet and a full private Bath
- Two additional bedrooms that share a full hall bath

MAIN AREA — 1,276 SQ. FT.
FINISHED STAIRCASE — 16 SQ. FT.
BASEMENT — 392 SQ. FT.
GARAGE — 728 SQ. FT.

TOTAL LIVING AREA:
1,292 SQ. FT.

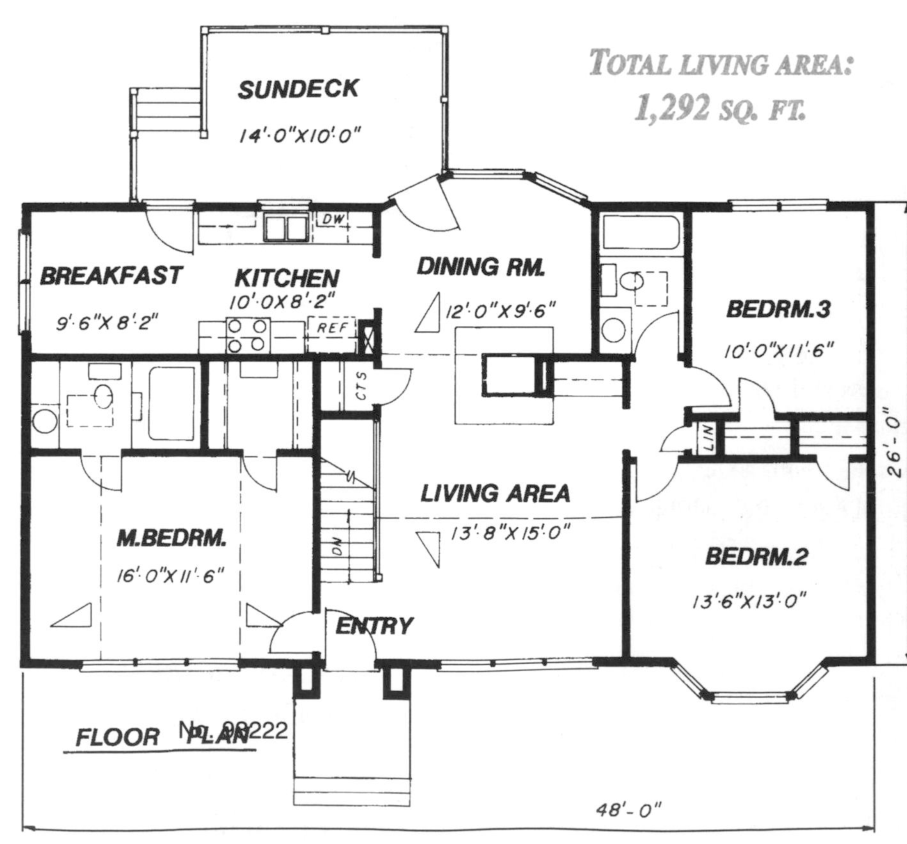

SUNDECK
14'-0"X10'-0"
DW
BREAKFAST
9'-6"X8'-2"
KITCHEN
10'-0X8'-2"
REF
DINING RM.
12'-0"X9'-6"
BEDRM.3
10'-0"X11'-6"
CTS
LIN
26'-0"
LIVING AREA
13'-8"X15'-0"
DN
M.BEDRM.
16'-0"X11'-6"
BEDRM.2
13'-6"X13'-0"
ENTRY
FLOOR PLAN
No. 93222
48'-0"

An EXCLUSIVE DESIGN
By Jannis Vann & Associates, Inc.

To order your Blueprints, call 1-800-235-5700

Refer to **Pricing Schedule D** on the order form for pricing information

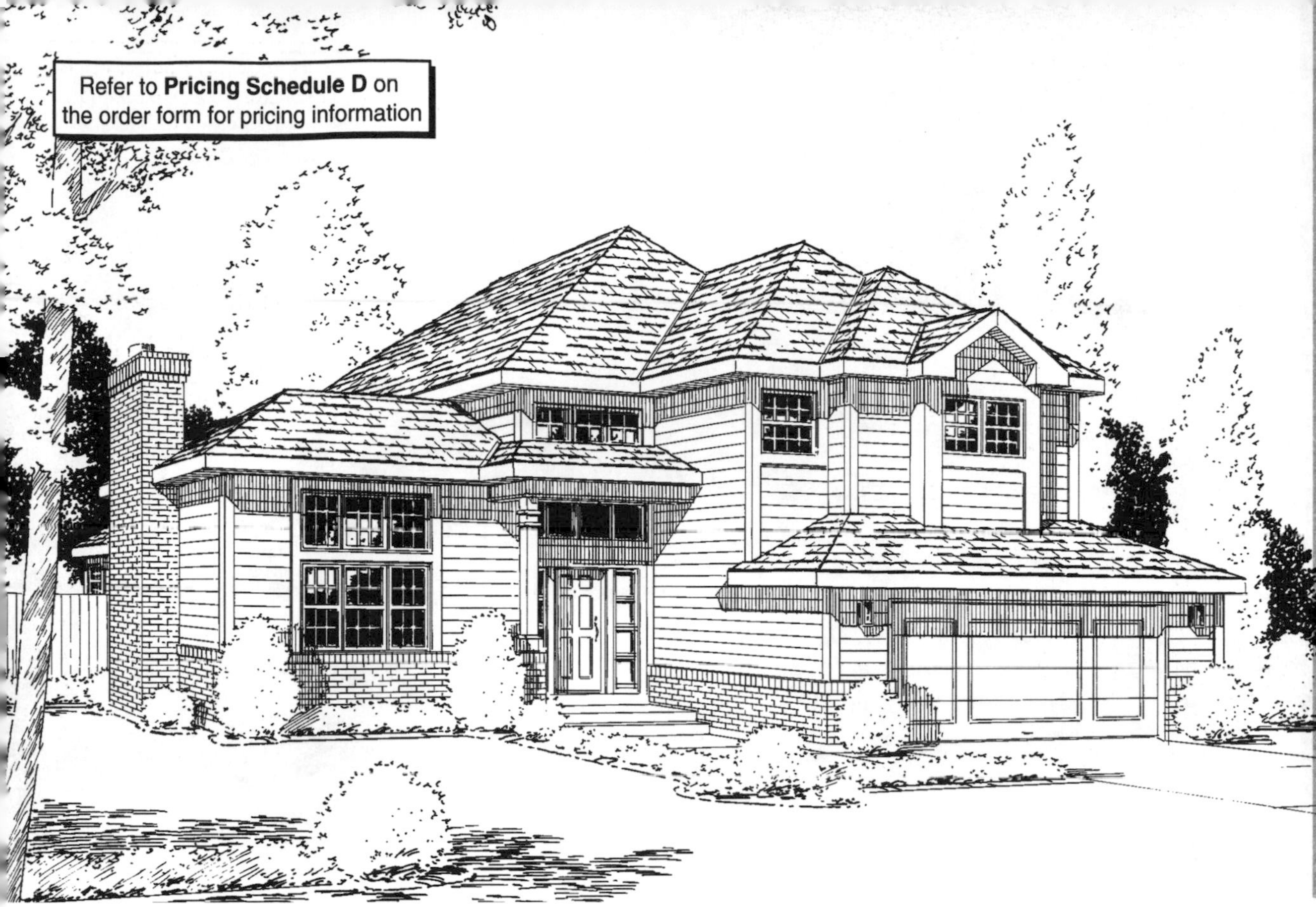

PLAN NO. 24323

An EXCLUSIVE DESIGN
By Marshall Associates

TOTAL LIVING AREA:
2,500 SQ. FT.

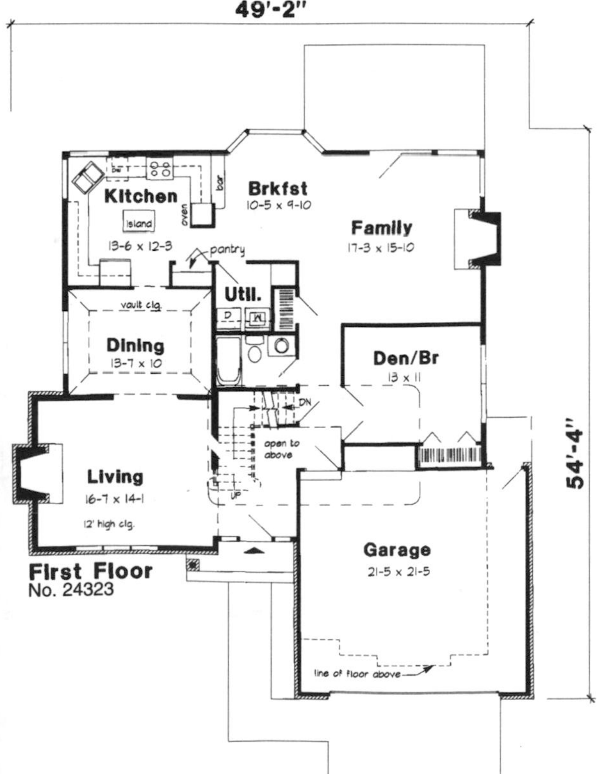

49'-2"
54'-4"
Kitchen
13-6 x 12-3
Brkfst
10-5 x 9-10
Family
17-3 x 15-10
Util.
Dining
13-7 x 10
vault clg.
Den/Br
13 x 11
Living
16-7 x 14-1
12' high clg.
open to above
Garage
21-5 x 21-5
line of floor above
First Floor
No. 24323

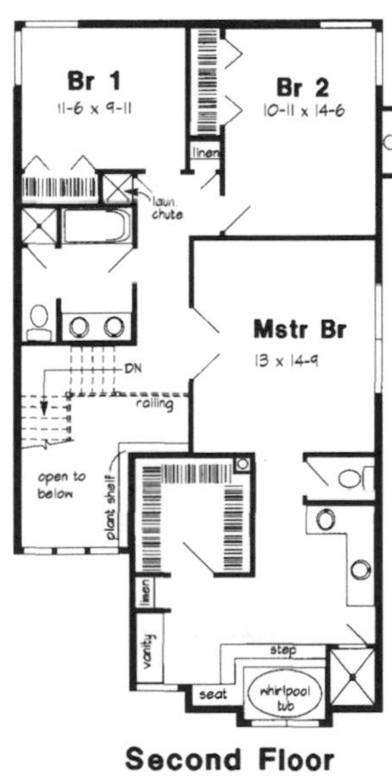

Br 1
11-6 x 9-11
Br 2
10-11 x 14-6
Mstr Br
13 x 14-9
open to below
whirlpool tub
Second Floor

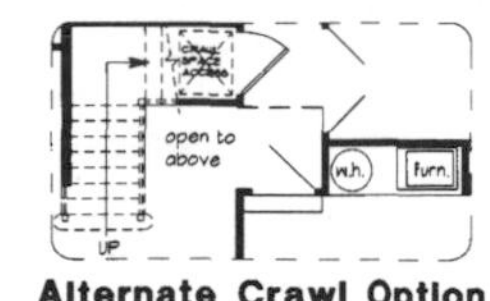

open to above
Alternate Crawl Option

Designed with Today's Active Family in Mind

- This plan features:
  - Three or four bedrooms
  - Three full baths
- An open layout between the Kitchen, Breakfast Bay and Family Room giving a feeling of spaciousness
- An island Kitchen with more than ample counter and storage space, a double sink, built-in pantry and an eating bar
- A fireplace in the Family Room which has direct access to the rear yard
- A vaulted ceiling adding a touch of elegance to the Dining Room
- A luxurious Master Suite with a lavish, private Master Bath
- Two additional bedrooms that share a full hall bath
- No materials list available

FIRST FLOOR — 1,420 SQ. FT.
SECOND FLOOR — 1,080 SQ. FT.
GARAGE — 477 SQ. FT.

PLAN NO. 90682

Refer to **Pricing Schedule A** on the order form for pricing information

Inviting Porch Adorns Affordable Home

- This plan features:
- — Three bedrooms
- — Two full baths
- A large and spacious Living Room that adjoins the Dining Room for ease in entertaining
- A private bedroom wing offering a quiet atmosphere
- A Master Bedroom with his-n-her closets and a private bath
- An efficient Kitchen with a walk-in pantry

MAIN AREA — 1,160 SQ. FT.
LAUNDRY/MUDROOM — 83 SQ. FT.

TOTAL LIVING AREA:
1,243 SQ. FT

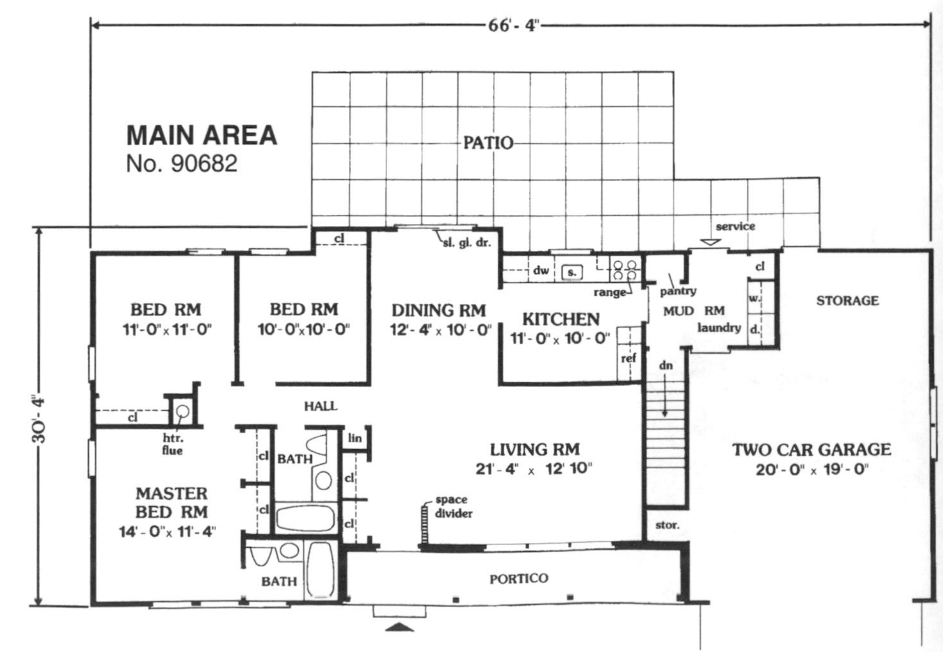

66'-4"
MAIN AREA
No. 90682
PATIO
service
cl
sl. gl. dr.
dw
s.
range
pantry
BED RM
11'-0"x11'-0"
BED RM
10'-0"x10'-0"
DINING RM
12'-4" x 10'-0"
KITCHEN
11'-0" x 10'-0"
MUD RM
laundry
w.
d.
STORAGE
ref
dn
HALL
htr.
flue
lin
BATH
LIVING RM
21'-4" x 12' 10"
space
divider
MASTER
BED RM
14'-0"x 11'-4"
TWO CAR GARAGE
20'-0" x 19'-0"
stor.
PORTICO
BATH
30'-4"

To order your Blueprints, call 1-800-235-5700

Refer to **Pricing Schedule A** on the order form for pricing information

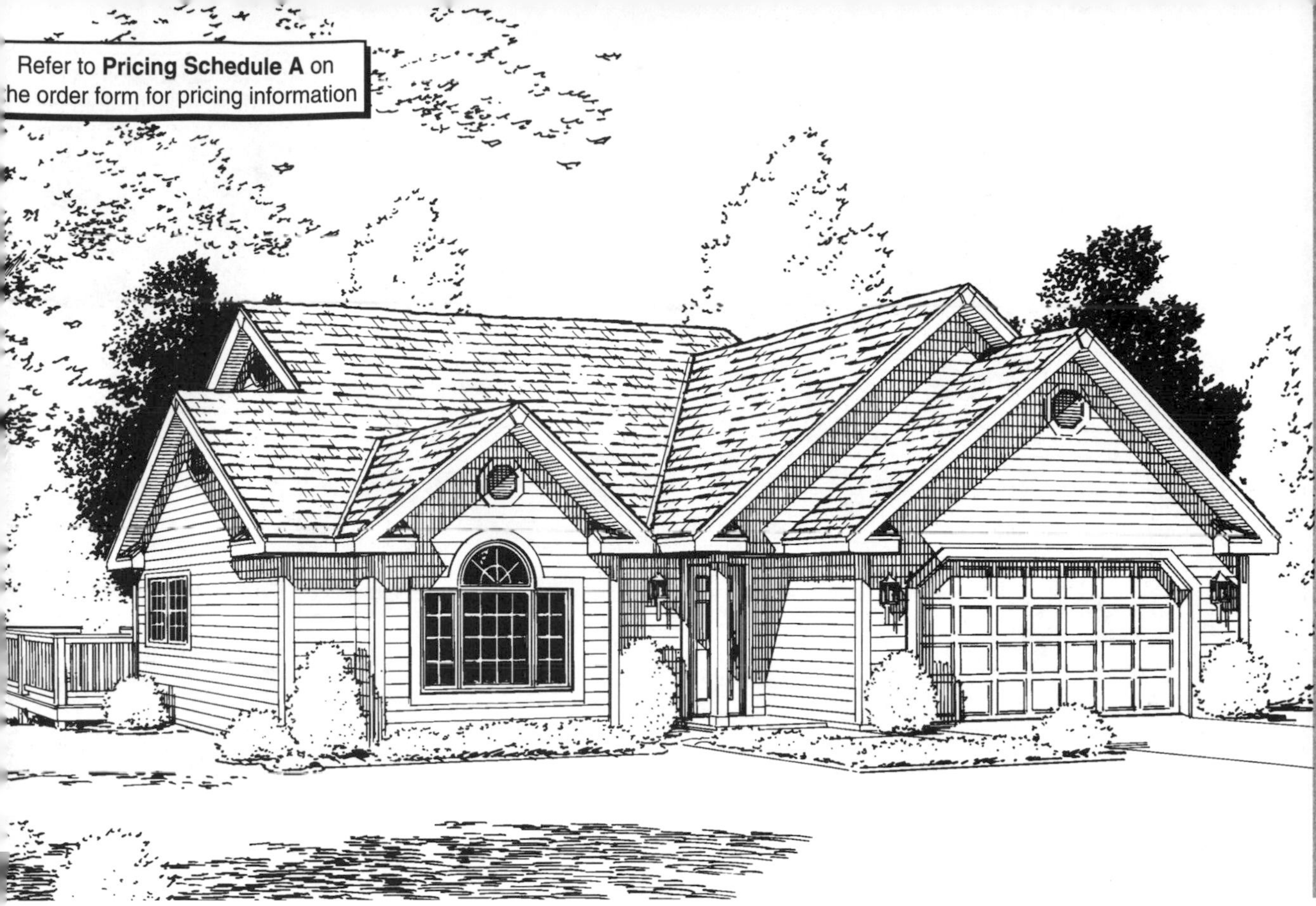

PLAN NO. 24402

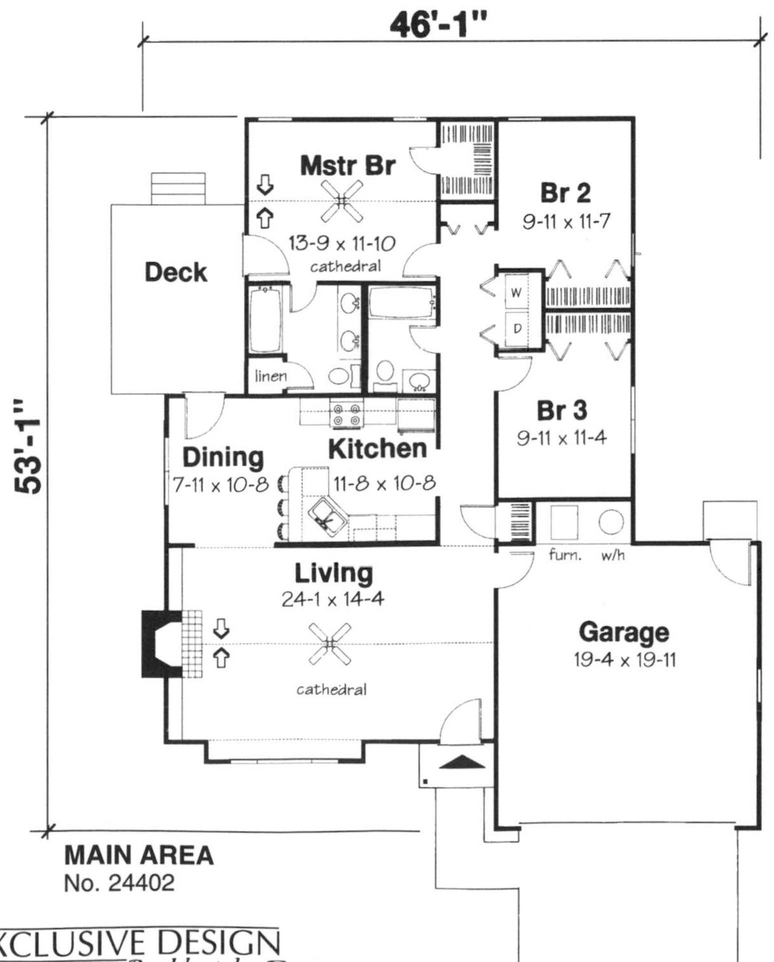
46'-1"
53'-1"
Mstr Br
13-9 x 11-10
cathedral
Br 2
9-11 x 11-7
Deck
W
D
linen
Br 3
9-11 x 11-4
Dining
7-11 x 10-8
Kitchen
11-8 x 10-8
furn.
w/h
Living
24-1 x 14-4
cathedral
Garage
19-4 x 19-11
MAIN AREA
No. 24402

An EXCLUSIVE DESIGN By Upright Design

Cathedral Ceiling in Living Room and Master Suite

■ This plan features:

— Three bedrooms

— Two full baths

■ A spacious Living Room with a cathedral ceiling and elegant fireplace

■ A Dining Room that adjoins both the Living Room and the Kitchen

■ An efficient Kitchen, with double sinks, ample cabinet space and peninsula counter that doubles as an eating bar

■ A convenient hallway laundry center

■ A Master Suite with a cathedral ceiling and a private Master Bath

MAIN AREA — 1,346 SQ. FT.
GARAGE — 449 SQ. FT.

TOTAL LIVING AREA:
1,346 SQ. FT.

PLAN NO. 91021

Refer to **Pricing Schedule A** on the order form for pricing information

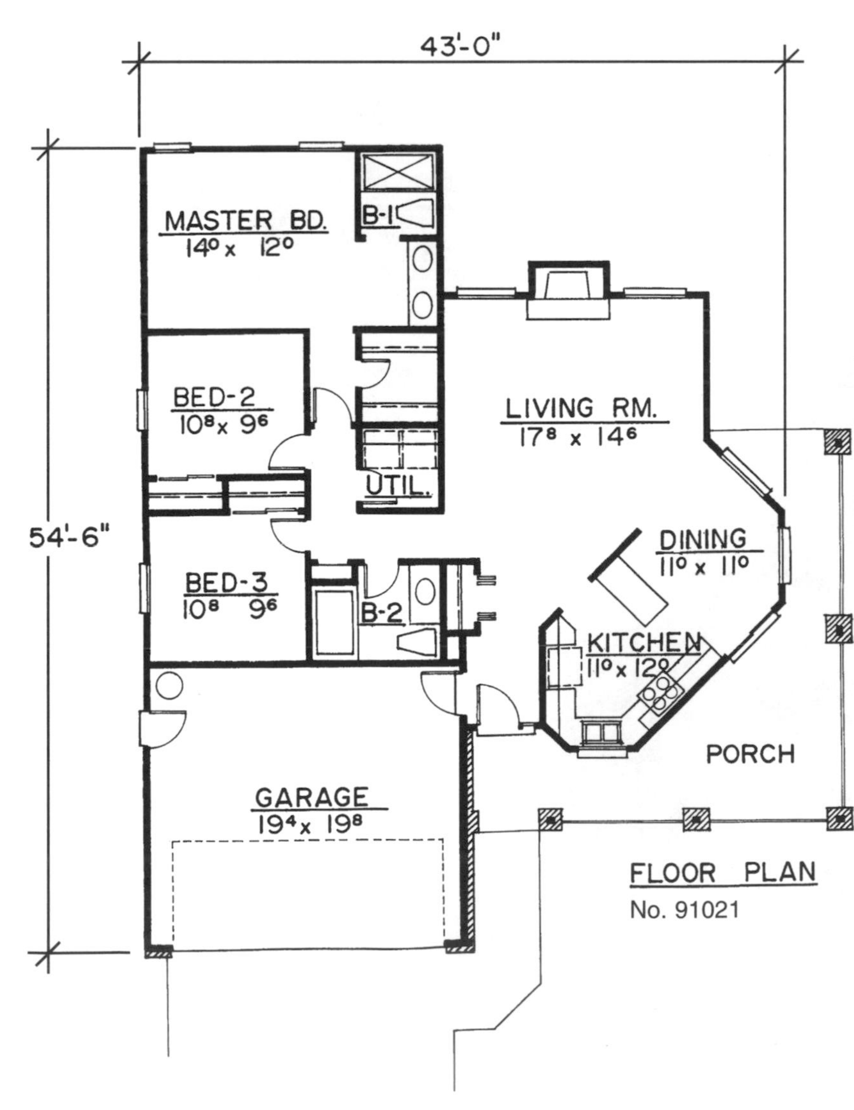

43'-0"
54'-6"
MASTER BD.
14⁰ x 12⁰
B-1
BED-2
10⁸ x 9⁶
UTIL.
LIVING RM.
17⁸ x 14⁶
DINING
11⁰ x 11⁰
BED-3
10⁸ 9⁶
B-2
KITCHEN
11⁰ x 12⁰
PORCH
GARAGE
19⁴ x 19⁸
FLOOR PLAN
No. 91021

Inviting Porch Has Dual Function

- This plan features:
- — Three bedrooms
- — Two full baths
- An inviting, wrap-around porch Entry with sliding glass doors leading right into a bayed Dining Room
- A Living Room with a cozy feeling, enhanced by the fireplace
- An efficient Kitchen opening to both Dining and Living Rooms
- A Master Suite with a walk-in closet and private Master Bath
- An optional basement, slab or crawl space foundation — please specify when ordering

MAIN FLOOR — 1,295 SQ. FT.

TOTAL LIVING AREA: 1,295 SQ. FT.

To order your Blueprints, call 1-800-235-5700

Refer to **Pricing Schedule B** on the order form for pricing information

PLAN NO. 90986

An EXCLUSIVE DESIGN *By Westhome Planners, Ltd.*

Surrounded with Sunshine

- This plan features:
  - — Three bedrooms
  - — Two full and one half baths
- An Italianate style, featuring columns and tile originally designed to sit on the edge of a golf course
- Tile used from the Foyer, into the Kitchen and Nook, as well as in the Utility Room
- A whirlpool tub in the elaborate and spacious Master Bedroom suite
- A Great Room with a corner gas fireplace
- A turreted Breakfast Nook and an efficient Kitchen with peninsula counter
- Two family bedrooms that share a full hall bath

MAIN AREA — 1,731 SQ. FT.
GARAGE — 888 SQ. FT.
BASEMENT — 1,715 SQ. FT.

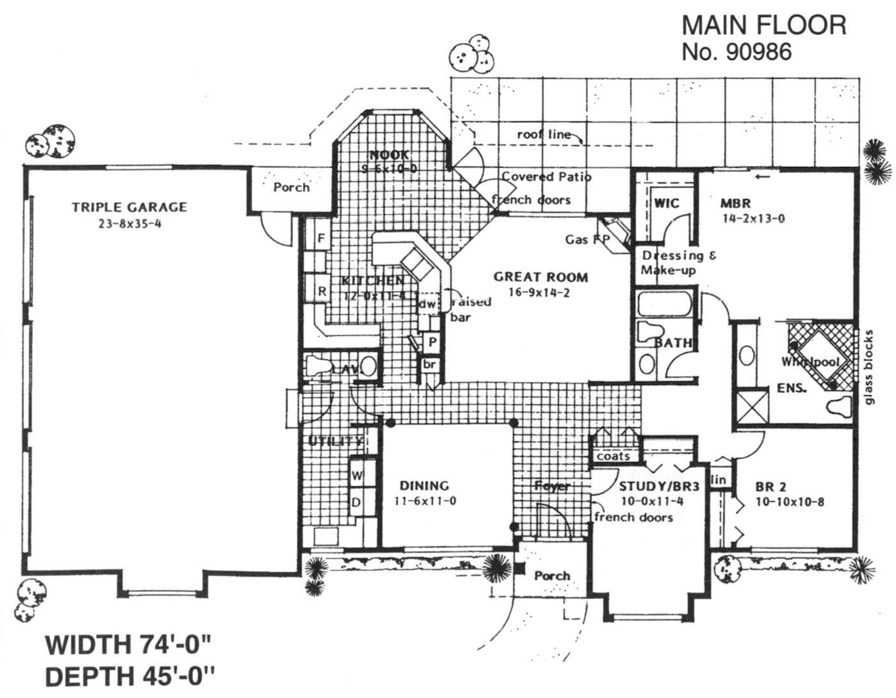
MAIN FLOOR
No. 90986
roof line
NOOK
Covered Patio
french doors
Porch
TRIPLE GARAGE
23-8x35-4
Gas FP
KITCHEN
GREAT ROOM
16-9x14-2
raised bar
WIC
MBR
14-2x13-0
Dressing & Make-up
BATH
Whirlpool
ENS.
glass blocks
UTILITY
DINING
11-6x11-0
Foyer
coats
STUDY/BR3
10-0x11-4
french doors
lin
BR 2
10-10x10-8
Porch

WIDTH 74'-0"
DEPTH 45'-0"

TOTAL LIVING AREA:
1,731 SQ. FT.

To order your Blueprints, call 1-800-235-5700

PLAN NO. 96513

Refer to **Pricing Schedule B** on the order form for pricing information

A Modern Slant On A Country Theme

TOTAL LIVING AREA:
1,648 SQ. FT.

- This plan features:

—Three bedrooms

—Two full and one half baths

- Country styled front porch highlighting exterior enhanced by dormer windows
- Modern open floor plan for a more spacious feeling
- Great Room accented by a quaint, corner fireplace and a ceiling fan
- Dining Room flowing from the Great Room for easy entertaining
- Kitchen graced by natural light from near by bay window and a convenient snack bar for meals on the go
- Master suite secluded in separate wing for total privacy
- Two additional bedrooms sharing full bath in the hall

FIRST FLOOR — 1,648 SQ. FT.
GARAGE — 479 SQ. FT.

68'-0"
9'-0" CEILINGS (TYPICAL)
50'-0"
SHOWER
BATH
MASTER SUITE
15 × 16
FAN
CLOSET
PORCH
DINING
10 × 11
F/P
GREAT RM
16 × 24
FAN
BEDRM
11 × 12
FAN
1/2 BATH
GARAGE
21 × 22
A/C
UTILITY
DRY
WASH
SNACK BAR
RANGE
KITCHEN
11 × 14
D/W
FOYER
LIN
CLOS
BATH
CLO
CLOS
BEDRM
12 × 12
FAN
PORCH

MAIN FLOOR
No. 96513

To order your Blueprints, call 1-800-235-5700

Refer to **Pricing Schedule A** on the order form for pricing information

PLAN NO. 94311

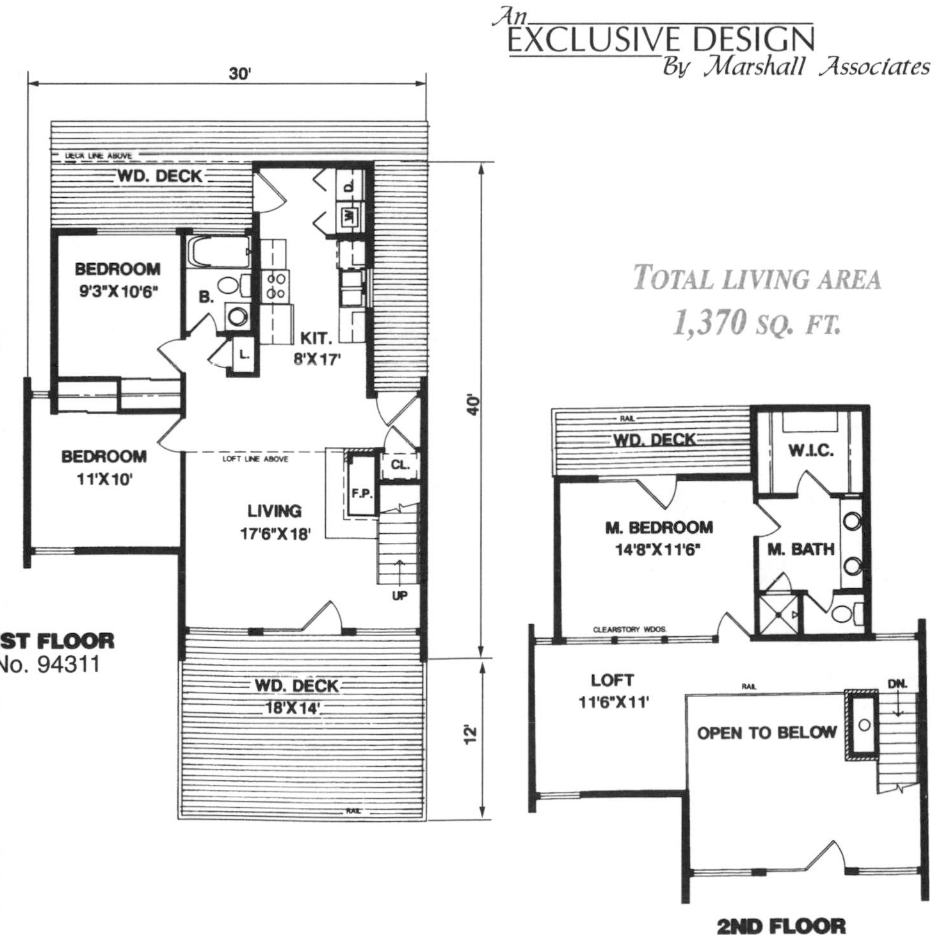

An EXCLUSIVE DESIGN By Marshall Associates
30'
DECK LINE ABOVE
WD. DECK
BEDROOM
9'3"X10'6"
B.
KIT.
8'X17'
L.
BEDROOM
11'X10'
LOFT LINE ABOVE
CL.
F.P.
LIVING
17'6"X18'
UP
40'
12'
WD. DECK
18'X14'
RAIL
1ST FLOOR
No. 94311
TOTAL LIVING AREA
1,370 SQ. FT.
RAIL
WD. DECK
W.I.C.
M. BEDROOM
14'8"X11'6"
M. BATH
CLEARSTORY WDOS.
LOFT
11'6"X11'
RAIL
DN.
OPEN TO BELOW
2ND FLOOR

Contemporary Styling

- This plan features:
- — Three bedrooms
- — One full and one 3/4 bath
- Perfect plan for a mountain side or lot with a view
- Front Deck gives far reaching view of surrounding vistas
- Cozy fireplace in the Living Room, illuminated by sunlight during the day through wall of windows
- Galley Kitchen with access to the rear deck
- Two first floor bedrooms sharing a full hall bath
- Loft overlooking the living room
- Master Bedroom suite with private deck, a private Master bath and a walk-in closet
- No Material List available

FIRST FLOOR — 810 SQ. FT.
SECOND FLOOR — 560 SQ. FT.

PLAN NO. 19863

Refer to **Pricing Schedule B** on the order form for pricing information

Prize-Winning Solar Home

- This plan features:

—Three bedroom

—Two full baths

- Flexible floor place to satisfy a wide variety of families and lifestyles
- Greenhouse where the sun's heat is collected, stored and shared with the rest of home
- Open spaces and partial ceilings maximizing air flow throughout
- Living room looking out onto the Greenhouse
- Kitchen with convenient pass-through to the Dining Room
- Bedrooms with ample storage and easy access to full bath

FIRST FLOOR — 1,000 SQ. FT.
SECOND FLOOR — 572 SQ. FT.

TOTAL LIVING AREA
1,572 SQ. FT.

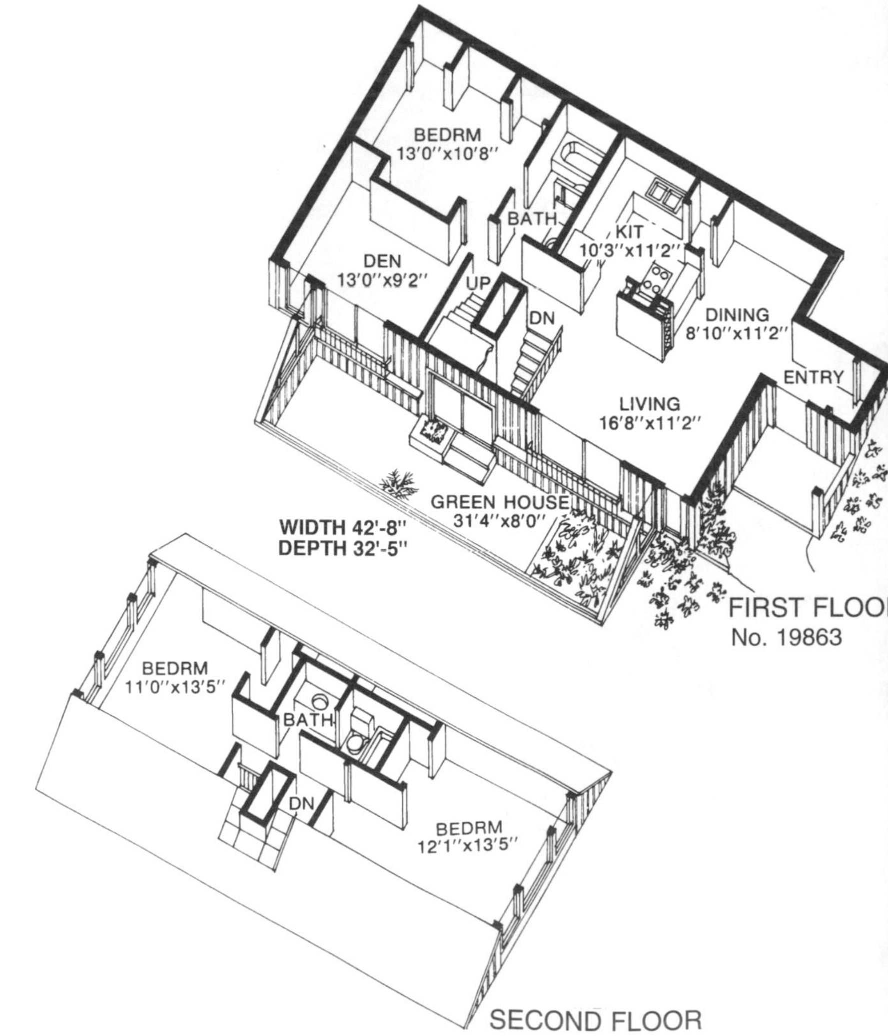

BEDRM
13'0"x10'8"
BATH
KIT
10'3"x11'2"
DEN
13'0"x9'2"
UP
DN
DINING
8'10"x11'2"
ENTRY
LIVING
16'8"x11'2"
GREEN HOUSE
31'4"x8'0"
WIDTH 42'-8"
DEPTH 32'-5"
FIRST FLOOR
No. 19863
BEDRM
11'0"x13'5"
BATH
DN
BEDRM
12'1"x13'5"
SECOND FLOOR

To order your Blueprints, call 1-800-235-5700

Refer to **Pricing Schedule A** on the order form for pricing information

PLAN NO. 90669

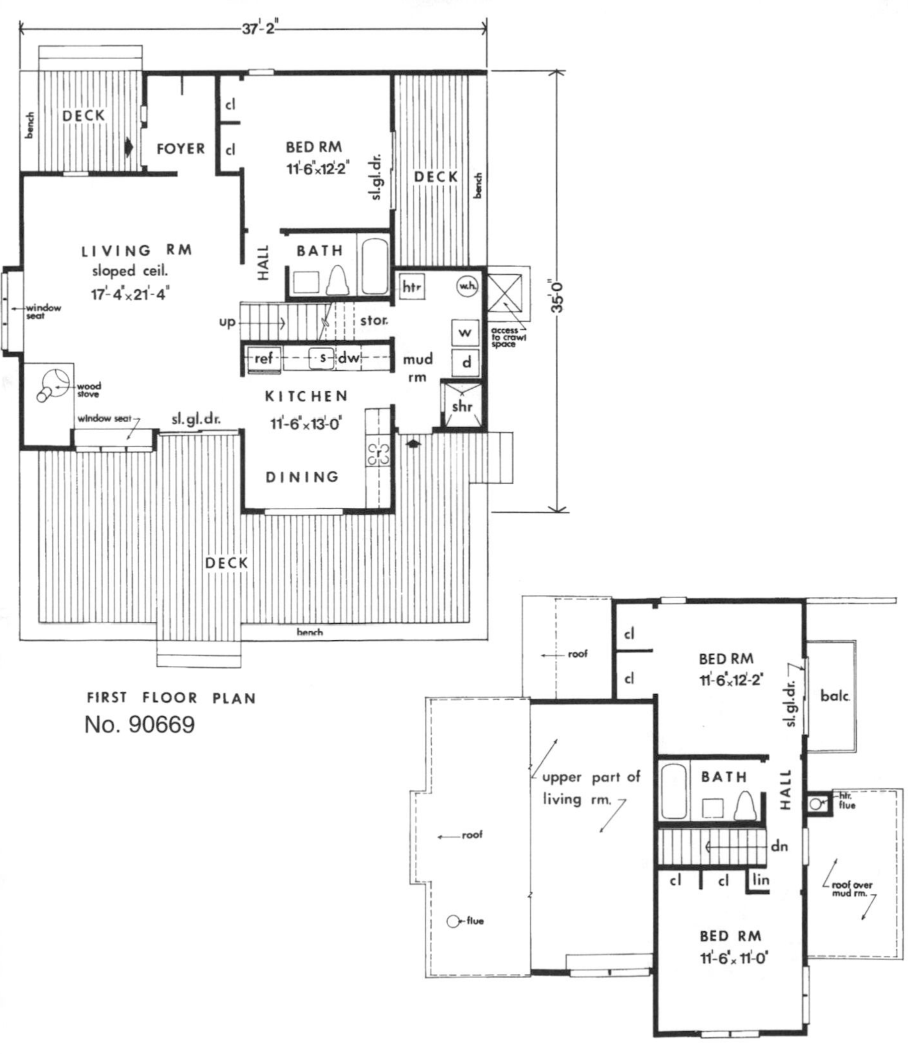

37'-2"
35'-0"
DECK
bench
FOYER
cl
cl
BED RM
11'-6"x12'-2"
sl.gl.dr.
DECK
bench
LIVING RM
sloped ceil.
17'-4"x21'-4"
HALL
BATH
htr
w.h.
access to crawl space
window seat
up
stor.
w
ref
s
dw
mud rm
d
wood stove
KITCHEN
11'-6"x13'-0"
shr
window seat
sl.gl.dr.
DINING
DECK
bench
FIRST FLOOR PLAN
No. 90669
roof
cl
cl
BED RM
11'-6"x12'-2'
sl.gl.dr.
balc.
upper part of living rm.
BATH
HALL
htr. flue
roof
dn
cl
cl
lin
roof over mud rm.
flue
BED RM
11'-6"x 11'-0"
SECOND FLOOR PLAN

Contemporary Energy-Saver

- This plan features:
  - — Three bedrooms
  - — Two full baths plus shower
- An enormous Deck, expanding living outdoors
- A spacious Living Room with a sloped ceiling and a wood stove flanked by windows with built-in seats
- An efficient, eat-in Kitchen with ample work space and easy access to all living areas
- A first floor Bedroom with a double closet and a private Deck adjoins a full hall bath
- Two additional bedrooms with double closets sharing a full hall bath

FIRST FLOOR — 877 SQ. FT.
SECOND FLOOR — 455 SQ.

TOTAL LIVING AREA: 1,332 SQ. FT.

PLAN NO. 24324
Refer to **Pricing Schedule B** on the order form for pricing information

Focus on the Family

- This plan features:
  - — Three bedrooms
  - — Two full and one half baths
- A fireplaced Family Room only divided from the Kitchen by an eating bar
- A U-shaped Kitchen with a pantry and ample cabinet space
- A pan-vaulted ceiling in the formal Dining Room adds a decorative accent
- A spacious Living Room, flowing easily into the Dining Room and viewing the front porch
- A Master Suite enhanced with a walk-in closet, a double vanity, a whirlpool tub, a step-in shower and a compartmentalized toilet
- Two additional bedrooms, one with a walk-in closet, share the second full bath
- No materials list is available

FIRST FLOOR — 916 SQ. FT.
SECOND FLOOR — 884 SQ. FT.
GARAGE — 480 SQ. FT.

TOTAL LIVING AREA:
1,800 SQ. FT.

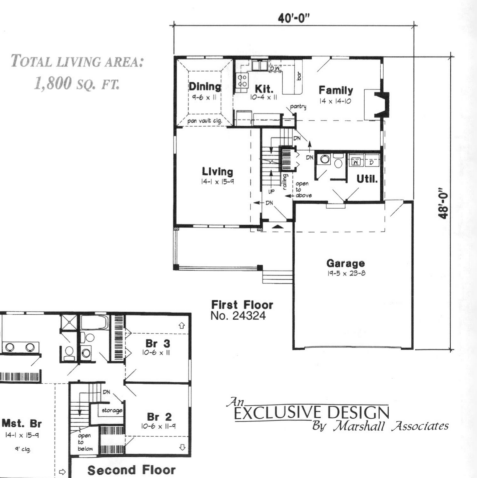

40'-0"
48'-0"
Dining 9-6 x 11
pan vault clg.
Kit. 10-4 x 11
DW
bar
pantry
Family 14 x 14-10
Living 14-1 x 15-9
DN
UP
railing
open to above
W D
Util.
Garage 19-5 x 23-8

First Floor
No. 24324

whirlpool tub
Br 3 10-6 x 11
DN
storage
Br 2 10-6 x 11-9
Mst. Br 14-1 x 15-9 9' clg.
open to below

Second Floor

An EXCLUSIVE DESIGN *By Marshall Associates*

To order your Blueprints, call 1-800-235-5700

Refer to **Pricing Schedule B** on the order form for pricing information

PLAN NO. 93261

Bay Windows and a Terrific Front Porch

An EXCLUSIVE DESIGN
By Jannis Vann & Associates, Inc.

TOTAL LIVING AREA:
1,778 SQ. FT.

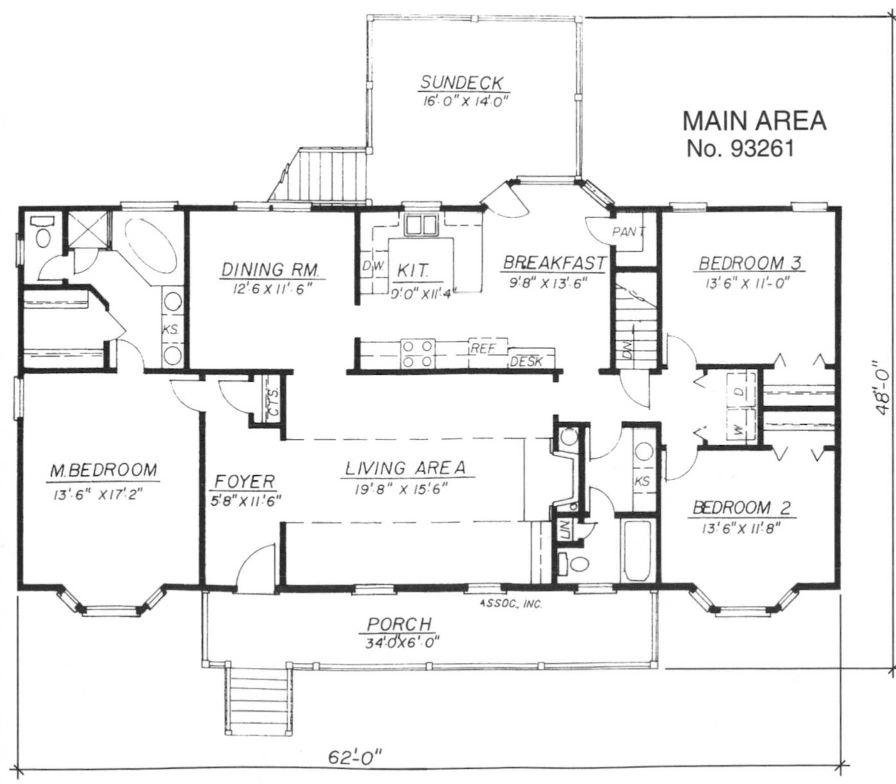

SUNDECK
16'0"X14'0"
MAIN AREA
No. 93261
DINING RM.
12'6X11'6"
KIT.
10'0"X11'4"
BREAKFAST
9'8"X13'6"
PANT
BEDROOM 3
13'6"X11'-0"
M.BEDROOM
13'6"X17'2"
FOYER
5'8"X11'6"
LIVING AREA
19'8"X15'6"
BEDROOM 2
13'6"X11'8"
PORCH
34'0X6'0"
48'-0"
62'-0"

- This plan features:
  - Three bedrooms
  - Two full baths
- A Country style front porch
- An expansive Living Area that includes a fireplace
- A Master Suite with a private Master Bath and a walk-in closet, as well as a bay window view of the front yard
- An efficient Kitchen that serves the sunny Breakfast Area and the Dining Room with equal ease
- A built-in pantry and a desk add to the conveniences in the Breakfast Area
- Two additional bedrooms that share the full hall bath
- A convenient main floor Laundry Room

MAIN AREA — 1,778 SQ. FT.
BASEMENT — 1,008 SQ. FT.
GARAGE — 728 SQ. FT.

PLAN NO. 93104

Refer to **Pricing Schedule B** on the order form for pricing information

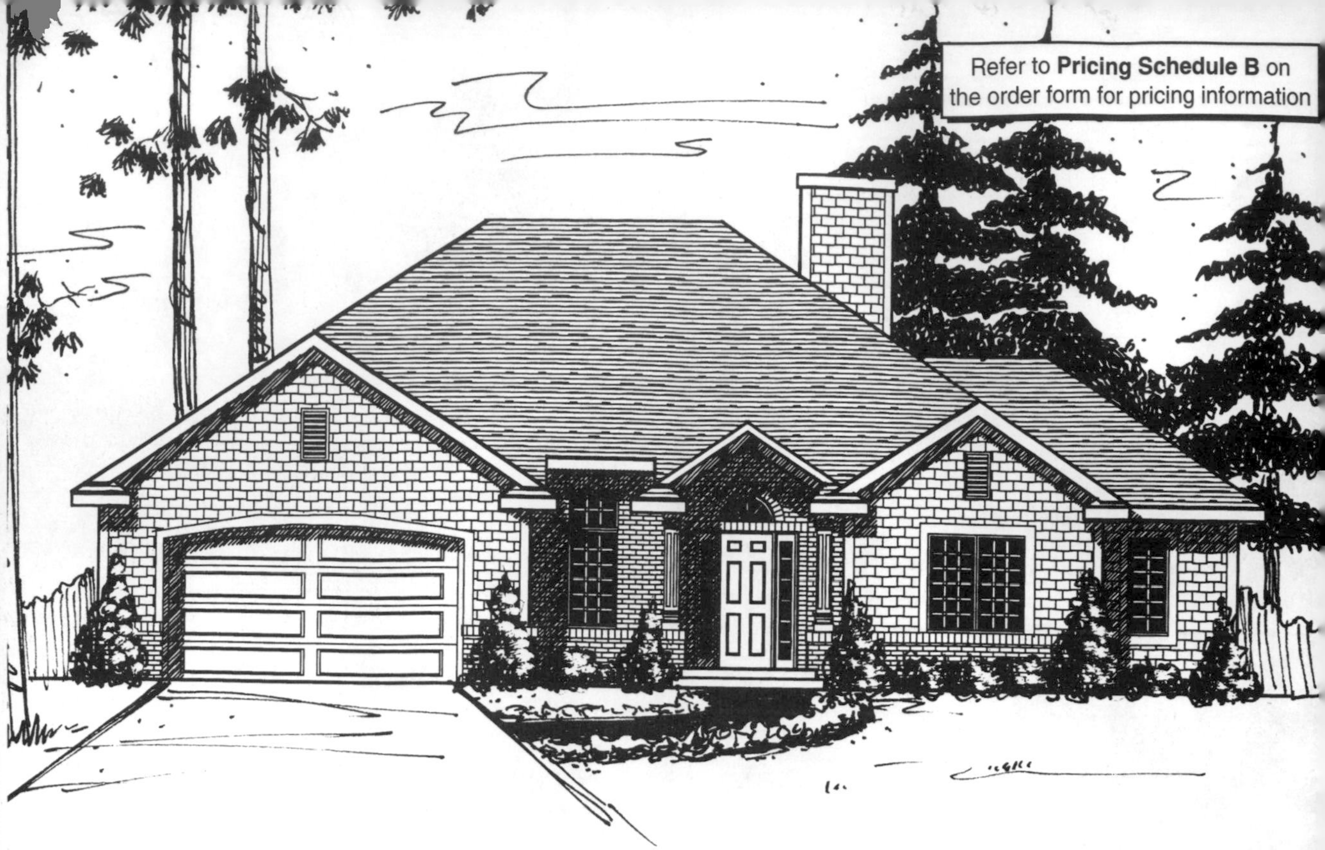

Unique Brick and Shake Siding

- This plan features:
  - — Three bedrooms
  - — Two full baths
- Sheltered entrance surrounded by glass
- Windows surround a cozy fireplace in the Great Room topped by a vaulted ceiling
- Kitchen with loads of counter and storage space, and a snackbar
- French doors lead into the Master Bedroom Suite with a huge walk-in closet and a double vanity bath
- Two additional bedrooms with ample closets, share a full bath
- No materials list available for this plan

MAIN FLOOR — 1,756 SQ. FT.
BASEMENT — 1,756 SQ. FT.
GARAGE — 536 SQ. FT.

An
EXCLUSIVE DESIGN
By Ahmann Design Inc.

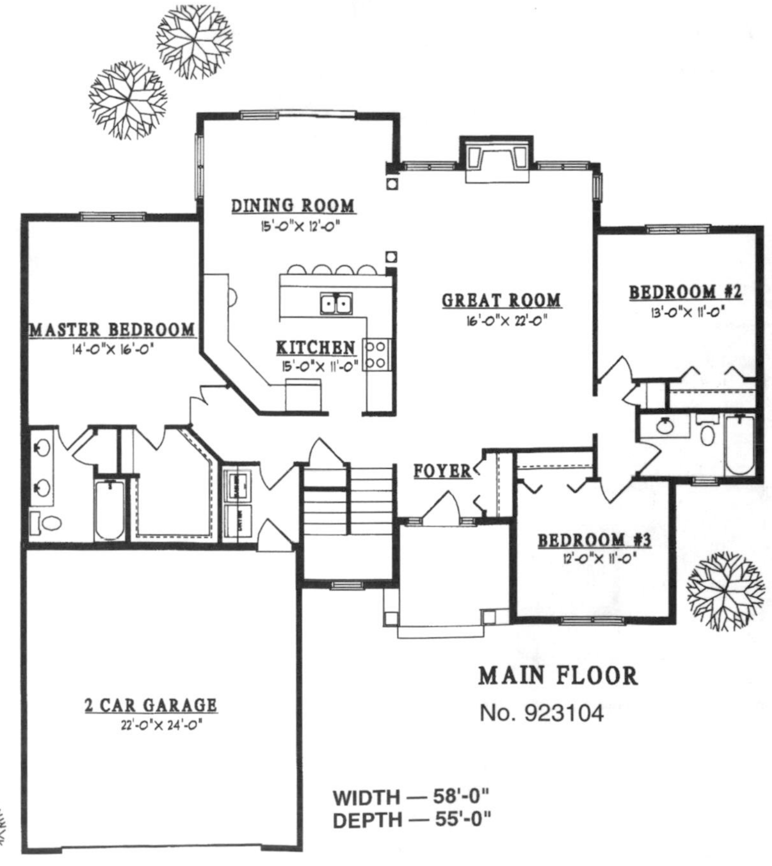
DINING ROOM
15'-0"X 12'-0"
GREAT ROOM
16'-0"X 22'-0"
BEDROOM #2
13'-0"X 11'-0"
MASTER BEDROOM
14'-0"X 16'-0"
KITCHEN
15'-0"X 11'-0"
FOYER
BEDROOM #3
12'-0"X 11'-0"
2 CAR GARAGE
22'-0"X 24'-0"

MAIN FLOOR
No. 923104

WIDTH — 58'-0"
DEPTH — 55'-0"

TOTAL LIVING AREA:
1,756 SQ. FT.

Refer to **Pricing Schedule A** on the order form for pricing information

PLAN NO. 94312

TOTAL LIVING AREA
1,024 SQ. FT.

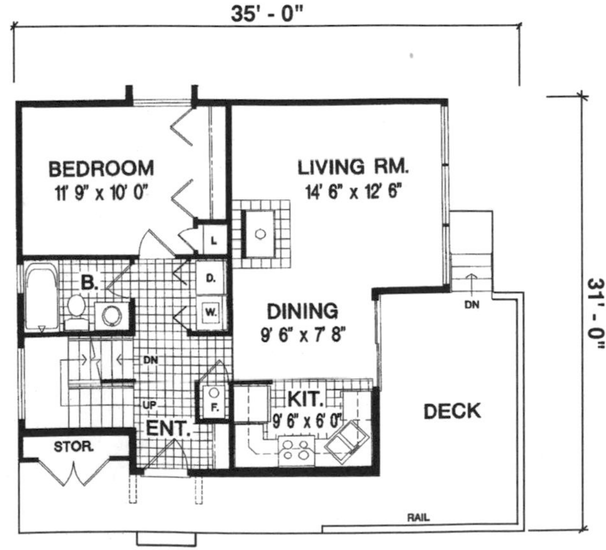

35' - 0"
31' - 0"
BEDROOM
11' 9" x 10' 0"
LIVING RM.
14' 6" x 12' 6"
L
B.
D.
W.
DINING
9' 6" x 7' 8"
DN
UP
F.
KIT.
9' 6" x 6' 0"
ENT.
STOR.
DECK
RAIL

MAIN LEVEL
No. 94312

BEDROOM
10' 0" x 11' 9"
L
B.
HW
LOFT
DN
Clearstory Wdos.
RAIL
open to below

UPPER LEVEL

Unique Design

- This plan features:
  - — Two bedrooms
  - — One full and one three-quarter baths
- Tiled entrance directing traffic into the Dining/Living Room, up the staircase or to the rear first floor bedroom
- Cozy wood stove warms the Living Room
- Sliding glass doors accessing the Deck from the Dining Room
- Efficient U-shaped Kitchen flows easily into the Dining Room
- First floor laundry center
- Second floor Bedroom has full access to the three quarter bath and ample closet space
- Optional Basement or Crawlspace foundation—please specify when ordering
- No Material List available

MAIN FLOOR — 710 SQ. FT.
UPPER FLOOR — 314 SQ. FT.
BASEMENT — 700 SQ. FT.

An EXCLUSIVE DESIGN *By Marshall Associates*

PLAN NO. 26112

Refer to **Pricing Schedule A** on the order form for pricing information

Contemporary Design Features Sunken Living Room

- This plan features:
- — Two bedrooms, with possible third bedroom/den
- — One and one half baths
- A solar design with southern glass doors, windows, and an air-lock entry
- A deck rimming the front of the home
- A Dining Room separated from the Living Room by a half wall
- An efficient Kitchen with an eating bar

FIRST FLOOR — 911 SQ. FT.
SECOND FLOOR — 576 SQ. FT.
BASEMENT — 911 SQ. FT.

TOTAL LIVING AREA:
1,487 SQ. FT.

Vest.
Entry
up
Kitchen
Cl
Lav
Dining
13'-0"x10'-0"
Bedroom/Den
12'-0"x12'-0"
dn
Deck
Living
20'-0"x16'-0"
34'
Deck
32'
FIRST FLOOR
No. 26112
Cl
Bath
Cl
Cl
Bedroom
12'-0"x12'-0"
dn
Bedroom
13'-0"x14'-0"
Balcony
Deck
Open to Living
Skylights
32'
SECOND FLOOR

To order your Blueprints, call 1-800-235-5700

Refer to **Pricing Schedule B** on the order form for pricing information

PLAN NO. 24708

Cozy Country Ranch

- This plan features:
  - — Three bedrooms
  - — Two full baths
- Front Porch shelters visitors and entrance into Living Room
- Expansive Living Room highlighted by a boxed window and hearth fireplace between built-ins
- Efficient, U-shaped Kitchen with direct access to the Screened Porch and the Dining Room
- Master Bedroom wing enhanced by a large walk-in closet and a double vanity bath with a whirlpool tub
- Two additional bedrooms with large closets, share a double vanity bath with laundry center
- No materials list available for this plan

MAIN FLOOR — 1,576 SQ. FT.
GARAGE — 576 SQ. FT.
BASEMENT — 1,454 SQ. FT.

TOTAL LIVING AREA:
1,576 SQ. FT.

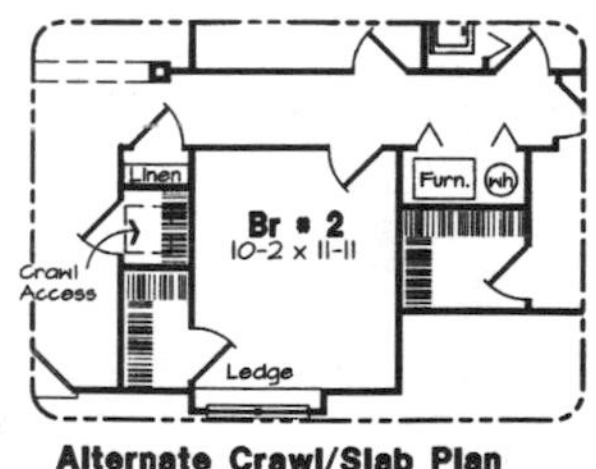

Linen
Br # 2
10-2 x 11-11
Furn.
Crawl Access
Ledge

Alternate Crawl/Slab Plan

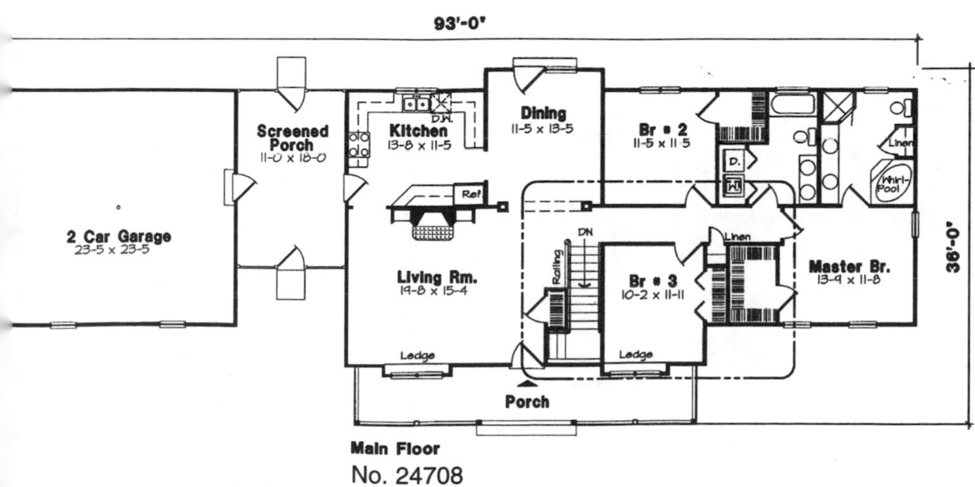

93'-0"
Screened Porch
11-0 x 18-0
Kitchen
13-8 x 11-5
D.W.
Dining
11-5 x 13-5
Br # 2
11-5 x 11-5
Linen
Whirl-Pool
2 Car Garage
23-5 x 23-5
Ref
Living Rm.
14-8 x 15-4
DN
Railing
Br # 3
10-2 x 11-11
Linen
Master Br.
13-4 x 11-8
36'-0"
Ledge
Ledge
Porch

Main Floor
No. 24708

PLAN NO. 93161

Refer to **Pricing Schedule B** on the order form for pricing information

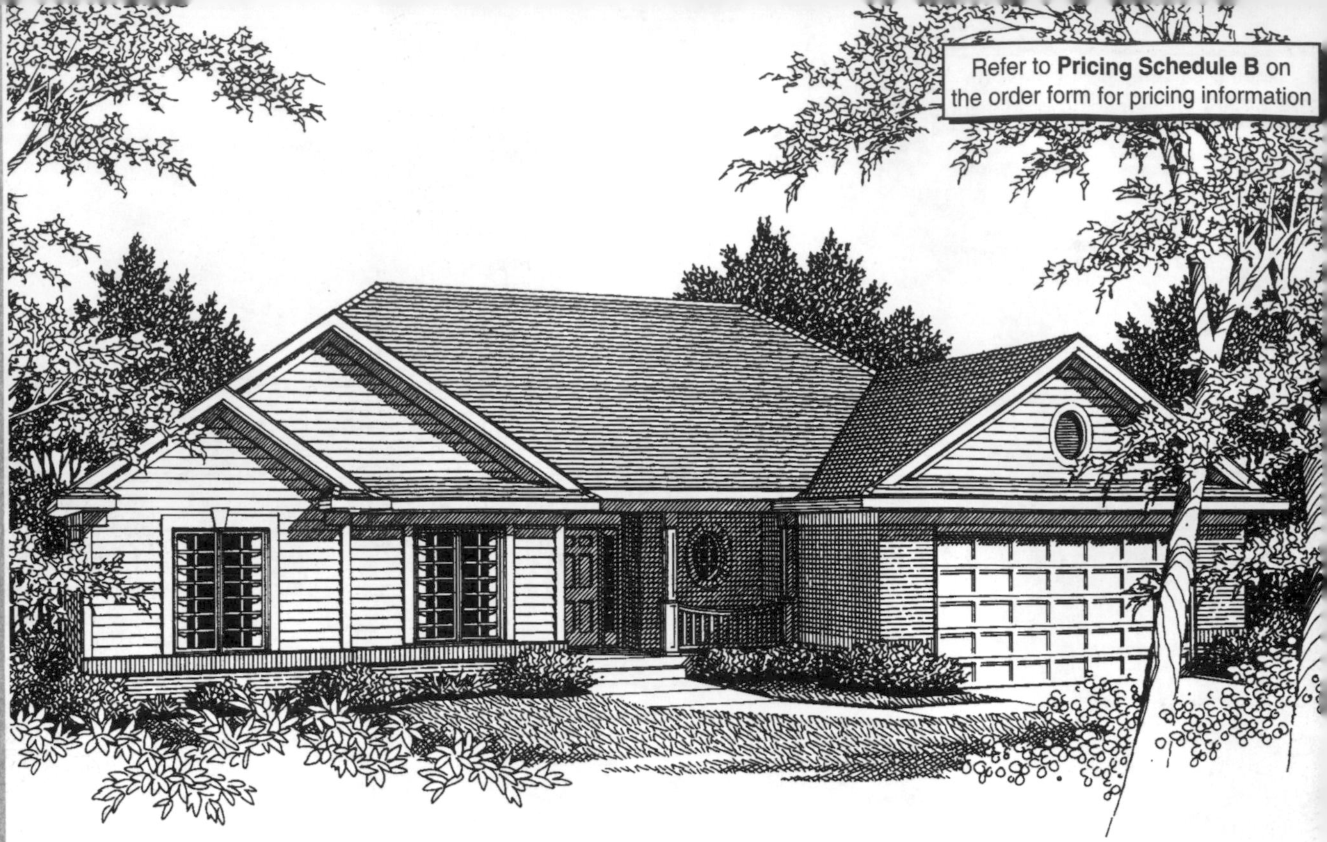

Hip Roof Ranch

An
EXCLUSIVE DESIGN
By Ahmann Design Inc.

- This plan features:
  - — Three bedrooms
  - — Two full baths
- Cozy front Porch leads into Entry with vaulted ceiling and sidelights
- Open Living Room enhanced by a cathedral ceiling, a wall of windows and corner fireplace
- Large and efficient Kitchen with an extended counter and a bright Dining area with access to Screen Porch
- Convenient Utility area with access to Garage and Storage area
- Spacious Master Bedroom with a walk-in closet and private bath
- Two additional bedrooms with ample closets, share a full bath
- No materials list available for this plan

MAIN FLOOR — 1,540 SQ. FT.
BASEMENT — 1,540 SQ. FT.

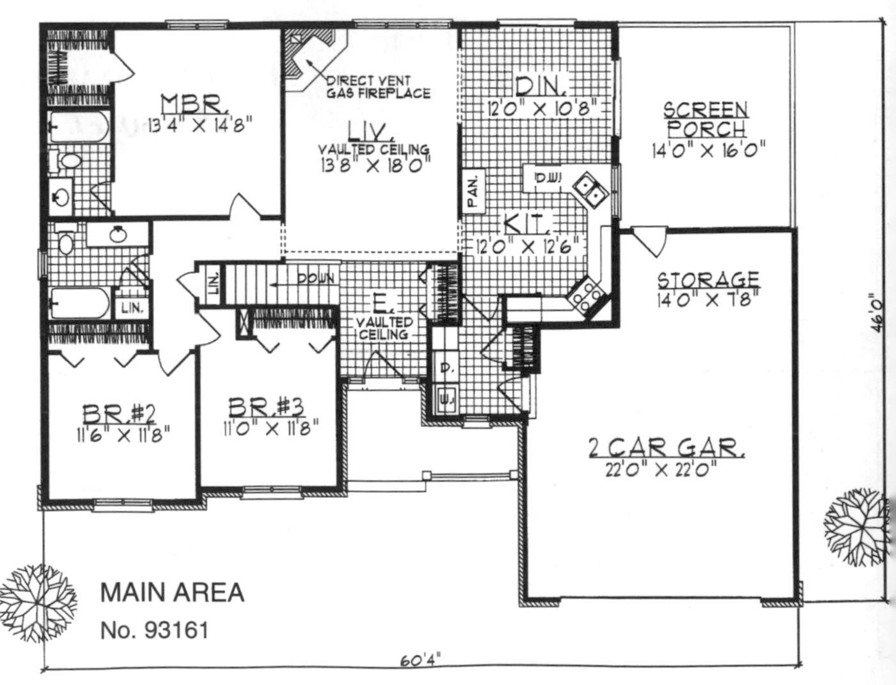
MBR.
13'4" X 14'8"
DIRECT VENT
GAS FIREPLACE
LIV.
VAULTED CEILING
13'8" X 18'0"
DIN.
12'0" X 10'8"
SCREEN
PORCH
14'0" X 16'0"
PAN.
D.W.
KIT.
12'0" X 12'6"
STORAGE
14'0" X 7'8"
LIN.
LIN.
DOWN
E.
VAULTED
CEILING
D.
W.
BR.#2
11'6" X 11'8"
BR.#3
11'0" X 11'8"
2 CAR GAR.
22'0" X 22'0"
46'0"
MAIN AREA
No. 93161
60'4"

TOTAL LIVING AREA:
1,540 SQ. FT.

To order your Blueprints, call 1-800-235-5700

Refer to **Pricing Schedule B** on the order form for pricing information

PLAN NO. 96506

TOTAL LIVING AREA
1,654 SQ. FT.

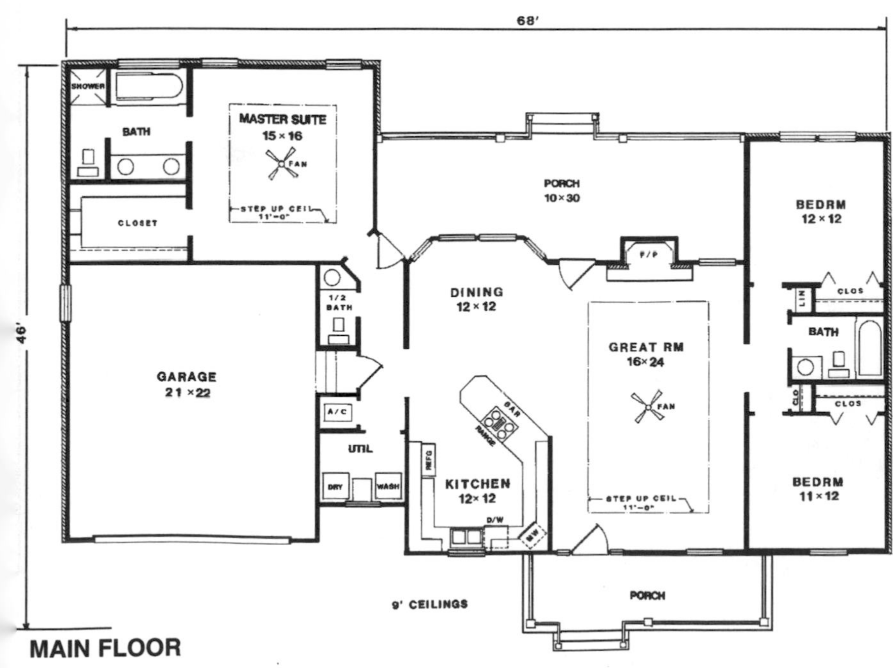

68'
46'
SHOWER
BATH
CLOSET
MASTER SUITE
15×16
FAN
STEP UP CEIL
11'-0"
PORCH
10×30
BEDRM
12×12
F/P
DINING
12×12
GARAGE
21×22
1/2 BATH
A/C
UTIL
DRY
WASH
BAR
RANGE
REFG
KITCHEN
12×12
D/W
GREAT RM
16×24
FAN
STEP UP CEIL
11'-0"
LIN
CLOS
BATH
CLO
CLOS
BEDRM
11×12
PORCH
9' CEILINGS

MAIN FLOOR
No. 96506

Attractive Ceiling Treatments and Open Layout

- This plan features:
- — Three bedrooms
- — Two full and one half baths
- Great Room and Master Suite with step-up ceiling treatments
- A cozy fireplace providing warm focal point in the Great Room
- Open layout between Kitchen, Dining and Great Room lending a more spacious feeling
- Five-piece, private bath and walk-in closet in the pampering Master Suite
- Two additional bedrooms located at opposite end of home

MAIN FLOOR — 1,654 SQ. FT.
GARAGE — 480 SQ. FT.

PLAN NO. 20100

Refer to **Pricing Schedule B** on the order form for pricing information

Wide Open and Convenient Plan

- This plan features:
- — Three bedrooms
- — Two full baths
- Vaulted ceilings in the Dining Room and Master Bedroom
- A sloped ceiling in the fireplaced Living Room
- A skylight illuminating the Master Bath
- A large Master Bedroom with a walk-in closet

MAIN AREA — 1,737 SQ. FT.
BASEMENT — 1,727 SQ. FT.
GARAGE — 484 SQ. FT.

TOTAL LIVING AREA:
1,727 SQ. FT.

An EXCLUSIVE DESIGN By *Karl Kreeger*

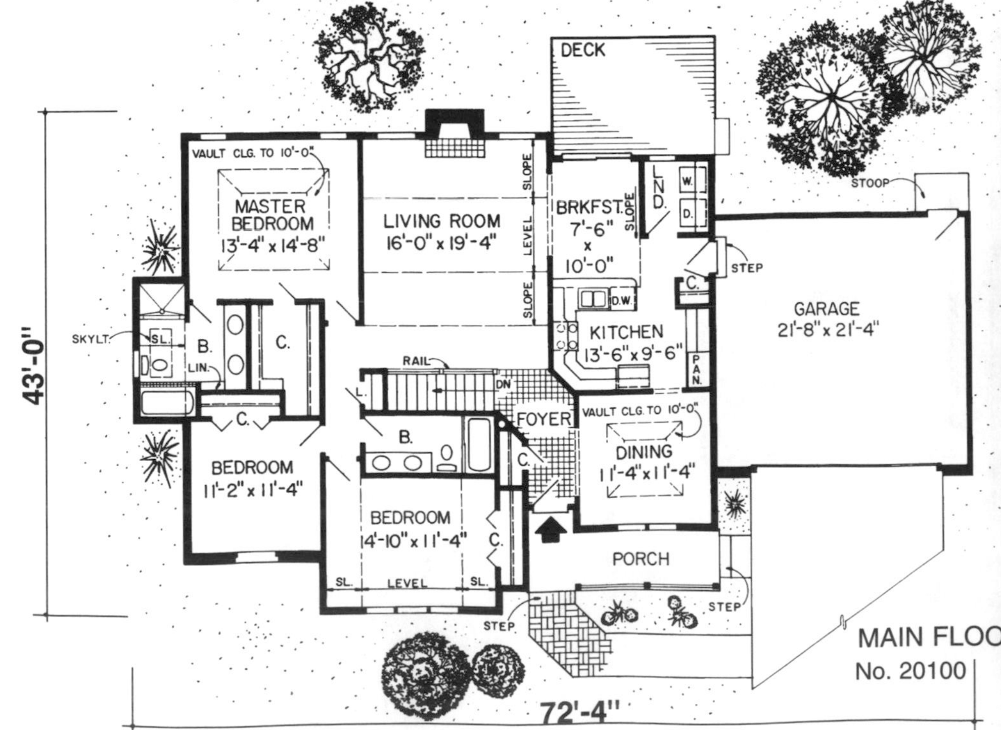

DECK
VAULT CLG. TO 10'-0"
MASTER BEDROOM
13'-4" x 14'-8"
LIVING ROOM
16'-0" x 19'-4"
SLOPE
LEVEL
SLOPE
BRKFST.
7'-6" x 10'-0"
SLOPE
LND.
W.
D.
STOOP
STEP
C.
GARAGE
21'-8" x 21'-4"
SKYLT.
SL.
B.
LIN.
C.
D.W.
KITCHEN
13'-6" x 9'-6"
PAN.
RAIL
DN
L.
C.
FOYER
VAULT CLG. TO 10'-0"
DINING
11'-4" x 11'-4"
B.
C.
BEDROOM
11'-2" x 11'-4"
BEDROOM
14'-10" x 11'-4"
C.
PORCH
SL.
LEVEL
SL.
STEP
STEP
43'-0"
72'-4"
MAIN FLOO
No. 20100

To order your Blueprints, call 1-800-235-5700

Refer to **Pricing Schedule B** on the order form for pricing information

PLAN NO. 90633

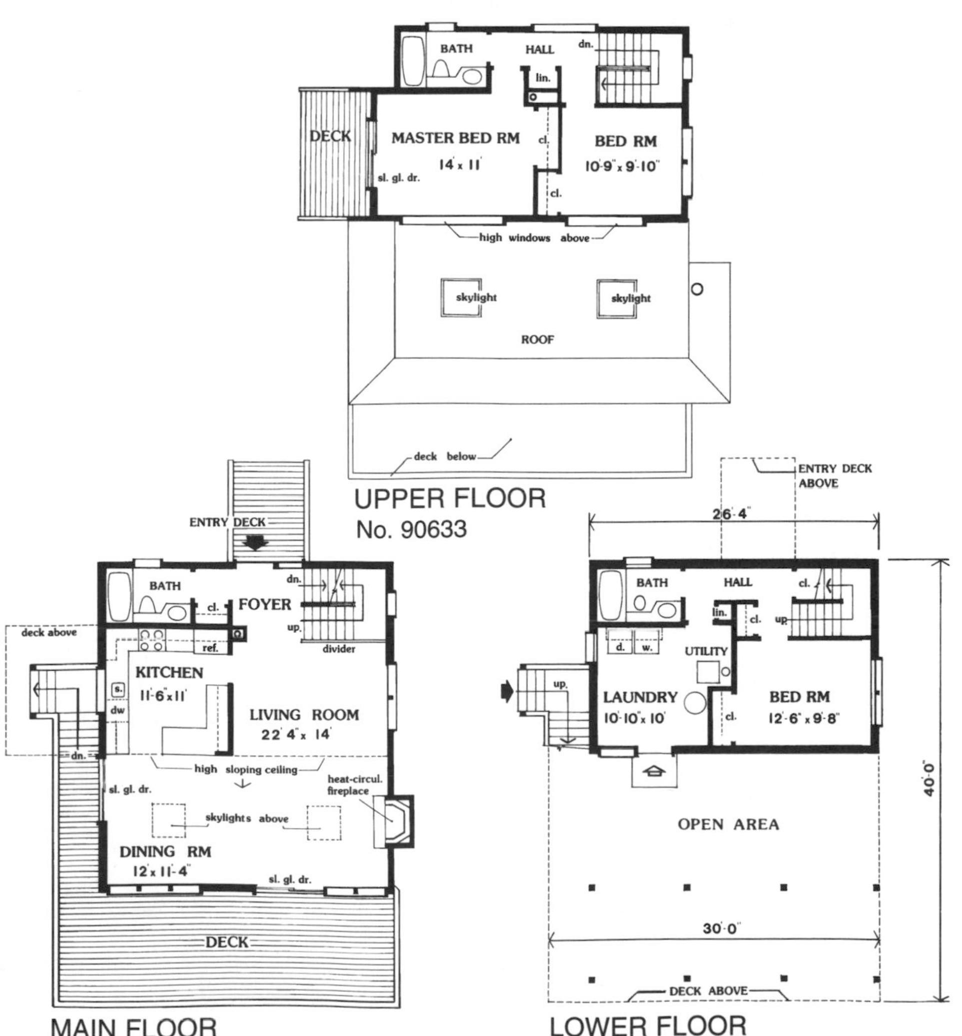
BATH
HALL
dn.
lin.
DECK
MASTER BED RM
14' x 11'
sl. gl. dr.
cl.
BED RM
10-9" x 9-10"
high windows above
skylight
skylight
ROOF
deck below
UPPER FLOOR
No. 90633
ENTRY DECK
BATH
cl.
FOYER
up.
deck above
ref.
divider
KITCHEN
11-6 x 11
dw
LIVING ROOM
22' 4" x 14'
dn.
high sloping ceiling
heat-circul. fireplace
sl. gl. dr.
skylights above
DINING RM
12' x 11'-4"
sl. gl. dr.
DECK
MAIN FLOOR
ENTRY DECK ABOVE
26'-4"
BATH
HALL
cl.
lin.
up
d.
w.
UTILITY
up
LAUNDRY
10-10" x 10'
cl.
BED RM
12'-6" x 9'-8"
40'-0"
OPEN AREA
30'-0"
DECK ABOVE
LOWER FLOOR

When There's a Hill

- This plan features:
  - — Three bedrooms
  - — Three full baths
- A design for a site that slopes down
- A sky-lit Dining Room with a high sloping ceiling and heat-circulating fireplace
- An efficient Kitchen with a peninsula counter and all the amenities
- A second floor Master Suite with a private balcony, deck and bath
- A basement foundation only

MAIN FLOOR — 790 SQ. FT.
UPPER FLOOR — 453 SQ. FT.
LOWER FLOOR — 340 SQ. FT.

TOTAL LIVING AREA:
1,583 SQ. FT.

PLAN NO. 24325

Refer to **Pricing Schedule C** on the order form for pricing information

Homey Country Porch

- This plan features:
- — Three bedrooms
- — Two full and one half baths
- A covered front Porch wraps around to connect with Patio that extends around back of home
- A spacious Living Room with a cozy fireplace, triple front window and atrium door to Patio
- A Family Room flowing into the Dining Room and Kitchen creates a comfortable gathering space
- An efficient Kitchen including a peninsula counter/snackbar, double sink, walk-in pantry and a broom closet
- A Master Suite with a walk-in closet, private Bath and a built-in audio/video center
- A Second floor Laundry Room
- Two additional bedrooms that share a full hall bath
- No material list available

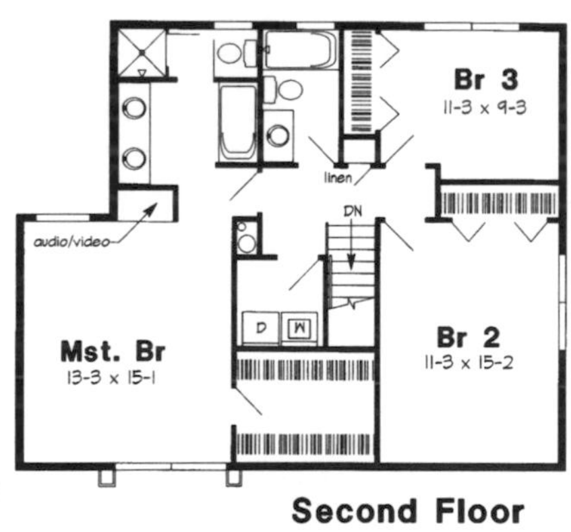

Br 3
11-3 x 9-3
linen
DN
audio/video
Mst. Br
13-3 x 15-1
D
W
Br 2
11-3 x 15-2

Second Floor

An EXCLUSIVE DESIGN By Marshall Associates

TOTAL LIVING AREA:
1,816 SQ. FT.

FIRST FLOOR — 908 SQ. FT.
SECOND FLOOR — 908 SQ. FT.
GARAGE — 462 SQ. FT.

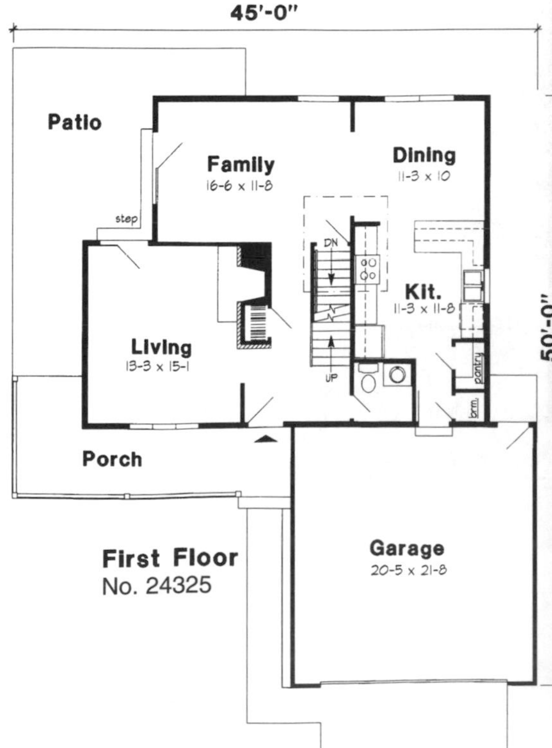

45'-0"
Patio
Family
16-6 x 11-8
Dining
11-3 x 10
step
DN
Kit.
11-3 x 11-8
Living
13-3 x 15-1
UP
pantry
brm
50'-0"
Porch
Garage
20-5 x 21-8

First Floor
No. 24325

To order your Blueprints, call 1-800-235-5700

Refer to **Pricing Schedule B** on the order form for pricing information

PLAN NO. 93133

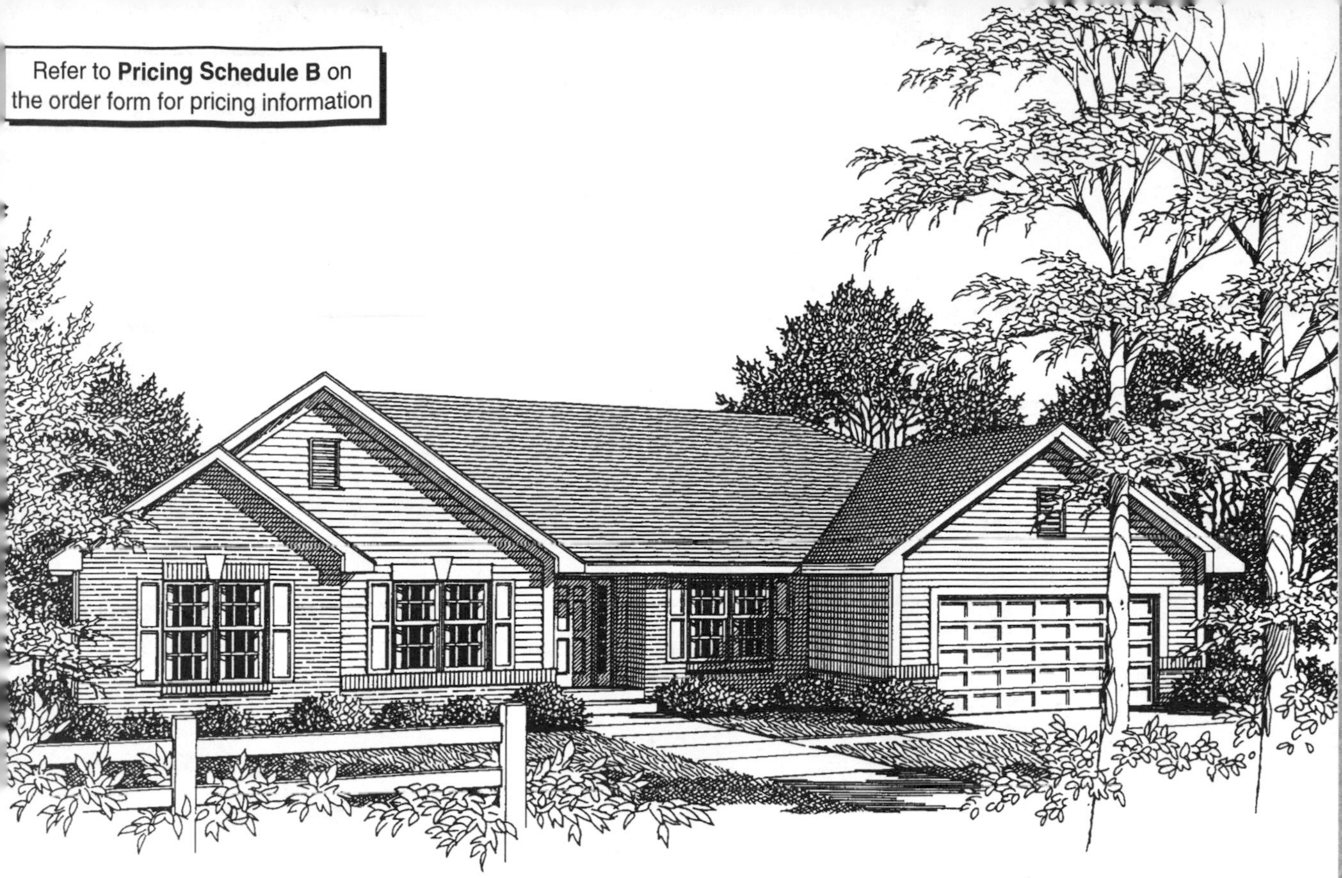

TOTAL LIVING AREA:
1,761 SQ. FT.

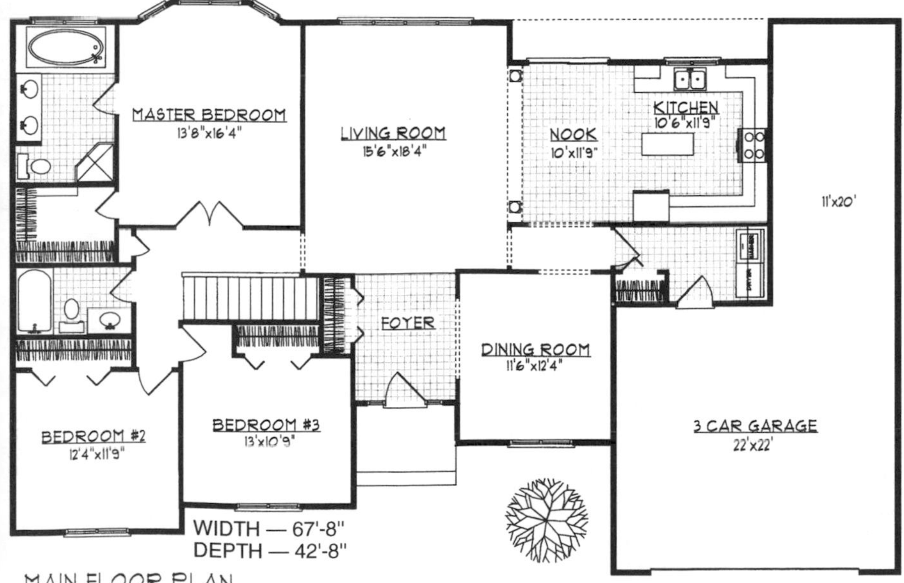

MASTER BEDROOM
13'8"x16'4"
LIVING ROOM
15'6"x18'4"
NOOK
10'x11'9"
KITCHEN
10'6"x11'9"
11'x20'
FOYER
DINING ROOM
11'6"x12'4"
3 CAR GARAGE
22'x22'
BEDROOM #2
12'4"x11'9"
BEDROOM #3
13'x10'9"
WIDTH — 67'-8"
DEPTH — 42'-8"
MAIN FLOOR PLAN

No. 93133

An EXCLUSIVE DESIGN By Ahmann Design Inc.

Triple Tandem Garage

- This plan features:
  - Three bedrooms
  - Two full baths
- A large Foyer leading to the bright and spacious Living Room
- A large open Kitchen with a central work island
- A handy Laundry Room with a pantry and garage access
- A Master Suite with a bay windowed sitting area and French doors, as well as a private Master Bath with a oversized tub, corner shower and room-sized walk-in closet
- Two additional front bedrooms that share a full bath
- A triple tandem garage with space for a third car, boat or just extra work and storage space
- No materials list available for this plan

MAIN FLOOR — 1,761 SQ. FT.
BASEMENT — 1,761 SQ. FT.
GARAGE — 658 SQ. FT.

PLAN NO. 34011

Refer to **Pricing Schedule B** on the order form for pricing information

Windows Add Warmth To All Living Areas

- This plan features:
  - — Three bedrooms
  - — Two full baths
- A Master Suite with huge his-n-her walk-in closets and private bath
- A second and third bedroom with ample closet space
- A Kitchen equipped with an island counter, and flowing easily into the Dining and Family Rooms
- A Laundry Room conveniently located near all three bedrooms
- An optional garage

MAIN AREA— 1,672 SQ. FT.
OPTIONAL GARAGE — 566 SQ. FT.

TOTAL LIVING AREA:
1,672 SQ. FT.

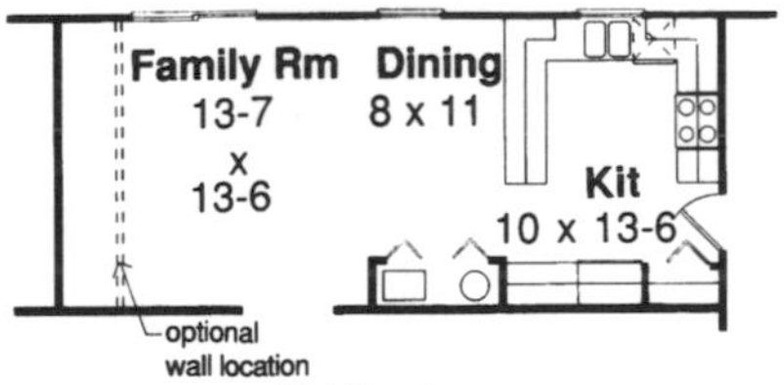

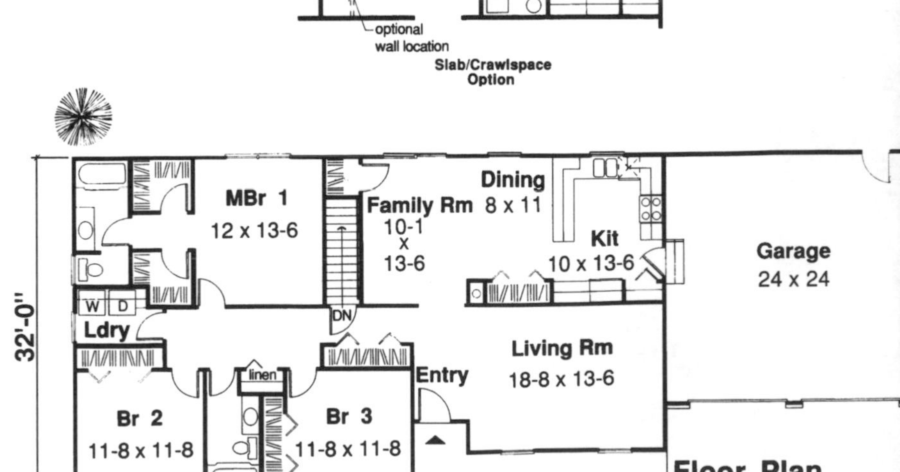

Family Rm
13-7
x
13-6
Dining
8 x 11
Kit
10 x 13-6
optional wall location
Slab/Crawlspace Option
MBr 1
12 x 13-6
Family Rm
10-1
x
13-6
Dining
8 x 11
Kit
10 x 13-6
Garage
24 x 24
W D
Ldry
DN
linen
Living Rm
18-8 x 13-6
Entry
Br 2
11-8 x 11-8
Br 3
11-8 x 11-8
32'-0"
80'-0"

Floor Plan
No. 34011

Refer to **Pricing Schedule Z** on the order form for pricing information

PLAN NO. 90934

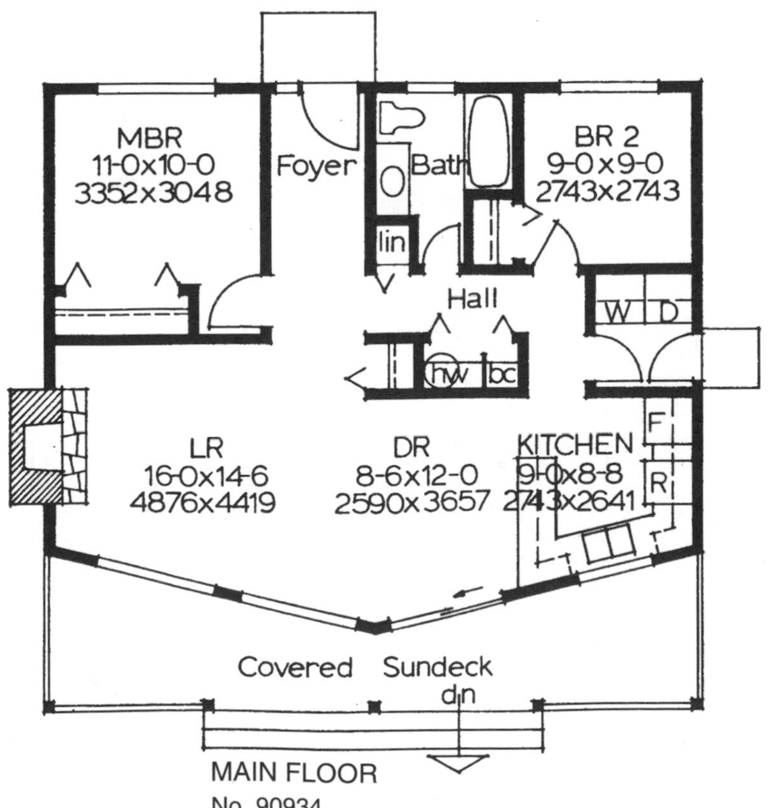

An EXCLUSIVE DESIGN By Westhome Planners, Ltd.
MBR 11-0x10-0 3352x3048
Foyer
Bath
lin
BR 2 9-0x9-0 2743x2743
Hall
W D
hw bc
F
R
LR 16-0x14-6 4876x4419
DR 8-6x12-0 2590x3657
KITCHEN 9-0x8-8 2743x2641
Covered Sundeck
dn
MAIN FLOOR
No. 90934

A Nest for Empty-Nesters

- This plan features:
  - — Two bedrooms
  - — One full bath
- An economical design
- A covered sun deck adding outdoor living space
- A mudroom/laundry area inside the side door, trapping dirt before it can enter the house
- An open layout between the Living Room with fireplace, Dining Room and Kitchen

MAIN FLOOR — 884 SQ. FT.
WIDTH — 34'-0"
DEPTH — 28'-0"

TOTAL LIVING AREA:
884 SQ. FT.

PLAN NO. 90684

Refer to **Pricing Schedule B** on the order form for pricing information

Window Boxes Add Romantic Charm

- This plan features:
  - — Three bedrooms
  - — Two full and one half baths
- A spacious Living Room and formal Dining Room combination that is perfect for entertaining
- A Family Room with a large fireplace and an expansive glass wall that overlooks the patio
- An informal Dining bay, convenient to both the Kitchen and the Family Room
- An efficient and well-equipped Kitchen with a peninsula counter dividing it from the Family Room
- A Master Bedroom with his-n-her closets and a private Master Bath

MAIN AREA — 1590 SQ. FT.
BASEMENT — 900 SQ. FT.

TOTAL LIVING AREA:
1,590 SQ. FT.

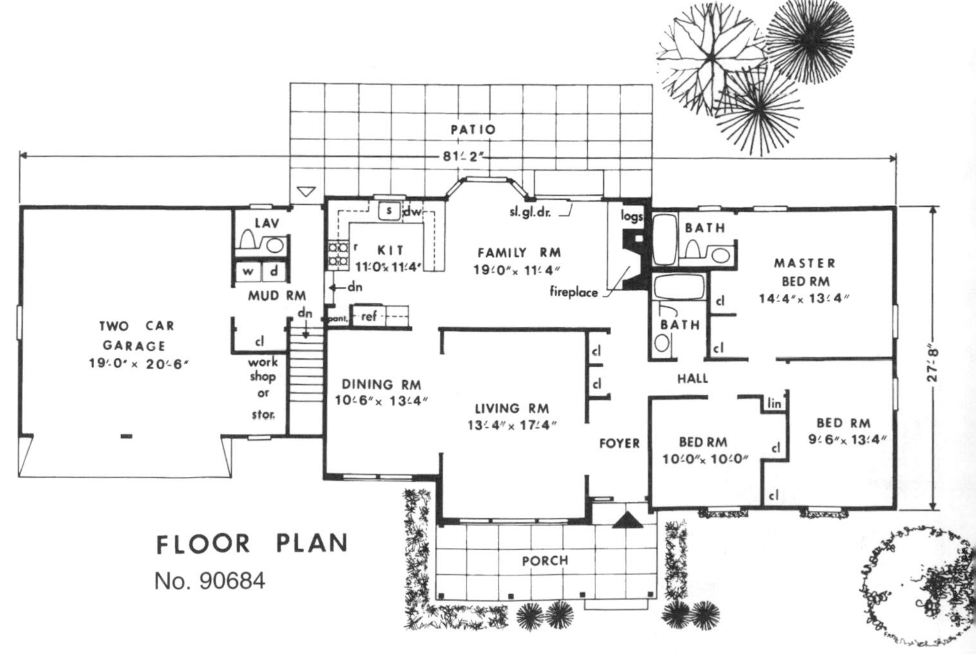

PATIO
81'-2"
LAV
w d
MUD RM
KIT
11'0"x 11'4"
FAMILY RM
19'0"x 11'4"
sl.gl.dr.
logs
fireplace
BATH
MASTER
BED RM
14'4"x 13'4"
TWO CAR
GARAGE
19'0"x 20'6"
work
shop
or
stor.
ref
DINING RM
10'6"x 13'4"
LIVING RM
13'4"x 17'4"
HALL
FOYER
BED RM
10'0"x 10'0"
BED RM
9'6"x 13'4"
27'-8"
PORCH

FLOOR PLAN
No. 90684

To order your Blueprints, call 1-800-235-5700

Refer to **Pricing Schedule A** on the order form for pricing information

PLAN NO. 24303

Affordable Living

- This plan features:
  - — Three bedrooms
  - — Two full baths
- A simple, yet gracefully designed exterior
- A sheltered entrance into a roomy Living Room graced with a large front window
- A formal Dining Room flowing from the Living Room, allowing for ease in entertaining
- A well-appointed U-shaped Kitchen with double sinks and adequate storage
- A Master Bedroom equipped with a full Bath
- Two additional bedrooms that share a full hall bath complete with a convenient laundry center
- A covered Patio, tucked behind the garage

MAIN AREA — 984 SQ. FT.
BASEMENT — 960 SQ. FT.
GARAGE — 280 SQ. FT.

An EXCLUSIVE DESIGN
By Marshall Associates

TOTAL LIVING AREA:
984 SQ. FT.

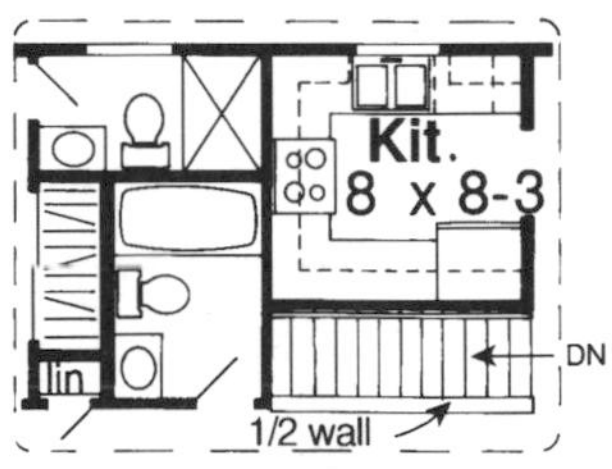
Kit.
8 x 8-3
DN
lin
1/2 wall

Basement Option

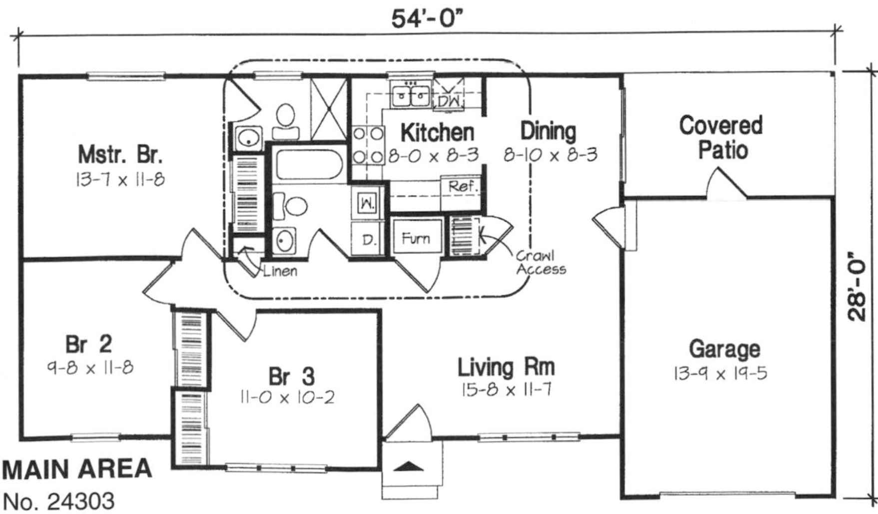
54'-0"
28'-0"
Mstr. Br.
13-7 x 11-8
Kitchen
8-0 x 8-3
DW
Ref.
W
D.
Furn
Dining
8-10 x 8-3
Crawl Access
Linen
Covered Patio
Br 2
9-8 x 11-8
Br 3
11-0 x 10-2
Living Rm
15-8 x 11-7
Garage
13-9 x 19-5

MAIN AREA
No. 24303

PLAN NO. 90638

Refer to **Pricing Schedule A** on the order form for pricing information

REAR ELEVATION

Build In Stages

- This plan features:
- — Three bedrooms
- — One full and one three quarter baths
- A covered entrance into spacious Living/Dining Area with a 13 foot cathedral ceiling, fireplace and two sliding glass doors to a huge Deck
- An efficient L-shaped Kitchen with separate counter space for dining is adjacent to Deck and Laundry/Utility room
- A Master Bedroom with a private shower bath
- Two additional bedrooms sharing a full hall bath
- An option to build in stages

MAIN FLOOR — 1,042 SQ. FT.

TOTAL LIVING AREA:
1,042 SQ. FT.

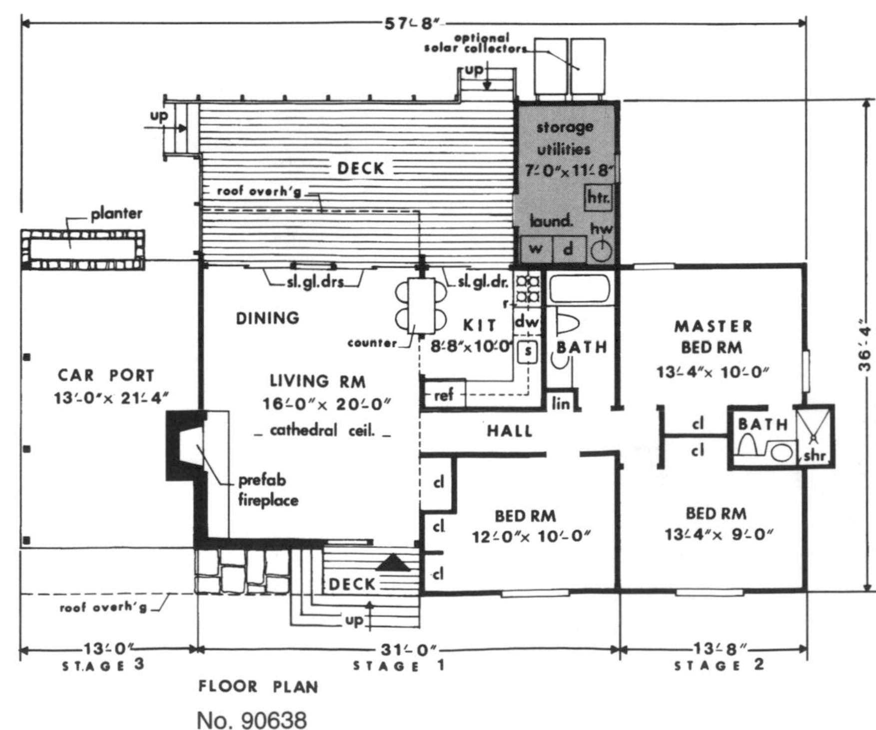
57'-8"
optional solar collectors
up
storage utilities 7'-0"x 11'-8"
htr.
laund.
hw
w d
DECK
roof overh'g
planter
sl.gl.drs.
sl.gl.dr.
DINING
counter
KIT 8'-8"x 10'-0"
dw
s
r
ref
BATH
lin
MASTER BED RM 13'-4"x 10'-0"
CAR PORT 13'-0"x 21'-4"
LIVING RM 16'-0"x 20'-0"
cathedral ceil.
HALL
cl
BATH
shr
prefab fireplace
BED RM 12'-0"x 10'-0"
BED RM 13'-4"x 9'-0"
DECK
up
roof overh'g
36'-4"
13'-0" STAGE 3
31'-0" STAGE 1
13'-8" STAGE 2

FLOOR PLAN
No. 90638

To order your Blueprints, call 1-800-235-5700

Refer to **Pricing Schedule B** on the order form for pricing information

PLAN NO. 10839

Perfect Compact Ranch

- This plan features:
  - — Two bedrooms
  - — Two full baths
- A large, sunken Great Room, centralized with a cozy fireplace
- A Master Bedroom with an unforgettable Bathroom including a skylight
- A huge three-car Garage, including a work area for the family carpenter
- A Kitchen, including a Breakfast Nook for family gatherings

MAIN FLOOR — 1,738 SQ. FT.
BASEMENT — 1,083 SQ. FT.
GARAGE — 796 SQ. FT.

TOTAL LIVING AREA:
1,738 SQ. FT.

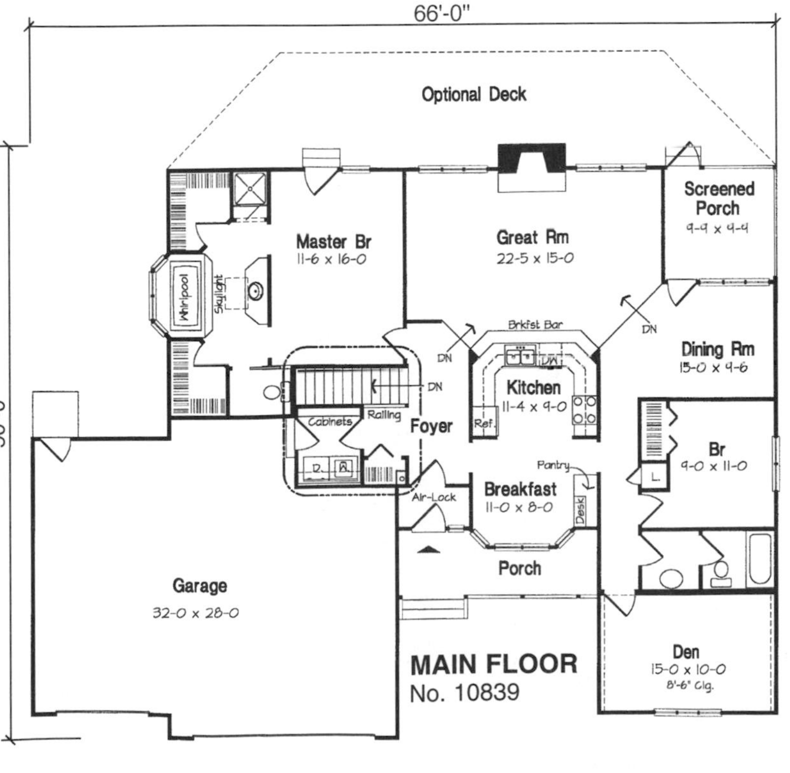

66'-0"
50'-0"
Optional Deck
Master Br 11-6 x 16-0
Whirlpool
Skylight
Great Rm 22-5 x 15-0
Screened Porch 9-9 x 9-9
Brkfst Bar
DN
Dining Rm 15-0 x 9-6
Kitchen 11-4 x 9-0
Ref.
Foyer
Cabinets
Railing
Br 9-0 x 11-0
Air-Lock
Pantry
Breakfast 11-0 x 8-0
Desk
Porch
Garage 32-0 x 28-0
Den 15-0 x 10-0 8'-6" Clg.

MAIN FLOOR
No. 10839

Furn.
WH
Crawl Space Access
Crawl / Slab Option

To order your Blueprints, call 1-800-235-5700

PLAN NO. 91031

Refer to **Pricing Schedule Z** on the order form for pricing information

Snug Retreat With A View

- This plan features:
  - — One bedroom plus loft
  - — One full bath
- A large front Deck providing views and an expansive entrance
- A two-story Living/Dining area with double glass doors leading out to the Deck
- An efficient, U-shaped Kitchen with a pass through counter to the Dining area
- A first floor Bedroom, with ample closet space, located near a full shower bath
- A Loft/Bedroom on the second floor offering multiple uses

MAIN FLOOR — 572 SQ. FT.
LOFT — 308 SQ. FT.

TOTAL LIVING AREA:
880 SQ. FT.

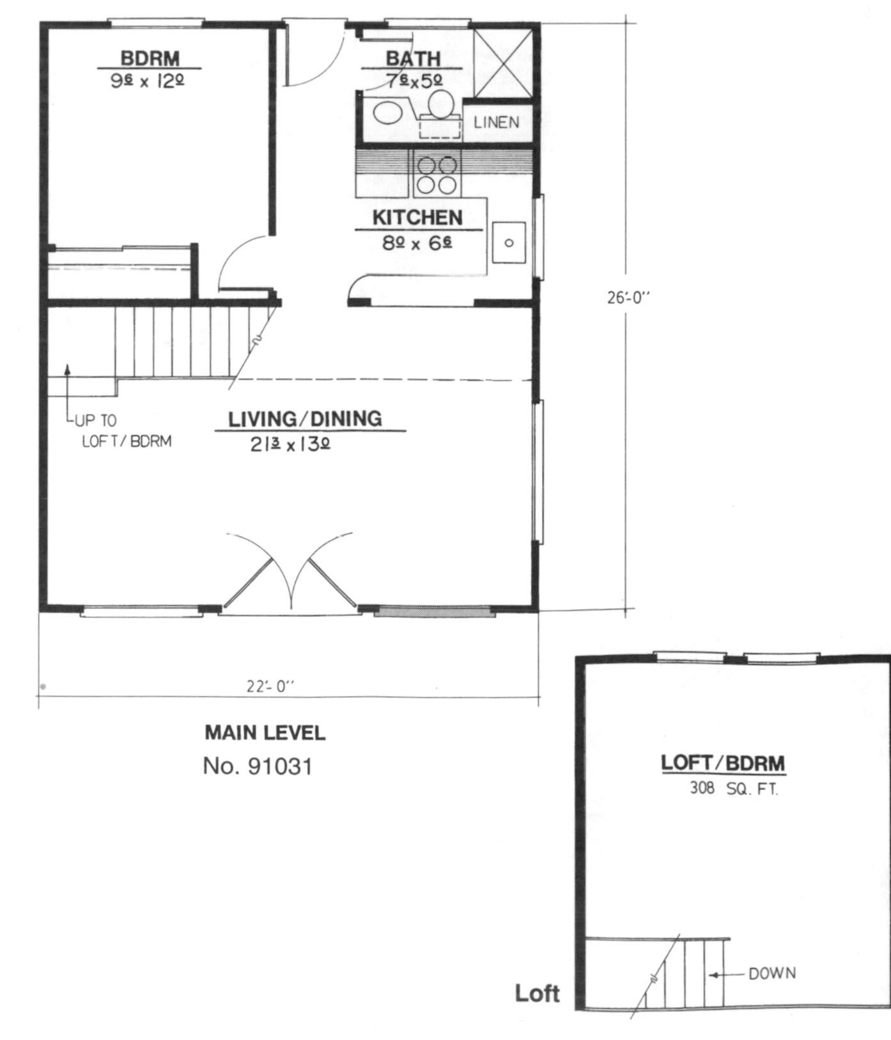
BDRM
$9^{6} \times 12^{0}$
BATH
$7^{6} \times 5^{0}$
LINEN
KITCHEN
$8^{0} \times 6^{6}$
UP TO LOFT/BDRM
LIVING/DINING
$21^{3} \times 13^{0}$
26'-0"
22'-0"
LOFT/BDRM
308 SQ. FT.
DOWN
Loft

MAIN LEVEL
No. 91031

To order your Blueprints, call 1-800-235-5700

Refer to **Pricing Schedule A** on the order form for pricing information

PLAN NO. 90990

An EXCLUSIVE DESIGN By Westhome Planners, Ltd.

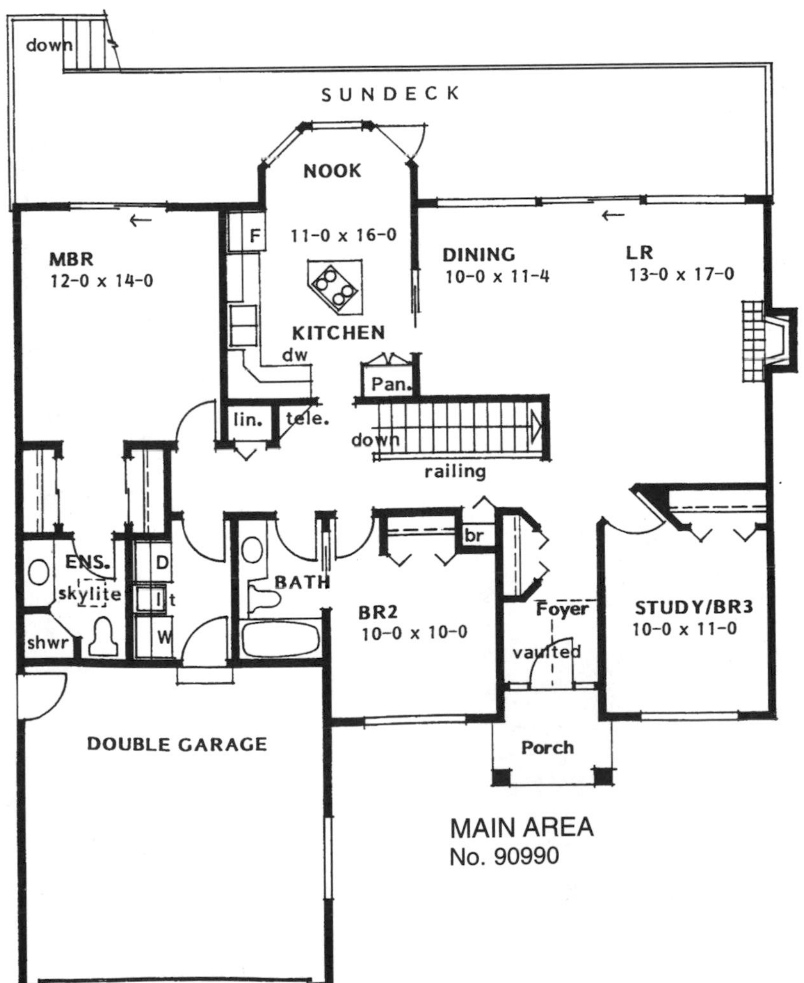

down
SUNDECK
NOOK
11-0 x 16-0
F
MBR
12-0 x 14-0
DINING
10-0 x 11-4
LR
13-0 x 17-0
KITCHEN
dw
Pan.
lin.
tele.
down
railing
ENS.
skylite
D
lt
W
shwr
BATH
br
BR2
10-0 x 10-0
Foyer
vaulted
STUDY/BR3
10-0 x 11-0
DOUBLE GARAGE
Porch

MAIN AREA
No. 90990

Comfort and Style

- This plan features:
  - — Two bedrooms with possible third bedroom/den
  - — Two full baths
- An unfinished daylight basement, providing possible space for family recreation
- A Master Suite complete with private bath and skylight
- A large Kitchen including an eating nook
- A sundeck that is easily accessible from the Master Suite, Nook and the Living/Dining area

MAIN AREA — 1,423 SQ. FT.
BASEMENT — 1,423 SQ. FT.
GARAGE — 399 SQ. FT.
WIDTH — 46'-0"
DEPTH — 52'-0"

TOTAL LIVING AREA:
1,423 SQ. FT.

PLAN NO. 20104

Refer to **Pricing Schedule B** on the order form for pricing information

Easy One Level Living

- This plan features:
- — Three bedrooms
- — Two full baths
- A sky-lit Kitchen
- Ample closet space
- Built-in storage areas in the Kitchen
- A Master bath with twin vanities, a raised tub, and a walk-in shower

MAIN AREA — 1,686 SQ. FT.
BASEMENT — 1,677 SQ. FT.
GARAGE — 475 SQ. FT.

TOTAL LIVING AREA:
1,686 SQ. FT.

An EXCLUSIVE DESIGN *By Karl Kreeger*

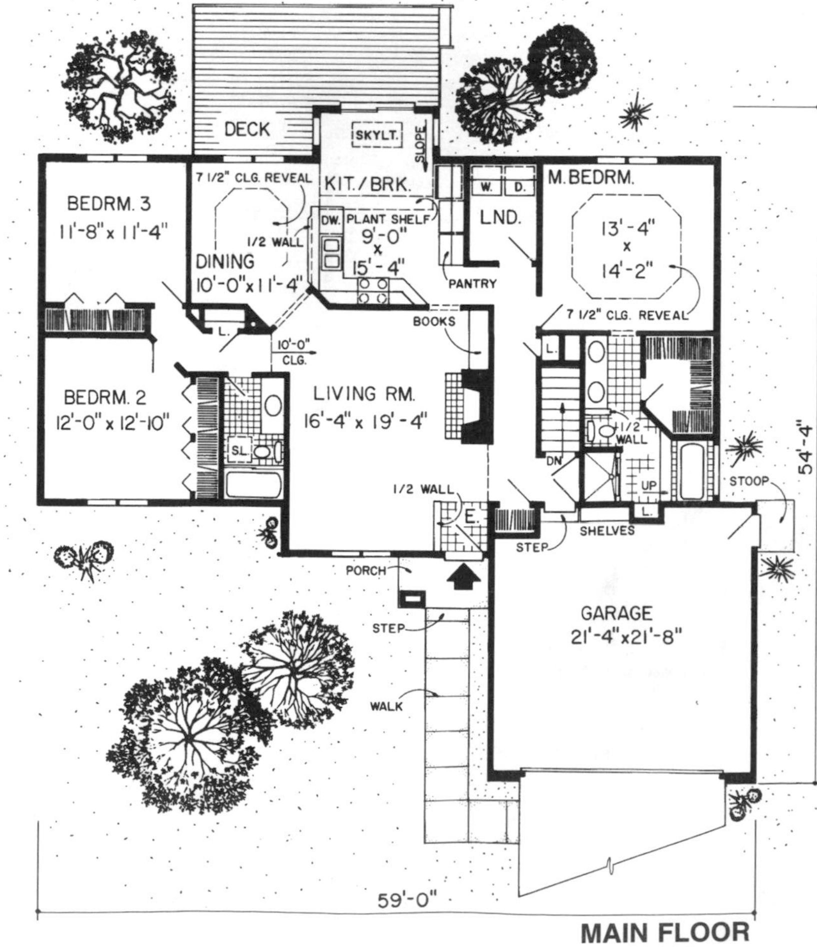

DECK
SKYLT.
SLOPE
7 1/2" CLG. REVEAL
KIT./BRK.
W.
D.
M.BEDRM.
BEDRM. 3
11'-8" x 11'-4"
DW.
PLANT SHELF
9'-0"
x
15'-4"
LND.
13'-4"
x
14'-2"
1/2 WALL
DINING
10'-0"x11'-4"
PANTRY
7 1/2" CLG. REVEAL
BOOKS
L.
10'-0" CLG.
BEDRM. 2
12'-0" x 12'-10"
LIVING RM.
16'-4" x 19'-4"
SL.
1/2 WALL
DN
UP
STOOP
1/2 WALL
E.
STEP
SHELVES
PORCH
GARAGE
21'-4"x21'-8"
STEP
WALK
54'-4"
59'-0"

MAIN FLOOR
No. 20104

To order your Blueprints, call 1-800-235-5700

Refer to **Pricing Schedule A** on the order form for pricing information

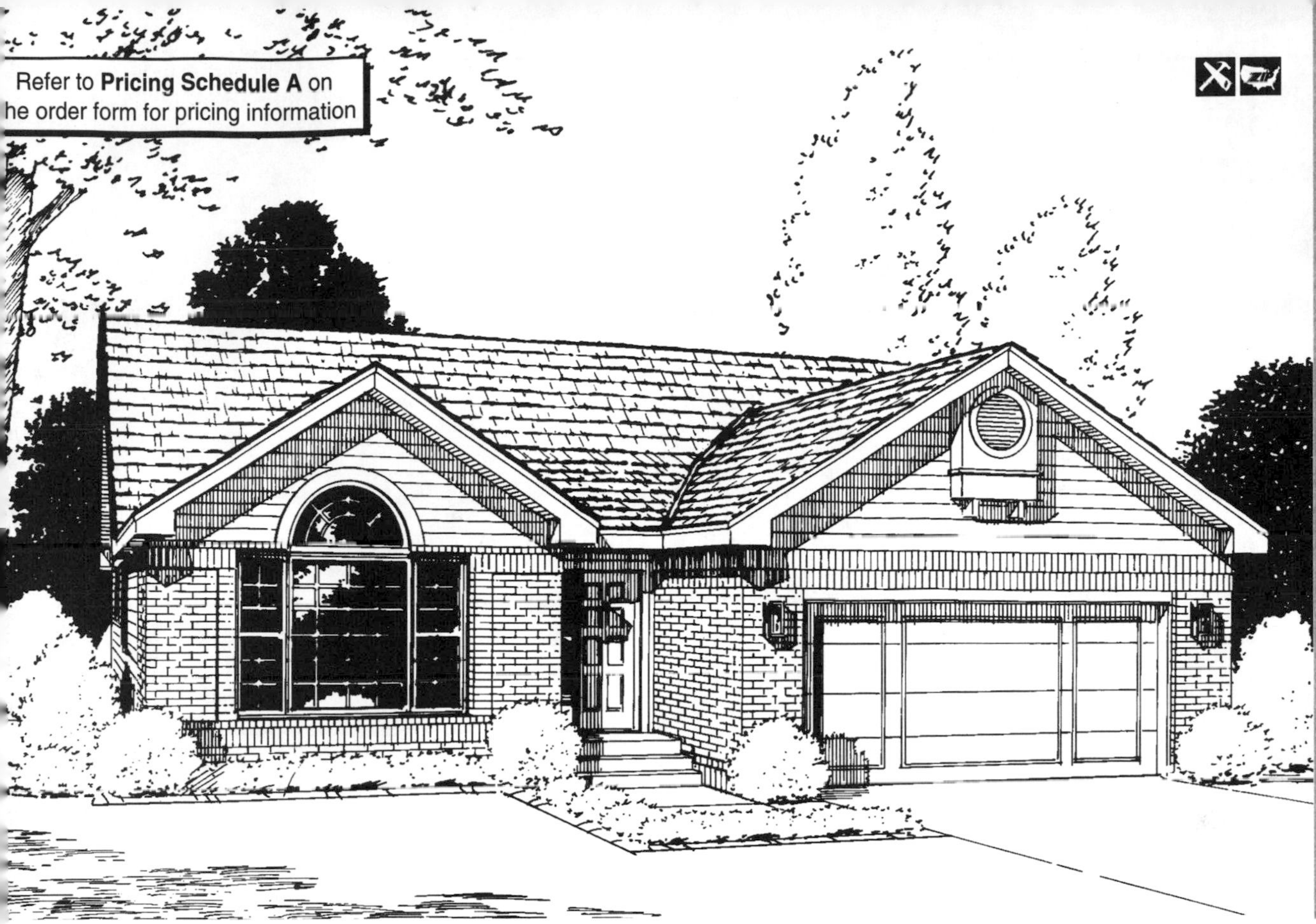

PLAN NO. 24327

An EXCLUSIVE DESIGN *By Marshall Associates*

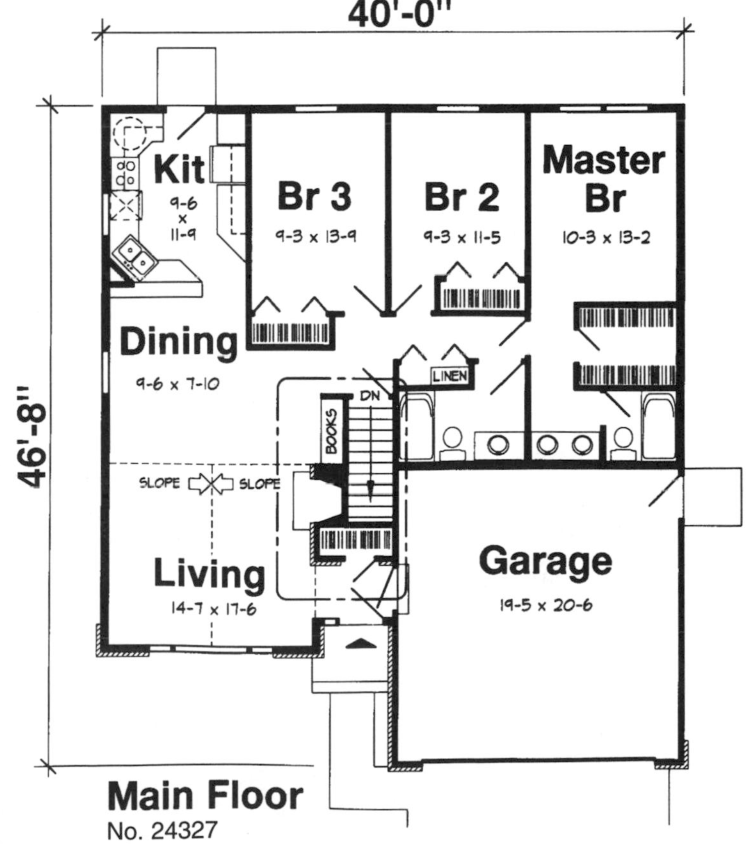

40'-0"
46'-8"
Kit
9-6 x 11-9
Br 3
9-3 x 13-9
Br 2
9-3 x 11-5
Master Br
10-3 x 13-2
Dining
9-6 x 7-10
LINEN
DN
BOOKS
SLOPE
SLOPE
Living
14-7 x 17-6
Garage
19-5 x 20-6

Main Floor
No. 24327

One Level Contemporary

- This plan features:
  - — Three bedrooms
  - — Two full baths
- A vaulted ceiling and elegant fireplace in the Living Room
- An open layout between the Living Room, Dining Room and Kitchen gives a more spacious feeling to these areas
- A well-equipped Kitchen with a double sink and a peninsula counter that may be used as an eating bar
- A Master Suite that includes a walk-in closet and a private bath with a double vanity
- Two additional bedrooms that have ample closet space and share a full hall bath

MAIN AREA — 1,266 SQ. FT.
GARAGE — 443 SQ. FT.
BASEMENT — 1,266 SQ. FT.

TOTAL LIVING AREA:
1,266 SQ. FT.

PRICE CODE A

TOTAL LIVING AREA:
1,373 SQ. FT.

No. 98411

Style and Convenience

- This plan features:
—Three bedrooms
—Two full baths
- Large front windows, dormers and an old-fashioned porch giving a pleasing style to the home
- A vaulted ceiling topping the Foyer flowing into the Family Room which is highlighted by a fireplace
- A Formal Dining Room flowing from the Family Room crowned in an elegant vaulted ceiling
- An efficient Kitchen enhanced by a pantry, a pass through to the Family Room and direct access to the Dining Room and Breakfast Room
- A decorative tray ceiling, a five-piece private bath and a walk-in closet in the Master Suite
- Two additional bedrooms, roomy in size, sharing the full bath in the hall
- Foundation options for Basement or Crawl Space — please specify when ordering

MAIN FLOOR — 1,373 SQ. FT.
BASEMENT — 1,386 SQ. FT.

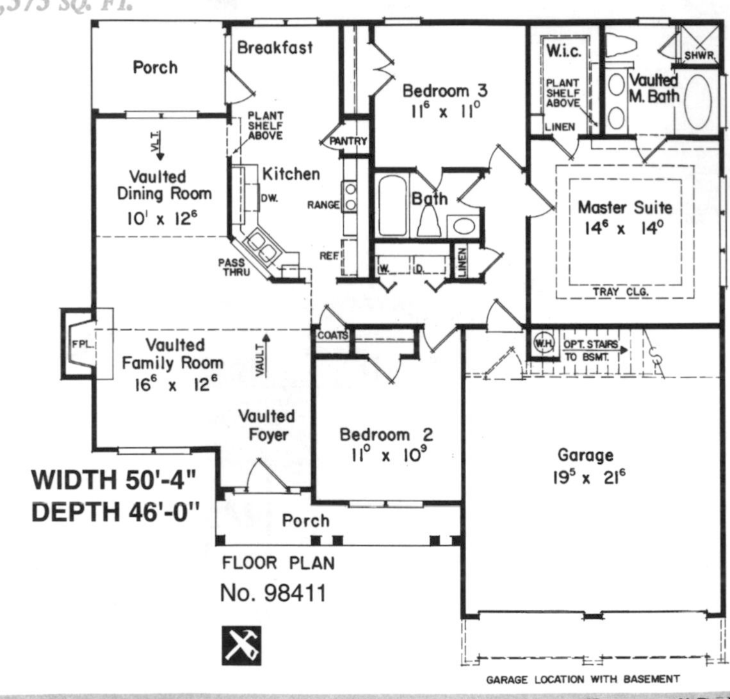
Porch
Breakfast
Bedroom 3
11⁶ x 11⁰
W.i.c.
PLANT SHELF ABOVE
LINEN
SHWR
Vaulted M. Bath
PLANT SHELF ABOVE
PANTRY
Vaulted Dining Room
10' x 12⁶
Kitchen
DW.
RANGE
Bath
Master Suite
14⁶ x 14⁰
TRAY CLG.
PASS THRU
REF
W. D.
LINEN
FPL
Vaulted Family Room
16⁶ x 12⁶
VAULT
COATS
W.H.
OPT. STAIRS TO BSMT.
Vaulted Foyer
Bedroom 2
11⁰ x 10⁹
Garage
19⁵ x 21⁶
WIDTH 50'-4"
DEPTH 46'-0"
Porch
FLOOR PLAN
No. 98411
GARAGE LOCATION WITH BASEMENT

No. 99303

Captivating Sun-Catcher

- This plan features:
— Two bedrooms
— Two full baths
- A glass-walled Breakfast Room adjoining the vaulted-ceiling Kitchen
- A fireplaced, vaulted ceiling Living Room that flows from the Dining Room
- A greenhouse window over the tub in the luxurious Master Bath
- Two walk-in closets and glass sliders in the Master Bedroom

MAIN AREA — 1,421 SQ. FT.

TOTAL LIVING AREA:
1,421 SQ. FT.

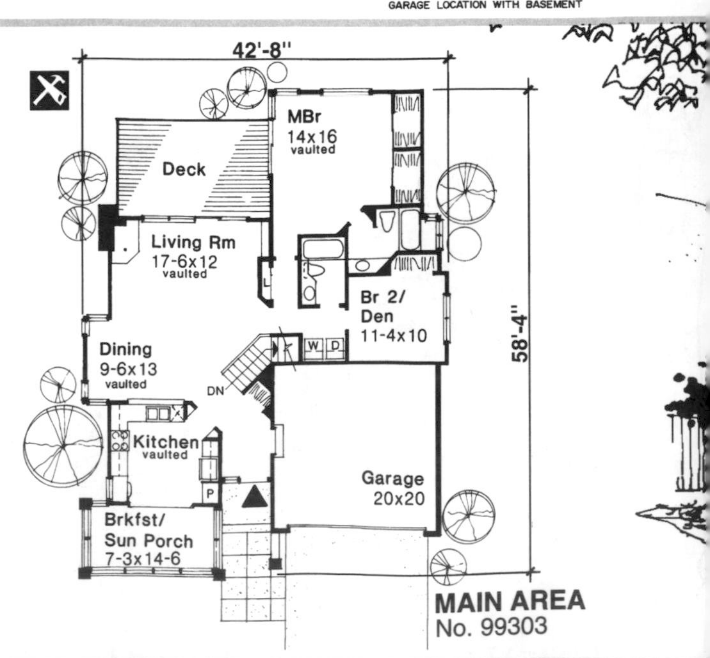
42'-8"
MBr
14x16
vaulted
Deck
Living Rm
17-6x12
vaulted
Br 2/
Den
11-4x10
58'-4"
Dining
9-6x13
vaulted
DN
W D
Kitchen
vaulted
P
Garage
20x20
Brkfst/
Sun Porch
7-3x14-6
MAIN AREA
No. 99303

PRICE CODE B

No. 99216

Easy One Floor Living

- This plan features:
  - Three bedrooms
  - Two full baths
- Living areas conveniently grouped in the right half of the home for everyday activities
- A Gathering Room with a sloped ceiling and a fireplace
- A Kitchen designed for easy cooking with a closet pantry, plenty of counter space, and cupboards
- A third bedroom making a perfect home office or study

MAIN AREA — 1,521 SQ. FT.
BASEMENT — 1,521 SQ. FT.

TOTAL LIVING AREA:
1,521 SQ. FT.

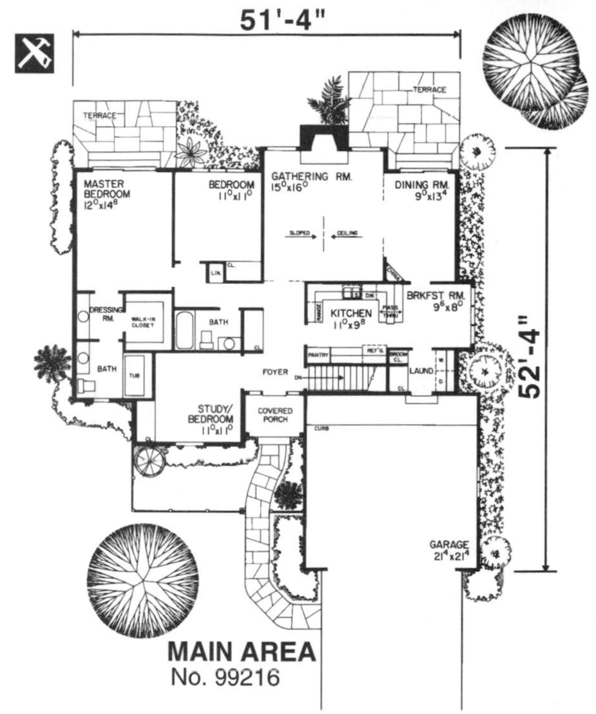
51'-4"
52'-4"
TERRACE
TERRACE
MASTER BEDROOM $12^{0}x14^{8}$
BEDROOM $11^{0}x11^{0}$
GATHERING RM. $15^{0}x16^{0}$
DINING RM. $9^{0}x13^{4}$
SLOPED CEILING
LIN.
CL.
DRESSING RM.
WALK-IN CLOSET
BATH
BATH
TUB
KITCHEN $11^{0}x9^{8}$
BRKFST RM. $9^{6}x8^{0}$
PANTRY
FOYER
LAUND
STUDY/ BEDROOM $11^{0}x11^{0}$
COVERED PORCH
CURB
GARAGE $21^{4}x21^{4}$
MAIN AREA
No. 99216

PRICE CODE A

PRICE CODE C

No. 99705

Flexible Floor Plan

- This plan features:
- — Two bedrooms plus loft
- — Three full baths and one half bath
- An entrance through the Sun Porch into the Kitchen and Utility area
- An efficient Kitchen with an island sink/eating bar, a built-in pantry and a broom closet, which opens into the Living Room area
- A expansive, two-story Living Room with a hearth fireplace and a wall of windows, providing access to a triangular Deck
- Two first floor bedrooms with over-sized closets, sliding glass doors to a Deck, and private baths
- A roomy Work Shop and a Garage providing multiple uses and ample storage space
- A Loft area with a full bath and a sliding glass door to a private Deck

FIRST FLOOR — 1,625 SQ. FT.
SECOND FLOOR — 466 SQ. FT.

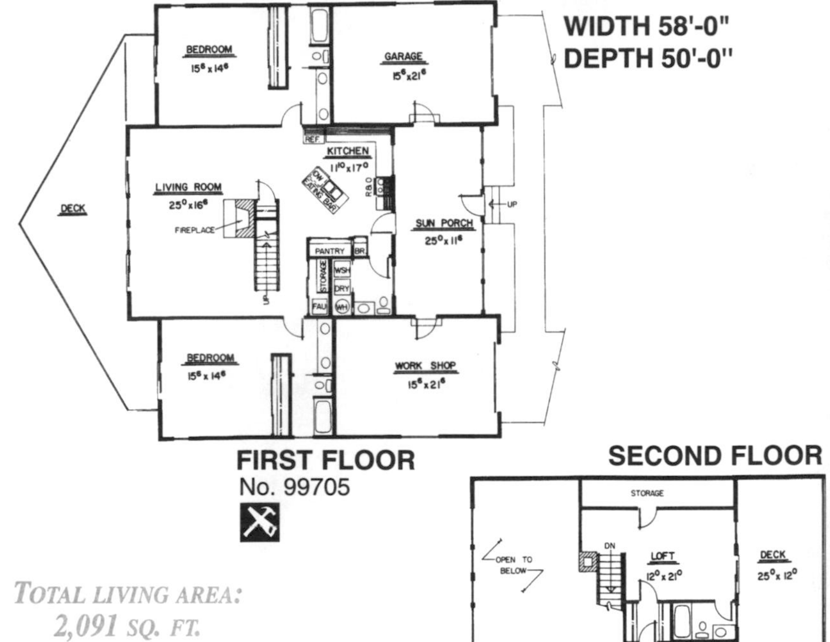
WIDTH 58'-0"
DEPTH 50'-0"
BEDROOM
GARAGE
KITCHEN
LIVING ROOM
DECK
FIREPLACE
SUN PORCH
PANTRY
BEDROOM
WORK SHOP
FIRST FLOOR
No. 99705
SECOND FLOOR
STORAGE
OPEN TO BELOW
LOFT
DECK
STORAGE

TOTAL LIVING AREA:
2,091 SQ. FT.

No. 99840

Beautiful From Front to Back

- This plan features:
- —Three bedrooms
- —Two full baths
- Porches front and back, gables and dormers providing special charm
- Central Great Room with a cathedral ceiling, fireplace, and a clerestory window which bringing natural light
- Columns dividing the open Great Room from the Kitchen and the Breakfast Bay
- A tray ceiling and columns dressing up the formal Dining Room
- Skylighted Master Bath with shower, whirlpool tub , dual vanity and spacious walk-in closet

MAIN FLOOR — 1,632 SQ. FT.
GARAGE & STORAGE — 561 SQ. FT.

TOTAL LIVING AREA:
1,632 SQ. FT.

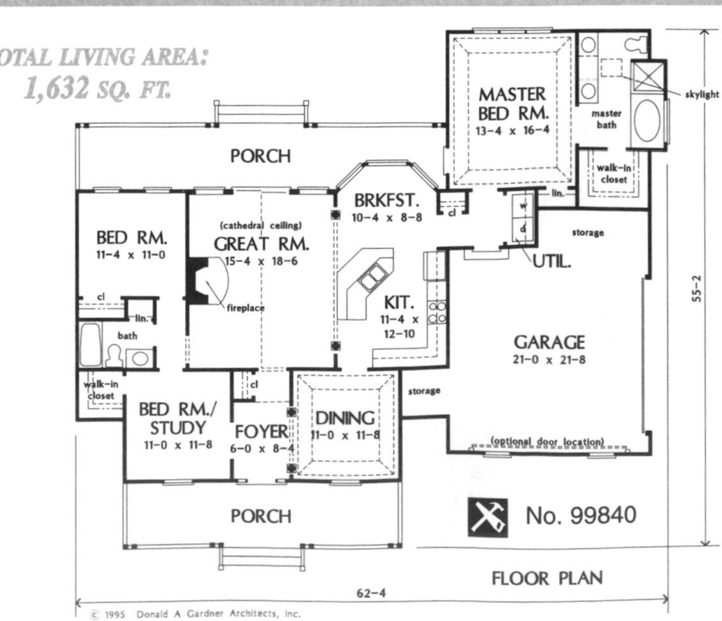
PORCH
MASTER BED RM. 13-4 x 16-4
skylight
master bath
walk-in closet
BRKFST. 10-4 x 8-8
BED RM. 11-4 x 11-0
(cathedral ceiling) GREAT RM. 15-4 x 18-6
fireplace
storage
UTIL.
KIT. 11-4 x 12-10
bath
GARAGE 21-0 x 21-8
walk-in closet
BED RM./ STUDY 11-0 x 11-8
FOYER 6-0 x 8-4
DINING 11-0 x 11-8
storage
(optional door location)
PORCH
No. 99840
55-2
62-4
FLOOR PLAN
© 1995 Donald A Gardner Architects, Inc.

B. NATHAN
© 1994 Donald A Gardner Architects, Inc.

PRICE CODE C

No. 99805

Exciting Three Bedroom

- This plan features:
- —Three bedrooms
- —Two full baths
- A Great Room enhanced by a fireplace, cathedral ceiling, and built-in bookshelves
- A Kitchen designed for efficiency with a food preparation island and a pantry
- A Master Suite topped by a cathedral ceiling and pampered by a luxurious bath and a walk-in closet
- Two additional bedrooms, one with a cathedral ceiling and a walk-in closet, sharing a sky lit bath
- A second floor bonus room, perfect for a study or a play area
- Foundation options for Basement or Crawl Space — please specify when ordering

MAIN FLOOR — 1,787 SQ. FT.
GARAGE & STORAGE — 521 SQ. FT.
BONUS ROOM — 326 SQ. FT.

TOTAL LIVING AREA :
1,787 SQ. FT.

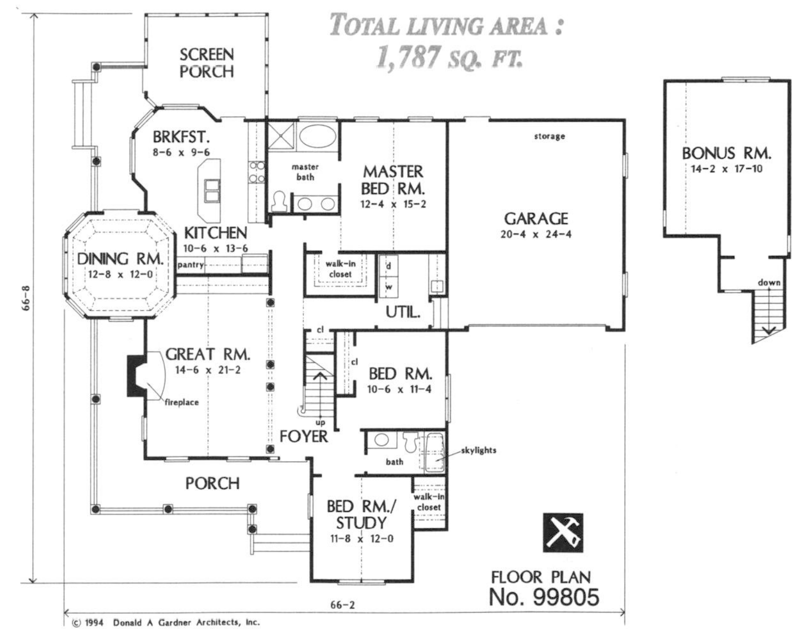
SCREEN PORCH
BRKFST. 8-6 x 9-6
master bath
MASTER BED RM. 12-4 x 15-2
storage
GARAGE 20-4 x 24-4
BONUS RM. 14-2 x 17-10
down
DINING RM. 12-8 x 12-0
KITCHEN 10-6 x 13-6
pantry
walk-in closet
UTIL.
66-8
GREAT RM. 14-6 x 21-2
fireplace
BED RM. 10-6 x 11-4
FOYER
bath
skylights
PORCH
BED RM./ STUDY 11-8 x 12-0
walk-in closet
FLOOR PLAN
No. 99805
66-2
(c) 1994 Donald A Gardner Architects, Inc.

PRICE CODE C

© 1995 Donald A. Gardner Architects, Inc.

PRICE CODE A

No. 99719

Let The Light Shine In

- This plan features:
- — Three bedrooms
- — Two full baths
- A main entry Deck, providing expanded living space
- A Solarium/Living area with windows and skylights surrounding a wood stove
- An efficient Kitchen with a built-in pantry, a garden window and a double sink island counter, convenient to the Dining area
- A first floor Bedroom with another skylight and ample closet space
- A Master Suite with private access to a full bath and an additional bedroom on the second floor

First floor — 852 sq. ft.
Second floor — 414 sq. ft.

Total living area:
1,266 sq. ft.

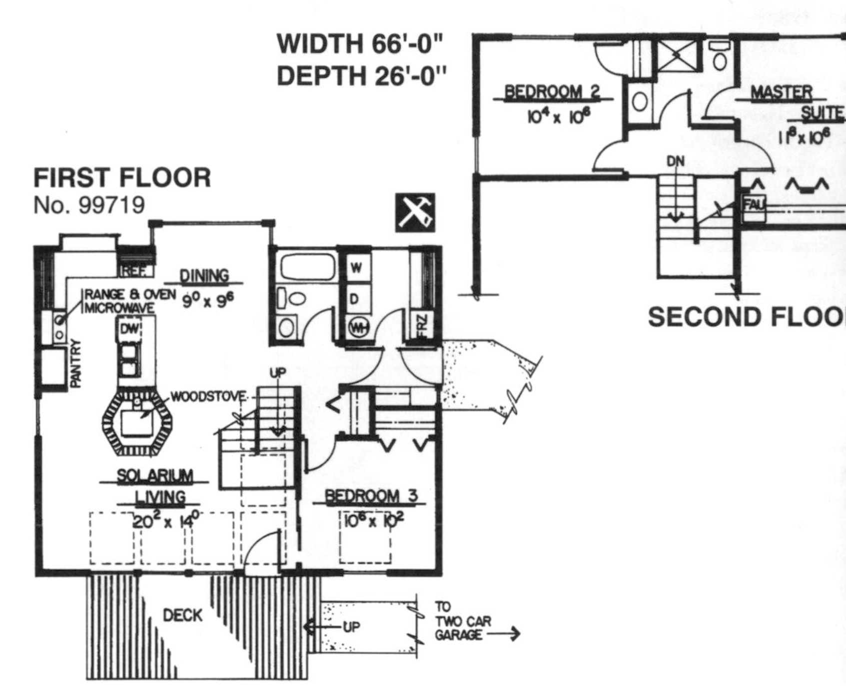
WIDTH 66'-0"
DEPTH 26'-0"
FIRST FLOOR
No. 99719
DINING
RANGE & OVEN
MICROWAVE
REF.
DW
PANTRY
WOODSTOVE
UP
W
D
WH
FRZ
SOLARIUM
LIVING
BEDROOM 3
DECK
UP
TO TWO CAR GARAGE
BEDROOM 2
MASTER SUITE
DN
FAU
SECOND FLOOR

No. 99321

Nostalgia Returns

- This plan features:
- — Three bedrooms
- — Two full baths
- A half-round transom window with quarter-round detail and a vaulted ceiling in the Great Room
- A cozy corner fireplace which brings warmth to the Great Room
- A vaulted ceiling in the Kitchen/Breakfast area
- A Master Suite with a walk-in closet and a private Master Bath
- Two additional bedrooms which share a full hall bath

Main area — 1,368 sq. ft.

Total living area:
1,368 sq. ft.

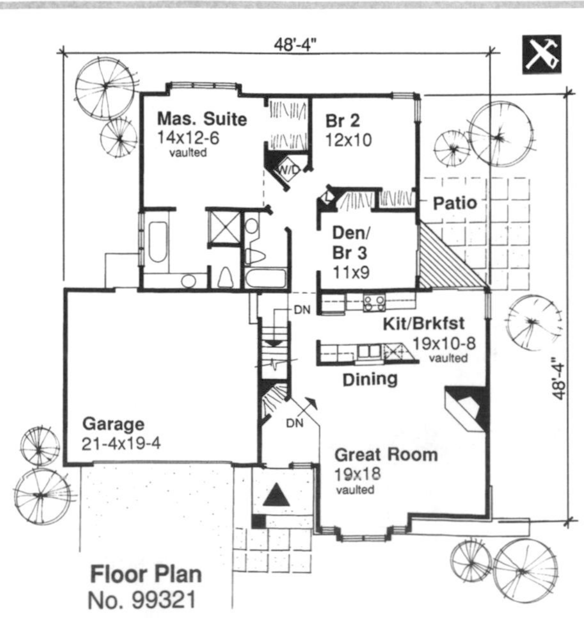
48'-4"
Mas. Suite
14x12-6
vaulted
Br 2
12x10
W/D
Patio
Den/
Br 3
11x9
DN
Kit/Brkfst
19x10-8
vaulted
Dining
48'-4"
Garage
21-4x19-4
DN
Great Room
19x18
vaulted
Floor Plan
No. 99321

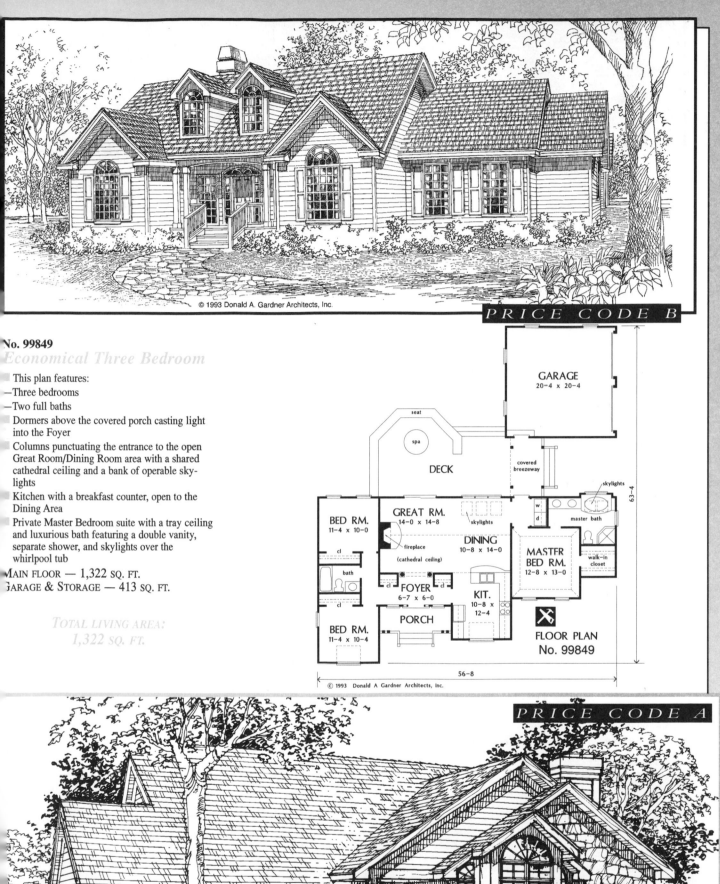

© 1993 Donald A. Gardner Architects, Inc.

PRICE CODE B

No. 99849

Economical Three Bedroom

- This plan features:
- —Three bedrooms
- —Two full baths
- Dormers above the covered porch casting light into the Foyer
- Columns punctuating the entrance to the open Great Room/Dining Room area with a shared cathedral ceiling and a bank of operable skylights
- Kitchen with a breakfast counter, open to the Dining Area
- Private Master Bedroom suite with a tray ceiling and luxurious bath featuring a double vanity, separate shower, and skylights over the whirlpool tub

MAIN FLOOR — 1,322 SQ. FT.
GARAGE & STORAGE — 413 SQ. FT.

TOTAL LIVING AREA:
1,322 SQ. FT.

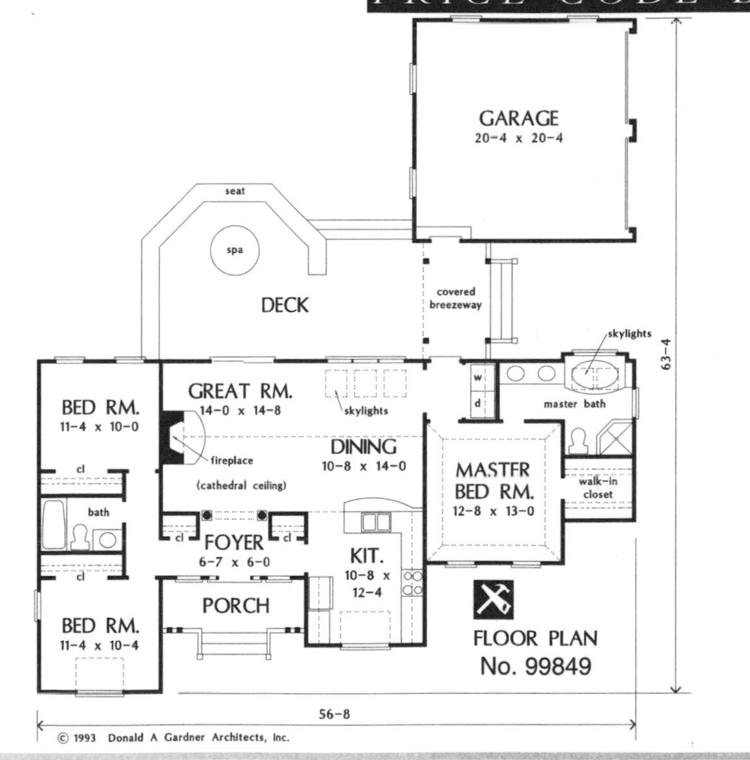
GARAGE
20-4 x 20-4
seat
spa
DECK
covered breezeway
skylights
63-4
BED RM.
11-4 x 10-0
GREAT RM.
14-0 x 14-8
skylights
w
d
master bath
fireplace
DINING
10-8 x 14-0
MASTER BED RM.
12-8 x 13-0
walk-in closet
cl
(cathedral ceiling)
bath
cl
FOYER
6-7 x 6-0
cl
KIT.
10-8 x 12-4
cl
PORCH
BED RM.
11-4 x 10-4
FLOOR PLAN
No. 99849
56-8
© 1993 Donald A Gardner Architects, Inc.

PRICE CODE A

PRICE CODE A

No. 98434

Expansive Living Room

- This plan features:
- —Three bedrooms
- —Two full baths
- Vaulted ceiling crowns spacious Living Room highlighted by a fireplace
- Built-in pantry and direct access from the garage adding to the conveniences of the Kitchen
- Walk-in closet and a private five-piece bath topped by a vaulted ceiling in the Master Bedroom suite
- Proximity to the full bath in the hall from the secondary bedrooms
- Foundation options for Basement, Slab or Crawl Space — please specify when ordering

MAIN FLOOR — 1,346 SQ. FT.
BASEMENT — 1,358 SQ. FT.
GARAGE — 395 SQ. FT.

TOTAL LIVING AREA:

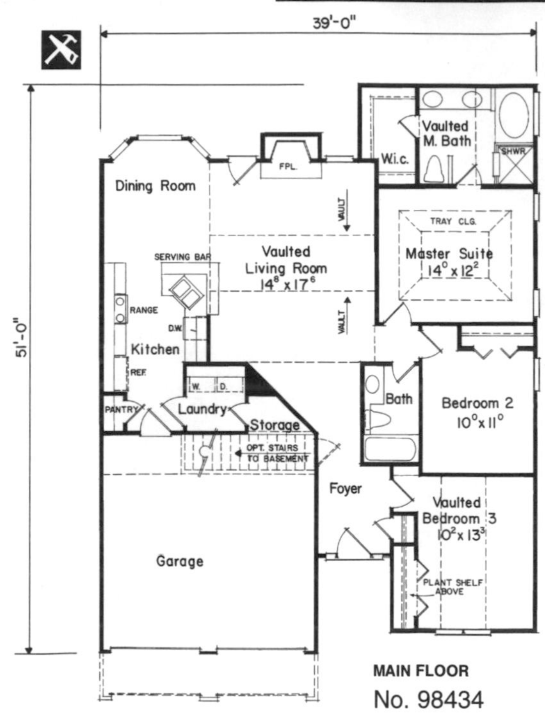
39'-0"
51'-0"
Dining Room
FPL.
W.i.c.
Vaulted M. Bath
SHWR.
SERVING BAR
Vaulted Living Room
14^{6} x 17^{6}
VAULT
TRAY CLG.
Master Suite
14^{0} x 12^{2}
RANGE
D.W.
Kitchen
REF.
W. D.
PANTRY
Laundry
Storage
OPT. STAIRS TO BASEMENT
Bath
Bedroom 2
10^{0} x 11^{0}
Foyer
Vaulted Bedroom 3
10^{2} x 13^{3}
PLANT SHELF ABOVE
Garage
MAIN FLOOR
No. 98434

No. 99858

Amenities Normally Found In Larger Homes

TOTAL LIVING AREA:
1,253 SQ. FT.

- This plan features:
- —Three bedrooms
- —Two full baths
- A continuous cathedral ceiling in the Great Room, Kitchen, and Dining Room giving a spacious feel to this efficient plan
- Skylighted Kitchen with a seven foot high wall by the Great Room and a popular plant shelf
- Master Bedroom suite opens up with a cathedral ceiling and contains walk-in and linen closets and a private bath with garden tub and dual vanity
- Cathedral ceiling as the crowing touch to the front bedrooms/study

MAIN FLOOR — 1,253 SQ. FT.
GARAGE & STORAGE — 420 SQ. FT.

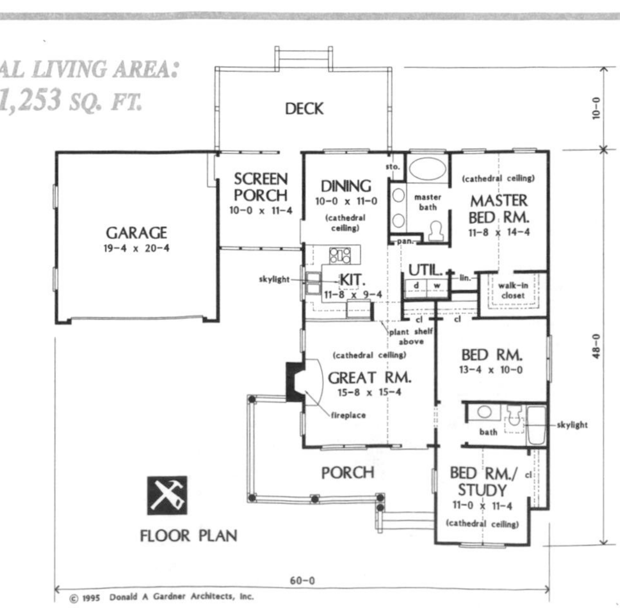
DECK
10-0
GARAGE
19-4 x 20-4
SCREEN PORCH
10-0 x 11-4
DINING
10-0 x 11-0
(cathedral ceiling)
sto.
master bath
(cathedral ceiling)
MASTER BED RM.
11-8 x 14-4
pan.
skylight
KIT.
11-8 x 9-4
UTIL.
d w
lin.
walk-in closet
cl
cl
plant shelf above
(cathedral ceiling)
GREAT RM.
15-8 x 15-4
fireplace
BED RM.
13-4 x 10-0
48-0
bath
skylight
PORCH
BED RM./ STUDY
11-0 x 11-4
(cathedral ceiling)
FLOOR PLAN
60-0
© 1995 Donald A Gardner Architects, Inc.

No. 99858

PRICE CODE A

No. 99345

Compact Ranch

- This plan features:
- — Three bedrooms
- — Two full baths
- A Great Room and Dining area with vaulted ceilings
- A Great Room with a fabulous fireplace
- A Kitchen and sunny Breakfast area with access to a rear deck
- A Master Suite with a private full bath and one wall of closet space

MAIN AREA — 1,325 SQ. FT.

TOTAL LIVING AREA:
1,325 SQ. FT.

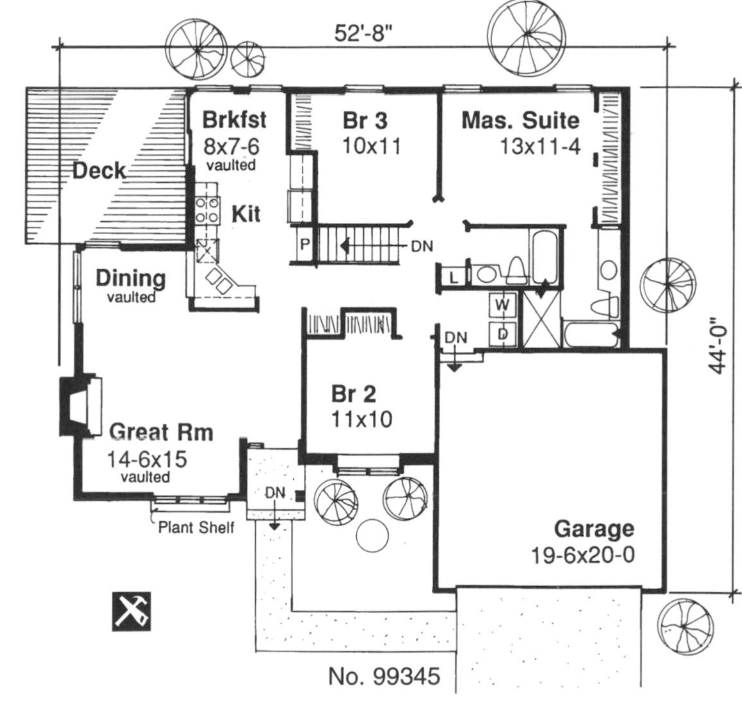
52'-8"
44'-0"
Brkfst
8x7-6
vaulted
Br 3
10x11
Mas. Suite
13x11-4
Deck
Kit
P
DN
L
W
D
DN
Dining
vaulted
Br 2
11x10
Great Rm
14-6x15
vaulted
DN
Plant Shelf
Garage
19-6x20-0
No. 99345

PRICE CODE B

© 1995 Donald A Gardner Architects, Inc.

PRICE CODE B

No. 99610

Greek Revival

- This plan features:
- — Three bedrooms
- — Two full baths
- A large front porch with pediment and columns
- A stunning, heat-circulating fireplace flanked by cabinetry and shelves in the Living Room
- A formal Dining Room enhanced by a bay window
- An efficient, U-shaped Kitchen with a peninsula counter and informal Dinette area
- A Master Suite with a private Master Bath and direct access to the private terrace
- Two additional bedrooms sharing a full hall bath

MAIN FLOOR — 1,460 SQ. FT.
LAUNDRY/MUDROOM — 68 SQ. FT.
BASEMENT — 1,367 SQ. FT.
GARAGE & STORAGE — 494 SQ. FT.

TOTAL LIVING AREA:
1,528 SQ. FT.

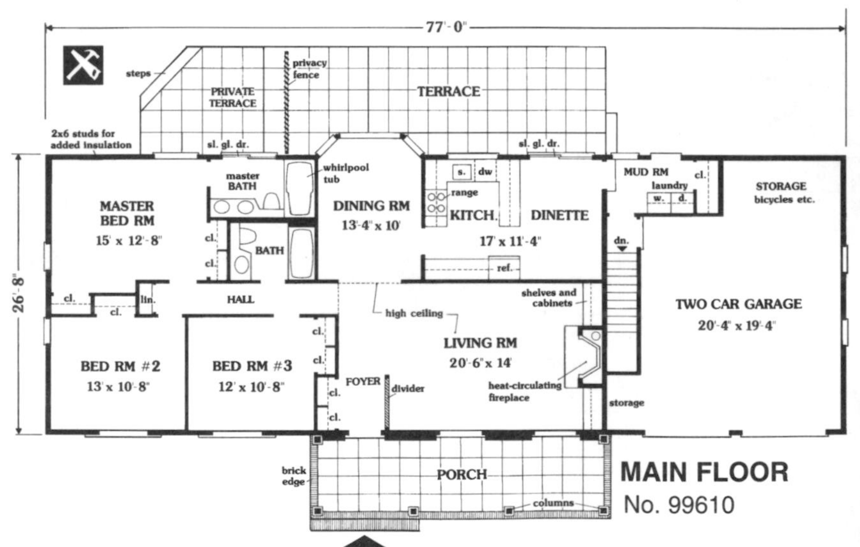
77'-0"
steps
privacy fence
PRIVATE TERRACE
TERRACE
2x6 studs for added insulation
sl. gl. dr.
whirlpool tub
master BATH
MASTER BED RM
15' x 12'-8"
DINING RM
13'-4" x 10'
range
dw
KITCH.
DINETTE
17' x 11'-4"
ref.
MUD RM
laundry
STORAGE
bicycles etc.
BATH
HALL
26'-8"
high ceiling
shelves and cabinets
LIVING RM
20'-6" x 14'
TWO CAR GARAGE
20'-4" x 19'-4"
BED RM #2
13' x 10'-8"
BED RM #3
12' x 10'-8"
FOYER
divider
heat-circulating fireplace
storage
brick edge
PORCH
columns
MAIN FLOOR
No. 99610

No. 98441

High Ceilings and Arched Windows

- This plan features:
- —Three bedrooms
- —Two full baths
- Natural illumination streaming into the Dining Room and Sitting area of the Master Suite through large, arched windows
- Kitchen with convenient pass through to the Great Room and a serving bar for the Breakfast Room
- Great Room topped by a vaulted ceiling accented by a fireplace and a French door
- Decorative columns accenting the entrance of the Dining Room
- Tray ceiling over the Master Suite and a vaulted ceiling over the sitting room and the Master Bath
- No materials list available

MAIN FLOOR — 1,502 SQ. FT.
GARAGE — 448 SQ. FT.

WIDTH 50'- 4"
DEPTH 45'-0"

TOTAL LIVING AREA:
1,502 SQ. FT.

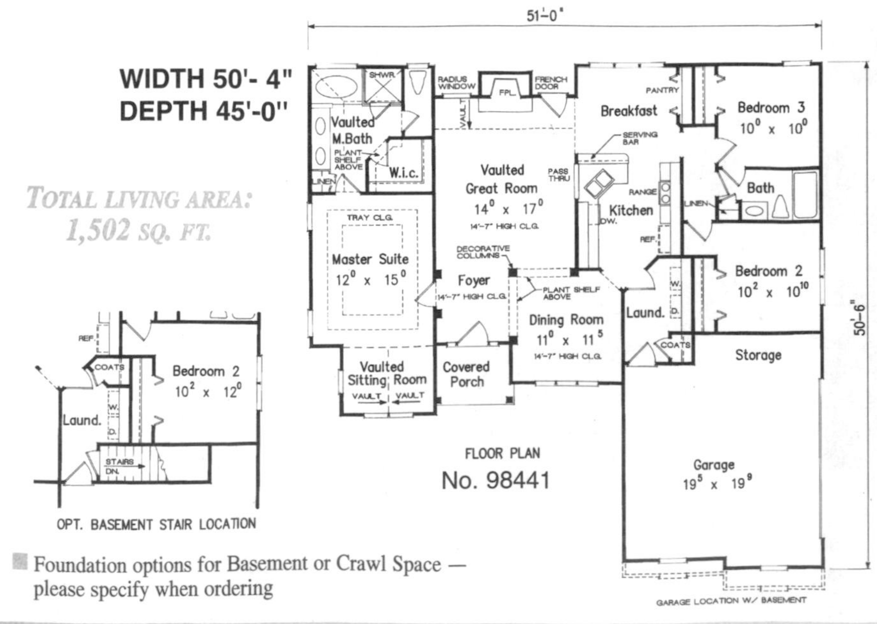
51'-0"
Vaulted M.Bath
W.I.c.
Breakfast
Bedroom 3
10^0 x 10^0
Vaulted Great Room
14^0 x 17^0
Kitchen
Bath
Master Suite
12^0 x 15^0
Foyer
Dining Room
11^0 x 11^5
Bedroom 2
10^2 x 10^{10}
Laund.
Storage
Vaulted Sitting Room
Covered Porch
Garage
19^5 x 19^9
50'-6"
Bedroom 2
10^2 x 12^0
Laund.
OPT. BASEMENT STAIR LOCATION
GARAGE LOCATION W/ BASEMENT
FLOOR PLAN
No. 98441

- Foundation options for Basement or Crawl Space — please specify when ordering

© 1996 Donald A. Gardner Architects, Inc.
PRICE CODE B

No. 99830

Compact Plan

- This plan features:
—Three bedrooms
—Two full baths
- A Great Room topped by a cathedral ceiling, combining with the openness of the adjoining Dining Room and Kitchen, to create a spacious living area
- A bay window enlarging the Dining Room and a palladian window allowing ample light into the Great Room
- An efficient U-shaped Kitchen leading directly to the garage, convenient for unloading groceries
- A Master Suite highlighted by ample closet space and a private a sky lit bath enhanced by a dual vanity and a separate tub and shower

MAIN FLOOR — 1,372 SQ. FT.
GARAGE & STORAGE — 537 SQ. FT.

TOTAL LIVING AREA:
1,372 SQ. FT.

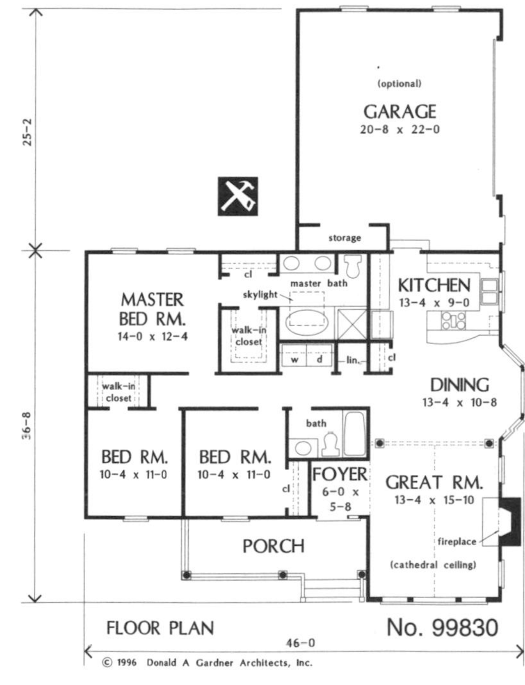
(optional)
GARAGE
20-8 x 22-0
storage
MASTER
BED RM.
14-0 x 12-4
cl
master bath
skylight
walk-in
closet
w
d
lin.
cl
KITCHEN
13-4 x 9-0
DINING
13-4 x 10-8
walk-in
closet
bath
BED RM.
10-4 x 11-0
BED RM.
10-4 x 11-0
cl
FOYER
6-0 x
5-8
GREAT RM.
13-4 x 15-10
fireplace
(cathedral ceiling)
PORCH
25-2
36-8
46-0
FLOOR PLAN
No. 99830
© 1996 Donald A Gardner Architects, Inc.

PRICE CODE B

© 1994 Donald A. Gardner Architects, Inc.

PRICE CODE B

No. 99826

Perfect for Family Gatherings

- This plan features:
- —Three bedrooms
- —Two full baths
- An open layout between the Great Room, Kitchen, and Breakfast Bay sharing a cathedral ceiling and a fireplace
- Master Bedroom suite with a soaring cathedral ceiling, direct access to the deck and a well appointed bath with a large walk-in closet
- Additional bedrooms sharing a full bath in the hall
- Centrally located utility and storage spaces

MAIN FLOOR — 1,346 SQ. FT.
GARAGE AND STORAGE — 462 SQ. FT.

TOTAL LIVING AREA:
1,346 SQ. FT.

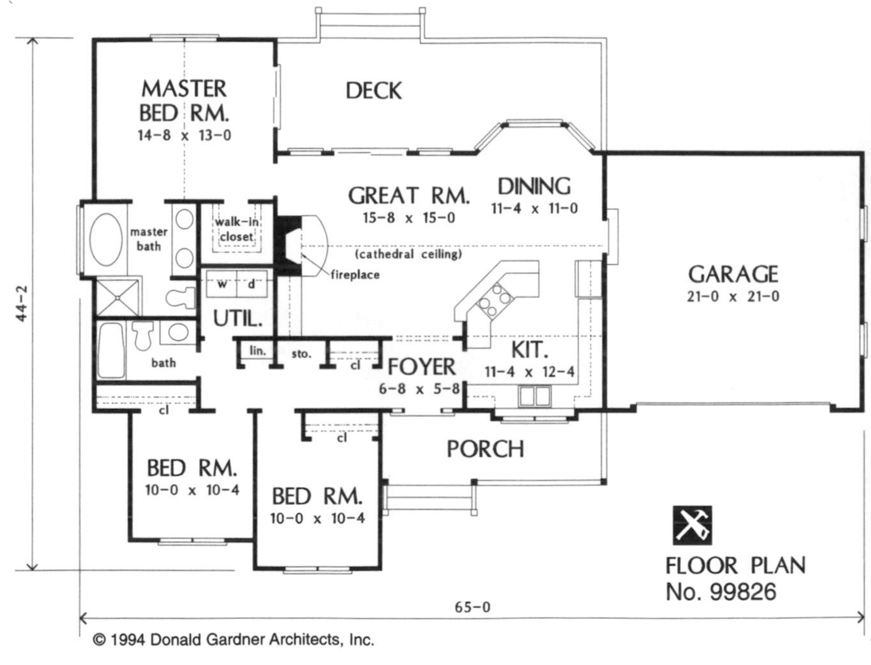
MASTER
BED RM.
14-8 x 13-0
DECK
GREAT RM.
15-8 x 15-0
DINING
11-4 x 11-0
(cathedral ceiling)
fireplace
walk-in closet
master bath
UTIL.
bath
lin.
sto.
cl
FOYER
6-8 x 5-8
KIT.
11-4 x 12-4
GARAGE
21-0 x 21-0
PORCH
BED RM.
10-0 x 10-4
BED RM.
10-0 x 10-4
44-2
65-0
FLOOR PLAN
No. 99826
© 1994 Donald Gardner Architects, Inc.

No. 99745

An Earth Sheltered Home

- This plan features:
- — Two bedrooms
- — Two full baths
- The living spaces are placed all on the open side
- A combined Kitchen/Living/Dining Room, with a semicircle of tall windows, catching light from three sides
- The Kitchen counters, sitting at the hinge of two wall angles, make a lazy bend to create space for a media nook and pantry
- A luxurious Master Suite having an oversized tub, walk-in closet, and vanity with a skylight in the ceiling
- An additional bedroom, with skylights, that has easy access to a full hall bath

MAIN AREA — 1,482 SQ. FT.
GARAGE — 564 SQ. FT.

TOTAL LIVING AREA:
1,482 SQ. FT.

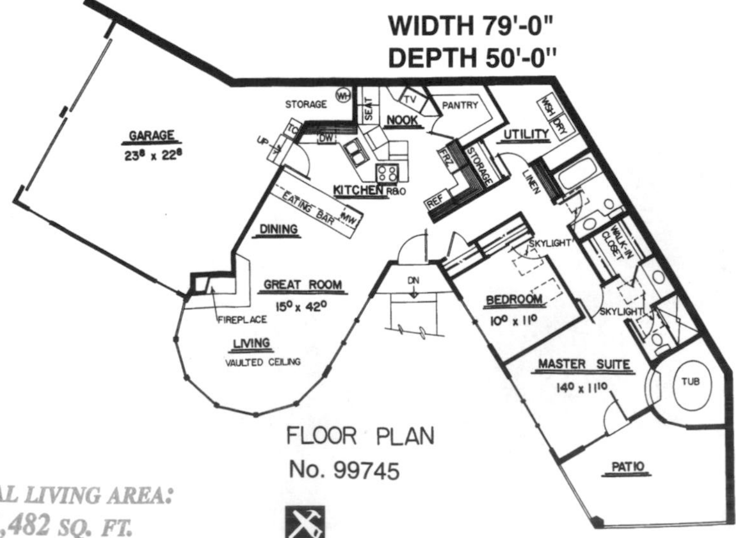
WIDTH 79'-0"
DEPTH 50'-0"
GARAGE
23⁸ x 22⁸
STORAGE
NOOK
PANTRY
UTILITY
KITCHEN
EATING BAR
DINING
GREAT ROOM
15⁰ x 42⁰
FIREPLACE
LIVING
VAULTED CEILING
BEDROOM
10⁰ x 11⁰
SKYLIGHT
MASTER SUITE
14⁰ x 11¹⁰
TUB
PATIO
FLOOR PLAN
No. 99745

PRICE CODE B

No. 99633

Angled Contemporary

- This plan features:
- — Three bedrooms
- — Two full and one half bath
- An angled shape that allows the house to be rotated on a site to give optimum orientation
- A spacious Foyer that opens to the Living Room
- A heat-circulating fireplace in the Living Room
- Sliding glass doors in the Living Room and the Dining Room that lead to a partially covered terrace
- A cathedral ceiling in the Family Room which also has a heat-circulating fireplace
- A Master Suite with a cathedral ceiling and private bath with double vanity and whirlpool tub
- Two additional bedrooms share a full hall bath with a double vanity and whirlpool tub

Main area — 1,798 sq. ft.
Basement — 1,715 sq. ft.
Garage — 456 sq. ft.

Total living area:
1,798 sq. ft.

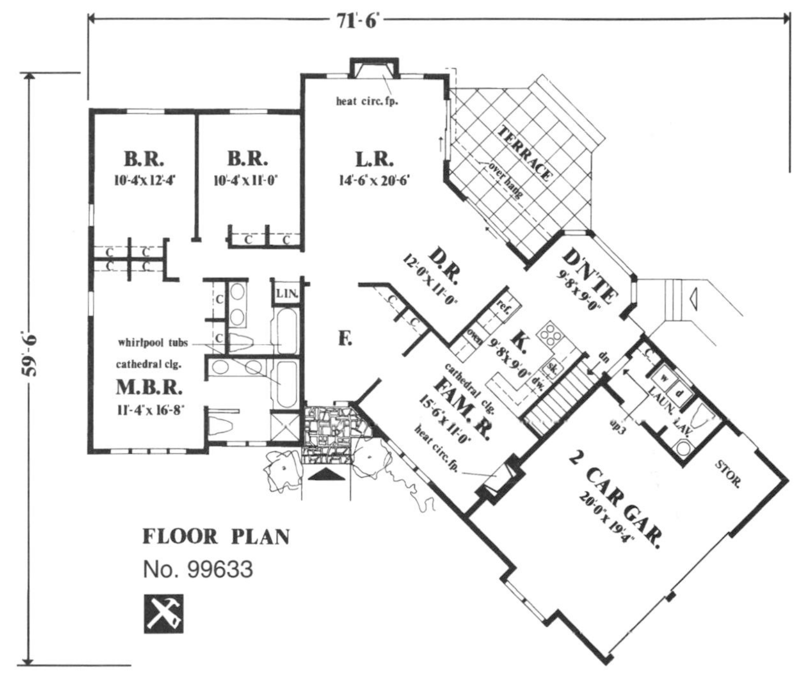
71'-6"
59'-6"
heat circ. fp.
B.R.
10'-4"x 12'-4"
B.R.
10'-4"x 11'-0"
L.R.
14'-6" x 20'-6"
TERRACE
over hang
D.R.
12'-0"x 11'-0"
D'NTE
9'-8"x 9'-0"
LIN.
whirlpool tubs
cathedral clg.
M.B.R.
11'-4" x 16'-8"
F.
K.
9'-8"x 9'-0"
ref.
oven
dn
cathedral clg.
FAM. R.
15'-6"x 11'-0"
heat circ. fp.
LAUN.
LAV.
2 CAR GAR.
20'-0"x 19'-4"
STOR.
FLOOR PLAN
No. 99633

PRICE CODE A

PRICE CODE C

No. 99208

Cozy Traditional with Style

- This plan features:
- — Three bedrooms
- — Two full baths
- A convenient one-level design
- A galley-style Kitchen that shares a snack bar with the spacious Gathering Room
- A focal point fireplace making the Gathering Room warm and inviting
- An ample Master Suite with a luxury Bath which includes a whirlpool tub and separate Dressing Room
- Two additional bedrooms, one that could double as a Study, located at the front of the house

MAIN FLOOR — 1,830 SQ. FT.
BASEMENT — 1,830 SQ. FT.

TOTAL LIVING AREA:
1,830 SQ. FT.

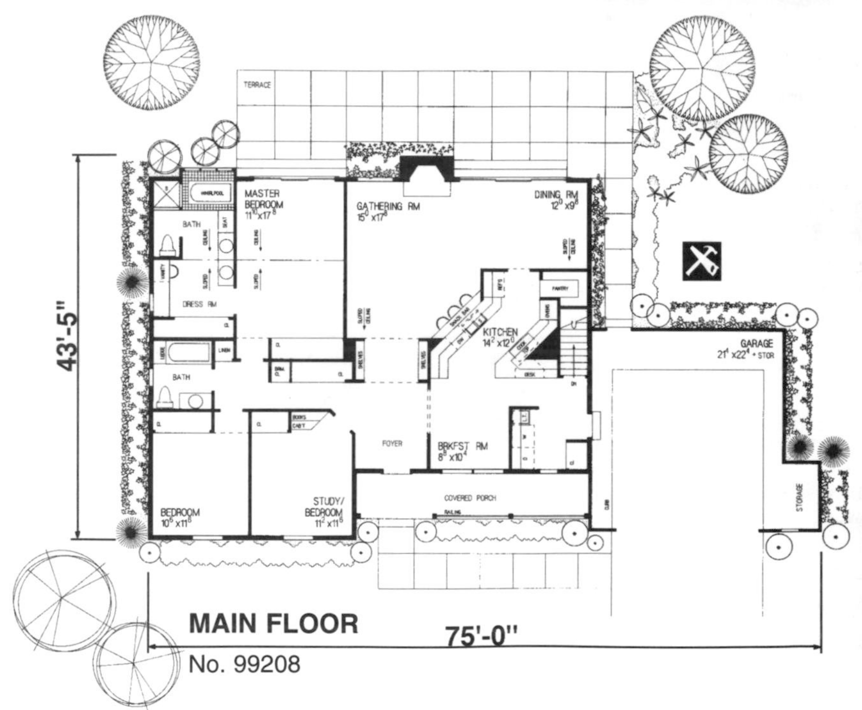
TERRACE
MASTER BEDROOM
GATHERING RM
DINING RM
BATH
DRESS RM
KITCHEN
GARAGE
FOYER
BRKFST RM
COVERED PORCH
BEDROOM
STUDY/ BEDROOM
STORAGE
43'-5"
MAIN FLOOR
75'-0"
No. 99208

No. 99812

Sunny Dormer Brightens Foyer

TOTAL LIVING AREA:
1,386 SQ. FT.

- This plan features:
- —Three bedrooms
- —Two full baths
- Today's comforts with cost effective construction
- Open Great room, Dining Room, and Kitchen topped by a cathedral ceiling emphasizing spaciousness
- Adjoining Deck providing extra living or entertaining room
- Front bedroom crowned in cathedral ceiling and pampered by a private bath with garden tub, dual vanity and a walk-in closet
- Skylighted Bonus Room above the garage offering flexibility and opportunity for growth

MAIN FLOOR — 1,386 SQ. FT.
GARAGE — 517 SQ. FT.
BONUS ROOM — 314 SQ. FT.

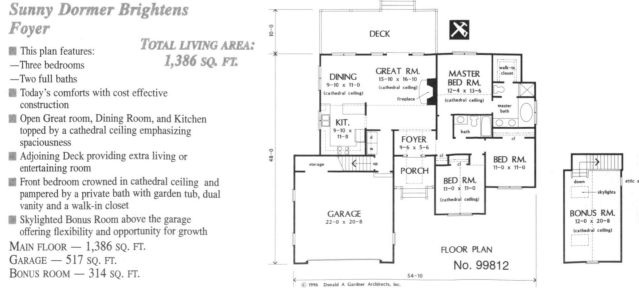

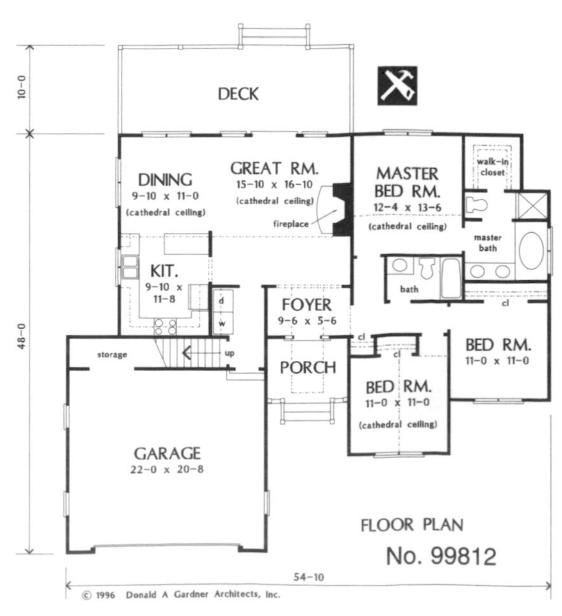
DECK
DINING
9-10 x 11-0
(cathedral ceiling)
GREAT RM.
15-10 x 16-10
(cathedral ceiling)
fireplace
MASTER
BED RM.
12-4 x 13-6
(cathedral ceiling)
walk-in closet
master bath
bath
KIT.
9-10 x 11-8
FOYER
9-6 x 5-6
storage
up
PORCH
BED RM.
11-0 x 11-0
(cathedral ceiling)
BED RM.
11-0 x 11-0
GARAGE
22-0 x 20-8
FLOOR PLAN
No. 99812
54-10
© 1996 Donald A Gardner Architects, Inc.

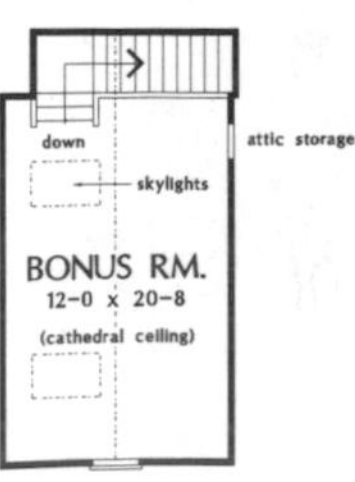
down
attic storage
skylights
BONUS RM.
12-0 x 20-8
(cathedral ceiling)

© 1993 Donald A Gardner Architects, Inc.
PRICE CODE C

No. 99802

Traditional Beauty

- This plan features:
- —Three bedrooms
- —Two full baths
- Traditional beauty with large arched windows, round columns, covered porch, brick veneer, and an open floor plan
- Clerestory dormers above covered porch lighting the Foyer
- Cathedral ceiling enhancing the Great Room along with a cozy fireplace
- Island Kitchen with Breakfast area accessing the large Deck with an optional spa
- Columns defining spaces
- Tray ceiling over the Master Bedroom, Dining Room and Bedroom/Study
- Dual vanity, separate shower, and whirlpool tub in the Master Bath

MAIN FLOOR — 1,576 SQ. FT.
GARAGE — 465 SQ. FT.

TOTAL LIVING AREA:
1,576 SQ. FT.

spa
DECK
MASTER
BED RM.
13-4 x 13-8
master
bath
skylights
fireplace
BRKFST.
11-4 x 7-8
w
d
walk-in
closet
storage
BED RM.
11-4 x 11-0
GREAT RM.
15-4 x 16-10
(cathedral ceiling)
KITCHEN
11-4 x 10-0
GARAGE
20-0 x 19-8
50-9
cl
bath
cl
FOYER
8-2 x 5-10
DINING RM.
11-4 x 11-4
BED RM./
STUDY
11-4 x 10-4
PORCH
FLOOR PLAN
No. 99802
60-6
© 1993 Donald A Gardner Architects, Inc.

© 1996 Donald A Gardner Architects, Inc.
PRICE CODE B

PRICE CODE A

No. 99701

Cabin with a Gambrel

- This plan features:
  - Three bedrooms
  - Two full baths
- An open-beam ceiling and six huge windows in the Living Room/Dining Room that includes a vaulted ceiling
- A private Master Suite with a full bath and two closets
- A compact Kitchen with plenty of cupboard and counter space
- Two additional small bedrooms that have the use of a full hall bath
- An average sized Utility Room with a laundry center

FIRST FLOOR — 864 SQ. FT.
SECOND FLOOR — 396 SQ. FT.

TOTAL LIVING AREA:
1,260 SQ. FT.

WIDTH 24'-0"
DEPTH 36'-0"

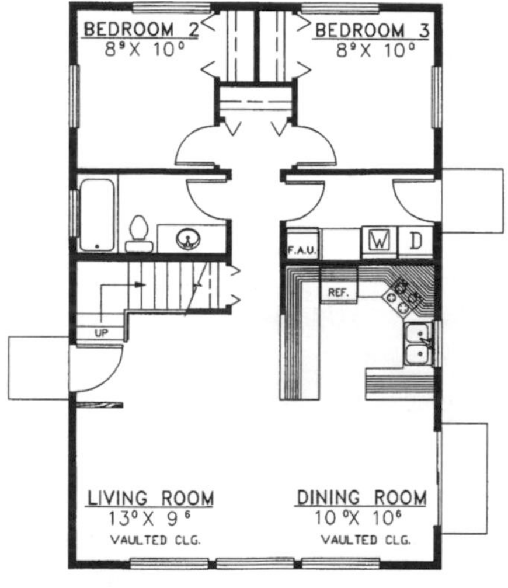

BEDROOM 2
8^9X 10^0
BEDROOM 3
8^9X 10^0
F.A.U.
W
D
REF.
UP
LIVING ROOM
13^0X 9^6
VAULTED CLG.
DINING ROOM
10^0X 10^6
VAULTED CLG.

FIRST FLOOR
No. 99701

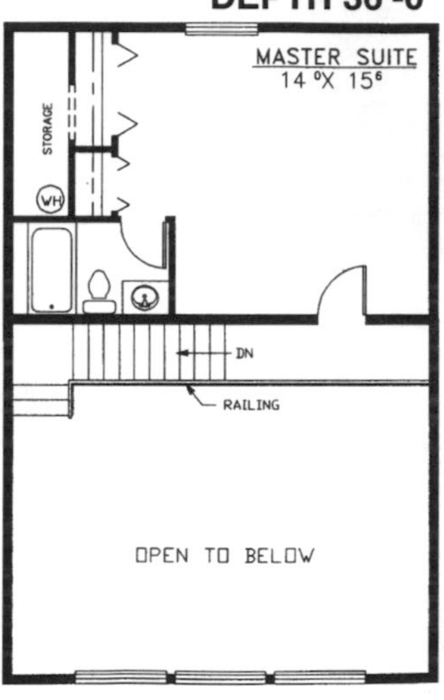

MASTER SUITE
14^0X 15^6
STORAGE
WH
DN
RAILING
OPEN TO BELOW

SECOND FLOOR

No. 99707

Chalet Hide-Away

TOTAL LIVING AREA:
1,476 SQ. FT.

- This plan features:
  - One bedroom
  - Two full baths
- A wrap-around Deck providing expanded living space outdoors and access into the Kitchen/Dining area
- An open Living Area with windows on three sides, a fireplace with an over-sized hearth and a Dining area
- An efficient, U-shaped Kitchen with ample counter space, convenient to the Dining area and the Laundry
- A first floor Bedroom with an over-sized closet, a private entrance, and adjacent to a shower bath
- A second floor Recreation Area with multiple uses, featuring a balcony at either end and a full bath

FIRST FLOOR — 864 SQ. FT.
SECOND FLOOR — 612 SQ. FT.

WIDTH 24'-0"
DEPTH 36'-0"

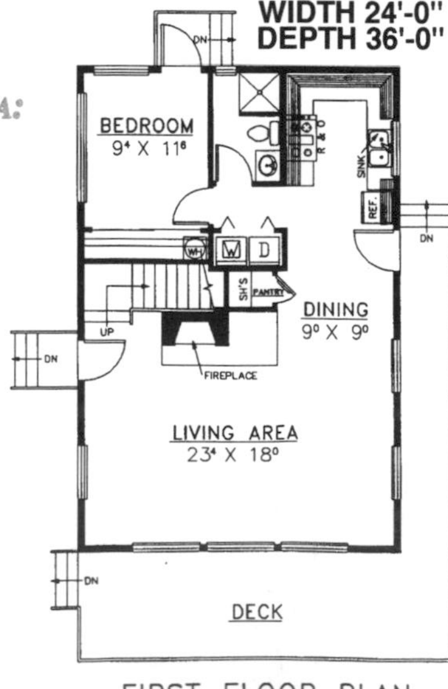

DN
BEDROOM
9^4 X 11^6
SINK
REF.
W
D
DN
UP
DN
DINING
9^0 X 9^0
FIREPLACE
LIVING AREA
23^4 X 18^0
DN
DECK

FIRST FLOOR PLAN
No. 99707

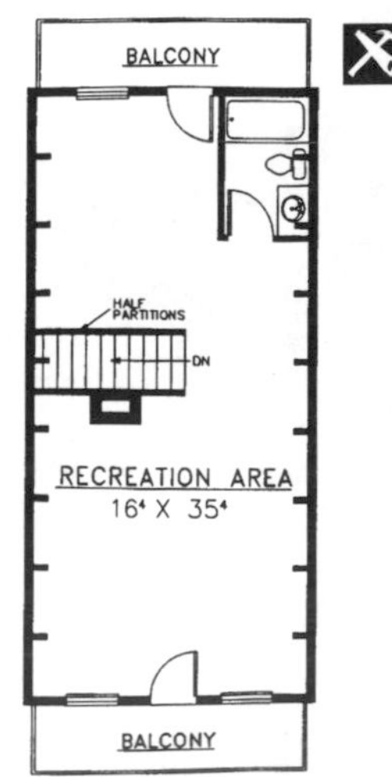

BALCONY
HALF PARTITIONS
DN
RECREATION AREA
16^4 X 35^4
BALCONY

SECOND FLOOR PLAN

PRICE CODE B

TOTAL LIVING AREA:
1,671 SQ. FT.

o. 98423

Easy One Floor Living

- This plan features:
- -Three bedrooms
- -Two full baths
- A spacious Family Room topped by a vaulted ceiling and highlighted by a large fireplace and a French door to the rear yard
- A serving bar open to the Family Room and the Dining Room, a pantry and a peninsula counter adding more efficiency to the Kitchen
- A crowning tray ceiling over the Master Bedroom and a vaulted ceiling over the Master Bath
- A vaulted ceiling over the cozy Sitting Room in the Master Suite
- Two additional bedrooms, roomy in size sharing the full bath in the hall
- Foundation options for Basement, Slab or Crawl Space — please specify when ordering

AIN FLOOR — 1,671 SQ. FT.
ASEMENT — 1,685 SQ. FT.
ARAGE — 400 SQ. FT.

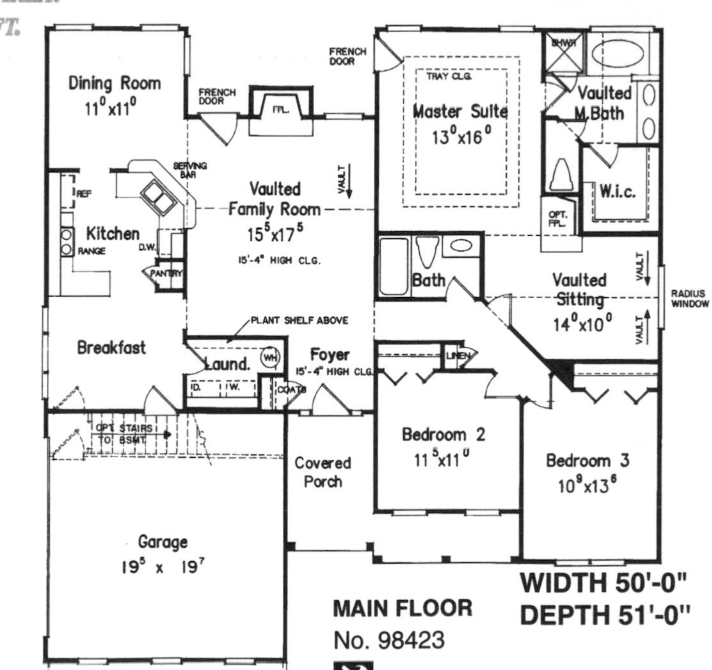

Dining Room
11^0x11^0
FRENCH DOOR
FPL.
FRENCH DOOR
TRAY CLG.
Master Suite
13^0x16^0
SHWR
Vaulted M.Bath
W.i.c.
SERVING BAR
REF
Kitchen
RANGE
D.W.
PANTRY
VAULT
Vaulted Family Room
15^5x17^5
15'-4" HIGH CLG.
OPT. FPL.
Bath
Vaulted Sitting
14^0x10^0
RADIUS WINDOW
PLANT SHELF ABOVE
Breakfast
Laund.
WH
Foyer
15'-4" HIGH CLG.
LINEN
COATS
OPT. STAIRS TO BSMT.
Covered Porch
Bedroom 2
11^5x11^0
Bedroom 3
10^9x13^6
Garage
19^5 x 19^7
WIDTH 50'-0"
DEPTH 51'-0"
MAIN FLOOR
No. 98423

PRICE CODE A

PRICE CODE A

No. 99639

One Story Country Home

- This plan features:
- — Three bedrooms
- — Two full baths
- A Living Room with an imposing, high ceiling that slopes down to a normal height of eight feet, focusing on the decorative heat-circulating fireplace at the rear wall
- An efficient Kitchen that adjoins the Dining Room that views the front Porch
- A Dinette Area for informal eating in the Kitchen that can comfortably seat six people
- A Master Suite arranged with a large dressing area that has a walk-in closet plus two linear closets and space for a vanity
- Two family bedrooms that share a full hall bath

MAIN AREA — 1,367 SQ. FT.
BASEMENT — 1,267 SQ. FT.
GARAGE — 431 SQ. FT.

TOTAL LIVING AREA:
1,367 SQ. FT.

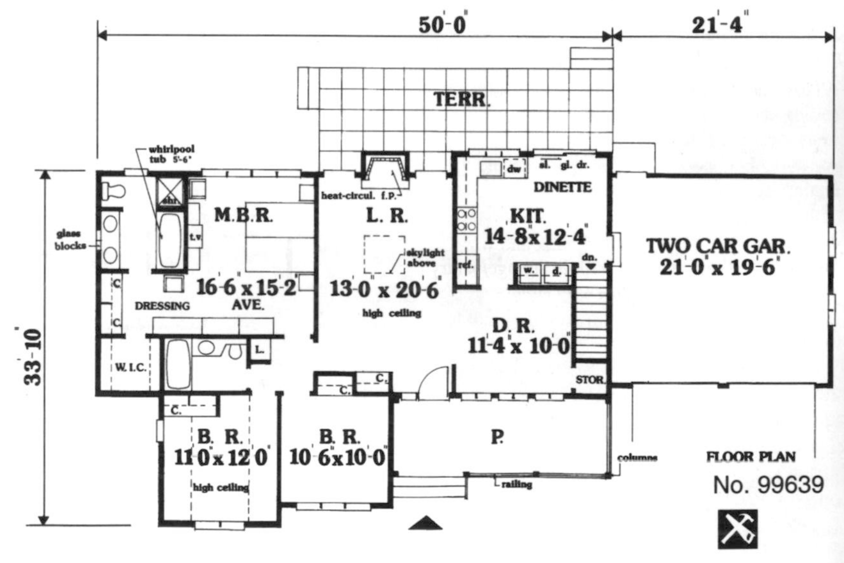

50'-0"
21'-4"
TERR.
whirlpool tub 5'-6"
heat-circul. f.p.
DINETTE
M.B.R.
L. R.
KIT.
14'-8"x 12'-4"
TWO CAR GAR.
21'-0" x 19'-6"
glass blocks
skylight above
16'-6" x 15'-2"
AVE.
DRESSING
13'-0" x 20'-6"
high ceiling
D. R.
11'-4" x 10'-0"
33'-10"
W.I.C.
STOR.
B. R.
11'-0" x 12'-0"
high ceiling
B. R.
10'-6" x 10'-0"
P.
columns
railing
FLOOR PLAN
No. 99639

No. 99810

Dramatic Dormers

TOTAL LIVING AREA:
1,685 SQ. FT.

- This plan features:
- —Three bedrooms
- —Two full baths
- A Foyer open to the dramatic dormer, defined by columns
- A Dining Room augmented by a tray ceiling
- A Great Room expanded into the open Kitchen and the Breakfast Room
- A privately located Master Suite, topped by a tray ceiling in the bedroom and pampered by a garden tub with a picture window as the focal point of the master bath
- Two additional bedrooms, located at the opposite side of the home from the Master Suite, sharing a full bath and linen closet

MAIN FLOOR — 1,685 SQ. FT.
GARAGE & STORAGE — 536 SQ. FT.

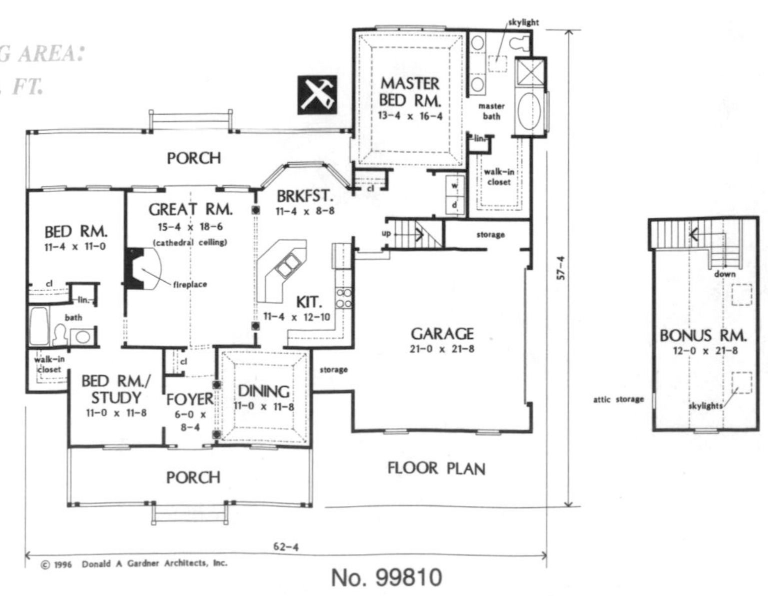

skylight
MASTER BED RM.
13-4 x 16-4
master bath
walk-in closet
PORCH
BRKFST.
11-4 x 8-8
BED RM.
11-4 x 11-0
GREAT RM.
15-4 x 18-6
(cathedral ceiling)
fireplace
storage
KIT.
11-4 x 12-10
bath
walk-in closet
GARAGE
21-0 x 21-8
57-4
BONUS RM.
12-0 x 21-8
attic storage
skylights
BED RM./ STUDY
11-0 x 11-8
FOYER
6-0 x 8-4
DINING
11-0 x 11-8
storage
PORCH
FLOOR PLAN
62-4
© 1996 Donald A Gardner Architects, Inc.
No. 99810

PRICE CODE C

No. 98714

Comfortable Vacation Living

- This plan features:
- — Three bedrooms
- — Three full and one half baths
- A wrap-around Deck offering views and access into the Living Room
- A sunken Living Room with a vaulted ceiling, and a raised-hearth fireplace adjoining the Dining area
- An open Kitchen with a corner sink and windows, an eating bar and a walk-in storage/pantry
- Two private Bedroom suites with sliding glass doors leading to a Deck, walk-in closets and plush baths
- A Loft area with a walk-in closet, attic access, and a private bath and a Deck

FIRST FLOOR — 1,704 SQ FT
SECOND FLOOR — 313 SQ. FT.

TOTAL LIVING AREA:
2,017 SQ. FT.

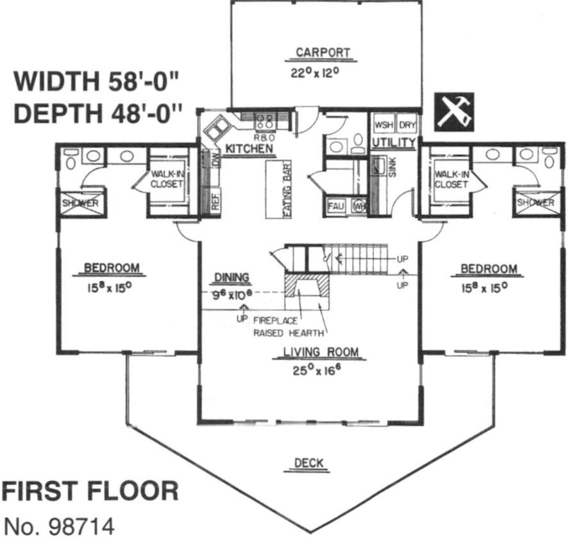
WIDTH 58'-0"
DEPTH 48'-0"
CARPORT
22⁰ x 12⁰
KITCHEN
UTILITY
WALK-IN CLOSET
SHOWER
BEDROOM
15⁸ x 15⁰
DINING
9⁶ x 10⁶
FIREPLACE
RAISED HEARTH
LIVING ROOM
25⁰ x 16⁶
DECK
FIRST FLOOR
No. 98714

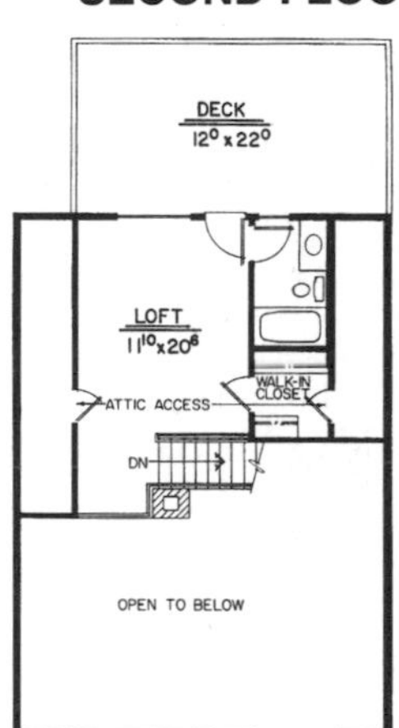
SECOND FLOOR
DECK
12⁰ x 22⁰
LOFT
11¹⁰ x 20⁶
ATTIC ACCESS
WALK-IN CLOSET
OPEN TO BELOW

PRICE CODE C

© 1996 Donald A. Gardner Architects, Inc.

PRICE CODE A

No. 98709

An Alpine Retreat

- This plan features:
- — 3 Bedrooms
- — 2 full Baths
- A wrap-around Deck providing views and access to the Living Room and the Dining area
- An expansive Living Room with windows on three sides, a hearth fireplace and a Dining Area
- An efficient Kitchen with ample counter and storage space serving the Dining area
- A first level Bedroom with a double closet and private access to the full bath
- Two additional bedrooms, one with a private Deck, sharing a half bath

FIRST FLOOR — 960 SQ. FT.
SECOND FLOOR — 420 SQ. FT.

TOTAL LIVING AREA:
1,380 SQ. FT.

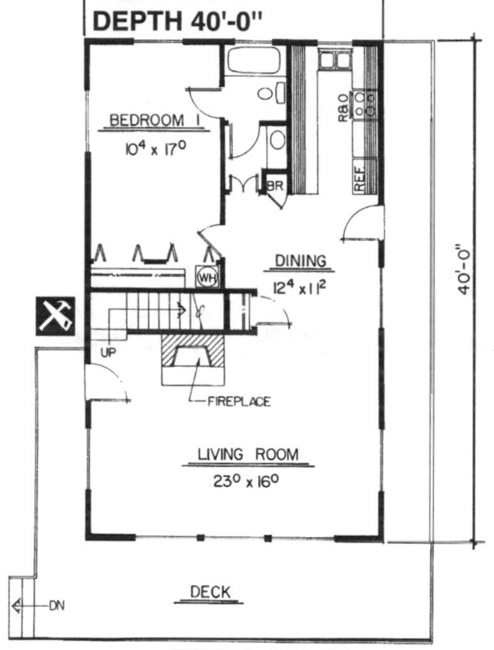
WIDTH 24'-0"
DEPTH 40'-0"
BEDROOM 1
10⁴ x 17⁰
R&O
REF.
BR
DINING
12⁴ x 11²
WH
UP
FIREPLACE
LIVING ROOM
23⁰ x 16⁰
40'-0"
DECK
DN

FIRST LEVEL
No 98709

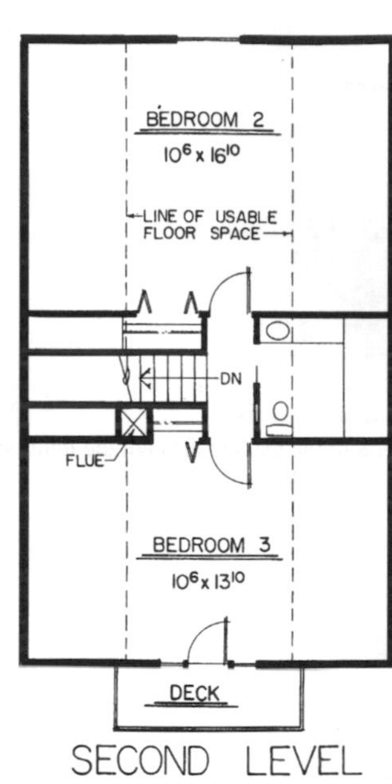
BEDROOM 2
10⁶ x 16¹⁰
LINE OF USABLE FLOOR SPACE
DN
FLUE
BEDROOM 3
10⁶ x 13¹⁰
DECK
SECOND LEVEL

No. 98415

Split Bedroom Plan

TOTAL LIVING AREA:
1,429 SQ. FT.

- This plan features:
- —Three bedrooms
- —Two full baths
- A tray ceiling giving a decorative touch the Master Bedroom and a vaulted ceiling topping the five-piece Master Bath
- A full bath located between the secondary bedrooms
- A corner fireplace and a vaulted ceiling highlighting the heart of the home, the Family Room
- A wetbar, serving bar to the Family Room and a built-in pantry adding to the convenience of the Kitchen
- A formal Dining Room crowned in an elegant high ceiling

MAIN FLOOR — 1,429 SQ. FT.
BASEMENT — 1,429 SQ. FT.
GARAGE — 438 SQ. FT.

- Foundation options for Basement, Slab or Crawl Space — please specify when ordering

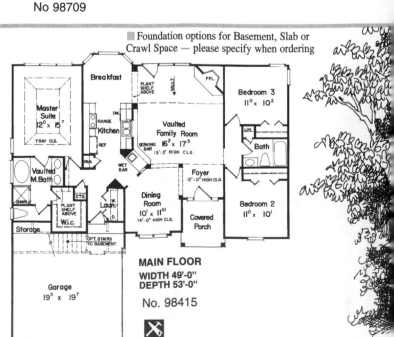

MAIN FLOOR
WIDTH 49'-0"
DEPTH 53'-0"

No. 98415

PRICE CODE B

No. 99635

Country Charm

- This plan features:
- – Three bedrooms
- – Two and one half baths
- A large heat-circulating fireplace
- A Master Bedroom with a private bath including a separate stall shower and whirlpool tub
- A comfortable lifestyle by separating the formal and informal areas
- Access to the Garage through the mudroom, which contains laundry facilities and extra closet space

MAIN AREA — 1,650 SQ. FT.
GARAGE — 491 SQ. FT.

TOTAL LIVING AREA:
1,650 SQ. FT.

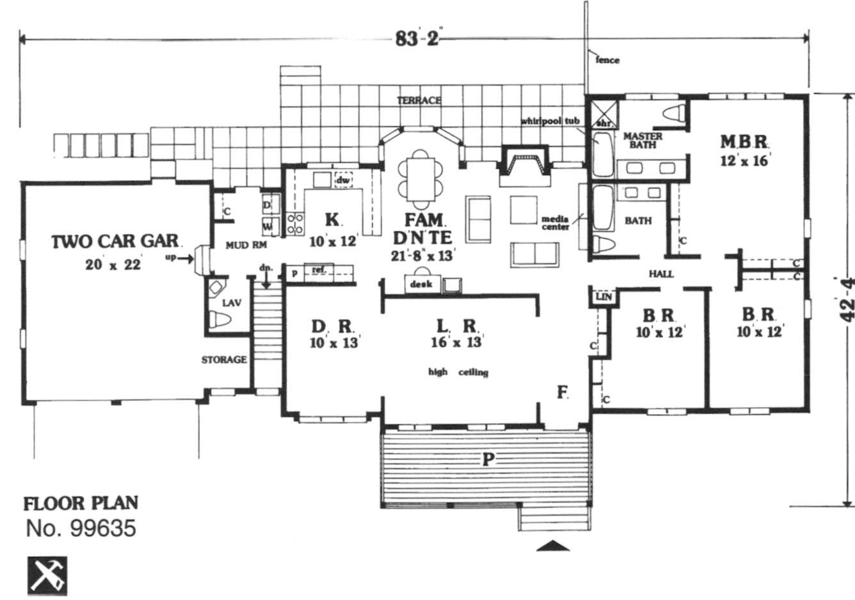
83'-2"
fence
TERRACE
whirlpool tub
shr.
MASTER BATH
MBR.
12' x 16'
dw
TWO CAR GAR.
20' x 22'
MUD RM
K.
10' x 12'
FAM. D'N'TE
21'-8" x 13'
media center
BATH
up
dn.
ref.
HALL
LAV
desk
LIN
D. R.
10' x 13'
L. R.
16' x 13'
B.R.
10' x 12'
B.R.
10' x 12'
42'-4"
STORAGE
high ceiling
F.
P

FLOOR PLAN
No. 99635

PRICE CODE A

Everything You Need...
...to Make Your Dream Come True!

You pay only a fraction of the original cost for home designs by respected professionals.

You've Picked Your Dream Home!

You can already see it standing on your lot... you can see yourselves in your new home... enjoying family, entertaining guests, celebrating holidays. All that remains ahead are the details. That's where we can help. Whether you plan to build-it-yourself, be your own contractor, or hand your plans over to an outside contractor, your Garlinghouse blueprints provide the perfect beginning for putting yourself in your dream home right away.

We even make it simple for you to make professional design modifications. We can also provide a materials list for greater economy.

My grandfather, L.F. Garlinghouse, started a tradition of quality when he founded this company in 1907. For over 90 years, homeowners and builders have relied on us for accurate, complete, professional blueprints. Our plans help you get results fast... and save money, too! These pages will give you all the information you need to order. So get started now... I know you'll love your new Garlinghouse home!

Sincerely,

EXTERIOR ELEVATIONS

Elevations are scaled drawings of the front, rear, left and right sides of a home. All of the necessary information pertaining to the exterior finish materials, roof pitches and exterior height dimensions of your home are defined.

CABINET PLANS

These plans, or in some cases elevations, will detail the layout of the kitchen and bathroom cabinets at a larger scale. This gives you an accurate layout for your cabinets or an ideal starting point for a modified custom cabinet design.

TYPICAL WALL SECTION

This section is provided to help your builder understand the structural components and materials used to construct the exterior walls of your home. This section will address insulation, roof components, and interior and exterior wall finishes. Your plans will be designed with either 2x4 o 2x6 exterior walls, but most professional contractors can easily adapt the plans to the wall thickness you require.

FIREPLACE DETAILS

If the home you have chosen includes a fireplace, the fireplace detail will show typical methods to construct the firebox, hearth and flue chase for masonry units, or a wood frame chase for a zero-clearance unit.

FOUNDATION PLAN

These plans will accurately dimension the footprint of your home including load bearing points and beam placement if applicable. The foundation style will vary from plan to plan. Your local climatic conditions will dictate whether a basement, slab or crawlspace is best suited for your area. In most cases, if your plan comes with one foundation style, a professional contractor can easily adapt the foundation plan to an alternate style.

ROOF PLAN

The information necessary to construct the roof will be included with your home plans. Some plans will reference roof trusses, while many others contain schematic framing plans. These framing plans will indicate the lumber sizes necessary for the rafters and ridgeboards based on the designated roof loads.

TYPICAL CROSS SECTION

A cut-away cross-section through the entire home shows your building contractor the exact correlation of construction components at all levels of the house. It will help to clarify the load bearing points from the roof all the way down to the basement.

DETAILED FLOOR PLANS

The floor plans of your home accurately dimension the positioning of all walls, doors, windows, stairs and permanent fixtures. They will show you the relationship and dimensions of rooms, closets and traffic patterns. Included is the schematic of the electrical layout. This layout is clearly represented and does not hinder the clarity of other pertinent information shown. All thes details will help your builder properly construct your new home.

STAIR DETAILS

If stairs are an element of the design you have chosen, then a cross-section of the stairs will be included in your home plans. This gives your builders the essential reference points that they need for headroom clearance, and riser and tread dimensions.

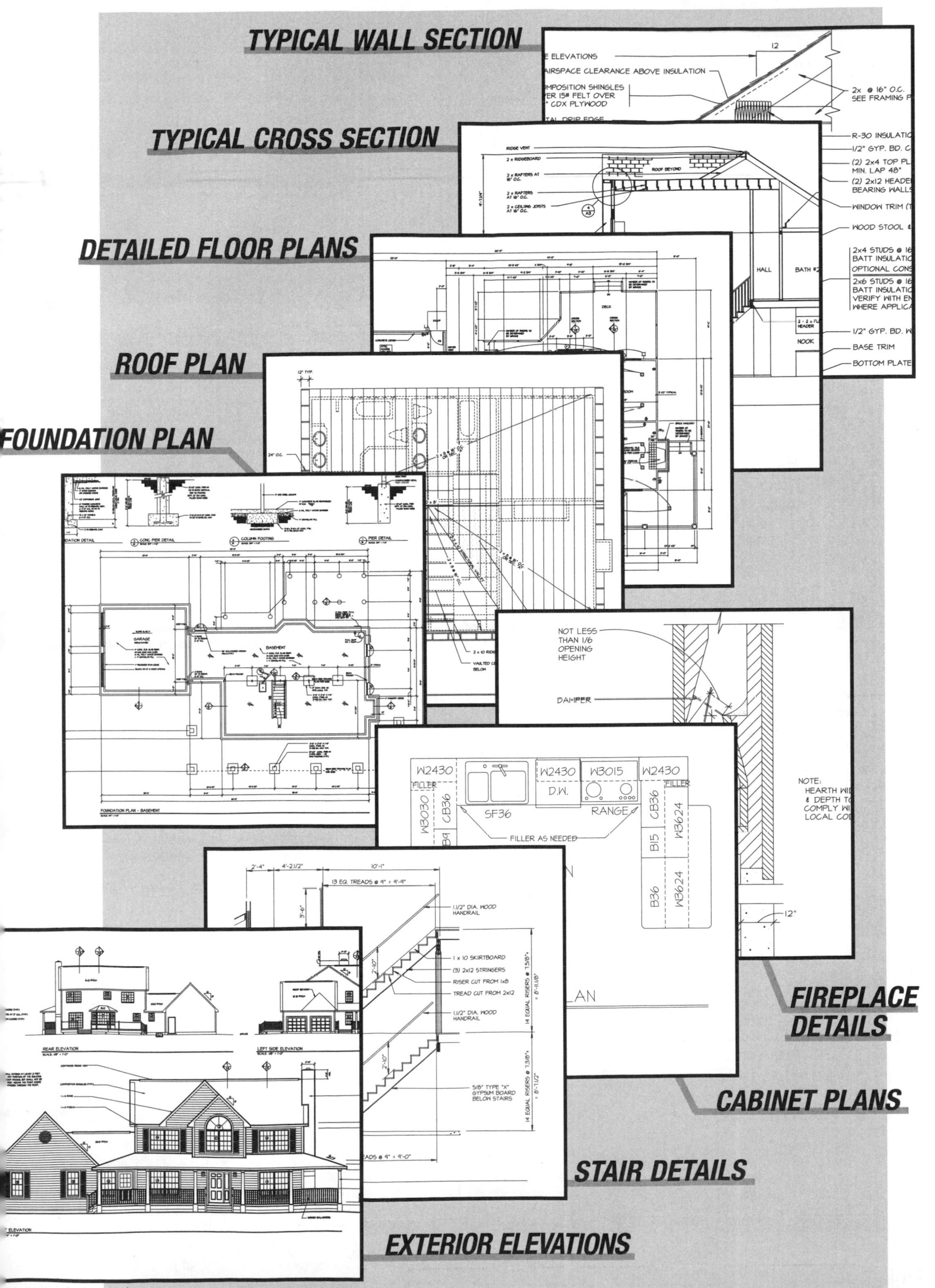
TYPICAL WALL SECTION
TYPICAL CROSS SECTION
DETAILED FLOOR PLANS
ROOF PLAN
FOUNDATION PLAN
FIREPLACE DETAILS
CABINET PLANS
STAIR DETAILS
EXTERIOR ELEVATIONS

Garlinghouse Options & Extras ...Make Your Dream A Home

Reversed Plans Can Make Your Dream Home Just Right!

"That's our dream home...if only the garage were on the other side!"

You could have exactly the home you want by flipping it end-for-end. Check it out by holding your dream home page of this book up to a mirror. Then simply order your plans "reversed." We'll send you one full set of mirror-image plans (with the writing backwards) as a master guide for you and your builder.

The remaining sets of your order will come as shown in this book so the dimensions and specifications are easily read on the job site...but most plans in our collection come stamped "REVERSED" so there is no construction confusion.

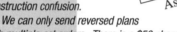

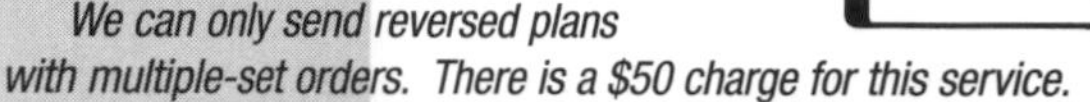
As Shown
Reversed

We can only send reversed plans with multiple-set orders. There is a $50 charge for this service.

Some plans in our collection are available in Right Reading Reverse. Right Reading Reverse plans will show your home in reverse, with the writing on the plan being readable. This easy-to-read format will save you valuable time and money. Please contact our Customer Service Department at (860) 343-5977 to check for Right Reading Reverse availability. (There is a $125 charge for this service.)

Specifications & Contract Form

We send this form to you free of charge with your home plan order. The form is designed to be filled in by you or your contractor with the exact materials to use in the construction of your new home. Once signed by you and your contractor it will provide you with peace of mind throughout the construction process.

Remember To Order Your Materials List

It'll help you save money. Available at a modest additional charge, the Materials List gives the quantity, dimensions, and specifications for the major materials needed to build your home. You will get faster, more accurate bids from your contractors and building suppliers — and avoid paying for unused materials and waste. Materials Lists are available for all home plans except as otherwise indicated, but can only be ordered with a set of home plans. Due to differences in regional requirements and homeowner or builder preferences... electrical, plumbing and heating/air conditioning equipment specifications are not designed specifically for each plan. However, non-plan specific detailed typical prints of residential electrical, plumbing and construction guidelines can be provided. Please see below for additional information. If you need a detailed materials cost you might need to purchase a Zip Quote. (Details follow)

Detail Plans Provide Valuable Information About Construction Techniques

Because local codes and requirements vary greatly, we recommend that you obtain drawings and bids from licensed contractors to do your mechanical plans. However, if you want to know more about techniques — and deal more confidently with subcontractors — we offer these remarkably useful detail sheets. These detail sheets will aid in your understanding of these technical subjects. ***The detail sheets are not specific to any one home plan and should be used only as a general reference guide.***

Finish Framing Details
Construction Detail Package

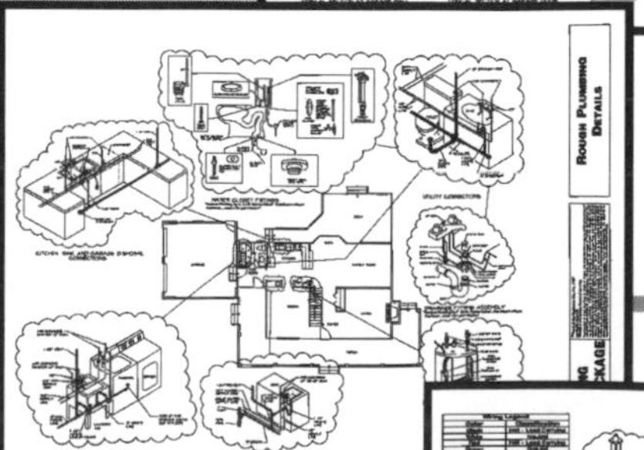
Rough Plumbing Details

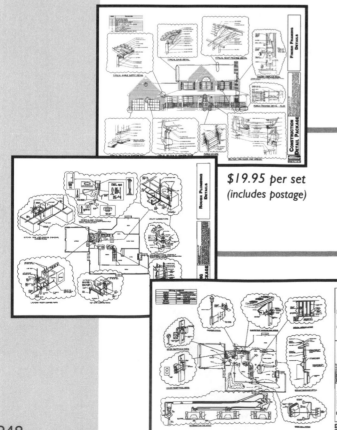

$19.95 per set
(includes postage)

RESIDENTIAL CONSTRUCTION DETAILS

Ten sheets that cover the essentials of stick-built residential home construction. Details foundation options — poured concrete basement, concrete block, or monolithic concrete slab. Shows all aspects of floor, wall and roof framing. Provides details for roof dormers, overhangs, chimneys and skylights. Conforms to requirements of Uniform Building code or BOCA code. Includes a quick index and a glossary of terms.

RESIDENTIAL PLUMBING DETAILS

Eight sheets packed with information detailing pipe installation methods, fittings, and sized. Details plumbing hook-ups for toilets, sinks, washers, sump pumps, and septic system construction. Conforms to requirements of National Plumbing code. Color coded with a glossary of terms and quick index.

RESIDENTIAL ELECTRICAL DETAILS

Eight sheets that cover all aspects of residential wiring, from simple switch wiring to service entrance connections. Details distribution panel layout with outlet and switch schematics, circuit breaker and wiring installation methods, and ground fault interrupter specifications. Conforms to requirements of National Electrical Code. Color coded with a glossary of terms.

Modifying Your Favorite Design, Made EASY!

OPTION #1

Modifying Your Garlinghouse Home Plan

Simple modifications to your dream home, including minor non-structural changes and material substitutions, can be made between you and your builder by marking the changes directly on your blueprints. However, if you are considering making significant changes to your chosen design, we recommend that you use the services of The Garlinghouse Co. Design Staff. We will help take your ideas and turn them into a reality, just the way you want. Here's our procedure!

*When you place your Vellum order, you may also request a free Garlinghouse Modification Kit. In this kit, you will receive a red marking pencil, furniture cut-out sheet, ruler, a self addressed mailing label and a form for specifying any additional notes or drawings that will help us understand your design ideas. Mark your desired changes directly on the Vellum drawings. NOTE: Please use only a **red pencil** to mark your desired changes on the Vellum. Then, return the redlined Vellum set in the original box to The Garlinghouse Company at, 282 Main Street Extension, Middletown, CT 06457. **IMPORTANT**: Please **roll** the Vellums for shipping, **do not fold** the Vellums for shipping.*

We also offer modification estimates. We will provide you with an estimate to draft your changes based on your specific modifications before you purchase the vellums, for a $50 fee. After you receive your estimate, if you decide to have The Garlinghouse Company Design Staff do the changes, the $50 estimate fee will be deducted from the cost of your modifications. If, however, you choose to use a different service, the $50 estimate fee is non-refundable.

Within 5 days of receipt of your plans, you will be contacted by a member of The Garlinghouse Co. Design Staff with an estimate for the design services to draw those changes. A 50% deposit is required before we begin making the actual modifications to your plans.

Once the preliminary design changes have been made to the floor plans and elevations, copies will be sent to you to make sure we have made the exact changes you want. We will wait for your approval before continuing with any structural revisions. The Garlinghouse Co. Design Staff will call again to inform you that your modified Vellum plan is complete and will be shipped as soon as the final payment has been made. For additional information call us at 1-860-343-5977. Please refer to the Modification Pricing Guide for estimated modification costs. Please call for Vellum modification availability for plan numbers 85,000 and above.

OPTION #2

Reproducible Vellums for Local Modification Ease

If you decide not to use the Garlinghouse Co. Design Staff for your modifications, we recommend that you follow our same procedure of purchasing our Vellums. You then have the option of using the services of the original designer of the plan, a local professional designer, or architect to make the modifications to your plan.

With a Vellum copy of our plans, a design professional can alter the drawings just the way you want, then you can print as many copies of the modified plans as you need to build your house. And, since you have already started with our complete detailed plans, the cost of those expensive professional services will be significantly less than starting from scratch. Refer to the price schedule for Vellum costs. Again, please call for Vellum availability for plan numbers 85,000 and above.

***IMPORTANT RETURN POLICY:** Upon receipt of your Vellums, if for some reason you decide you do not want a modified plan, then simply return the Kit and the unopened Vellums. Reproducible Vellum copies of our home plans are copyright protected and only sold under the terms of a license agreement that you will receive with your order. Should you not agree to the terms, then the Vellums may be returned, **unopened,** for a full refund less the shipping and handling charges, plus a 15% restocking fee. For any additional information, please call us at 1-860-343-5977.*

MODIFICATION PRICING GUIDE

CATEGORIES	ESTIMATED COST
KITCHEN LAYOUT — PLAN AND ELEVATION	$175.00
BATHROOM LAYOUT — PLAN AND ELEVATION	$175.00
FIREPLACE PLAN AND DETAILS	$200.00
INTERIOR ELEVATION	$125.00
EXTERIOR ELEVATION — MATERIAL CHANGE	$140.00
EXTERIOR ELEVATION — ADD BRICK OR STONE	$400.00
EXTERIOR ELEVATION — STYLE CHANGE	$450.00
NON BEARING WALLS (INTERIOR)	$200.00
BEARING AND/OR EXTERIOR WALLS	$325.00
WALL FRAMING CHANGE — 2X4 TO 2X6 OR 2X6 TO 2X4	$240.00
ADD/REDUCE LIVING SPACE — SQUARE FOOTAGE	QUOTE REQUIRED
NEW MATERIALS LIST	$.20 SQUARE FOOT
CHANGE TRUSSES TO RAFTERS OR CHANGE ROOF PITCH	$300.00
FRAMING PLAN CHANGES	$325.00
GARAGE CHANGES	$325.00
ADD A FOUNDATION OPTION	$300.00
FOUNDATION CHANGES	$250.00
RIGHT READING PLAN REVERSE	$575.00
ARCHITECTS SEAL	$300.00
ENERGY CERTIFICATE	$150.00
LIGHT AND VENTILATION SCHEDULE	$150.00

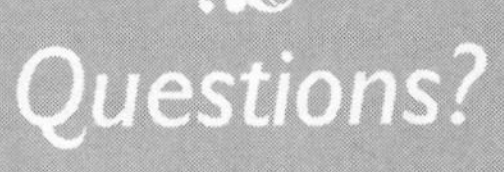

Questions?

Call our customer service department at **1-860-343-5977**

"How to obtain a construction cost calculation based on labor rates and building material costs in your Zip Code area!"

ZIP-QUOTE!

HOME COST CALCULATOR

GARLINGHOUSE

ZIP QUOTE

HOME COST CALCULATOR

WHY?

Do you wish you could quickly find out the building cost for your new home without waiting for a contractor to compile hundreds of bids? Would you like to have a benchmark to compare your contractor(s) bids against? ***Well, Now You Can!!,*** with **Zip-Quote** Home Cost Calculator. Zip-Quote is only available for zip code areas within the United States.

HOW?

Our new **Zip-Quote** Home Cost Calculator will enable you to obtain the calculated building cost to construct your new home, based on labor rates and building material costs within your zip code area, without the normal delays or hassles usually associated with the bidding process. Zip-Quote can be purchased in two separate formats, an itemized or a bottom line format.

Zip-Quote is available for plans where you see this symbol.

"How does **Zip-Quote** actually work?" When we receive your **Zip-Quote** order, we process your specific home plan building materials list through our Home Cost Calculator which contains up-to-date rates for all residential labor trades and building material costs in your zip code area. "The result?" A calculated cost to build your dream home in your zip code area. This calculation will help you (as a consumer or a builder) evaluate your building budget. This is a valuable tool for anyone considering building a new home.

All database information for our calculations is furnished by Marshall & Swift, L.P. For over 60 years, Marshall & Swift L.P. has been a leading provider of cost data to professionals in all aspects of the construction and remodeling industries.

OPTION 1

The **Itemized Zip-Quote** is a detailed building material list. Each building material list line item will separately state the labor cost, material cost and equipment cost (if applicable) for the use of that building material in the construction process. Each category within the building material list will be subtotaled and the entire Itemized cost calculation totaled at the end. This building materials list will be summarized by the individual building categories and will have additional columns where you can enter data from your contractor's estimates for a cost comparison between the different suppliers and contractors who will actually quote you their products and services.

OPTION 2

The **Bottom Line Zip-Quote** is a one line summarized total cost for the home plan of your choice. This cost calculation is also based on the labor cost, material cost and equipment cost (if applicable) within your local zip code area.

COST

The price of your **Itemized Zip-Quote** is based upon the pricing schedule of the plan you have selected, in addition to the price of the materials list. Please refer to the pricing schedule on our order form. The price of your initial **Bottom Line Zip-Quote** is $29.95. Each additional **Bottom Line Zip-Quote** ordered in conjunction with the initial order is only $14:95. **Bottom Line Zip-Quote** may be purchased separately and does NOT have to be purchased in conjunction with a home plan order.

FYI

An **Itemized Zip-Quote** Home Cost Calculation can ONLY be purchased in conjunction with a Home Plan order. The **Itemized Zip-Quote** can not be purchased separately. The **Bottom Line Zip-Quote** can be purchased seperately and doesn't have to be purchased in conjunction with a home plan order. Please consult with a sales representative for current availability. If you find within 60 days of your order date that you will be unable to build this home, then you may exchange the plans and the materials list towards the price of a new set of plans (see order info pages for plan exchange policy). The **Itemized Zip-Quote** and the **Bottom Line Zip-Quote** are NOT returnable. The price of the initial **Bottom Line Zip-Quote** order can be credited towards the purchase of an **Itemized Zip-Quote** order only. Additional **Bottom Line Zip-Quote** orders, within the same order can not be credited. Please call our Customer Service Department for more information.

SOME MORE INFORMATION

The Itemized and Bottom Line Zip-Quotes give you approximated costs for constructing the particular house in your area. These costs are not exact and are only intended to be used as a preliminary estimate to help determine the affordability of a new home and/or as a guide to evaluate the general competitiveness of actual price quotes obtained through local suppliers and contractors. However, Zip-Quote cost figures should never be relied upon as the only source of information in either case. The Garlinghouse Company and Marshall & Swift L.P. can not guarantee any level of data accuracy or correctness in a Zip-Quote and disclaim all liability for loss with respect to the same, in excess of the original purchase price of the Zip-Quote product. All Zip-Quote calculations are based upon the actual blueprint materials list with options as selected by customer and do not reflect any differences that may be shown on the published house renderings, floor plans, or photographs.

Ignoring Copyright Laws Can Be A $1,000,000 Mistake

*Recent changes in the US copyright laws allow for statutory penalties of up to **$100,000** per incident for copyright infringement involving any of the copyrighted plans found in this publication. The law can be confusing. So, for your own protection, take the time to understand what you can and cannot do when it comes to home plans.*

•••WHAT YOU CANNOT DO•••

You Cannot Duplicate Home Plans

*Purchasing a set of blueprints and making additional sets by reproducing the original is **illegal**. If you need multiple sets of a particular home plan, then you must purchase them.*

You Cannot Copy Any Part of a Home Plan to Create Another

*Creating your own plan by copying even part of a home design found in this publication is called "creating a derivative work" and is **illegal** unless you have permission to do so.*

You Cannot Build a Home Without a License

*You must have specific permission or license to build a home from a copyrighted design, even if the finished home has been changed from the original plan. It is **illegal** to build one of the homes found in this publication without a license.*

What Garlinghouse Offers

Home Plan Blueprint Package

By purchasing a single or multiple set package of blueprints from Garlinghouse, you not only receive the physical blueprint documents necessary for construction, but you are also granted a license to build one, and only one, home. You can also make simple modifications, including minor non-structural changes and material substitutions, to our design, as long as these changes are made directly on the blueprints purchased from Garlinghouse and no additional copies are made.

Home Plan Vellums

By purchasing vellums for one of our home plans, you receive the same construction drawings found in the blueprints, but printed on vellum paper. Vellums can be erased and are perfect for making design changes. They are also semi-transparent making them easy to duplicate. But most importantly, the purchase of home plan vellums comes with a broader license that allows you to make changes to the design (ie, create a hand drawn or CAD derivative work), to make an unlimited number of copies of the plan, and to build one home from the plan.

56'-0"
Deck
Dining
Living Rm
Master Br
Br #2
Den/Br #3
Kit.
Garage
MAIN FLOOR
Slab/Crawlspace Option

License To Build Additional Homes

With the purchase of a blueprint package or vellums you automatically receive a license to build one home and only one home, respectively. If you want to build more homes than you are licensed to build through your purchase of a plan, then additional licenses may be purchased at reasonable costs from Garlinghouse. Inquire for more Information.

Order Code No. **H8VL5**

Order Form

Plan prices guaranteed until 1/30/99 —After this date call for updated pricing

_____set(s) of blueprints for plan # __________ $ ______

_____Vellum & Modification kit for plan # __________ $ ______

_____Additional set(s) @ $30 each for plan # __________ $ ______

_____Mirror Image Reverse @ $50 each $ ______

_____Right Reading Reverse @ $125 each $ ______

_____Materials list for plan # __________ $ ______

_____Detail Plans @ $19.95 each

❑ Construction ❑ Plumbing ❑ Electrical $ ______

_____Bottom line ZIP Quote@$29.95 for plan # __________ $ ______

_____Additional Bottom Line Zip Quote

@ $14.95 for plan(s) # __________

__________ $ ______

_____Itemized ZIP Quote for plan(s) # __________ $ ______

Shipping (see charts on opposite page) $ ______

Subtotal $ ______

Sales Tax (CT residents add 6% sales tax, KS residents add 6.15% sales tax) (Not required for all states) $ ______

TOTAL AMOUNT ENCLOSED **$** ______

Send your check, money order or credit card information to:
(No C.O.D.'s Please)

Please submit all United States & Other Nations orders to:

Garlinghouse Company
P.O. Box 1717
Middletown, CT. 06457

Please Submit all Canadian plan orders to:

Garlinghouse Company
60 Baffin Place, Unit #5
Waterloo, Ontario N2V 1Z7

ADDRESS INFORMATION:

NAME: __________

STREET: __________

CITY: __________

STATE: __________ ***ZIP:*** __________

DAYTIME PHONE: __________

Credit Card Information

Charge To: ❑ Visa ❑ Mastercard

Card # __________

Signature __________ Exp. ___/___

Payment must be made in U.S. funds. Foreign Mail Orders: Certified bank checks in U.S. funds only

TERMS OF SALE FOR HOME PLANS: *All home plans sold through this publication are copyright protected. Reproduction of these home plans, either in whole or in part, including any direct copying and/or preparation of derivative works thereof, for any reason without the prior written permission of The L.F. Garlinghouse Co., Inc., is strictly prohibited. The purchase of a set of home plans in no way transfers any copyright or other ownership interest in it to the buyer except for a limited license to use that set of home plans for the construction of one, and only one, dwelling unit. The purchase of additional sets of that home plan at a reduced price from the original set or as a part of a multiple set package does not entitle the buyer with a license to construct more than one dwelling unit.*

IMPORTANT INFORMATION TO READ BEFORE YOU PLACE YOUR ORDER

How Many Sets Of Plans Will You Need?

The Standard 8-Set Construction Package

Our experience shows that you'll speed every step of construction and avoid costly building errors by ordering enough sets to go around. Each tradesperson wants a set — the general contractor and all subcontractors; foundation, electrical, plumbing, heating/air conditioning and framers. Don't forget your lending institution, building department and, of course, a set for yourself.

The Minimum 4-Set Construction Package

If you're comfortable with arduous follow-up, this package can save you a few dollars by giving you the option of passing down plan sets as work progresses. You might have enough copies to go around if work goes exactly as scheduled and no plans are lost or damaged by subcontrators. But for only $50 more, the 8-set package eliminates these worries.

The Single Study Set

We offer this set so you can study the blueprints to plan your dream home in detail. As with all of our plans, they are stamped with a copyright warning. Remember, one set is never enough to build your home. In pursuant to copyright laws, it is illegal to reproduce any blueprint.

Our Reorder and Exchange Policies:

If you find after your initial purchase that you require additional sets of plans you may purchase them from us at special reorder prices (please call for pricing details) provided that you reorder within 6 months of your original order date. There is a $28 reorder processing fee that is charged on all reorders. For more information on reordering plans please contact our Customer Service Department at (860) 343-5977.

We want you to find your dream home from our wide selection of home plans. However, if for some reason you find that the plan you have purchased from us does not meet your needs, then you may exchange that plan for any other plan in our collection. We allow you sixty days from your original invoice date to make an exchange. At the time of the exchange you will be charged a processing fee of 15% of the total amount of your original order plus the difference in price between the plans (if applicable) plus the cost to ship the new plans to you. Call our Customer Service Department at (860) 343-5977 for more information. Please Note: Reproducible vellums can only be exchanged if they are unopened.

Important Shipping Information

Please refer to the shipping charts on the order form for service availability for your specific plan number. Our delivery service must have a street address or Rural Route Box number — never a post office box. (PLEASE NOTE: Supplying a P.O. Box number only will delay the shipping of your order.) Use a work address if no one is home during the day.

Orders being shipped to APO or FPO must go via First Class Mail. Please include the proper postage.

For our International Customers, only Certified bank checks and money orders are accepted and must be payable in U.S. currency. For speed, we ship international orders Air Parcel Post. Please refer to the chart for the correct shipping cost.

Important Canadian Shipping Information

To our friends in Canada, we have a plan design affiliate in Kitchener, Ontario. This relationship will help you avoid the delays and charges associated with shipments from the United States. Moreover, our affiliate is familiar with the building requirements in your community and country. We prefer payments in U.S. Currency. If you, however, are sending Canadian funds please add 40% to the prices of the plans and shipping fees.

An Important Note About Building Code Requirements:

All plans are drawn to conform to one or more of the industry's major national building standards. However, due to the variety of local building regulations, your plan may need to be modified to comply with local requirements — snow loads, energy loads, seismic zones, etc. Do check them fully and consult your local building officials.

A few states require that all building plans used be drawn by an architect registered in that state. While having your plans reviewed and stamped by such an architect may be prudent, laws requiring non-conforming plans like ours to be completely redrawn forces you to unnecessarily pay very large fees. If your state has such a law, we strongly recommend you contact your state representative to protest.

The rendering, floor plans, and technical information contained within this publication are not guaranteed to be totally accurate. Consequently, no information from this publication should be used either as a guide to constructing a home or for estimating the cost of building a home. Complete blueprints must be purchased for such purposes.

BEFORE ORDERING PLEASE READ ALL ORDERING INFORMATION

Please submit all Canadian plan orders to:
Garlinghouse Company
60 Baffin Place, Unit #5, Waterloo, Ontario N2V 1Z7
Canadian Customers Only: 1-800-561-4169/Fax #: 1-800-719-3291
Customer Service #: 1-519-746-4169

ORDER TOLL FREE — 1-800-235-5700
Monday-Friday 8:00 a.m. to 8:00 p.m. Eastern Time
or FAX your Credit Card order to 1-860-343-5984
All foreign residents call 1-800-343-5977

Please have ready: 1. Your credit card number 2. The plan number 3. The order code number ⇨ H8VL5

rlinghouse 1997 Blueprint Price Code Schedule

Additional sets with original order $30

PRICE CODE	A	B	C	D	E	F	G	H	Z
8 SETS OF SAME PLAN	$375	$415	$455	$495	$535	$575	$615	$655	$200
4 SETS OF SAME PLAN	$325	$365	$405	$445	$485	$525	$565	$605	$250
1 SINGLE SET OF PLANS	$275	$315	$355	$395	$435	$475	$515	$555	$300
VELLUMS	$485	$530	$575	$620	$665	$710	$755	$800	$340
MATERIALS LIST	$40	$40	$45	$45	$50	$50	$55	$55	$40
ITEMIZED ZIP QUOTE	$75	$80	$85	$85	$90	$90	$95	$95	$75

Shipping — (Plans 1-84999)

	1-3 Sets	4-6 Sets	7+ & Vellums
Standard Delivery (UPS 2-Day)	$15.00	$20.00	$25.00
Overnight Delivery	$30.00	$35.00	$40.00

Shipping — (Plans 85000-99999)

	1-3 Sets	4-6 Sets	7+ & Vellums
Ground Delivery (7-10 Days)	$9.00	$18.00	$20.00
Express Delivery (3-5 Days)	$15.00	$20.00	$25.00

International Shipping & Handling

	1-3 Sets	4-6 Sets	7+ & Vellums
Regular Delivery Canada (7-10 Days)	$14.00	$17.00	$20.00
Express Delivery Canada (5-6 Days)	$35.00	$40.00	$45.00
Overseas Delivery Airmail (2-3 Weeks)	$45.00	$52.00	$60.00

Option Key

- ZIP — Zip Quote Available
- Duplex Plan
- RR — Right Reading Reverse
- ML — Materials List Available

Index

GARAGE PLANS

Save money by Doing-It-Yourself using our Easy-To-Follow plans. Whether you intend to build your own garage or contract it out to a building professional, the Garlinghouse garage plans provide you with everything you need to price out your project and get started. Put our 85 years of experience to work for you.

Order now!!

ITEM NO. 06016C — $86.00
Apartment Garage With One Bedroom

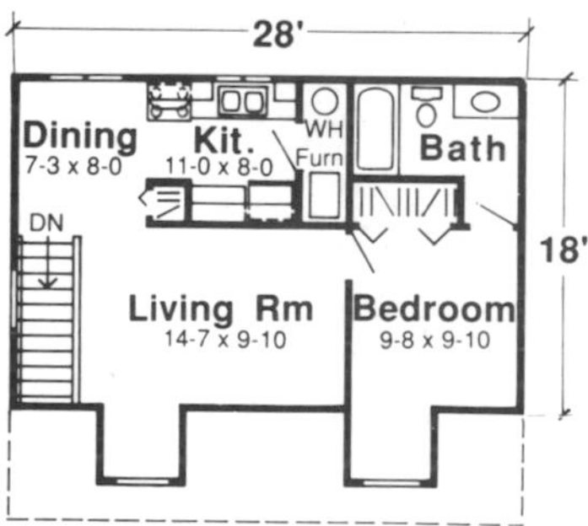
28'
Dining
7-3 x 8-0
Kit.
11-0 x 8-0
WH
Furn
Bath
DN
18'
Living Rm
14-7 x 9-10
Bedroom
9-8 x 9-10

- 24' x 28' Overall Dimensions
- 544 Square Foot Apartment
- 12/12 Gable Roof with Dormers
- Slab or Stem Wall Foundation Options

ITEM NO. 06015C — $86.00
Apartment Garage With Two Bedrooms

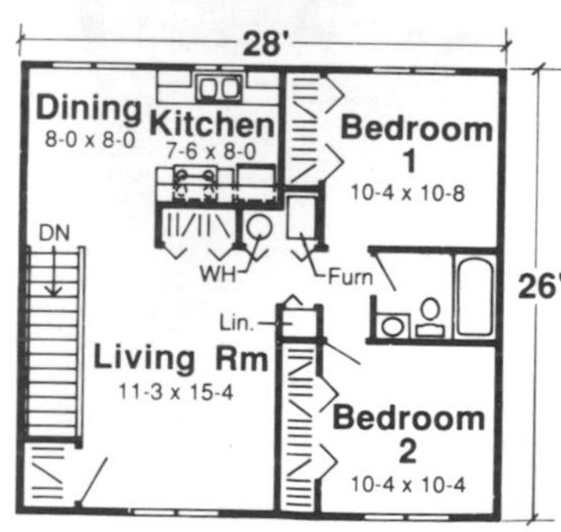
28'
Dining
8-0 x 8-0
Kitchen
7-6 x 8-0
Bedroom
1
10-4 x 10-8
DN
WH
Furn
Lin.
26'
Living Rm
11-3 x 15-4
Bedroom
2
10-4 x 10-4

- 26' x 28' Overall Dimensions
- 728 Square Foot Apartment
- 4/12 Pitch Gable Roof
- Slab or Stem Wall Foundation Options

ITEM NO. 06012C — $54.00
30' Deep Gable &/or Eave Jumbo Garages

- 4/12 Pitch Gable Roof
- Available Options for Extra Tall Walls, Garage & Personnel Doors, Foundation, Window, & Sidings
- Package contains 4 Different Sizes
- 30' x 28' • 30' x 32' • 30' x 36' • 30' x 40'

ITEM NO. 06013C — $68.00
Two-Car Garage With Mudroom/Breezeway

- Attaches to Any House
- 24' x 24' Eave Entry
- Available Options for Utility Room with Bath, Mudroom, Screened-In Breezeway, Roof, Foundation, Garage & Personnel Doors, Window, & Sidings

ITEM NO. 06004C — $48.00

24' Deep-Eave 2-Car Garages

- Can Be Built Stand-Alone or Attached to House
- Available Options for Roof, Foundation, Garage & Personnel Doors, Window, & Sidings
- Package contains 4 Different Sizes
- 24' x 22' • 24' x 24' • 24' x 26' • 24' x 28'

ITEM NO. 06005C — $48.00

20' x 22' Deep-Eave 2-Car Garages

- Can Be Built Stand-Alone or Attached to House
- Available Options for Roof, Foundation, Garage & Personnel Doors, Window, & Sidings
- Package contains 6 Different Sizes
- 20' x 20' • 20' x 24' • 22' x 24'
- 20' x 22' • 22' x 22' • 22' x 26'

ITEM NO. 06010C — $60.00

Eave 2 & 3-Car Cape Cod Garages

- Loft Dormer Windows
- Interior Side Stairs to Loft Workshop
- Available Options for Engine Lift, Foundation, Garage & Personnel Doors, Window, & Sidings
- Package contains 4 Different Sizes
- 24' x 28' • 24' x 30' • 24' x 32' • 24' x 36'

ITEM NO. 06014C — $54.00

Single-Story 2-Car Saltbox-Style Garages

- Decorative Round Gable Vent
- Available Options for Storage Loft, Foundation, Garage & Personnel Doors, Window, & Sidings
- Package contains 6 Different Sizes
- 24' x 24' • 24' x 32' • 26' x 28'
- 24' x 28' • 26' x 24' • 26' x 32'

ITEM NO. 06009C — $60.00

Eave 2 & 3-Car Saltbox-Style Garages

- Interior Side Stairs to Loft Workshop
- Available Options for Engine Lift, Foundation, Garage & Personnel Doors, Window, & Sidings
- Package contains 3 Different Sizes
- 24' x 28' • 24' x 32' • 24' x 36'

ITEM NO. 06011C — $54.00

26' Deep Jumbo Garages

- Available Options for Eave, Gable Entry or 8', 9', 10' Walls, Foundation, Garage & Personnel Doors, Window, & Sidings
- Package contains 4 Different Sizes
- 26' x 28' • 26' x 32' • 26' x 36' • 26' x 40'

Here's What You Get

- Three complete sets of drawings for each plan ordered.
- Detailed step-by-step instructions with easy-to-follow diagrams on how to build your garage (not available with apartment/garages).
- For each garage style, a variety of size and garage door configuration options.
- Variety of roof styles and/or pitch options for most garages.
- Complete materials list.
- Choice between three foundation options: Monolithic Slab, Concrete Stem Wall or Concrete Block Stem Wall.
- Full framing plans, elevations and cross-sectionals for each garage size and configuration.
- And Much More!!

Order Information For Garage Plans:

All garage plan orders contain three complete sets of drawings with instructions and are priced as listed next to the illustration. Additional sets of plans may be obtained for $10.00 each with your original order. UPS shipping is used unless otherwise requested. Please include the proper amount for shipping.

GARLINGHOUSE
Build-It-Yourself
PROJECT PLAN

Garage Order Form

Please send me 3 complete sets of the following GARAGE PLAN:

Item no. & description ____________ Price $________

Additional Sets

_____ (@ $10.00 each) $________

Shipping Charges: UPS-$3.75, First Class- $4.50 $________

Subtotal: $________

Resident sales tax: KS-5.9%, CT-6% *(Not Required For Other States)* $________

Total Enclosed: $________

Send your order to:
(With check or money order payable in U.S. funds only)
The Garlinghouse Company

P.O. Box 1717
Middletown, CT 06457

No C.O.D. orders accepted; U.S. funds only. UPS will not ship to Post Office boxes, FPO boxes, APO boxes, Alaska or Hawaii. Canadian orders must be shipped First Class.

Prices subject to change without notice.

Order Code No. **G8VL5**

My Billing Address is:

Name ________________

Address ________________

City ________________

State ________________ Zip ________

Daytime Phone No. ________________

My Shipping Address is:

Name ________________

Address ________________
(UPS will not ship to P.O. Boxes)

City ________________

State ________________ Zip ________

For Faster Service...Charge It!

U.S. & Canada Call
1(800)235-5700

All foreign residents call 1(860)343-5977

❑ Mastercard ❑ Visa

Card # | | | | | | | | | | | | | | | |

Signature ________________ Exp. ___/___

If paying by credit card, to avoid delays: billing address must be as it appears on credit card statement

or FAX us at (860) 343-5984